King of the Empty Plain

The Tsadra Foundation Series

published by Snow Lion Publications

Tsadra Foundation is a U.S.-based non-profit organization that was founded in 2000 in order to support the activities of advanced Western students of Tibetan Buddhism, specifically those with significant contemplative experience. Taking its inspiration from the nineteenth-century nonsectarian Tibetan scholar and meditation master Jamgön Kongtrül Lodrö Tayé, Tsadra Foundation is named after his hermitage in eastern Tibet, Tsadra Rinchen Drak. The Foundation's various program areas reflect his values of excellence in both scholarship and contemplative practice, and the recognition of their mutual complementarity.

This publication is part of Tsadra Foundation's Translation Program, which aims to make authentic and authoritative texts from the Tibetan traditions available in English. The Foundation is honored to present the work of its fellows and grantees, individuals of confirmed contemplative and intellectual integrity; however, their views do not necessarily reflect those of the Foundation.

Tsadra Foundation is delighted to ally with Snow Lion Publications in making these important texts available in the English language.

King of the Empty Plain

The Tibetan Iron-Bridge Builder
Tangtong Gyalpo

Cyrus Stearns

Snow Lion Publications
Ithaca, New York
Boulder, Colorado

Snow Lion Publications
P. O. Box 6483
Ithaca, NY 14851 USA
(607) 273-8519
www.snowlionpub.com

Printed in Canada on acid-free recycled paper.
Designed & typeset by Gopa & Ted2, Inc.

ISBN-10 1-55939-275-4
ISBN-13 978-1-55939-275-4

Library of Congress Cataloging-in-Publication Data

'Gyur-med-bde-chen, Lo-chen, b. 1540.
[Dpal grub pa'i dbaṅ phyug chen po Lcags zam pa Thaṅ stoṅ rgyal po'i rnam par thar pa ṅo tshar kun gsal me loṅ gsar pa. English]
King of the empty plain : the Tibetan iron-bridge builder Tangtong Gyalpo / Cyrus Stearns.
p. cm. — (Tsadra Foundation series)
Includes bibliographical references and index.
ISBN-13: 978-1-55939-275-4 (alk. paper)
ISBN-10: 1-55939-275-4 (alk. paper)
1. Thaṅ-stoṅ-rgyal-po, 15th cent. 2. Lamas—China—Tibet—Biography—Early works to 1800. I. Stearns, Cyrus, 1949- II. Kun dga' bsod nams grags pa dpal bzaṅ. Grub thob chen po'i rnam thar phyi ma mya ṅan las 'das pa'i skor. English & Tibetan. III. Title.

BQ990.H367G8813 2007
294.3'923092—dc22
[B]

2007013655

Contents

Preface ix
List of Illustrations xiii
List of Plates xix
Introduction
1. The Life and the Lifespan 1
2. King of the Empty Plain 14
3. Iron-Bridge Man 33
4. Madman of the Empty Valley 58

A Jewel Mirror in Which All Is Clear
by Lochen Gyurmé Dechen 81
Prologue 83
1: Hundreds of Thousands of Lifetimes 87
2: A Mental Emanation of Padmasambhava 95
3: Crazy Tsöndru Is Insane 103
4: The White Light of Profound and Vast Instructions 133
5: Five Names of Suitable Meaning 149
6: Uḍḍiyāna, the Land of Ḍākinīs 169
7: Appearances Are Like Dream and Illusion 191
8: A Situation in Which a Yogin Needs Iron 215
9: Fine Pathways of Precious Iron 243
10: A Relic of the Buddha Blazing with Light 277
11: Five-Peaked Mount Wutai 309

12: A Geomantic Focal-Point to Suppress the Mongol Armies 333
13: The Auspicious Stūpa of Many Doors 363
14: To the Palace of the King of Kāmata in India 391
15: A Yogin Departs into the Basic Space of Phenomena 421
Colophon 439

THE FINAL STORY CONCERNING THE NIRVĀṆA OF THE GREAT ADEPT
by Kunga Sönam Drakpa Palsang
Tibetan Text and English Translation 441

Notes 465
Bibliography
Sources in Tibetan Language 587
Sources in European Languages 607
Index 615

This book is humbly dedicated to my teachers:
Dezhung Rinpoché (1906–87),
Dilgo Khyentsé Rinpoché (1910–91),
and Chogye Trichen Rinpoché (1919–2007).

. . .

Preface

One day in 1974 I was sitting with my teacher Dezhung Rinpoché in the living room of his home in Seattle. I had been enthralled by Rinpoché's eloquent, profound, and hilarious stories about the renowned Tibetan master Tangtong Gyalpo for the last year or so. He often told these tales in private conversation, or while explaining Tangtong's practice for meditation on Avalokiteśvara, or when bestowing the great adept's ritual blessing for longevity. Tangtong's biography had been one of Rinpoché's favorite books in Tibet, although he had not seen the work since fleeing his homeland in 1959. I had recently come across the biography among the uncatalogued microfilm collection of Tibetan works at the University of Washington. When I mentioned this to Rinpoché, he began to quote from memory a long series of verses from the text. Then he wrote for a moment in a small notepad, tore off the sheet, and handed it to me, saying, "Look for this!"

> On the mountain of the illusory body
> of four elements
> is the monastery of uncontrived mind.
> It's the sublime place where
> bliss and lucidity arise.
> Be single-minded in that place of practice![1]

Thus began my infatuation with Tangtong Gyalpo, which has finally come to fruition in the form of this book more than thirty years after that misty morning in Seattle. Dezhung Rinpoché never told me to translate Tangtong's biography, but he certainly inspired me to do so.

In the late 1970s I had the incredible good fortune to meet two other wonderful teachers. From Dilgo Khyentsé Rinpoché in India I was able to receive the initiations and some meditation instructions for the Heartdrop of the Great Adept, a cycle of mental treasures that Tangtong Gyalpo had transmitted in a vision to Jamyang Khyentsé Wangpo. When I met Chogye Trichen Rinpoché for the first time at the Buddha's birthplace of Lumbini, he kindly gave to me the gift of his own copy of Tangtong's biography, which is the book I have used ever since.

Since first learning from Dezhung Rinpoché about the life and teachings of Tangtong Gyalpo, I have continued to gather information about him whenever possible. Through the blessing of my teachers, certain auspicious connections came into alignment, and I was contacted several years ago by Lama Drupgyu (Anthony Chapman), Director of Programs for the Tsadra Foundation, whom I had first met about the time I began to study with Dezhung Rinpoché. I am truly grateful for the generous support of the Tsadra Foundation and its founder and president, Eric Colombel, which has enabled me to finally return to this project and bring the amazing story of Tangtong Gyalpo's life and accomplishments into English.

Geshé Ngawang Nornang, Turrell V. Wylie, David Seyfort Ruegg, and T.G. Dhongthog Rinpoché were very helpful when I first began to study the Tibetan biography and work on my 1980 M.A. thesis about Tangtong Gyalpo. Michael Aris and Janet Gyatso also gave me valuable information and encouragement long ago. David Jackson, Roberto Vitali, and Franz-Karl Ehrhard kindly helped obtain rare texts from the Nepal-German Manuscript Preservation Project in Kathmandu. Matthieu Ricard and a Bhutanese attendant (whose name I have shamefully forgotten) of Dilgo Khyentsé Rinpoché both brought me copies of Tangtong Gyalpo's Collected Works from Bhutan. Khenpo Jamyang Tenzin patiently answered my endless questions about the biography. My daughters Sofia, Anna, and Tania (who have heard about Tangtong Gyalpo all their lives) helped transfer old typed information into the computer. John Frederick commented on a very early version of the translation. For many of the photographs that enrich this book, I am grateful to Ulrich von Schroeder, Hildegard Diemberger, Maria Antonia Sironi, Jon Garfunkel, Jerry and Betty Ann Sensabaugh, John McKinnon, Andy Quintman, Wolf Kahlen, Ani Lodrö Palmo, Hubert Decleer, Kunzang Olivier Brunet, David Jackson, and Moke Mokotoff. Decades apart, Jeff Watt, Jon Garfunkel, and Sarah Harding gave me precious gifts of Tangtong Gyalpo images that have inspired me along the way. I am particularly grateful to Sarah for reading parts of the nearly complete manuscript of the book and making helpful suggestions. My thanks also go to Steven Rhodes for his very skillful editorial suggestions and corrections, Gopa & Ted2 for the beautiful design of the book, and James Steinberg for the comprehensive index.

The translation of Tangtong Gyalpo's biography has been made from the standard Dergé edition of the Tibetan text. I have used a microfilm copy of the original eighteenth-century xylograph edition, the 1976 Indian traced reprint, and the 1982 typeset Tibetan reprint. The page numbers from the 1976 Indian reprint are included in the translation in brackets. With some exceptions (such as the Kangyur and Tengyur), citations from Tibetan works in the endnotes are identified by the arabic page numbers of published editions and the Tibetan folio numbers (1a, 1b, 2a, 2b, etc.) of unpublished texts. The Tibetan biography is a continuous narrative without any section or chapter divisions. I have divided the translated text into chapters and used appropriate phrases from the text itself as chapter headings.

Both the Tibetan text and a translation of the unique manuscript describing Tangtong Gyalpo's amazing death and the events that followed have been included at the end of this book. The original Tibetan text was in cursive *dbu med* script, which has been changed here to printed *dbu can* script using Sambhota software. Some obvious spelling mistakes have been corrected in the new edition, and the folio numbers from the original manuscript have been inserted into the text in brackets.

Many stories and much additional information about Tangtong Gyalpo that is found in other Tibetan sources have been put into the endnotes with the hope that they will enrich the reader's understanding of the translated biography. Familiar topics receive brief treatment (or none at all) in the endnotes, but unfamiliar subjects are explained in some detail. Some of the most significant spelling mistakes in the Tibetan text are corrected in the endnotes.

In the endnotes the various references from classical Indian works in the Kangyur and Tengyur are identified according to the numbers in the Tohoku catalogue of the Dergé edition of these collections: *A Complete Catalogue of the Tibetan Buddhist Canons (Bkaḥ-ḥgyur and Bstan-ḥgyur),* edited by Hakuju Ui, Munetada Suzuki, Yensho Kanakura, and Tokan Tada (Sendai: Tohoku Imperial University, 1934).

During this project, when rare texts and photographs have seemed to appear from nowhere just when needed, I have often thought of Edvard Radzinsky's telling comment: "How many times, working on these documents, have I encountered their mystical quality. It's like that saying 'The beast ran into the hunter.' I call it 'evoking documents.'"[2]

List of Illustrations

Number *Page*

1. The great adept Tangtong Gyalpo (1361?–1485). Fifteenth-century copper alloy image consecrated by the great adept himself. He holds a medicinal pill and a longevity vase. Published in Weldon and Singer (1999), p. 185. xx

2. Old woodcut print of Tangtong Gyalpo holding a chain and longevity vase. The most famous verse in praise of the great adept, written by the venerable lady Chökyi Drönmé (1422–55), is printed below. Private collection. 3

3. An iron link of the bridge over the Tsangpo River at Puntsok Ling. Photograph by Maria Antonia Sironi. Courtesy of Hildegard Diemberger. 5

4. Lochen Gyurmé Dechen (1540–1615) teaching the Six-branch Yoga to Yölmo Tulku (1598–1644). After a drawing by Yölmo Tulku himself. In Tenzin Norbu, Yölmo Tulku (Bstan 'dzin nor bu, Yol mo sprul sku), *Lute of Vajra Sound*, p. 48. 10

5. Tenzin Nyima Sangpo (b. 1436), Tangtong Gyalpo's son and Dharma heir. After a frontispiece in Gyurmé Dechen, Lochen ('Gyur med bde chen, Lo chen), *Beautiful Forms of Pure Faith*. 16

6. The great yoginī Machik Labdrön. Tangka published in Linrothe (2006), p. 173. 20

7. Four-armed Avalokiteśvara. Published in *Bod kyi thang ka*. Rigs dngos dpe skrun khang. N.p. n.d., p. 96. 22

8. A group of Aché Lhamo dancers. Photograph by Alexandra David-Néel, 1921–22. Published in Lhalungpa (1983), p. 99. 24

9. The upholder of pure awareness Gökyi Demtruchen (1337–1408). After Dudjom Rinpoche (1991), p. 781. ... 27

10. Hayagrīva. Tangka published in Jackson (1996), p. 274. ... 29

11. The iron bridge over the Kyichu River. Photograph by Hugh Richardson. After Tucci (1973), illustration 59. ... 34

12. Tangtong Gyalpo with alms bowl and iron chain. Fifteenth- or sixteenth-century copper image. Published in Kazi and Bartholomew (1965), plate 7. ... 35

13. Iron bridge over the Tsangpo River at Puntsok Ling. Photograph by Sven Hedin, 1907. Published in Lhalungpa (1983), p. 83. ... 36

14. Iron bridge at Toling. Photograph courtesy of John McKinnon. ... 39

15. The iron bridge at Chukha, Bhutan. Illustration by Lieut. Samuel Davis, 1793. After Turner (1971), facing p. 54. ... 43

16. Chains from an iron bridge in Paro, Bhutan. Photograph courtesy of Betty Ann and Jerry Sensabaugh. ... 44

17. The monastery and iron bridge at Chaksam Chuwori. Photograph by J. Claude White, 1904. Published in Lhalungpa (1983), p. 114. ... 45

18. Iron bridge at Chung Riwoché. After Kahlen (1990), p. 92. ... 47

19. The iron bridge at Dosum, eastern Bhutan. Photograph courtesy of Hubert Decleer. ... 49

20. Chung Riwoché. After Vitali (1990), plate 75. ... 52

21. Drawing of the Chung Riwoché complex before damage. After Kahlen (1990), p. 96. ... 55

22. Tachok Norbugang Monastery, Bhutan. Photograph courtesy of Kunzang Olivier Brunet. The iron bridge is a reconstruction of the original bridge that was washed away by a flood in 1969. ... 57

23. Tangtong Gyalpo holding an alms bowl, with a chain by his knee. Published in Linrothe (2006), p. 66. ... 59

24. Images of Tangtong Gyalpo awaiting consecration. Photograph courtesy of Jon Garfunkel. Drapchi Monastery, Lhasa, 1996....... 63

25. Dolpopa Sherab Gyaltsen (1292–1361). Early twentieth-century tangka. After front flyleaf of *Jo nang pa'i gdan rabs mdor bsdus drang srong rgan po'i zhal lung*, Beijing: Mi rigs dpe skrun khang, 2005........ 67

26. Tangtong Gyalpo holding a chain. Photograph courtesy of Wolf Kahlen........ 71

27. Tsang Nyön Heruka (1452–1507). Sixteenth-century gilt image. Published in Linrothe (2006), p. 373........ 73

28. Guru Padmasambhava. After Jackson (1996), p. 347........ 85

29. The great stūpa of Jonang. After Tucci (1973), illustration 79. Mistakenly identified as the Gyang stūpa........ 93

30. Guru Padmasambhava at the Copper-Colored Mountain. Tangka published in Jackson (1996), p. 374........ 99

31. Thousand-armed Avalokiteśvara. Published in *Bod kyi thang ka*. Rigs dngos dpe skrun khang. N.p. n.d., p. 98........ 113

32. The northern temples of Sakya Monastery. Photograph by Hugh Richardson. After Jackson (1996), p. 72........ 115

33. The great stūpa of Gyang. After Tucci (1967), p. 70........ 117

34. The Kyirong Jowo. Photograph courtesy of Andy Quintman........ 122

35. Svayambhūnāth Stūpa in Nepal. After Slusser (1982), vol. 2, plate 217........ 134

36. Cakrasaṃvara. Brass image, eastern India, twelfth century. Published in Singer and Denwood (1997), p. 247........ 135

37. The Vajrāsana, or Vajra Seat, at Bodhgayā. About mid-third century B.C. After Huntington (1985), p. 51........ 139

38. Ruins of a temple and stūpa at the ancient monastery of Nālandā. Late sixth-early seventh century. After Huntington (1985), p. 225........ 140

39. The Satmahal Pāsāda in Polonnaruva, Ceylon. Twelfth century. Photo by J. Lawton, 1870. Published in von Schroeder (1990), p. 654. 141

40. The great adept Śavaripa. Detail of an illuminated manuscript. Published in Huntington and Huntington (1990), plate 112. 142

41. The great adept Kukkuripa. After Tshe dbang rin chen, *Grub chen brgyad cu'i rnam thar dang zhal thang.* Lhasa: Bod ljongs mi dmangs dpe skrun khang, 2005, illustration 34. 144

42. Niguma, the ḍākinī of primordial awareness. Detail from a modern drawing by the artist Gega. 151

43. The great stūpa at Jonang. After Tucci (1973), illustration 78. Mistakenly identified as the Gyang stūpa. 162

44. The golden spires and pagoda roofs of the Rasa Trulnang, or Jokhang, temples. After Richardson (1998), plate 19. 168

45. White Tārā. Photograph by M. Ricard. Detail of a tangka published in Jackson (1996), p. 267. 170

46. The lord of yogins, Virūpa. Detail of a tangka published in Linrothe (2006), p. 29. 173

47. Vajradhara. After Jackson (1996), p. 131. 175

48. Mahākāla Pañjaranātha. Tangka published in Rhie and Thurman (1991), p. 222. 183

49. The holy Jowo image of Śākyamuni Buddha in Lhasa. After Batchelor (1987), p. 86. 193

50. The great stūpa of Tsel Gungtang. After Ferrari (1958), plate 11. 195

51. Eleven-faced Avalokiteśvara. Published in Rhie and Thurman (1991), p. 143. 199

52. The hermitages of Yerpa. After Batchelor (1987), p. 193. 205

53. The Samyé monastic complex. After Tucci (1956), facing p. 74. 207

54. Vajrapāṇi. Published in Singer and Denwood (1997), p. 113. 212

55. Vajrayoginī. Detail of an eleventh-twelfth-century tangka. Published in Kossak and Singer (1998), p. 98. 224

56. Chakpori Hill, Lhasa. Photograph by Brooke Dolan, 1942–43. Published in Lhalungpa (1983), p. 51. 249

57. Six-armed Mahākāla. Published in Rhie and Thurman (1991), p. 296. 251

58. The hermitage of Taktsang, Bhutan. After Bell (1968), facing p. 6. 253

59. The Dumtsé Stūpa of Paro, Bhutan. Photograph courtesy of Betty Ann and Jerry Sensabaugh. 255

60. Small stone image of Tangtong Gyalpo. Published in Aris (1980), p. 189. 258

61. The ruler Rabten Kunsang Pak (1389–1442). After the frontispiece in Jikmé Drakpa ('Jigs med grags pa), *Rain of Attainments for a Crop of Faith*. 260

62. Mount Kailash. Photo courtesy of John McKinnon. 264

63. The great yogin Milarepa. Detail of a late-eighteenth- to early-nineteenth-century tangka. After Rhie and Thurman (1991), p. 245. 272

64. The iron bridge of Chung Riwoché. Photograph courtesy of Wolf Kahlen. 274

65. The great adept Tilopa. After Jackson (1996), p. 305. 278

66. Ngorchen Kunga Sangpo (1382–1456). After Jackson (1996), p. 77. 279

67. Crossing the Tsangpo River in a coracle. After Tucci (1956), facing p. 34. 299

68. Four-armed Mahākāla. Published in Jackson (1996), p. 189. 303

69. Drigung Monastery. Photograph by Hugh Richardson. After Jackson (1996), p. 339. 305

70. Mahottara Heruka. After Dudjom Rinpoche (1991), p. 484. 313

71. Five-Peaked Mount Wutai. Tourist map of Wutaishan looking from the south. After Tuttle (2006). 316

72. The monastic complex of Pal Khorlo Dechen, Gyantsé. After Batchelor (1987), p. 280. 349

73. The great Kalkī Namgyal Draksang (1395–1475). Published in Pal (2001), p. 297. 356

74. Amitāyus. Published in Rhie and Thurman (1999), p. 464 369

75. The venerable lady Chökyi Drönmé (1422–55). Detail of a mural in the small gallery of Nyemo Monastery. Photograph courtesy of Hildegard Diemberger. 379

76. The great stūpa of Chung Riwoché before recent repairs. After Vitali (1990), plate 76. 381

77. The Great Temple of Sakya. After Jackson (1996), p. 72. 413

List of Plates

Between pages 332 and 333

1. The great adept Tangtong Gyalpo (1361?–1485). Fifteenth-century copper alloy image consecrated by the great adept himself. He holds a medicinal pill and a longevity vase. Published in Weldon and Singer (1999), p. 185.
2. Tangtong Gyalpo's great stūpa at Chung Riwoché after repairs. Photograph by Maria Antonia Sironi. Courtesy of Hildegard Diemberger.
3. Tangtong Gyalpo holding an iron chain. Detail of a tangka of the fifteenth-century Taklung Kagyü master Sangyé Drakpa. Photograph courtesy of Ulrich von Schroeder.
4. The iron bridge over the Tsangpo River at Puntsok Ling. Photograph by Maria Antonia Sironi. Courtesy of Hildegard Diemberger.
5. Image of Tangtong Gyalpo holding a longevity vase. Fifteenth-century bronze image. After Christie's Indian and Southeast Asian Art catalogue, New York, September 17, 1999, p. 61.
6. Chung Riwoché. After Vitali (1990), plate 75.
7. Tangka of Tangtong Gyalpo in the tradition of the Heartdrop of the Great Adept. Photograph courtesy of Ani Lodrö Palmo.
8. Tangtong Gyalpo's iron bridge and great stūpa at Chung Riwoché. Photograph by Maria Antonia Sironi. Courtesy of Hildegard Diemberger.
9. Image of Tangtong Gyalpo holding a medicinal pill and longevity vase. Fifteenth-century image in the Potala collection. Photograph courtesy of Ulrich von Schroeder. Published in von Schroeder (2001), plate 276-D.
10. Iron suspension bridge near Shang, in Tsang. Photograph courtesy of Moke Mokotoff.

1. The great adept Tangtong Gyalpo (1361?–1485). Fifteenth-century copper alloy image consecrated by the great adept himself.

Introduction

1. The Life and the Lifespan

Countless Buddhist teachers and practitioners have appeared over the centuries in the snowy land of Tibet. None have made a deeper impact on the combined religious, artistic, and technological history of the country than the great adept *(mahāsiddha, grub chen)* Tangtong Gyalpo, "King of the Empty Plain" (Thang stong rgyal po, 1361?–1485). This heroic figure became legendary because of his contributions to the mystical traditions, his exceptionally long life, and his innovative achievements in the fields of art, architecture, and metallurgy. Tangtong's life and teachings are intertwined with divine madness, visionary revelation, demon exorcism, the quest for immortality, the relationship of human beings with their environment, and the process of ultimate enlightenment. He is famous in Tibet and the Himalayan regions for building many iron suspension bridges and is thus known by the epithet "Iron-Bridge Man" (Lcags zam pa). The great master also constructed many stūpas—architectural symbols of enlightened mind—that were strategically located according to geomantic principles in order to control the wild energy of the landscape. Several of his monasteries in Tibet and Bhutan are still famous at the beginning of the twenty-first century.

Tangtong Gyalpo is said to have lived 125 years as a result of his perfection of meditative techniques for achieving longevity.[3] These methods have been passed down as the most efficacious and popular such practices in Tibetan Buddhism. His other systems of meditation, in particular those of Avalokiteśvara and Vajravārāhī, are still practiced after more than five hundred years. He is known as a mental emanation of Guru Padmasambhava and is believed to have recovered numerous caches of hidden treasure teachings *(gter ma)* concealed by the Indian master. His nonsectarian activities and teachings have earned him a special position in all the Buddhist traditions of Tibet.

Tangtong Gyalpo was also called "Madman of the Empty Valley" (Lung stong smyon pa), one of five names given to him by the ḍākinīs in recognition of his spiritual attainments. This title indicates that he was one of the most important of the "mad adepts" who have been prominent in Tibetan history. He is remembered today as a charismatic figure of dark maroon complexion with long white hair and beard, dressed only in a single cloak, provocative in both appearance and behavior. His reputation as a formidable sorcerer is clearly retained in the popular Gesar legends, where he is identified with the White Old Man, while the tradition of his attainment of immortality is reflected in the opera performances of the Aché Lhamo, which he is said to have created as entertainment for the people while his iron bridges were being built.

This book is divided into two sections. The introductory section contains four parts. The first part focuses primarily on the various biographical sources concerning Tangtong Gyalpo and then examines the question of his incredible lifespan. The second part investigates his widespread Dharma legacy. The results of research into Tangtong's unprecedented bridge-building career are presented in the third part, along with a discussion of his various stūpas, monasteries, and other architectural and artistic achievements. The final part seeks to explain his eccentric behavior in the context of the tantric tradition of "crazy wisdom" that came to full flower in Tibet during his lifetime.

The second and major section of the book contains a complete translation of the most famous biography of Tangtong Gyalpo, written in 1609 by his descendant Lochen Gyurmé Dechen (1540–1615). The biography is followed by the Tibetan text and English translation of a unique manuscript describing Tangtong's amazing death, written by Kunga Sönam Drakpa Palsang, who was the son of the only witness to the great adept's nirvāṇa.

Biographical Sources

The wealth of information in Tibetan literature about the life of Tangtong Gyalpo is nearly overwhelming. The main biographies contain more than eighteen hundred pages of stories and historical material that is always fascinating, but often contradictory. Some writings of Tangtong himself that have been preserved in the oldest biographies written by three of his students are particulary significant. Several other brief biographical sketches by other disciples are available, and many later writers composed summaries of his life.

2. Old woodcut print of Tangtong Gyalpo holding a chain and longevity vase.

The earliest text concerning Tangtong Gyalpo's life, ostensibly first spoken by Guru Padmasambhava in the eighth century, is the *Bright Lamp of Prophecy (Lung bstan gsal ba'i sgron me)*, also referred to as a "biographical prophecy."[4] This work is one of the treasure texts that Padmasambhava is believed to have left in Tibet for Tangtong to discover. Padmasambhava spoke some portions of the *Bright Lamp* when he appeared in a vision while Tangtong was in a six-year meditation retreat from 1422 until 1428. By the end of the retreat, Tangtong had written a long scroll recording many of the visions and prophecies he had received concerning his future activities.

But when he read the scroll aloud to more than five hundred people, they all looked into each other's eyes, clapped their hands in amusement, and rolled from side to side howling with laughter. Everyone thought he had gone insane during the retreat and dismissed any possibility of the prophecies being true.[5] Tangtong later recovered the original text of the *Bright Lamp* from a treasure trove in the holy region of Tsari sometime after 1444. Although the *Bright Lamp* is often quoted in later works concerning Tangtong and his teachings, the text itself has been preserved in large part only in the biography of Tangtong written by his disciples Könchok Palsang and Dewa Sangpo.[6] Perhaps this prophetic treasure text was among the prophecies that Tangtong instructed Dewa Sangpo to memorize and only write down later after his return to Bhutan.[7] This would explain why the *Bright Lamp* is never quoted in the other early biography written by Tangtong's disciple Sherab Palden.

The fascinating edicts *(bka' shog)* of Tangtong Gyalpo are the original sources for other details that appear in the biographies. Tangtong made these declarations to kings and ministers, monks and patrons, gods and demons. A number of the edicts are found in complete form, including colophons, in the major biographies by his disciples that will be discussed separately below.[8] Another is preserved in the biography of Tangtong's consort Jetsun Chökyi Drönmé (1422–55).[9] Taken as a whole, these edicts are the largest group of his writings, but only a few of the least significant are actually copied or quoted in the biography that is translated in this book. Unique information about Tangtong's early life and travels, his building activities, and his thoughts about the times in which he lived are found in the edicts. These extraordinary documents are also where his character is most vividly revealed, and contain penetrating and informal comments about human nature and the essential teachings of Buddhism.

The edicts were used for various purposes. As described in the translated biography, Tangtong Gyalpo once gave a written edict, an iron link, a banner of the Dharma protectors, and an image of the bodhisattva Avalokiteśvara to each of a group of disciples and sent them to collect offerings for the building of iron bridges. On another occasion he gave disciples an image of himself, a model of an Auspicious Stūpa of Many Doors, and an edict, and sent them with a prayer to recite at Sakya to dispel an epidemic. The edict he gave to his consort Chökyi Drönmé began with two lines of Tangtong's actual handwriting and ended with two more lines. Presumably the rest of the text was written by a scribe. Three small

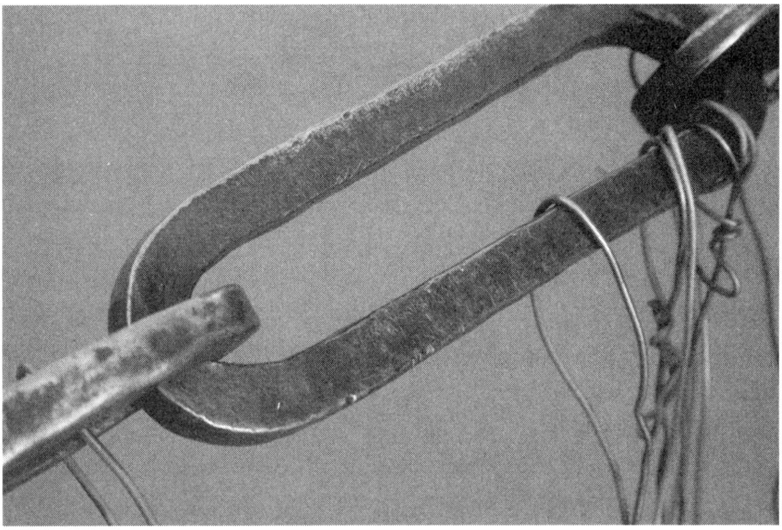

3. An iron link of the bridge over the Tsangpo River at Puntsok Ling.

pieces of gold, turquoise, and coral were attached to the bottom of the sheet of paper, which was wrapped in a silk scarf. Along with the edict, Tangtong also gave Chökyi Drönmé the gift of a blessed iron link from the chain of an iron bridge, which he had hammered and forged himself from a large quantity of needles and carried around Kongpo twice during his travels.[10]

In other edicts, Tangtong Gyalpo specifically mentions that he made twenty-eight distant journeys, ranging from Mount Wutai (Wutaishan) in China to the east, Tāmradvīpa (Ceylon?) and the famous pilgrimage site of Śrīparvata (Śrīśailam?) to the south in India, the area of Kashmir to the west, and four border regions to the north of Tibet. He also describes his visit to the region of Kāmata (Kāmarūpa) in eastern India and says he traveled around many parts of the Indian subcontinent, going even as far as the Turkic Qarlug (Gar log) areas on the way home to his monastery of Riwoché in western Tibet.[11] Tangtong is traditionally believed to have been the most widely traveled person in Tibetan history.

Several of Tangtong Gyalpo's disciples wrote about their teacher's life.[12] The most important and extensive biographies were written by three major disciples: Könchok Palsang, Dewa Sangpo, and Sherab Palden. The *Bright Lamp (Gsal ba'i sgron me)*, a name obviously borrowed from the biographical prophecy mentioned above, was originally written at Tangtong's monastery of Riwoché by Könchok Palsang, who was from nearby Ngamring in the same district of Latö Jang in western Tsang.[13] In about 1433, Tangtong had left Könchok Palsang to supervise the completion of the Samdrup Temple at Pari. Much later, Könchok Palsang and another disciple named Dewa Sangpo were sent at the head of a delegation to represent Tangtong in the Indic region of Kāmata and to continue the work of converting the King of Kāmata to Buddhism.[14] The biography initially composed by Könchok Palsang was later supplemented and revised by Dewa Sangpo, who was from Paro in Bhutan. Dewa Sangpo's descendants became the leaders of Tangtong's Chaksam (Lcags zam) or "Iron Bridge" tradition in Bhutan,[15] based at the monastery of Tachok Norbugang, where Dewa Sangpo also completed the revised biography. This work does not mention Tangtong's death, although it does describe his son Nyima Sangpo's construction of the iron bridge at Nyago, which took place in 1485.[16] Thus the biography must have been written after 1485, but before 1517, when it was finally revealed at Riwoché that Tangtong had died thirty-two years before. According to the colophon of the sole surviving manuscript, Dewa Sangpo supplemented Könchok Palsang's original work with the personal statements of Tangtong and his consort Chökyi Drönmé, specifically those of a visionary and prophetic nature and those concerning Tangtong's memories of previous lifetimes.[17] The text also contains much autobiographical information that Tangtong told the two authors. This is explicitly mentioned at several points, and Dewa Sangpo sometimes refers to himself by name as the recipient of Tangtong's autobiographical comments.[18]

The anonymous work entitled *All-Illuminating Lamp (Kun gsal sgron me)* is almost certainly the original biography composed by Könchok Palsang that was later edited and enlarged by Dewa Sangpo under the new title of *Bright Lamp (Gsal ba'i sgron me)*. Although the *All-Illuminating Lamp* is anonymous, the colophon does specify that it was written at Riwoché according to the command of Tangtong Gyalpo himself, as "a great wind to blow away" other unreliable biographies.[19] When this text is compared to the *Bright Lamp*, it is easy to see what additional information was included in the new work by Dewa Sangpo. For example, the original *All-Illuminating Lamp* is a straight narrative of Tangtong's life, whereas Dewa Sangpo divided the revised work into 108 chapters and gave each a title. The original work does not include any quotations from Padmasambhava's *Bright Lamp of Prophecy (Lung bstan gsal ba'i sgron me)* or Chökyi Drönmé's biographical supplication to Tangtong, around which Dewa Sangpo's expanded text was later structured. Dewa Sangpo also added seventy-eight pages of material to the beginning of his revised biography, which he describes in the colophon as "the oral transmission of the dharmakāya reality body of Amitabha." These pages are filled with prophetic and visionary teachings related to the Nyingma treasure tradition, and may yet prove to be from some of Tangtong's own lost treasure teachings. The original *All-Illuminating Lamp* also does not mention the woman Khandroma Sengé (Tangtong's consort who gave birth to his son Nyima Sangpo), nor does it tell the story of his consort Chökyi Drönmé's visit to Riwoché and final trip to Kongpo.[20] Nearly the entire *All-Illuminating Lamp* has been retained in the *Bright Lamp*, but there are some tidbits of information in the earlier work that are not found anywhere else.[21]

The other early and indispensable biography of Tangtong Gyalpo, entitled *Ocean of Marvels (Ngo mtshar rgya mtsho)*, was composed by his disciple Sherab Palden.[22] Sherab Palden, like Könchok Palsang, was from the Jang capital of Ngamring. He belonged to a prominent family of physicians and studied with the famous physician and Kālacakra expert Namgyal Draksang (1395–1475), who was the ruler at Ngamring.[23] As a young boy, Sherab Palden also received the Kālacakra initiations from Paṇḍita Vanaratna (1384–1468) during the Indian master's third trip to Tibet in 1453–54. Sherab Palden went to Riwoché when he was twenty-six years old and met Tangtong Gyalpo. For sixteen years he served Tangtong as personal attendant and, presumably, physician, and was the only witness to his death. According to Tangtong's instructions, Sherab Palden and the great adept's son, Tenzin Nyima Sangpo (b. 1436), concealed his death for the next thirty-two years. During this period Sherab Palden served as Tangtong's regent at Riwoché. Finally, in the Fire Ox Year (1517), Tangtong's remains were placed in a silver stūpa as their final resting place.[24] Since the last date mentioned in Sherab Palden's work is 1484,[25] he almost certainly wrote his biography of Tangtong during the period between 1485 and 1517, while it was generally believed that the master was still alive.

Sherab Palden's biography of his teacher contains a large amount of crucial information that must have come directly from Tangtong Gyalpo.[26] He repeatedly refers the reader to other sources that he says contain more detail on specific points, and mentions the existence of many biographical writings by different experts concerning Tangtong's life. He also mentions Tangtong's extensive personal statements (a reference to the edicts?), prophecies, and other writings contained in the "great collected works" *(bka' 'bum chen mo)*, which does not seem to have survived. Sherab Palden says he wrote the biography at Riwoché when he was thirty-six years old.[27] The last date he mentions in the biography is 1484, the year before Tangtong's death. However, Gyurmé Dechen and Sangyé Gyatso both say that Sherab Palden was twenty-six years old when he came to Riwoché and that he served as Tangtong's attendant for sixteen years. So Sherab Palden would have presumably been forty-one years old at the time of Tangtong's death in 1485, which is not mentioned in his biography. One of the sources about Sherab Palden's age is obviously incorrect, and it does not seem possible to resolve this conflict without access to further information.

At some point after 1517, when the news that Tangtong Gyalpo had died in 1485 finally became general knowledge, Sherab Palden's son, Kunga Sönam Drakpa Palsang, wrote the *Final Story Concerning the Nirvāṇa of the Great Adept (Grub thob chen po'i rnam thar phyi ma mya ngan las 'das pa'i skor)*, an extremely important supplement to his father's biography of Tangtong.[28] The Tibetan text and a translation of this unique work are provided at the end of this book. Kunga Sönam's supplement is a detailed description of Tangtong's death, the thirty-two-year period of secrecy that followed, and the events in 1517 after the announcement of the master's passing. Kunga Sönam must have received most of this information directly from his father, Sherab Palden, who was the only witness to Tangtong's miraculous death. All later stories of Tangtong's nirvāṇa are based only on Kunga Sönam's work, which is also the original source for the date of Tangtong's death and his age at the time. Kunga Sönam wrote his supplement at the request of a certain Lodrö Gyaltsen, who was a descendant of Tangtong Gyalpo. Although this work is not dated, it was perhaps written between 1517 and 1528, or shortly thereafter, because a versified biographical supplication summarizing the major events in Tangtong's life as described in Sherab Palden's biography was written by Kunga Sönam in 1528 and also mentions Tangtong's wondrous nirvāṇa.[29]

The last major biography of Tangtong Gyalpo, which is translated in this book, was completed at Riwoché by his descendant Lochen Gyurmé Dechen (1540–1615) in 1609, 125 years after Tangtong's death. *A Jewel Mirror in Which All Is Clear (Kun gsal nor bu'i me long)* is the only biography of Tangtong that was ever cut onto woodblocks and published in Tibet. Almost everything written about Tangtong during the last four hundred years seems to have been based on Gyurmé Dechen's work. The earlier biographies by Tangtong's disciples were very rare manuscripts and were never widely available until two of them were finally published in Bhutan in 1984. Gyurmé Dechen's work is essentially an edited and abridged synthesis of these early works. In this respect, he has tried to make sense of the extremely different accounts in the ancient sources and create a coherent story. When comparing his work with the earlier biographies, it is clear that the sequence of many events is extremely different. Some episodes in the older works have also been combined, and dates have been made more explicit. The most important of these points will be addressed in the notes to the translation. Gyurmé Dechen also had access to other sources that further informed his account. For example, his description of Tangtong's death is derived from the original record written by Kunga Sönam Drakpa Palsang, although Gyurmé Dechen does not acknowledge this earlier work. Gyurmé Dechen does say that he based his account on ancient works written by five different people who had asked Tangtong himself about his life, but does not identify these sources.[30] Three of the people must have been Könchok Palsang, Dewa Sangpo, and Sherab Palden. Since the work of Könchok Palsang and Dewa Sangpo is structured around the versified biographical supplication to Tangtong written by Chökyi Drönmé, she is probably the fourth person. If Sherab Palden's son, Kunga Sönam Drakpa Palsang, met Tangtong, he may have been the fifth. Gyurmé Dechen's biography was first cut onto woodblocks and printed at the monastery of Riwoché, perhaps in the seventeenth century. In the late eighteen century, this original Riwoché edition was proofread and substantially edited by Tenzin Gyaltsen (fl. 1759–71), a famous Sanskrit scholar of Shechen Monastery in eastern Tibet. The new edition was published by the printing house of Dergé and became the standard biography.[31]

Lochen Gyurmé Dechen was recognized as an emanation of the Indian master Maitrīpa and was one of the most respected teachers of his time, especially of the Kālacakra practices and the teachings of the Shangpa Kagyü tradition.[32] According to his versified autobiography written at Riwoché, Gyurmé Dechen's most important master was Lochen Ratnabhadra (1489–1563), from whom he received many transmissions, such as the Path with the Result (Lam 'bras) according to the Sakya tradition and, in particular, the Six-branch Yoga of the Kālacakra, probably according to the Jonang system.[33] He meditated on the Six-branch Yoga in retreat for four years and eight months. Gyurmé Dechen studied and meditated extensively on the teachings of the Sakya tradition in general under the

4. Lochen Gyurmé Dechen (1540–1615) teaching the Six-branch Yoga to Yölmo Tulku (1598–1644).

guidance of Jetsun Tsemo, from whom he received the Path with the Result of the Sakya lineage and the Shangpa teachings of Niguma. He also completed the Hevajra retreat according to the Path with the Result. He studied with many other teachers of different Tibetan traditions, such as Jonang Kunga Drolchok (1507-66), who taught him the instructions of Niguma, and Lhatong Lotsāwa Shenyen Namgyal (b. 1512). As indicated by his epithet "Lochen" (Great Translator), Gyurmé Dechen was a master of Sanskrit language and the various fields of scholastic knowledge. He also became the royal preceptor *(ti shri)* of Namkha Tsewang Puntsok Wangi Gyalpo, the governor of the Jang district in which Riwoché was located.[34]

Gyurmé Dechen passed various teachings to a number of special disciples who continued the lineages. Among his most important students were the Sakya master Panchen Ngawang Chödrak (1572-1641) and the Nyingma master Yölmo Tulku Tenzin Norbu (1598-1644). Gyurmé Dechen recognized Ngawang Chödrak as his main heir for the Six Dharmas of Niguma and other transmissions of the Shangpa Kagyü tradition. Ngawang Chödrak later wrote instruction manuals on the various Shangpa practices according to Tangtong Gyalpo's teachings.[35] Yölmo Tulku received many teachings from Gyurmé Dechen, especially the practices of the Six-branch Yoga of Kālacakra. Gyurmé Dechen also gave Tangtong's monastic complex at Riwoché to Yölmo Tulku.[36] Gyurmé Dechen's main heir in the fields of scholastic knowledge was Taktsang Lotsāwa Ratna Sengé.[37] Although Gyurmé Dechen wrote many texts, his most enduring literary composition would turn out to be his biography of Tangtong Gyalpo, which was the last major study of the master's life.[38]

A Tibetan Methuselah

The dates for Tangtong Gyalpo's birth and death and the tradition of his lifespan of 125 years have long been controversial. Like the Biblical patriarch Methuselah, who is said to have lived 969 years (Genesis 5:27), Tangtong has become the archetype for longevity in Tibetan lore. The great adept himself obviously promoted and cultivated the idea that he had gained control of his lifespan and was immortal. The following exchange occurred late in his life when he was asked a direct question about his age:

> A powerful scholar of dialectics said, "The initiation was a great blessing. O great adept, how many years old are you?"
>
> "From when I was born to my mother, up until now," the great adept replied. "I can be old and I can be young. I haven't counted the years since I was born to my mother. To display emanations that are old, young, or in the prime of life, it doesn't matter how many years have passed."[39]

The fact that Tangtong Gyalpo either did not know his exact age or purposely declined to tell people how old he was certainly makes it very difficult to determine when he was born. However, the date of his death can now be known with certainty. The first writer to mention Tangtong's death was Kunga Sönam Drakpa Palsang, the son of Tangtong's disciple and biographer Sherab Palden, who says Tangtong was 128 years old at his death.[40] The lifespan of about 138 years mentioned by the Ngor abbot Sangyé Puntsok (1649–1705) seems to be the longest attributed to the great adept.[41] The Sakya master Shuchen Tsultrim Rinchen (1697–1774) wrote that some people believed Tangtong was still alive in the eighteenth century, while others thought that he had ascended to the paradise of Khecara without discarding his body.[42] No classical Tibetan source says he lived less than 125 years, which is the figure given in Gyurmé Dechen's biography. Almost every Tibetan writer since that time has simply accepted this number, although there has been some disagreement about the specific dates of birth and death.[43] Among European and American scholars, the generally accepted dates for Tangtong Gyalpo have been 1385–1464.[44]

The biography by Gyurmé Dechen says Tangtong Gyalpo was born in an Iron Female Ox Year (1361) and died in the Wood Female Snake Year of the eighth cycle of the Tibetan calendar (1485). Gyurmé Dechen specifically says Tangtong lived for two sixty-year calendar cycles plus five single years, and that if the extra months and days of the irregular Tibetan calendar were counted, it could be considered that he lived to be 128 years old.[45] This biography established the dates for the birth and death of the great adept, and the tradition of the 125-year lifespan. But how did Gyurmé Dechen reach his conclusions?

None of the oldest biographies of Tangtong Gyalpo give a date for his birth or mention his death. But in the old biography by Sherab Palden, the Earth Male Dragon Year of 1484 is specifically mentioned twice when presenting a final list of Tangtong's accomplishments.[46] This is significant because Sherab Palden had first-hand knowledge of many events and was the only witness to the great adept's death. Gyurmé Dechen also mentions the dates of 1484 and 1485,[47] and says that in the beginning of a Snake Year—clearly 1485—Tangtong sent his son and heir Tenzin Nyima Sangpo (b. 1436) to begin the construction of an iron bridge at Nyago. The last date in the biography is for Tangtong's miraculous death in the Wood Snake Year of 1485.[48]

All this information is found only in Tangtong Gyalpo's biographies, but other independent sources also contain important material. All three biographies of the mad yogin Tsang Nyön Heruka (1452–1507), written by his direct disciples, mention that he traveled as a young man to Riwoché to meet Tangtong.[49] The biography by Lhatsun Rinchen Namgyal (1473–1557) specifies that Tsang Nyön was twenty-five years old (twenty-four according to Western calculation) at the time. Tsang Nyön was born in 1452, and so the meeting must have occurred in 1476. The scene described in these accounts fits very well with the descriptions found in Tangtong's biographies, where the old master is shown spending his last years at Riwoché in near seclusion.

Gyurmé Dechen seems to have based his computations concerning the dates of Tangtong Gyalpo's birth and death on one crucial piece of information. In the early sixteenth century, Kunga Sönam Drakpa Palsang had written that the great adept died at the age of 128, on the fourth day of the first month of a Snake Year.[50] Kunga Sönam must have received this information directly from his father, Sherab Palden, who was the only witness to Tangtong's death. A Snake Year occurs every twelve years in the Tibetan calendar, so without further information it is not possible to be certain about this date. However, Kunga Sönam also mentions that Tangtong's son Tenzin Nyima Sangpo returned to Riwoché after building the iron bridge at Nyangpo (Nyang po)—a common variation for Nyago (Nya mgo)—only to find that his father had died during his absence.[51]

One of the oldest biographies of Tangtong Gyalpo describes, but does not give a date for, the construction of the Nyago bridge during the master's lifetime.[52] It is absolutely certain that this bridge was built in the Wood Snake Year of 1485. According to an early history, the Pakmodru ruler Ngagi Wangpo (1439–91) built the long iron bridge at the ferry crossing at Nyangpo (=Nyago).[53] The modern Tibetan historian Losang Trinlé clarifies this point by saying Ngagi Wangpo provided the necessary assistance for Tangtong to build the iron bridge.[54] The Pakmodru ruler Ngagi Wangpo, who was present at the completion of the bridge, did not come to power until 1481, and died in 1491. The only Snake Year during his reign was the Wood Snake Year of 1485,[55] which is also the date given for Tangtong's death in the biography written by Lochen Gyurmé Dechen.

The question of Tangtong Gyalpo's birth is much more difficult. It seems probable that Gyurmé Dechen used three key pieces of information to determine the birth date. The first and most important point is that Tangtong was 128 years old (as explained above) when he died in 1485. The second is that Padmasambhava's *Bright Lamp of Prophecy* (recovered by Tangtong himself), says he was born in an Ox Year.[56] The third point is that Tangtong once said, "In my last life I was called Dolpopa the Omniscient, but in this life I am called Crazy Tsöndru."[57] Tangtong's declaration is important because he was speaking to an audience that was well aware of when the famous Jonangpa master Dolpopa Sherab Gyaltsen (1292–1361) had died.

According to Gyurmé Dechen, the age of 128, which is found in the original description of Tangtong Gyalpo's death, was calculated by including the extra months and days of the irregular Tibetan calendar. Without counting those extra months and days, which is not usually done, Tangtong lived for 125 years. By counting back 125 years (instead of 128) from 1485, Gyurmé Dechen arrived at the Ox Year of 1361. In the biography, he specifically says Tangtong was born on the tenth day of the first month of the Iron Ox Year (1361). Dolpopa Sherab Gyaltsen died on the sixth day of the eleventh month of the Iron Ox Year (1361). According to these dates, Tangtong was born almost ten months before the death of Dolpopa, whose rebirth he claimed to be! According to Dezhung Rinpoché, this is referred to as an "emanated body prior to passing away" *(ma 'das sprul sku)*. For Gyurmé Dechen, the combination of the death date of 1485, the lifespan of 125 years, the prophecy of Tangtong's birth in an Ox Year, and his own statement that he was the rebirth of Dolpopa, meant he had definitely been born in the Iron Ox Year of 1361.

Without further evidence concerning when the great adept was born, the only reason to question the dates presented by Gyurmé Dechen in the biography translated in this book is simply the difficulty of accepting a 125-year lifespan. Whatever the case, it is obvious that Tangtong Gyalpo did live an exceptionally long life. This is frequently mentioned in all of his biographies. The tradition of his longevity should not be dismissed by using the argument that such a long life was attributed to him simply to instill confidence in practitioners of his longevity techniques (such as the *Glorious Giver of Immortality*) that they too could live to a ripe old age. It is more probable that his teachings were treasured and passed down through the centuries in Tibet precisely because of his longevity. It is traditionally believed that certain auspicious connections were brought into alignment because Tangtong achieved control of his own lifespan, as a result of which many of his disciples also lived very long lives.[58]

2. King of the Empty Plain

With maroon and wrathful body,
you destroy the hordes of Māra.
With charismatic gazes,
you maintain deliberate behavior.
A hidden yogin,
you are the protector of all beings.
Prophesied by the Teacher of Uḍḍiyāna,
you are the best of men, an emanated body.
I pray at the feet of Tangtong Gyalpo,
King of the Empty Plain.[59]

—Chökyi Drönmé

Tangtong Gyalpo is said to have mastered the practices of all the religious systems in Tibet, and the transmission of his teachings reflects this eclectic approach. His own blend of the various traditions he inherited, influenced by his numerous visions of the divine, came to be known as the Chaksam, or Iron-Bridge, Tradition (Lcags zam lugs). Tangtong's tradition was centered at his main monasteries of Chuwori in Central Tibet and Riwoché in Tsang, but also existed as an even more independent school in Bhutan, where the Chaksam was listed side by side with the major orders such as the Sakya, Nyingma, and Kagyü. However, the Chaksam tradition in Bhutan remained cohesive and powerful only until the time of Shabdrung Ngawang Namgyal (1594–1651), the founder of the Drukpa Kagyü tradition in that country, who had it suppressed for political reasons. The tradition has survived in Bhutan under the leadership of the Tachok Chöjé, but with nothing approaching the influence of bygone centuries.

The teachings of Tangtong Gyalpo's Iron-Bridge tradition have come down to the present day as currents found in virtually all the major Buddhist schools in Tibet. After Tangtong, the tradition was led by hierarchs bearing the title Tenzin (Bstan 'dzin, Upholder of the Doctrine) or Iron-Bridge Man (Lcags zam pa), who have made their seat at Chuwori in Central Tibet.[60] On the basis of prophecies by his teacher Rendawa (1349–1412) and the advice of various deities and humans, Tangtong entrusted the transmission of his system of Dharma and the responsibility for the upkeep of his many artistic and architectural accomplishments to his hereditary descendants.[61] In 1456 Tangtong Gyalpo enthroned his son the monk Tenzin Nyima Sangpo as his successor at Riwoché Monastery. He placed his hopes for a continuation of the family line in his son Döndrup Sangpo, and sent another son, Kyabpa Sangpo, to occupy the monastic seat of the Tsagong Monastery in Kongpo. His nephew and disciple, Jampa Nyendrak, was appointed as general administrator of the network of bridges, monasteries, and stūpas that Tangtong had constructed. Therefore, it is puzzling to find that his Dharma teachings were not passed down through Tenzin Nyima Sangpo or any other family members.[62] The precise role of his descendants in regard to the transmission of his teachings is somewhat nebulous.

The line of Tenzin title-holders had their ecclesiastical residence at Chaksam Monastery on Chuwori in Central Tibet, a more convenient location for the main monastery than that of Riwoché in the far west. Almost nothing is known about Tangtong Gyalpo's son and designated

5. Tenzin Nyima Sangpo (b. 1436), Tangtong Gyalpo's son and Dharma heir.

heir, Tenzin Nyima Sangpo (b. 1436), except what is found in his father's biographies. Although a biography of him once existed,[63] it has apparently been lost. Nyima Sangpo's mother was an extraordinary woman, a ḍākinī called Khandroma Sengé, whom Tangtong met when he was studying with Ka Ngapa Paljor Sherab.[64] According to the Fifth Dalai Lama, Tenzin Nyima Sangpo's body was later enshrined in a golden reliquary in the inner sanctuary of Tangtong's temple on Chakpori Hill in Lhasa.[65]

Because Tangtong Gyalpo specifically designated Nyima Sangpo as his Dharma heir, and because the title *Tenzin* is often found preceding his name, it might be assumed that the later Tenzin title-holders at Chuwori were Nyima Sangpo's reincarnations. This does not seem to have been the case. Jamyang Khyentsé Wangpo (1820–92), who studied with the eighth Chaksam Tulku, Tenzin Khyenrap Tutob, and would certainly have known about his teacher's incarnation line, is extremely clear about their identity:

> The practice center of Tsechu at Chaksam Chuwori was founded by Tangtongpa. The monastic seat has been successively held by the Chaksam Tulkus, who are reincarnations of the spiritual son Kyobpa Sangpo. Many great learned and realized masters such as Tenzin Yeshé Lhundrup have appeared.[66]

As mentioned above, Kyabpa (or Kyobpa) Sangpo was not only Tangtong Gyalpo's spiritual son *(thugs sras)*, but one of his physical sons *(sku'i sras)*. Khyentsé Wangpo's statement leaves no room for doubt that the leaders of the Chaksam tradition were recognized as the rebirths of Tangtong's son Kyabpa Sangpo, not the great adept himself or his son Nyima Sangpo. And yet, Situ Chökyi Gyatso (1880–1925) mentions a series of images at Chuwori depicting "the nine lives of the spiritual son Tenzin Rinpoché," which is how Nyima Sangpo is often named in Tangtong's biographies.[67] Until more detailed information appears, this question still remains troublesome.

Only one of the Tenzin title-holders at Chuwori was definitely a descendant of Tangtong Gyalpo. Tenzin Nyida Sangpo, who studied with the Jonang master Kunga Drolchok (1507–66), is referred to as an "upholder of the adept's hereditary line" *(grub rigs 'dzin pa* and *grub rigs 'chang),* a phrase often used to indicate Tangtong's descendants. The greatest figure of the later lineage was the seventh Chaksam hierarch Tenzin Yeshé Lhundrup (b. 1738), who was also the heir to the treasure tradition of Drimé Lingpa (d. 1775).[68] For the three-hundred-year period between Tenzin Nyima Sangpo and Tenzin Yeshé Lhundrup information about the leaders of the Chaksam tradition is very scarce. No histories of the tradition have survived (if any were ever written) and no biographies of anyone after Tangtong except Yeshé Lhundrup.[69] The names of different Chaksam hierarchs are mentioned in various histories and biographies, but little else is known about them.[70]

Tangtong Gyalpo's western monastery of Riwoché also continued to be an important center for the propagation of his teachings, and his disciple Sherab Palden lived there as Tangtong's first regent. In the following centuries, Tangtong's descendants such as Gyurmé Dechen and Ngawang Yongdrak (1714–67) continued to live and teach at Riwoché, which was the main residence of the great adept's hereditary line. At least one of the Tenzin title-holders at Chuwori, Tenzin Nyida Sangpo, was also recognized from among these paternal descendants. Guru Tashi's history of the Nyingma tradition, mostly written in the early nineteenth century, contains a crucial statement about Riwoché:

> Chung Riwoché was initially founded by the great adept Tangtong Gyalpo. Then it was successively upheld by his hereditary line until Lochen Gyurmé Dechen offered it to the Yölmo treasure revealer Tenzin Norbu. After that, the monastic seat was successively held by the treasure revealer's younger brother, Gam Nyön Chakdor Norbu, and the Gam Nyön Tulkus.[71]

This passage shows that Tangtong Gyalpo's descendants were in charge of Riwoché until Gyurmé Dechen offered the monastery to his disciple, the third Yölmo Tulku, Tenzin Norbu (1598–1644), in the early seventeenth century. Then the monastic seat was held by Yölmo Tulku's brother Gam Nyön Chakdor Norbu and his successive reincarnations. However, Tangtong's hereditary line remained unbroken, and Gam Nyön's incarnation line must have died out or lost control of Riwoché at some point, because Tangtong's descendants are found presiding there again in the early eighteenth century. For example, the Sakya master Kunga Lekpai Jungné (1704–60) visited Riwoché in 1745 and exchanged many teachings with the Riwoché throne-holder Ngawang Yongdrak and his brother the abbot Losang Tobden Paljor, who were paternal descendants of Tangtong Gyalpo.[72]

Tangtong Gyalpo's surviving teachings are mostly connected with the Shangpa Kagyü, the Northern Treasure tradition of the Nyingma, and the practices of Severance or Chöd. It is not surprising to find that his tradition developed in a nonsectarian way, since Tangtong himself studied under some five hundred masters from India, Nepal, and every tradition in Tibet. In particular, the teachings of the ḍākinī Niguma, sister of the Indian master Nāropa, were of special importance to him. Niguma bestowed her teachings on the eleventh-century Tibetan master Khyungpo Naljor, the founder of the Shangpa tradition. Tangtong received the transmission of her instructions from the master Jangsem Jinpa Sangpo, passed down through the lineage of the "Seven Jewels" and Jagchungpa Tsangma Shangtön (1234–1309).[73] He may also have studied the same instructions under the guidance of Dorjé Shönu and Müchen Namkhai Naljor, both disciples of Gyaltsen Palsang.[74] Tangtong went into retreat after receiving the transmission from Jinpa Sangpo. During a profound visionary experience, the ḍākinī Niguma herself bestowed upon him the four initiations, specific instructions concerning the esoteric significance of her *Vajra Lines*, and an extraordinary technique for transference of consciousness through meditation on the white and red forms of Khecarī.[75] Tangtong's mastery of these practices is said to have given him the ability to instantly emanate many forms, to know what other people were thinking, and to perform the transference of consciousness from afar for the benefit of another person. This was the first of his three visionary encounters with Niguma.[76]

Some years later Tangtong Gyalpo was traveling from his birthplace to Lhasa soon after he had returned to Tibet from Uḍḍiyāna. In a grove of juniper trees at a place called Sinpo Dzong (Demon Fort), he was approached again by the ḍākinī Niguma, this time in the form of a fifteen-year-old shepherd girl.[77] On this occasion she gave him special instructions concerning the sequence of visualizations during meditation, and bestowed the blessing of the illusory body.[78]

The esoteric instructions Tangtong Gyalpo received from Niguma were not written down until many years later, in 1458. In that year he finally received, in a third vision, permission to write down what Niguma had previously given him. This event occurred at Riwoché, and the instructions were recorded by Tangtong's disciple Lodrö Gyaltsen, through whom the major lineage was subsequently transmitted. These instructions, known as the *Collection of the Essentials (Snying po kun 'dus),* and a group of related teachings, have been passed down as the Tangtong Tradition (Thang lugs) of the Shangpa Kagyü lineage, and are among the few texts actually signed by the great adept.[79] His Shangpa teachings have been transmitted through a line of teachers distinct from those of his other traditions. This tradition, like all of Tangtong's extant teachings, was later received by Jamyang Khyentsé Wangpo, both from his teachers and in a direct visionary meeting with Tangtong Gyalpo in 1834, when Khyentsé was fifteen years old.[80]

The most closely guarded esoteric teachings of Tangtong Gyalpo concern the practice of Chöd, or Severance, about which he never wrote. During the course of his studies and travels, Tangtong studied all the systems of Chöd in Tibet. From Lhadongpa Sönam Chokpa, he received the transmission of the Chöd practices taught by Padmasambhava and passed down in the Northern Treasure tradition of the Nyingma School, which were based on the treasures of Gökyi Demtruchen (1337–1408). However, it was a vison of Vajravārāhī appearing to Tangtong as Machik Labdrön (eleventh–twelfth centuries) in the Kashmiri cemetery of Rāmeśvara that was to be most significant.[81] Machik Labdrön was the mother of the most influential Chöd system in Tibet, and the visionary teachings she transmitted to Tangtong form the basis of *Tangtong's Oral Transmission (Thang stong snyan brgyud),* also known as the *Oral Transmission of Machik's Secret Behavior (Ma gcig gsang spyod snyan brgyud),* which has been passed down without interruption to the present day.[82] Tangtong specifically practiced Chöd to bring the local spirits under his control long before beginning his first construction projects.[83]

The practice of *Tangtong's Oral Transmission* focuses on Vajravārāhī and the deities of her maṇḍala. These techniques can be generally classified as Chöd and Shijé (Pacification) practices according to the systems of Machik Labdrön and Padampa Sangyé (d. 1105). Tangtong Gyalpo considered the

6. The great yoginī Machik Labdrön.

specific blend of these teachings he received in the vision at Rāmeśvara to be so secret that he only taught them to one disciple, Namkha Lekpa, whom he called "King of the Chöd Practitioners" (Gcod mkhan gyi rgyal po).[84] Tangtong taught Namkha Lekpa orally and bound him to a strict oath, requiring that the teachings be passed down in a single, unique transmission in Namkha Lekpa's family for three generations. The seal of secrecy could be lifted in the third generation, and if the teachings were widely spread from that time they would be very beneficial. The instructions were then passed down in a single oral transmission from Namkha Lekpa to his nephew Khedrup Shākya Shenyen (d. 1549), who spoke them to his nephew Phagö Gyaltsen Palsang (1519?–1592?), who in turn taught them only to his nephew Shongchen Khetsun Tenpai Gyaltsen.[85] Shongchen, who was a major figure in this lineage, then wrote down the teachings for the first time and, according to Tangtong's prophecy, the tradition was no longer restricted to a single transmission. In later years many great teachers upheld this lineage, such as Tangtong's descendant Ngawang Yongdrak at Riwoché and Tenzin Yeshé Lhundrup at Chuwori. Yeshé Lhundrup and Jamyang Khyentsé Wango both revived the embers of the tradition when it was in danger of dying out in the eighteenth and nineteenth centuries.

Tangtong's Oral Transmission is an extremely esoteric collection, but the great adept's method for meditative realization of Avalokiteśvara, known as *Infinite Benefit for Living Beings ('Gro don mkha' khyab ma)*, has become one of the most popular practices in Tibetan Buddhism.[86] Tangtong Gyalpo is believed to have been an emanation of Avalokiteśvara, and so his teachings have the same status as those of the bodhisattva himself. Commenting on Tangtong's text, the Fifteenth Karmapa, Khakhyap Dorjé (1871–1922), said, "The accomplished lord Tangtong Gyalpo was really Avalokiteśvara appearing for the benefit of humanity."[87] Many of the prophecies about Tangtong identify him with Avalokiteśvara, and throughout his life he was guided by visions and teachings bestowed directly by the bodhisattva.

Tangtong Gyalpo first studied the Avalokiteśvara practices of the *Compendium of Maṇis* and the ancient systems of practical instruction under the guidance of his elder half-brother, the Dharma lord Draksangpa.[88] Although Tangtong studied these traditional teachings and received a special refuge formula that Avalokiteśvara had given to his teacher Ka Ngapa Paljor Sherab specifically for him, *Infinite Benefit for Living Beings* is believed to be based on his many visions of Avalokiteśvara.[89] Nevertheless, certain aspects of the meditation liturgy are obviously borrowed from the earlier traditions of practical instruction.[90] Tangtong's text continues to be very popular, and has been the subject of several commentaries, beginning with the beautiful summary by Kunga Drolchok (1507–66), who was a central figure in most lineages connected with the great adept.[91] *Infinite Benefit for Living Beings* was also selected by modern teachers such as the Sixteenth Karmapa, Rangjung Rikpai Dorjé (1923-81), Kalu Rinpoché (1905–89), and Dezhung Rinpoché as one of the best practices for introducing Buddhist meditation to non-Tibetan students in the 1970s when Tibetan Buddhism began to spread into Europe and North America.

7.Four-armed Avalokiteśvara.

Tangtong Gyalpo's biography is full of episodes involving Avalokiteśvara in various situations.[92] Many teachings are connected to the bodhisattva, such as the one Tangtong gave to a *maṇi* devotee *(ma ṇi pa)* that begins with a simple statement: "The word of Vajradhara, the transmission of Mahākaruṇika, the writing of Tangtong Gyalpo."[93] Several instances illustrate Tangtong's connection with the tradition of the *maṇi* devotees, who received that name because of their dedication to the repetition of Avalokiteśvara's mantra, *Oṃ maṇi padme hūṃ*.[94] This connection is significant because of traditional ties between the wandering *maṇi* devotees, who put on shows of mime and dance to illustrate the teachings of Avalokiteśvara, and the popular opera traditions of dance and theatrical performance known as the Aché Lhamo, believed to be Tangtong's creation. Although the Aché Lhamo is not mentioned in any of Tangtong's biographies, his influence in these operas and other popular traditions such as the Gesar epic is clear.[95] Tangtong's traditions for making blessed *maṇi* pills *(ma ṇi ril sgrub)*, and white and red medicinal pills known as "One Medicine for a Hundred Ills" *(nad rgya sman gcig)*, were also inspired by Avalokiteśvara.[96] In the realm of popular tradition and religion, Tangtong's ties with Avalokiteśvara are strengthened even further by the exorcistic Breaking of the Stone (Pho bar rdo gcog) ceremony that is attributed to him.[97]

Tangtong Gyalpo holds a special place in the Nyingma tradition. Jamgön Kongtrul's sketch of Tangtong's life begins with the following words:

> The accomplished lord Tangtong Gyalpo was the united emanation of Avalokiteśvara and glorious Hayagrīva, Guru Padmasambhava appearing as though born from a womb.[98]

Guru Padmasambhava, father of the Nyingma tradition, is believed to have been born from a lotus flower, and Tangtong Gyalpo is often mentioned as his mental emanation. In Tangtong's biographies, he is said to have been a second Padmasambhava returning in the degenerate age, and to have recovered hidden treasures left by the Teacher of Uḍḍiyāna during the first spread of Buddhism in Tibet. Only the names of Tangtong's original treasure texts have survived, except for substantial quotations from the *Bright Lamp of Prophecy*. Apparently, his five mental treasures (*thugs gter* or *dgongs gter*) were intended for five specific individuals who would achieve buddhahood and leave no bodies behind.[99] Tangtong is also thought to have rehidden several treasure teachings that were not suitable

8. A group of Aché Lhamo dancers.

for the people of his time.[100] The essential content of all these teachings was later revealed to Jamyang Khyentsé Wangpo, who revived Tangtong's treasure tradition.[101]

Tangtong Gyalpo mostly learned the Nyingma teachings from four masters. Two of these teachers belonged to the Northern Treasure tradition and two he met during his studies in India. These latter two, Kunga Nyingpo and Kalden Dorjé Drakpa, are otherwise unknown. Since Sanskrit names are given in the biographies for all the other masters that Tangtong met in Nepal and India, these two Nyingma teachers with Tibetan names were perhaps Tibetan masters living in India at the time of his visit.[102] His teachers in Tibet, Kunpang Dönyö Gyaltsen and Lhadongpa Sönam Chokpa, were both disciples of Gökyi Demtruchen (1337–1408), the founder of the Northern Treasure branch of the Nyingma tradition. From these two masters Tangtong received all the Nyingma teachings that had been passed down in a sequential lineage, and in particular the visionary teachings of the Northern Treasure tradition.

Without texts of his own composition, it is difficult to know how much Tangtong Gyalpo continued the Northern Treasure tradition, although it is obvious that he was extremely involved with the Nyingma teachings. He is sometimes referred to as Urgyen Tangtong Gyalpo, signaling his identity with Padmasambhava of Uḍḍiyāna (Urgyen), and when his mother became a nun near the end of her life, Tangtong taught her the Nyingma teachings of the Great Perfection. His journey to Padmasambhava's paradise in Uḍḍiyāna, his visionary encounter with the great adept Hūṃkara, and his numerous treasure recoveries all illustrate the importance of the Nyingma tradition in his life.[103] Furthermore, other masters and his own disciples had visions of Tangtong as Dorjé Drakpotsel, or actually saw him in this form when meeting him. Dorjé Drakpotsel is the terrible form of Padmasambhava found in Gökyi Demtruchen's treasure teachings. Tangtong often gave Nyingma teachings such as the Great Perfection, especially according to the Northern Treasure tradition, and lineages from him were passed down.[104]

The Nyingma master Jamyang Rinchen Gyaltsen (b. 1446?), who was the father of Ngari Panchen Pema Wangyal (1487–1542) and Rikzin Lekden Dorjé (1500–1577), met Tangtong Gyalpo toward the end of the great adept's life. Jamyang Rinchen Gyaltsen went to Riwoché at the advice of the treasure revealer Kunkyong Lingpa (1396–1477), and the episode provides a wonderful glimpse of the old ascetic's lifestyle from an independent source.[105]

> Lord Jamyang Rinchen Gyaltsen went to meet the great adept Tangtong Gyalpo at Palchen Riwoché. The great adept was in retreat, during which his body, speech, and mind could be met for one year; his body could be met during the next year; and his body and speech could not be met at all for the next year. Because Jamyang Rinchen Gyaltsen arrived during the period when the great adept's body could be met, during the day he beheld the maṇḍala of his face and was given food, although the great adept did not speak. But during the night he did speak, giving complete teachings such as the Ten Royal Sūtras, the Six Dharmas of Niguma, the Mahāmudrā, three types of Mahākaruṇika, and the Heart Practice and the *Penetration* of the Northern Treasures.[106] For half a month the great adept gave many prophecies of the future and numerous oral instructions and advice, such as how Jamyang Rinchen Gyaltsen's lifespan would be 113 years.
>
> On the day of Jamyang Rinchen Gyaltsen's departure, the great adept gave him thirty-three long-life pills and shouted "*Phaṭ*!" three times while completely flinging out his arms.

> A close attendant explained, "Your previously accumulated residual karma has awakened to the Dharma. Clear the precipitous pathway of combined Dharma and worldly obstacles! Practice until your hair becomes an armspan in length! Then be very careful when you are thirty-three and sixty-four years old! Father and son will meet in the paradise of Akaniṣṭha. There will be no obstacles on any path you travel. I'll clear away that slight affliction of displeasure in your mind about going home."
>
> The great adept struck him nine times with his staff. That cleared away a minor problem in his mind. Then Jamyang Rinchen Gyaltsen left, wandering through Jang and arriving home in Mustang without problems and obstacles.[107]

This description matches the biographical portrayals of Tangtong Gyalpo remaining in long retreats during his final years at Riwoché. In a Dragon Year, perhaps corresponding to 1484, Tangtong himself wrote that he had sat immobile on the same meditation cushion for twenty-three years and been silent for fourteen of those years.[108] Moreover, the close attendant who interpreted Tangtong's cryptic behavior and played such an important role in the meeting was almost certainly Sherab Palden, his biographer and eventual regent at Riwoché, who was his close attendant for the last sixteen years of his life.

The most significant master connecting Tangtong Gyalpo with the Northern Treasure tradition was Kunpang Dönyö Gyaltsen. Before Tangtong first came to request the Northern Treasures, Dönyö Gyaltsen prophesied that he would gain the ability to extend his lifespan through the practice of the *Iron Tree (Lcags kyi sdong po)*, a section of Gökyi Demtruchen's hidden treasure teachings.[109] The *Iron Tree* is the section in the Heart Practice cycle of Gökyi Demtruchen's treasures for sustaining the essence of life through meditation on Amitābha, Amitāyus, and Hayagrīva.[110] This treasure text is believed to have been written in the symbolic language of the ḍākinīs by Padmasambhava's secret consort, the goddess Caṇḍālī, and hidden in a casket of maroon rhinoceros hide until rediscovered by Gökyi Demtruchen.[111] The Sakya master Ngawang Kunga Tashi, in his explanatory text for bestowing initiation into these teachings, says Tangtong perfected the attainment of immortality through practice of the *Iron Tree*.[112]

9. The upholder of pure awareness Gökyi Demtruchen (1337–1408).

The *Iron Tree* is believed to be the specific technique that Padmasambhava himself used to achieve immortality. It is said that Amitāyus actually appeared to Padmasambhava when he was in Maratika Cave meditating with his consort, the Indian princess Mandarava. Padmasambhava requested many teachings from Amitāyus, including the *Iron Tree*, which both he and Mandarava used to achieve the immortal, indestructible, vajra body.[113] Padmasambhava's *Bright Lamp of Prophecy*, the biographical prophecy of Tangtong Gyalpo, says:

> His lifespan will be eighty-one,
> but if he practices the elixir

of the life-sustaining goddess,
he will be able to live longer than that.[114]

Having a tantric partner is nearly a requirement among revealers of treasure teachings because it is the ḍākinīs who deliver attainments and guard the secrets of esoteric knowledge.[115] Tangtong Gyalpo practiced life-sustaining techniques throughout his life, and perhaps through the tantric methods of meditation practiced with women such as Khandroma Sengé, who was the mother of his son Tenzin Nyima Sangpo, and Jetsun Chökyi Drönmé, he lived an exceptionally long life.

From among the many teachings of Tangtong Gyalpo that have been passed down until the present day, his life-sustaining techniques are the most famous. These methods, known as the *Glorious Giver of Immortality ('Chi med dpal ster)*, focus on Amitāyus, who is the Buddha of Infinite Life, and Hayagrīva, who is a terrible form of Avalokiteśvara.[116] Tangtong is believed to have actually visited Padmasambhava's Palace of Lotus Light on Cāmara Island or in Uḍḍiyāna and received the teachings directly from the Lotus-Born Guru.[117] According to some sources, he later retrieved the same teachings as a portion of the five treasure scrolls that he discovered in the cave of Chimpu near Samyé in the 1420s.[118] The *Glorious Giver of Immortality* is thus considered to be based both on pure visionary revelation and hidden treasure teachings. The Northern Treasure tradition and the Chaksam tradition each claim that Tangtong's long life was a result of meditation on the life-sustaining practices of their respective systems. Tangtong had practiced the Northern Treasure teachings of the *Iron Tree* for many years before receiving the teachings of the *Glorious Giver of Immortality* from Padmasambhava on Cāmara Island and then rediscovering the treasure texts at Chimpu. It would not be surprising to find some links between the Northern Treasure techniques and Tangtong's own, but this does not seem to be the case.[119]

The *Glorious Giver of Immortality* is a ritualized version of the original visionary teachings of Tangtong Gyalpo that focus on the realization of immortality. These methods are for the achievement of longevity, but the ultimate aim is to realize that "death" is a mistaken concept. If one knows that the mind is birthless, one will also realize that it does not die. The teachings were transmitted orally for three generations, first by Tangtong to both the Sakya master Kunpang Doringpa (1449–1524) and Shenyen Tashi Sangpo, and from them to Kunga Drolchok (1507–66),

10. Hayagrīva.

who taught the Chaksam hierarch Tenzin Nyida Sangpo. Nyida Sangpo first wrote down Tangtong's original words and composed a history of the techniques and manuals for their practice. This is what came to be known by the name *Glorious Giver of Immortality.*[120] Related practices were later developed by the Fifth Dalai Lama based on his repeated visions of Tangtong, and the nineteenth-century treasure revealer Chöjé Lingpa Dzamling Dorjé also received a visionary revelation from Tangtong that is still widely used as a life-sustaining practice.[121] For such popular practices as the *Glorious Giver of Immortality* and *Infinite Benefit for Living Beings,* many divergent lineages spread throughout the old and new traditions in Tibet. In the late sixteenth century the transmission of these teachings began to diversify after the time of Tenzin Nyida Sangpo, through whom virtually everything passed. The *Glorious Giver of Immortality* is now the most widespread and influential longevity practice in Tibetan Buddhism.

Tangtong Gyalpo is regarded as an upholder of the pure awareness of immortality *('chi med rig 'dzin)* and is thought to be always present, although only accessible to persons with pure vision and a connection of karma. In addition to those already mentioned, many stories are told of visionary meetings through the centuries.[122] The Sakya master Kunga Lekpai Jungné (1704–60) had dreams and visions of Tangtong throughout his life. On one occasion a dazzling Tangtong Gyalpo gave him a jeweled bowl containing a fresh, wet human heart, cut open for him to see. Kunga Lekpai Jungné understood this to be a symbolic revelation of the ultimate meaning of the *shentong (gzhan stong),* or "emptiness of other," a view that he deeply appreciated.[123] Another Sakya master, Shuchen Tsultrim Rinchen (1697–1774), was once afflicted by a severe eye disease and was going blind. He describes the following event in his autobiography:

> At that point, in a dream, I gazed out the window, and the adept Tangtong Gyalpo was mounted on a white mule in a meadow on the far mountain. When I also arrived there instantly from my residence, he said, "You seem to have an obstacle." I did not see him urinate, but he gave me a cup full of what appeared to be urine.
>
> I thought, "Whatever obstacle I have will be removed by drinking this."
>
> I drank it, woke up, and the great adept also vanished.[124]

Many people have been graced by Tangtong Gyalpo's body of primordial awareness in visions, dreams, and other circumstances. However, Tangtong's teachings have survived into the twenty-first century primarily due to his special link with Jamyang Khyentsé Wangpo, who received, practiced, and transmitted them all in the nineteenth century. Khyentsé Wangpo was regarded as an incarnation of Tangtong Gyalpo, and when people came to meet him he sometimes appeared to actually be Tangtong.[125] Jamgön Kongtrul certainly heard the following story directly from Khyentsé Wangpo himself.

> When Jamyang Khyentsé Wangpo or, according to his secret name, Ösel Trulpai Dorjé, was fifteen years old, he had a dream at dawn on the fourteenth day of the middle month of autumn in the Wood Male Horse Year [1834] of the fourteenth cycle. A finely decorated mansion in a place he did not recognize contained a large, red, circular maṇḍala. Above it was an extremely beautiful white cloud, in the middle of which was the great adept Tangtong Gyalpo, with the five types of ḍākinīs. The initiation implements were arranged in front of him, and he bestowed initiation and instructions. When Jamyang Khyentsé Wangpo awoke from the dream, he actually met the great adept, who bestowed a single couplet of instructions introducing him to the essential nature and then dissolved into him, which caused the cycle of ripening and liberating instructions to shine brilliantly in his mind. Thus he transcribed the practice manuals and so forth of the Heartdrop of the Great Adept during the fifteenth day.[126]

In the same dream-vision, Khyentsé Wangpo also received a direct transmission of the Amulet Mahāmudrā and the Six Dharmas of Niguma, the most important Shangpa teachings for which Tangtong Gyalpo had composed meditation manuals. Khyentsé Wangpo practiced the Heartdrop of the Great Adept himself in secret, and not until 1866, when he was forty-seven years old, did he first teach it to Jamgön Kongtrul, Chokgyur Lingpa (1829–70), and Tupten Gyaltsen.[127] These teachings were later taught to other worthy disciples, and Jamgön Kongtrul, who also met Tangtong in a vision, included them in his *Treasury of Precious Treasure Teachings*, a massive collection of all the treasure literature in Tibet.[128] In addition to these visionary revelations, Khyentsé Wangpo was the holder of all existing lineages passed down from Tangtong, and became the major transmitter and preserver of his tradition in modern times.

The Heartdrop of the Great Adept represents the quintessence of the reconcealed treasures *(yang gter)* that Tangtong Gyalpo hid in a cave in Lhatsé, near his birthplace, and in a rock crevice near Samyé Chimpu.[129] While in retreat in the cave near Lhatsé, Tangtong had realized that it was not the time to teach many of the profound instructions he had received from his masters in India and Nepal. He gathered a large quantity of slate and recorded the instructions by scratching them on the slate until he had worn out two thick iron needles. He left these tablets for the time when a karmically endowed individual would discover them and they would benefit future generations.[130] But the Heartdrop of the Great Adept is not a group of treasure texts discovered in the earth *(sa gter)*; it is a cycle revealed as "mental treasure" (*dgongs gter* or *thugs gter*), which Tangtong taught in the form of his "body of primordial awareness" to Khyentsé Wangpo. Tangtong concealed the quintessence of all these instructions in the ultimate depths of his mindstream, and, because Khyentsé Wangpo was his emanation, these realizations dawned again in Khyentsé's mind when the proper conditions were complete.

The Heartdrop of the Great Adept is particularly significant because Tangtong Gyalpo's original treasure texts are lost and their contents almost a complete mystery. It is composed of three groups of teachings. The basic text is a guruyoga practice focusing on Tangtong and used for unification with his profound awareness.[131] A set of five methods for accomplishment focus on the master as Padmasambhava in a tranquil and a terrible form, the four-armed Avalokiteśvara, Hayagrīva, and Vajravārāhī.[132] The final set of texts is a collection of methods for propitiation of the eight major herukas of the Nyingma tradition.[133] The practices centered on the eight herukas are linked with Tangtong's journey to Padmasambhava's paradise where he beheld them directly and received the techniques. Several texts are also concerned with strengthening and sustaining the essence of life, and a cryptic set of *Vajra Lines* summarize the key points of the entire cycle.[134]

Direct transmission of this kind transcends the level of normal historical events and bypasses the more ordinary chronological transmission of teachings from master to disciple. Tangtong Gyalpo received all of his most significant teachings in direct communion with the divine world, and, in a similar way, the legacy of this compelling visionary continues to be transmitted to the present day. After five centuries, one can still be the direct disciple of this master who is only chronologically "in the past."

3. Iron-Bridge Man

> As prophesied by Padmasambhava,
> you opened the gates to sacred places,
> made sublime representations of enlightened body,
> speech, and mind,
> and constructed countless boats, ferries,
> iron bridges, and so forth,
> becoming the glory of all living beings—
> to you I bow.[135]
>
> —Kunga Sönam Drakpa Palsang

Tangtong Gyalpo built his first iron suspension bridge over the Kyichu River near Lhasa in 1430, and from that time was famed throughout Tibet and the Himalayan regions as the "Iron-Bridge Man" (Lcags zam pa). His exploits in Bhutan and in Kongpo in southeast Tibet, from where the iron for most of his bridges was transported, as well as in the uncivilized regions of Lo, gained him the reputation of being a formidable subduer of barbarian people and demonic forces.[136] In addition to iron bridges, he built many stūpas to tame hostile influences, prevent natural disasters, protect against disease, and avert invasion by Mongol armies. These stūpas were constructed in Tibet and the borderlands according to geomantic principles, and were situated at strategic locations to serve as environmental focal-points *(sa'i me btsa')*. A number of Tangtong's monasteries and temples were placed according to the same theory, such as Riwoché in Latö Jang in western Tibet and Lhundrup Teng in Dergé in eastern Tibet.

In two of his edicts, Tangtong Gyalpo speaks of what was probably a legendary oral version of the origin of ferries and bridges in Tibet. He says that at the time of the founding of Samyé Monastery (in the late eighth century) there were no boats, coracles, or ferries with which to cross the rivers. One day a weasel climbed onto a flattened dung pattie, grabbed flat pieces of wood in his paws, and paddled across a river. A shepherd saw this happen, and using the clever animal's feat as an example, boats, coracles, ferries, and so forth were first made in Tibet. Wooden bridges were also

11. The iron bridge over the Kyichu River.

built over small streams.[137] However, actual historical accounts tell of iron bridges in Tibet even earlier than the setting of this folk tale.

Iron bridges were extremely rare in Tibet before the fifteenth century, although the technology had existed for hundreds if not thousands of years. According to Tibetan tradition, the smelting of gold, silver, copper, and iron was mastered by Tibetan craftsmen perhaps two thousand years ago, during the reign of the king of the Yarlung dynasty usually known as Pudé Gungyal. Bridges (but not of iron) were also constructed during the same period over the impassable rivers of Tibet.[138] The consummate skill of Tibetan ironworkers nearly two thousand years ago was famous even in China at the time of the Tibetan king Drigum Tsenpo, whose craftsmen made iron swords and armor that were much admired. The most skillful of these ironworkers are said to have come from the area of Markham in southeastern Tibet.[139]

12. Tangtong Gyalpo with alms bowl and iron chain.

A legendary iron bridge is said to have been built in approximately 635 C.E. to connect the two castles of the king Songtsen Gampo and his Nepalese queen, but no evidence has come to light concerning the use of iron bridges at this early date to span any rivers.[140] Nevertheless, Tibetan craftsmen were definitely capable of building iron bridges in the seventh century, because ancient sources say the army of the Tibetan king Tridé Tsukten built an iron bridge over a large river at the beginning of the eighth century.[141] Perhaps the earliest Tibetan author to mention the construction of an iron bridge was the treasure revealer Nyang Nyima Öser (1136–1204), who said the Tibetan king Ralpachen had an iron bridge built over the lower Yellow River (Rma chu) in Minyak in the early ninth century during a period of military conflict with Tang dynasty Chinese forces.[142] In the generation just before Tangtong Gyalpo, the Third Karmapa, Rangjung Dorjé (1284–1339), built an iron bridge in 1328.[143] Other

13. Iron bridge over the Tsangpo River at Puntsok Ling.

references to iron bridges between the ninth and fourteenth centuries in Tibet may also exist. Tangtong was well educated in the ancient literary and oral traditions, and would have known of the previous existence of iron bridges. Perhaps the ruined remains of ancient iron bridges were still to be seen during his youth.

In this context, it is particularly fascinating to learn that an iron suspension bridge actually existed precisely at Rinchen Ding, Tangtong Gyalpo's birthplace in the region of Ngamring, long before his birth. With the sole exception of the bridge mentioned above that was built by the Third Karmapa, the various references to this specific iron bridge at Rinchen Ding are the only definite literary evidence of the existence of iron bridges anywhere in Tibet after the early dynastic period. This seems very significant. The fact that an iron bridge had existed at his birthplace must have been known to Tangtong, even though the bridge itself had been dismantled about thirty years before his birth. And it is startling to find that the iron bridge of Rinchen Ding had been dismantled by none other than Dolpopa Sherab Gyaltsen (1292–1361), the famous Jonang master of whom Tangtong claimed to be the immediate rebirth.

According to Dolpopa's disciple and biographer, Kunpang Chödrak Palsang, each iron link[144] of this bridge was worth one twentieth of an ounce of gold, which may partially explain why iron bridges were so scarce in Tibet. The bridge originally belonged to the governor of Ngamring, but malicious spirits were believed to have taken control of it and no one even dared to touch it. The governor offered the bridge to Dolpopa, saying that his iron bridge of four chains was now useless. Dolpopa gave the ruler a large amount of silver in gratitude and sent about twenty men with horses and mules to haul the iron bridge back to Jonang. Dolpopa sent an edict with the men—much as Tangtong Gyalpo would later do on many occasions—which they attached to the rock cliff with five-colored silk streamers and a tenth of an ounce of gold. The men slept there that night, and everyone dreamed of a black man with yellow hair who said that he offered the 450 iron links of the bridge as material for the huge stūpa that Dolpopa was building at Jonang. The next morning the men took down the iron chains, loaded them on the horses and mules, and hauled them back to Jonang, where they were used for the padlocks of the stūpa, the iron supports (*lcag 'jer/'dzer?*) of the Dharma wheels, to stabilize the main body of the stūpa, and to pull up the great pinnacle.[145] As a final note to this story, Tangtong Gyalpo later built another iron bridge at his birthplace of Rinchen Ding, perhaps at the exact location of the original ancient bridge.[146]

No specific information about other iron bridges before the time of Tangtong Gyalpo has been located, but some circumstantial evidence indicates that earlier iron bridges did still exist during his lifetime. For example, during his early wanderings as an eccentric yogin, he once sat overnight in the river under a bridge at Jonang. Although this bridge is not specifically identified as an iron bridge, the well-known iron bridge that spans the Tsangpo River at nearby Puntsok Ling could have been the same bridge. A large bridge at Toling in Gugé is believed to have been constructed during the reign of the king Namgyal Dé (1372–1439), sometime before the king's abdication in 1424. Again, the original sources do not specify that this was an iron bridge, but a famous iron bridge did exist at Toling. According to the biography by Gyurmé Dechen, Tangtong did not travel to Gugé until about 1435. None of the biographies mention that he built iron bridges near Jonang or Toling, although later sources and the oral tradition do consider them to be his work.[147] In 1949 Dezhung Rinpoché visited the ancient iron bridge in Gugé on the Langpoché Khabap and the one in front of Puntsok Ling on the Tsangpo, but declined to cross them because of their precarious condition.[148]

Iron bridges were very scarce in Tibet before Tangtong Gyalpo, but many other types of bridges obviously existed. For example, the Pakmodru ruler Tai Situ Jangchup Gyaltsen (1302–64) is known to have built a marvelous bridge in front of his castle of Nedong in the mid-fourteenth century.[149] One of the most impressive of the early bridges must have been the one built over the Nyangchu River in front of Gyantsé in 1414 by the governor Rabten Kunsang Pak (1389–1442). This bridge was specifically built to symbolize that sentient beings who wished to escape from the sea of existence would finally reach the shore of enlightenment if they followed the path of the six perfections. The construction materials used for the bridge are not mentioned anywhere, but it must have been made from stone, mortar, wood, and plaster. This massive bridge had six piers, with a Stūpa of Great Enlightement built in the middle above the pathway. The upper part of the stūpa was filled with nine large maṇḍalas and the walls were covered with paintings of various deities. Tangtong Gyalpo was certainly familiar with this bridge, since he visited Gyantsé and met Kunsang Pak several decades after its construction.[150]

The use of the bridge and boat as symbols for liberation is quite old in Buddhist literature, and it is even said that these are two of the forms that a buddha can manifest to benefit living beings.[151] Tangtong Gyalpo repeatedly emphasized in his edicts that the Buddha had said that much merit was accumulated by constructing images, even more merit than that by writing out the scriptures, even more merit than that by creating representations of enlightened mind (such as stūpas), even more merit than that by building boats and bridges, and even more merit than that by saving the lives of sentient beings.[152] Tangtong's construction of bridges and ferries was motivated by his concern for the welfare of others. This altruistic intention was first linked with the building of iron bridges while he was living in India. During a meditation retreat he had a vision in which he lowered long jeweled ladders into four gaping pits and rescued many living beings trapped below. His teacher, the Indian master Dharmaratna, explained that the four pits were the lower forms of existence in saṃsāra and that Tangtong's extending of the ladders to higher forms of existence indicated that he would later construct unprecedented iron bridges over turbulent rivers.[153]

A further interpretation was provided in another vision when Tangtong

14. Iron bridge at Toling.

Gyalpo saw a large crowd of people crossing an expanse of water on iron bridges and ferries. He took this to symbolize that he would be able to save all living beings from the four rivers of birth, old age, sickness, and death. Moreover, he would liberate them from the sufferings of the ocean of saṃsāra by means of the ferries and bridges of skillful means and wisdom. The ḍākinīs of Uḍḍiyāna also urged him to build ferries and iron bridges to symbolize the liberation of sentient beings. Tangtong further emphasized this himself by often referring to his bridges as "iron-bridge pathways to enlightenment" *(byang chub kyi rgyu lam lcags zam).*[154] In the words of his consort Chökyi Drönmé: "As symbols of the liberation of all living beings from the ocean of existence, you cast a net of iron over the great rivers."[155] It was also believed that work on these projects purified the sins of the laborers and contributed to their eventual attainment of liberation.

Tangtong Gyalpo's construction of iron bridges can be divided into three categories.[156] An example of the first is the iron bridge built in 1430 over the Kyichu River in Lhasa, where Tangtong personally planned and supervised the construction and was present from start to finish. An example of the second is the iron bridge completed at Chuwori in 1444, where he was actually present for the crucial planning, laying of the abutments, and raising of the iron chains, but delegated the interim construction work to his followers while he remained in retreat. An example of the third category is the iron bridge built in 1485 at the Nyago ferry crossing in Yarlung, when Tangtong sent his son and heir Tenzin Nyima Sangpo to do all the actual construction. By the end of his life, Tangtong had constructed fifty-eight iron bridges, sixty wooden bridges, and 118 ferries.[157] His biographies clearly mention only about a dozen of these iron bridges by name and location, but many more have survived in different regions of Tibet and Bhutan to the present day.[158]

The first expedition Tangtong Gyalpo made in search of iron was motivated by an event at the Lhadong ferry landing on the Kyichu River near Lhasa.[159] Tangtong wanted to cross the river, but because of his ragged appearance the ferryman struck him on the head with an oar and threw him into the water. This impressed on him the plight of poor and disadvantaged people, and he vowed to build a bridge there so that everyone could easily cross the river. The ḍākinīs of Uḍḍiyāna had previously told him that he could find iron at Tsagong in Kongpo with which to construct iron bridges, and so during the 1420s he traveled through the aboriginal areas in the extreme southeast of Tibet. There he discovered iron being worked at such places as Tengtsar and Bhakha. He managed to gather a quantity of iron and also establish a monastery at Tsagong in Kongpo, where he forged four long iron chains with local blacksmiths. With the eventual cooperation of the Kongpo people these chains were transported to Central Tibet and used for the bridge that he built over the Kyichu River in 1430.

Many of Tangtong Gyalpo's bridges, ferries, stūpas, and monasteries were built to subdue demonic influences and to bring Buddhism into barbarian regions. Quite early in Tangtong's life, the Sakya master Rendawa told him to gain control over the eight kinds of worldly gods and demons before attempting to exert his influence on the environment.[160] Tangtong then compassionately practiced Chöd (Severance) where various demonic spirits lived. During this process he transformed his body of flesh and blood into blessed nectar and offered it to the Three Jewels. When the spirits partook of this offering, they were delighted and satisfied with the sacrifice, and offered him their lives and support for his virtuous work. On other occasions, he did not hesitate to use more threatening methods to deal with the most intransigent spirits and demons.

When Tangtong Gyalpo first went to Kongpo searching for iron, he received the invitation of the earth spirits and the protective goddess Kongtsun Demo.[161] This was an essential prelude to his removal of iron from the domain of the local spirits, without whose permission the violation of soil and the removal of its wealth from the area would have been a dangerous act. To build bridges and ferries on the water, it was also necessary for Tangtong to obtain the cooperation of the nāgas or water spirits. At Waru Namtsel in Kongpo he confronted the nāga king Varuṇa, gained his allegiance, and built a stūpa and temple there.[162]

When Tangtong Gyalpo returned to Central Tibet, he built the bridge over the Kyichu River in 1430, but only after subduing the demon Kharnak. In the same year, Lady Kalden Rinchen Sangmo[163] built a residence for him on Chakpori Hill in Lhasa, where he later established a temple and nunnery. According to the Fifth Dalai Lama, in 1645 the inner sanctum of the temple on Chakpori contained an image of Tangtong that had been blessed with barley from his own hand,[164] and many images of precious substances he had made himself (and which are described in the biographies). Among these were a conch-shell image of Mahākaruṇika, an Amoghasiddhi from turquoise, a turquoise Tārā that was said to be able to speak, an Amitābha of coral, and a Vajrapāṇi of lapis lazuli. A number of other special objects are also mentioned by the Dalai Lama, among them an image of Padmasambhava made from white sandalwood, and various relics from Tangtong himself.[165] Jamyang Khyentsé Wangpo (1820–92) later visited this temple and noted that the coral statue of Amitāyus, the conch-shell Avalokiteśvara, and the turquoise Tārā were made by Tangtong himself.[166] In 1918, Katok Situ also mentioned the presence of many statues made from coral, conch shell, silver, and gold.[167] Dezhung Rinpoché paid a visit to the temple in 1950 and saw some of the precious statues and a large image of Tangtong that was enshrined there at the time.[168]

In 1433–34 Tangtong Gyalpo again traveled south with the specific intention of gathering iron to build bridges along the western Tsangpo River. During the journey through Bhutan he was given a large amount of iron and other offerings that he exchanged for more iron. At Ochu Gadrak in the Paro Valley blacksmiths forged seven thousand links of iron for him. By the time he returned to Tibet he had accumulated fourteen hundred manloads of iron chain, each composed of fifteen links. The people of Paro supported him because an iron bridge at Chuwori on the Tsangpo River would make it easier for them to visit the holy city of Lhasa. During his stay in Bhutan, Tangtong built eight iron bridges,[169] some of which still exist. In 1793 Samuel Turner visited the iron bridge at Chukha, south of Paro, and the bridge Tangtong built in front of his monastery at Tachok Norbugang was still standing until washed away in a 1969 flood.[170] The bridge he constructed at Bardrong near Wangdü Podrang is no longer standing, but in the 1980s a pile of chains remained on the riverbank where it once stood.[171]

When Tangtong Gyalpo returned to Tibet, the Paro people carried the fourteen hundred loads of iron as far north as the Tibetan town of Pari. While staying at Pari, he laid the foundations for the Samdrup Temple in 1433 and left his disciple and biographer Könchok Palsang to supervise the construction work. When Tangtong was ready to leave Pari and return to Central Tibet, the Gyantsé ruler Rabten Kunsang Pak (1389–1442) provided laborers to transport two hundred loads of iron links to Chuwori.[172] Tangtong himself took eleven hundred loads into Latö Jang in western Tsang, and from there traveled as far as Kashmir (Kha che), building more bridges. He also collected iron in the vicinity of Kyirong, and became known in the Ladakh area as the "Iron-Bridge Man," perhaps from the time of this journey. Returning toward Central Tibet, he arrived at his monastery of Riwoché in Latö Jang and completed the construction of an

15. The iron bridge at Chukha, Bhutan.

iron bridge there in 1436. This iron bridge is still standing at the beginning of the twenty-first century, although it has been extensively repaired several times.

During Tangtong Gyalpo's second visit to Bhutan in about 1437, the bridge work at Chuwori suffered a setback when all but eighty-six of the two hundred loads of iron sent there from Paro were stolen by the people of Gongkar, a valley near Chuwori, and used to make weapons and tools. But Tangtong's monks were sent into the countryside to gather more iron and building materials, and after some delay the Chuwori bridge was finally completed in 1444. The governor of Gongkar eventually offered a large quantity of goods in penance for the previous theft of the iron by his people.[173]

The iron suspension bridge at Chuwori was Tangtong Gyalpo's most famous bridge, and the monastery on the southern banks of the river came to be known as the "Iron-Bridge Monastery" (Lcags zam dgon). This iron bridge finally broke in about 1594 and many pilgrims from Yamdrok on a pilgrimage to Lhasa died.[174] It was later repaired and was still used regularly until 1878. At the beginning of the twentieth century, the bridge was made of two double-chain cables composed of one-inch thick iron links

16. Chains from an iron bridge in Paro, Bhutan.

that were each one foot long. It was about 150 yards in length, with the abutments on both banks built in the shape of stūpas. The chains were fastened into the abutments and the rocks below them. Yak-hair ropes were suspended from the chains at about one-yard intervals, and boards lashed end to end in their loops.[175] The bridge was finally destroyed in the 1960s during the Chinese "Cultural Revolution" and all that remains is a pile of chains on an island that was previously its northern abutment.

Tangtong Gyalpo created a wide range of artistic works. This aspect of his genius was first expressed when his mother passed away and he built a stūpa in her memory, wrote a copy of the *Condensed Verses on the Perfection of Wisdom* with gold and precious materials, and made a tangka painting of the eight sugatas. He said that these were the first iconographic representations he made.[176] However, it was not until about 1445 that he started a large scale project of statue construction. At that time he was approached by three young women on the road from Drigung to Lhasa. They offered him a relic of the Buddha blazing with light, seven pieces of turquoise, and many other types of precious substances. These ḍākinīs asked him to make statues of the buddhas and bodhisattvas from the precious materials and place relics inside the images as their hearts. And they promised to help construct the images, since statues created from such substances

17. The monastery and iron bridge at Chaksam Chuwori.

were unheard of at that time. Tangtong gathered many offerings of precious stones and gold, prayed to the famous Jowo image of the Buddha in Lhasa, and received visionary instructions to construct first a large image of Vajradhara with an interior of finest silver covered with old turquoise. He summoned about fifty sculptors the next day, but they said they were unable to make images from turquoise, coral, amber, conch shell, and similar substances. Tangtong slept in the courtyard of the Jokhang Temple that evening and received inspiration from a ḍākinī who taught him how to make the unprecedented images.[177] The next day he scolded the sculptors by reminding them that they knew how to make jewelry from the same materials. He told them to make the framework for the Vajradhara from unadulterated silver. Then he cut the turquoise himself and showed them how to correctly place and attach it to form the statue. They made many unusual images, such as Amoghasiddhi and Tārā from turquoise, seven statues of Avalokiteśvara from conch shell, Amitāyus and Amitābha from coral, a Vajrapāṇi from silver and lapis lazuli, and the ḍākinīs of the five spiritual families from coral, lapis lazuli, conch shell, amber, and turquoise. Some of the statues were left on Chakpori Hill.

According to the Fifth Dalai Lama, several of these statues and the images of the five ḍākinīs that Tangtong Gyalpo made from precious substances offered to him by the ḍākinīs were still kept at Chakpori in 1645.[178] Other images that Tangtong made with his own hands were kept at the Jokhang Temple in Lhasa, including statues of himself, the great Indian adepts Padampa Sangyé and Virūpa, the famous Kashmiri paṇḍita Śākyaśrī, and the buddhas of the past, present, and future.[179] By the end of his life, Tangtong is said to have made many hundreds of large and small images from precious materials, five thousand large and small clay images, innumerable paintings, and to have built 120 assembly halls and temples.

Following the completion of the bridge at Chuwori in 1444 and the creation of the unique images of precious substances in Lhasa, Tangtong Gyalpo traveled to Dokham and Minyak by way of Kongpo.[180] After gathering a large quantity of iron from all sections of Kongpo, he proceeded to one of his monasteries in Tsagong. There he established an iron factory composed of eight smitheries where he worked, praying to Avalokiteśvara as he forged iron links with the blacksmiths.[181] When he returned from Dokham to Tsagong several years later, the monks of the monastery had prepared three hundred manloads of iron, each containing fifteen iron links, for him to take back to Central Tibet. While touring Dokham during the years 1445–46 he had built iron bridges over such rivers as the Dzachu, Drichu, and Nyakchu, but the Kongpo area remained his primary source of iron. His consort Jetsun Chökyi Drönmé gathered a large quantity of iron from the Kongpo area in about 1455. This iron was eventually used for the bridge built thirty years later by Tangtong's son Tenzin Nyima Sangpo at the ferry crossing of Nyago near Densatil.

Due to Tangtong Gyalpo's pervasive legacy, any iron bridge existing in Tibet today will almost certainly be attributed to him, even though some were certainly built by other people after his time. His son Tenzin Nyima Sangpo continued the tradition of iron-bridge construction, raising the iron bridge at Nyago in the last year of his father's life, repairing the bridge at Chökhor Gang, and building new bridges at Drakralkha in Penyul and at the ferry crossing of Shar Drukha. The Nyago iron bridge over the main part of the Tsangpo River had thirty-two stone piers *(zam mig)* on the north side that allowed people and cattle to get to the bridge during flood season. This was the longest bridge ever built in Tibet.[182] Nyima Sangpo also continued to build other iron bridges and ferries during the period of 1485–1517, while Tangtong's death was being kept secret, but their specific locations are not known.[183] The Taklung Kagyü master Jikten Wangchuk

18. Iron bridge at Chung Riwoché.

(1454–1542) also built many wooden and iron bridges, probably inspired by Tangtong's recent example.[184]

A number of Tangtong Gyalpo's original iron bridges have also been repaired or rebuilt in the last several hundred years. His hereditary line continued to live at Riwoché, and one of his descendants, Orgyan Tenzin Norbu, was the father of Losang Tobden Paljor and Ngawang Yongdrak (1714–67), both important masters of the Chaksam tradition.[185] Orgyan Tenzin Norbu completely rebuilt *(gsar du btsugs)* the double-span iron bridge that Tangtong had originally constructed at Riwoché in 1436. Following his father's example, Losang Tobden Paljor repaired the bridge pier *(zam 'bum)* of the iron bridge at Tangtong's birthplace of Rinchen Ding and built a new guesthouse on the northern shore of the river.[186] During this same period, the Iron-Bridge Man Losang Paldrup also repaired many old iron bridges and built many new ones in Central Tibet and Tsang. One of the bridges Losang Paldrup repaired was at Rakdzong, and one of the new iron bridges he built was at Gamodrang in Lhasa.[187] In 1824, about six hundred monks under the direction of Shabkar Natsok Rangdrol (1781–1850) spent several days raising the iron bridge at Riwoché, which had sagged into the river.[188] This iron bridge has survived into the twenty-first century.[189] In the 1940s, a man named Dekyi replaced the iron chains and extensively rebuilt the old iron bridge at Lhawang Tsé, but after several years it became unstable again and collapsed.[190] This is the bridge that Tangtong had originally completed in 1436 at Tashi Tsé in Jé Bodong.

Chemical analysis made in 1970 of a chain link from one of Tangtong Gyalpo's Bhutanese bridges showed that the chains are actually steel composed of a remarkably high percentage of iron. According to one scientific opinion, the chain was manufactured by oxidizing the iron in a dough-like state, which was the only steel-manufacturing method known when high temperatures capable of smelting steel were still unattainable. It is apparently the unusually high content of arsenic in the steel that has kept the chains from corroding over the last 550 years.[191] Dezhung Rinpoché once crossed an old iron bridge believed to have been built by Tangtong in Minyak, made prayers at the side of the bridge, and placed ceremonial white scarves over the chains. According to Rinpoché, the original bridges that Tangtong built can be distinguished from the later ones by the small vajras that he stamped on each link of the chains. The bridge in Minyak that Dezhung Rinpoché visited still had some of the original links marked with vajras.[192] However, surviving bridges do not seem to bear such marks.

According to eyewitness accounts from the mid-1980s, the longest of the iron suspension bridges now surviving in Tibet are somewhat more than one hundred meters in length and the shortest are about fifty meters in length. Some are about two meters wide, but most are about one and a half meters in width. Where the Tsangpo River is wide, not very deep, and the current is not too swift, a bridge pier of stones has been piled up in the middle of the river and the bridges have two spans. At sites where the water is deep and the river current is very swift and powerful, the bridges have only a single span with no pier in the middle. In those cases, both ends of the chains are anchored into bridge abutments *(zam rngur)* on the shores. Otherwise, one or both ends of the chains are attached to two iron spikes that are about two meters long and six centimeters in diameter, which have been driven into a stone cliff.[193] These present-day observations correspond very well to the descriptions of bridge construction found in Tangtong Gyalpo's biographies.

19. The iron bridge at Dosum, eastern Bhutan.

Tangtong Gyalpo's iron bridges transformed the environment, but did not provide lasting spiritual power. For this purpose he built a large number of stūpas—symbolic representations of enlightened mind—in strategic locations throughout the Tibetan cultural regions. These stūpas served as geomantic focal-points *(sa'i me btsa')* in the environment and, depending on their location and type, aided in the control of demonic intrusion, disease, warfare, and various other destructive forces. Monasteries and temples were also constructed along the same principles. Tibetan medical practice maintains that the human body contains a number of vital focal-points *(me btsa')* around which is structured the subtle body of the individual. Chinese acupuncture also employs a similar system of vital points in the body, where needles are inserted for specific remedies. Ancient legends say the landscape of Tibet is the prone body of a gigantic demoness and the points on the earth corresponding to the vital focal-points in her body must be controlled in order to bring harmony to the environment, just as treatment is applied to the specific point of ailment in the body of a human patient. The *Compendium of Maṇis* contains an account of the seventh-century King Songtsen Gampo constructing 108 temples in Tibet and border lands that were situated on the focal-points of the demoness' body in order to prevent natural catastrophe and foreign invasion.[194]

Tangtong Gyalpo was first involved in the construction of a stūpa when he assisted the Sakya master Dakchen Sönam Tashi (1352–1407) in building the huge stūpa of Gyang near Lhatsé. This stūpa was constructed close to one of the temples that had been built centuries before by King Songtsen Gampo for the purpose of protecting Tibet from external threats.[195]

However, the first stūpa that Tangtong planned himself as an environmental focal-point was at Waru Namtsel in Kongpo. Several years later, while he was in the Paro area of Bhutan in 1433–34, he built the stūpa of Dumtsé to subdue a malignant earth spirit, and said the stūpa's power would wipe out the disease of leprosy in the area. The original structure of this monument is still standing today. The twenty-fifth head-abbot of Bhutan, Sherab Gyaltsen (1772–1847), later commissioned beautiful wall paintings on its three floors, expanded the ground floor with a larger outer wall, and reinforced the basic structure with huge pillars carried from neighboring villages.[196] Among the other stūpas Tangtong built that were situated on focal-points was the one at Dartsedo in Minyak to prevent earthquakes and the one at Jé Bodong in Tsang to stop fighting among the people. The most magnificent of all these projects was the massive Auspicious Stūpa of Many Doors at Riwoché in Latö Jang in western Tsang, which was Tangtong's main residence. Another large stūpa was at Chuwori, which is one of the four main mountains of Central Tibet. During his long life Tangtong built a total of 111 stūpas.[197]

The construction of stūpas was Tangtong Gyalpo's primary method for taming the hostile forces of a given area, but on several occasions the founding of a monastery or temple was based on the same theory. He was deeply interested in understanding the physical environment as an external expression of inherent psychic and divine energy. As mentioned above, he had studied the *Compendium of Maṇis*, one of the basic sources describing this relationship, and some events in his life seem to be related to the theories found there. In this ancient text the Chinese wife of the Tibetan king Songtsen Gampo, through her visionary powers and skill in Chinese astrology, is said to have advised the king that the Lhasa area was the heart of a prone demoness who formed the land of Tibet, and that the subterranean Otang Lake was her heart-blood. To the west, the two mountains of Marpori and Chakhar formed her heart-bone. It was necessary to suppress these areas in order to control the environment, and so the Jokhang Temple was built over the lake and the king's palace was constructed at the side to suppress the heart-bone. Around it to the four directions were four scorpion-shaped mountains forming the demoness' mouth, which also had to be controlled.[198]

Tangtong Gyalpo was clearly inspired by at least two of the grand stūpas built in Tibet before his lifetime. When he visited the monastery of Tropu, he saw the stūpa and Maitreya image constructed by Tropu

Lotsāwa Jampa Pal (1172–1236) from 1230–34, and at Jonang he visited the stūpa built by Dolpopa Sherab Gyaltsen from 1330–33, itself probably modeled on the stūpa at Tropu. At both of these monuments he made prayers and exclaimed, "Let's see if I can build a stūpa like this!"[199] As mentioned in his biographies, Tangtong was also involved in the construction of the famous stūpa at Gyang around the beginning of the fifteenth century.[200] He also received many prophecies from his teachers and the deities that he should build stūpas in Tibet. When he traveled to the island of Tāmradvīpa (Ceylon?), he visited an ancient Auspicious Stūpa of Many Doors and had visionary meetings with the legendary adepts Śavaripa and Kukkuripa, who both told him to construct an Auspicious Stūpa of Many Doors in Tibet. Śavaripa specifically told him to build it on the peak of a scorpion-shaped mountain in Tibet.[201] Such a monument was essential for preventing foreign invasion and for controlling the focal-point necessary to subdue the four base elements of earth, water, fire, and air. When Tangtong was circumambulating the stūpa in Tāmradvīpa, he carefully memorized the architectural details such as its two-level dome.[202]

After returning to Tibet, Tangtong Gyalpo saw a scorpion-shaped mountain (as in the legends of the *Compendium of Maṇis*) on the northern shore of the Tsangpo River in the valley of Chung in Latö Jang in western Tsang. He realized that it was the prophesied site for his monastery and stūpa and named it Pal Riwoché (Glorious Great Mountain).[203] His ability to locate such focal-points and construct monasteries or stūpas had been prophesied by Padmasambhava, one of whose stūpas Tangtong caused to be repaired in 1447 to protect Tibet against Mongol invasion. As described in the translated biography, his monks and the workers of the Jang district labored from 1449 to 1456 at Riwoché to construct a gigantic stūpa of the style called Auspicious Stūpa of Many Doors *(bkra shis sgo mang).* This monument was later surrounded by many temples containing a magnificent collection of murals and large images.[204] The Riwoché stūpa was built at the base of the scorpion-shaped mountain to crush the forehead of the scorpion. The location of Tangtong's meditation hut was specifically selected to suppress this mountain and river that were believed to embody the spiritual energy of armies that were hostile to Tibet. The stūpa and complex of temples below and on the mountain were built as a geomantic focal-point to counter any harm from the Mongols.[205] The artistic style and structure of the Riwoché stūpa is specifically said to match that of the ancient stūpa that Tangtong had visited on the

20. Chung Riwoché.

island of Tāmradvīpa during his Indian travels.[206] Nevertheless, obvious architectural and artistic similarities also connect the Riwoché monument and the earlier stūpas at Jonang and Gyang.[207]

The Gungtang princess Jetsun Chökyi Drönmé (1422–55) first met Tangtong Gyalpo at Riwoché in about 1455 as work on the immense stūpa was nearing completion.[208] This great yoginī was the daughter of Tri Lhawang Gyaltsen (1404–64), the king of Ngari Gungtang, and his queen Dodé Gyalmo (d. 1463?). Chökyi Drönmé was believed to be an emanation of the goddess Vajravārāhī. When she was seventeen years old, she had been forced to marry the Bönpo prince Tsewang Tashi (d. 1454/55), son of the Latö Lho governor Lhatsen Kyab. When she was nineteen years old she gave birth to a daughter, who died while still very young.[209] In spite of much opposition, Chökyi Drönmé soon left her husband, renounced her royal heritage, and became a fully ordained nun and one of the main disciples of Bodong Panchen Cholé Namgyal (1376–1451). Paradoxically, she also became Bodong Panchen's consort and, after his death, one of the main teachers of the Bodong tradition. Chökyi Drönmé's biography contains marvelous details of her brief time with Tangtong at Riwoché in about 1455. Her main companion and attendant, the nun Delek Chödrön, had previously visited Riwoché and carried letters between Tangtong and Chökyi Drönmé, but the two teachers had never met. Tangtong knew she was coming to visit, but did not know when. This is how Chökyi Drönmé's biographer describes their first meeting:

> As the venerable lady was about to arrive at Chung Riwoché and was sitting on a ridge of the mountain for a moment to rest and prepare a meeting-scarf, the adept himself leaned his upper body out of his meditation hut and was waving with his hand.
>
> The venerable lady asked, "Delek, who is that up there?"
>
> "It is the adept," she replied.
>
> "The master himself is so joyful!" she exclaimed, and smiled.
>
> Then she went up and offered prostrations before him and presented the offering of a meeting-scarf. The adept was wearing a new cloak and summer-hat and sat with his mouth covered by the cloak while she prostrated.[210]
>
> She offered the pearl earrings that the Dharma lady of Taktsé had offered to her, bootstraps woven from brocade thread, a plate full of white sugar, and various medicinal herbs.
>
> When she prostated again, the adept said, "Have you come with everyone's knowledge or are you fleeing?"
>
> "I asked my father and brother's advice and have come with everyone's knowledge," she replied.
>
> "That someone like you has become a renunciant with everyone's knowledge is incredible. I rejoice! Now, please take a seat right here where I can see you."
>
> Delek asked the adept, "Why did you wave just before?"
>
> "I waved because I was impatient for you, teacher and disciples, to arrive," he replied.[211]

As described in the translated biography, after receiving a prophecy by Tangtong Gyalpo, Chökyi Drönmé went to his monastery of Tsagong Nesar in Kongpo. She also expanded the Menmogang monastery and gathered a large quantity of iron for the bridge Tangtong wished to build at the ferry crossing of Nyago. She died soon after, and her rebirths have been known ever since as the Yamdrok Jetsünma, the famous abbesses of the Samding monastery overlooking Yamdrok Lake near Kongpo. These women were famed as incarnations of Vajravārāhī, and became the most important female religious figures in Tibet.[212] In the 1420s, when Tangtong had first traveled to the Kongpo area, Vajrayoginī had prophesied that Vajravārāhī would leave there an "authentic skull-cup" *(mtshan ldan dbu thod),* which would become a special relic bestowing joy on those who beheld it. This prophecy was fulfilled when the skull-cup made from the cranium of Chökyi Drönmé was enshrined at Tsagong.[213]

Riwoché Monastery became the seat for Tangtong Gyalpo's activities in Tsang and his main residence for the last part of his life. It continued for centuries to be one of the main centers of his Iron-Bridge tradition and the home of his descendants. Some of the first restorations to Riwoché may have been those carried out in 1558 by Lochen Ratnabhadra (1489–1563), who was the main teacher of Tangtong's descendant and biographer, Gyurmé Dechen. Ratnabhadra also built two retreat centers at Riwoché in the same year.[214] In 1824, the master Shabkar Natsok Rangdrol (1781–1850) made extensive repairs to the Riwoché stūpa. The thirteen rings of the upper part of the structure had been destroyed by fire. The restoration of the entire stūpa, from top to bottom, inside and out, was begun with a work force of about six hundred monks, nuns, and pilgrims. At one point more than a thousand people were engaged in the project. The thirteen rings were replaced, along with a new pinnacle, all of gilt copper.[215] About a hundred years later, in 1929, the Thirteenth Dalai Lama, Tupten Gyatso (1876–1933), appointed Dzatrul Ngawang Tenzin Norbu (1867–1940) to be the abbot of Riwoché, and ordered him to repair the damage that time had caused to the stūpa and the various other temples. This restoration work was begun in 1933.[216] Ngawang Tutob Wangchuk (1900–50), the head of the Sakya tradition, visited the monastery for several weeks in 1946 and paid his respects in front of the small reliquary stūpa containing the preserved body *(sku dmar gdung)* of Tangtong Gyalpo. At that time the monastery and the stūpa Tangtong had built were in good condition.[217] Unfortunately, this was not to last.

Tangtong Gyalpo's huge stūpa and the monastic complex at Riwoché suffered severe damage in the 1960s during the Chinese "Cultural Revolution." A native of Chung Riwoché who revisited his home in 1979 was told by local people that the monasteries, precious images, and manuscripts had all been destroyed over a period of ten days by a gathering of four hundred people from fifteen regions. The metal images were taken by the Chinese for small payments according to their weight, and the clay images were mixed with manure and burnt along with the manuscripts. Stone

21. Drawing of the Chung Riwoché complex before damage.

carvings were broken and laid on the roads. However, the iron bridge was not destroyed and, although nearly buried under debris, the magnificent stūpa was still standing.[218]

It was not until 1988 that detailed information and photographs of Riwoché emerged. Although severely damaged, the main structure of the stūpa has survived intact. The upper spire was completely smashed. The roofs of the inner temples were mostly collapsed and many murals destroyed, although some examples of the original paintings do remain. The surrounding monasteries were obliterated. Restoration had begun sometime before 1988. The iron suspension bridge was not singled out for destruction, and still spans the Tsangpo River.[219]

On Chuwori Mountain in Central Tibet, Tangtong Gyalpo built two monasteries, one at the foot of the mountain and one on the peak. He also constructed an iron bridge over the Tsangpo River in front of the lower establishment and a stūpa containing a small portrait-image *(nga 'dra ma)* that he made of himself. The Tenzin Rinpochés or Chaksam Tulkus reigned at this monastery, which became the main center of Tangtong's tradition in Central Tibet. The monastery and the Stūpa of Enlightenment at Chuwori were still in excellent condition in 1919 when visited by Katok

Situ Chökyi Gyatso (1880–1925). Situ describes in detail the buildings and their contents at the time of his visit. The entombed remains of four of the Chaksam hierarchs were preserved in splendor, as well as many other exquisite statues and tangka paintings made during Tangtong's lifetime. Among them were a set of metal images that Tangtong himself made, a set of the Translated Scriptures from his lifetime, and works of art illustrating the nonsectarian nature of his teachings.[220] This monastery was also visited by Giuseppe Tucci in 1948 and by virtually every European traveler to pass through Central Tibet.[221] Sadly, the monastery, stūpa, and bridge at Chuwori were totally destroyed during the "Cultural Revolution." Not even a trace remains.

In Kongpo, Tangtong Gyalpo founded the monastery of Palgyi Nesar in Tsagong, which was the seat of his activities in the southeast, and placed his disciple Riksum Gönpo on the monastic seat as the first abbot. Tangtong's consort Chökyi Drönmé later went there to supervise various projects, and toward the end of his life he sent his son Kyabpa Sangpo there to be his heir in the Kongpo area.[222]

Tangtong Gyalpo also built various monasteries in Bhutan, the most important of which was Tachok Norbugang, which became the seat of the Chaksam tradition in that country. This monastery was destroyed by Shabdrung Ngawang Namgyal (1594–1651) because it was the main seat of the Chaksam tradition that, along with four other sects in Bhutan, was opposed to his rule. It was restored later by the Fourth Druk Desi, Tenzin Rabgyé (reign: 1680–95).[223] Tachok Norbugang is presided over by the Tachok Chöjé, who have been the hereditary leaders since the time of Tangtong's visit, although by the 1980s no community of monks remained in the establishment.[224]

The most historically significant of the many monasteries Tangtong Gyalpo founded was probably at Dergé in eastern Tibet. When Tangtong visited Dergé in 1446, the king Potar Tashi Sengé became his patron and he became the king's teacher. It is said that he saw that a lake at the foot of the northern mountain in the upper valley of Ngu was inhabited by a powerful nāga spirit. He tamed this spirit and bound it to the vow not to harm people and to create harmonious conditions in the area. Then he magically covered over the lake in a manner reminiscent of the legends in the *Compendium of Maṇis* and laid the foundation for a monastery where the shores had been. When the construction was complete, he performed the rites of the Dharma protector Caturmukha. Because all the conditions

22. Tachok Norbugang Monastery, Bhutan.

necessary for the prosperity of the monastery were accomplished without any effort, as though spontaneously, it was given the name Lhundrup Teng.[225] This center would become perhaps the most important monastery in all of eastern Tibet, and the seat of the Dergé rulers and of the Sakya tradition in Kham. It is believed to have become a Ngor monastery of the Sakya sect as a result of the connection between Tangtong and the founder of the Ngor subsect, Ngorchen Kunga Sangpo (1382–1456).[226] One of the inner sanctums of the monastery is the Tangtong Temple (Thang stong lha khang) that houses a famous special clay image of Tangtong Gyalpo.

Only Tangtong Gyalpo's most famous iron bridges, monasteries, and stūpas have been briefly discussed here. Many more are mentioned in biographies and histories. Others are attributed to him in the oral tradition. For example, according to Dezhung Rinpoché, a local tradition in Kham says that when Tangtong was ready to leave a place called Yilhung Shi, where he had been staying for some time, the people prayed for him to remain, and so he made a clay statue of himself that was a perfect likeness. In fact, it was so similar that the people could not tell them apart, because the statue was miraculously able to teach Dharma and travel about like a person. Everyone said there were two Tangtong Gyalpos. When Tangtong left the area, the figure he had made was used as the model for a huge one-story-high image. The smaller clay figure was then placed inside the large image to embody its primordial awareness *(tsha tsha ye shes dpa')*. In the 1920s a band of thirty to forty bandits terrorized the town and burned down many homes and the temple. The large statue was destroyed, but the smaller original in its interior was unharmed. The spiritual energy of the image therefore remained intact. One of Dezhung Rinpoché's teachers, Gangkar Rinpoché Chökyi Sengé (1891–1957), rebuilt the temple and the large statue and placed the small image within it. This master also rebuilt the Stūpa of Great Enlightenment that Tangtong had constructed at Dartsedo, which had been reduced to ruin by an earthquake in the early twentieth century.[227]

Tangtong Gyalpo was the greatest engineer in Tibetan history, one of its most prolific architects, and an innovative artist. His many iron bridges, monasteries, and stūpas have enriched Tibetan culture for over five hundred years. The extent to which he changed his country's spiritual topography through concrete activities based on mystical theory remains unparalleled in Tibetan history.

4. Madman of the Empty Valley

> Crazed by the disease of realizing
> emptiness as the ground,
> crazed by the demon of destroying
> confusion on the path,
> and crazed by the force of discarding
> any thought of achieving a result,
> lord, Madman of the Empty Valley,
> I bow at your feet.[228]
>
> —Gyaltsen Sangpo

Tangtong Gyalpo was widely known as Lungtong Nyönpa (Lung stong smyon pa), "Madman of the Empty Valley," one of the five names given to him by the ḍākinīs. He is famed as one of the great "mad yogins" of Tibetan history, along with three of his younger contemporaries: Tsang Nyön Heruka (Madman of Tsang, 1452–1507), Druk Nyön Kunga Lekpa (Madman of Bhutan, 1455–1529), and Ü Nyön Kunga Sangpo (Madman of Central Tibet, 1458–1532).[229] These eccentric masters and their predecessors based their behavior on the scriptures of the Guhyasamāja, Hevajra, Cakrasaṃvara, Catuḥpīṭha, and other traditions of Indian tantric Buddhism, and followed the examples of the great adepts *(mahāsiddha, grub*

23. Tangtong Gyalpo holding an alms bowl, with a chain by his knee.

chen) of ancient India and Tibet. Based on the contents of the tantric scriptures, some of the most famous heroes in Vajrayāna Buddhism are believed to have achieved enlightenment using methods that also shocked their contemporaries from worldly slumber. The Buddhist traditions in India that were the sources for the tantric Buddhism that developed in Tibet are full of stories and teachings of masters such as Padmasambhava, Saraha, Virūpa, and Nāropa, whose actions sometimes earned them the epithet "mad" *(smyon pa)*. According to one tradition, 101 Indian masters were known for their practice of peculiar styles of deliberate behavior, from among whom six are said to have perfected it: Mañjuśrīmitra, Mañjuśrībhadra, Virūpa, Kṛṣṇacārin, Ḍombi Heruka, and Padmasambhava.[230]

The specific behavior recommended in tantric literature for testing and enhancing the realization of the advanced practitioner is a fascinating and complex subject.[231] A general term often used for this conduct is *deliberate behavior (vratacaryā; brtul zhugs spyod pa)*. The original range of meaning for this expression is extremely wide, sometimes denoting any type of religious behavior in general and at other times indicating a specific disciplined style of conduct. The literal meaning of the Tibetan translation of the Sanskrit term is *behavior (spyod pa) of taming (brtul) and entering (zhugs)*. According to the explanation of Dezhung Rinpoché, this means "taming worldly behavior and entering into the behavior of the buddhas. Or else, taming bad behavior and entering into perfect behavior."[232] The varieties and levels of tantric deliberate behavior cannot be discussed in detail here. In the biographies of Tangtong Gyalpo and his contemporaries, eccentric acts of a religious nature are usually just referred to as *deliberate behavior*, and sometimes as *secret behavior*, which in this context is a synonym. The use of feigned madness is just one of the many facets of deliberate or prescribed behavior advocated in the tantric treatises.

In brief, deliberate behavior is essentially a special type of physical, verbal, and mental conduct used to enhance an already stable meditative concentration that has been achieved though practice of the creation and completion stages of Vajrayāna meditation.[233] In general, this special conduct can only be practiced at an advanced point on the tantric path, when *warmth (drod)* has been obtained. *Warmth* is the term used to indicate a foretaste of the attainments, in the sense that warmth is the initial sign that appears before fire. For example, a person has obtained *warmth* when he or she is not affected by inner or outer harm, nothing whatever can disturb meditative concentration, he or she is equanimous toward the eight worldly concerns,[234] and all apparent objects in general and sensory objects in particular only serve to increase meditative concentration. *Warmth* is the first of the four stages of the Path of Application. The practices of deliberate behavior are forbidden until at least this stage has been reached.

A person must also have the correct motives for engaging in deliberate behavior, which must be used only for the purpose of liberating oneself and others, without any selfish interests. The practitioner must also have no attachment to material possessions, deep compassion for sentient beings, and complete dedication of body and mind to the benefit of others.

In general, three of the main categories of deliberate behavior are called *avadhūti*, *totally good (kun tu bzang po)*, and *completely victorious (phyogs las rnam rgyal)*. In this context, the Sanskrit term *avadhūti* was translated into Tibetan as *sinful behavior (sdig pa spyod pa)*, *nondual behavior (gnyis spangs)*, or *behavior that makes everyone tremble (kun 'dar)*. The basic meaning is that it purifies sins, destroys dualistic thinking, and destabilizes and expels conceptual notions and clinging to things as true. The second behavior is called *totally good* because the essence of the behavior is always good, whether it appears externally to be good or bad. The third is known as *completely victorious* because the person has actually achieved victory over the afflictions, the four māras have been subdued, he or she has the power to benefit sentient beings, and the obscuration of knowledge has also been destroyed.

When a practitioner engages in deliberate behavior according to the teachings of the tantras, the first phase of the conduct is done in secret to determine whether or not stability of mind has been achieved. This is done at night in places such as charnel grounds or cemeteries, wandering with a consort or utilizing a visualized consort, and engaging in various kinds of socially unacceptable behavior. If this type of conduct indicates that a person's awareness is not stable, then the behavior should not yet be performed, and the practitioner should concentrate on meditation to stabilize the yoga. If the awareness is stable, then the person practices in this way for a month to become accustomed to it. With a prophesied consort, and after requesting permission from his or her teacher, the *avadhūti* behavior is begun, which is to publicly pretend to be a crazy person, a fool, or another type of despised individual. Together with the consort or ḍākinīs, the practitioner does various kinds of unpredictable acts, such as singing, dancing, babbling, scolding, playing, laughing, running and leaping about in public, and engaging in prohibited sexual activities. The mind is kept focused in meditation at all times while doing these things that actually serve to further meditative concentration. Overt religious acts that might be recognized by other practitioners and reveal the nature of what is really going on are not done at this time. This *avadhūti* behavior is mostly utilized while the person is at the level of *lesser warmth* on the Path of Application.

When the ordinary conceptual process has ceased, and a practitioner has advanced to the level of *middling warmth*, the *totally good* behavior is practiced. If permission was not requested from a teacher before, it is imperative that it be requested now. At this point the person reveals to the public that he or she is practicing a yogic discipline. Various miraculous deeds are performed to change the minds of those who lack faith, and techniques such as the charismatic gazes and so forth that are taught in the tantras are used to benefit sentient beings in different ways. Numerous ḍākinīs are effortlessly attracted. At least one of Tangtong Gyalpo's disciples specifically noted that his master sometimes practiced the *totally good* behavior.[235]

When a person reaches the level of *greater warmth*, the *completely victorious* behavior is appropriate. While some conditions may have been slightly harmful before, nothing is harmful anymore. The same consort as before may still be relied upon here, but since vast ability has been gained, various female spirits and ḍākinīs are also attracted. By means of practices with the appropriate consort, the Path of Seeing is actualized.

The behavior of a madman and other unusual styles of action can be deliberately chosen according to the formulas described in the tantric treatises, or can also arise in a spontaneous and ecstatic way. A vision of a deity or some similar experience can serve as the catalyst for an ecstatic outburst of apparent madness or the assumption of a specific deliberate behavior. In the Nyingma tradition most of the mad yogins were treasure revealers. One of the most important of these, Nyang Nyima Öser (1136–1204), was called insane as a young boy because of his strange behavior following a visionary initiation by Padmasambhava.[236] At the age of thirteen, the treasure revealer Kunkyong Lingpa (1396–1477) acted insane when a ḍākinī revealed to him where a treasure text was hidden. He was called crazy by his father following his ecstatic display.[237] Orgyan Lingpa (1323–ca.1360), the discoverer of the *Five Chronicles (Bka' thang sde lnga)*, was known as a "madman of the treasures" *(gter smyon)*.[238] Many other examples could be mentioned, such as the Bhutanese revealer of treasures, Pema Lingpa (1450–1521), who sometimes referred to himself as "Pema Lingpa, the crazy revealer of treasures."[239] Pema Lingpa's aunt, Ashi Drubtob Sangmo, was also a consort of Tangtong Gyalpo during his travels in Bhutan.[240]

Tangtong Gyalpo practiced and taught the Northern Treasure teachings of the Nyingma tradition. The first of the Northern Treasure masters was Ngödrup Gyaltsen (1337–1408), who was sometimes called "a crazy yogin with hair-feathers."[241] When he was twelve years old, three protuberances resembling vulture feathers sprouted from the crown of his head, signifying that he had been graced by Padmasambhava.[242] He was therefore known as Gökyi Demtruchen, "Vulture Feathered." One of Tangtong's most important masters, Kunpang Dönyö Gyaltsen, had actually studied under Gökyi Demtruchen, and passed all of his treasure tradition to Tangtong. The Chöd, or Severance, teachings also have a place in the Northern Treasure tradition, although the Nyingma lineages of Chöd originate with Padmasambhava and not Machik Labdrön. The treasure revealer Dawa

24. Images of Tangtong Gyalpo awaiting consecration.

Gyaltsen, who was one of the successors of Gökyi Demtruchen in the Northern Treasure and Chöd lineages, is also described as "adopting the deliberate behavior of a Chöd practicer, or an insanelike manner."[243]

Mad yogins are known in virtually every tradition in Tibet, but most often in the Nyingma and Kagyü lineages, and also in the Shijé (Pacification) and Chöd traditions. The Nyingma, Kagyü, and Chöd traditions are the three with which Tangtong Gyalpo had the closest ties. One of the texts in Tangtong's Oral Transmission, a collection of teachings originally passed down from Tangtong, quotes the great yoginī Machik Labdrön's statement concerning proper yogic conduct following realization. In response to a question by one of her sons, Machik recommended that a practitioner act like a child with unfeigned spontaneity, like a lunatic with no regard for what is conventionally acceptable, like a leper with no attachment to his or her own physical health, and like a wild animal wandering in isolated and rough terrain.[244]

The tradition of mad yogins seems to have flowered in Tibet during the fifteenth century and to have been most pronounced among adherents to the Kagyü schools.[245] The crazy masters Tsang Nyön Heruka, Druk Nyön, and Ü Nyön all had their strongest ties with Kagyü traditions.

Tsang Nyön in particular was deeply influenced by the life and teachings of Milarepa (1040–1123), who was in many ways the perfect mad yogin. For example, when Milarepa met Padampa Sangyé, the Indian master tried to disguise himself from Milarepa and called him crazy when the Tibetan yogin paid his respects. In response Milarepa sang this eloquent definition of his madness.

To my wise lord and master,
I pray as a beggar, grant me your blessings!

Please listen, Indian yogin.

When struck by the demon of ignorance,
all living beings of the six realms in general are crazy.

Realizing appearances are illusory,
Milarepa in particular is crazy.

With clairvoyant knowledge of others' minds,
my old father Marpa the Translator is crazy.

Courageous in austerities for the sake of Dharma,
my grandfather Nāro the great scholar was crazy.

With inconceivable abilities of emanation and transformation,
my great-grandfather Tilo Prajñābhadra was crazy.

Bestowing simultaneous bliss,
Vajrayoginī is crazy too.

Dwelling in union with taintless great bliss,
great Vajradhara, [the source of] the lineage, is crazy.

Not clearly showing your form to me,
Dampa, the object of my respect, you're crazy too!

Father's crazy, son's crazy, grandfather's crazy!
You're crazy, I'm crazy, everyone's crazy!

Some are crazed by ignorant deeds.
Some are crazed by the water of desire.
Some are crazed by the fire of hatred.
Some are crazed by the darkness of ignorance.
Some are crazed by the poison of pride.

You're crazed by knowing other's minds.
I'm crazed by realizing the fundamental nature.

You're crazed by realizing the meaning
of the vowels and consonants.
I'm crazed by realizing the unborn truth.

You're crazed by the practice of Pacification.
I'm crazed by realizing the meaning of Mahāmudrā.

This song sung at an intimate meeting of lunatics
is audible yet empty Mahāmudrā.[246]

Milarepa sings about his "madness" with profound humor, but a yogin was most often called "mad" if he displayed extremely eccentric behavior. Guru Padmasambhava himself prophesied that Tangtong Gyalpo would care for living beings by means of unpredictable actions.[247] Tangtong's unusual conduct began to manifest at an early age, and resembled traits noted in the lives of other mad yogins. He was first called insane by his father and the members of his village when, as a child, he subdued a malicious spirit responsible for an epidemic. Several other early incidents are mentioned in the biographies. When he went to take scholastic examinations at the renowned monastery of Sakya he earned the nickname Tsöndru Nyönpa (Crazy Tsöndru) because of his disinterest in explaining the scriptural definitions of the highest states of realization. He preferred to spend his time absorbed in actually experiencing these states.[248] When he was later practicing deliberate behavior secretly in a vast and empty wasteland, the ḍākinīs gave him five names indicating his high realization, one of which was Lungtong Nyönpa (Madman of the Empty Valley).

In the valley of equanimity free of conceptual elaboration,
you have the view of appearance

> and emptiness as indivisible.
> A madman free of accepting and rejecting,
> we name you Madman of the Empty Valley.[249]

The feigning of madness and other modes of deliberate behavior prescribed in the Buddhist tantras are always chosen in order to benefit others. The pivotal event convincing Tangtong Gyalpo that he should employ the various forceful means of tantric behavior occurred when he received the treasure teachings of Gökyi Demtruchen from Kunpang Dönyö Gyaltsen. Tangtong was still young, and as a newly ordained monk he felt some misgivings concerning the various fierce methods advocated in the teachings that had been concealed by Padmasambhava. As he pondered whether these techniques were in conflict with the lifestyle of a monk, he was graced with a terrifying vision of Padmasambhava in the sky surrounded by rainbow light and yogins and yoginīs. Padmasambhava indicated the yogins to his right eating a human corpse, the yoginīs to his left drinking from a skull-cup filled with beer, and finally himself in sexual union with the goddess Vajravārāhī. Tangtong considered this vision to be a symbolic command that if the good of others was accomplished through reliance on the sacramental substances and deliberate behavior, he should perform even the four defeating acts.[250] He immediately went into strict seclusion for three years, at the end of which Padmasambhava appeared again and directly urged him to assume the lifestyle and dress of a tantric yogin and engage in deliberate behavior. Before this retreat, Tangtong had dressed as a monk, but now he began to wear only a simple cloak in keeping with the yogic lifestyle, and often used the unusual techniques of deliberate behavior to heighten his own realization and to benefit others.[251]

The following early episodes in the life of Tangtong Gyalpo are from the biography written by his disciple and close attendant Sherab Palden, who certainly learned of them directly from the great adept himself.

> Then the great adept traveled to Lhatsé and Dechen. "Come listen to Dharma!" he called.
>
> "Greedy renunciant!" a woman said. "If you've got Dharma to teach, teach it to this donkey!"
>
> A donkey was going along the path burdened with a load. When the great adept carefully explained the advantages and disadvantages of actions according to the relationship of cause

25. Dolpopa Sherab Gyaltsen (1292–1361).

and result, the donkey understood the Dharma and lay in the road and could not get up.

"This bad renunciant has abused the donkey!" people cried.

A dog had defecated, and that woman said, "If you're a good yogin, eat this shit!"

When the lord ate it, the people exclaimed, "He's a crazy renunciant!"

The lord said that the thought arose in his mind that foolish people have less understanding than animals.

Then the great adept traveled to glorious Jonang. The practitioners were performing the rite of accomplishment and offerings to Kālacakra. One practitioner who had good experience in meditation actually saw the sovereign master as the Omniscient Dolpopa,[252] offered countless prostrations, circumambulated, and placed the great adept's feet on his head.

The great adept sat on the Dharma throne of the great Omniscient Dolpopa that night. The steward came carrying the steps [for the throne] and exclaimed, "Who put this mad-

> man on the Dharma throne? He won't get away!" He beat him with his staff and threw him down.
>
> Then, without any clothing, for three days the great adept circumambulated the Auspicious Stūpa of Many Doors during the night and sat on a flat white boulder during the day. To each of the several male and female practitioners who came to look at him he gave a writing slate[253] that said, "You'll see, I'll build a stūpa like this too."
>
> The steward and everyone else gathered there said, "Renunciant, you're crazy. The Omniscient Dolpopa, who was the actual embodiment of the buddhas of the three times, inspired the gods, demons, and human beings, and spent his entire life in virtuous actions, but did not complete more than this stūpa. You're an old renunciant who doesn't have food to eat, doesn't have clothing on his back, and doesn't even have a hole in the ground to live in. To say that you'll build a stūpa like this is really crazy!"
>
> That night the great adept sat in the middle of the waves under the bridge, with the water up to his neck. In the morning, people came to draw water and cried, "Oh, this stupid madman. Poor thing!"
>
> They had not developed any pure perception.
>
> The lord said he thought it was incredible that they practiced only conceptual meditation, without having learned what is to be discarded and accepted in regard to actions and their results.[254]

The eccentric acts of the mad yogins serve to enhance their realization, which is sometimes referred to as a state of *sameness* or *equal taste (samarasa; ro snyoms/ro mnyam).* The realization of equal taste was a goal articulated by the adepts of ancient India and is mentioned in the tantric scriptures. The view that all phenomena are of equal value or "taste the same" because of their lack of self-nature is a basic tenet. The expression of this through a lifestyle that directly shows the fragility of normal distinctions and value judgments is precisely what sets the mad yogin apart from his more conventional contemporaries. The behavior used to further the realization of equal taste is aimed at breaking down the habitual functioning of dualistic consciousness and developing equanimity toward the eight worldly concerns. This realization was emphasized in another of the names given to Tangtong Gyalpo by the ḍākinīs:

> Whatever various conditions occur,
> realizing they're like a dream or an echo,
> you overpower the eight worldly concerns,
> which for you have an equal taste.
> We name you One for Whom Conditions
> Have an Equal Taste.[255]

The iner development of equal taste is vividly portrayed by Tangtong Gyalpo himself in the following verses:

> The zombies of the eight worldly concerns
> stalk through the charnel ground
> of confusing thoughts.
> This inescapable, terrifying place,
> is the spot to practice equal taste.[256]

Total control over the ordinary, random flow of thoughts, achieved through experiencing the equal taste of all mental formations, is tested and proven through external acts that mirror the internal conquest. This is illustrated in an episode soon after Tangtong built his first iron bridge in 1430.

> As he traveled the road to Tölung[257] the great adept met several men of Minyak. They requested Dharma and offered him many personal possessions such as a helmet, a sword, and a bow and arrows. He wore these on his body and continued to the border of Sakha Nakpa and Gyeré Tsarpa.
>
> A blood feud had broken out between the people of Minyak and Gyeré. The Gyeré people thought the great adept was a Minyak man from Kham and robbed his personal possessions. When they stuck him with arrows, staffs, knives, and so forth, he experienced the equal taste of pleasure and pain and did not strike back or say anything. They thought he was a suitable victim, tied a rope to his penis, weighted it with a stone, and left him hanging on a fence that night.

At daybreak the next morning they cried, "This is the Adept of Iron Bridges! We have committed a grave sin!"

They took him down from where he was hanging on the fence. He was not at all angry, but when they offered their confessions with great regret, he was overjoyed and commented, "It was a profound practice for longevity."[258]

A yogin conventionally sought attainments such as equal taste through a wandering or secluded life style, poverty, and strenuous physical and mental training. However, some chose to follow the path of deliberate behavior, and many charlatans must have given the genuine yogin choosing this route a bad name. In various situations Tangtong Gyalpo was taken for an idiot, a madman, a beggar, a thief, and even a demon. A scholarly monk once accused him of being a fake who deceived faithful people by dressing like a yogin. Tangtong replied to these insults in an effort to correct mistaken opinions and conduct toward "yogins who maintain the practice of deliberate behavior and wear cloaks." He explained his own cloak, endowing every clasp and thread with an esoteric meaning, and referred to himself sarcastically as "a fake clad in my cloak."[259]

Almost all the descriptions of Tangtong Gyalpo's eccentric behavior are found in his own biographies, but some independent verification has come to light. He once spent a year at the famous Kaṃṇi Goshi stūpa in Lhasa without moving his body, and his deeds during this time clearly left a deep imprint on the collective memory of the citizens. Many decades later Tsang Nyön Heruka spent time at the same place, and, because of his eerie appearance, some people thought he was a rākṣasa demon and some said he was Tangtong Gyalpo. When Tsang Nyön was acting crazy on the road from Gungtang just before going to Lhasa, people had also mistaken him for Tangtong, exclaiming, "We take refuge! It could be Tangtong Gyalpo!"[260]

A meeting between Tangtong Gyalpo and the Sakya master Rongtön Sheja Kunrik (1367–1449) is very briefly described in Tangtong's biographies.[261] But in the biography of Rongtön written by his student Panchen Shākya Chokden (1428–1507), who also knew Tangtong, the same episode is more detailed and revealing. The meeting was at Rongtön's monastery of Nālendra, probably in about 1444.

26. Tangtong Gyalpo holding a chain.

When Rongtön was once on the Dharma throne teaching an early session of Dharma, the Iron-Bridge Man, in the costume of a Minyak man with braids, burst in unexpectedly and made three circumambulations around the Dharma throne without dismounting from his horse.

"I'm boiling up a tea for everyone. Blow the conch shell!" he shouted, setting up a little stove in the corner of the teaching arena and producing a bowl full of delicious tea. The conch shell was not blown, but about five hundred of the Sangha gathered on their own. He poured a spoonful of tea into the hand of each member of the Sangha and said, "There, I've made tea for everyone. Bring me a plate! Dharma lord, if you have clairvoyance, what am I serving on the plate?"

Lord Rongtön replied, "Could it be some lumps of brown sugar?"

Just as Rongtön had said, the Iron-Bridge Man offered the plate full of brown sugar and commented, "Isn't it incredible to hold a tea for everyone with one bowl full of tea? Dharma lord, if you can take that plate full of brown sugar and distribute a lump to each one of all the Sangha, Dharma lord, you would be a real man!"

Lord Rongtön replied, "Well, hand it out to everyone!"

When a geshé from Kham handed it out, there was a quantity of about twenty lumps of brown sugar, but one was distributed to each of the five hundred members of the Sangha.

Lord Rongtön asked, "Isn't that even more amazing?"

The Iron-Bridge Man replied, "Well, will I return from Mount Wutai, or not? Will I build an iron bridge on the Nyakchu River, or not?"[262]

During the time when the Iron-Bridge Man had been building the iron bridge of Lhasa before, lord Rongtön had been staying at Sangpu.[263] Because the prophecies requested at that time had been accurate, it appears that the Iron-Bridge Man believed in him.

At this time, the Iron-Bridge Man did not generally go inside buildings, but that day he went into the residence.[264] Master and disciple had a brief conversation in private, and then he left.

This was said by Rongtön's personal attendants.[265]

Riding a horse into the main hall of a monastery during a teaching session is an outrageous act, and Tangtong Gyalpo was stoned by monks on several occasions when he did the same thing at other monasteries. But this and the other behavior in the Nālendra episode are relatively mild. Deliberate behavior is often much more extreme. The most shocking examples are found in the biographies of Tsang Nyön Heruka, who was the author and editor of the famous biography and collected mystical songs of Milarepa. Tsang Nyön knew that the people of his time were afflicted with coarse passions, had short lives, many diseases, and completely wrong ideas about the nature of reality. According to his student Natsok Rangdrol, Tsang Nyön had already achieved perfection for his own benefit, but understood that the most effective way to tame others was to pretend that he was a yogin on the path. Thus he wandered about engaging in deliberate behavior while totally concealing all of his own exceptional qualities. He did this only for the benefit of the Buddhist doctrine and all sentient beings. With these altruistic motives in mind, he

27. Tsang Nyön Heruka (1452–1507).

once danced about in a crowd of people at Tsari, holding a lump of brown sugar in his right hand and a piece of shit in his left, taking a bite from one and then the other, while urinating on everyone and striking out at them. On other occasions Tsang Nyön smeared his naked body with ash, blood, and grease from a cremated corpse, used a corpse's intestines for a garland, bracelets, and anklets, cut off the fingers and toes and strung them on a thread to tie up his hair, and wandered through a huge religious assembly, sometimes laughing and sometimes weeping. He also flayed the skin from a corpse and wore it as a cloak, while eating human flesh and brains. Taking a bloody skull that was about one third full of brains, he filled it with beer, drank some, and then offered it to Tashi Dargyé, the powerful ruler of the district of Ja. When the governor drank the rest of the dreadful mixture, he experienced a blazing of warmth in his body and a freedom from the usual dualistic state of mind for ten days.[266] It is not surprising that Tsang Nyön Heruka became known as the "Madman of Tsang" following these episodes.

Tangtong Gyalpo once came upon the body of a dead horse by the side of a road and searched for its heart to use for a ritual feast, but could not find it. So he just took the pus-filled lungs, which he blessed and ate during the feast. People cried, "This man is a rākṣasa demon!" and all ran away. The next day, the ruler of the Yargyab district brought a huge quantity of fine food and drink, which Tangtong used for a ritual feast. But he later commented, "I thought the ritual feast yesterday was perfect, but nobody was able to eat it. Today's wasn't like that."[267]

When Ü Nyön Kunga Sangpo (Madman of Central Tibet) once visited the Kathmandu Valley of Nepal, he saw the king of Bhaktapur in a large public audience. The king was seated on a jeweled throne, surrounded by silk parasols, musicians, and so forth. With fearless intensity, Ü Nyön jumped on the king's head, grabbed him by the hair, beat him with his fists, and urinated on his head. Everyone was so terrified by this deranged behavior that they listened to him like slaves, and he was presented with lavish offerings. A severe epidemic was raging in Nepal at the time, and Ü Nyön later picked up many corpses of people who had died from contagion and carried them to the charnel grounds.[268]

The outrageous behavior of Tangtong Gyalpo, Tsang Nyön, Ü Nyon, and other mad yogins cannot be viewed according to the criteria found in the Hinayāna or Theravada traditions, to which they do not belong. Furthermore, these methods are not advocated in the tantric context except for those who have already reached a very high degree of realization. Of course, it is extremely difficult to discern the validity of deliberate behavior chosen by another person. Only that person and his or her teacher can judge whether or not the assumption of unconventional behavior is appropriate. However, according to Dezhung Rinpoché, it is taught that a person who performs the extreme actions of deliberate behavior without being sufficiently mature will be reborn in vajra hell.[269]

The yogin who is acting to accelerate his awareness of the ultimate nature of all phenomena may seem to others to be a madman or fool with none of the normal value judgments guiding his activities. But it is only from the conventional viewpoint that the behavior of the mad yogin is aberrant. A scholarly monk once remarked to Tsang Nyön Heruka, "It's said there is a crazy renunciant around. Are you him?" Tsang Nyön replied, "There are different ways to see it. When I look, it's you who's crazy!"[270]

For Tangtong Gyalpo and these other special masters, ordinary people seem to be sleepwalking, already dead, or mad in their insane quest after ephemeral pleasures. The mad yogin has gained freedom from the limitations and bonds of saṃsāra, while worldly people are trapped by the stringent ties of their narrow viewpoints. The mad yogin is totally uncompromising, both in lifestyle and the content of his teachings, and directly confronts existence in saṃsāra by the employment of dynamic methods in the search for liberation. The realization of equal taste is sustained and heightened through the application of deliberate behavior as the method. Tangtong often confronted negative situations, and sometimes dealt with them in ways difficult to interpret. One episode illustrating his use of deliberate behavior for the common good, and demonstrating his attainment of equal taste, occurred during a trip through Penyul, a valley north of Lhasa.

> To form an auspicious connection to relieve the severe famine that existed at that time, the great adept announced, "I'm going to Penyul."
>
> The Iron-Bridge Man traveled to Penyul with six disciples. "No matter whom we meet today," he ordered, "rob whatever they have!"
>
> When traveling from Gyalchen Tsé in Penyul, he met a woman coming along carrying a load of barley for which she had gone into debt.
>
> "Give me that barley!" he demanded.
>
> "O Patron! Master from Kham, please! Our family is large and has nothing but this to eat," she cried.
>
> But he robbed her barley and fled, whipping his horse.
>
> The woman called for help to many men from Kham and Minyak who were passing by, and they chased and caught him. Not recognizing the great adept, they thought he was an Amdo man.[271] They bound and beat him. They dunked him in the water and threw him down on his back. They stuck their assholes in his face, sprayed excrement on him, and so forth. But the great adept thought, "It's a fine auspicious connection," and was delighted.
>
> The Minyak chieftain thought, "Those dimwitted servants have carried the beating too far. They may have killed him."
>
> When he mounted his horse and raced over, he recognized the great adept. He leapt from his horse, prostrated, and exclaimed, "Great master, are you in trouble?"

"A fine auspicious connection has happened to me today," the great adept replied. "From the day after tomorrow the famine among the common people will cease."

Showing the Minyak chieftain the barley he had robbed from the woman, he said, "Send this barley with some of my monks who are following!"

Laying his whip to the horse, he cried, "I'm returning to Lhasa!" and left.

The Minyak chieftain repaid the woman with barley and gave the original to the Iron-Bridge Man's monks. It was exchanged with the old barley in the alms bowl of the Jowo, and the great adept made prayers.[272]

Tangtong Gyalpo's most eccentric or "insane" deeds can be comprehended in small measure only if his motivation is understood. He certainly realized that this would not be possible for many people, and on one occasion remarked, "Half of Tibet will see me as an actual buddha. Half will see me as a demon."[273] Once, while in seclusion at Riwoché, he wrote down a series of verses pointing out that things are not always as they seem, and passed them out to a group of monks and laborers gathered in front of his meditation hut.

Faithful workers on the projects of virtue!
Listen to whether this is crooked or straight!

All straight isn't straight.
A fool's straight is crooked.

All crooked isn't crooked.
A wise man's crooked is straight.

All benefit isn't benefit.
A fool's benefit is harm.

All harm isn't harm.
A wise man's harm is benefit.

All pleasure isn't pleasure.
A fool's pleasure is suffering.

All suffering isn't suffering.
A wise man's suffering is pleasure.[274]

The actual intention of Tangtong Gyalpo's actions, regardless of their appearance, was always to do the most possible good. He sometimes achieved this by doing precisely the opposite of what might be expected. His manipulation of a situation for the good of others through the use of actions that were negative in appearance but positive in essence and result was the pragmatic application of theories expressed in tantric scriptures such as the *Hevajra Tantra*:

Using the very same poison,
a little of which would kill all living beings,
the person who knows the nature of poisons
dispels that poison.

If endowed with the means,
people are liberated from the bonds of existence
by precisely those evil deeds by which they are bound.

The world is bound by desire
and is liberated by passionate desire.
Buddhists and non-Buddhists do not know
this meditation of reversal.[275]

In Mahāyāna Buddhism the primary emphasis is placed on awakening the enlightened state of mind in which all activity is motivated by compassion for other living beings. This concern is the deciding factor in determining the moral validity of any specific deed and may outweigh the negative force of what appear to be vile acts. The problem of defining virtue and sin in the tantric tradition is discussed in Tangtong's Oral Transmission. All actions are seen to be manifestations of a person's state of mind. Therefore, it is the state of mind that ultimately defines whether a virtuous or nonvirtuous act is performed. If, for instance, a person is not acting with selfish and nonvirtuous intent, but for the purpose of turning others away from nonvirtue, then lying and using harsh words are not a vocal fault. These acts, if impelled by a virtuous mind, are virtuous. The same applies to physical acts, even killing, which if done under the power of the passions, are sins. If done with genuine love and compassion, they are not sinful, but virtuous.[276] Therefore, the true nature of any act is determined by whether or not self-centered, dualistic consciousness has been transcended. Tangtong once emphasized this to a disciple:

> The purity of your own mind is buddha.
> Appearances are the ephemeral
> images of a dream.
>
> When phenomena are understood in that way,
> there are no karma and no result of karma.
> There are no ripening of karma
> and no cause and result.
> There is no experiencing individual.
>
> The reason for that is no self-clinging.
>
> There is no result of positive and negative karma.
> The reason for that is no confusion.
>
> In the relative, confused perception
> of a person with no realization,
> there is karma and there are results of karma.
> There is ripening of karma
> and there are pleasure and suffering.
> There is an experiencing individual.
>
> The reason for that is self-clinging.
>
> There are positive and negative karma,
> and there are results.
>
> In conventional, relative, confused perception,
> accept cause, result, and karma as true!
>
> Act with the thought of enlightenment
> and great compassion!

> Be careful, mindful, and attentive!
>
> Strictly guard the three vows
> and the sacred commitments![277]

Most of the famous mad yogins lived during the fourteenth and fifteenth centuries, and several actually met each other. Tangtong Gyalpo and Tsang Nyön Heruka were the most important of these eccentric masters in terms of their lasting influence on Tibetan culture and religion. The account of their meeting portrays the continuity of the tradition of religious madness in Tibet and heralds the appearance of Tsang Nyön as the next great mad yogin. The year was 1476 and Tangtong was perhaps 115 years old.

> Tsang Nyön had reached twenty-five years of age and with his nephew for an attendant traveled through Latö Jang in western Tsang to the foot of glorious Riwoché. The precious lord sent his nephew ahead, and following behind, arrived when the great adept Tangtong Gyalpo was performing the tenth-day ritual feast on the peak of Riwoché. He came straight in, and just in front of the great adept was an enormous bowl covered both inside and out with barley paste and filled with beer. The lord took it in his hands and drank it. All the people were stunned, and even the great adept stared at him for a moment. Then the lord grabbed and bit the great adept's beard.
>
> The great adept jerked his head back and cried, "Ow! Ow!"
>
> The lord remarked, "What kind of great adept is this? He cries out in pain, unable to bear even the sting of his beard."
>
> The great adept laughed and said with embarrassment, "A fine auspicious connection. Offer me that garment of yours."
>
> The lord replied, "It's a fine auspicious connection, but since you've got a lot, I'll take this," and grabbed the great adept's cloak.
>
> "Delightful deliberate behavior!" the great adept exclaimed, "I don't need you and you don't need me, so get out! I'll see that you have no obstacles."[278]

Tangtong Gyalpo lived in a social environment that was willing to accept the incredible behavior of the mad yogins once it had been established that they were genuine masters putting the tantric teachings into practice, and not spurious imitators. He purposely cultivated his image as a mad yogin by emphatically signing his surviving works with the name Lungtong Nyönpa, Madman of the Empty Valley.[279] His cultural legacy in the form of iron bridges, stūpas, and monasteries is still evident today, and his religious teachings have spread throughout every lineage in Tibet. As Emily Dickinson once wrote, "Much Madness is divinest Sense—To a discerning Eye."[280]

A Jewel Mirror in Which All Is Clear

The Biography of the Glorious Accomplished Lord Tsöndru Sangpo

by

Lochen Gyurmé Dechen

Prologue

In the sublime place of truth,
which is the basic space of phenomena,
the syllable *e* blooms with a hundred petals,
while introspective awareness,
which is the syllable *vaṃ*,
is eternally present as its pistil
unmoved by the winds of subject and object.

The innate light of the dharmakāya reality body
appears as the rūpakāya bodies of form,
and the fragrance of unceasing,
enlightened activities spreads.
Sole savior of living beings in degenerate times,
sublime accomplished lord,
please grant your blessings.[281]

The single clear crystal
of discriminating primordial awareness
adopts the lustrous hue of the inclinations
of various disciples,
and any one of a sea of conquerors,
calm and wrathful,
such as Padmapāṇi and Hayagrīva,
may appear.[282] [3]

The calm, basic space of phenomena,
nonreferential Mahākaruṇika,
while not straying from
the spacious sky of reflexive awareness,
appears as the body of glorious Hayagrīva

to tame the malevolent,
and so his physical appearance is semiwrathful.[283]

The immortal lord Padmākara himself
returned again with affection
for miserable beings in degenerate times,
and the sky was filled with the fame
of his emanated body,
known as the Iron-Bridge Man.[284]

Like a spreading sandalwood tree,
his maroon color [4]
and sublime fragrance stop anxiety,
and with an easy disposition
and dynamic pure awareness,
he cares for various disciples
through unpredictable behavior.[285]

Reaching the pinnacle
of the sixteenth coemergent joy,
he was embraced by sixteen sublime lovers,[286]
ḍākinīs of primordial awareness,
and happily enjoyed the pleasure of great bliss
by means of the nine dance moods
of wrath and passion.[287]

If his enlightened actions equaling the sky
are not precisely understood
even by sublime noble beings,
they are not an object for childish minds.
Nevertheless, I will write a little based
on what several former masters have recorded.

WITH HIS COMPASSION, Padmasambhava, the Teacher of Uḍḍiyāna, the One Who Knows the Three Times, did not abandon those distressed by the harshness of suffering during the spread of fivefold degeneracy in the final five hundred years of the age of strife.[288] He returned

28. Guru Padmasambhava.

once again to this glacial land and was known everywhere by the name Glorious Iron-Bridge Man, Tangtong Gyalpo. He threatened and intimidated human beings, his primary disciples here on Jambudvīpa, and the malevolent, nonhuman, eight tribes of gods and demons.[289] Then, to present a path to the higher realms and definitive excellence, he constructed representations of enlightened body, speech, and mind, opened the gateways to sacred places, founded monasteries, and built ferries and iron bridges. To expand the Dharma and prosperity in the Land of Snows, he [5] retrieved treasures of many profound Dharma teachings and various precious substances, and, with the pleasant Dharma melody of the six syllables,[290] he filled a vast area with the pristine enlightened activities of the conquerors.

Here I have taken as a basis the ancient historical texts recorded by some five different petitioners who had asked the great adept himself.[291] I will only briefly describe the miraculous images of the ornamental wheel of his inexhaustible enlightened body, speech, and mind that will easily appear in the mirrors that are the minds of us ordinary people. These are enlightened actions that, when heard in our ears, will cause our body hairs to tremble with faith, and are able to plant the seeds of liberation.

1: Hundreds of Thousands of Lifetimes

This great accomplished lord actualized the full qualities of the dharmakāya reality body for his own benefit, yet took birth in infinite, ephemeral, rūpakāya form bodies for the benefit of others. He said:

> I'm a Tibetan, the Iron-Bridge Man.
>
> For many hundreds of thousands of lifetimes,
> I've done what was to be done for the Buddhist doctrine.
>
> I've prayed for the benefit of sentient beings.[292]

The cause for this accomplished lord to work for the benefit of sentient beings during this time when they experience fivefold degeneracy and are extremely difficult to tame occurred in his fifth lifetime prior to this one.[293]

In the city Siden in the noble land of India, the father, King Drakyong Sangpo, had two hundred queens led by Drakdenma, sixty inner ministers, five hundred provincial rulers, three hundred thousand subject households, and an infinite treasury, but no son to inherit the kingdom. [6]

When he pleased with offerings everyone worthy of offerings, primarily the precious Three Jewels, and made prayers, a son who was fascinating to gaze upon was born to Drakdenma.

Showing his son to a brahmin soothsayer, the king commanded, "Examine well the signs and marks on this child!"

The brahmin replied, "This son is one who awakened his mind toward enlightenment many lifetimes ago. Because attachment to the glory of a kingdom would bind him to saṃsāra, he will wander alone in extremely isolated, unpredictable places, and be nourished by the nectar of meditation."

"He must assume the throne," the king said. "So he will not be free to have unpredictable residences. Brahmin, you must give him a fine boy's name!"

The brahmin gave the king's son the name Drakpa Öser, Light Rays of Fame. Then all the people of the city gathered, and a vast name celebration was held. The prince was raised.

~

When the prince then reached thirteen years of age, the father ordered his son, "My son, take the daughter of King Kuntu Ö as your queen. And then, my son, I will give you power over the glory of a great kingdom."

The son said this to his father and mother:

> That which is famous as a kingdom,
> is an ocean of suffering in saṃsāra.
> The great one called a king
> is the sole bearer of everyone's suffering.
> This authority over those called serfs
> is to be surrounded by retribution and debt. [7]
>
> This human body like a daytime star
> is found only once.
> I, the son of a king,
> am seeking enlightenment.
> Father, please keep the kingdom.
> Allow me, your son, the Dharma!

He respectfully prostrated to his father and mother, and requested permission to practice the Dharma.

His mother replied, "At first, lacking a son, we worried like a thirsty person searching for water. Without being miserly with our possessions, we pleased with offerings the excellent objects of worship such as the precious Three Jewels. We thought we had a son to uphold the lineage. The subjects, the provincial rulers, and the ministers were satisfied, and we thought that you would take a queen and be given all the power and glory of the kingdom. You must not speak of practicing the Dharma!"

The ministers and provincial rulers pleaded, "The command of your father and mother is sacred, like the Three Jewels. If you break it, your practice of Dharma will not be successful. A prince who does not take the throne will not accomplish the welfare of living beings with Dharma when [his refusal] plunges the subjects into despair. These subjects, retinue, and servants have no one to turn to except you, our prince. So you must accept the throne now! Please make vast prayers to work for the benefit of living beings in your future lives."

When all the ministers and subjects urgently offered prostrations along with this request, the son thought, "My father and mother have no son except me. I could practice Dharma, but if I break the command of my parents, whose [8] sanctity is equal to that of the Three Jewels, and ignore the hopes of the subjects, retinue, and servants, it would conflict with the intention to benefit sentient beings that I have awakened for many lifetimes. During this lifetime, according to the command of my father and mother, I will rule the kingdom with the Dharma and please limitless subjects, retinue, and servants. It would be wrong to do other than use all material possessions for the benefit of the doctrine and sentient beings, and make vast prayers."

When he agreed to act according to the words of his father and mother, as well as those of the retinue and subjects, they were all overjoyed and rejoiced. Chöden Dzema, the daughter of the great king Kuntu Ö, was accepted as the prince's queen.

To then rule the kingdom according to the Dharma, the young prince admitted all the young children of the population into the precious doctrine of the Conqueror, a source of benefit and happiness. For explication of the Tripiṭaka,[294] he founded an establishment known as Siden Dharmacakra, where a Sangha of three thousand gathered. After gathering together disciples of superior fortune from among his subjects, he also founded a great meditation establishment known as Ösel Dechen Ling for the purpose of study and reflection on the scriptures of the four classes of tantra, and for penetrating the key points of the channels, essential constituents, and vital winds.

At those monastic establishments he constructed an infinite number of temples and representations of enlightened body, speech, and mind. When he provided them with provisions to rival [9] a mass of noble Samantabhadra's clouds of offerings, the powerful blessings of the precious Three Jewels caused the prosperity of all the subjects to increase.

Without even a word for conflict, their happiness came to rival the happiness of the god realms.

Then King Drakpa Öser, with his father, mother, and queen, as well as the ministers and five hundred provincial rulers with their retinues and servants, carried boundless offerings and visited the source of the thousand conquerors of a good aeon, the Bodhi tree and Mahābodhi at the Vajrāsana [of Bodhgayā].[295] With fine and lavish honors, he pleased the Sangha of two hundred thousand who lived there.

Then the king and his retinue performed the seven-branch offering, such as prostrating to all the representations of the precious Three Jewels, presenting offerings such as a golden maṇḍala arrayed with heaps of the seven types of precious substances, and confessing their sins.[296]

Following that, the king and his retinue knelt upon the ground. He placed the palms of his hands together and made this prayer: "All buddhas and bodhisattvas appearing and residing throughout the three times, please give your attention to me, King Drakpa Öser, together with my father, mother, and retinue.

"Without breaking the command of my father and mother, whose kindness is unequaled, I have ruled the kingdom with Dharma, founded establishments for explication and practice, and then [10] constructed temples and representations of enlightened body, speech, and mind, and presented offerings.

"Until saṃsāra is emptied, by the force of this basic virtue may I be of a high family line and endowed with good physique and perfect prosperity!

"May I be endowed with the faculties of birth in a human body with the freedoms and endowments,[297] and endowed with the profound and vast wisdom of listening, reflection, and meditation!

"May I receive absolutely all the initiations and oral instructions of the new and old secret mantra traditions, and then bring experience and realization to perfection!

"May I master absolutely all the meaning and words of the scriptures of sūtra and tantra, together with the commentaries on their intention!

"According to the inclinations of disciples, may I be able to widely teach the Dharma of scripture and realization that I have mastered!

"May everyone else carry me like an ornament on their heads!

"May I pervade all directions like the sky!

"May I be constantly as bright as the sun and the moon!

"May I be worshipped by all like a precious [wish-fulfilling] gem!

"May everyone gather to be my subjects, like those of a Universal Monarch!

"May I realize the fundamental nature of the mind, be able to bear physical circumstances, and attain a rainbow body!

"May I show all living beings the path to liberation!

"May I attain self-control of unpredictable lifespan!

"May I be able to emanate and transform the body of flesh and blood!

"May my enlightened actions spread throughout Jambudvīpa!

"May an innumerable retinue and disciples gather!

"May the gathered retinue practice according to the scriptures! [11]

After he had spoken, his father, mother, queen, ministers, provincial rulers, and subjects all also prayed in unison, "May it be accomplished just exactly as King Drakpa Öser wishes!"

≈

The great adept himself said that the result of these prayers ripened into the form of the body of Tangtong Gyalpo, the Iron-Bridge Man.

• • •

Since the force of making vast prayers
had been established during many
hundreds of thousands of lifetimes,
who could prevent him from also placing
the living beings of the age of strife,
during which degeneracy is rampant,
in the glory of benefit and happiness?

When the auspicious connections of a seed,
warmth, and moisture are accumulated,
the leaves and branches
of a heavenly tree fully expand,
and fine fruit with a sublime taste
completely ripens naturally,
which is the nature of things.

• • •

During the lifetime as King Drakpa Öser, the great adept had to accept the kingdom without breaking the command of his father and mother and disappointing the subjects. This wearied him, and it is apparent that in future lifetimes he performed the sealike conduct of enlightenment from a middle-class family.

This accomplished lord was then reborn as a fully ordained nun, and upheld infinite, excellent Dharma teachings of scripture and realization. The *Prophecy* says:

> This present realized person
> will take the body of a fully ordained nun,
> and engage in the Dharma of the piṭakas.[298]

Then his next life is mentioned:

> In the borderland of Bhutan and Tibet,
> a great meditator called Rongtön will appear.[299] [12]

He took birth as the one known as the great master Rongtön, who was first the excellent spiritual son of Gomtsul.[300] To the south of Jayul[301] he filled temples such as Goma Tsekar and Mangyel with scriptures piled up like mountains and with infinite representations of the Tathāgatha's enlightened body and mind, and founded great establishments for explication and practice.

In the *Prophecy*, it seems as though he was born as the great adept immediately after that lifetime as the great Rongtön.[302] But the great adept himself said, "In my last life I was called the Omniscient Dolpopa, in this life I am called Crazy Tsöndru, and in the next I will be called the overlord Sangwa Düpa. This is proof that I have achieved self-control over appearances."[303]

Between Rongtön and the great adept, he took birth as the great expert adorned with the sublime attainment, known everywhere by the name Omniscient Dolpopa. He built the Stūpa of Glorious Qualities at Jonang, and caused the Sage's doctrine of scripture and realization to shine like the sun upon glacial mountains, performing vast benefit for sentient beings.[304]

29. The great stūpa of Jonang.

2: A Mental Emanation of Padmasambhava

The great adept's next life was as this Iron-Bridge Man, Tangtong Gyalpo. His birthplace was in the domain of the glorious Yeru Jangpa, where kings endowed with Dharma successively appear.[305] This is mentioned even more specifically in the *Prophecy* of the Great Teacher of Uḍḍiyāna:

> In a valley called Owa,
> is a mansion called Lhatsé,
> surrounded in all directions
> with places for practice.[306] [13]

From the east, in front of the sacred site of Owa Lhatsé, a river flows from the right like a fluttering white silk scarf. On the left bank of the great Tachok Khabab River[307] is a rock like a black snake slithering down, with a treasure of various precious substances in its throat, naturally created as a solid stone object in the shape of a vase.

The village known as Owa was close below Rinchen Ding, a great court where the wheels of both traditions[308] were kept turning. It was completely surrounded by fine fields in which various grains ripened, various trees were beautiful with fruit, and all the mountains were adorned with fine grasses, blue like a peacock's throat. There were various birds and wild creatures roaming peacefully, and a variety of cattle bearing udders swollen full with milk.

This place with no lack of great material prosperity was the birthplace of the great adept's mother, Gyagar Lhamo. His mother was endowed with the signs and marks of a ḍākinī. Slight facial hair grew on her upper lip and chin. She had three furrows of wrinkles at her forehead and a white hair the color of a jasmine flower in a clockwise curl between her eyebrows.

She was beautified with moles like a tiara of the five spiritual families and like a long necklace. She delighted in all virtues, such as reciting the [Sanskrit] vowels and consonants and making offerings to the precious Three Jewels. With her gentle disposition and great compassion, she acted as a parent to the destitute.

Her adoptive bridegroom[309] was the great adept's father, Önpo Dorjé Gyaltsen, who was from Jindré Valley. [14] As the *Prophecy* says:

> A son of the Dong clan,
> a Minyak upholder of pure awareness.[310]

His clan was the Lhadong Karpo, who had migrated from Minyak. He was handsome, of patient disposition, and alternately acted virtuous and sinful. Everyone trusted his beneficial attitude and great general service for the people of the area.[311]

Six sons and daughters were born to these two parents: Sero Pal, Lopön Paltsul, Trowo Palden, Penpo, Ngadar, and their sister Palzin Dorjema. The great adept was the fifth child, Trowo Palden, "Wrathful Glory."[312]

When the Teacher of Uḍḍiyāna, the One Who Knows the Three Times, had concealed many profound Dharma teachings as treasures in the Mansion of Secret Mantra at Tsari,[313] King [Mutri Tsenpo] had asked, "Who is the person that will retrieve this profound Dharma and benefit living beings? How will he help living beings? When will he become enlightened?"

The Great Teacher of Uḍḍiyāna had smiled and replied:

> In the final age of the last five hundred years,
> the person with the karma,
> the emanated body who extracts and uses this,
> will be my mental emanation to benefit living beings.[314]

Thus the Teacher of Uḍḍiyāna's own mental emanation, the Iron-Bridge Man Tangtong Gyalpo, would take the mental treasures of profound Dharma from the Mansion of Secret Mantra at Tsari. Especially, the great adept would also take the *Bright Lamp* from the treasure, in which he himself was prophesied by means of outer, inner, and secret signs. This very text mentions the outer sign, the way he was physically semiwrathful:

Emanating indivisibly as one,
both calm Mahākaruṇika
and the terrible Great Wrathful Lord, [15]
his physical appearance will be semiwrathful.[315]

His body was maroon in color, with a very pleasant fragrance, and adorned with moles. Mentally, he had an easy disposition and dynamic pure awareness. He displayed various unpredictable appearances and behavior. This is the meaning of the statement in the *Prophecy*:

Maroon in color, with a pleasant fragrance,
and adorned with moles,
he will have an easy disposition,
dynamic pure awareness,
and care for various living beings
through unpredictable behavior.[316]

The great adept assumed the manner of a śrāvaka, a fully ordained monk in the doctrine of the Śākya, but since he practiced the four initiations[317] of secret mantra, he brought absolutely all the ḍākinīs under his control. He was invested with power over the great Dharma kingdom of all the conquerors, but worked for the benefit of living beings while concealing his qualities concerning scripture and realization, and practiced the profound and vast excellent Dharma. The *Prophecy* says:

While upholding the Śākya manner,
he will practice secret mantra,
bringing absolutely all ḍākinīs under control.
The conquerors will initiate him from basic space,
and he will work in secret for the benefit of living beings,
practicing the profound and vast Dharma teachings.[318]

These statements explain the outer and the secret signs indicating that the great adept would be a mental emanation of Padmasambhava of Uḍḍiyāna.

The inner signs were that his mother had a very marvelous dream on the tenth day of each of the ten months following the great adept's entry into her womb. These inner signs are mentioned in the *Prophecy*:

The inner signs will occur as omens in dreams.[319] [16]

Accordingly, the fine dreams his mother had will just be roughly mentioned.[320] In the first month after the great adept had entered his mother's womb, she had a dream. In the center of a forest grove of various spreading trees with perfect leaves, branches, flowers, and fruits, was Amitābha, whose body was fascinating to gaze upon, on a vast and spacious throne of five kinds of precious substances.[321] He pronounced a benediction and scattered flowers upon the mother.

In another dream, she gazed down from the summit of Mount Meru and clearly saw the sun shining on the four continents and the subcontinents.

[In yet another dream,] those in this mundane realm who were blind, those with crippled limbs, and those with incomplete sense faculties all gathered together. She made them happy by bestowing sight, healing their crippled limbs with medicine and mantras, and giving various foods, wealth, and possessions to those who were poor and destitute.

[In yet another dream,] a rainbow of five colors shone from the southwest, making a path upon which she traveled. At what she thought was the Glorious Copper- Colored Mountain,[322] a yogin of peerless grandeur and majesty was seated on the crossed forms of a male and a female athlete. Adorned with various ornaments, he held a sacred dagger and skull-cup in his two hands, and was accompanied by an assembly of spiritual heroes, ḍākinīs, and rākṣasa demons.

To the right and left of the yogin were two beautiful women. She asked, "Who is this assembly leader of yours?"

"Gyagar Lhamo from the land of Tibet," they replied, "have you forgotten since you've wandered through the gate of a human womb? This naturally arisen emanated body is the great master Padmasambhava. [17] Prostrate and request attainments!"

When she prostrated, circumambulated, and requested attainments, he gave her a jewel sparkling with various colors and said, "I give you this wish-fulfilling gem, a relic of the body of all the buddhas, but you must carry it to the land of Tibet on Jambudvīpa! By that auspicious connection, living beings will be satisfied by Dharma and the land of Tibet will be established in happiness."

The two ḍākinīs also said, "Bliss Sustaining Queen, on your journey to the land of Tibet, take this impressive ornament," and gave her a gold vajra inlaid with turquoise.

30. Guru Padmasambhava at the Copper-Colored Mountain.

The mother [had another dream in which] many spiritual heroes and ḍākinīs presented her with offerings. As her happiness increased, she flew into the upper reaches of space and arrived at Akaniṣṭha Khecara.[323]

Vajravārāhī was there like a ruby mountain in the sunshine, adorned with bone and jewel ornaments and surrounded by many spiritual heroes and ḍākinīs. In front of them was a vast ritual feast of food and drink she had never tasted before. The mother was also given a portion of the feast, and her happiness increased. From the heart of Vajravārāhī, who was the central figure, a lovely casket emerged, which she gave to her and said, "A wish-fulfilling gem is inside this. Any contact with it is meaningful. You must take good care of this! Vast benefit will appear in the human and nonhuman world, and future sentient beings of lesser fortune, who will be difficult to tame, will be tamed by this." [18]

The mother awoke and thought, "Am I dying? Or is a special person going to appear in this body? In any case, by asking the master for blessings, obstacles are cleared away."

The great repository of the excellent Dharma of the Northern Treasures, the anchorite and recluse Dönyö Gyaltsen,[324] was living at Dorjédan. She invited him, and received many initiations and blessings of the Guru Calm and Wrathful.[325]

When she told him how the dreams had occurred, he exclaimed, "How marvelous! It is also in the *Prophecy* of the Great Teacher of Uḍḍiyāna: 'To the east in front of Owa, one with the name Tsöndru will appear. He is my mental emanation.'[326] It is very important that you take special care of this body of yours."

In another dream, the mother went to the top of a temple she thought was the Lhasa Dharmacakra. She dreamed that the sun and moon shone upon her body, she blew a white conch shell three times, raised a victory banner above her head, waved a great silk banner to her right, a rainbow touched down at her left, she beat a great drum in front of her, and explained the Dharma in the market behind her.

The perfect Buddha remained in his mother's womb for ten months in order for the [major and minor] marks and the sense faculties to mature. Likewise, on the night this accomplished lord had completed ten months in his mother's womb, she had a dream: "I sat on the seats of a lotus, sun, and moon atop a high throne inside a perfect heavenly palace. My son was in my lap, emitting an aroma of incense [19] and adorned with moles. Many divine boys and girls were bathing the infant, putting ornaments on him, and offering fine clothing. Many nonhuman beings from the ten directions were offering various gifts to us, mother and son."[327]

• • •

That mother who was able
to hold the priceless jewel
of the accomplished lord
in her belly for ten months
was certainly a ḍākinī of primordial awareness,
and the precious container for a buddha.

As soon as the orb of the sun
of the sublime son
shone over the shoulder
of the eastern mountain
of the mother of wisdom,
the flight of the hordes of Māra's
assemblies of darkness
and the blooming of a hundred petals
of benefit and happiness
occurred simultaneously.

• • •

3: Crazy Tsöndru Is Insane

The *Prophecy* also says the great adept would be beautified by fine physical marks and mentions the year in which he would be born:

> In an Ox Year, a person with fine marks,
> and with the body and face
> of a bodhisattva in his final lifetime,
> will be compassionately born
> from his mother's womb.[328]

Accordingly, the great adept was born feet-first as the sun rose on the tenth day of the month of miracles[329] in the Iron Female Ox Year [1361]. He immediately said, "*Oṃ maṇi padme hūṃ*," and repeated "*A*" many times.[330]

A servant girl saw his eyes in the gaze used when sitting in the sevenfold posture of Vairocana.[331] "As soon as he is born, the infant has staring eyes!" she exclaimed.

He replied, "Hey, sister! Not only do I sit with staring eyes, I know how to do this," and sat with the posture of a relaxed king, the index finger of his right hand pointing to the sky and the left resting in the gesture of meditative equipoise.

On that occasion, [20] there was a sound of music in the sky, a wafting pleasant aroma of incense, and a falling rain of flowers. At the court of the king in Rinchen Ding the conversation was pleasant and silk banners fluttered. The trader Tashi Gyaltsen had returned from trading in Nepal and arrived with many goods from the south. A guest from Mangkar arrived at the door with eighteen bags of oil.

Even though there was a natural alignment of such fine auspicious omens, the father said, "Gyagar Lhamo, while this son of ours was in your womb you spoke about so many dreams of seeing gods and seeing demons. He also stayed in your body for ten months and came out feet first when he was born. As soon as he was born he demonstrated various body positions and said all sorts of things. I don't know that I like this."

The great adept then spoke again, saying this:

Father and mother, there's no need to dislike
those omens in the dreams of recent past months.

Listen, while I explain and unravel the symbolism.

Going to the top of the temple
was a sign of successively traversing
the spiritual levels and paths.

The sun and moon shining on your body
was a sign of dispelling the darkness of ignorance.

Blowing the white conch shell three times
was a sign of fame to come
from benefiting living beings.

The victory banner raised above the crown of your head
was a sign of upholding the victory banner of the doctrine.

The waving of the great silk banner to the right
was a sign of performing powerful virtue.

The rainbow touching down to the left
was a sign of bringing ḍākinīs under control.

Beating the great drum in front
was a sign of proclaiming the melodious sound of Dharma.

Explaining the Dharma in the market behind you
was a sign of subduing gods, demons, and humans. [21]

So they were not bad dreams, but good dreams,
which there's no need to dislike, father and mother.

His mother remarked, "We may not exactly dislike them, but there's no harm in doing a ritual. Since we must request a name for this infant and a method for increasing his inclination toward wisdom, please send an invitation to the anchorite Dönyö Gyaltsen."

The great anchorite came and was told about how the previous dreams had occurred and how the child had acted after birth.

He replied, "This is so marvelous! Last night I also had a dream in which it was said that, for the benefit of sentient beings, Padmasambhava of Uḍḍiyāna was coming to Jambudvīpa from the Land of Demons in the southwest. Many people gathered and a vast ritual feast of various kinds of food was arranged. They were acting joyful, praying and dancing around. When I also went there, prayed, and enjoyed portions of the feast, a great feeling of joy arose. When I awoke from sleep, a feeling of infinite mental joy and physical pleasure unlike before arose. This infant of yours will be able to benefit living beings."

He gave the name Trowo Palden and performed many rites, such as the initiation of Amitāyus, the lustration ritual of Vidāraṇa, and a method for increasing the inclination toward wisdom.

~

The child grew. When he was one month old, his father and mother were distracted with activities and the little boy dressed his own naked body in clothing. He was easier to nurture than other children and grew faster. [22]

When he was about five months old, his mother put him down by a very high cliff at the edge of a field she was weeding. He fell from the cliff and for a while she did not know. When she thought, "Is he dead now?" and ran to look, he was sitting unharmed in the midst of a bunch of nettles and said that no harm had occurred.

About seven or eight months after he was born he sat observing the key physical points for meditative concentration, performed many hand gestures for presenting offerings while gazing with his eyes into space, and accepted no food or drink for about twenty days.

When he was about eleven months old, he drew on the ground the figures of gods, the forms of stūpas, maṇḍalas, and so forth. He looked at them from the right and from the left, and smiling over and over made prostrations and circumambulations.

When he was one year old, his father and mother left the child by a window and went to work outside. When they came back in again, they saw the little boy playing with many birds.

When he was two years old, a white vulture came, took the little boy on its back, flew high in the sky, and performed three circumambulations.[332] Then it gently brought him back and left him where he had been sitting before.

When he was about three or four years of age, he made several figures of deities from dough and mud. Then he announced to everyone, "This is a gold deity, this is a turquoise deity, this is a coral deity. Prostrate and request blessings!"

When the great adept was five years of age, his father and mother sent him to tend the goats and sheep, but he went [23] to the Dharma place of the anchorite Dönyö Gyaltsen. While he was receiving many initiations, instructions, and ritual blessings, the people listening to the Dharma said, "This little boy doesn't understand Dharma."[333]

But the master declared, "This is an amazing child. It's uncertain whom the Dharma will benefit."

Sometimes the great adept ate many poisonous and filthy things himself, and, using the food his mother sent with him for sacrificial cakes and ritual feasts, performed initiations and ritual feasts for the goats and sheep. When he explained the Dharma he was able to get the goats and sheep to meditate.

Once during that period he stayed for five days without any clothing, food, or drink in a nest of white-tailed eagles on the Shasho Cliffs to the east of Men Valley. When he taught Dharma, they became calm and listened respectfully without causing harm. It was very marvelous to be able to teach Dharma to animals, so he intended to remain for several days. But he saw that his mother and relatives were weeping and very worried. He went to his mother and said, "Why do you have to worry so much? I went to teach Dharma to the birds."

After the birth of the great adept, the wealth and prosperity of the village increased effortlessly. The goats and sheep in particular became a huge herd that could hardly be rounded up. His father and mother said, "We sent this little boy to tend the goats and sheep when he was five, and none were lost. Trowo Palden, go be the shepherd!"

When he was herding, he wrapped in his robe as many black pebbles as there were goats and as many white pebbles [24] as there were sheep, and tied it up with a bootstrap. From a high spot on top of a hill he shouted, "Local gods, earth spirits, tend my goats and sheep!" Then he sat in meditation.

Sometimes he let the goats and sheep wander away, and he led many children in pretending to construct representations of enlightened body, speech, and mind, build iron bridges, launch ferries, consecrate them, and so forth. During those times he distributed to the children mushrooms that had not yet sprouted in the meadows, and ears of rice and many fruits they had never eaten before. People said, "This son of Gyagar Lhamo gives away types of food that even his parents don't have, and he has good habits. If he was made to enter the door of Dharma he might become a fine Dharma person."

One day, in addition to tending the goats and sheep, he went to the monastery of Jangding and begged food from all the villagers. About fifty villagers were there, and all gave him a meal each. He ate them all in one day. When he distributed three mushrooms to each of the villagers the next day, they asked, "Where does this child find mushrooms during the spring season?"

On another day he picked garlic from the cliffs on the south side of the great river and distributed it to the scribes who were copying the Translated Scriptures for the Dharma lord Ka Ngapa at Jangding.[334]

"There is no place for this child to cross over the water," they said. "He probably flew to get this garlic from the other side of the river."

He displayed many such magical feats.

When he was tending the livestock he would give the cooked food sent with him by his parents [25] to whomever came to beg, and to the insistent beggars he gave unsparingly his own parent's roasted barley flour, barley, and so forth. Then he would make many prayers: "May I and all sentient beings complete the perfection of generosity!"

He was a shepherd for several years, and even when his livestock became mixed with that of others, because of the auspicious connection of using the white and black pebbles [to count the sheep and goats], and because of his command to the earth spirits, they did not remain mixed with the others. Unharmed by wild beasts such as wolves, the livestock vastly increased.

Then he was sent to the Jangding Monastery to study reading and writing under the master Chökyong Palwa.[335] He knew how to read as soon as the letters were shown to him. When the teacher told him to practice writing the letters, he replied, "Reciting the verses of taking refuge is more beneficial than practicing the writing of the letters."

When he recited the fourfold taking of refuge[336] continuously, day and night, the teacher exclaimed, "You really don't listen! If you won't practice writing the letters, go back to your parents' place! If taking refuge is more important at your parents' place, take refuge! If writing is more important, write the letters!"

"If you need writing, that's no problem," he replied, and wrote in *lañcana, vartula,*[337] the symbolic script of the ḍākinīs, and five different kinds of Tibetan script.

The teacher and the scribes were astounded and said, "This son of Gyagar Lhamo acts unruly but is very wise. If he enters the gate of Dharma, he will become endowed with good qualities."

~

Once, about eighteen women who were led by the great adept's mother, Gyagar Lhamo, were weeding.[338] [26] "Trowo Palden," she said. "Run off and pick some garlic! When you come back, we'll have lunch."

While they were distracted, the great adept walked on the surface of the Tsangpo Yeru River and arrived on the far shore of the river without his feet sinking into the water. Picking garlic and loudly singing songs among the cliffs, he was seen by a person of the area. With the lap of his robe full of garlic from the cliffs, he arrived back on the near side of the Tsangpo. He met the person who had seen him, who asked, "Son, just now you were on the far side of the Tsangpo. How did you arrive here all of a sudden? It's not possible that you're able to walk on the water. You weren't led by a demon?"

"I went to pick garlic," the great adept replied. "I wasn't led by a demon, but don't let yourself be led by a demon!"

~

On another occasion the great adept was lost and could not be found for about three months. His father and brothers were very worried, but his mother said, "Trowo Palden isn't lost. You don't have to worry. He'll come back."

After three months had passed, he arrived carrying various different fruits that did not exist in the land of Tibet. He gave them to many people, primarily his mother, but when they asked where amazing food like this came from, he would not explain.

Then a severe epidemic broke out at the great adept's birthplace. Various means were tried without benefit and many people died. In particular, his own brothers Penpo and Ngadar and his sister Palzin Dorjema also passed away. [27] A prediction by the astrologers said to throw the corpses into the river and not to perform the basic virtues. So they were unable to even scatter the hundred sacrificial cakes. The survivors were terrified.

When the great adept rested his mind evenly in meditation and carefully looked for the cause from which the epidemic had arisen, he realized that the harm had been done by the malevolent nāga-māra[339] of Tsalu. He went to graze the donkeys in the place where that earth spirit lived. He sheared the hair from the manes and tails of the donkeys, and the inconceivable number of snakes that were in that place wrapped themselves around the donkeys' necks, limbs, ears, and tails. He took the very largest snake in his hand, mounted a donkey, and fearlessly rode through all the ravines and gorges. The donkeys also joined him, and they went to the village.

His father and everyone else yelled, "Madman! You've brought harm to the earth spirit. Now harm will come from the earth spirit."

They were terrified, but the great adept told his father and the local people, "That you are not mourning for the dead people and not performing basic virtues in this way isn't according to custom, so I've put the donkeys in mourning. Now, for the benefit of everyone living and dead, offer a sacrificial cake as atonement! Those who can read should recite Dharma. Those who can't read should recite *maṇi*s, make clay molds, and repair the pathways. I guarantee the sickness will end after five days." [28]

A huge black snake was at the place where the earth spirit lived. The great adept stuck it into his boot, which he tied shut with the bootstrap. Then he sat in a meditative concentration that tormented the nāga, who revealed his own form and pleaded, "Please don't act like this now. I won't harm the people and wealth of Rinchen Ding. Master, I offer what wealth I have to you." He offered a promise not to harm sentient beings.

The great adept guided the transmigration of the dead and made prayers. His father and other local people said it was crazy behavior and offered no sacrificial cakes and so forth. But his mother, Gyagar Lhamo, took whatever he said to be true and made great positive efforts, so the epidemic came to an end.

Through the compassion of the great adept, those who died during that time reached the pleasant realms. Especially, his younger brother, Penpo, was reborn as a neighbor's son and clearly remembered his past life. He was admitted through the gate of the Dharma and, engaging in listening and reflection, became the great scholar known as Lekchok, who lived to be seventy-three years old.

~

The great adept then took many white tails and musk pods and went to trade them in Dölka. The King of Dölka was preparing to flay at the stake seven Nyishang men who had broken the law. Unable to bear it, the great adept offered the man-load of white tails and musk pods to the Dölka king and spoke, "It is said that no other sin is greater than that of taking a life. Please don't harm the bodies and lives of these seven men." [29]

The king replied, "This unselfish ransom of life and rescue from punishment has no rival among all basic virtues. It is amazing that a Tibetan bodhisattva offers a payment and ransoms these human lives."

He did not harm the bodies and lives of the seven men, and sent them happily to their homes.

When the great adept returned to his own home, his father and brothers asked, "What did you get for the white tails and musk pods?"

"I got seven human lives."

He explained what had happened, but they said, "This inept madman has lost the white tails and musk pods."

They quarreled with him, not thinking it was the truth.

During that period, government agents demanding military conscription and taxes appeared at the door. The father and two older brothers were very upset about the military tax. Since his mother had to pay the military tax[340] she was very worried and said, "Father and the two older brothers won't help by going. Trowo Palden can't be a soldier because he is young in years."

The great adept said, "Mother, I have a larger body and greater physical strength than my two older brothers, so I can be in the army. It's all right for me to go into the army. Mother, don't worry about it. Load some things on the ram with the white blaze on its forehead and send me off!"

His mother served beer to the local people and sent him off with words of advice. It was determined that he had quick feet and a sharp intellect, and thereafter he had to go countless times to fulfill the compulsory military tax, and many signs of the purification of sins appeared. Thus the great adept said.[341]

~

Then the father and mother discussed which son was fit to inherit the property.[342] [30] His father said, "This son Trowo Palden has energetic behavior and bright intelligence, so he is fit."

But his mother said, "A vigorous man will be vigorous in Dharma, so Trowo Palden should enter the Dharma."

Since they didn't agree, they asked Gugum Rinchen Gyaltsen,[343] who told them, "Let your son Trowo Palden enter the Dharma."

This agreed with the intention of his mother, but the great adept heard talk that his father was arranging a marriage for him with a young girl.

"I may act worldly," he told his father, "but I won't take over our property. Let my two older brothers take the property. But I do also need a share of the wealth."

~

[In the past,] the great teacher Śāntideva [dreamed that] noble Mañjuśrī sat on the throne where he was to be crowned as king the next day and said:

> My only son, this is my seat,
> and I am your spiritual friend.
> You and I both have the same seat,
> and this is totally wrong.[344]

In a similar way, when the great adept decided to take ordination and go from having a home to being homeless, he stacked many cushions in the east of the house, and also took and stacked several cloths upon them. But an extremely calm, noble Avalokiteśvara appeared before him in the sky for three nights and said, "Son, the cushions covered with cloth are for me, and it is improper for you to use them."

One night, when he took a sheet of cloth and sat without a cushion, Avalokiteśvara [31] said these words to him with a wide smile on his face:

> Hey! Absolutely all living beings,
> who have been your parents,
> must be liberated from the great sea of suffering.

To exhaust existence and attain perfect joy,
you should respectfully resort to an excellent friend.

The finest things in existence
are momentary and impermanent,
like a dream, an illusion, and a spirit town.

Carefully realize that, while they appear,
they are not established as real,
and are your own mind,
son of good fortune and family!

In order to not spoil the vow
of the sublime intention
that you have awakened
during many aeons for the benefit of others,
and to completely fulfill your vast prayers,
renounce sensory objects and resort to solitude.

With the behavior of an animal,
such as a dog or a pig,
one cannot achieve unexcelled enlightenment.

With the desire for liberation,
reject the distraction of activities
and meditate correctly
on the excellent oral instructions.

Since the great adept had received permission from his father, his mother, and even the king, the obstacles to maintaining the vows had been completely removed. He had even been urged by noble Avalokiteśvara to take ordination. So he went to the monastery of Jangding to obtain ordination from the master Nyima Sengé.

The master said, "Will this young boy be one to benefit the doctrine? In my dream last night all directions were filled with sunlight. I dreamed that many monks cleaned this Dharma throne of past masters, displayed decorations, arranged various offerings, [32] and announced, 'The lord of the doctrine will ascend the throne.'"

31. Thousand-armed Avalokiteśvara.

When the hair was shaved from the great adept's head, a great rain of flowers fell. Rainbow light filled the directions where the hair was scattered. He beheld the abbot, the teacher, the master of ceremonies, and the row of Sangha members to be the Lord of Sages [Śākyamuni] surrounded by the sixteen noble sthaviras. While the pleasant fragrance of the incense of the gods spread, he was given the name Tsöndru Sengé, "Lion of Diligence." Then he received the method for accomplishment of Amoghapaśa,[345] together with the collection [of texts] for the activities, the reading transmission of the tantra, and the ritual for fasting practice.

~

The great adept then decided to fill the pure vessel of precious moral discipline with the nectar of listening, reflection, and meditation. Under the scholars Lodrö Dorjé and Könchok Dar at the great monastery of Jang Ngamring,[346] he assumed the guise of studying the *Pramāṇavārttika*, the basic texts and commentaries of the Five Dharmas of Maitreya, such as the *Abhisamayālaṃkāra*, and the vinaya and abhidharma.[347] When he told the teachers, "I understand the meaning in this way," they said he had understood and were very pleased.

When repeatedly reciting the treatises and commentaries he became immersed in the meaning. Several times, with no thought of food and drink, for three or four days in a row he remained in a vajralike meditative concentration on the nature of the mind, clear light always shining and present, yet empty and free of [the extremes of] permanence or nonexistence and limit or center.

~

Then the great adept went to the great monastic seat of glorious Sakya for further scholastic studies and examinations on the four fundamental subjects.[348] His companions who had also come for study and examination made extensive outlines of each of their assigned portions of the treatises and closely analyzed the commentaries. [33] They had great conceited pride in their scholarship.

The great adept thought, "These people who declare their qualities and understanding are articulate, but they cannot tame the coarseness of their own mindstreams without understanding the meaning. To tame our own mindstreams we must work for the benefit of sentient beings. Furthermore, *Engaging in the Conduct of a Bodhisattva* says:

> Perform these with the body.
> What is accomplished by just saying the words?[349]

While he was thinking that he would use this body for the benefit of all sentient beings, experience the eight worldly concerns such as happiness and suffering[350] as equal in taste, and become able to withstand circumstances, the headmaster gave him this quotation from a treatise:

32. The northern temples of Sakya Monastery.

Here there is absolutely nothing to remove.
And nothing at all to establish.
Perfectly observe perfection itself.
If perfection is seen, you will be free.[351]

Within this vajra of the mind there are absolutely no faults such as afflictions to be removed and previously absent qualities to be newly established. None of the conquerors of the three times are able to show any beings who are to be tamed the nature of their own mind, *evaṃ*, unity, the king of sublimely immutable bliss, a coemergent bliss with a taste like nectar. The great adept, also unable to speak, sat for a moment gazing with staring eyes.[352]

Concerning this, here are Dohās or vajra songs sung by the great adepts Saraha and Tilopa, and then a summary of the previous points expressed in verse:

May what even the omniscient ones lack words for,
the sole king of bliss, be victorious![353] [34]

It is not what is taught by the master,
and not understood or obtained by the disciple.

Who tells whom about that nectar
of coemergent bliss?[354]

Amazing! This is reflexive primordial awareness,
beyond the path of speech and not within the range
of conceptual mind.
I, Tilopa, have absolutely nothing to present.
Show it to yourself and understand![355]

• • •

Unspeakable, unthinkable,
inexpressible, Prajñāpāramitā,
unborn and unceasing,
the very essence of space
within the range of individual,
reflexive, primordial awareness—
the meaning of the Mother of the Conquerors
of the three times arose in his mind.[356]

The nectar of coemergent joy,
unexpressed by the master
and unheard by the disciple,
is consumed,
and just like the bliss of a maiden,
is experienced,
but is beyond the range of expression.

Those who sing mere words in song
are like the blind explaining the nature of form,
or those pursuing the sound of an echo
and the water in a mirage.
Those conceited about their scholarship
were parrot paṇḍitas.

• • •

33. The great stūpa of Gyang.

At that point, when the great adept did not elaborate on the words of the treatise, some people remarked, "This young monk from Latö has a sharp intellect. Why is he poor in the treatises?"

Some people said, "This young monk becomes immersed in clear light when he studies. We can't tell if it's good or bad."

Special qualities were born within the great adept at that time. Therefore, with a deliberate behavior to equalize the eight worldly concerns, like an elephant intoxicated with beer, he did not even act ashamed when people said, "This little monk is poor in the treatises."

So he was known as Crazy Tsöndru. [35]

~

When the great adept was returning from the great monastic seat, he saw from the road the massive compulsory labor force gathering earth and stones to build the Great Stūpa of Gyang for Dakpo Sönam Tashi,[357] and he rejoiced again and again.

He arrived back home and, to prevent his father and older brothers from being born as hungry spirits because of their greed, told them, "By offering the possessions we have in common as contributions to the great stūpa so that all sentient beings may reach enlightenment, the wealth would not be wasted."

But they did not have the courage to give it up. The *Tantra* says, "You should take it even when it is not given."[358] He put the meaning of those vajra words into practice by pretending to be crazy, and pleased Dakchen Jampaiyang Sönam Tashi by offering an ounce of gold, two hundred loads of barley, and so forth.[359]

When he came home, his mother said, "Geshé Tsöndru, please take this food and beer for ten people, and these axes and ropes, and go tomorrow to gather poplar logs. The day after tomorrow, I will send your older brother and Gewo Tashi Gyaltsen with twenty donkeys to fetch the wood."

He went to the thick forest called Tsakhur in Men Valley. When he had finished enjoying the food and beer in a rock cave, he thought, "I'll be embarrassed if I don't cut the trees. I should summon the earth spirits of this valley for help."

He called, "Earth spirits of this valley, led by Shalsang, come cut my trees!" As soon as he had spoken, the valley was filled with an army of axes. [36] In an instant there were about an equal number of cut and uncut trees.

"All the people call me Crazy Tsöndru and despise me," he thought, "but the local gods and earth spirits love me."

Then his older brother and Gewo Tashi Gyaltsen appeared driving the twenty donkeys. His older brother said, "Many trees have been cut. Where have your helpers gone?"

"I enjoyed the food and beer by myself. And I cut the trees by myself."

His older brother was very happy and said, "This younger brother of mine sometimes causes trouble for the village with his crazy behavior, but this time he has done work equal to that of ten men."

~

Then no one knew where the great adept had gone, but his mother said, "Geshé Tsöndru will arrive when the time comes."

His father and brothers said, "We haven't lost a beloved person. That rotten guy has been trouble since birth. Just recently he caused trouble with all that gold and barley."

They did not even consider searching.

From the great adept Darma Palwa[360] at Khangbulé, the great adept requested the austere practice of survival with only water, and then meditated naked in a rock cave. For one year no one knew where he had gone.

~

The great adept returned home. Then, on a tenth day, his parents, brothers, and others went out to work in the fields. The great adept made "glorious sacrificial cakes" from what roasted barley flour they had in the house, and arranged a ritual feast with what meat, butter, yogurt, and beer they had. Nonhuman beings gathered, filling the house, and when he prayed to the Great Teacher of Uḍḍiyāna, the house almost burst apart from the sound of his hand-drum, bell, and cymbals. [37]

When his mother came to get lunch for the workers, there was not enough roasted barley flour and beer to take. "Geshé Tsöndru," she said, "there are many workers. What should we do now?"

"Mother," he replied, "our workers today have pure sacred commitments. Give them this meat and beer that has been blessed."

He gave her a bowl full of beer, a head-sized piece of kneaded dough, and a single side of meat. When his mother gave that to the thirty workers, they were all satisfied.

~

Then one day, to go do something on the far side of the Tsangpo River, the great adept drove two donkeys to the boat crossing at Ngagpuk. He told the boatman, "Please row the boat."

"You're stout," he replied. "You put the donkeys in the boat and I'll row the boat."

The great adept put the two donkeys under his arms and jumped into the boat. Water splashed into the boat, and the boatman yelled, "The pranks of a madman don't work on the water! You're crazy! I'm not going the same time as you!" and refused to row the boat.

From within the boat the great adept pointed a finger at the mountains on the far side of the water, and the boat went straight across. And later, when he and the two donkeys came back to cross the Tsangpo, from within the boat he pointed a finger at the northern mountains, and the boat returned easily to its original spot.

During that period the great adept was living as a novice monk, but with unpredictable behavior he displayed a variety of magical physical forms. When the young man Yeshé Dren, his paternal uncle, said, [38] "Come tomorrow to dig manure," he agreed. And he also agreed when his father said, "Please go build a wall around the field in Men Valley," and when his elder half-brother, master Draksangpa, said, "Come to the Dharma."

Those who knew said, "Don't act deceitful like that. You can't accept the requests of three people!"

The great adept replied:

> With my illusory body,
> this heap of flesh and blood,
> I've created a rainbow body,
> a vajra body.
>
> Thus the maṇḍala of mantra
> recitation arose as the nature
> of my speech, created from sound.
>
> The immutable dharmakāya reality body
> arose as the nature of ignorant, confused mind.
>
> I've never broken the words of a promise.
>
> If I'm able to display ten million emanations,
> two or three don't worry me.

As he had said, he emanated one body to listen to Dharma from the Dharma lord Draksangpa, one to dig manure for the young man Yeshé Dren, and one to prepare the wall around the field in Men Valley, thereby pleasing all three of them.

~

Then the great adept served as the retreat attendant during the retreat of his paternal relative, his elder half-brother Draksangpa, at Tarpa Ling. He received the Mind Training,[361] the initiation of Mahākaruṇika Who Tames Living Beings,[362] and the reading transmission for the *Compendium of Maṇis* and the practical instructions.[363] When he served the proper proportions of roasted barley flour and water, just enough food to tame the vital winds, the master said, "Geshé Tsöndru, this food you have given me is balanced and nutritious, so that my pure awareness is clear and my spiritual practice has improved. Has your spiritual practice improved?" [39]

The great adept replied, "The Mind Training was very effective. During the practical instructions, many people appeared in an experiential vision and said that they were renunciants, Nepalese, from Mön and Kongpo, and from Lo Khatra.[364] They acted as my patrons, and I also had cordial relations with them. What was that?"

The Dharma lord Draksangpa spoke a prophecy: "It is a sign that, although you are now called Crazy Tsöndru, you will be given a name by the ḍākinīs of primordial awareness because you have seen the meaning of the true nature of phenomena. That name will become known everywhere, because India, China, Nepal, Mön, Kongpo, and Lo Khatra are the lands where you will tame living beings."

Then the great adept joined company with many people of glorious Rinchen Ding who were going to trade in Kyirong.[365] He loaded his merchandise on two donkeys, and they set off. When they reached the foot of the Kha and Cha Passes at the beginning of the Tratang Plain, a place from which it is a single day's journey to reach Ngari Dzongka,[366] it snowed enough to almost bury a man. For thirteen days and nights the men and beasts shuddered in the middle of the snow, tormented by intense suffering that threatened their lives. The great adept sat on a square ledge up on a high ridge. Without being cold for even an instant, he sat in the sevenfold posture of Vairocana.[367] The fallen snow around him receded for about eight feet and steam rose.

To save the lives of the men and beasts, he then displayed three [40] physical emanations. One stayed where the traders were, one went to offer prayers before the Jowo [in Kyirong], and one went to search for grass and wood from Tangpoché. He distributed as much grass and wood as they wanted and saved their lives. But without recognizing it as a sign of his attainment, they just said, "Crazy Tsöndru is very sharp."[368]

Then the road became open and they went to Kyirong. He told his companions, "It will be difficult for us to attain precious human bodies again and again, and since we've come from far away and are visiting a naturally arisen statue of the Noble One[369] such as this, we should use

34. The Kyirong Jowo.

our possessions for what is essential. Therefore, it would be best to each offer butter lamps, do circumambulations, and make good prayers that are always beneficial, now and in future lives."

They replied, "Recent days were bad and our merchandise was severely damaged, so after offering butter lamps there would be nothing to take for trading. You don't have to support a family. If you have that much faith, then you offer the butter lamps and make the circumambulations."

He thought, "Fools who don't understand actions and their result take encouragement toward virtue to be harmful. Each time they get something to bring home for their families, they don't think for even an instant of the needs of others. To make my own illusory wealth meaningful, I will buy butter with what merchandise I have, offer butter lamps, and make prayers for the benefit of the doctrine and living beings. While they linger to trade, I must be energetic in circumambulations."

He bought butter with his merchandise, got a huge amount of butter lamps, and offered them. He performed single-minded circumambulations and prayers, and on the morning of the fourth day [41] came to the Jowo image to request blessings. He touched his head to the naturally arisen Noble Wati's right hand, which was making the gesture of granting the sublime attainment. From the five fingers of the Noble One, streams of nectar in five colors dissolved into the great adept's head, blessing him with vajra body, speech, mind, and primordial awareness. All sentient beings touched by the white, yellow, red, and green colors of the four enlightened actions[370] that shone from the Jowo's heart became the great adept's disciples. Then the indestructible sweet sound of the six syllables of the naturally arisen Noble One was spoken, alternating with these six phrases:

Oṃ maṇi padme hūṃ
Mahākaruṇika, and Hayagrīva sublime in power.[371]
Oṃ maṇi padme hūṃ
My son, a guide for living beings.
Oṃ maṇi padme hūṃ
As far as was covered by the light
of the four enlightened actions.
Oṃ maṇi padme hūṃ
You will spread the doctrine
of the six-syllable *dhāraṇī-mantra.*
Oṃ maṇi padme hūṃ
Holder of the pure awareness of longevity,
Iron-Bridge Man.
Oṃ maṇi padme hūṃ
You will establish living beings
of the age of strife in happiness.
Oṃ maṇi padme hūṃ

Once again, when circumambulating the Jowo and single-mindedly reciting *maṇi*s, he realized that, from the auspicious connections of his extremely clear visualization of the three carry-over practices,[372] his lineage and assembly of disciples would accomplish vast enlightened actions of the conquerors in reliance on the six syllables of enlightened speech.

After eleven days had passed,[373] the traders finished trading and asked, "Are you also going?"

"I'm going," he replied, and came driving two empty donkeys.

His companions [42] cried, "It's said that Crazy Tsöndru is insane, and it's true. So you won't have come to the Kyirong area and returned home with empty donkeys, put some of our loads on your two donkeys. We'll each give you a piece of iron."

He replied, "You're exhausted from losing sleep over the gain and loss of each measure. We came to trade, and you have greater loads of merchandise. But I, Crazy Tsöndru, have greater trade profits."

He sang a song about this way of profiting in trade:

> May the Dharma lord,
> the master who embodies all sources of refuge,
> the precious Three Jewels,
> which are the ever infallible sources of refuge,
> and noble Avalokiteśvara,
> who guides the six kinds of living beings,[374]
> gaze with compassion on the sentient beings
> of this degenerate, evil time.
>
> Clever men, listen to this song of mine!
>
> You may gather wealth,
> but there's no certainty of keeping it.
> You may even keep it,
> but there's no certainty of enjoying it.
> Don't gather sins for the sake of wealth!
>
> In the sublime bazaar of Kyirong in Mangyul,[375]
> the residence of the Noble One
> and the source of fulfillment,
> dwells the great merchant,
> powerful Avalokiteśvara.
>
> The seven riches of a Noble One
> are spread out as merchandise.[376]
> Many want these, but there are few buyers.

I dealt in this, the trade share of a madman.

I measured out single-minded faith
and devotion in payment.
I took the precious jewel
of inexhaustible contentment.
Understanding all things of illusory value
in this world to be deceptive,
I exchanged them for inexhaustible treasure.
I didn't lose in trade, my friends, I profited.
My profit in trade is forever,
and my mind is at ease.

In the great bazaar
of the immutable [universal] ground, [43]
dwells the merchant of your own mind,
perfect buddhahood.
The jewels of emptiness and compassion
are arranged as merchandise.
Many need these, but they're difficult to obtain.

I dealt in that, the trade share of Crazy Tsöndru.
I measured out objectless compassion in payment.
I took the precious jewel of inexhaustible enlightened activity.

I exchanged all enjoyment of the five coemergent poisons[377]
for the jewel of emptiness and lucidity, free from grasping.
I didn't lose in trade, my friends, I profited.
My trade profit is forever, and I'm content.

In the great bazaar of virtuous body, speech, and mind,
dwells Mahākaruṇika, the merchant of benefit for others.
The jewels of the ten virtues[378] are spread out as merchandise.
Many strive for these, but few obtain them.

I dealt in this, the trade share of Crazy Tsöndru.
I measured out unattached love in payment.
I took the precious jewel of fivefold primordial awareness.[379]

I exchanged the three poisons,
the sterile wealth that produces suffering,
for the jewel of the spontaneous three bodies
of enlightenment.[380]
I didn't lose in trade, my friends, I profited.
My trade profit is for all lifetimes, and my mind at ease.

An aimless madman
scared of wandering in endless saṃsāra,
I realized the root of confusion,
this clinging to a self, to be harmful,
and threw it away.

I took the jewel that fulfills all needs and desires.
The caravan leader who has taken that is always happy.
To return empty-handed
with the merchandise of your lifetime spent
is a mistake.
Very few recognize wealth.

Thus he sang a vajra song, and then spoke further to his trading companions about how the results of happiness and suffering come from virtue and sin as their causes. [44] Especially, he said, "Contemptuous of the relationship between sin and suffering, you strive for wealth, but it's difficult to obtain if you lack the result of generosity. The possessions you obtain are used for your own food, clothing, and drink, as well as for manifesting your arrogance in this world. Even if you aren't capable of strong virtue now, each time you get up and each time you go to sleep, direct three prostrations to the precious Three Jewels, and recite five hundred *maṇis* without interruption. When a beggar appears at your door, don't turn him away with an empty mouth. Offer the Three Jewels a bit of whatever you eat and whatever you drink. Give pieces of food to the dogs. This is cumulative virtue, so be constantly diligent."

But the time for their taming had not come, so without devotion and pure perception they just remarked, "He speaks well for someone who came to Kyirong just to drive back empty donkeys without merchandise to load on them."[381]

The great adept thought, "Even when the Dharma is explained to these fools who have faith in wealth, they don't understand. I'll have to perform a miracle."

On the morning that the traders departed from Dzongka, he emanated four fine loads of conch shell, indigo, brown sugar, and cotton. Loading them on two donkeys, he started off.

They cried, "How is it possible that this Crazy Tsöndru, who has faith in wealth, was offering butter lamps and making circumambulations? While we were occupied in trading, he gave the innkeeper a bribe, engaged in smuggling, and the loads were delivered to Dzongka. Now, after coming to trade together, we have nothing except iron, but Crazy Tsöndru [45] has indigo, conch shell, brown sugar, cotton goods, and so forth. Our families will probably complain about our trading, and the neighbors will ridicule us."

They were suffering a lot, so he said, "Sometimes you suffer when I don't have wealth, and sometimes you exhaust yourselves with such suffering as this when I do have wealth. Fine, I won't take this wealth of mine home."[382]

He made the four loads disappear.

When he arrived home, his father and brothers complained, "This rotten fellow has completely wasted our wealth."

They criticized him, but his mother observed, "It's good that Geshé Tsöndru used the merchandise to offer butter lamps to the Noble One."[383]

Then the great adept thought, "I have met the Buddhist doctrine that is difficult to meet. The *Root Tantra* says, 'Among the three lifestyles, it is maintained that the fully ordained monk is superior and the novice monk is middling. The householder is inferior.'[384] It is said that the lifestyle of a fully ordained monk is superior for the performance of any initiation, consecration, burnt offering, or ritual feast of the secret mantra tradition. Therefore, I will aspire to the state of complete ordination as a monk. Ka Ngapa Paljor Sherab[385] is noble Avalokiteśvara assuming the role of a fully ordained monk and living in the Dotö Gyara Monastery. I will go to meet him."

That night, the Dharma lord Ka Ngapa had an experiential vision of clear light in which a young novice monk riding a lion [46] and surrounded by a retinue of many nonhuman beings appeared up in the sky and announced,

"I am the Indian great adept Kukkuripa.[386] I need my things that were entrusted to you." Taking the three representations,[387] books, and offering articles, he said, "I'm going to care for disciples in the three areas of Central Tibet, Tsang, and Kham," and departed through space to the east. And the master also briefly escorted him through space.

As soon as it was daybreak, the master said, "A fine person is coming to our monastery today, one with whom any degree of contact is meaningful, one for whom all appearances arise as auspicious connections, and who will perform vast benefit for living beings by means of auspicious connections. Bring the finest auspicious connections into alignment everywhere, inside and out!"

The attendant arranged fine offerings before the three representations and the master. He raised a multi-colored silk banner on top of the master's residence, and placed in front of the door to his room a load of barley upon which was a vase filled with pure water. On top of that was a white conch shell with a five-colored silk ribbon attached. After the sun had risen, he asked the master for excellent foodstuffs.

While the attendant was preparing a meal in the kitchen, three clear blasts of a conch shell were blown. When he looked through a window, there was someone in the robes of a monk, holding the load of barley in the lap of his robe, carrying the full vase of water in his left hand, holding the white conch shell in his right, and with a radiant smile upon his face.

"This is the special person the master spoke about," the attendant thought, and went to tell him. But [47] without the door having been opened, that monk had arrived in the presence of the master before the attendant.

The attendant exclaimed, "How did you come up the ladder and through the door?"

The great adept replied, "Appearances have no value for me, so I came straight on in."

The attendant became filled with faith, prostrated, and placed the great adept's feet upon his head.

In the midst of the Dharma lord Ka Ngapa, the master of ceremonies, and the Sangha, the great adept received complete ordination. He was beautified by the dress of the three Dharma robes, and given the name Tsöndru Sangpo, "Good Diligence."

He stayed with the Dharma lord Ka Ngapa for some time and received, like one full vase being poured into another, many maturing initiations, and the liberating instructions of the path for many systems, such as the Fivefold Mahāmudrā, the Coemergent Union, the *Ganges Mahāmudrā*, [the Six Dharmas of] Nāropa and of Niguma, the Practical Instructions, and the Six-branch Yoga.[388]

Especially, this outer, inner, and secret taking of refuge, known as "Mothers Infinite As Space,"[389] had been given to Ka Ngapa by Avalokiteśvara, who had said, "Give this Dharma to the fully ordained monk Tsöndru Sangpo. He will proclaim it to all the people of Jambudvīpa. Removing their temporary illnesses, demons, and obstacles, he will save them from the sufferings of the three lower realms."

According to that prophecy, the Dharma lord Ka Ngapa gave it to him and said that he was an emanation of the great adept Kukkuripa.[390]

Then he met the Dharma lord Lhadongpa Sönam Chokpa. He received many Dharma teachings, such as the Mountain Dharma, the Severance Cycle, the entire Great Perfection retrieved as a treasure by the upholder of pure awareness Gökyi Demtruchen,[391] [48] the Heartdrop of the Ḍākinī,[392] the Cycle of the Great Perfection of Aro,[393] the initiations of Vajrapāṇi such as Mahācakra, the One with the Blue Robe, and the Subduer of Demons, and the ritual permission and entrustment of the great guardian Vaiśravaṇa together with his retinue.

Many men and women wearing tiger and leopard skins then heaped many kinds of food and drink such as meat and beer in front of the great adept and said, "Fully ordained monk with the three vows, great vajra holder, please bless these in a ritual feast and happily enjoy our offering gifts." And they offered limitless kinds of precious substances, such as gold and silver. When he gave them the food and drink that had been blessed, they all acted very pleased.

"Who are you?" he asked. "What do you want in return for the offerings and honors?"

"We are the eight yakṣa horsemen,[394] together with our sisters," they replied. "The great master Lhadongpa commanded us to create favorable conditions for you to perform vast virtuous acts, and so we will offer whatever you need. We don't want anything else in return, but we would request the initiation and tantra of Vajrapāṇi with the Blue Robe."

He gave that, and the eight yakṣa spirits each offered their life-mantras, made prostrations and circumambulations, and disappeared.

~

During that period, the anchorite Dönyö Gyaltsen was living at the sacred place of Riwo Drasang.[395] Ekajaṭī and other treasure-owners[396] [49] actually came before the anchorite hermit one evening while he was performing the tenth day rituals. "The owner of the Dharma is coming to get it," they said. "So give him absolutely everything in the texts."

In the middle of the night Ṛṣī Rāhula[397] appeared and announced, "A great strongman, the Iron-Bridge Man who is a mental emanation of the Teacher of Uḍḍiyāna, is coming straight to this sacred place on the tenth day of next month. Prepare well!"

At about daybreak, the Great Teacher of Uḍḍiyāna with a crystalline radiance appeared surrounded by many ḍākinīs and said, "I am the one who hid the Dharma teachings you have as treasures. I am staying in this land of Tibet for up to 180 years to care for disciples. Give me the Dharma treasures." Then he vanished.

The anchorite told his attendants, "The fully ordained monk Tsöndru will soon come here to receive the treasure teachings. He will become an upholder of the pure awareness of longevity gained from the *Iron Tree*, the longevity practice within this treasure trove, and will attract disciples equal in number to the host of stars, who will offer him boundless possessions."[398]

With the pure conduct of a fully ordained monk, the great adept then arrived at the sacred place of Riwo Drasang on the tenth day. "Great anchorite," he requested, "Please bestow upon me the entire profound Dharma of the canonical lineage and the treasures.[399] To practice the Dharma, I will perform meditation at this sacred place for three years."

"You are the Great Teacher of Uḍḍiyāna," he replied. "You probably don't need to perform meditation. For the entire night of the tenth day last month [50] pure appearances that were a mixture of dream and clear light occurred to me." He told in detail how they arose and then said, "Of course I will offer whatever Dharma I have to the owner."

The great anchorite bestowed the *Magical Net* and so forth of the canonical lineage, and the complete initiations, reading transmissions, and esoteric instructions of the Dharma treasures of Gödrochen, the upholder of pure awareness.[400]

On that occasion the great adept thought, "Considering degenerate future times, the Great Teacher of Uḍḍiyāna provided a variety of profound Dharma teachings—calm, enriching, powerful, terrible, murderous, frightening, dulling, and petrifying—that are incompatible with the dress of a fully ordained monk. Especially, I think the main practice of a śrāvaka is to be contented with few desires. Since I have not taken possessions for myself, I have nothing to arrange for a ritual feast and nothing to offer for having received profound Dharma and initiation such as this."

Then music and a loud "*hūṃ*" resonated in space and the earth was covered with the pleasant fragrance of incense. He looked to the sky, and in a pavilion wrapped in rainbow light on top of a mass of clouds he saw the Great Teacher of Uḍḍiyāna on a lotus, adorned with terrifying things, and surrounded by many spiritual heroes and ḍākinīs.

The great teacher gestured with his finger to the right, and when the great adept looked he saw a whole corpse placed in the middle of eight yogins who were enjoying the flesh. He gestured with his finger to the left, and when he looked he saw a skull-cup full of beer placed in the middle of five yoginīs who were humming "*hūṃ*" and enjoying the beer. Guru Padmasambhava gestured with his finger at himself, and when the great adept looked [51] he saw that he was seated in union with mother Vajravārāhī, surrounded by many spiritual heroes and ḍākinīs, and performing a ritual feast.

He understood this to be a sign that, from within the Mahāyāna, once he had entered the practice of unexcelled secret mantra, he must resort to the sacramental substances and, if deliberate behavior would be beneficial to others, he must perform even the four defeating acts.[401]

When the great adept had stayed for three years in very strict retreat in the Mansion of Lotus Light at the sacred place of Riwo Drasang, the Great Teacher of Uḍḍiyāna arrived before him in the sky surrounded by many ḍākinīs and spoke, urging him to engage in the behavior of a yogin:

> Emanated body,
> yogin endowed with Dharma,
> you should maintain and engage
> in deliberate behavior!
>
> Your enlightened activities
> for disciples will be vast.
>
> Saraha and Virūpa, Tilopa and Nāropa
> had the dress of yogins.

4: The White Light of Profound and Vast Instructions

At the completion of the retreat, the great adept then made the twenty-ninth-day offering of sacrificial cakes to the Dharma protectors.[402] At the passing of midnight, a black man with the face of a raven appeared and announced, "I have knowledge of the area and the route, and have arranged what favorable conditions are necessary. Paṇḍita Mahābodhi,[403] a master with whom you have a prior karma connection, is living in Nepal, so please come now."

The great adept's body hairs rose with faith, and leading the great raven-faced Dharma protector as a servant, he magically traveled in an instant to noble Svayambhūnāth in Nepal. [52] On the fifth day there, the Newar aristocrat Manudhara presented him with offering articles such as gold, silver, cotton goods, finger-cymbals, and a large quantity of rice. Using these supplies, he whitewashed Svayambhūnāth and carefully weeded Bodhnāth.[404] He went on pilgrimage to all the sacred places such as Asura Cave,[405] and made vast prayers. He held a fine puja for the Indian and Tibetan pilgrims, distributing seven mangoes[406] to each. Then he decided to visit the paṇḍita the next day.[407]

That night Paṇḍita Mahābodhi had an experiential vision. A path like an extended bolt of cloth appeared, upon which a Tibetan yogin, maroon in color, with a pleasant fragrance and beautified by the marks and characteristics, was coming toward him with a parasol of five-colored rainbows floating by itself above his head. The paṇḍita himself also honored him well, and all the Nepalese people, led by the King of Bhaktapur,[408] showed great faith and devotion to the Tibetan yogin.

The next day, as soon as the paṇḍita and the great adept met, the paṇḍita said, "You are the yogin who appeared in my experiential vision last night. I will construct the maṇḍala of glorious Cakrasaṃvara and perform the creation and offerings."

35. Svayambhūnāth Stūpa in Nepal.

The great adept then prostrated, saying, "After bestowing the maturing initiation in the maṇḍala of the chosen deity whom the master himself considers to be his own special deity, you must bestow a variety of liberating paths that I can use for the benefit of sentient beings in Tibet." [53]

Paṇḍita Mahābodhi bestowed the initiations of Cakrasaṃvara and the reading transmissions of many tantras.

Then the great adept thought, "At the Vajrāsana [of Bodhgayā] in Magadha,[409] the center of Jambudvīpa, I will see the Bodhi tree that supports the backs of a thousand conquerors in the fortunate aeon. I will drink the white light of profound and vast instructions from the moon-faces of many learned and realized masters, causing the moon-lilies[410] of my own and others' liberation and omniscience to blossom."

The paṇḍita, knowing the thoughts of others, told him, "Tibetan yogin,

36. Cakrasaṃvara.

if you travel to India, at a place called Yari Go Nga on the border of India and Nepal, there is a disciple of Mitrayogin,[411] a great expert who has become an upholder of the pure awareness of longevity. A gathering of the upholders of pure awareness will be there, and he will also give you a prophecy of vast enlightened actions in the future, so please go there first."

Accordingly, when the great adept decided to go, the master Dharmaratna had an experiential vision in which he saw a white man with a calm and radiant smile appear leading a dark reddish-colored yogin who was semiwrathful and smiling. The white man said, "Completely give the concentrated essence of the enlightened mind of Vajradhara, the quintessence of all tantras, to this lamp for the Land of Snows, who is my mental emanation and the heir of the teacher Padmasambhava."

The white man dissolved into the yogin. The master's guardians of the teaching and the spirits of the place welcomed the yogin and were delighted. [54] "What kind of an exceptional person is coming?" the master wondered.

The next day a Tibetan yogin emitting the aroma of moral discipline made prostrations and said, "For me to tame the malevolent beings of the Land of Snows who are to be tamed, please bestow the vast collected practices for enlightened activities according to the tantras, and the liberating path according to various vehicles."

"You should stay here for five years," the master replied.

So the great adept stayed for five years, during which he received all the Dharma techniques.

Afterwards, Dharmaratna, the great upholder of pure awareness, said, "Now I have no Dharma that you have not received, so please observe a strict retreat for five months. Every month a marvelous omen will occur, each prophetic of the future."

According to that advice, he practiced for five months, during which buddhas, bodhisattvas, and the assembled deities of the four classes of tantra appeared, surrounded by many upholders of pure awareness and limitless spiritual heroes and ḍākinīs, and bestowed initiations and prophecies.

During the first month of retreat, a vision occurred in which hawks, wolves, and crocodiles prostrated and behaved with great respect in front of the great adept.[412]

During the second month of retreat, a vision occurred in which many people he had never seen before, who were wearing tree leaves, eating fruit, and drinking sap, made prostrations and presented limitless offerings.[413]

During the third month of retreat, a vision occurred of a pot full of poisonous water hidden under the ground, on top of which he [55] stacked a large cairn of white stones.[414]

During the fourth month of retreat, an experiential vision occurred in which one person's body was blazing with fire in the midst of many people. When the great adept poured four vases of water on him, all the fire blazing on his body was extinguished, but fire still blazed on the big toe of his left foot.

During the fifth month of retreat, a vision occurred in which he placed a jeweled ladder with a hundred rungs into each of four great pits whose depths were difficult to comprehend, and brought many sentient beings that were inside the pits up to the surface.[415]

When the great adept finished the five months of retreat he told the master the way the experiential visions had occurred. Dharmaratna, that great upholder of pure awareness who clearly knew the three times, spoke this interpretation of the symbols in the experiential visions:

Listen, for I will explain in prophecy
the future enlightened actions
of the great emanated body,
the upholder of pure awareness,
the Iron-Bridge Man,
based on his experiential visions
in the clear light of meditation
during five months of profound
meditative concentration.

The malevolent trio of hawks, wolves, and crocodiles,
having faith in you, a man, and prostrating,
is a sign that the murderous, sinful sentient beings
of savage Khatra will be tamed by your methods,
O emanated body.

In the experiential vision of the second month,
the people dressed in tree leaves,
eating fruit from trees, and drinking sap,
who made offerings to you,
are a sign that you will bring
the emperor of China under your control.

In your third experiential vision,
the hiding of poisonous water beneath the earth
and then your stacking up of a cairn of white stones, [56]
is a sign that you will build a great stūpa
to suppress the Mongols,[416]
the common enemy of the Land of Snows.

Using the water of the vases
of the four enlightened actions
to cool off the king of Kāmata,

who will be burnt by hellfire
because he has wrong view,
is a sign that you will stop him
from making offerings of the blood
of hundreds of human bodies.

Placing a ladder with a hundred rungs
to the higher realms into each
of the four pits of the birthplaces
of the lower realms,
the depths of which are difficult to calculate,
is a sign that you will build unprecedented,
precious iron bridges over great rivers
that are difficult to cross.[417]

• • •

From the powerful learned
and realized master Ratnakāra,[418]
the great upholder of pure awareness
who was victorious in battle over the Lord of Death,
he received profound and vast initiations, tantras,
and oral instructions in the Sanskrit language,
like one full vase being poured into another.

From the symbols in the experiential visions,
his future was clearly indicated:
the taming of the savages,
offerings by the emperor of China,
the suppression of the Mongols,
breaking a barbarian king's stream of sins,
and the building of iron bridges.

• • •

In that way, after obtaining a prophecy of the future from the symbols of the experiential visions, the great adept traveled to the Mahābodhi of the Vajrāsana [at Bodhgayā] without his vajra body being harmed by

37. The Vajrāsana, or Vajra Seat, at Bodhgayā.

tigers, leopards, poisonous snakes, impassable rivers, and the heat of the Indian plains. He made vast prayers for the benefit of the doctrine and sentient beings.

When he spent the night in front of the Stūpa of Descent from the Gods, resting evenly in the meditative concentration of fire, the people of Ushuri said, "It isn't good to make a fire by the Vajrāsana."[419]

When they came to look, they just said, "It's a Tibetan yogin meditating on the vital wind of fire," and went back.[420] [57]

During that time at the Vajrāsana he received absolutely all the Dharma and initiations possessed by the master known as Siddhiratna, an expert in the profound key points of secret mantra. From that master's consort, a brahmin woman of good family, he also received many secret key points of the mother tantras. She advised him, "Tibetan yogin, you have reached attainment. Without giving these profound instructions to everyone, make them a unique transmission."[421]

Then he traveled to Mount Kukkuṭakapāda, where he met the renunciant Kunga Nyingpo and gained proficiency in the three yogas.[422]

Then the great adept went to Nālandā.[423] He met the adept Atikara, who had reached 230 years of age and could emanate and transform his physical

38. Ruins of a temple and stūpa at the ancient monastery of Nālandā.

body. When the great adept requested the initiation of Amitāyus, he saw in the master's heart Amitāyus [figures] of the five spiritual families embraced by their consorts. At his wrists and ankles,[424] he saw the deities of enlightened action, the four goddesses of the gates, and in the center of the bliss-sustaining cakra at the genitals he saw Hayagrīva, the king of the wrathful beings, with one face and four arms, adorned with terrifying things. They were all beautiful and endowed with the nine dance moods.[425] He made farewell prostrations with faith that the master was actually a buddha.

The great adept traveled to Tāmradvīpa in India.[426] Tāmradvīpa was surrounded in all directions by water, so many people were boarding a boat, but he went to Tāmradvīpa by magical means.[427] Various wild creatures were peacefully wandering in attractive meadows and forest groves of various herbs. Many birds with brilliant plumage and pleasant calls were soaring in flight, [58] and numerous seers with magical abilities were bathing in bathing pools.

In the mountains, noble sthaviras were teaching Dharma to gatherings of arhats, and many boys and girls of the great marketplaces in the towns

39. The Satmahal Pāsāda in Polonnaruva, Ceylon.

and cities were performing various songs and dances and leaping about in play. In the frightful charnel grounds, many yogins and yoginīs who had reached attainment were using various types of behavior to benefit living beings.

In the center [of the island], surrounded with flowers in all directions, was an Auspicious Stūpa of Many Doors created from various precious substances. It had a bodhi tree for a central pole, an assembly of the deities of the four classes of tantra on the four levels, and from the dome upward, an assembly of the deities of the four enlightened bodies of the master. It was fascinating to gaze upon. Many types of meditative concentration arose just by requesting blessings, and it had been consecrated by the Buddha.

He circumambulated it for twenty-one days. During that time he met

40. The great adept Śavaripa.

the glorious lord Śavaripa,[428] who was in the prime of life, with flowing hair and a headdress of flowers. He had peacock feathers for a lower garment, and above his head a parasol of peacock feathers floated by itself. He carried a bow and arrows in his two hands, and a jeweled vase filled with nectar stayed before him unsupported in the sky. To the right, a yoginī was blowing a trumpet, and to the left, a yoginī was carrying the body of a deer. The trio of master and disciples had extremely happy, smiling faces.

The great adept prostrated to them with devotion, [59] mentally emanated a cloudbank of offerings to fill the sky, and said:

> From the vast space of nonduality,
> this offering free of subject and object
> is presented as a mere illusion
> to the rainbowlike master—
> please accept it.

Lord Śavaripa replied, "Fortunate Tibetan yogin, it is good that you have come here." By means of the symbols of various physical displays, he presented limitless techniques of profound and vast Dharma.[429] At the end, he suddenly took into his hand the jeweled vase filled with the nectar of primordial awareness that was before him in midair. Placing it on the head of the great adept, he said, "May the genuine, coemergent primordial awareness, the unborn nature of all phenomena, enter your heart!"

The great adept was instantly freed from the obscuring veil of ignorance, and, as he saw with primordial awareness the fundamental nature of everything knowable just as it is, the initiation was bestowed. Śavaripa told him, "Great performer of the enlightened actions of all the conquerors of the three times, you must build a great stūpa with a shape and size like this one on the peak of a scorpionlike mountain on the banks of a great river in the northern Land of Snows. That will protect the people of the Land of Snows from fear of foreign armies, and, because the shadow of that stūpa will fall on the great river, the creatures that live in the water will quickly be born in the higher realms."[430]

After giving the prophecy and praise, Śavaripa blessed the flesh of pigs, deer, and so forth into the nectar of primordial awareness, [60] and held a vast ritual feast. The trio of father Śavaripa and his consorts dissolved into that stūpa and disappeared.

• • •

He actually met glorious Śavaripa,
the lord of yogins in whom
method and wisdom are united,
and who always happily enjoys the taste
of the indestructible, vajralike sublime.

From the symbols of unity,
he actualized the symbolized Mahāmudrā,
the fundamental nature beyond mental activity,
and received a prophecy telling him
to build in the Land of Snows
a sublime representation of enlightened mind,
in which space and pure awareness
are indivisible.

• • •

41. The great adept Kukkuripa.

When he circumambulated the Auspicious Stūpa of Many Doors again, he met the great adept Kukkuripa.[431] When he looked at Kukkuripa's dress and behavior, Kukkuripa said:

Yogin free from viewed
and viewing,
you won't see by viewing me.

The view without seeing
is sublime seeing.

Kukkuripa became a five-pronged golden vajra radiating light rays and said this:

> In the country of the northern Land of Snows,
> on the bank of a great river,
> build an Auspicious Stūpa of Many Doors like this.
>
> Make a representation of the enlightened mind of the Sugata,
> space and primordial awareness indivisible,
> with a shape and structure like this.
>
> The bad karma of sentient beings
> who are connected with the work that forms
> the cause and circumstances for that [stūpa]
> will be extinguished in this life,
> and they will take magical births
> in the hearts of lotus flowers
> in the pure land of Sukhāvatī.[432]
>
> The creatures [61] living in the river
> upon which the shadow of the stūpa falls
> will gain free and opportune human bodies,
> and grasp the beginning of the path to liberation.
>
> By the blessing of that stūpa,
> excellent bliss and happiness will spread
> in the country of the Land of Snows.

After saying this, the golden vajra vanished like a rainbow.

~

When the great adept returned from Tāmradvīpa, he traveled magically over the surface of the water.[433] At the Vajra Cave, a secret, isolated place near the Vajrāsana, he met Kalden Dorjé Drakpa,[434] an adept of the Nyingma tradition of secret mantra. He received absolutely all the Nyingma Dharma cycles from him. During the time of the general initiation as a regent,[435] the great adept said this to the master:

Saṃsāra is primordially pure
and primordially free,
and the uncontrived universal ground
is primordial buddhahood.
There is nothing
except the dharmakāya reality body,
Samantabhadra.

The master replied:

I, Kalden Dorjé Drakpa,
have lived for 320 years.

From opening the door of Dharma, until today,
I have performed about seven hundred initiations.

Those who received the initiation of the words
are countless.
One hundred received the vase initiation;
eighty received the secret initiation.
You, an emanated body,
received the absolute initiation.

The bestowed and the bestowing
are empty by nature.
The received and the receiving
are pure from the beginning.

Emanated body, Tsöndru Sangpo,
you have gained self-control
of your own pure awareness.

You have seen the very face
of the unborn dharmakāya reality body.
Propensities for confusion
have been purified at the ground.

Now go to the glacial land of Tibet
and [62] care for the doctrine
and infinite living beings
by means of the three wheels.[436]

Your enlightened actions
will be victorious over obstacles
and the māras.

After the initiation, prophecy, and encouraging praise, the great adept presented an extensive offering of meditative concentration to the master.

5: Five Names of Suitable Meaning

In three days the great adept magically arrived at his birthplace, Rinchen Ding. His brothers and all the local people exclaimed, "Venerable monk Tsöndru Sangpo, we haven't laid eyes on you for almost eighteen years. Where did you go?"

"I went to Nepal and India," the great adept replied. "I received Dharma, profound and vast. An exceptional experiential realization has arisen in my mindstream, so now there is no Dharma that I don't know and need to study."

All the local people commented, "This madman went off as a wandering bum. He has come home only to tell lies. If he had met learned and realized masters of India and Nepal and an exceptional realization had arisen, he would be different from this!"

Engaging in nothing except the wrong view, they were not at all faithful and amazed.

~

The great adept then went before Jangsem Jinpa Sangpo to receive the Six Dharmas of Niguma.[437] At that time the master announced, "An exceptional person who will uphold the Dharma lineage is coming to our place today. Last night all the spiritual heroes and ḍākinīs went to welcome him. Prepare a vast ritual feast!"

The attendants made the arrangements and waited. Then they told the master, "No one else has arrived except Crazy Tsöndru, the monk from Rinchen Ding who says he has come to meet you. [63] Should he be granted an audience?"

"Oh, that's him!" the master cried. "Spread out fine cushions! Invite him in right now and offer the ritual feast!"

So they offered a fine ritual feast to the master and disciple. The master was very pleased and said, "Oh, a vigorous son has been born to an old father. An upholder of the doctrine of the practice lineage has come. In my old age I will give the Dharma to its owner."

He continued, "I will give you the entire Dharma of the Shangpa, such as the Six Dharmas, the Amulet Mahāmudrā, the Three Ways to Carry the Practice on the Path, the Immortal and Infallible, the White and Red Khecarīs, and the Master and Protector Indivisible,[438] instructions such as this that have come through a lineage that is like a rosary of pearls, transmitted in a unique transmission through the Seven Jewels and from Jagchungpa Tsangma Shangtön."[439]

As soon as the ritual feast was over, the master began teaching the Dharma, and completely filled the fine vase of the great adept's comprehension with the nectar of the profound path.

The great adept then practiced these profound instructions in an isolated and pleasant wilderness hermitage. Many types of meditative concentration arose in his mind, so that he considered spreading this profound oral transmission in these glacial mountain ranges. At that moment a clear voice from the sky called out, "Son! Yogin!"

When he looked up into midair, in the center of a bunch of clouds, the famous Niguma, the ḍākinī of primordial awareness [64] endowed with the power to traverse space and with the immortal form of a rainbow body, directly revealed her face to the great universal emperor of attainment known as Tangtong Gyalpo, "King of the Empty Plain," the thunder of whose fame totally fills the expanse of space. When she completely bestowed the four initiations in a great sublime maṇḍala, he was filled with the youthful vitality of the four joys. At that time they fully engaged in the great secret practices, such as questions and responses, symbols and return symbols, and happily enjoyed the miraculous sensory objects of a ritual feast.

On that occasion, Niguma deciphered and fully instructed the great adept in each of the *Vajra Lines*[440] by means of actual, implied, and hidden oral instructions. In particular, she bestowed the extremely profound transference practices of the infallible White and Red Khecarīs, together with instructions for enhancing them by means of two examples sealed by her command. When he put these into practice, he gained an inconceivable repertoire of attainments, such as the instantaneous display of countless physical forms in just a single moment, a clairvoyant knowledge of others' minds, and the ability to actually transfer [the consciousness] when he performed the transference for another person.[441]

42. Niguma, the ḍākinī of primordial awareness.

Later, on the peak of the famous glorious Riwoché in Latö Jang that was the adept's home, he was given permission by the ḍākinī and placed in writing the guidance manual for this profound path, the *Collection of the Essentials*, together with the affiliated texts.[442] [65] But the oral instructions for the transference practices of the White and Red Khecarīs, together with the illustration of the two examples, he taught with the tune of the indestructible *nāda*.[443]

• • •

From the sublime maṇḍala of the ḍākinī
with the brilliance of a moon-lily
that drinks the moonlight,

he extracted the desirable
great bliss of coemergence
and obtained absolutely all the instructions
of the great secret and rapid path.

The ḍākinī's oral transmission,
a great sea of milk,
he placed in writing without dilution
with the water of his own fabrications,
and from that kindness,
future generations of disciples
also became fortunate.

• • •

The great adept's mother, Gyagar Lhamo, entered the door of Dharma and was given the name Palmo Gön. He taught her the Great Perfection and she lived together with his maternal aunt Jangsang. She practiced single-mindedly for several years, directly beheld the true nature of phenomena, and then passed away peacefully into her own realm, the land of Uḍḍiyāna.

After his mother passed away, the great adept completed the basic acts of virtue during twenty-one days. Then he kept silent for seven days, sitting without moving his body from the sevenfold posture of Vairocana.[444]

When the body of his mother was cremated, there was a rain of heavenly flowers and the pleasant aroma of incense. Without dispersing her bones, he molded them into the forms of many buddhas and bodhisattvas, placing within them the five great *dhāraṇīs*[445] and so forth, relics of the dharmakāya reality body, and the many five-colored relics like mustard seeds that had come from her body.

The great adept [66] created by himself, with his own hands, a Kūṭāgāra Stūpa, the *Condensed Verses on the Perfection of Wisdom* written with jewels and gold as a representation of enlightened speech, and a tangka painting of the eight sugatas as a representation of enlightened body.[446] He consecrated the representations of enlightened mind, speech, and body at the same time, saying, "These are the first of the representations I will construct."

After his mother had passed away, all his relatives became very contemptuous, saying, "Crazy Tsöndru doesn't distinguish between Dharma and the world."

So he brought a lawsuit, both general and specific, against his two elder brothers and many paternal relatives.[447]

He [later] commented, "Due to the power of past karma and the truth of my statements, I won and was awarded many fields."

He appointed two honest persons to care for the buildings, fields, and cattle that he controlled. He gave orders, saying, "Until I return, perform without fail the regular agricultural labor during the four seasons. Save what barley you can, treat the animals with love, and never do anything to harm them."

~

The great adept then practiced meditation single-mindedly in a clay grotto[448] on the mountain behind his birthplace, on the west slope of Owa Lhatsé. At that time there were no fortunate disciples who were inspired with faith in the profound instructions of the new and old secret mantra traditions that he had received from learned and realized upholders of pure awareness in Nepal and India. In order for a person with the karma to encounter [those instructions] in the future and benefit sentient beings, he searched for many pieces of slate, wrote the words on the stones until he had worn out two thick iron needles, and hid them as treasures. [67] He appointed a great genyen spirit as the Owa Lhatsé treasure-owner.[449]

He then dwelt single-mindedly in the "river-flow yoga," living inside a cave with a small opening but a spacious interior and a spring, a clay grotto on the east slope of Owa Lhatsé.[450] On one occasion the eighty-four great adepts of India magically arrived before him in the sky and blessed him. They bestowed this prophecy that he would accomplish vast virtuous acts:

> Up until the present time,
> through a hundred thousand lifetimes,
> you have been a person who has prayed
> to benefit infinite sentient beings.
>
> By the power of that accomplishment,
> you will be able to build unprecedented
> precious iron bridges and large ferries

spanning the great rivers that are
extremely difficult to cross,
and to lead creatures from the sea of existence
to the isle of liberation.

Therefore, you must now take responsibility
for the benefit of sentient beings!

You will be able to tame the sinful savages
who have never even heard the words
"precious Three Jewels,"
and to establish pleasant monastic centers
providing refuge from the fears
of the mountains, rivers, thieves, and robbers.

Thus he received a prophecy of accomplishing vast virtuous acts.

During that time, by the blessing of his precious enlightenment mind, about ten springs that were not there before sprang up close to his meditation shelter. Various flowers grew. Even sentient beings such as snow leopards, wolves, wild dogs, and hawks, who take the lives of sentient beings and then eat their flesh, lived peacefully on that mountain eating grass and grain without harmful thoughts.[451] [68]

At the completion of the retreat, after seven years[452] had passed in that spot, a shepherd heard the sound of the great adept's hand-cymbals, came to the door of the cave, and asked for a blessing. That evening the shepherd told the local people, "We didn't know before that a fine yogin was living in a clay grotto on our Owa Lhatsé. Wouldn't it be best[453] for us to now offer some foodstuffs and barley flour for sacrificial cakes and ask for a blessing?"

They all agreed, saying, "It would be best for us to take some useful things to offer, such as barley flour for sacrificial cakes, and go request a blessing."

The shepherd guided them on the path and they came to the door of the cave. They offered barley flour for sacrificial cakes and various foodstuffs and said, "We need Dharma and a blessing."

He blessed them with his hand and bestowed a Dharma connection of taking refuge, awakening the thought of enlightenment, and reciting *maṇis*. All the people were filled with faith and were making prayers when the chieftain of that area, called Sengé Sangpo, arrived. He made prostrations and requested a blessing, but when the great adept extended his hand and blessed him, he exclaimed, "This isn't the hand of a fine master! It's the hand of Crazy Tsöndru. We're dimwits! But Tsöndru, he's really clever. So it's not true that he died."

When everyone took the wrong view, the great adept understood this faithfulness of the people in the morning and their taking of the wrong view by the afternoon as an example of the falsehood of appearances.[454]

~

Then, to the east of the great adept's birthplace, at the boat crossing of Ngampuk, a large bunch of chestnut trees had grown on an extension of rock where the water crashed against the cliffs. [69] A malicious demon lived there, whom the boatmen resorted to as their god. By the harm of that demon, many boats had capsized and the lives of 128 people had been lost. The great adept saw with the eye of primordial awareness that they had been reborn in the lower realms. He set fire to the bunch of chestnut trees in order to subdue the demon, who offered a promise to cause no harm thereafter. When the great adept sat in meditation to extract from the lower realms the people who had died in the boats, three boatmen carrying swords and spears chased but did not catch him.

~

Then the great adept went to the place of the couple to whom he had entrusted his buildings, fields, and cattle. There had been a great increase of barley and cattle, so he was also able to pay off those to whom his mother owed debts.

He sponsored the recitation of two sets of one hundred million *maṇis*. For the first, he commissioned his elder half-brother Draksangpa as leader, honored him, and made fine offerings. Because it was said to be very dangerous to act as the leader for a recitation of one hundred million *maṇis*, the great adept did not find anyone for the next [recitation]. So he acted as the group leader himself. When he began the one hundred million *maṇis*, the local people said, "The likes of Crazy Tsöndru is leading the group. It's an excuse for him to not give offerings to another person."

But when sprouts grew from the vase and the meditative sacrificial cakes and ears of grain appeared on them, the people wondered, "What method did he use to make ears of grain appear during the month of miracles?"[455]

Then, at dawn on the eighth day of the month of miracles, the great adept beheld in the sky before him the noble lord Avalokiteśvara with one face and two arms, [70] and above him, in ascending order, the one with four arms, the one with eleven faces and eight arms, and the one with a thousand arms and a thousand eyes, surrounded by an inconceivable assembly of buddhas and bodhisattvas.

He offered the seven branches,[456] such as prostrations by countless bodies that he emanated and offerings that filled the sky, and made a prayer: "Please look with compassion upon sentient beings in degenerate, evil times."

The Noble One replied by saying this:

> Since I am your spiritual friend,
> it is excellent that you use illusory food,
> wealth, and possessions for the recitation
> of the six-syllable mantra of pure awareness,
> expanding the two assemblies[457]
> into an ocean for yourself and others.
>
> Firmly build ferries and precious iron bridges
> on the great rivers of the Land of Snows,
> and construct representations of the enlightened body,
> speech, and mind of the Conqueror,
> increasing the merit of sentient beings
> of the degenerate age.
>
> Fill all the vast country with the sound
> of the royal six-syllable mantra of pure awareness,
> the mere seeing, hearing, memory,
> and touch of which shuts the doors
> to lower realms and shows
> the path to higher realms.

The great adept then took full advantage of the increased food, wealth, and possessions from the buildings and fields he controlled. He gave each of his two assistants what wealth they desired, told them to be energetic as before, and left them in control of the estate. Taking a tenth of an ounce of gold to gild its face, he decided to go for a while to visit the precious

Jowo[458] of Lhasa [71] and to request Dharma from what fine masters there were in the land of Tibet.

When the great adept set off from home, the guardians of primordial awareness, the twelve tenma spirits and so forth who protect the land of Tibet, and all the eight tribes[459] that are the subjects of the Great Teacher of Uḍḍiyāna also set off after him. They announced, "Great man, the time is now gradually coming for you to tame living beings. Therefore, we will also go, so that you, a mental emanation of the Teacher of Uḍḍiyāna, may accomplish your enlightened actions in all the regions of Central Tibet and Tsang, the geomantic focal-points of Lho,[460] Mön, and Sodruk, and in Dokham, India, China, and so forth."

The great adept told the primordial-awareness beings, "Since you have feet of magical ability and eyes of primordial awareness, you must uphold, protect, and spread the precious doctrine. You of the eight tribes should each stay in your own places without causing harm to sentient beings."

~

First the great adept traveled to Tarpa Ling to request Dharma from Choksang Lekpai Lodrö.[461] That night the master had a dream. He dreamed that a yogin arrived holding in his two hands a parasol and a victory banner, and riding on a lion. When asked, "Who are you?" the yogin replied, "Kukkuripa of India, come to care for disciples in the land of Tibet."

The master wondered what kind of omen it was.

When the great adept arrived the next day, the master asked, "Venerable monk Tsöndru, why have you come?"

"I have come to request Dharma."

"You are more profound in Dharma than I," the master said.

But when the great adept insisted, he received [72] many systems of guidance, initiations, reading transmissions, and instructions, such as the Mahāmudrā teachings of the *Ganges Mahāmudrā*, the Amulet, the *Unwritten*, the Coemergent Union, and the Fivefold.[462]

~

The great Rendawa[463] himself was then at the Yilung Gandentsé of Gangbulé, resting evenly in meditation on perfect reality and seeing the three times without obscuration. The great adept met him during that period and offered as gifts a plate full of myrobalan plums, nutmeg, and brown sugar, upon which were a gold nugget, a turquoise, a coral, and a whole piece of cotton cloth with uncut fringe. Then he said, "I need a Dharma in which appearances arise as auspicious connections."

The Dharma lord Rendawa examined the auspicious connections concerning the great adept and the gifts, and granted this prophecy:

"You, a great emanated body, will extend the duration of the precious doctrine, the source of benefit and happiness, on this Jambudvīpa.

"Since you are like this gold, the best among precious substances, you will perform great enlightened actions for the doctrine and become very famous.

"From the auspicious connection of this turquoise, you will attain the immutable dharmakāya reality body, and from the auspicious connection of this coral, your sons and nephews will uphold the lineage and work for the benefit of sentient beings.

"There are fifty-eight pieces of myrobalan plum, nutmeg, and brown sugar, and by the auspicious connections of this you will have fifty-eight major disciples connected by karma and prayers, who are of different clans and families, and who will have different costumes and behavior. They will bring [73] infinite sentient beings of Jambudvīpa into contact with virtue.

"This immaculate white cotton cloth indicates that you will establish the victory banner of the doctrine and gather an assembly of disciples equal to the number of its warps and wefts, and because its fringe is uncut, you will perfectly complete virtuous acts just as you intend."

The Dharma lord Rendawa bestowed initiation in the maṇḍalas of the trio of Red Yamāri, Black Yamāri, and Bhairava.[464] Then he said, "Since appearances are the mind, if confusion is purified into space, your own mind is seen to be the dharmakāya reality body. See the essence of whatever appearances arise. Do not negate and affirm or reject and accept in regard to conduct. First bring under control the eight tribes of gods and demons in apparent existence."

According to the prophecy and advice, the great adept practiced Severance with great love and compassion at places where malicious gods and demons lived. When he blessed the flesh and blood of his physical body into nectar, offered it to the Three Jewels, and dedicated it to the six types of living beings, the eight tribes were satisfied and pleased. They each devotedly offered the great adept their life essence, and, for his performance of virtuous acts, all the dangerous places, dangerous trees, dangerous rivers, and dangerous rocks that they owned.

• • •

Upholding the manner of an intelligent
young spiritual son of the conquerors,
Rendawa perfected study and reflection,
and spread forth fine explanations
for a sea of clear minds.

Then they met while he was resting evenly
in single-minded meditation
on the slope of a glacial mountain.

In the clear mirror of his primordial awareness,
Rendawa saw instantly and without obscuration
all that is knowable in the three times.

He made an extremely clear prophecy,
stating, "This and that excellent attribute
of existence and quiescence will come to you." [74]

This had just the same meaning as the prophecy
by the Knower of the Three Times, Padmasambhava.

Therefore, the great venerable lord Rendawa
undoubtedly dwelt on the spiritual level of accomplishment.

• • •

Then the great adept traveled to the edge of the river at Yongru, went across the surface of the ice that was like an unrolled woolen cloth, and arrived on the north of the great river. He then went before Lekhawa Sherab Sangpo and received the higher initiations of Kālacakra and the complete Six-branch Yoga according to the Jonang tradition.[465]

Moreover, he received limitless Dharma from many excellent teachers in the land of Tibet. By means of austerities in isolated places and secret behavior[466] in numerous dangerous mountain sites such as charnel grounds, he accomplished infinite direct and indirect benefit for living beings, human and nonhuman disciples.

~

The great adept then engaged in secret behavior at the foot of Gyedé Plain in Tsang. Many girls of human form appeared to him again and again, singing songs and stomping their feet in dance.[467] Foremost among these were the five white, yellow, red, blue, and green ḍākinīs of primordial awareness,[468] fascinating to gaze upon, adorned with various bone and jewel ornaments and silk garments, and surrounded by a retinue of the ḍākinīs of sacred commitment and the carnivorous ḍākinīs, filling the sky while playing hand-drums and bells. Pleasant fragrances covered the earth, together with various sounds of music. The leading white one was calm, the yellow one was enriching, the red one was powerful, and the blue one was terrible. In the center, the green ḍākinī of the buddha spiritual family said, "We five sisters will accomplish for you, a great emanated body, [75] any of the four enlightened actions you require."

All the ḍākinīs joined their voices together as one and bestowed these five names in sweet melodious song:

> We five girls gathered here
> will each give a name,
> with suitable meaning,
> to this most astonishing man
> staying on the Gyedé Plain.
>
> On a great plain of immense expanse,
> the yogin who has realized emptiness
> dwells like a fearless king.
> Therefore, we name you Tangtong Gyalpo,
> King of the Empty Plain.
>
> In the valley of equanimity
> beyond conceptual elaboration,
> you have the view of appearance
> and emptiness as indivisible.
> A madman free of accepting and rejecting,
> we name you Madman of the Empty Valley.

Whether food and drink of a hundred tastes,
or vile and disgusting filth,
you are one who extracts the nutriment,
beyond benefit and harm.
We name you Alchemist of Foods.

Realizing that whatever various conditions arise
are like a dream or an echo,
you overpower the eight worldly concerns,
which for you have an equal taste.
We name you One for Whom Conditions
Have an Equal Taste.

Since you fully understand,
without disgust toward or reliance on them,
that absolutely all phenomena in saṃsāra
and nirvāṇa may appear,
but are like the moon reflected in water,
we name you Free from Disgust toward
or Reliance on Phenomena.

Peerless yogin,
to expand your measureless
enlightened activities,
the time has come to now lead
living beings upon the plain of joy.

After bestowing five names of suitable meaning, the five ḍākinīs of primordial awareness magically traveled in a single instant to their home, Uḍḍiyāna, the land of ḍākinīs. [76]

From then on, the great adept was known everywhere in the three worlds[469] by the name Accomplished Lord Tangtong Gyalpo, "King of the Empty Plain."

~

The great adept then went to Drampa Gyang.[470] From a treasure trove in the Red Temple he extracted the Dharma Cycle of the Extremely Secret

43. The great stūpa at Jonang.

and Unexcelled Realization of Enlightened Mind, the great adept's own Dharma inheritance.

When he traveled to Jonang, the practitioners were performing the rite of accomplishment and offerings to Kālacakra. One practitioner who had good experience in meditation actually saw the great adept as the Omniscient Dolpopa, offered prostrations, and placed the great adept's feet upon his head.[471]

The great adept slept on the Dharma throne that night, but the steward came the next day, carrying the steps [for the throne], and yelled, "Who put this madman on the Dharma throne?" beat him with his staff, and threw him down.

Then he circumambulated the great stūpa for three days.[472] He then slept one night in the middle of the waves under the bridge. In the morning, people came to draw water, and cried, "Oh, this stupid madman.[473] Poor thing!"

During that period the great adept made the vows that until he had finished reciting two hundred million *maṇis* he would not engage in ordinary talk except if a request was made for a Dharma connection, that he would not seek food or clothing other than what there was, that he would not cross the thresholds of doors other than those of a master's residence and a temple, and that he would never give up the good of the doctrine and living beings.

During that time at Jonang he stayed [in retreat][474] for seven months under a boulder shaped like a garuda with outstretched wings. Once, at the first break of dawn, venerable Tārā appeared in the sky in front of the great adept. In the midst of rainbow light, with a form fascinating to gaze upon, [77] she said this:

> Hey! Fortunate son of good family,
> without clinging to the taste
> of the nectar of meditative concentration,
> build, build, build for the benefit
> of sentient beings!
>
> Go quickly before
> the Jowo Śākya in Lhasa,
> and swiftly construct an iron bridge
> to easily cross a turbulent river
> of cascading waves!
>
> Make prayers to tame the sinful savages
> to the southeast of the snowy land of Tibet.
>
> Since the time has now come
> to benefit living beings,
> take now the great responsibility
> to bring them benefit and joy
> by means of representations
> of the enlightened body, speech, and mind
> of the conquerors and their spiritual children,
> and with ferries and iron bridges!

Thus she spoke, and departed like a cloud in the sky.

~

The great adept traveled from Jonang to Bodong Jagö Shong, and made prostrations and circumambulations around the Jowo. He offered a sacrificial cake to the Vaiśravaṇa with a Red Lance.[475] When he came to take away the old dough of the sacrificial cake, it had changed into the nature of the five precious substances.[476]

He knew that the adept Japurwa, who was said to be staying at Chiwolé, was Tsenden Namkhai Naljor,[477] his master's master, and decided to go and ask for blessings. In an experiential vision of clear light, Tilopa, the lord of yogins, appeared to the master at dawn, traveling in midair adorned with charnel ground garments, ringing a hand-drum and bell, and proclaiming the sound of *hūṃ*.

The great adept arrived shortly after sunrise, and Tsenden Namkhai Naljor asked, "By what name are you known?"

"I am called Tangtong Gyalpo. Have good signs not appeared to you?" [78]

"Extremely favorable signs have appeared. It seems that you are Tilopa," he remarked, and they requested Dharma from each other.

~

The great adept traveled from Bodong to Shab. At the top of the Dakla Pass he met about seven thousand people making the great pilgrimage from Sakya to Lhasa,[478] and joined company with the pilgrims. Sometimes he urged them to take refuge and recite *maṇis*. Sometimes he explained Dharma. Sometimes he sang songs and performed Dharma dances.

The people on the great pilgrimage said, "This crazy renunciant definitely isn't an ordinary person. We feel content merely to see him, and our afflictions and sufferings are naturally calmed. When we look at where he's sleeping at night, there is a bunch of light."

He arrived at Nartang and said to the noble sthavira Aṅgaja,[479] who was sitting in the midst of beggars, "You must give me Dharma."

"A beggar has nothing to explain."

When he pleaded for him to teach, Aṅgaja said, "Let's go into seclusion."

They went, and he bestowed once an explanation of the *Perfection of Wisdom in Eight Thousand Lines*.[480]

The next day he went to Tsongdu Gurmo[481] with those on the great pilgrimage. Those on the great pilgrimage circumambulated Shalu[482] and traveled on. The great adept offered the seven branches to the Avalokiteśvara,[483] and made extensive prayers for the benefit of the doctrine and living beings. He spent the night there in front of the Dharma throne, and a crystal-colored youth[484] appeared before him in the sky and said this:

> As a qualified person [79]
> and a yogin with perfect realization,
> you are endowed
> with the confidence of equal taste.
>
> Thus you will meet face-to-face with a ḍākinī
> of the primordial awareness
> of the dharmakāya reality body,
> be taught the Dharma, and receive a prophecy.
>
> Stay in this place for three days.

Having spoken, the crystal-colored youth faded away like a rainbow.

The next day the great adept walked in circumambulation around the outer wall. When he arrived at Obkha[485] to the north, there was a girl about fifteen years old reciting the *Two-Part [Hevajra] Tantra*. Beneath her loom was placed a skull-cup filled with beer and covered with a saucer. When he saw that she was weaving in a state of mind free from conceptual elaboration, he thought, "Last night that crystal-colored youth prophesied that I would meet a ḍākinī of primordial awareness. This is the one. I must ask for a Dharma connection."

In front of her, he said, "I request a Dharma connection."

The girl replied, "To give attainments to fortunate yogins, I have stayed in the great gathering places of people, such as Lhasa, Samyé, Tradruk, Shalu, Nartang, Sakya, and Ngari Gungtang. None but you have recognized me. To request the profound Dharma of secret mantra it is necessary to have a vast ritual feast. Arrange one!"

To request the complete four initiations from the maṇḍala of the enlightened body, speech, and mind of Vajrayoginī, the great adept searched for the sacramental substances. In the center of Ob there was the corpse of a horse that had been torn open by three dogs, and whose entrails were spilled out. He cut it up. Carrying in the folds of his cloak the five kinds of flesh[486] from the inside of the horse's corpse, and its head, [80] he arranged a ritual feast.

In the instant it takes to snap the fingers three times, that girl became like a mountain of ruby wreathed in the radiance of the sun, adorned with the five bone ornaments,[487] and holding a curved knife and skull-cup. She bestowed the four initiations of great bliss simultaneously, and performed the ritual feast. She gave a detailed explanation of equal taste, and then spoke:

> Hey, yogin!
> Overcome unwanted conditions!
> All impure food is great nectar.
> Conceptual thoughts will be naturally freed
> and the dharmakāya reality body discovered.

Venerable Khecarī became a mass of light and dissolved into the great adept, greatly enhancing his experience of equal taste.

While again circumambulating the Mahākaruṇika of Shalu and single-mindedly reciting the six-syllable mantra of pure awareness, he came to a place where a realized yogin and his two wives, who were leading a monkey, had each pitched their tents.

"Where have you come from?" the great adept asked. "For what reason do you go around the country?"

"I am the master of a great monastery," the yogin replied. "I know much Dharma, but I had intercourse with these two women. I go around the country out of shame."

"What are you doing leading this monkey?"

"It's a way to seek food."

"You must give me Dharma."

"Ask the two of them."

He asked, but they replied, "First the master must give it. Then it can happen."

Again he asked the master, who said, "If you need a Dharma connection, stay three days."

"I'll stay," he replied.

That night the master gave the initiation of glorious Hevajra, together with the reading transmission of the Tantra Trilogy.[488] The next night, one woman gave the initiation of Vajrayoginī and the reading transmission of the *Tantra of the Direct Emergence of Vajravārāhī.*[489] [81] The last night, one yoginī gave the initiation of the fifteen goddesses of Nairātmyā and the initiations and reading transmissions of Avalokiteśvara as the Protector from the Eight Fears, as the One Who Dredges the Pit of Saṃsāra, as the Wish-fulfilling Gem, and as the Lord of the Dance.[490]

While the master and consorts sat in one spot performing a vast ritual feast, the great adept devotedly prostrated, offered a maṇḍala, and implored them to bestow the four initiations. That lord of yogins himself became glorious Hevajra, his two wives became Vajravārāhī and Nairātmyā, and they directly bestowed the initiations with vajra body, speech, mind, and primordial awareness.

~

The great adept went magically from Shalu to Ngurmik in the lower valley of Rongchen and stayed for three days. When he visited the image in the Tārā Temple,[491] a voice like the sound of hand-cymbals came forth from the figure, speaking this prophecy: "On the border of India and Tibet there is a large region where only sin is practiced, stretching from Lo Khatra, Sharmön, Bumtang, Layak Losum, and Paro in Bhutan, down to the country of the sinful king of Kāmata.[492] You are a person who, through the power of your prayers, must display skillful compassion and magical bodies in whatever way necessary to tame them. By building monasteries, iron bridges, and representations of enlightened body, speech, and mind, make the Buddhist doctrine like the rising sun in a dark and sinful land!"

Traveling from Ngurmik, he caught up to those on the great pilgrimage at about midday, between the palace and the Malchak of the Lhasa Dharmacakra.[493] [82] Just at the sight of the golden spires and pagoda roofs of the Rasa Trulnang temples,[494] he became exhilarated and rushed forward. Unhindered by the gates, the iron gate of the precious [Jowo], and so forth, he went straight up to the Jowo. Tossing a tenth of an ounce of gold like a flower to the Jowo, he requested blessings. The reflexive great primordial awareness of the Jowo blended with his mind as one, and the flesh and blood mass of his body fell down unconscious.

When the iron gates of the top floor were opened, the steward came inside and cried, "A person has died here! When I went out of the temple there was no person or corpse here."

Some of the people on the great pilgrimage arrived at that time and commented, "That crazy renunciant arrived before the Jowo and died, but it's a fine place to die."

When five rays of light shone from the heart of the precious Jowo and dissolved into the great adept's body, he suddenly sprang up and made

44. The golden spires and pagoda roofs of the Rasa Trulnang, or Jokhang, temples.

countless prostrations, saying, "Please bless me to be able to bring infinite disciples to maturation and liberation."

The voice of the Jowo, sweet like the melody of a four-stringed lute, uttered this prophecy, urging him to benefit living beings:

As one who acts on behalf
of all the conquerors of the three times
and is a sublime individual,
a mental emanation of Padmasambhava,
your fame will fill all the ten directions,
and your disciples will spread through
this land of glacial peaks.

To establish these infinite disciples in happiness,
remember the prayers you made before,
and bring benefit and joy to the Land of Snows
with representations of enlightened body, speech,
and mind, and with ferries and iron bridges. [83]

At that time the great adept decided that he should examine the length of his lifespan through the omen of how long a butter lamp would last. He begged butter from all the residents and foreigners in Lhasa, and one person gave him a fist-sized lump of butter. When he offered it in a butter lamp and it lasted for a month and eighteen days, everyone was astonished.

6: Uḍḍiyāna, the Land of Ḍākinīs

The great adept traveled from Lhasa to Rinchen Ding in seven days. It had been a good year and there was much barley. He needed to pay off the debts left by his father and mother, but many remained. He paid off most of them and bought gold and salt with what was left, which he loaded on eight donkeys. He joined together with traders from the area and went to trade in Lhorong.[495] He had the finest success in trading.

On the return trip he arrived in the lower valley of Chung Yulpoché. When they asked to be taken across at the Dongshur ferry, a disagreement broke out over the fare and his companions were sent to make an appeal before the governor of Jang.[496] The great adept took care of the loads and pack animals. While sitting in meditation on the bank of the river, he saw venerable Tārā in front of him in the sky, fascinating to gaze upon in the center of a mass of clouds and surrounded by her retinue. When he prostrated and offered prayers, the Noble One spoke: "Courageous man, remember the many lifetimes in which you completely gave up your body and all possessions for the benefit of sentient beings and then awakened the thought of enlightenment and made prayers! First bring the sentient beings of the barbarian borderlands to maturation! Then, when you build representations of the conquerors and their spiritual children [84] here on the bank of the great river, they will appear in a naturally arisen way. There will be a stable iron bridge over which to easily cross the great river, and on the side of the mountain many will live while cultivating meditation, and meditative concentration will arise."

When the prophecy sounded as nectar to his ears, he looked in the northern direction. He saw many sons and daughters of the gods presenting offerings to an assembly of buddhas and bodhisattvas on the peak of the mountain, many meditators sitting in meditative concentration on the

45. White Tārā.

mountainside, and, at the base, many representations of enlightened body, speech, and mind resting in midair, and treasuries of grain and jewels.

The great adept thought, "As prophesied by Tārā, the goddess of the enlightened activities of the conquerors of the three times, the great scorpion-shaped mountain over to the north of this river is the spirit-mountain of foreign armies who are the common enemy of Tibet, the Land of Snows, and the river is their spirit-river. These will be suppressed by my own meditation hut, where I will cultivate vajralike meditative concentration. The forehead [of the scorpion][497] will be suppressed by the great stūpa prophesied by the learned and realized masters and upholders of pure awareness in India and Nepal. The sentient beings involved in the circumstances and work of founding a vast temple and monastic center will also be established temporarily in the glory of the higher realms and then take magical birth in lotus flowers in the pure lands. Vast benefit for living beings will be accomplished." He was overjoyed.

He then crossed over in a boat with his companions and arrived on the north bank of the river. He took three companions as assistants and walked on foot around Dongshur Mountain in these areas now used for the outer pilgrim's circuit. [85] He spent one night, and named this mountain Glorious Riwoché.

• • •

As he rested evenly in meditation
on the bank of the great river,
before him in the sky
appeared the enchanting figure of noble Tārā,
from whose lotus-mouth
flowed such honeycombs of prophecy.

At that moment, in the pure mirror
of primordial awareness,
he saw buddhas and bodhisattvas
on the peak of this place,
meditators seated in meditative
concentration on the slopes,
and many representations of enlightened body,
speech, and mind at the base.

So he placed his lotus-feet
upon this site and blessed it,
named it Glorious Riwoché,
and said that a monastic center,
representations of enlightened body, speech,
and mind, and a stable iron bridge
would appear here.

I think that even Lochen's[498] *construction*
of practice centers to fulfill
the great adept's intentions
was clearly prophesied

in the statement that meditators
would appear and meditative concentration
would arise in this place.

• • •

The great adept then traveled to his birthplace. He paid off the debts with the goods from Lho,[499] and no debts remained.

"Now I don't have to repay the debts of my parents anymore," he thought. "I must abandon bad activities such as trading, and meditate single-mindedly on the Dharma teachings that I received from the masters of India and Nepal."

In the Shalkar Lhadong meditation hut at the isolated site of Tarpa Ling, he lived on the milk of two female goats. Without even a single measure of any other provisions, he practiced for six years.[500] During that period the two female goats each gave birth to young goats twice a year, so that the goats greatly multiplied. The goats came and slept in front of the meditation hut at night and went to eat grass when the sun rose. There was always milk, in summer and in winter. [86]

Then one day at the first light of dawn, the lion-faced ḍākinī Siṃhamukha appeared in the sky before him and announced, "The lord of yogins, Virūpa, is staying at the Charnel Ground of Blazing Skeletons in India.[501] Go there and request initiation and instructions! It will benefit infinite sentient beings."

Immediately after the prophecy, he flew from the meditation hut. In all directions of the Charnel Ground of Blazing Skeletons many human corpses were scattered and vicious carnivores roared. There was a forest of sandalwood, gugula, and so forth. The mere scent of the trees caused demons and obstructing spirits to flee. In the cool shade of a great sandalwood tree, around which spiritual heroes and ḍākinīs were gathered like clouds, he met the glorious lord of yogins, Virūpa,[502] an incredibly majestic figure seated on a kṛṣṇasara antelope skin after having drawn all the environment and its inhabitants into a single skull-cup.

Just at the sight of him, deep faith automatically arose and the great adept made countless prostrations and offered mentally emanated gifts filling the sky. Then he said, "Please have compassion for our kind parents who have experienced unbearable suffering throughout beginningless time."

The great adept was granted initiation in an emanated maṇḍala and

46. The lord of yogins, Virūpa.

given a skull-cup filled with nectar. When he completely drank it he became able to rest evenly in many hundreds of meditative concentrations and to emanate a billion magical physical forms. When three nectar pills of the secret initiation were placed on his tongue, the impure sediments were extinguished, and so, as it appeared to other disciples, his excretions ceased.[503] He received an analysis of infinite tantras by means of the six limits and the four styles, and completely received the esoteric instructions of the Path with the Result.[504] Again, he [87] magically returned to the meditation hut.

. . .

When the moon climbed to the summit
of the cranial dome,

the flow of the Ganges reversed,
and with the solar particle bound
in the secret place,
Virūpa held the sun immobile.

He gave the food of immortality,
and when it was consumed,
the vital winds in the rasanā and lalanā stopped,
and the clear essences of Vairocana and Akṣobhya
were devoured by the mouth of the dhūtī.[505]

With the residue being used for a burnt offering
to the fire of the syllable A *in the form of a vertical line,*
what chance had any impure sediment to fall outside?

• • •

Also, in an experiential vision one night, a manifestion arose of building an iron bridge on a great river and of putting many people into several ferries and crossing a large river. He became overjoyed at the thought that from the temporal auspicious connection of crossing over the element of water, he would be able to liberate all sentient beings from the four great rivers of suffering: birth, old age, sickness, and death. Moreover, with the ferries and bridges of method and wisdom he would be able to liberate the six types of living beings from the sea of the sufferings of saṃsāra.

Also, on one occasion at Tarpa Ling, the great adept met Vajradhara surrounded by the buddhas of the five spiritual families with their consorts, the eight bodhisattvas, the ten wrathful beings, and the five goddesses. He received a variety of vehicles—techniques of Dharma required to grace degenerate sentient beings—the foremost of which was a guruyoga of the profound path, an unexcelled skillful method for the automatic arising of coemergent primordial awareness.[506]

When he had spent four years in that meditation hut, [88] all the gods and demons of glacial Tibet gathered and announced, "You are a mental emanation blessed by the Great Teacher of Uḍḍiyāna, a great lord of yogins equal to Avalokiteśvara because of your lack of despondency and fatigue in benefiting sentient beings, a great adept fearless in subduing the malevolent savages of the final five-hundred-year period[507] of the age of

47. Vajradhara.

strife. For you to benefit sentient beings, we offer a plan for the building of stūpas and temples and the construction of ferries and iron bridges at geomantic focal-points that will impartially benefit the sentient beings of China, Tibet, and Mongolia, and of Paro and the four areas of Mön[508] and so forth. We will fulfill the activities of your family line, major disciples, and monks who have dedicated themselves to virtuous tasks, using the six-syllable mantra to inspire virtue. We will even clear away the hindering conditions and obstacles of those who, for the support of their own wives and children, act as though they are inspiring virtue."

Then they each returned to their own places.

One day he heard many people on the main road below his meditation hut praying to the Jowo as they returned from Lhasa. He thought, "The people below pray to meet the outer physical form of the Jowo, while I have met the inner Jowo of reflexive pure awareness. If I do not perform benefit for living beings that can be seen, heard, remembered, and felt, it will be a pity for sentient beings."

As a basis for emanations, the great adept sat with his body immobile in the sevenfold posture of Vairocana, while projecting emanated great adepts out through the square handspan-sized hole in the door. These assumed the physical forms of human beings and, together with sixteen hidden and secret consorts, accomplished vast benefit, actual and invisible, for living beings throughout Tibet. [89] How he did this is not clearly known, but the *Prophecy* of the Great Teacher of Uḍḍiyāna says:

> Together with sixteen hidden ḍākinīs,
> he will accomplish actual and indirect
> benefit for living beings.[509]

Also, at dawn one morning in the meditation hut of Shalkar Lhadong, the foremost lion-faced ḍākinī Siṃhamukha appeared in the expanse of space surrounded by a boundless retinue of nonhuman beings and said this:

> Best of men, to carry out the enlightened activities
> of past and future conquerors
> and their spiritual children,
> you awakened the thought of enlightenment
> in order to tame sentient beings
> who would be difficult to tame
> in a degenerate future time.
> Now the time has come to benefit living beings.
>
> Display whatever various forms
> will tame the savages of this evil age
> in which fivefold degeneracy is rampant,
> and spread benefit and joy
> by means of geomantic focal-points
> to suppress the four elements
> that are out of balance.
>
> After your previous training
> and prayers fully ripen,
> the exact intentions of the sūtras and tantras
> will appear in your mind.
>
> According to the intentions
> of the great teacher Padmasambhava,
> you will repel a foreign army
> and long preserve the doctrine of the Sage.

You will accomplish benefit for living beings
by building many iron bridges and ferries
to cross over the rivers of suffering.

You will construct images from turquoise,
coral, amber, lapis lazuli, and conch shell,
which will appear in a naturally arisen way.

After urging him to perform vast virtuous acts, she faded away like a rainbow.

The great adept then decided that because he was now able to bring vast numbers of disciples to maturation and liberation, and because he had been repeatedly urged to do so by the masters, chosen deities, ḍākinīs, and even by the eight tribes, [90] he should bring those of highest good fortune to maturation and liberation by means of the profound path. As for people in general, the *Prophecy* of the Great Teacher of Uḍḍiyāna says:

Fifty-eight have the karma,
and whichever of those persons meet him,
and whoever practices precisely
this profound Dharma,
will actually go to Sukhāvatī.

Five hundred will never regress,
a million will have Dharma connections with him,
and by means of those connections,
a hundred thousand will definitely go to Sukhāvatī.[510]

According to the prophecy, in order to make prayers to a blessed image, to search for disciples with the karma, and especially because he was afraid that the time would pass for a disciple who was in front of the Jowo of Kyirong[511] and with whom he had a prior connection of karma and prayers, he broke open the hole in the door when his six-year vow had expired and went out into the courtyard, leaving perfectly clear footprints in the stone.[512]

~

The great adept then magically traveled to the Charnel Ground of Ramadoli to practice secret behavior.[513] He established a connection with the sacred place for three days, and many spiritual heroes and ḍākinīs presented a fine ritual feast. At first, he was almost eaten by jackals, like dogs meeting a beggar, but because he felt great compassion, the jackals became like watchdogs meeting their master, sniffing the fragrant body of the great adept and showing their happiness even though they did not know how to speak. Because they enjoyed flesh and blood, they were only interested in killing and eating, which caused them to constantly wander from lower realm to lower realm. [91] He felt compassion for them and the hairs on his body rose and he was moved to tears. Joining the palms of his hands together he offered this prayer to the Noble One:

I respectfully beg
the sovereign of compassion,
lord Avalokiteśvara,
who has awakened the thought of enlightenment
for countless aeons and agreed
to save infinite living beings
—please give me your loving attention!

Although the kind mothers
who have benefited us again and again
through beginningless time
are experiencing suffering,
I do not have the ability to protect them.

Lord of Love, please protect them
with your compassion!

Have pity on my kind parents.

I dare not abandon them;
what should I do?

Deity endowed with skillful methods
and compassion,

you must grant the unmistaken,
sublime path right now!

Because he offered the prayer with intense force, noble Khasarpaṇa instantly appeared before him in the sky and spoke this prophecy: "Son of good family, those to be tamed by you in the barbarian Land of Snows will be extremely difficult to tame because the environment and its inhabitants are filled with evil. However, from the force of past prayers you will tame them by constructing representations of enlightened body, speech, and mind, building ferries and iron bridges, and with magical abilities that will actually repulse the unfaithful."

~

Then the great adept traveled to Kyirong. Three jackals and two wolves followed as his attendants and listened to Dharma with respectfully bowed postures. But he met several people from Nyeshang who chased the jackals and wolves with arrows and stones, [92] robbed the great adept's robe and so forth, and beat him.

He thought, "Foolish people. They aren't amazed at carnivorous animals listening to Dharma and bowing with respect. May even this evil connection of starting to kill them and robbing and beating me become a cause for the enlightenment of the people from Nyeshang!"

He went before the Jowo of Kyirong and made prayers for the sake of the doctrine and living beings. When he went to make circumambulations, there was an eighty-five year old woman on the circumambulation path.[514] When she was young, she had committed various sins for the sake of her children and husband. When she was old, her husband passed away and her children threw her out of the home. The great adept realized that she had cleansed the impurities of her vessel-like mind through prostrations and circumambulations after arriving before the Jowo, and that a connection of prayer existed between master and disciple. He approached the cushion where she had her head.

"Old woman!" he called.

She raised her head from the cushion.

"Who is the master to whom you are devoted?" he asked. "To which chosen deity are you devoted? If I explain an oral instruction to extract you from saṃsāra, a Dharma for the moment of death, will you be able to meditate?"

"Renunciant master," the old woman replied. "The master to whom I am devoted is now living in Central Tibet and Tsang. That master is not coming here. I have not made it to Central Tibet and Tsang, so I have not met that master. The chosen deity to whom I am devoted is the golden image of Jowo Śākya,[515] whom I have not met. There is nothing to do but make prayers to meet in the next life. If you have profound oral instructions, please look upon me with compassion and bestow them!"

The great adept asked, "What is the name of that master living in Central Tibet and Tsang to whom you are devoted?" [93]

"He is known as the adept Tangtong Gyalpo," she replied, "who is actually the Uḍḍiyāna Guru.[516] If I met him, I would not wander in saṃsāra."

The great adept lifted up the old woman and taught her the key physical postures. He gave her the pleasant practice of a guruyoga that he had received from Vajradhara at the isolated site of Tarpa Ling.[517] After that, he meditated on Jowo Śākyamuni, and when he made the Jowo's prayer of *Fivefold Benefit for Living Beings*,[518] the old woman saw the body of the great adept as Jowo Śākyamuni. She recognized that he was the great adept and a feeling of immeasurable joy arose. When she meditated single-mindedly with clear, undistracted visualization, although she had reached eighty-five years and was old and feeble, her body became vigorous.

This is just as mentioned in an oral instruction of the great adept, in the *Two-Part [Hevajra] Root Tantra*, and by Saraha, the forefather of all adepts:

(An oral instruction of the great adept:)

Old woman,
everything composite
is impermanent and destructible,
with not even an atom worthy of belief.

If your own uncontrived mind
beyond conceptual elaboration
is correctly realized,
you will be liberated.

That profound guruyoga is the unique path
traveled by all the conquerors.

If you pray with undistracted devotion
you will be liberated.
There is no doubt about this.

(From the *Two-Part Root Tantra*:)

Inexpressible by another,
coemergence is not found anywhere,
and is to be known
by resorting to the means
of the time of the master,
and from your own merit.[519]

(By Saraha:)

Just as the moon shines
in the midst of great darkness,
so also [94] a single instant
of the immutable sublime
vanquishes absolutely all
accumulated sins.[520]

Then the great adept went to a large area in Mön where fire blazed in the earth, water, and stone. Since that place was a palace of Saṃvara,[521] he stayed for one month to propitiate and make offerings to the divine assembly of Saṃvara, the spiritual heroes and ḍākinīs of enlightened mind, speech, and body below the earth, on the earth, and above the earth. The five classes of the ḍākinīs of primordial awareness appeared, surrounded by infinite ḍākinīs of sacred commitment and carnivorous ḍākinīs, and said, "Great adept, please go to actually meet the great teacher of the ḍākinīs of Uḍḍiyāna and request a prophecy about just how to tame the living beings who are to be tamed in the Land of Snows. We will create favorable conditions."

Then they disappeared.

~

The great adept then went to the Charnel Ground of the Grove of Terrifying Darkness,[522] where the wailing cries of zombies caused fear and trembling. There he met the brahmin master Vararuci[523] in the middle of a sea of spiritual heroes and ḍākinīs, surrounded by a retinue of yogins and yoginīs who had reached attainment. Vararuci gave him the initiation, the ritual permission, and the entrustment of glorious Pañjaranātha.[524] When they performed a ritual feast during the early evening, the great adept saw in the expanse of space a bunch of clouds the color of smoke and a mass of blazing fire, in the center of which were the eight deities of Pañjaranātha surrounded by the eight tribes of the gods and demons of apparent existence.

The great brahmin master said, "Pañjaranātha, surrounded by a sea of oath-bearing deities, you must accomplish the enlightened actions of this upholder of pure awareness!"

With that command, [95] he gave Pañjaranātha to the great adept as a Dharma protector.

~

Then the great adept decided to travel to the land of Uḍḍiyāna. When he faced the southwest and prayed to the Great Teacher of Uḍḍiyāna, he became exhilarated and in an instant arrived in Singala, the Land of Demonesses, near Uḍḍiyāna.[525] About a thousand demonesses gathered and made a great display of desire. The great adept emanated a thousand physical bodies. From a state of discriminating primordial awareness that is the pristine nature of desire, he kindly satisfied the demonesses with bliss in the temporary sense and established them in the sublime, immutable great bliss in the ultimate sense.

When he traveled about a league[526] from that land he met traders who were going to get jewels from the ocean.

"Please take me across, too." he requested.

"We're getting jewels," the captain said. "Where are you going?"

"The great Teacher of Uḍḍiyāna lives to the northwest of this land," he replied. "I am going there to study Dharma."

"That country is a land filled with demons and carnivores," the traders said. "You can't travel there without magical abilities. A person with some magical abilities may arrive in that place, but will have nothing except obstacles to body and life. You should turn back here."

They would not let him in the boat. The great adept sat on a dogskin at the ocean shore and cultivated an illusionlike meditative concentration. When he saw countless sentient beings experiencing suffering in the ocean, [96] he made a prayer.

48. Mahākāla Pañjaranātha.

May I place on the path
to freedom and liberation
those who, by the force of their evil karma
accumulated through beginningless time,
are tortured by many sufferings
difficult to bear in this great,
bottomless, boundless hell.

May those screaming in misery
without protection as they are fried
in a boiling ocean of poison
and constantly burned by hellfire
difficult to bear be cooled
by a rain of benefit and joy.

After this body has been discarded,
may the many tens of thousands
who live in this ocean tormented by much
heat, cold, hunger, and thirst
be born in the pure realms, in good families,
and in places where Dharma exists.

When he said that, the eight great nāga kings[527] with an inconceivable retinue circumambulated him and prostrated. They offered many kinds of jewels and a promise not to cause harm to sentient beings. With the nāgas as his attendants, he traveled to Uḍḍiyāna, the Land of Ḍākinīs, at the edge of which were fragrant and beautiful trees such as sandalwood. On their tips were birds with beautiful plumage, such as peacocks and cranes, dancing and singing with pleasant calls. Vicious carnivores such as tigers, leopards, tawny bears, and red bears roared, but did not harm sentient beings. Upon the rivers and ponds of water with eight qualities,[528] various aquatic birds sang pleasant calls and soared in flight. Uḍḍiyāna, the Land of Ḍākinīs, was filled in all directions with the aroma of flowers and incense, and completely surrounded by villages, cities, and great marketplaces. [97]

He was immediately welcomed from in front by many ḍākinīs, the moons of whose faces were beautified by the colors of the four enlightened actions, and who were adorned with bone ornaments and garlands of human heads. They brandished small skull-drums, human-thighbone trumpets, parasols and victory banners of tiger and leopard skins, flags of entire flayed human skins, and carried tail-hair fans.

In the northwest of that land was a mountain of three peaks, with the eastern slope made of conch shell, the southern of beryl, the western of ruby, and the northern of sapphire. On the right and left peaks, in palaces created from various precious substances, were Amitābha and lord Avalokiteśvara, teaching various vehicles according to the inclinations of disciples.

On the vast and spacious peak of the central heart-shaped mountain[529] was the Palace of Lotus Light, created from various precious substances. It was square, with four gates and four turrets, the tip of the pagoda roof adorned with a precious jewel pinnacle, and completely transparent, inside and out. Surrounding it were inconceivable numbers of ḍākinīs carrying various articles for offerings, making offering dances, and singing vajra songs. In the center of the palace, the Great Teacher of Uḍḍiyāna was on a jeweled throne, with the costume of a king and wearing a double cloak of fine brocade. Light rays that outshone the sun and moon radiated from his body.

The great adept went before him, prostrated, and presented inconceivable mentally emanated offerings. When he made prayers, [98] the Great Teacher assumed the form of Heruka in an emanated maṇḍala of [the Deities of] the Eight Transmissions of Great Attainment.[530] He blessed the great adept with vajra body, speech, mind, and primordial awareness, so that he directly beheld each of their faces.

In the robes of ordination, the Great Teacher of Uḍḍiyāna sat on an eight-petalled red lotus on the great lake there, surrounded by a five-colored rainbow. To his left was a red lotus with a thousand petals, on which sat the thousand buddhas of a fortunate aeon, with the eight close sons seated on eight branches.[531] To his right was a five-branched variegated lotus, with Vajravārāhī on the center one and the ḍākinīs of the four spiritual families on the other four. In the sky in front was Teacher Vajrasattva. With the Great Teacher of Uḍḍiyāna acting as the requester, the great adept received without any omission the unexcelled quintessence, the Dharma methods of the Great Perfection.

Then he traveled around the vast land teaching Dharma in the marketplaces and sidestreets to various disciples according to each of their inclinations. They were all filled with faith and devotion and made boundless offerings of jewels and so forth. When he lingered a while for the sake of disciples in Uḍḍiyāna, the Great Teacher of Uḍḍiyāna spoke this to inspire him to benefit living beings in the Land of Snows:

> Recipient of names from the ḍākinīs,
> upholder of pure awareness, Tangtongpa.
>
> You have mastered absolutely all
> the meaning of the rūpakāya form bodies;
> the dharmakāya reality body, pure as space;

and indestructible vajra speech, audible yet empty;
which are beyond conceptual subject and object
and forever noncomposite. [99]

For the sake of sentient beings
whose fivefold degeneracy is rampant,
repair a geomantic focal-point that I built
at the border of Mongolia and the Land of Snows,
and benefit and happiness will long prevail in Tibet.

You must complete the firm establishment
of the geomantic focal-point
on the tenth day of the first summer month
of the Earth Dragon Year [1448].[532]

If you delay, it will be like a levee
where the water has already escaped.

If you are early, it will be like setting
a trap where wild animals do not go.

Benevolent man,
upholder of pure awareness,
return to the snowy land of Tibet,
and benefit living beings with emanations
in whatever way necessary
to tame the sentient beings of Tibet,
whose fivefold degeneracy is rampant.

The Great Teacher of Uḍḍiyāna gave that prophetic advice about a method to repulse the Mongol armies and then announced, "Great adept, the five treasures that are your own Dharma inheritance, and also the biographical prophecy of how you will work for the sake of living beings, are in Tibet. Go now to the Land of Snows and urge those beings, who are connected by sinful karma, toward virtue with the pleasant sound of the royal six-syllable mantra of pure awareness. Then build representations of enlightened body, speech, and mind, and construct stable ferries and precious iron bridges!"

Then he spoke again with these verses:

Upholder of pure awareness,
man of Tibet, you came here
by the power of magical abilities,
but your Dharma inheritance
of five treasures is in Tibet,
and I left a biographical prophecy in Tibet.

Mental emanation of Padmasambhava,
the Knower of the Three Times,
you should now build iron bridges.

According to the omens,
you should swiftly travel to the Land of Snows
in order to tame living beings. [100]

After being repeatedly urged by the commands of the Great Teacher of Uḍḍiyāna to benefit the boundless sentient beings of Tibet, the land of glacial mountain ranges, the great adept thought, "Now I will go to Tibet."

At that moment, the ḍākinīs presented a vast ritual feast and joined their voices together as one to speak this pleasant vajra song:

Wonderful!
Fortunate child of good family,
single son of all the conquerors,
only brother of all the ḍākinīs,
remember your previous oath,
for the time has come to tame disciples.

If you do not gaze compassionately
on malevolent people
who are difficult to tame in an evil time
when fivefold degeneracy is rampant,
who can they hope for as a protector?

In the land of Tibet,
where perverted practices are widespread,

the ten virtues have declined
and nonvirtue is practiced.

An aeon of disease, weapons,
and famine has dawned—
who will remove those sufferings?

In the lands of the barbarian savages,
where even the sound of the excellent Dharma
is not heard, only nonvirtue is practiced.

Save them from fear of the lower realms!

In particular, there is a marvelous land
called the great holy site of Tsagong,
a place where Vajravārāhī dwells,
a palace where the sugatas gather.

Just by going to that holy place,
the gates will each open themselves,
the chosen deities will give prophecy,
the ḍākinīs will remove obstacles,
and the protectors of the word
will carry out your enlightened actions.

In a nearby area
is a source of precious iron.

The mouth of the mine
will open with no need for effort.

With various methods,
you will tame absolutely all
the barbarians who are to be tamed,
and spread measureless enlightened activities
in the ten directions.

Wonderful! [101]
As symbols of the liberation of miserable
beings from the sea of suffering,
build ferries, boats, and precious iron bridges
on the great rivers.

To suppress the external four elements,
construct sublime representations
of the Sugata's dharmakāya reality body.[533]

In particular, carefully establish
a geomantic focal-point
to suppress foreign armies
and prolong joy and happiness
in the land of Tibet.

Furthermore, to multiply vast merit
for boundless sentient beings,
construct representations
of the enlightened body, speech, and mind
of the conquerors and their spiritual children,
created from various precious substances.

Masses of obstacles will not be able to move them.

As a person with the karma,
you must display many tens of millions
of emanations,
extensively turn the wheel of Dharma,
and fill Jambudvīpa with Dharma!

The doctrine will long remain,
and we will carry out your enlightened activities.

Since the ḍākinīs also urgently appealed to him for the sake of those in snowy Tibet, the great adept prepared to go to the land of glacial peaks. The ḍākinīs pitched a tent of five-colored rainbows on the shore of the lake and arranged a throne and tapestries, together with a ritual feast to increase the enjoyment of the five senses.

The ḍākinīs placed the palms of their hands together as a physical gesture of respect and, speaking again with pleasant voices, said this: "At first, the Great Teacher of Uḍḍiyāna traveled to the land of Tibet and bound the malevolent deities and demons to oaths. He constructed many temples and stūpas, introduced the system of the doctrine, [102] brought the kingdom under control, established the code of the ten virtues, concealed inconceivable major and minor treasures, and then departed.

"In the interim period, many speech-emanations of the Great Teacher of Uḍḍiyāna opened many treasure troves of their own Dharma inheritances and spread the wealth of the Dharma, from the King of Tibet down to all the common people.

"Now, during this time when the final five-hundred-year period of the doctrine has dawned, the malevolent disturbances of the deities and demons are great, and human beings have short lives and great wrong views. Therefore, you, a great agent of the enlightened activities of the conquerors of the three times, please go now by means of various methods, and do not abandon the beings of the Land of Snows who are to be tamed."

The ḍākinīs prostrated to him, placed his feet upon their heads, and returned to their own places. According to the words of the Great Teacher of Uḍḍiyāna and the ḍākinīs, the great adept decided to go to tame the devilish savages in the eastern land of Kongpo and to search for iron to build precious iron bridges on the great rivers.

7: Appearances Are Like Dream and Illusion

The great adept first went to his birthplace. He got ten ounces of gold for his things, which he took and traveled toward Lhasa. At the foot of Sinpo Dzong in Domé he sat for a moment beside a grove of three great juniper trees. Many of the earth spirits of that area came and honored him well. They even offered him the juniper trees where they lived. Then a girl about fifteen years old arrived in front of him, singing and driving a large herd of goats and sheep.

"Where is your home?" he asked. [103] "What is your name? Why were you singing?"

"I have no home, relatives, or name," she replied. "Since I am a woman, I cannot actually benefit sentient beings. So I thought about what would be best, and became the shepherd of this village. I felt sad about this saṃsāra and sang, but no one listened and no one understood. I have come now to make a Dharma connection with you, yogin."

"By all means," the great adept replied, "I request a Dharma connection."

"You stay right here tonight," the girl said. "I'll deliver the livestock and get provisions for a ritual feast." She left.

At about midnight, the girl along with many girls like her brought various kinds of food. "I sent my friends to India and Nepal to get provisions," she said. "Did you have a long wait?"

Niguma, the queen of khecarīs, gave him the entire visualization sequences of the profound path, unspeakable, unthinkable, and inexpressible, which appeared in the mirror of his primordial awareness, and the blessing of the illusory body in an emanated maṇḍala.[534] She prophesied that he would establish boundless disciples in maturation and liberation.

~

Then the great adept continued traveling. On the road leading to Gyeré Tsarpa he met a woman with tangled hair, a black face, and a weak voice. Her eyes were filled with tears and she was sobbing.

"Who are you?" he asked. "What are you doing sitting here? What's the matter?"

"Our family are the butchers of this area," she replied. "My husband got a bad disease and passed away. His last testament said, 'Leave my body for twenty-one days. [104] Then someone will come to burn it.' The time has now elapsed this morning. I haven't found anyone to collect the corpse of a lower-class man who died from a bad disease."

"If you have so much suffering, I can collect it," he said.

She was pleased and invited him inside a small house. He saw that the man's shoulder was braced against the side of his bed, his hair was tied with a rope and attached to the ceiling, and a yellow flower had emerged from his mouth.

"Why did he die like this?" he asked. "What spiritual practice was he doing? Who performed the transference of consciousness?"

"He was afraid that he would fall asleep at night," she replied. "So he tied his hair to the ceiling. His spiritual practice was to recite the *Litany of the Names of Mañjuśrī*[535] one hundred times every day without break. I performed the transference."

When he cremated the corpse, the bones burned in an instant and many relics remained. She offered much wealth, but he said, "I'm a renunciant, so I don't need anything."

"You have been a great help," she said. "What good would you like me to do in return?"

"If you have profound oral instructions that will benefit sentient beings, I need them."

"I know many instructions, but do not actually benefit sentient beings greatly. If I give them to you, vast benefit will come to sentient beings."

She completely gave the outer, inner, and secret initiations and blessings of venerable Vajrayoginī, blessed the sacramental substances of meat, beer, and so forth into nectar, and held a ritual feast.

49. The holy Jowo image of Śākyamuni Buddha in Lhasa.

Then the great adept went before the precious Jowo [in Lhasa].[536] He offered a lumpy[537] two-and-one-tenth-ounce gold nugget for the throat of the Jowo. [105] To the precious Jowo, the Mikyö Dorjé, and the Fivefold Naturally Arisen One,[538] he tossed [gold] flakes without restraint, filling the sky with golden flowers. The deities also caused the sweet aroma of incense to spread and a great rain of flowers to fall. He made prayers for the sake of the doctrine and sentient beings, and performed many circumambulations, bringing into alignment the auspicious connections for the appearance of boundless disciples.

He then sat at the Kaṃṇi Goshi for a year without moving his body.[539] During that time, the aristocrats were embarrassed to prostrate in the market and to eat his gifts of food. At night, people made up their minds and prostrated, asking for tales of India and Tibet, and requesting Dharma connections and clairvoyant prophecies. They tied pieces of his robe to their throats, and boundless offerings occurred. People told various tales about him, making comments such as, "This person has profound knowledge of how to bring things under control."

~

Then the great adept joined together and traveled with people going to a flower offering at Tsel Gungtang. When he gave the ferryman a handful of warmth-producing medicine that a woman had offered, he happily rowed the ferry to the far shore. Then he arrived at Tsel Gungtang.[540] A great number of amazing representations of enlightened body, speech, and mind were in all the temples, but as a result of fighting between the rulers, the upkeep was very bad. As an auspicious connection to improve the upkeep of the three representations, he offered to gild the Lhachen Palbar image of the Great Sage[541] with two tenths of an ounce of smelted gold that had been offered to him by the Nepalese yoginī Tödreng Tsel, which he had as the strikers on his hand-drum. [106] When the two tenths of an ounce of gold spread over the entire image, people said, "The renunciant has much gold." He was even known to be wealthy.

During that period, for seven days he made offerings of fine gifts such as rows of butterlamps, food, and incense. He made prayers for the spread of the doctrine of the Sage and for the good health of the upholders of the doctrine. When he rested evenly with his mind—the dharmakāya reality body—indivisible from the masters, chosen deities, ḍākinīs, and Dharma protectors, and offered prayers without moving his body from the sevenfold posture of Vairocana, the great Shang Yudrakpa[542] appeared before him in the sky in the costume of Vajradhara, surrounded by numerous chosen deities, and said this:

> Mental emanation of the conquerors,
> upholder of pure awareness,
> Iron-Bridge Man,
> when the end of the doctrine is near
> and people's teeth fall out when they are sixty,
> you will live for 118 years,
> taming malevolent beings who are to be tamed
> in China, Tibet, and barbarian lands.

50. The great stūpa of Tsel Gungtang.

By the force of your prayers,
disciples will spread to distant places,
and with the name Tsöndru,[543]
since you rejected depression and laziness,
a rain of everything desired will fall
and you will accomplish infinite virtue.

With equanimity and no clinging
to the eight worldly concerns,
you will destroy confusion,
obstacles will be naturally removed,
and evil omens become auspicious.

Best of men, emanated body,
you and I are inseparable
in the palace of Khecara.

After speaking, master Shang departed amid various sounds and music.

~

Returning from Gungtang to Lhasa, the great adept arrived at the boat crossing on the Kyichu River and sat in the boat. [107] The ferryman became angry at the other people and cried, "Why did you put him in the ferry without asking me? If aristocrats are lost in the water, will you take responsibility?"

He hit the great adept three times on the head with an oar and threw him out of the ferry into the water.[544]

The great adept thought, "We are under the control of those with sharp tongues and wealth. Humble people are not allowed in the boat and are unable to cross the river. How pitiful! The masters, chosen deities, and ḍākinīs of India and Tibet such as the Great Teacher of Uḍḍiyāna, have repeatedly urged me to build precious iron bridges. So I will go and search for iron to first build an iron bridge on the Kyichu River, and go to tame the barbarian savages."

"I am a yogin who has realized the meaning of reality and gained self-control over the elements," he said. "However I go on the water, it will work."

Without moving his body from the sevenfold posture of Vairocana, he spoke these verses of good fortune as he traveled across the surface of the water on a dog skin he had spread on the riverbank:

> In reality there is no birth,
> but for the living beings of the six realms,
> the doors of birth into the lower realms
> exceed the imagination.
>
> From today on, may all living beings
> in every lifetime
> have the good fortune to realize
> unborn reality!
>
> In reality there is no growing old,
> but the sufferings of old age
> exceed the imagination.

From today on,
may all living beings
in every lifetime
have the good fortune to realize
ageless reality!

In reality there is no illness,
but the sufferings of the four elements in turmoil
exceed the imagination. [108]

From today on,
may all living beings
in every lifetime
have the good fortune to realize
reality free of illness!

In reality there is no death,
but we don't have the power
to remain on this earth forever.

From today on,
may all living beings
in every lifetime
have the good fortune
to realize deathless reality!

May we have the good fortune
of experience and clear light
blended together!

May we have the good fortune
of the mother and child clear light
blended together!

May we have the good fortune
of doing what benefits us!

May we have the good fortune
of spontaneous benefit for others![545]

As he finished these verses, he arrived on the far shore of the Kyichu River and looked back.[546] Since the ferry was not more than about halfway across the water, the people said, "He is the rebirth of the adept Samten Palwa,[547] but we didn't recognize him as an adept. Now we had better offer an apology and request Dharma."

~

In just an instant, the great adept arrived before the Jowo, unimpeded by the gates, such as the iron gate of the precious [Jowo]. He made supplications and prayers to tame the barbarian savages and to build precious iron bridges just as he intended. When he climbed into a hole dug in the earth in the middle of the Lhasa market and sat with his head sticking out, all the residents and visitors in Lhasa paid him great respect and honors.[548]

"Before, no one requested Dharma except in secret," he thought. "Now, from the auspicious connections of which Dharma is actually requested first and what offerings are made, [109] I must determine which of the three turnings of the Dharma wheel[549] and which chosen deity I should rely on to benefit living beings here in the Land of Snows."

At that moment, three nuns came before him and requested the vows of ritual fasting and the *maṇi* transmission.[550] He told them, "There are large offerings and there are small offerings. It depends on your faith and wealth. Each of you should bring whatever offering comes to mind."

One nun offered a piece of wood she found. One offered a nice stone she found. One did not bring any offering, saying, "I offer my body, speech, and mind."

He explained, "Because I received profound and vast methods of Dharma, like an ocean, from learned and realized upholders of pure awareness in India and Tibet, I have thought to fill all the isolated mountain gorges of this land of glacial peaks with monasteries and to plant a victory banner of the doctrine of the practice lineage that would be unrivaled above, upon, and below the earth. The omens of the Dharma connection and offerings right now indicate that, on the basis of the sublime speech of the six syllables, I should join the sentient beings I see, hear, know, and touch with the glory of the higher realms in the temporary sense, and establish them in the definitive excellence of unexcelled enlightenment

51. Eleven-faced Avalokiteśvara.

in the ultimate sense. Therefore, the auspicious connections have come into alignment for me to work with earth, stone, and wood, constructing geomantic focal-points that will bring benefit and happiness to those in the Land of Snows. The auspicious connections have also come into alignment for me to build as many temples and representations of enlightened body, speech, and mind as I can in the monastic establishments that give protection from fear of thieves, robbers, gods, and spirits on the precipitous pathways and waterways, the places frequented by gods, demons, and humans, and to build stable ferries and precious iron bridges [110] for creatures to move easily across the great rivers. That statement offering body, speech, and mind brought into alignment the auspicious connections for disciples following me to, on the basis of composite virtue, realize the meaning of the noncomposite true nature of phenomena."

Then, before the precious Jowo, the great adept made prayers to accomplish the benefit of living beings just as he intended. With single-minded devotion he performed a hundred thousand circumambulations in seven days and then slept in the Lhasa plaza. At daybreak, the Naturally Arisen Eleven-faced Avalokiteśvara[551] gave this prophecy of how his enlightened actions would occur:

Excellent mental emanation
of the second Conqueror,
the Teacher of Uḍḍiyāna,
your loving intentions
for the benefit and happiness
of the doctrine and sentient beings
are amazing.

The time has come for you
to build that precious iron bridge
on the blue waters of the Kyichu River.
Please accomplish it without sadness and exhaustion.

By the truthful words of your pure prayers
and the compassion of the conquerors
and their spiritual children,
you will accomplish the benefit
of living beings just as you intend,
helping the doctrine and living beings.

Although he had been told to quickly construct a precious iron bridge on the Kyichu River for the benefit of living beings, he thought about whether he should first tame the border area of Lo, open the gates to sacred places, or build the iron bridge. As he was hesitating a little, Machik Palha,[552] youthful and adorned with jewels [111] and silks, offered prostrations, placed his feet upon her head, and said this: "Excellent protector of all gods and human beings, please listen. From the period of the three ancestral Dharma kings in the past up until the present, the doctrine has expanded and declined several times. However, the Great Teacher of Uḍḍiyāna touched the entire earthly expanse of this glacial land with the auspicious cakras on the soles of his feet and constructed the individual geomantic focal-points. At that time you were the individual known as Dorjé Drolö.[553]

"During the later expansion of the doctrine, your own emanations, the individuals Yeshé Dorjé, and Nyö, Gar, and Gyaré,[554] beheld the mountains, cliffs, and trees of the Secret Mantra Mansion of Tsari to be the chosen deities, ḍākinīs, and guardian Dharma protectors. They opened the gate of the sacred place of the Tsari Tra Sphere of Primordial Awareness.

"Great emanated body named Tangtong Gyalpo in this final five-hundred-year period of the doctrine, the time has come for you to open the gate to the sacred place of Tsagong as prophesied by the Great Teacher of Uḍḍiyāna: 'The sacred place for benefiting living beings is Tsari Tsagong.'[555] The time has also come for you to build an iron bridge over these waters of the blue Kyichu River as prophesied by the Naturally Arisen Eleven-faced Avalokiteśvara. My sister Kongtsun Demo[556] is arranging the favorable conditions for that virtuous work. Please go quickly to the area of Kongpo in the east."

The great adept then thought, "When I was a child I displayed magical abilities, but since the time had not come for those beings who were to be tamed, nothing happened except that everyone took me to be crazy. [112] But now all the masters, chosen deities, ḍākinīs, and Dharma protectors, and the trio of gods, demons, and humans,[557] all agree and only urge me to construct representations of enlightened body, speech, and mind, build ironclad ferries, and open the gates to sacred places. So I will travel to the Kongpo area first."

At that time a Drepung scholar of the ten fundamental subjects[558] asked, "Where have you come from? Where are you going now? What qualities of knowledge do you have? For what purpose have you come?"

"I come from a place of transcendence and no attachment," he replied. "I go to seek disciples. I have the quality of knowing how to tame my own mindstream. My purpose is to benefit the doctrine and sentient beings."

"What Dharma do you have to explain to disciples?"

"I show that these outside appearances are like dream and illusion. I know how to directly show the true nature of mind inside. The practice depends on the disciple."

Again the scholar of the ten fundamental subjects asked, "You are someone who knows how to bring things under control. What is profound about bringing things under control?"

"This precise practice of Dharma is profound," he replied.

"Of course, that is profound. What else is profound?"

"This giving up of self-clinging is profound."

"It is. What else is profound?"

"This taking control of how things appear to myself is profound."

The scholar of the ten fundamental subjects was overcome with faith, prostrated, placed the palms of his hands together, and said this: "Master, great adept. I was ordained as a youth. I studied the ten fundamental subjects. [113] With the pride and arrogance of my own partial knowledge, I had no pure perception of others, and so my own mind became rigid. Now, master, I too will follow you. So I would ask about going, staying, food, clothing, the way to relate to companions, and for something with which to grasp the key point of the essence through meditation on the master and chosen deity."

The great adept spoke this oral instruction:

Hey! Listen to me, geshé,
scholar of the ten fundamental subjects.

You may be expert in the words
of the canonical Dharma collections,
but if you don't gain self-control
of your own mind,
you won't find the entrance
of the path to the sacred site of liberation.

So, if you want to travel
the spiritual levels and paths,
abandon your home
and roam the country.

Quit craving food,
wealth, and possessions.

If it benefits others,
go out even at night.[559]

If it benefits the doctrine,
stay even in a pit of thorns.

If you go to a ritual feast,
eat, even though it may
have come from wrong livelihood.

Constantly meditate
on the master of reflexive
primordial awareness.

Clearly imagine
the chosen deity
of naturally arisen spontaneity.

Continually recite
the heart-mantra that destroys
eruptions of wrong thought.

For a companion,
constantly associate with
naturally arisen primordial awareness.

For a son,
adopt the child of pure awareness
as a disciple.

If you have experience of these Dharma teachings,
the eight tribes[560] will act as your servants.

You'll be free from signs
of obstacles and impediments.

Whatever appears,
meditate that everything is the master.
Partiality concerning masters
will naturally be forgotten.

Whatever appears,
meditate that everything is the chosen deity. [114]
Clinging to the chosen deity as a thing
will naturally be forgotten.

Whatever appears,
meditate that everything is your parents.
The duality of enemy and friend
will naturally be forgotten.

Whatever circumstances arise,
experience everything as equal in taste.
The duality of pleasant and painful sensations
will naturally be forgotten.

Whatever food appears,
accept everything as nutriment.
Donated food and deadly poison
will naturally be forgotten.

If you live up to your name,
act like that!

If you follow me,
strive to be like this![561]

~

On the road going to Yerpa, the great adept then met some hunters who were stalking wild animals. "Offer me your traps!" he demanded. When they would not offer them, he seized the traps and said:

Knowing that confused living beings
are like wild animals caught in traps,
the wise move about like birds in the sky.[562]

When he said that, the hunters turned back.

The great adept arrived at Yerpa.[563] He emanated a body into each of the 108 meditation cells and sat there. In a pavilion of five-colored rainbows on a cloud in the sky in front of him, he saw the dharmakāya reality body, Vajradhara, surrounded by the eight great adepts.[564] A woman appeared in a dress of white clouds with a hem of five-colored rainbows and a tiara, carrying in her hands a vajra and a skull-cup. She announced, "Your Dharma inheritance left by the Great Teacher of Uḍḍiyāna is in Dawa Puk.[565] Retrieve the Dharma treasure!"

52. The hermitages of Yerpa.

Then she disappeared.

He went into where a geshé from Latö was making a retreat at Yerpa, and told him, "You must follow me!"

The geshé went as his attendant. Because he was the first of the retinue, [115] the great adept said, "I name you Ngaripa, 'First One.'"[566]

While the great adept was staying for several days at Chaktsal Gang, a monk of the Drom clan said he would go as an attendant. He was appointed spokesman of the writing slate and was known as Lama Lotsāwa, "Master Translator."[567]

Also, a geshé said he would go as an attendant, and the great adept asked, "What knowledge of routes do you have?"

"I have some knowledge of Central Tibet and Tsang," he replied, and was given the name Sanawa, "Guide."[568]

Also, a geshé with the three religious robes, alms bowl, and monk's staff appeared. He was given the name Lama Dülwapa, "Master of Monastic Discipline."[569]

The great adept held a ritual feast with those gathered there, performed virtuous acts, urged them to recite *maṇis*, and so forth. Leaving his retinue there, he magically traveled to Dawa Puk. From a treasure trove, he extracted the *Essential Droplet of the Enlightened Mind of the Teacher of Uḍḍiyāna, A Single Summation of the Intention of Samantabhadra.*

~

The great adept traveled with his retinue to Drakral in the lower valley of Penyul.[570] He sat on a large stone cairn there on the clay ledge where the road and the water met. In front of the great adept appeared a hundred beings who had human torsos and the lower bodies of snakes; a black man with three eyes, braids of flesh, and a snake tied around his waist; a woman wearing a dress of peacock feathers and leading beside her a scorpion the size of a yak; and a white man riding a white horse, carrying a white spear, and leading seven white yaks with long belly-hair. These nāgas and earth spirits of that place [116] offered various jewels, prostrated, circumambulated, and announced, "Great adept, whatever virtuous work such as a stūpa, temple, or ironclad ferry you establish as a geomantic focal-point on this clay ledge, we will carry out the activities for any favorable conditions you need." They dissolved into the lake below the path just as the monks arrived before him.

~

The great adept went from Drakral to Samyé. A large gathering of gods, demons, and humans appeared, and he gave the initiation and entrustment of pure awareness for Avalokiteśvara. Then he practiced meditation for eight months at Drakmar in Samyé Chimpu.[571] A radiant red light shaped like a shield appeared inside the rock cave, with the brilliant *dhāraṇī-mantras* of Amitāyus the Destroyer of the Lord of Death in a clockwise circle. It dissolved into the rock, and when he stared at it, a piece of rock about the size of a human head popped open. Inside that treasure door were inconceivable Dharma treasures. From among them, five scrolls of the great adept's own Dharma inheritance were extended into his hands: *Condensed General Practice of the Masters of the Three Times*, *Compilation of All Chosen Deities That Is a Tool for Attainments*, *Secret Treasury of the*

53. The Samyé monastic complex.

Ḍākinīs That Yields Spontaneous Enlightened Activities, Oathbound Protectors of the Word Who Eliminate the Arrogant, and *Enslavement of the Eight Tribes That Brings Apparent Existence Under Control.* That rock about the size of a human head slipped into place as before, with no trace of it evident.

Then he left a footprint in the stone so that there would be no harm from the sands in the lower valley of Samyé. [117] He put a very blessed hand-drum as a sanctified object in a Kūṭāgāra Stūpa and performed the consecration. He gave this edict to the two deities of earth and wind:

Homage to Lokeśvara

> This is from the master Tangtong Gyalpo to the yellow earth goddess and the blue wind god.
>
> This great Immutable and Spontaneous Temple of glorious Samyé was constructed by the mental emanation of the conquerors of the three times and the Dharma king, priest and

> patron.[572] It was constructed to spread the Buddhist doctrine in all directions and for happiness to arise in the entire land of Tibet.
>
> Blue wind god, bind the mouth of your great bag of wind, except for the wind that balances the four elements. Yellow earth goddess, do not let the bad earth and sands move. Do not let them pass the footprint of the yogin Tangtong Gyalpo. Do not let them approach in the direction of Samyé!

After giving the edict, he traveled straight from Samyé to Sheldrak[573] on the surface of the Yeru Tsangpo River without his feet sinking into the water. On the day he observed the tenth-day celebration, everyone saw the body of the great adept seated in midair.

~

From Sheldrak the great adept went to Nedong Peak. The sovereign Drakpa Gyaltsen made fine offerings, honored him, and requested a Dharma connection.[574] But the great adept replied, "As the ruler, you agreed to be the legal authority, but you act with lawless behavior. Since those who are malicious and shameless in their arrogance of being great and venerable themselves are unable to keep the sacred commitments, [118] no Dharma connection can occur."

"I can definitely keep the sacred commitments," the ruler said.

"If you can keep the sacred commitments, do not listen to slander and lies," he replied. "For the people's sake, do not let the law slip away for wealth and power. Do not make war in order to seize the fortresses and estates of others and with the aim of gaining wealth. Do not draft monks who are your subjects into the army. If you are able to keep these oaths, the sovereigns will have long lives and their subjects will greatly increase. If you are unable to keep the oaths, the meetings of the people of Central Tibet will be like dogfights."[575]

The great sovereign agreed to keep the oaths and was granted the initiation and the entrustment of pure awareness for Avalokiteśvara.[576]

~

Then the great adept traveled to Tselmin to grace a disciple who had the karma. He met Nyakpuwa Sönam Sangpo, who asked him to come inside.[577]

"I won't come in because I have renounced crossing thresholds," he replied. But when an insistent request was offered, he went in because he saw that if he did it would be a good auspicious connection for Sönam Sangpo.

Lord Sönam Sangpo said, "Because of miracles such as walking on the surface of the water, and because your clairvoyance is unimpeded, you are known as an indisputable adept. Please say that you are an adept of the profound path of the Vajrayoga! It would benefit our Jomonang doctrine."[578]

"I'm not telling a lie like that."[579]

"Well, I'm offering you a set of monk's robes, so please use it."

"Tilopa, Nāropa, and so forth also had the dress of yogins," [119] he replied.[580]

Then a layman asked to practice Dharma.

"Do Dharma right now!" the great adept exclaimed, shaved the man's head, and gave him the monk's robes offered by Tselminpa. After bestowing the vows, the great adept recited the benediction of the lords of the three spiritual families beginning with "Golden Blessed One."[581] When he scattered barley with his hand, three grains of barley stuck on the man's forehead and everyone was astounded. He was given the name Lama Riksum Gönpo, "Master who is Lord of the Three Spiritual Families."[582]

"Well," Nyakpuwa said. "Do you take anyone who appears into your retinue?"

"I'll take anyone who appears today," he replied.

He even accepted people who came to offer goats and dogs. As he left he also took a nun, a layman, and a woman who said they would go as attendants.

~

Together with a retinue of about fifty, the great adept used the corpse of a horse to hold a ritual feast at Yangal in Dra.[583]

Along with a few strict monks, he held a fine ritual feast with the meat, butter, roasted barley flour, beer, and so forth that were offered by the governor of Yargyab.[584] He asked the great crowd that had come, "Is there a woman here who has never had relations with a male other than her own man?"

A woman stood up and said, "Me."

"If that is true, you will achieve a great goal. Take off your clothes and jewelry and walk around this crowd."

She accepted whatever the master said to be authoritative, and with equanimity toward the eight worldly concerns, she walked naked around the crowd. A great rain of flowers fell. He realized that she was a disciple with the karma. When he gave her Dharma, she meditated and [120] became a naturally liberated yoginī.

~

Then the great adept traveled to Densatel,[585] which was veiled in mist. When he made prostrations and offerings to the Kagyü forefathers, the mist cleared. He went into the triangular teaching yard. A person came before him and said, "Chen Nga Sönam Gyaltsen[586] is about to die. You must come inside."

"I won't come because I have renounced crossing thresholds," he replied. But Chen Nga's servants picked him up and he arrived at the bedside.

"You are a good yogin," Chen Nga said. "I need an auspicious connection not to die right now."

"Illness is a purification of obscurations, so be happy. You will not die right now, but you will not have a long life. This is the result of meeting me a little too late. The mist cleared after[587] I made prostrations and offerings, so several of my followers will benefit the Kagyü doctrine."

He gave the Fivefold Mahāmudrā to Chen Nga and gave the initiation and entrustment of pure awareness for Mahākaruṇika to the assembly.[588]

~

The great adept then went to Sangri Khangmar.[589] A very beautiful girl about fifteen years old offered him five measures of white rice.

"Great man, you are kind to come to this place," she said. "I also blessed this place.[590] It is good that you have now created this auspicious connection for the benefit of sentient beings." Then she disappeared.

~

The great adept traveled to Ölkha Taktsé, taking Ané Tsomo as an attendant.[591] He told his retinue not to carry valuables, but they did not listen. They were robbed by Taktsé nomads at the entrance to the pass. [121] He also gave the bandits what they did not find, and sang this song:

> The illusory valuables
> you monks and disciples gathered here

sought with such energy,
you were unable to enjoy
when under your control.

Now you've got it; now it's lost.

May the robbers, the good teachers
who demonstrate impermanence,
be satisfied and collect the debt
that has been owed through lifetimes
of beginningless saṃsāra.

After making that prayer he traveled to Gampo. He engaged in deliberate behavior at the encampment of the Karmapa Tongwa Dönden.[592] The monks beat him with stones and staffs until they were tired. The realized yogin Tokden Drakgyal rushed before the Karmapa and cried, "Our monks have killed a blameless man!"

The Karmapa came quickly and exclaimed, "This many stones were thrown at this yogin, but he did not die. I am certain he is not just an ordinary person."

The great adept said, "*Phaṭ*!" three times. He held his breath and sat for a while with a special gaze. With one inhalation of breath he performed the thirty-two yogic exercises for immortality.[593] Invited into the residential tent [of the Karmapa], he gave the initiation and entrustment of pure awareness for Mahākaruṇika Who Tames Living Beings and for Mahākaruṇika Who Dredges the Pit of Saṃsāra, and taught the profound key points concerning the vital winds and visualizations of the yogic exercises for immortality.[594] The Karmapa made fine offerings of tea, clothing, silk, horses, and so forth.

At a place just within earshot from the Karmapa's encampment, seven men and women afflicted with leprosy saw the great adept to be dark blue in color, [122] with a vajra blazing with fire in his right hand and holding a snake-lasso in his left hand with a threatening gesture.

"Master," they said. "You are Vajrapāṇi, so we request a blessing to cure this disease."

When he pressed with his feet on the seven male and female lepers, creatures such as frogs, snakes, and scorpions actually emerged from the openings of their sense organs and they were freed from the earth demons.

54. Vajrapāṇi.

Also, there at the edge of the [Karmapa's] encampment, he met a single greedy woman who had been very wealthy, but as a result of being deprived of her wealth by thieves she had gone insane and was running about naked.[595] The great adept looked with a special gaze at the madwoman and said this:

You've helplessly been parted
from those possessions called "wealth."

Let the debt that was owed be collected!

Mindful awareness,
that fundamental nature of the mind,
resting without being mindful,
is emptiness.

Now splice together
the rope of mindful attention!

Look at the essence of mind
without distraction!

When the great adept spoke, the madwoman recovered her senses. He directly introduced her to the essence of the mind, and she became a realized woman who prayed single-mindedly, staying in the mountain ranges.

From the Karmapa's encampment, he traveled to Daklha Gampo and visited the shrines. When he prostrated, made offerings, and circumambulated the image of lord Gampopa with great devotion, these words came from the precious image:[596]

Protector of living beings
in the glacial land of Tibet
in degenerate times, best of men,
mental emanation of Padmasambhava,
the upholder of pure awareness,
because you have benefited sentient beings
for a hundred thousand lifetimes,
you have seized the throne of mind,
reflexive pure awareness. [123]

During this degeneracy of lifespan,
one among the five degeneracies,[597]
you will easily live a life of seventeen decades.[598]

Because of you, the doctrine of the practice lineage
will spread, and the sphere of your activities
will increase benefit and happiness
in the Glacial Land.

Especially, it was prophesied that vast activities and Dharma connections would occur here in the Dakpo region, such as the constructing of iron bridges and ferries and the building of representations of enlightened body, speech, and mind.

At that time, Kongtsun Demo, surrounded by the earth spirits of Sodruk, appeared to welcome the great adept.[599] When they played musical instruments unseen by the temple steward and so forth, it became known that the musical instruments had played by themselves.

8: A Situation in Which A Yogin Needs Iron

Then the great adept traveled to the pilgrimage circuits of Tsari. Inside a very bright tetrahedron of white clouds at the center of Lake Yutso, Vajravārāhī, endowed with the nine dance moods,[600] spoke this prophecy: "Southeast of this place is an area known as Lo, where a human body is used only for sin. Therefore, the time has come to tame those who have no opportunity to practice Dharma."

Leaving his retinue behind at Tsari, he traveled to a place known as Waru Namtsel,[601] where the rivers formed a triangle and the earth formed a triangle. There was a very dense forest of yew trees and a travel route for carnivores and wild men. Many malicious demons lived there, and, in particular, the nāga king, the water lord Varuṇa.[602] Realizing that it was a place prophesied[603] by noble Avalokiteśvara, [124] the great adept stayed there for three days. The nāga-māra was extremely vicious, and on that great travel route of creatures he ate the life essence of black horses, dogs, goats, sheep, and so forth who were not covered with white and red blankets, and of shepherds who merely raised their voices.

The great adept decided to stop that savagery and to construct a stūpa-temple as a geomantic focal-point. At about midnight, he went on top of Waru Seso[604] and rested evenly in meditative concentration for seven days. That earth spirit fought him for three days with an army of snakes the size of yokes and scorpions the size of yaks. But the great adept just remarked, "How pitiful. In general, everything composite is like a dream and an illusion. In particular, your hope to frighten me with this kind of magic is hilarious."

He sang this song:

From great Vajradhara
down to my root masters,

108 masters endowed with the three vows[605]
are constantly seated
on the crown of my head.

Don't you see that I'm swollen
with the view?

I've studied the Words [of the Buddha],
the treatises on sūtra and tantra,
scripture, reasoning, esoteric instructions,
and the special teachings of the profound
Dharma of emanation and transformation.[606]

Don't you see that I'm swollen
with experience?

I know the stages of both
creation and completion
for the assembled deities of enlightened body,
speech, and mind.

My vocal recitations
have never been interrupted.

Don't you see that I'm swollen
with blessings?

The oath-bearers who guard the doctrine,
a thousand black
and a hundred thousand carnivorous,
accompany me like a body and its shadow. [125]

Don't you see that I'm swollen
with powerful energy?

Hey, hey!
I'm really just joking with you!

If you're an infertile field for devotion,
I may eloquently plant seeds,
but there's little point.

If you don't have the powerful energy of truth,
there's little point in making
a small sacrificial cake,
beating an old drum, and shouting,
"Come! Kill!" and "*Hūṃ hūṃ*! *Phaṭ phaṭ*!"

Do you know how
to tame the enemy within you?

As a yogin who's realized truthlessness,
I put the saddle and bridle of compassion
on the stallion of emptiness,
and applied the whip of no distraction.

How could anyone causing obstacles
prevent me from arriving at
the intent of the Conqueror?

Earth spirit, how pitiful you are!

Instead of this, it would be better
if you revealed your own form
and then listened to words of truth.

After speaking, he felt uncontrived compassion for the malicious earth spirit. When he shed many tears, the snakes and scorpions disappeared. A brief moment passed, and then a creature with a human torso and the lower body of a snake appeared, with a black snake wrapped around his head, holding a ritual-dagger in his right hand and a snake-lasso in his left, and surrounded by a large retinue of similar types. They offered prostrations and respect. The earth spirit said this with a pleasant voice:

Lord, you are a wish-fulfilling gem
in human form,

the single embodiment of the intentions
of all the buddhas of the three times,
and the crown ornament of gods and humans.

My retinue and I each offer you
the essence of our lives,
and pay homage [126] with devoted body,
speech, and mind.

Until we reach the essence of enlightenment,
O great adept,
we promise to act as lay practitioners
according to your oral instructions.

After making the promise of a lay practitioner, the water lord Varuṇa offered this appeal: "Southeast of here, where the Drakchu and Nyangchu Rivers meet and form a triangle of earth and sky, lives a single-faced water demon of the Lord of Death who devours the breath of every creature he sees. Please make him a lay practitioner.

"In the eastern of the two upper valleys of the Drakchu River is my sister, the lumen spirit[607] of Lake Dangma Dangtso, who was the consort of the Great Teacher of Uḍḍiyāna. If it pleases you, please grace her.[608]

"Especially, I, the water lord Varuṇa, and my retinue renounce the creation of disturbing conditions and will create whatever favorable conditions are necessary for any work done upon the water by your lineage and monks, O master, O great adept, such as the building of boats, barges, levees, large ferries, and wood and iron bridges along the waterways such as the Yeru Tsangpo that flow into Kong Ralsum.

"If people who are terrified when traversing the great rivers by means of the boats, ferries, iron bridges, and so forth, remember the name of the master, the great adept, and take refuge and make prostrations and prayers, we offer the promise of no harm from the water."

Saying this, each offered their life essence. Then Varuṇa continued:

"This great forest called Namtsel is the place where we eight tribes of gods and nāgas[609] gather to curse the three-thousandfold world systems [127] and eat flesh and drink blood. From this day we offer it to you, O great adept. The Great Teacher of Uḍḍiyāna's prophecy of the future says:

If you build representations of enlightened body,
speech, and mind,
and an image of me, the Guru,
at that great crossroads
in the lower portion of three valleys
known as Sumpa,
the land of Tibet will be happy
and foreign armies will be repelled.[610]

"Therefore, please build representations of enlightened body, speech, and mind, and perform vast benefit for living beings here."

As a result of the earth spirit Waru Seso[611] having offered this urgent appeal, the great adept would build a large stūpa and a temple as a geomantic focal-point to repel foreign armies according to the prophecy of the Great Teacher of Uḍḍiyāna. At that time, the great adept agreed to be the lord of Waru Namtsel.[612]

∼

Then, at the confluence of the Nyangchu and Drakchu Rivers, where waves as tall as a single-story house would suddenly arise and many people had died, the great adept said one night, "Row me out in the boat!"

"If I row at night," the boatman replied, "both of us will die."

"I guarantee we won't die. It's very important, so row now!" he ordered.

Recognizing the great adept, he accepted the order. When the great adept scattered barley on the waves, the water became smooth and calm. The single-faced water demon of the Lord of Death took the vows of a lay practitioner. Everyone agreed that it became a very pleasant boat landing.

∼

Then, invited by the female nāga[613] of Dangma Dangtso Lake, [128] the great adept traveled to the Great Teacher of Uḍḍiyāna's place of meditation at Tsozong. He knew that the source of benefit and happiness, the doctrine of the Sage, had reached the final five-hundred-year period, and that lifespans had decreased to a low point because of rampant fivefold degeneracy. He said that he would try to repulse the celestial planetary demons, the intermediate gyalgong demons, and the subterranean earth spirits, nāgas, and nyen demons[614] who ravenously devoured the life essence of living beings, mainly humans.

With the ornamental wheel of inexhaustible enlightened body, the great adept suppressed Jambudvīpa by sitting in the vajra position. With inexhaustible enlightened speech, he proclaimed fierce mantras like a thousand dragons roaring at the same time. With inexhaustible enlightened mind, he emanated endless Vajrapāṇi karma-garudas to fill the sky.[615] While he threatened the malevolent eight tribes, seven days passed. Beneath his right foot and left knee, the earth spirits, nāgas, and nyen demons were mashed and packed together in the form of turtles, tadpoles, fish, snakes, scorpions, and so forth. Beneath his left foot and right knee, the gyalgong demons panted for breath in the form of baboons, monkeys, dogs, birds, and so forth. When he looked to the sky with a terrible gaze, the planets and stars became frightened and terrified inside their palace of five-colored clouds and lost their sparkle and became dim. He taught Dharma about the subtle details of cause and result, and gave this edict [129] to the eight tribes:

Take your own body as an example,
and do not cause harm to others!

If you harmful demons and obstructing spirits,
who are the mental embodiments
of the habitual propensities for
confusing appearances that lead people astray,
do not obey a promise of peace,
I will snag you with the iron hook
of unimpeded enlightened actions,
bind you with the noose of infinite compassion,
lock you in infallible vajra shackles,
drive you mad with the fierce sound of *hūṃ*,
shut you in the vast corral of emptiness,
and surround you with the fire
of self-manifesting primordial awareness.

Confusing appearances, harmful thoughts,
and wrong behavior will vanish.

He also said, "If you do not instantly release the bodies of those people with little merit who have become paralyzed, deaf, and blind, and those you have made mute, given speech impediments, and driven insane, I will use the vajra sword of meditative concentration to sever the limbs and digits of any among the eight tribes who is harming others. Don't let it come to that!"

After the great adept had given that edict, the eight tribes that he had threatened and tormented dispersed and were happy and delighted. At that time, the bodies and minds of people in the three regions of Central Tibet, Tsang, and Kham who had been possessed by demons blazed with the light of flourishing health and happiness, like the sun and moon released by Rāhu.[616] He established the female nāga of Dangma Dangtso Lake and her retinue in maturation and liberation, and they each offered him their life essence and many nāga jewels.

~

Then the great adept traveled to Tengtsar in the Kongpo region, a place where many people were working with iron. Since appearances arise as auspicious connections [130], he thought, "How can I make an iron bridge? I'll examine whether the words from these people are auspicious or bad."

He told the people, "Bring a yogin gifts of iron and much food and drink!"

"Renunciant," they replied, "you are a mature and vigorous man. If you are able to do iron work, you can take your wages in iron and get a lot."

"If I do iron work, can I make a lot of iron?"

"If you are able to do the work, even if you need a mountain of iron, you can make it."

At that moment a person offered him an iron chain and said, "I had an excellent dog that died. Yogin, do a fine dedication."

He did the dedication. He took the iron chain in his hands and asked, "Can iron chains be longer than this?"

"If you are able to work with iron, they can be longer than this, even if they must reach from the near to the far side of the Yarchab Tsangpo River."

"If I make them that long, won't they break?" the great adept asked.

Just as they were replying, "If you are skillful . . . ," a girl about eight years old, who was endowed with the marks of a ḍākinī, showed him her wrist and said, "If you make the iron chains about this thick, I guarantee they will not break."

"She's right," the people said. "About this thickness is definitely necessary. If you make them about like this, how could they break?"

He realized he could build iron bridges as prophesied by the masters and chosen deities and was overjoyed.

⁓

The great adept traveled on and arrived at Kongpo Bhakha.[617] [131] While he examined the omens, a great ritual feast was held and many offerings of iron were made.

"As a renunciant, what will I do with this much iron?" he asked.

The Kongpo people replied, "This iron is really good. If you go to Central Tibet and Tsang, you can do anything with it."

As he was thinking that it was a good omen, again a girl about fifteen years old, who was endowed with the marks and signs of a ḍākinī, said, "This is a situation in which a yogin needs iron." She got up and left, and the crowd also dispersed.

Then, after a while, that girl brought four companions like her and presented a fine ritual feast to the great adept. After offering prostrations and their respects, they combined their extremely pleasant voices together as one and sang this song:

A yogin like the sky
encompasses everything without distinction.

We are delighted to meet in this place
with a great all-encompassing master.

A yogin like the sun and moon
circles the four continents[618] without sadness
and fatigue.

We are delighted to meet in this place
with a master who endures hardship.

A yogin like a mountain
cultivates unchanging meditative concentration.

We are delighted to meet in this place
with an undistracted master.

A yogin like a [wish-fulfilling] gem
grants attainments to devoted disciples.

We are delighted to meet in this place
with a master who fulfills hopes.

A yogin like an Indian tiger
wanders fearlessly in charnel grounds. [132]

We are delighted to meet in this place
with a master free from arrogance.

A yogin like a lion
roams the glacial ranges without freezing.

We are delighted to meet in this place
with a master blazing with blissful heat.

Sir, wherever we stay and wherever we go,
we will benefit living beings as you wish.

Please take as consorts we five girls
who have arrived here,
and grace us with compassion.

We pray to meet you again and again.

May we have the good fortune
that you achieve your aims!

After presenting the offering of dance and song they pleaded, "Please bestow the sublime attainment."

"To which of the five spiritual families do you five girls belong?" the great adept asked. "Do you have control of both sublime and common attainments or control of one?"

55. Vajrayoginī.

"As for the reason we offered a ritual feast to the lord who embodies the buddhas of the three times, it was offered as an auspicious connection for gathering the riches of the common attainments. We five are of the five spiritual families—vajra, ratna, padma, karma, and buddha. If we present the offering of bliss and emptiness with our voices as one in song and dance, since we have realized our own minds as the unborn dharmakāya reality body, we are also able to offer the sublime attainment. We are the guardians of this great sacred place. We will carry out any of the four enlightened activities that are necessary for you, O adept, to construct unprecedented, precious iron bridges for the benefit of living beings as prophesied by the masters of India and Tibet."

When the five beautiful young ḍakinīs of primordial awareness gracefully performed a dance [133] and presented the offering of united *evaṃ*,[619] the great adept was pleased.

Except for that ḍākinī of primordial awareness who had assumed the guise of a human girl, the other four vanished like rainbows in the sky. The one in the form of a human girl made three prostrations, seven circumambulations, and went into a village there. He stayed in that area for thirteen days, but did not learn anything about the girl's family. When he prayed to venerable Vajrayoginī, Dorjé Nangzema[620] appeared at daybreak and spoke this prophecy:

> Spiritual son of the conquerors,
> bodhisattva who considers only
> the benefit of others,
> it is good that you have come
> to this place with compassionate intentions
> for the entire three realms.[621]
>
> I have never recited words before.
>
> This time I will clarify the meaning.
>
> The five radiant and fragrant girls
> who presented a ritual feast to you yesterday
> belong to my retinue.
>
> It is excellent that you enjoyed their gift
> made with partial control of the sublime
> and common attainments,
> and the offering of unity—realize it to be so.
>
> At a place one day's journey
> continuing up the mountain range from here,
> is the great sacred site known as Tsagong.

Since the masters, chosen deities, ḍākinīs,
and oath-bearing Dharma protectors
and guardians
continually gather there
like dense clouds and mist,
their blessings fall,
granting attainments to the fortunate [134]
and causing obstacles for the unfortunate.

If you practice meditation in that place,
without doubt you will reach attainment.

Know that anyone devoted to it
and anyone who gathers there are vajra relatives!

You will get the sublime and common attainments.

It is an unexcelled great sacred place.

In the future, Vajravārāhī will also
leave there an authentic skull-cup.[622]

It is no different from a wish-fulfilling gem,
and will remain in that place.

To see, hear about, remember, or touch it
will bring bliss.

Proceed swiftly to that special,
sublime, sacred site,
for it is time to open the gate of the place.

Then the great adept went to Naktang Pang in Drakyul. When he made camp, many people gathered. He sat on top of a pile of rocks and said, "Bring great offerings and a fine ritual feast."

"What offerings do you need?" one person asked.

"Bring whatever you have."

"Well, I offer you that big pile of rocks beneath you."

"A fine auspicious connection. My monks will now build a Dharma throne on these rocks."

When it had been built, a person appeared from the village and demanded, "Who offered the rocks? These are rocks that I piled up!"

He struggled with the monks and moved those rocks away.

The great adept declared, "Because he struggled over the rocks, this region of Kongpo will not keep sacred commitments. But because of the auspicious connection of being able to build a Dharma throne, I will build a vast establishment at Tsagong. It is an auspicious connection for opening the gate to the sacred place." [135]

Then he sat on top of the Dharma throne for three days. At about daybreak of the last night, the earth spirit of Tsagong, who had a tall body, one eye in the center of his forehead, and was dressed in blue and yellow garments, appeared surrounded by many of his retinue. Offering various kinds of food, as well as many different welcoming beverages such as honey beer and barley beer, the earth spirits said this in a single voice: "Dorjé Drakpotsel,[623] single embodiment of the wisdom, love, and energy of the conquerors of the three times, having come here, please have compassion on us! Trapa Ngönshé,[624] Dzagom Jodar, the renunciant Ngönpo Yöndar,[625] and Lama Dampa of Sakya[626] stayed in this sacred place for a long time to get the texts about the sacred place and treasure texts previously concealed by the Great Teacher of Uḍḍiyāna. They gave us sacrificial cakes and said they needed the keys and guidebooks for opening the gate to this sacred place, but we are not able to give them to anyone other than you, an emanation of the Teacher of Uḍḍiyāna. The time of your return was almost too late, but now the time has come to take the treasure texts, guidebooks, and keys, and to open the gates to sacred places in the regions of Kongpo and Lo, and to perform vast benefit for living beings."

The great adept replied, "Lords of the sacred places, I ask for your advice. How do I open the gates of the sacred places? Where in the east, west, north, and south are the guidebooks, keys, and texts about this sacred place, and the locations at which to establish geomantic focal-points? [136] Are there not lords of sacred places and protectors other than you? To what families and tribes do you belong?"

The earth spirits said this: "O great adept. The guidebooks, keys, and texts about this great sacred place, and the prophecies and advice about how to establish geomantic focal-points, are in the secret organ of Vajravārāhī, a naturally arisen cave of stone. After you have first seen it to be the palace of the five types of ḍākinīs of primordial awareness, without you having to make any effort, the ḍākinīs will offer you, excellent man, whatever you need, such as guidebooks, keys, texts about the sacred places, prophecies, and advice on how to establish geomantic focal-points."

~

The great adept then traveled to Gomnak Drak, and the protectors of the word offered their life essence and promises to accomplish whatever he ordered.

Then he went to Menmogang. When he held a vast ritual feast, [the spirits said,] "We will open all the visionary gates. Our races are the Mu and the Tsan.[627] Since the chief lord of all the sacred places in the mountain ranges of Tsari, Tsanang, and Tsagong is the field-protector Kunga Shönu, we belong to his tribe."[628]

~

The great adept then took both Sangri Bawachen and Riksum Gönpo as attendants and went to Khandro Sangpuk, the Secret Cave of the Ḍākinīs.[629] When he saw the cave itself to be the essence of the masters, chosen deities, ḍākinīs, and Dharma protectors, and especially of myriads of ḍākinīs in the vajra, ratna, padma, karma, and buddha spiritual families, [137] he was exhilarated. The three of them, master and disciples, joined hands and performed this dance with a song of experience:

> To the east is the ḍākinī
> of the vajra spiritual family,
> white in color, rattling a hand-drum,
> and surrounded by a retinue
> of a hundred thousand who are white.
>
> We dance in step, stomping and stomping
> —grant us sublime and common attainments!
>
> To the south is the ḍākinī
> of the ratna spiritual family,
> yellow in color, holding a jewel,

and surrounded by a retinue
of a hundred thousand who are yellow.

We dance in step, stomping and stomping
—grant us sublime and common attainments!

To the west is the ḍākinī
of the padma spiritual family,
red in color, holding a lotus,
and surrounded by a retinue
of a hundred thousand who are red.

We dance in step, stomping and stomping
—grant us sublime and common attainments!

To the north is the ḍākinī
of the karma spiritual family,
green in color, holding a crossed vajra,
and surrounded by a retinue
of a hundred thousand who are green.

We dance in step, stomping and stomping
—grant us sublime and common attainments!

In the center is the ḍākinī
of the buddha spiritual family,
indigo in color, holding a wheel,
and surrounded by a retinue
of a hundred thousand who are indigo.

We dance in step, stomping and stomping
—grant us sublime and common attainments!

The lords who show the path to liberation,
and who are actually buddhas,
jewels the memory of whom brings satisfaction,
are the sole infallible refuge.
May the good fortune of the root
and lineage masters, come to us! [138]

May the good fortune of the assembly
of chosen deities come to us!

May the good fortune of the spiritual heroes
and ḍākinīs come to us!

May the good fortune of the protectors
and guardians of Dharma come to us!

May the good fortune of friends
and companions practicing Dharma come to us!

May the good fortune of the area gods
and earth spirits come to us!

When they performed that dance with a song of experience, the ḍākinīs of primordial awareness were also pleased. Then a copper amulet emerged from a crack in the rock. The Great Teacher of Uḍḍiyāna had left everything necessary inside it, such as the guidebooks and keys to the sacred places and advice and prophecies of how to benefit living beings in the regions of Kongpo and Lo.

≈

Then the great adept traveled to Gomnak. He placed his vajra of sacred commitment on the gems at the crowns of the heads of a sea of protectors of the doctrine, such as the Six-armed Protector of Primordial Awareness, the Four-armed Protector, and Pañjaranātha, famed in India and Tibet.[630] In brief, they agreed to guard the entire legacy of whatever enlightened actions the great adept did in any area for the benefit of the doctrine and infinite sentient beings, such as building monastic establishments with temples and representations of enlightened body, speech, and mind, and constructing ferries, boats, and iron bridges on the great rivers. They offered the life essence of each of their families, and firm pledges.

The naturally arisen image of the Raven-faced Karmanātha[631] that emerged from the rock and is now in the assembly hall of Tsagong appeared at that time in Gomnak.

The great adept then traveled to Menmogang. On top of a Dharma throne [139] that the people had constructed, he made prayers and created the auspicious connections for the founding of an establishment for the explanation and practice of Dharma. At that time he made a prophecy in which he saw the future without obscuration and said that the authentic skull-cup and the mountain man of Ngari would come to this place.[632]

The Kongpo people said, "If the authentic skull-cup comes here, Tsari Machen would be vacant. How could such be possible?"[633]

He held a ritual feast and opened and looked at the guidebooks and keys for opening the gates to the sacred places, which said, "The outer gates to the sacred places will be opened by five fully ordained monks. The inner gates to the sacred places will be opened by five women. The secret gates to the sacred places will be opened by the great adept himself."

When he sent off five fully ordained monks such as Dülwapa and five women such as Kalden Rinchen Tsomo,[634] the gates to the sacred places were opened.

He sent off Riksum Gönpo and Sangri Bawachen[635] to search for a place to establish a monastery, saying, "Take a complete set of cooking materials, with flint and so forth that will be immediately necessary, and stay in a pleasing and delightful spot in this valley!"

When the two of them arrived in the middle of the valley descending from Menmogang, a great, violent rainstorm occurred. Unable to go anywhere, they stayed inside a rock cave there and ate roasted barley flour. Wherever the great adept searched in the upper and lower parts of the valley, he did not find them, so he called out. They did not reply because they were in the rock cave with their mouths stuffed with roasted barley flour.

The great adept [140] arrived at the rock cave and said, "Are you two staying here? This land is either too high or it's too low."

With mouths stuffed with roasted barley flour and eyes bulging, they shook their heads and defended themselves, saying, "In violent rain like this how can we travel around a large area? The sun will also dawn tomorrow, so we'll have time to search for a pleasant and delightful place."

From such omens, he gave this prophecy of the future: "The patrons and meditators at this site for a monastery where your mouths are stuffed with roasted barley flour will be extremely prosperous, but since you did not respond, they will have no learned qualities. Because you defended yourselves, there will be only tough and obstinate people. Because you said, 'We will have time to search for a pleasant and delightful place tomorrow,' a most amazing person will arrive from afar."[636]

At the place where the two of them had stayed, they then completed in one month a residence and an assembly hall with twelve pillars that would hold two thousand people. Then a very rich deposit of iron was discovered.

The great adept thought, "I must use the offerings by the Kongpo people as the means, gather many blacksmiths in this assembly hall, and forge an iron bridge."

At that moment, the rich Kongpo man Döndrup Gyalpo offered thirteen man-loads of iron and said, "Master, my father who has died must not be reborn in the lower realms."

Then a man appeared and the great adept said, "Good, Kunga the blacksmith has arrived."

Another man came, and he said, "Has Sangyé the blacksmith come?"

A girl came, [141] and he said, "The girl Tashi has come. It is a good omen."

"Who told our names?" the three of them asked.

When it was explained that no one had told him, they realized he had unimpeded clairvoyance, and became filled with faith. The girl Tashi offered five lumps of iron. Moreover, a great number of persons offered iron. The two blacksmiths single-mindedly assisted the great adept in forging the iron. When he extracted it from the mine himself and many blacksmiths forged the iron that was offered by the people, in eighteen days they finished four iron chains that were eighteen armspans in length.

At that point several people whose hearts were possessed by the māras told the blacksmiths, the workers, and those who had offered riches of iron and so forth, "This master is really a fake. We've never heard of iron bridges anywhere in India or Tibet before. Iron is rare in Tibet, so we'll be blamed when it's manufactured and taken away."

Everyone became doubtful. Many people of Kong Ralsum gathered together and demanded, "You must show proof of your attainment! If believable proof of your attainment doesn't occur, we won't transport the iron to Central Tibet."

"I have no proof of attainment to show," he replied. "Come at sunrise tomorrow."

The people dispersed.

That night he joined the four iron chains together and fastened them to the top of a very tall fir tree with their four ends hanging down in the four directions. On a high rock cliff of Gomnak that no one could climb, [142] he drove an iron spike the size of an arrow, with an iron chain ten armspans in length. He attached a long piece of cotton cloth to its end and sat down.

All the people of the Kongpo region gathered at sunrise and demanded, "You must show proof of attainment!"

He replied, "All of you pray to the four iron chains for liberation from the sufferings of birth, old age, sickness, and death!"

"That won't do. We need handprints and footprints [in stone]."

At that moment he met a single man from Lo who had come to trade. The man thought, "Is it possible that a prayer could work?" He grabbed the four iron chains and his prayers were fulfilled exactly.[637]

Then, because the Kongpo people were idiots, they did not recognize that the great adept's fastening of the iron chains by himself on the mirrorlike rock cliff of Gomnak and the top of the tall fir tree was proof of his attainment. "If you have no handprints or footprints in stone to show for us to believe in," they said, "each person will throw a rock and fire an arrow, and we will kill you right now!"[638]

The great adept looked into their eyes with an angry glare and replied in a terrible voice, "Destructive demons, only fakes have appeared here in your land before. Still I have come. If you can't hit me, you're not men. If I can't take it, I'm not a man. Strike now!"

The monks fled and the people of Kongpo were petrified and remained staring at him.

That night some thieves of Drakyul gathered and talked, "We can take the iron that fake fastened to the tree yesterday, and sell it for meat and beer. His fakery is too much. All [143] the powerful and the meek of Kongpo are disgusted. Not a single supporter will come."

They went to take the iron. When they grabbed the iron at the base of the tree, they could not move it.

"We had better cut the tree," they said, but when they chopped with their axes, a branch of the tree fell and struck the thieves. They received serious wounds and were in agony, but through the compassion of the great adept their lives were not threatened.

During that period the time had not come for disciples in Kongpo. The great adept decided, "Now I will go to tame Lo first."

Furthermore, Karmapa Rangjung Dorjé[639] had intended to tame Lo in the past, but when he did not tame it he said, "It will be tamed in the future by an emanation of noble Avalokiteśvara."

When the great adept decided to go tame the cannibals of Lo as had been prophesied, the earth spirits of the Lo area actually appeared to him at about midnight and announced, "Excellent source of refuge, you are very kind to come and tame disciples with your compassion that does not fade away with time. We have come to invite you because we protectors have in our hands the gates to the sacred places where attainments occur because the spiritual heroes and ḍākinīs gather there. Menmogang and the sacred places in our region of Lo are our summer and winter spots, but by all means please come now to the sacred places in our region of Lo to open the gates of the sacred places and subdue the borderland."

Then they disappeared. The great adept thought, "I didn't ask the [144] earth spirits just now about what supplies are necessary for auspicious connections when I come there."

At the first break of dawn, the earth spirit from the upper valley of Drakyul came and said, "The earth spirits of the Lo area and I are relatives. I can invite you on the path. As supplies for traveling there, please bring a white conch shell, seven axes, a bow and seven arrows, ritual objects, offerings, a full set of cooking utensils, and seven monks with pure sacred commitments."

Daybreak came and the great adept told seven attendants such as master Riksum Gönpo, "Come, and do not forget the white conch shell, the axes, the arrows, the bow, the ritual objects, the offerings, the cooking utensils, and so forth. Kongpo Pöndruk, you be the guide!"[640]

Surrounded by the earth spirits of Lo, the great adept mounted a white mule and went ahead into midair without impediment. At about mealtime he met in Taktsang with shepherds from Drakyul. They offered much yogurt and butter and said, "Master, it is not good for you to go to the Lo region. You will be killed. But if you go, we will guide you."

"The omens are mostly favorable," he replied. "Let's go!"

The master traveled to Lo with eight disciples.

Then they arrived at Khadö Hena in the region of Lo. The great adept went into a thick forest without any paths. When his attendants followed wherever he went, in the midst of the forest there were nothing but carnivorous animals such as tigers and bears, birds such as parrots and peacocks, and no paths traveled by human beings. [145] It was a thick forest of acacia trees so dense that it was like during a rainstorm, and there was nowhere to go.

"Now we need the bow, the arrows, and the axes we have been carrying," he said. He shot arrows to the right, to the left, and to the center. The three arrows opened up three clear paths.

When they went on the right path, the arrow had hit the trunk of a sandalwood tree at the entrance to a rock cave shaped like the mouth of a lion.

"Now, cut that tree with the axes!" he ordered.

When the tree had been cut about halfway through and the monks were resting, about a hundred baboons and monkeys prostrated to the great adept, made circumambulations, and offered various fruits. Some happily did other things such as finishing the work of cutting the tree.

When the tree had been cut, the gate was opened to the sacred place, a rock cave shaped like the mouth of a lion, inside of which were the brilliant, naturally arisen nine deities of Hevajra[641] created from crystal. He performed the rite of accomplishment and offerings to Hevajra there for one month.

When they followed the path of the arrow to the left, the arrow was sticking in the trunk of a huge white eaglewood tree. The great adept pointed his finger and the tree fell over by itself, opening the gate to the sacred place, a rock cave shaped like an ox horn, inside of which were the brilliant, naturally arisen five deities of Amoghapaśa.[642] For one month there he performed the practice of the *dhāraṇī* of Amoghapaśa.

When they followed the path of the arrow to the center, the arrow was sticking in the trunk of a poisonous thorn tree.

"Cut that tree!" he ordered. [146]

When the tree had been cut about halfway through, the axe broke because they were clumsy in chopping. From the midst of the forest a tree nymph with a flower headdress and dressed in tree leaves offered the great adept a sharp axe and then went back. They cut the trunk of the poisonous tree, opening the gate to the sacred place, a rock cave shaped like a tetrahedron. Inside of it were a brilliant trio: the ḍākinī of the primordial awareness of the dharmakāya reality body in the center and the ḍākinīs

Siṃhamukha and Tröma Nakmo[643] to her right and left. He performed the offering of ritual feasts to the ḍākinīs there for one month.

Leaving the monks hidden there in the middle of the forest, the great adept went to a place where there was a river in front of a huge number of villages in the land of Lo. On the bank of the river about a hundred naked, charcoal-colored savages were cooking and eating any creature they saw, such as fish, turtles, and tadpoles. All the other Lo people had gathered at a large wedding and were making a loud noise.

The great adept held an image of the Buddha that was one handspan tall in his right hand and grasped the flange of the white conch shell with his left hand. When he blew a very fine sound from the conch shell, all the people of Lo yelled, "A fat man[644] who has never come before has arrived, carrying in his hand a baby demon!" They fled in terrror.

Then the Lo people agreed, saying, "This person was going to another area, but got confused and arrived here. We'd better kill him."

They all brought swords and spears.

When the great adept [147] pointed a finger at the Lo people, they saw him as a terrifying black man with all his teeth bared and his eyes glaring. They were all petrified, and the swords, spears, and other weapons held in their hands fell to the ground.

Then he climbed to the top of a very tall fir tree. The Lo people regained their senses and yelled, "The fat man has gotten to the top of the tree! Shoot arrows!"

When they all shot, the arrows returned and almost struck each of the archers.

"Cut the tree!" they cried. When they cut the tree with as many axes as they could bring, the tree trunk magically turned into iron and the axes turned into wood.

"The fat man is good. Start a fire!" they exclaimed. When they piled up a stack of fir wood two stories high and lit the fire, the great adept rose from the top of the tree into the sky about as high as seven palmyra trees. His countless different physical apparitions held various frightening weapons in their hands. When they proclaimed the sounds of *hūṃ* and *phaṭ* like the roar of a thousand dragons at once, and four great thunderbolts struck the mountains in the four directions, all the mountains were smashed into pieces. Furthermore, terrifying magical apparitions such as earthquakes, falling trees, and churning waters made the Lo people faint and they were dumbfounded and petrified.

At that point the monks such as Riksum Gönpo also arrived. [148] And at that time the great adept blessed the single man from Lo whom he had met in Kongpo, so that the man remembered his previous lifetime.[645] When he remembered that the great adept had been his master in the previous lifetime, he became filled with faith and devotion without fear of the magical apparitions.

The great adept told the monks and the single Lo man, "Quickly build a Dharma throne here."

As soon as it was finished, he climbed on top of the Dharma throne. He made his body beautiful and fascinating to gaze upon and said, "*Oṃ maṇi padme hūṃ*," causing the Lo people to regain their senses.

At that moment the single Lo man said, "No one can match this master. He is the leader of all the people in Kongpo and so forth. I also listened to him, and when I made a prayer it turned out well. If you also accept him as your leader and listen to whatever he says, you will be happy."

"You are right," they replied. "No matter what we did to the master, we could not defeat him. So now we have no choice but to do whatever he says."

The great adept established the code of the ten virtues.[646] To those who had a little potential for the Mahāyāna, he taught that among all embodied beings none can remain without dying, and that death is not enough because everyone must be reborn. He taught Dharma with many examples and reasons for how the place of rebirth, the body, and all experiences appear as consequences of good and bad actions. The great adept and his disciples taught about taking refuge, awakening the thought of enlightenment, reciting *maṇis*, and the tenth-day rituals.[647] These customs have not died out even up to the present day.

On one occasion, when he was making the Buddhist doctrine shine [149] like the sun in the barbarian border regions, a land of darkness, he told those who were gathered there, "In this land there are many gates to be opened to amazing sacred places. Bring the arrows and axes!"

"We haven't brought but one axe," the monks replied.

"Three gates to sacred places are to be opened, but this is a sign that there will be none except this one for now. Watch where this arrow of mine goes!"

When he shot the arrow, it went into the middle of a thick forest. The monks and everyone else searched, and after a while they saw the arrow buried up to its feathers in a huge sandalwood tree on the bank of a great waterfall.

"Here it is," they told him.

"Cut that tree down with the axe!" he ordered.

They chopped, and it was cut down in about half a day. Beneath it was a large flat stone. They turned it over, opening the great gate to a sacred place shaped like the mouth of a lion. It was spacious, vast, and beautiful, and the mere sight of it caused meditative concentration to arise. Inside it were infinite images of glorious Samantabhadra, Vajrasattva and consort, the lords of the three spiritual families,[648] the eleven-faced Avalokiteśvara, and buddhas and bodhisattvas. As representations of enlightened mind, there was a Stūpa of Enlightenment, an Auspicious Stūpa of Many Doors, and a stūpa to bless the conditioning factors for the great adept's long life. There was also a maṇḍala platform on which the Great Teacher of Uḍḍiyāna had previously bestowed initiation, [150] a white conch shell with a clockwise spiral, the eight auspicious symbols such as the victory banner and lotus, and worldly wealth without omission, such as a pleasure garden, a bathing pool, a heavenly tree, and a spring of nectar.

He held a ritual feast there, taught Dharma, made prayers for the benefit of the doctrine and sentient beings, and told the people of Lo, "Arrange vast ritual feasts in this sacred place! Supplicate the Great Teacher of Uḍḍiyāna! Make prayers for your happiness in this and future lives!"

Then the people of Lo offered him various kinds of wealth, such as sentient beings and grains. He dedicated toward enlightenment the virtue from offering the infinite kinds of other wealth, and, except for the three types of creatures—dogs, water buffaloes, and wild oxen, returned them to each person who had offered them.

After staying in the Lo region for two years, the great adept and his disciples prepared to return to Tibet. The people of Lo offered an appeal: "No one was able to come here to our land before. We had not heard the name of the Buddha. We engaged only in sin, with the sound of the Dharma unknown. Nevertheless, O master, you established the people of the Lo region in the Dharma. By making this land happy and pleasant, you have been extremely kind. We will do whatever you say, so please do not go elsewhere."

Tears flowed from their eyes and they made countless prostrations.

"Our [151] meeting now is due to the force of prayers in previous lives," the great adept replied. "Pray from your own places for us to also meet in future lives! A monk will come as my representative every year to make prayers and offer sacrificial cakes to the naturally arisen crystal stūpa at the border of Lo and Tibet. Serve him! It is no different from doing so to me. Your land will grow and flourish."

The people of Lo said, "We don't know when your disciple will arrive. If we know, we will perform whatever service is necessary."

"As a sign that my monk is coming, two ravenlike birds will come and caw. At that time, you should bring offerings and materials for sacrificial cakes."

The people of Lo were overjoyed. They circumambulated him and offered prostrations by throwing their bodies on the ground. With tears streaming from their eyes, they cried, "We have no other source of hope than you for this life, the next life, and the intermediate state. Hold us with compassion!"

They placed his feet upon their heads and each made whatever prayers they knew.

Those events may be recounted in verse:

• • •

After a prophecy by venerable Tārā ,
the goddess of enlightened action
for the conquerors of the three times
and their spiritual children,
he caused the barbarians of the borderland
who had never heard even the name
of the precious Three Jewels,
and who had no opportunity for Dharma,
to turn away from engaging only in sin.

In establishing the royal code of the ten virtues,
Tangtong Gyalpo in the barbarian land
was the same as Songtsen Gampo
here in the Land of Snows.[649]

Binding [152] *the strong barbarians*
beneath the earth with the magical stride of Viṣṇu
and illuminating all directions with the light
of the Conqueror's doctrine,
he could easily be respected as Cakravartī.[650]

• • •

Then the people of Lo, the single Lo man and so forth, escorted the great adept as he traveled to the site of the naturally arisen crystal stūpa at the top of the pass on the border of Lo and Tibet. The Lo people arranged a fine ritual feast, and everyone enjoyed it.

When he left, he met the shepherds from Kongpo.[651] "Master, you are good," they said. "It is wonderful that the Lo people made offerings without killing you."

They arranged a fine ritual feast, and the shepherds offered a hundred measures of butter and curd, twenty-one hybrid yak-cows, and seven kettles. They agreed to offer butter lamps every year to the shrines at Tsagong.

"Please do something so that the Lo people will not overpower us and the tigers will not harm our hybrid yak-cows and yaks," they requested.

"Long life to the tigers!" he replied.

"That won't do. We need a prayer for the tigers to die."

"May the tigers live in love!"

He scattered barley from his hands in the valley and built a stūpa as a geomantic focal-point. Even if the tigers mingled with the hybrid yak-cows and yaks, they did no harm, and trouble from the Lo people ceased.

~

The great adept then traveled to Drakyul and stayed in Khandro Sangpuk, the Secret Cave of the Ḍākinīs.[652] The people of Kong Ralsum gathered and one Kongpo person said, [153] "It is impossible to stay that long in the Lo region and not be killed by the Lo people. Did you go to another place? You must give us food."

They offered him five buckwheat cakes and a full cup of beer. He blessed these into nectar and, when they were distributed, about four hundred people each received a buckwheat cake the size of the palm of the hand and enough beer to satisfy each of them. But the Kongpo people did not recognize it as proof of his attainment.

He told those who were gathered there, "I need to borrow hybrid yak-cows, yaks, horses, and mules to transport the iron to Tibet."

Some Kongpo people said, "No one came to offer you this much iron. Since it was mined from our valley, the earth's essence will be lost. Taking it to Tibet is not good."

Kong Lhakyab also told them, "We could gather men with strong arms and be unsparing with food and beer, but how could we get this much iron? This master subdued even the cannibals of Lo. If he had no magical abilities, he would not have subdued Lo. In Tibet it is said that he even goes serenely across the surface of the water. For two years, many dimwits such as our own thieves have come to bring down these iron chains he fastened to the top of the tree, but they have not been able to bring them down. If the master himself brings down the iron, he is definitely an adept. If he is not, the earth spirit of the valley will also not release this much iron."

The Kongpo people announced with one voice, "Master, if you are able to bring down these iron chains by yourself, you may transport the iron to Tibet."

The great adept then climbed to the top of the tree. Breaking the chains into sections of fifteen iron links, [154] he brought them down.

They exclaimed, "Even a hundred of us, the young, husky men of Kongpo, were not able to move them. The master broke them into fifteen sections without separating the links, and brought them down. If he was not an adept, he could not do this with the iron. It is great merit to meet this master."

They arranged a fine ritual feast, made various offerings, and announced, "From today, you are the master of Kongpo in the east. We know you are the one who will defeat difficult situations in this life and lead us upward in the next. Now, master, we will do whatever you say."

The iron was loaded on 240 hybrid yak-cows and sent off.

9: Fine Pathways of Precious Iron

A stūpa at Tselagang was harmful to Tibet in general. When the great adept sat on top of it for a day in the meditative concentration that suppresses the māras, the servants of the Karmapa said, "Tangtong Gyalpo is famous in Kongpo and the region of Lo as an indisputable adept. His retinue and possessions are enviable, but he's a madman who doesn't understand the results of actions, and sleeps on top of a stūpa!"

They struck him with swords, spears, staffs, and so forth, and rained stones upon him so that it seemed he had been killed under a pile of stones. But when sunrise came the next day, the great adept was sitting on top of the pile of stones, with his body even more majestic than before, performing the sūtra ritual of the Medicine Buddha. They all became filled with faith and offered confessions. Karmapa Tongwa Dönden rebuked his servants, telling them they had committed an inexpiable act.[653] Then he pleased the great adept with great offerings such as tea, clothing, and silk.

Then [155] the great adept traveled to Orshö. The master Dorjé Shingpa said, "My temple is completed. Come for the consecration."

"I don't need to come there," he replied. "I can scatter barley from here."

He scattered barley from Orshö, and everyone saw it reach the entire temple, top to bottom, inside and out.

~

The great adept arrived in Lhasa. When he was seventy years old, in the Iron Male Dog Year [1430], he decided to build an iron bridge over the Kyichu River.[654] While he sat on the bank of the river, a man arrived carrying three arrows and a bow.

"Would you loan me the arrows and this bow?" the great adept asked.

They were offered into his hands. When he shot an arrow, it was lost in the water. When he shot an arrow again, it sailed over the top of the mountain. When he shot an arrow again, it stuck in a rock.

"The time and the signs are good," he said.

The auspicious connections for building an iron bridge had come into alignment. The great adept told the Nepa governor and his subjects, and all the lay persons and clergy of Kyishö,[655] "I will build an iron bridge over these blue waters. You must gather rocks!"

When all the people did not want to do the work, they voiced various opinions. But the thoughtful people noted, "Even though he does not build an iron bridge as he says, to gather rocks on the north side will be beneficial for the levees of the Jowo.[656] Gathering them on the south side will be beneficial for the embankment of the Nengser."

The Nepa governor and his subjects provided assistance. After the rocks were gathered, the great adept built the bridge abutment on the north side of the river. He drove two iron spikes the size of arrows into the rock that his arrow had stuck into on the south side, and fastened the two ends of the iron bridge.[657] Twenty-one days had passed. [156]

The patroness Kalsang[658] and others provided assistance, and about three hundred lay persons and clergy attached ropes to the iron and pulled. But the ropes broke every time and the people pulling them fell down. Many people were there, but when their strength was insufficient, they dispersed.

That night the great adept sat above the iron spikes and made the monks take refuge by chanting the "Mothers Infinite As Space."[659] When the eight tribes [of gods and demons] pulled the chains, the iron bridge was up in an instant.[660]

The sun rose and many people gathered, saying, "Yesterday so many people were not able to pull it. As proof of his attainment, the master built the iron bridge himself last night."

There then was no rope to fasten onto the iron bridge. He told the people of Kyishö, "I brought this much iron from the Kongpo region in the east, but you haven't even given one of your ropes. How thoughtless! I need rope to fasten it."

But no one came to offer.

The great adept ordered, "You two monks, go! In the middle of a pile of stones in the center of the grove of trees where the nyen demon Kharnak[661] lives, there is an elongated blotched stone eighteen inches long. Tie it with a string and bring it!"

They took it as they had been told and offered it before him. He appointed a nun as its keeper and advised her, "Until I take it, beat it with a staff thirteen times each morning, noon, and night! At night, put it in a hole dug in the earth and place this vajra on top!"

The demon possessed a person of Nam and begged, "The Adept of Iron Bridges [157] is holding me in prison. During the day, I'm beaten with a staff. At night, I'm put in a hole in the earth and crushed with a vajra. It's really bad. You people of the upper and lower Kyishö Valley, please ransom me!"

Since he was miserable, the people of Kyishö came before the great adept and said, "This Kharnak is the god who protects us. We will offer whatever ransom price is necessary. Please release him from prison."

Released from the hole, the god-demon made himself into a handsome young man. When he prostrated together with the people, the great adept said, "This demon doesn't pay much attention to the orders of the Great Teacher of Uḍḍiyāna. He has hurt many people visiting the precious Jowo, so he should not be left in this place. He was to be delivered to the edge of the ocean, but due to your urgent request, I will not banish him from the region. Fasten the rope on the iron bridge by tomorrow!"

Accordingly, the people collected a hundred man-loads of rope and fastened them to the iron chains. The great adept gave them the stone to take back to its place. Kharnak appeared before him in his real form and offered a confession. He took the vows of a lay practitioner and was assigned to be the caretaker of the ironclad ferry. From that time, the reputation of the peerless emanated body, the Iron-Bridge Man, filled all directions.

~

The great adept [158] built the iron bridge on the face of the rock of Drib as an auspicious connection for the moon of the precious Jowo's face to always shine as the unexcelled shrine for human beings on the surface of the earth in the vast Land of Snows. Thereafter, when the great river of Kyishö turned to the south, the subterranean nāgas had no opportunity to invite the Jowo into the water.

At that time, when he looked toward Tsang from the end of the iron bridge of Lhasa and shot two arrows, one landed at Shu Nyemo and was retrieved by a man on the great pilgrimage.[662]

"By that auspicious connection," he declared, "I will build many iron bridges and large ferries along the Tsangpo River."

When one arrow stuck in Chakpori Hill, he understood it as an auspicious connection for building a residence and center for practice at that place.[663]

~

To form an auspicious connection to relieve the severe famine that existed at that time, the great adept announced, "I'm going to Penyul."[664]

The Iron-Bridge Man traveled to Penyul with six disciples. "No matter whom we meet today," he ordered, "rob whatever they have!"

When traveling from Gyalchen Tsé in Penyul, he met a woman coming along carrying a load of barley for which she had gone into debt.

"Give me that barley!" he demanded.

"O Patron! Master from Kham, please! Our family is large and has nothing but this to eat," she cried.

But he robbed her barley and fled, whipping his horse.

The woman called for help to many men from Kham and Minyak who were passing by, and they chased and caught him. Not recognizing the great adept, they thought he was an Amdo man.[665] They bound and beat him. They dunked him in the water and threw him down on his back. They stuck their assholes in his face, sprayed excrement on him, and so forth, [159] but the great adept thought, "It is a fine auspicious connection," and was delighted.

The Minyak chieftain thought, "Those dimwitted servants have carried the beating too far. They may have killed him."

When he mounted his horse and raced over, he recognized the great adept. He leapt from his horse, prostrated, and exclaimed, "Great master, are you in trouble?"

"A fine auspicious connection has happened to me today," he replied. "From the day after tomorrow the famine among the common people will cease."

Showing the Minyak chieftain the barley he had robbed from the woman, he said, "Send this barley with some of my monks who are following!"

Laying his whip to the horse, he cried, "I'm returning to Lhasa," and left.

The Minyak chieftain repaid the woman with barley and gave the original to the Iron-Bridge Man's monks. It was exchanged with the old barley in the alms bowl of the Jowo, and the great adept made prayers.

That year, the patroness Kalsang, who had come from Sharkha in upper Nyang, built a circular residence for the great adept on the peak of Chakpori Hill.[666] She offered him ten ounces of gold and a complete set of orange robes dyed with saffron. He spoke this about the subtle process of actions and results:

The masters, chosen deities, and ḍākinīs,
and the triad of Buddha, Dharma, and Sangha,
constantly reside as an ornament
on the crown of my head.

Listen, qualified woman of good family,
and grasp this with the faculties
of mind and hearing.

Listen to me for a moment
without distraction.

If you haven't sincerely practiced
what is beneficial at this time
while you have now obtained a human body
and achieved great wealth and power,
when [160] you are born in *naraka* hell,[667]
where even cool water is hotter than fire,
could you bear suffering like that?

When born in the realm of the hungry spirits,
with no chance to use wealth
even were you to have it,
could you bear the sufferings of hunger and thirst?

When born in the realm of the animals,
unable to speak even though the mind is clear,
could you bear the inconceivable sufferings
of having your fur shaved, being milked,
burdened, exploited for plowing, and so forth?

In general, if you do not understand
that the choice is right now—the sufferings
of the three lower realms or the pleasures
of the three higher realms,
is anything else more foolish than that?

Look inward and think about it!

This son of yours was also the influential minister
of a great Dharma king in the past.

By the force of pure prayers
he now rules the kingdom with Dharma.[668]

By the power and blessing of the Dharma,
his intentions are accomplished as he wishes.

When you die and depart from here,
you will meet me in the presence
of the Teacher of Uḍḍiyāna.

Thus he spoke on Chakpori Hill, giving Lady Shakhama[669] prophetic advice about cause and result.

~

Taking a head-sized ball of manure from the cows of Lhasa, the great adept walled up the door to his circular residence and did not meet anyone, even to receive food or to speak. As he sat in a single session of meditative concentration until the next autumn came, people were certain that he had died.

The great adept said that with his ornamental wheel of inexhaustible enlightened body, speech, and mind, [161] he received the teachings of various vehicles from an ocean of buddhas in infinite buddha fields such as Tuṣita, Abhirati, and Sukhāvatī.

During that period, all the people outside saw a white rainbow continually touching the window of his residence on Chakpori Hill. From Drepung, Jamyang Tashi Palden[670] saw a rain of whatever they desired fall upon the boundless sentient beings of the three regions of Central

56. Chakpori Hill, Lhasa.

Tibet, Tsang, and Kham, sent by noble Avalokiteśvara from the peak of Chakpori. So Jamyang Chöjé had great devotion.

During that Iron Female Pig Year [1431], two iron bridges were built due to the great adept's enlightened activity.[671]

~

In the Water Male Mouse Year [1432],[672] using the ten ounces of gold that had been offered by the patroness Kalsang as the basis, the great adept offered a gold maṇḍala before the precious Jowo, along with what gold he had in hand, and made vast prayers.

Also during that year, the great adept and the patroness Kalsang acted as the sponsors and commissioned a gold image of noble Avalokiteśvara and thirty volumes of sūtras. When he performed the consecration for them, the rains fell at the right time, causing the finest of harvests.

~

The great adept went from Lhasa to Tölung.[673] A woman offered him a full cup of fine tea, and he said, "By this merit, [162] may prosperity fall like rain!"

That woman became rich enough to rival Vaiśravaṇa.[674]

As the great adept traveled the road to Tölung he met several men of Minyak. They requested Dharma and offered him many personal possessions such as a helmet, a sword, and a bow and arrows. He wore these on his body and continued to the border of Sakha Nakpa and Gyeré Tsarpa.

A blood feud had broken out between the people of Minyak and Gyeré. The Gyeré people thought the great adept was a Minyak man from Kham and robbed his personal possessions. When they stuck him with arrows, staffs, knives, and so forth, he experienced the equal taste of pleasure and pain and did not strike back or say anything. They thought he was a suitable victim, tied a rope to his penis, weighted it with a stone, and left him hanging on a fence that night.

At daybreak the next morning they cried, "This is the Adept of Iron Bridges! We have committed a grave sin!"

They took him down from where he was hanging on the fence. He was not at all angry, but when they offered their confessions with great regret, he was overjoyed and commented, "It was a profound practice for longevity."

~

The great adept reached the age of seventy-three in the first month of the Water Female Ox Year [1433].[675] At the great sacred place of glorious Chuwori[676] he laid the foundations of a temple for the Translated Scriptures and the Translated Treatises, two monasteries at the peak and base of the mountain, and a great stūpa. He left people to maintain the place and gave them detailed advice. Then he decided to build many iron bridges along the course of the great Tachok Khabab River.[677]

He traveled to Nakartsé on the road leading to Paro in Bhutan. [163] The governor of Yamdrok requested many Dharma cycles of Avalokiteśvara and presented great offerings and honors.[678] The great adept spoke a prayer: "May all the sentient beings cooked in the governor's hearth quickly attain buddhahood!"

Then he went to Ralung.[679] Many dedicated meditators came to request blessings in front of the Pökya residence, and he taught the removal of impediments and the enhancement of meditation involving the channels, drops, and vital winds. The yakṣa spirit Gangwa Sangpo and his retinue emanated human forms with attractive faces and figures, presented a fine ritual feast, and climbed the glacial mountain there.[680]

The great adept left Ralung at daybreak and arrived at Nénying about

57. Six-armed Mahākāla.

sunrise. When he knelt at the Stūpa of a Thousand Lotuses, a woman offered him a plate full of roasted barley flour. He sprinkled it on the water of the pool and performed the threefold outer, inner, and secret offerings of sacrificial cakes to the Protector of Primordial Awareness. When he gave the ritual permission of the Six-armed Protector of Primordial Awareness[681] to many geshés, the four yakṣa spirits of the retinue also came to listen to the ritual permission.

Then he went to the entrance of Pari.[682] He felt special compassion for these people of Pari who tricked people for a living and cheated in the measure of produce, accumulating only karma that would cause birth in the three lower realms without a virtuous state of mind having arisen for even an instant.

When he sat in meditation at the Kaṃṇi,[683] by means of clear light he saw many people of different races and languages dissolving into the lower realms. The intention arose to build a temple for their benefit. [164] At that moment appeared the trio of the extremely beautiful Jomo Lhari, Drakyé of Paro, who was mounted on a large snake, and Kyungdu of Ha, who was a black man riding a horse. "Great master," they declared, "we will accomplish your actions of building iron bridges, so please come to Lhokha Shi," and disappeared.[684]

~

The great adept then traveled to Paro. At Taktsang, the meditation place of the Great Teacher of Uḍḍiyāna, he performed the rite of accomplishment and offerings to Vajrakīla, and the divine assembly of the Deities of the Eight Transmissions of Great Attainment actually came.[685]

The nine-headed nāga-māra that was the lord of the sacred place of Taktsang appeared and said, "Great adept, your Dharma inheritance was left by the Great Teacher of Uḍḍiyāna. So please extract it from the treasure trove."

From the rock face of Taktsang, the great adept withdrew from the treasure trove a paper scroll ten armspans in length, in which the profound key points of all the sūtras and tantras were compiled together as one.

Then, with magical feet, he circumambulated Namkha Dzong in Mönyul and met many chosen deities. At the Charnel Ground of Ngampa Dradrok, where the water and birds proclaimed the sound of *hūṃ*, there was a cave in a tree trunk in which even many thousands of people could fit when gathered during the day. It was also pleasant with no more than one person. All the malicious demons gathered there at night. He stayed for five days, and when he taught a variety of Dharma to boundless bhuta demons and nonhumans, they agreed to accomplish what he told them.

Then, on the road going to the Viśuddha Stūpa at Singri in India, he arrived in the town known as Tirikha. He saw that a naturally arisen stūpa in the center of that large city [165] had great blessings. When he circumambulated and made prayers for three days, he beheld the faces of the nine deities of Vijayā and received the attainment of immortal life.[686]

When he performed prostrations, offerings, and circumambulations at the Viśuddha Stūpa, where the son of Śuddhodana had renounced his

58. The hermitage of Taktsang, Bhutan.

home for homelessness, he heard a variety of special instructions from Mahāvairocana and many adepts such as Tringyi Shukchen.[687] When the townspeople of Tirikha offered fine gifts and honors, he used them to perform the practice of the *dhāraṇī* of the nine deities of Vijayā, whose faces he beheld. When he taught Dharma in the language of the Tirikha people, they were devoted and respectful.

The great adept then went to the Charnel Ground of Tumdrak.[688] He was welcomed by malicious demons, and the zombies and ḍākinīs requested initiation. He manifested as the enlightened body of Vajrabhairava, the principal deity of the maṇḍala, and bestowed the initiation.[689]

Intending to travel to Tibet, he went to the valley of Té. A young girl whose hair, nails, and so forth even had a red radiance asked, "Yogin, where did you come from? Where are you going? What is your purpose?"

"I came from Tibet," he replied. "I went on pilgrimage. I am going back home where my parents and children are."

"Don't tell such lies, yogin. Your parents have passed away. You have no children now. Before you travel home, bring Lhokha Shi under control, and vast benefit will come to others. [166] We will make a Dharma connection. Stay here tonight."

She went into the middle of the town. Then, in the early evening the coral-colored Vajravārāhī appeared, surrounded by ten million ḍākinīs, and performed a blessing and a ritual feast. She prophesied that he would build an iron bridge at Chuwori, bringing great benefit to living beings.

~

Then, because the mountain range from Sengé Puk at Taktsang ran down like a venomous black snake to bisect the main Paro Valley, the great adept made a geomantic survey for erecting a stūpa at its end to suppress the earth spirit. He drove an iron spike in each of the four directions. The people built a Dharma throne on top of a rock that was shaped like many turtles stacked up on the shoulder of that mountain, and he made it his evening sitting place.[690]

"When this stūpa is finished," he announced, "these settlements of male and female lepers that are now in Lhokha Shi will become empty. Disciples of mine will bring benefit to living beings in Kāmata in India.[691] Even the king of Kāmata will present offerings at this stūpa. Furthermore, because many stūpas, temples, iron bridges, and so forth will be completed, know that you people of Lhokha Shi will gather attainments!"

At night he only sat on top of the Dharma throne. During the day, when he emanated many bodies in different regions and encouraged virtue, he found much iron and charcoal and many blacksmiths to forge iron links. When manufacturing them, he emanated eighteen bodies at the shops of eighteen blacksmiths in Torbopu, Dungkar, Cheu, Malpu, and Lholingka.[692] [167] He inflated the bellows, pounded the hammer, stoked the charcoal, and so forth. When the blacksmiths met, they individually boasted, "The Dharma lord stayed only at my place." But later they realized he had come by means of different emanations, and they all gained total faith.[693]

Especially, the great adept was very pleased with eight blacksmiths at

59. The Dumtsé Stūpa of Paro, Bhutan.

Ochu Gadrak. He gave them each an anvil stone that could not be broken no matter which strong man pounded hot or cold iron on it with a hammer, and a very special vessel filled with beer. In three months they finished seven thousand links, and strong stone hammers, stone chisels, and iron tools.

The people of Paro said, "Master, if you build this iron bridge of yours in front of Chuwori, it will also benefit our pilgrimages to Lhasa."

He agreed to build it as they requested.

At Wam Tengchen, the rich man Alek offered a birth-turquoise worth seventy loads of silver coins[694] and said, "Here in my area, water is scarce. So please create an auspicious connection for the water to improve."

The great adept placed a large kettle on three lap-sized stones and filled it with water. When he threw in various grains, and dedicated it to the earth spirits, nāgas, and nyen demons, the people had more water than what sustained the humans and cattle of that region, even enough to irrigate the fields.

From Tengchen he went up the rock face of a mountain to the east of Umdur that could not be climbed by any human being. After one month he declared, "In the hollow interior of the mountain is [168] a miraculous sacred place known as Tashi Gomang. It is no different from Shambhala[695] in the north, but no one can go there without magical abilities. As a sign of the presence of a sacred place, the shape of a gate can be seen in the rock. Look!"

When they looked, all the people saw a gate that had not been there before in the mirrorlike surface of the rock.

Then he traveled to Umdul. A bridge of ice one armspan thick stretched straight across the great river. He crossed it, and the local people on the bank of the river exclaimed, "Other than now, we have never seen a bridge of ice on the river here in Lhorong."[696]

When they went to look at the ice bridge the next day, only the turbulent waves of the Rong River were there.

He then traveled to Gyaldung and Langmar in Mön, and to upper and lower Ha.[697] He exchanged the offerings for iron and brought it to Paro. When he sat with his body immobile for three months on top of the Dharma throne of Kyewang Pakné, which had been prophesied by Avalokiteśvara, he became known as an indisputable adept in Lhokha Shi and all the regions of Mön.

~

Although no one was able to physically harm the great adept, three greedy fools of Mön had a discussion. "The master is sleeping alone on the Dharma throne on top of the rocks. A lot of silver coins and turquoise have come to him. We should throw him into the gorge and take the valuables."

When they came about midnight, threw the great adept into the rock gorge, and searched for valuables, they did not find any. When they heard the great adept, on top of the same throne, say, "*Hūṃ*! *Phaṭ*!" [169] they thought that where they had thrown him before had not been sufficient. So they lifted the great adept's body and threw him off the high rock cliff there. Intending to take everything valuable, they searched the entire surface of the throne. When they saw the great adept's body again, even more majestic than before, the three thieves were terrified and went back to their homes.

The great adept had emanated three bodies, and a body was sitting in each of the Mön men's homes. One Mön man picked up an axe and struck the great adept. But another figure came in the door and said, "Mön fool, don't kill the pig!" The man saw that the ax had struck the head of a pig.

Also, one Mön man shot an arrow at the body of the great adept that was in his home. Again the great adept said, "Mön fool, don't kill the pig!" When the man looked, he saw that the arrow had struck the belly of a pig.

Also, one Mön man stabbed the great adept that was in his home with his sword. Again the great adept appeared and said, "Mön fool, don't kill the cow!"

That night the three Mön men were regretful, but there was nothing they could do about it. The next day they offered many valuables such as iron to the great adept and made a confession.

~

Then the great adept traveled to Tembu in Té. He built the Dzom iron bridge and the Bakdrong iron bridge. In east Mön, about ten men from west Mön saw the huge offerings of gold and turquoise. Greedy for it, they decided to kill him with an attack of poisoned arrows at the entrance to the bridge in the area of Tembu, [170] and to rob what was kept on the bodies of those in east Mön. They attacked with poisoned arrows from both directions at the bridge, but the arrows scattered beneath his feet without even touching his robes. Many people from different regions had gathered to meet the great adept, and they presented various offerings of horses, oxen, and so forth. Those who had fired the poisoned arrows fled and disappeared without a trace.

~

At a geomantic focal-point of Lhokha Shi and the Mön region, the great adept constructed the stūpa at Kyewang Pakné[698] to suppress the earth spirit. Chiefly at the places of Changyul Rawakha, Nyal Pakmodrong, Tachok Gang,[699] Umdul Dogar, Bakdrong, Binang Khaché, Daklha, and Gyerling Nyishar, he performed vast virtuous work, such as constructing representations of enlightened body, speech, and mind, iron bridges, and meditation centers.

Fourteen hundred loads of iron, with each bundle consisting of fifteen iron links, and seven hundred loads[700] of Bhutanese goods such as paper and ink were transported to the entrance of Pari through faithful volunteer work by the monks and patrons of the newly established monastery at Paro.

No faithful volunteers or compulsory laborers appeared from Pari, but

60. Small stone image of Tangtong Gyalpo.

the monk Ami Gön gained total faith and offered a growing field of green grain. Fossil shells and a special type of soil were extracted from a treasure.[701]

An emanation of the great adept carried seventy iron links and went from Pari to Nénying between mealtimes.[702] [171] He placed the load of iron on a flat stone at the main gate and sat down. A geshé asked, "Where have you come from?"

"I came from Pari this morning," he replied.

"Did you carry this iron?"

"Yes," he replied, and lifted it on to his shoulders with one hand.

Realizing it was proof of his attainments, the geshé said, "Please come to accept my gifts and respect."

They went to Ulung. "Bring clay," the great adept said, and while eating a meal he fashioned with his hands an image of himself and gave it to the geshé.

Eight mules carried the iron as far as the Nénying bridge. From on the bridge, the great adept threw the iron into the water and cried, "You nāgas, get it there before me!"

Traveling the Yamdrok Ridge, he arrived at Chuwori in one day. He hid the seventy links of iron in the sand and left them.[703]

≈

When the great adept made the return journey, at Gampa Pass the yakṣa spirit Gangsang, who was riding a white horse and leading another, said, "Please ride on this one."[704]

They climbed up the glacial mountain, and inside a beautiful mansion he placed the great adept on a throne of five types of jewels and offered various kinds of food.

"Master," he said, "after meeting you at Pökya, because of your great blessing I have not been affected by injury from scorching and have been happy.[705] When you build the iron bridge at Chuwori, I will also come to serve you. I have carried out your enlightened activities by having compulsory laborers come quickly for the iron at Pari."

Gangsang and his retinue escorted the great adept during the journey to the entrance of Pari. [172]

When the great adept, who was the source of that emanation,[706] was laying the foundation for the Samdrup Temple, the Dharma king Kunsang Pak arrived at the entrance to Pari. The great adept requested an official seal conscripting workmen from as far as the mountains of upper Nyang for the construction of the temple. He also left his spiritual son Könchok Palsang to supervise the work thereafter.[707]

The great adept said, "On the occasion of the consecration, I will come myself." Accordingly, everyone would [later] see a vulture that was an emanation of the great adept scatter flowers from under its wings.

When lord Rabtenpa saw the bundles [of iron and Bhutanese goods], he exclaimed, "I have heard it said that in the past Drogön Pakpa[708] arrived bringing much wealth from Mongolia. But it is incredible to bring this much wealth from the borderlands of the Mön region."

He issued an order for compulsory labor and attached his official seal.

≈

Two hundred loads of iron links, together with most of the other bundles, were sent off to glorious Chuwori. The great adept took one thousand loads of iron and traveled to Latö Jang in western Tsang.[709] During the

61. The ruler Rabten Kunsang Pak (1389–1442).

Wood Male Tiger Year [1434], when the great adept was seventy-four years old, he stayed in meditation in the Shalkar Lhadong meditation hut at the isolated site of Tarpa Ling.[710] He gave orders to the disciples and, because an iron bridge would bring vast benefit to living beings, they completed in nine months an iron bridge and two stūpas that contained magical diagrams for the Dharma king of Jang to bring Latö Lho under his control.[711]

From the meditation hut, he scattered flowers for the consecrations. The artisans and workers saw them reach from the tops to the bottoms of the stūpas and the iron bridge, and they became deeply faithful. [173]

∾

In the Wood Female Rabbit Year [1435], the great adept made some journeys in the western regions.[712] Riding on a mule, he came to a great precipice at the foot of Gyaltang. The monks saw it and said, "There is no way across if you do not take the path."

"If I do not get across," he replied, "I'll die. If I do get across, it's shorter than the path."

He used the whip three times, and left clear mule tracks on the cliff that was like the surface of a mirror. The monks traveled on the path. He was sitting on top of a rock protruding at the edge of the hot springs on the south bank of the Tsangpo River. Something with a human body, but the face of a wolf, was holding his mount. Many kinds of people were transporting rocks on the near and far sides of the Tsangpo, strong workmen were piling up the bridge pier, and so forth. Three very beautiful women riding white hybrid yak-cows were serving various foods in front of the great adept. The iron bridge of Gangla Longka was built, and he left a bridge keeper.[713]

He then stayed for seven days before the Noble One of Kyirong.[714] During the day, he gave many Dharma connections to the people of Kyirong, such as the awakening of the thought of enlightenment and the oral transmission of *maṇis*, and made circumambulations and prayers. While he stayed there, a rain of flowers constantly fell. At night he stayed on a flat stone to the east of the Jowo. He prophesied, "If a great drought occurs in Kyirong, rain will fall when [the Jowo image] is washed on this stone."[715] [174]

He built a Lhungsé Kabub Stūpa[716] at Madun Pangka in order to stop fighting and harm in Kyirong. Since he made disciples in the monasteries of the Kyirong area, many offerings of iron and so forth came. Three nuns from Kyirong, such as Ané Paldren, followed him as attendants.

∾

When the great adept sat on the broad Dharma throne at Ngari Dzongka, the Ngadak king and all the other powerful and meek people requested Dharma and made great offerings.[717] When they pleaded with him to stay for a while, Chöpal Sangpo, who was the master of the Ngadak king, became jealous.[718] Deciding to murder the great adept, he gave four tenths of an ounce of gold to his own consort [Semo Remo].[719] He sent her with a large dose of deadly poison, saying, "Put this in beer and you should be able to kill the realized yogin!"

She put the poison in a full cup of beer and offered it to the great adept. He took it in his hand and told her, "If I don't drink this beer, you won't like it. If I do drink it, I won't like it. Which is best?"

She was mortified and fled. The great adept told the monks, "You, my very faithful disciples, take these links for the iron bridges and, within seven days, reach a place from where you cannot see this area. Those who are not disciples should not carry them. This is for an auspicious connection. While I make a retreat for seven days, no one may come inside the boundary markers of the retreat. Either I will die inside the retreat hut or I will live. I will fulfill the intentions [175] of the great master."[720]

Drinking absolutely all of the beer, he spoke this prayer invoking words of truth:[721]

In many past lives,
I have given away
food, clothing and jewelry,
horses and elephants,
and even my body and life
for the benefit of others.

May this truth quickly cure
sickness from the poison!

If I am without biased thoughts
for even an instant
concerning both a dear child
and a harmful enemy,
and if I am without thoughts
of pleasure and pain or benefit and harm
concerning food of a hundred tastes
and deadly poison,
then just like a peacock
that has eaten deadly poison,[722]
may no harm come to my body and life,
may I be healthy and strong,
my sense faculties lucid,

and may I gain control of my lifespan
for the benefit of living beings.

He had consumed every bit of the poison. The next day, the great master [Chöpal Sangpo], Semo Remo, and those belonging to her family saw the great adept to be the color of charcoal and desperately ill. The patroness Darma Kyi presented offerings of butter lamps, food, incense, and so forth and offered many prostrations from the boundary markers of his retreat. When she looked, she saw him as Avalokiteśvara. People had various viewpoints: some saw a mass of light from which came the sound of *maṇis*, several saw the Medicine Buddha, and so forth. But most people agreed that they saw a semiwrathful great adept, even more majestic than before, conversing with a spiritual friend in front of him [176] who was light blue in color and held an alms bowl and a tree branch with leaves, on the tip of which was a myrobalan plum. On that occasion the great adept gave the blessing for creating the medicinal nectar of the Medicine Buddha, and these exceptional instructions for benefiting all diseases, which are known as the White and Red Pills of the Iron Bridge Tradition.[723]

∾

Then the great adept traveled to the glacial Mount Kailash and stayed in Dzumdrul Pukmoché, the Great Cave of Miracles.[724] Just at the passing of midnight, Dzongtsen, the earth spirit of Mount Kailash, appeared and announced, "Tomorrow I will offer a meal to the master and disciples." Then he disappeared.

The next day the earth spirit delivered the plump body of a deer. The great adept said, "I am a yogin who can survive even without eating food, but the earth spirit has killed a deer to nourish us, master and disciples. If we bless it in a ritual feast and then enjoy it, great benefit will come to the deer."

He pleased and delighted his retinue, such as Ané Paldren,[725] and all the spiritual heroes and ḍākinīs.

Then the master and disciples circumambulated Mount Kailash on foot. In each of the four directions around Mount Kailash, he also built a Dharma throne, a stūpa, and a meditation hut in which one person could fit. He also left a handprint in stone at each one. When he requested blessings at the eight stūpas constructed by Tsangpa Gyaré,[726] he clearly remembered back through seventeen hundred of his lifetimes.

62. Mount Kailash.

He then went to circumambulate Lake Mapam Yutso.[727] The water had dried up in the valley [177] and many tens of thousands of fish had died. When he saw that those that had not died were also suffering without water and were experiencing the misery of being eaten by carnivores and birds and so forth and having their eyes plucked out, a compassion arose that moved him to tears. He chanted many names of the buddhas, spit on the fish, and spoke this prayer:

May the unexcelled
precious Three Jewels,
and the special deity,
the protector Avalokiteśvara,
lord of compassion,
kindly consider miserable living beings
with your compassion,
and please fulfill your vast prayers.

When the Great Sage [Śākyamuni]
became a waterfall in the past,

he liberated the fish
by chanting the names of the sugatas.

Likewise, may I also satisfy
with a rain of Dharma
the animals who are experiencing
unbearable suffering.

When these bodies are discarded,
may those beings avoid the lower realms,
obtain the sublime bliss of the gods and humans,
be energetic in listening to
and practicing the excellent Dharma,
and achieve unexcelled enlightenment.

Then he traveled to Gugé and Purang. Avalokiteśvara, the middle of the Three Silver Brothers of Khachar,[728] declared, "Yogin with the karma, benefit living beings through the various methods that tame degenerate sentient beings in whatever way necessary!"

He went to the Gyalti Palace of Purang[729] and sat on top of a flat rock for thirteen days. When no one came to request Dharma connections and to offer respect and gifts, he thought there was probably no karma connection. [178] When he pushed down his two fists and stood up, clear imprints of his crossed legs and two fists appeared in the flat rock.

"Adepts who squeeze rock like mud are rare even in India!" the people cried. "He's an adept!"

Many came to request Dharma connections and make offerings.

At that time several of the great adept's monks went out on an excursion and met traders from Mangyul.[730]

"Where are you from?" the traders asked. "What news do you have?"

"The Great Adept of Iron Bridges is teaching much Dharma. You traders should go request Dharma," the monks replied.

"You are great liars," the traders from Mangyul said. "The Adept of Iron Bridges is staying in Mangyul. We met him. He hasn't come here."

While the traders from Mangyul and the Iron-Bridge Man's monks were talking, seven renunciants on pilgrimage from Shang appeared and said, "When we came, the great adept was staying at Samdrup Tsé in Tsang.[731] He didn't go to Mangyul."

They realized that he had displayed individual physical forms and worked for the benefit of living beings. All who were gathered there placed the feet of the great adept on the tops of their heads and made prayers.

~

Then, at the Charnel Ground of Rāmeśvara in the land of Kashmir, the great adept held a vast ritual feast for Vajravārāhī surrounded by many ḍākas and ḍākinīs, and received many profound key points of secret mantra [179] with which to grace disciples.[732] He went to where an elephant skull with the naturally arisen *lañcana* syllables *oṃ āḥ hūṃ* was and told the monks, "That is the skull of my ninth lifetime."

"What other types of births have you taken, during which you worked for the benefit of sentient beings?" they asked.

"I have worked for the benefit of sentient beings during one hundred thousand lifetimes. In particular, I took three animal births that brought great benefit to sentient beings."

Then the great adept told his retinue, "Seven hundred and thirty lifetimes before this one, I took birth as a fully ordained monk called Padmākara."

He showed his retinue the stone cave of Karita, in which he had meditated on noble Avalokiteśvara while subsisting merely on the three white milk products[733] from a patron's buffalo. Inside was a naturally arisen image of the Noble One, in front of which was a soft mat of peacock feathers spread out on green kuśa grass that had been blessed to not grow old. The surroundings of the stone cave were beautified with various flowers and fruits, and it was a meditation site adorned with extremely clear and cool water that had appeared from meditation practice.

Then he said, "I stayed in this place observing the fasting ritual from the time I was twenty years old until I was eighty, repeating the mantra of pure awareness and making this single-minded prayer to the Noble One:

> I pray to you,
> master Avalokiteśvara.
>
> I pray to you,
> chosen deity Avalokiteśvara.
>
> I pray to you, [180]
> noble, sublime Avalokiteśvara.

I pray to you,
sublime refuge Avalokiteśvara.

I pray to you,
loving protector Avalokiteśvara.

Compassionate conqueror,
hold us with your compassion!

For countless living beings
wandering in endless saṃsāra
and experiencing unbearable suffering,
there is no other refuge than you, O protector.

Bless them to obtain omniscient buddhahood!

By the force of their evil karma
accumulated through beginningless time,
they have been born in the hells
due to their hatred.

May the sentient beings experiencing
the sufferings of heat and cold
be born in your presence, O sublime deity!

Oṃ maṇi padme hūṃ

By the force of their evil karma
accumulated through beginningless time,
they have been born in the realm
of the hungry spirits due to their greed.

May the sentient beings experiencing
the sufferings of hunger and thirst
be born in the sublime realm of Potala!

Oṃ maṇi padme hūṃ

By the force of their evil karma
accumulated through beginningless time,
they have been born as animals
due to their ignorance.

May the sentient beings experiencing
the sufferings of being stupid and mute
be born in your presence, O protector!

Oṃ maṇi padme hūṃ

By the force of their evil karma
accumulated through beginningless time,
they have been born in the realm
of the demigods due to their jealousy.

May the sentient beings experiencing
the sufferings of combat
be born in the realm of Potala!

Oṃ maṇi padme hūṃ

By the force of their evil karma
accumulated through beginningless time,
they have been born in the god realm
due to their pride. [181]

May the sentient beings experiencing
the sufferings of falling transmigration[734]
be born in the realm of Potala!

Oṃ maṇi padme hūṃ

In all births and in all lifetimes,
with enlightened actions
equal to those of Avalokiteśvara,
may I liberate the living beings
of impure realms

and spread the six syllables
of sublime speech in the ten directions!

By the force of my prayer to you,
noble and sublime deity,
may my disciples take responsibility
for the results of their actions,
be energetic in virtuous deeds,
and be endowed with Dharma
for the sake of living beings![735]

He then said, "That patron who offered me the three white products for sustenance was born in Sukhāvatī. The patroness was born as a god in the heaven of the thirty-three gods. That buffalo who provided me with yogurt and milk has continually taken birth in a human body. Now she is a person of Minyak in Dokham who will quickly come to be a patron for my construction of images of the buddhas and bodhisattvas from turquoise, coral, lapis lazuli, conch shell, amber, and so forth."

He made many statements in which he showed that he saw the three times without obscuration.

~

Then, during the return trip, due to the expansion of the great adept's jasmine-flowerlike enlightenment mind,[736] even the cold sensation of the frigid winter wind appeared as bliss to him, so he wore a single cloak for clothing and walked with bare feet. When he arrived at the Ulek[737] [Monastery] of Namgyal Lhatsé, from faith in the blissful warmth of the great adept's body, fine honors and offerings were made. [182]

"By what name are you known?" people asked.

"I am called the Iron-Bridge Man, Tangtong Gyalpo."

"Renunciant, you probably have some experiential realization, but it isn't right to impersonate an adept."

"What is the Adept of Iron Bridges, Tangtong Gyalpo, like?" he asked.

"The Adept of Iron Bridges is an emanation of the Uḍḍiyāna Guru, whose fame has reached even as far as India and China. He is more dignified than you and has gathered a great retinue and riches."

Then the many monks, horses, mules, hybrid yak-cows, yaks, bundles, and so forth that were behind him, arrived.

The people exclaimed, "We do not suspect that you are lying. You are certainly the Adept of Iron Bridges."

There were huge offerings of gold, copper, and so forth.

~

The great adept then traveled to the Dradun Temple.[738] Many Meshang nomads were making huge offerings of butter lamps in the temple. More nomads than could fit on the circumambulation path were circumambulating and reciting *maṇis* when they saw the great adept come serenely across the surface of the lake. When he joined together with the nomads and performed three circumambulations, the nomads said, "We saw you from the circumambulation path. Master, yogin, you seemed to come across the surface of the lake. Was that a hallucination or proof of attainment?"

The great adept replied, "If the faithful look, it is proof of attainment. If those with wrong view look, it is a [183] hallucination."

The nomads presented fine offerings and honors.

~

Then the great adept went to the upper valley of Surtso. He thought about what would be the best method he could use to spread the doctrine of the Sage, the source of benefit and happiness, in the kingdom of Latö Lho. When he looked carefully by means of clear light, he realized that a stūpa built by a capable Bönpo at the Bönpo monastery of Yungdrung Ling[739] during a period in the past when Bön had declined would certainly harm the expansion of the doctrine. In just an instant he magically went to the top of the stūpa and sat in the meditative concentration that suppresses the māras.

Three Bönpos appeared and asked, "Where did you come from?"

"*Oṃ maṇi padme hūṃ*," he replied.

"It's wrong to recite *maṇis* on top of a blessed stūpa," the Bönpos said.[740] They threw him from the top of the stūpa and beat him until the three of them were exhausted.

When they were exhausted and gasping for breath, he asked, "Now do you believe?"

"To speak like this is unacceptable," they replied, and a great many Bönpos beat his prone body with stones and staffs. They rained stones upon him, burying him under a pile of stones equal to the stūpa.

The next day the great adept was sitting on top of the pile of stones, his body even more majestic than before. He had destroyed the energy of that stūpa to harm the doctrine. The Bönpos offered apologies and made many offerings. [184]

~

The great adept then met the Tsanda chieftain Gyaltsen Pal with seventeen horseman attendants at the entrance to the bridge at Tedung.[741]

"Renunciant master, where have you come from?" they asked.

"I came from behind," he replied.

"Where are you going now?"

"I'm going forward."

"You're a very coarse-mouthed person."

"I've smeared on my mouth whatever oily stuff there was. If it's still coarse now, there's nothing to do about it."[742]

The chieftain and attendants attacked him with stones like they were killing a mad dog, but he was not at all injured. They bound him like a criminal and set him up as a target. When they shot arrows, they shot from close range where they were certain to hit him, but they did not hit his body and the arrows did not even stick in the ground. They made the bonds even tighter than before and threw him in the river. When he was not carried away, they said, "He is either a demon or an adept."

The chieftain and his attendants went away.

The great adept rose from the middle of the river and went to Dingri Langkor. From the great mirror of primordial awareness famed as the White Mausoleum of Dampa, he beheld infinite apparitions of vast purity.[743]

~

Then the great adept traveled to Lapchi. He met the Drigungpa Dharma lord Namkha Gyaltsen. They gave explanations to each other of the teachings of Nāropa and Niguma. The great adept saw the Dharma lord Drigungpa as a mass of light. Drigungpa saw the Iron-Bridge Man as Guru Drakpotsel.[744]

He then decided to go to Drin Chuwar. At that moment Tashi Tseringma appeared.[745] "I will go make a path [185] and call the people of Drin," she said, and left.

When he arrived, there was a narrow valley with a raging river, above

63. The great yogin Milarepa.

which was a very thick snake with a circumference of about three armspans, extending in midair across the valley. He knew it was Tseringma's welcome, and when he traveled on top of the snake he quickly arrived at Drin Chuwar. He stayed for three days. He beheld Vajradhara surrounded by the Kagyü masters, and a white, red, and indigo *oṃ āḥ hūṃ* on the rock wall that had supported the corpse of the venerable lord Milarepa. When he offered prayers, light rays dissolved into his body, speech, and mind. The Five Sisters of Long Life[746] presented a fine ritual feast. Then he traveled across the valley again on the snake-bridge.

When he stayed for three months in the sacred places of Lapchi, a huge snowfall occurred, and even the dedicated meditators who were near each other could not meet. He sat on top of a large boulder and the fallen snow receded as far away as a stone could be thrown. First many wild animals such as burrhel sheep came to the glistening moist earth. Then many carnivores arrived, such as snow leopards, lynxes, and wild dogs. But the great adept had perfected the force of this bodhisattva prayer for a hundred thousand lifetimes: "May animals become free from the fear of being eaten by each other!" Therefore, the carnivores lived peacefully among the wild animals, [186] sniffing their scent, licking them with their tongues, and so forth. On that occasion, the Five Sisters of Long Life served him various kinds of fruit and food, and he completely fulfilled their wishes with whatever initiations and instructions they requested.

~

Then the great adept traveled to glorious Riwoché in the first month, when he had reached the age of seventy-six [1436].[747] The bridge pier was finished, but when they pulled the iron chains, the ropes broke and one of the iron chains fell into the river. Many people pulled on it, but the iron chain was tangled in the mud and rocks and they could not pull it out. He made many people take refuge by chanting the "Mothers Infinite As Space." The great adept brought the bright, glistening end of the iron chain, which had been tangled in the rocks underwater, from out of the turbulant ice floes and waves of the river in that first month. Then the iron bridge, a pathway to enlightenment, was easily built in front of glorious Riwoché. During the consecration, he scattered flowers so that it would not be destroyed for as long as the precious doctrine, the source of benefit and happiness, remained.

Furthermore, no adept who previously appeared in Central Tibet and Tsang, Dokham, Lhokha Shi, and the regions of Mön impartially gave fine pathways of precious iron above the turbulent waves of the rivers to all beings. But the Great Adept of Iron Bridges himself constructed fifty-eight iron bridges, before and after this.

• • •

In the middle of great rivers
turbulent with violent waves,
piles of small, single rocks

64. The iron bridge of Chung Riwoché.

were transformed into stone mountains
that rival Mount Meru. [187]

I think that he made rosaries
of iron chains in beautiful rows,
impartially welcoming and leading
by the hand countless living beings
as his guests.

What else could this loving gift,
in which even inanimate objects bring
benefit and joy to living beings, come from,
except the blending of all phenomena
into a single taste in great primordial awareness?

The magical abilities of powerful
adepts are countless,
but I wonder whether,
not seeing any except this
to be for the enjoyment of everyone
here on the surface of the earth,
they have gone to Khecara in shame?

• • •

10: A Relic of the Buddha Blazing with Light

Then the great adept decided to go visit the Dharma lord Ka Ngapa Paljor Sherab,[748] who was staying in the monastery of Kyara in upper Dok. At that moment, the Dharma lord Ka Ngapa had an experiential vision of clear light in which an enormous boat appeared on the shore of a great lake, and many human and nonhuman sentient beings gathered at the edge of the water. He went to where many people were taking refuge by chanting the "Mothers Infinite As Space." He met a white man and asked, "What is this lake?"

"This lake is called saṃsāra, the ocean of suffering. This boat is Avalokiteśvara's boat of compassion. These sentient beings are going to cross the lake, but they are waiting because the person who will take them across has not yet arrived."

"What is the name of the person who will take them across on the boat?"

"In India, he is known by the name Tilopa. Here in the land of Tibet, he is known as the Iron-Bridge Man. He is coming to your place tomorrow." [188]

"Where have you come from? Why are you staying here?"

"I came from Potala.[749] I am helping them cross this lake."

Ka Ngapa woke from the experience of clear light and realized, "The venerable monk Tsöndru has accomplished infinite and impartial virtuous acts and is coming here."

The next day, the great adept came riding a mule straight up the precipitous path of Kyara. He prostrated and requested blessings before Ka Ngapa, who said, "Venerable monk Tsöndru, we have not met for a long time. Where have you gone during the last year?"

"During the last year I have gone impartially around the land to carry out vast virtuous actions. I have come at this time to request a blessing."

65. The great adept Tilopa.

"You have the greater blessing. You are a holy man whose prayers are fulfilled and who is expert in the key points of auspicious connections. So please make a prayer and create the auspicious connections for calming the internecine quarrels of the Jangpa brothers. Please make your main residence Yeru Jang in general and, within it, since this Chungpa patron has also been very kind to me, please live at glorious Riwoché where your iron bridge has been built."[750]

He agreed to do so, and also made the prayer and created the auspicious connections.

The Dharma lord Ka Ngapa told all the monks and patrons, "This monk Tsöndru is no different from Tilopa, so present offerings and request Dharma."

Many people gathered, [189] and the great adept taught the taking of refuge by means of the "Mothers Infinite As Space," the awakening of the thought of enlightenment, and the meditative recitation of Mahākaruṇika. Many offerings came, and he made a prayer at each one. He offered them to his master and said, "I have great fears for your life this year, so please make a one-month retreat."

Ka Ngapa replied, "I'm an old man and can die without regret because I have passed all the Dharma to its owner. Your lineage and group of disciples will bring unceasing benefit to living beings by means of taking refuge using the 'Mothers Infinite As Space,' and by means of the six syllables of sublime speech."

66. Ngorchen Kunga Sangpo (1382–1456).

~

Then the great adept went to Dok Logkya. With master Lhagyal Sangpo in charge, he sent the mules and monks to pile up the bridge pier for the iron bridge that was to be built at Tashi Tsé in Jé, and to encourage virtue. The great adept practiced the austerity of subsisting only on water for twenty-one days at Tolé Lhé, the meditation site of Tsenden Ridröma.[751] He beheld the faces of the precious Teacher and the two sublime śrāvakas,[752] offered the seven-branch prayer, and received Dharma. He bound four powerful yakṣa spirits to vows. Then many people saw him go across the surface of the Dok River, and various tales were told.[753]

~

The great adept then traveled to Ngor Gönsar and met the Dharma lord Kunga Sangpo.[754] A tsen demon lived in a grove of yew trees down below the monastery. He was a malevolent demon that entered into the mindstreams of monks who had little merit, took the lives of horses, mules, and donkeys that arrived at the monastery, and was very unhappy about the growth of the monastery. [190]

When Ngorchen asked the great adept to liberate the demon, he shot an arrow from the pinnacle of the master's residence and much blood poured from the bunch of trees. Because the minds of the Sangha members were in harmony and their moral discipline was pure from then on, the monastery vastly expanded. He received much Dharma from Ngorchen, such as the Hevajra initiation.[755] Their minds blended together as one and they met many times.

~

Then, with feet of magical ability, he traveled to Bumtso Dong. Many men and women wearing the skins of tigers and leopards arranged many ritual feasts of various kinds of food.

"Precious Master," they said, "we gods and demons of apparent existence are servants who will accomplish whatever you say. So please care for us with your great love."

Then they disappeared.

~

The great adept then went to Uyuk Gong Ngön. The oath-bound Dorjé Lekpa[756] honored him well with various kinds of food, and declared, "My retinue and I will protect and care for the representations of enlightened body, speech, and mind, and the boats, ferries, and iron bridges that you build."

Thus he offered the promise to serve as a caretaker for the great adept.

~

Then the great adept made a detailed pilgrimage to the sacred places of Shang Sambulung. Genyen Dölpa and the others held a ritual feast and made boundless offerings before him.[757] Then they said this:

> Mental emanation of the Teacher of Uḍḍiyāna,
> great adept, ornament of Jambudvīpa,
> source of refuge for the trio of gods, demons,
> and humans of the Land of Snows, [191]
> excellent field for accumulating merit,
> we take refuge in you—
> please hold us with your compassion!
>
> According to the command
> of the Great Teacher of Uḍḍiyāna,
> we twenty-one genyen spirits
> of Dölpa Nakpo protect Dharma practitioners,

destroy the breakers of sacred commitments,
and will also act as your servants and messengers.

Therefore, according to your command,
great holy man, we will protect and guard
the stūpas and temples
that are geomantic focal-points,
and the boats and ferries
that impartially benefit living beings.

Genyen Dölpa and his retinue prostrated and agreed to be caretakers.

~

In that way, with his actual body, the great adept brought immediate and long-term benefit and happiness to many incorporeal gods and demons. To construct an iron bridge as a pathway to enlightenment that would actually benefit corporeal human beings without distinction, he went to Tashi Tsé when it was time to pull up the iron bridge. This was after Shabpa Lhagyal Sangpo and his spiritual brothers had completed the piling up of the bridge abutment according to the great adept's command.

Lhagyal Sangpo said, "The patrons and spiritual brothers have listened to me with great attention, and so the virtuous work has been completed even better than you hoped. You should give a dedication and a gift."[758]

The great adept spoke in dedication: "Led by the monks and workers, may those who have made positive or negative karma connections with this iron bridge quickly attain buddhahood!" [192]

"I have no food to give," he said. "If this rock were butter-cheese, I would cut it and give it to you."

He pressed down with his left hand on the rock in front of him, extended the fingers of his right hand, and acted like he was cutting it. When he squeezed the rock with both hands, a clear imprint of both hands appeared in the rock. By urging all the powerful and the meek people of Jé Bodong toward virtue, and collecting offerings, the iron bridge of Tashi Tsé was built at the end of the Fire Male Dragon Year [1436].[759] He performed the consecration and left a bridge keeper there.

In the naturally arisen rock cave to the right of the isolated site of Tarpa Ling, the spiritual son of the conquerors, Nyima Sangpo, was born in this year amidst many marvelous signs.[760]

~

In the Fire Female Snake Year [1437],[761] the great adept saw that people would lose their lives from hunger and thirst because of a severe famine in Central Tibet. He was moved with unbearable compassion. When he looked for a way to help, an idea occurred: "If I, Tangtong Gyalpo, with the perfect motive of awakening the thought of enlightenment for the benefit of sentient beings impartially, as I have done for a hundred thousand lifetimes in the past, fill the pure object of a precious golden alms bowl with barley and offer it to the special field for merit, the precious Jowo who is equal to the actual perfect Buddha, by the great force of that action with a pure field, motive, and object, the sufferings of human beings caused by hunger will be immediately relieved."

He decided to directly illustrate that truth, [193] and the idea arose to solicit gold for virtue in Latö Lho and Latö Jang in western Tsang, and in Rinpung.

First, he went to Mü Sanak. Among a great crowd that had gathered was a woman of good family who had several gold nuggets attached to her excellent jewelry and clothing.

"I have come to encourage the virtue of presenting an offering-object of gold in Lhasa," he declared. "Offer gold!"

The woman offered a small gold nugget with five-colored silk threads attached. The great adept remarked, "Patroness, wearing this much gold and turquoise, you should produce the courage to dare and give away a treasury of riches, and make a better offering than this."

"O great adept. You encourage virtue in China, Tibet, and Mongolia. Please use that little gold of mine as the basis for an auspicious connection, and create a golden alms bowl, a small cup, and a maṇḍala for the Jowo."

"It is a fine auspicious connection," he replied.

At that time the great adept announced, "An invitation is coming from someone who will make a huge offering."

The next day, Gyaltsen Pal of Tsanda, who had made the awful attack on the great adept at the entrance to the bridge at Tedung, but who then felt intense regret, came with an invitation in which he offered an apology.[762] The man from Tsanda offered thirty ounces of gold and a huge amount of other things. He made countless prostrations and begged, "Master, please prevent my rebirth in the three lower realms as the maturation of my awful attack upon your person." [194]

Since he had apologized with intense regret, the great adept replied, "Your recent sins are mostly purified. A slight maturation of them will come at the end of your life. Be happy, for you will take the path to liberation in the next life!"

Furthermore, the eighteen men who had made the attack at Tedung each offered a golden ear ornament beaten from four tenths of an ounce of gold.

~

Then the great adept traveled to the large court of Ngamring in Jang, a second Shambhala. The Kalkī Puṇḍarīka, Namgyal Drakpa Sangpo, presented a huge offering of fine turquoise, gold, and so forth.[763]

Then he went to Shelkar Gyantsé in upper Nyang. Tai Situ Sönam Pak offered many silver bowls and porcelain cups.[764]

Then he traveled to Rinpung, and Governor Norsangpa presented fine offerings and honors.[765]

~

The great adept then returned to Lhasa. The famine was extremely severe, and it took one tenth of an ounce of gold to get one-and-a-half loads of barley.[766] As a way to relieve this suffering, he decided to quickly make a golden alms bowl for the precious Jowo.[767] In front of the patroness Kalsang,[768] he piled up many goods from Latö in western Tsang, such as medicine, copper, and cloth.

"Please sell these for barley," he said, "and break the official seals on barley. The major merchants should do what they can."

She accepted his orders and the merchants made purchases, offering huge loads of barley. Then the great adept [195] went to the center of the market. He arranged the loads of barley behind him and to the right and the left. He put a large copper tub in front of him and told those in the market, "I will offer a golden alms bowl to the precious Jowo, and then make a prayer to relieve the famine. I will perform a dedication for those who offer gold. I will raise the price of gold for sellers and give barley in payment, so please sell!"

A huge number of people offered and sold gold. In particular, when the ten ounces of gold offered by the patroness Kalsang had been weighed, there was a total of 130 ounces of gold. He summoned the goldsmiths and told them, "Make an alms bowl from this."

The smiths replied, "If we mix silver with this huge amount of gold, it will be a gigantic alms bowl."

"In general, there is little point in faking virtue," he said. "In particular, it is necessary to have a pure object as the basis for making prayers for the benefit of the doctrine and sentient beings, so do not alloy it. Make it well, like refined gold!"

When refined, it was reduced by three ounces. They crafted an alms bowl from 127 ounces of gold, quickly completing a golden alms bowl that would hold thirteen measures.[769] When the monks were sent to beg for barley to fill the alms bowl, they were almost unable to fill it due to the famine, but because of the great number of monks, it was just filled.

He asked the people of Lhasa, "Will anyone offer a complete set of new monk's robes for me to make the prayer?"[770] [196]

Again, the patroness Kalsang offered a complete set, such as the Dharma robes dyed with saffron. She also made prayers and asked the great adept for a prayer. He spoke this:

> In the past, with pure altruistic intent,
> Sister Gangādevī[771] carefully offered flowers
> to the completely perfect Buddha
> and made prayers.
>
> Likewise, may the pure prayers made
> by Kalden Rinchen Sangmo of good family
> be fulfilled by the force of her offering
> of the Dharma robes with saffron sheen,
> which are the victory banner of liberation,
> and precious gold, turquoise, grain, and so forth.
>
> By your single-minded faith and devotion to me,
> and by the force of taking my words to be authentic,
> after your departure from here at death,
> may you become the foremost of my retinue
> in the pure land of Uḍḍiyāna.

The great adept wore on his body the saffron victory banner, the robes of all the conquerors of the three times, and, holding the golden alms bowl filled with barley in both hands, made this prayer before the precious Jowo:

O compassionate Conqueror,
to definitely liberate infinite living beings,
you awakened the sublime thought
of unexcelled enlightenment
and completed the two assemblies.

Gaze with love upon the living beings
of this degenerate age who lack a protector,
and to definitely protect these embodied beings
who are tortured by the miserable sufferings
of hunger and thirst,
cause a rain of all possessions,
attractive and necessary,
such as jewels, food, wealth,
grain, and bedding, [197]
to fall on the Land of Snows on Jambudvīpa!

May harm from the four elements,
such as untimely winds, fires, droughts, and rains,
come to an end,
and may harvests and so forth of nutritious grains
and fruits ripen and flourish as in the perfect aeon!

By the force of making this vast prayer,
deeply inspired by the power of love and compassion,
may the aeon of disease, weapons, and famine
come to an end,
and may we have long life, freedom from illness,
and happiness!

By the compassion of the conquerors
and their spiritual children,
and the power of the infallible truth
of actions and results,
may the doctrine of the conquerors

spread and flourish,
and may all living beings
quickly reach unexcelled enlightenment!

From the force of making the prayer, he freed all living beings from the sufferings of thirst and hunger. At that time, several individuals with the karma saw noble Avalokiteśvara cause a rain of grain to fall from the sky onto the land of Tibet.

During that period, about seven thousand people had arrived on the great pilgrimage from Sakya.[772] Because of the total economic failure, even though possessions had been sold at a loss, the residents and foreigners had all been tormented by hunger and thirst. As an auspicious connection to make it easier to get food, the great adept had an announcement made: "Tomorrow the Iron-Bridge Man will host a ritual feast for those on the great pilgrimage."

The great adept took a leather bag full of roasted barley flour that he had kneaded into dough, five lumps of butter, and a bunch of garlic [198] and went at sunrise to where those on the great pilgrimage were.

"There's no need to worry that there won't be enough," he said. "Distribute an iron-bowl-full of dough, a piece of butter, and a bunch of garlic to each of the seven thousand foreigners and five thousand residents."

It was distributed as he said and the leftovers were heaped in the center of the Lhasa market. All the people and dogs of Lhasa were liberated from the sufferings of hunger. Then he created an auspicious connection for famine not to occur in Lhasa and for those on the great pilgrimage to get provisions easily.

When he taught much Dharma in the market—such as the recitation of *maṇis*, and the three texts of the *Litany of the Names of Mañjuśrī*, the *Condensed Verses on the Perfection of Wisdom*, and the *Prayer of Good Conduct*—those with pure karma saw the body of the great adept in various forms, such as the precious Jowo, the lords of the three spiritual families, and Tārā.[773]

That year, Governor Drakwang of Neu Dzong offered a complete set of brocades [for the Jowo] and the patroness Kalsang offered her necklaces.[774] Using those as the basic material, the great adept offered a butterlamp, the vessel of which was made of sixty-three ounces of gold and inlaid with four fine pieces of turquoise, and made prayers for the darkness of the ignorance of all sentient beings to be cleared away.

Then the great adept emanated a body in each of the three places of Guru Lhakhang, Layak in Lho,[775] and Drodingma, which are in Drok Megyu, and benefited living beings. At the foot of [the mountain of] the local spirit Kulahari, he visited the handprints of the Teacher of Uḍḍiyāna that had been left in the stone and water at the center of Drultso Pemaling, which is one of the four famous great lakes.[776] He prophesied that although there were not dedicated meditators always living in this holy place now, [199] a meditation center would appear in the future.

From the side of a rock mountain that was like a heart-shaped sacrificial cake, he extracted *A Jewel-Heap of Oral Instructions*[777] from a treasure trove.

He then stayed for three days at Sekhar Gutok. One night he met Marpa Lotsāwa, who bestowed the initiation of Mahāmāyā and the explanation of the tantra.[778] Saying, "I have passed it to the owner of the Dharma," Marpa departed into the sky.

Then the great adept traveled to Mön Bumtang.[779] He left a footprint in a boulder on the far side of the river from the village of Sipal. When he stayed for thirteen days in a temple of Mön in the south where the Great Teacher of Uḍḍiyāna had left a bodyprint in a rock, the many people who came to circumambulate that sacred place saw him as the [Uḍḍiyāna] Guru himself and offered prayers.

During that time, three men from Bumtang and one from Central Tibet went to trade at Sapuk. As they were traveling on the glacier, one man fell into a crevasse in the ice. When his three companions looked, his cry rang out from about ten stories below. The man thought, "I'm certainly going to die." With intense longing he thought, "Adept of Iron Bridges, please be aware of me in this life, the next, and the intermediate state!"

The man fell asleep for a while and dreamed that the great adept extended a bolt of cloth from the peak of the mountain. When the man grabbed it, he arrived at the peak of the mountain. He woke up and had actually arrived on the surface of the glacier. When he went down to Sapuk he met his three companions carrying many ropes and leading several people. [200] "Who pulled you out from the deep bottom of the glacial crevasse?" they cried.

When he explained about his prayer and the dream, his three companions exclaimed, "Such compassion is incredible!"

~

The great adept walked from Bumtang Deshi up to Mön Gurulung. He arrived at Kharchu in Lhodrak. An emanation stayed in each of the three places of Chakpurchen, Dungi Shalyé, and the rock cave of Palgyi Samyé.[780] He spoke in prophecy: "In the future, masters will make war at Kharchu."

Then he traveled through eastern Lhodrak and arrived at Darmagang in upper Nyal. He told his retinue, "An Avalokiteśvara appeared on the bone of my foot when I took birth as a dog. It's in this temple. Should we visit it?"

The retinue asked, "What caused the image of a deity to appear on a dog? What fatal circumstance caused the death of the dog? How did the naturally arisen relic come to this temple?"

"The cause of the image's appearance was that I never parted from the thought of enlightenment. Even with the body of a female dog, I kept the vows of renewal and purification[781] unbroken. The fatal circumstance was that when the dog's owner, Kunga Kyi, finished milking a cow and was in the company of a close friend, the dog lapped up the milk. The owner became angry and threw a stone that broke her ribs and caused her death. When children saw the miracle of a rainbow touching the dog's corpse, they repeatedly brought the bone of a foot into the assembly hall. This foot gets thrown out, but comes back in. They don't know what it is."

When the abbot washed it, the great adept showed the retinue a footbone that sparkled like a heap of jewels, with the eleven-faced Avalokiteśvara, [201] the four-armed Avalokiteśvara, Tārā, naturally arisen syllables, and so forth. They became vigilant in regard to actions and results.

The great adept remarked, "Although I didn't become angry at that time, the owner of the milk was reborn in hell because of her hatred. But when I appeared in front of her in the sky and spoke the name of noble Avalokiteśvara, she was reborn in the pleasant realms."

~

The great adept then went to the stūpa of Serché in lower Nyal.[782] He was sitting with his cloak pulled over his head when Yönten Nyingpo, who was a scholar of the ten fundamental subjects,[783] and six disciples arrived to circumambulate the stūpa. They unwrapped the cloak that was pulled over his head and said, "Since you haven't studied, you don't know what is prescribed and what is prohibited in the monastic code. For the cultivation of meditation you must stay in an isolated place. It is a great fault to wear a cloak and trick people around the country in order to get food. This cloak is not the clothing prescribed by the Buddha. Explain the need to wear this!"[784]

They were very abusive, but the great adept remained patient without his mind wavering at all. However, they were accumulating the karma of rejecting the Dharma with their wrong views and contempt for all types of renunciant yogins, so he sang this song as a way to dispell that.

Listen, geshé, teacher and disciples!

A fake wearing a cloak,
I went for scholastic studies and examinations
with faith and diligence.

I severed outer doubts through learning,
and reached a decisive conclusion
about external appearances.

I went to hermitages for renunciation
and practice. [202]

Through meditation,
I was freed from inner bondage.

I have no terror of the three lower realms.

I've never traveled around the country for food.

The reason I travel around the country
is to trick people toward virtue[785]
and guide the six types of living beings
onto the path of liberation.

I'll explain the need to wear a cloak.

This cloak worn on my body
is smooth and nice—
conceptual elaborations have been eliminated.

This joining of the inside and outside as one
is the realization of the nonduality
of saṃsāra and nirvāṇa.

This white and red striped
pattern on the cloak
is the acquisition of the four styles
of enlightened action.[786]

This decoration with two iron clasps
is the union of method and wisdom.

This piece held together with thread
is the three realms brought under control.

This three-piece collar
is the spontaneous three bodies
of enlightenment.

This complete physical outfit
is a sign of having taken control
of how things appear to myself.

My clothes transcend human calculation.

Take that as an explanation of my cloak!

His words caused the teacher and disciples to become extremely respectful. They prostrated, lifted his feet onto their heads, and said, "Master, you are an adept. We apologize and confess our wrong views. Now we request a Dharma connection."

He spoke this:

If whatever happens is acceptable,
you'll be happy in anything you do.

If the mind stays where it's put,
it's all right for you to move about.

If your mind has turned to Dharma,
even dying is easy.

If you realize mind is unborn,
there is nothing to die.[787]

Make that your Dharma connection!

At his words, an uncontrived faith arose in the minds of the teacher of the ten fundamental subjects and his disciples. "We pray to the master [203] cloaked in the dharmakāya reality body," they said, and left.

~

Then the great adept traveled to the forest monastery of Jarpo, the venerable lord Rechungpa's meditation place. Performing the rite of accomplishment and offerings to Amitāyus, he attained self-control over his lifespan.[788]

He then went to Karpo Dönden, the stūpa of Loro.[789] He gave the vows for ritual fasting to many people who gathered. At that time, he had in his hand a fine white conch shell. One person said, "Let me handle the conch shell," and stole it. The conch shell clearly trumpeted by itself. Unable to conceal it no matter what he did to hide it, he returned the conch to the great adept.

From there he gradually traveled into Central Tibet and arrived at the rock cave of Drakyang Dzongshel.[790] When he gave the initiations and ritual permissions of the Dharma protectors to many people, many of the requesters of the ritual permissions, initiations, and reading transmissions saw the Six-armed Protector actually standing to the right of the great adept, Pañjaranātha to the left, the Four-armed Protector and Lekden behind him, and Vaiśravaṇa with the eight horsemen in front of him.[791]

~

Then, except for eighty-six loads of iron, the two hundred loads of iron that had been forged and packaged into bundles of fifteen links at Paro in Bhutan for transportation to glorious Chuwori were used without consideration by the people of Gongkar[792] to make swords, spears, farming tools, and so forth. It was a great obstacle to the virtuous work, but without impairing his disposition as a great bodhisattva, the great adept did not do anything such as sue them, call on the Dharma protectors, and so forth.

The great adept then decided to definitely construct an iron bridge for the benefit of the doctrine and sentient beings in general, [204] and for people who visited the precious Jowo in particular. He sent off the monks to encourage virtues such as searching for iron, making charcoal, digging stone, manufacturing iron links, and seeking out supplies.

On the first day of the first month of the Earth Male Horse Year [1438],[793] the great adept made a vow from his residence on glorious Chuwori, declaring, "Until the iron bridge is built, I will not pass through this door, no matter what damage is caused from above by lightning, from below by lakes, and from in between by men and the eight tribes."

During that period, he displayed many acts of clairvoyance and magical ability. While making the twenty-ninth-day offering of sacrificial cakes, he realized that the alloted lifespan of a Jonangpa Dharma practitioner[794] who had studied at the lotus-feet of the Iron-Bridge Man for more than a year was coming to an end. He asked the many people gathered before him, "Is anyone capable of going to a distant place?"

The Jonangpa said, "I could go if I had a pair of boots."

"You won't need boots. There is a great goal to achieve," he replied, and made prayers.

He gave the initiation of Opening the Door to the Sky[795] to the people gathered there. When struck by the visualization, on the first of the three *phaṭ* that were spoken, the Jonangpa's body and consciousness separated, and everyone gathered there saw white light about the size of a goose egg eject from the crown of his head and rise into the sky. At that time, when his body was cremated, very marvelous signs appeared, such as a rain of flowers and a lattice of rainbows.

~

The bridge abutment had collapsed three times. People said it was impossible to build the iron bridge. The monks were lazy. [205] In particular, most of the monks such as [Lama] Lotsāwa and so forth gathered and talked.[796]

"This work of ours never ends," they said. "He is a fine master, but he doesn't teach Dharma. This isn't virtuous work on the image of a deity and so forth. The food of this life doesn't just come from whatever happens. We don't know where we will go in the next life. Perhaps it would be better if we went around the country and visited the three representations[797] instead of working like this."

Some said, "Let's go request Dharma from whichever masters are best."

Some said, "Let's roam around dangerous places in the mountain ranges and practice Severance."

Some said, "Let's return home, and subdue our enemies and protect our friends."

The great adept knew about this with his clairvoyance and said, "Gather all the monks and craftsmen!"

When they had gathered in front of his dwelling, an elaborate ritual feast was arranged and he bestowed the instructions and reading transmission for *Taking Happiness and Suffering as the Path.*[798] Then he said this:

> You who are gathered here,
> listen respectfully without distraction.
>
> As a support, the human body
> with the freedoms and endowments[799]
> is difficult to obtain.
>
> As a path, the Buddhist doctrine
> is rarely met.
>
> As for karma, you can only do
> virtuous acts right now.
>
> Worldly actions are endless.
> More must be done
> than you've done already.

If the foe of hatred has not been subdued,
it's impossible to withstand the enemy.

If you don't know
that all beings are your parents,
you'll be uncertain who is enemy or friend.

If without the fruit of generosity,
you may want prosperity,
but it won't happen.[800]

If you don't understand
the fundamental nature of phenomena,
what use is wishful thinking?

What confidence do you have
of no regrets even at death?

Look into your mind! [206]

When creating benefit and happiness
for yourself and others,
depression and laziness are obstacles.

I will carefully explain
the instructions that clear away obstacles,
so keep them in mind!

In the palace of the immutable
universal ground,
the Mahābodhi image
of the dharmakāya reality body
is astonishing and incomparable.[801]
Offer it the gifts of body, speech, and mind.

In the village of the five senses
are the illusory minstrels
of the sensory objects.

They have various shows to watch.
Watch them without distraction!

On the mountain of the illusory body
of four elements
is the monastery of uncontrived mind.
It's the sublime place where
bliss and lucidity arise.
Be single-minded in that place of practice!

In the hermitage where
unawareness has been dispelled
dwells the master of reflexive
primordial awareness.
None are better than that master.
Ask him for Dharma and instructions.

The zombies of the eight worldly concerns
stalk through the charnel ground
of confusing thoughts.
This inescapable, terrifying place
is the spot to practice equal taste.[802]

In this faultless vajra body
reside the twenty-four great sacred places
and the assemblies of spiritual heroes
and ḍākinīs.[803]
Offer them a ritual feast.

In general, if you don't know
the way to practice Dharma,
whatever you do
will be a cause of bondage.

You may go around the country,
but so does a beggar.

You may be a skillful speaker,
but so is a singer.[804]

You may live in the mountains,
but so does a wild animal.

You may live in a cave,
but so does a marmot.

It's crucial to recognize
your very essence,
and to be expert in rejection
and acceptance concerning cause and result.

If you aren't energetic
in positive actions now
while you've gained self-control, [207]
you'll regret it when reborn
in the three lower realms,
but won't be able to do anything about it.

Without virtuous karma of your own,
you animals in human form who make
others have doubts—the time has come
to take heed!

By virtuous acts without belief,
disdainfully crushing the hopes of others,
and religious hypocrisy
that discards moral discipline,
you can't achieve even your own goals.

An aimless madman,
I've made prayers
for a hundred thousand lifetimes.

I accept the teachings of the Buddha
to be authentic.

I apply body, speech, and mind
to virtuous activity.

I could die now and have no regrets.

I trick people in the direction of virtue.

I work impartially for the benefit of living beings.

I pray to the triad of master,
chosen deity, and demons and obstructing spirits
as one and indivisible.[805]

If you want to follow me,
throw the pretensions of this life away,
and rely on just whatever
food and clothing appear.

Submit your body and mind
to virtuous activity
for the benefit of all sentient beings.

Recite the essential six-syllable mantra!

Meditate constantly on impermanence and death!

Think carefully about the evils of saṃsāra!

Trust in the precious Three Jewels!

If you act like this,
the great goal will be achieved.

At these words, all became filled with faith and diligent in the virtuous work. Without accumulating wealth, they went directly wherever the great adept sent them in India and Tibet, saying, "I will give up this life and offer my body, speech, and mind," and so forth. [208]

The great adept sent Tsangpa Chökyi Gyaltsen to Nyal in Ja to search for paper.[806] He sent Yarlungpa Chödrak Palsang to the great adept's birthplace of Rinchen Ding to commission a copy of the Translated Treatises.[807]

While the other monks were diligently at work on the iron bridge, the Shiga Neupa ruler and his subjects had launched a coracle ferry on the Kyichu River and many people had died because of harm from Kharnak.[808] Later, when unable to launch the coracle ferry, they appealed to the great adept to launch it. So he decided to build one large ferry at Drak Lhadong[809] and one at glorious Chuwori.

He told Kharnak, "You harmed many coracle ferries before, and other people are unable to launch one. For me to build the large ferries, you will cut down the trees you live in yourself!"

Led by the great tree trunk where Kharnak lived, many trees fell over by themselves. The monks saw that the pathways of people and cattle were blocked, and told the great adept, "No one else is able to touch them. Would it be best for us to throw them in the river?"

"A fine auspicious connection," he replied. "Trees, get down here!"

The monks threw the trees into the Kyichu River and they arrived at glorious Chuwori. The great adept instructed the monks in using that [great] tree trunk for the keels of two fine large ferries. Then he told them, "Tow one ferry up the Kyichu River and place it together with the ironclad boat at Drak Lhadong."

They towed it, but could not get it out of the inlet in front of Kharnak. When they told the great adept the situation, he issued this edict. [209]

Homage to Lokeśvara

This is from Tangtong Gyalpo to the nyen demon Kharnak

> You have brought harm to coracle ferries in the past. You have taken the lives of many sentient beings and are holding a ferry there. This is not right. I will punish you later. As soon as this letter reaches you, bring the ferry yourself and get to Drak Lhadong! It won't go well if you resist!

That night the large ferry was delivered to Drak Lhadong and tied to a big boulder. Then the great adept declared, "Nepa governor and subjects, whatever coracle ferries you launch on the Kyichu River will not be harmed, so do as much benefit for living beings as you can in all the great

67. Crossing the Tsangpo River in a coracle.

gathering places! Especially, do not impose tolls on people who are visiting the precious Jowo. I guarantee no harm will come from Kharnak."

Then, as instructed by the great adept himself, the monks and major disciples, with a great gathering of energy, also urged everyone throughout the country to virtuously donate toward the links for the double iron chains. After completing the preparations for pulling up the iron bridge, and also completing the building of the bridge pier, they asked, "Now, how should the bridge be pulled up?"

The great adept sent the monks out to urge people toward virtue in Se Chushul, Gongkar, Nyukla, and so forth with the message, "It will purify your sins, so come to pull up the bridge!"

Many hundreds of people gathered and attached ropes to the ends of the iron chains. They pulled for three days, but when the ropes repeatedly broke and the people fell down, they said, "This mountainous heap of iron chains [210] can't be pulled up by human beings," and everyone dispersed.[810]

On the evening of the ninth day of the second month of the Wood Male Mouse Year [1444], the monks and craftsmen gathered in front of the great adept's residence and said, "The people pulling up the iron bridge were unable to pull it up for three days and have dispersed. Now, how will we, master and disciples, pull up the iron bridge by ourselves?"

The great adept gave these orders, "We, master and disciples, together with the craftsmen, must hold an elaborate ritual feast tonight, with offerings and sacrificial cakes for the masters, chosen deities, ḍākinīs, and Dharma protectors. Stay right here without breaking ranks until the sun rises over the top of the mountain tomorrow. This is for an auspicious connection."

Then he dedicated sacrificial cakes to the masters, chosen deities, ḍākinīs, Dharma protectors, and the eight tribes of gods and demons. He blessed a ritual feast, and while they were enjoying the feast, the monks and craftsmen repeatedly heard the clanging of iron. It was so intimidating that they could not even go defecate or urinate.

In dreams and experiential visions that night, the monks with good channels and essential constituents saw the great adept sitting in his residence while one [emanated] body went on top of the bridge abutment and gave orders to the eight tribes of the gods and demons of apparent existence. The next day, when the monks broke ranks and looked, on the morning of the tenth day the iron bridge was freely standing.[811]

During six years, one month, and ten days, the iron bridge and two large ferries had been constructed. Within a period of twelve years, from the first month of the Water Ox Year [1433], when the great adept left people to uphold the place, [211] until the tenth day of the second month of the Wood Male Mouse Year [1444],[812] the work was completed on representations of enlightened body, speech, and mind, such as the temple of glorious Chuwori with its contents, the great stūpa, and countless volumes of the Words of the Conqueror and the treatises of commentary on their intention, everything translated in the glacial land of Tibet. Then he completed an extensive consecration for its stable duration.[813]

At that time, a white man who had a hood of snake heads and was riding a white horse placed the palms of his hands together, kneeled on the ground, and said, "Compassionate adept, I have come to invite you for the benefit of sentient beings. If you build a great stūpa on top of the mountain of Tashi Dung with the aim of happiness for Jambudvīpa, I will offer my life essence and accomplish whatever you say."

"Where is your palace?" the great adept asked. "To what race do you belong?"

"My palace with walls of blazing jewels is in Lake Namtso Chukmo.[814] I am of the race of lords, the foremost of the eight great nāga races. By all means, please come now."

He invited an emanation of the great adept and at the same time said, "In the center of the terrifying lake that is like a ground of sapphire, we nāgas offer you this palace that is like a white conch shell with a clockwise spiral. If you build an Auspicious Stūpa of Many Doors here, the merit of the glacial land of Tibet will gather here."

The great adept knew that if he founded a monastic establishment there, [212] he would become the priest of the emperor of China and Mongolia and that his family line and monks would become peerless in power and riches. However, because it would be harmful to the offering lamps of Lhasa and not be a geomantic focal-point that would benefit the glacial land in general, he did not accept.

~

When the great adept was released from his vow of retreat,[815] more people than could fit inside came from Se Chushul, Nyukla, and so forth to request blessings and make offerings. He said, "Less benefit will come to living beings if a toll is taken for the ironclad ferry. You who are gathered here should offer an arable field."

But no one offered. So he gave the order, "No stable continuity will occur if the bridge and ferry have no caretaker, so use an iron bowl and take from each person a toll of two cupped handfuls [of grain]."[816]

Lhawang Paljor of Gongkar felt intense regret for having carelessly used up 1,860 links of iron.[817] He offered prostrations, placed the great adept's feet upon his head, and begged, "Please don't let me be reborn in the lower realms as the maturation of the terrible, bad karma I have accumulated."

He made large offerings. As an apologetic gift, he offered lands from which to take provisions for five meditators on glorious Chuwori for as long as the Buddhist doctrine remains in Lhasa.

~

The great adept constructed the iron bridge of Tölung.[818] He traveled to Nālendra and met Rongtön Sheja Kunrik.[819] The great adept said, "Dharma Lord Rongpo, what is in the fold of my robe?"

The Dharma lord replied, "Thirty lumps of rock sugar that you intend to give me."

Then Rongtön held up a cloth bundle [213] in his hands and asked, "What is in this?"

The great adept replied, "A complete roll of pale yellow cloth and some tea that you intend to give me."

They both spoke with unimpeded clairvoyance.

~

Then the great adept made prayers before the shrines at Ratreng.[820] Many people made various offerings in front of the temple. When he gave the *Kadam Volumes*[821] as a Dharma connection for those who were gathered there, a great rain of flowers fell. Most of the assembly saw the great adept as Avalokiteśvara.

When he went on the outer circumambulation path, he heard the *Prayer of Good Conduct* ringing out in Sanskrit in the midst of the juniper trees. When he looked, he beheld Atiśa teaching Dharma in a high juniper tree, Dromtön and Kutön with folded hands in two slightly lower ones, and countless ḍākinīs in the branches listening to Dharma.[822]

~

The great adept then traveled to Taklung.[823] Many dedicated meditators made offerings and requested Dharma. He told the life stories of the Kagyü masters and taught techniques for the removal of impediments and the enhancement of Mahāmudrā. Furthermore, he told the many assembled lay persons and clergy, "Here in Tibet I am doing some powerful virtuous work at geomantic focal-points to suppress the four elements. Everyone should each present a bold offering."

When one man playfully offered the crossbar and key to the main gate, the great adept said, "A fine auspicious connection. The gate to an inexhaustible treasury is opened." [214]

When the great adept gave the vows for ritual fasting the next day, Geshé Drakpa Pal saw him as the thousand-armed thousand-eyed Avalokiteśvara.

~

Then, as the great adept traveled on the road to Drigung,[824] some robbers talked: "The great adept has gold, because many people made offerings."

They circled around and came to seize him. He approached while reciting the *śāsana* mantra, but not as the Adept of Iron Bridges. When they

68. Four-armed Mahākāla.

saw him as a grimacing black man holding a curved knife, sword, lance, and trident in his four hands, and surrounded by a retinue of black men, the robbers fell down unconscious.[825]

He then arrived at Drigung. Walking on the outer circumambulation path, he met the Dharma lord of Drigung with his disciples, who said,

"Since you are known as an indisputable adept, I need a Dharma connection and an auspicious connection for my family line."[826]

"It is very important that everyone be open-minded and trust in the rare and precious Three Jewels," he replied. "In the future, disaster will come from being carried away by divisive opinions."[827]

He observed the tenth day there. Three practitioners saw the great adept as Drigung Jikten Gönpo.[828] One saw him as the Great Teacher of Uḍḍiyāna. One from Gomo Chöding saw him as Hayagrīva with three faces and six arms. He gave a Dharma connection to the Dharma lord of Drigung, who made boundless offerings of gold and so forth.

~

Then, as the great adept traveled along the road, three young women appeared and offered a relic of the Buddha blazing with light, seven pieces of turquoise in the shape of jewels, and also many other kinds of precious substances. [215]

"Lord of the three realms," they said, "in order to increase the merit of living beings, if you make images of the conquerors and their spiritual children from these precious substances, with relics for their hearts, vast benefit will occur."

Thinking, "These aren't ordinary women. I should seek their help for the virtuous work," he said, "I haven't seen images of the buddhas created from turquoise, conch shell, and so forth anywhere in India and Tibet before. How should they be made? These precious substances are probably not quite sufficient. Will you help?"

"We will also accomplish any activities you need," they replied. "There is no previous tradition in India and Tibet for crafting images of the conquerors and their spiritual children from turquoise, coral, amber, conch shell, and so forth. But from the force of your prayers, the precious substances will be obtained without the need of effort. The images will also appear in a naturally arisen way and bring benefit to living beings. By all means, please make them."

He then took the many offerings of precious substances such as gold, turquoise, conch shell, and lapis lazuli, and clothing, silk, grain, and so forth that he had received when making disciples in Kyishö, Penyul, and so forth, and traveled to Lhasa.

When he collected offerings in the market, the people offered about two measures[829] of fine turquoise. Especially, Lady Kalsang offered four large

69. Drigung Monastery.

gold reliquaries adorned with extremely fine turquoise inlay. Furthermore, he completely filled a copper tub with the heap of precious substances that had come from his encouragement of virtue. This he offered into the hands of the precious Jowo and [216] requested a prophecy: "Which of these three will benefit the doctrine and sentient beings: to construct images from these substances, to present an offering object to the Jowo, or to give food to the beggars?"

The prophecy was to build images. The great adept sat on top of a dark stone maṇḍala. When he prayed to the masters and chosen deities, the chosen deity Vajrayoginī, apparent yet without self-nature, manifested at the break of dawn in front of the image of the precious Jowo. "If you construct images," she said, "please first construct one of the sixth [buddha]

Vajradhara,[830] the lord of all the tantras. Make the inside of white silver and the outside of old turquoise. Construct one of him first, with accurate proportions and eighteen inches tall."

The Jowo spoke in prophecy: "After the completion of a Vajradhara from precious turquoise, by also creating many images from other precious substances that cannot be smelted, the doctrine that is the source of benefit and happiness will long endure, and happiness and joy will impartially come to sentient beings."

Then the great adept told the patroness Kalsang, "I will construct various images from these precious substances, so send a message to whatever craftsmen you have."

About fifty craftsmen had gathered before noon the next day. The great adept said, "You will please fashion images from these precious substances."

The craftsmen conferred and then replied, "We have never heard it said that images of deities crafted from turquoise exist anywhere in India or Tibet, and have never laid eyes on any. So how can we know the technique? Please don't show off the wealth of turquoise and many jewels that you have."[831]

The great adept [217] slept on the verandah, and at dawn a woman came and said, "The sculptors already know ornaments for men and women, such as lotuses, utpala flowers, and crossed vajras. And they know images. So please give them emphatic orders tomorrow. We will also carry out your activities."

The next day the craftsmen gathered before him. "You know the crossed vajra, jewels, and so forth, for men and women's ornaments," he told them. "Insisting that you don't know images is unacceptable. First make a finely proportioned image of Vajradhara from this white silver!"

When they had finished crafting the framework of the Vajradhara from white silver, the great adept himself instructed them in cutting, grinding, and arranging the old turquoise with white and red hues. An eighteen-inch turquoise Vajradhara with proper proportions that was inspiring on sight was quickly finished as though it were naturally arisen.

Then they constructed a Medicine Buddha, an Amoghasiddhi, and a venerable Tārā created from turquoise; seven large and small images of Avalokiteśvara created from conch shell; images of the buddhas Amitābha and Amitāyus created from coral; images of the ḍākinīs of the five families from coral, lapis lazuli, conch shell, amber, and turquoise; an image of Vajrapāṇi created from silver and one from lapis lazuli; and a golden image of Mañjuśrī in the Gar style,[832] using the large gold reliquaries of the patroness Kalsang as the basis.

For the inner contents of those images, the great adept used as their hearts the relic of the Buddha about the size of a lark's egg that had been offered to him by the ḍākinīs, [218] and those that had multiplied from it. He filled the images with bones and relics of great noble śrāvakas; hair, fingernails, and toenails of many learned and realized masters of India and Tibet; and boundless blessed substances from great sacred places. The bottoms of the images were beautified with crossed vajras. After the image work was completely finished, when he cast flowers for the consecration, miraculous signs caused by many sons and daughters of the gods, such as a rain of flowers, the spreading of the sweet aroma of incense, and the playing of the pleasant sound of music, were perceived through the senses of all who were gathered there.

Then the great adept told the crowd, "An image of noble Avalokiteśvara, who is even more loving than all the conquerors toward beings in snowy Tibet, must be constructed from precious substances. Is there a donor of precious substances?"

A person from the area of Dam in Kham offered a huge load of conch shells.[833] The great adept summoned the sculptors and instructed them, "Make a finely proportioned noble Avalokiteśvara from these conch shells."

With the handiwork of five sculptors it was quickly finished. When the great adept performed the consecration, miraculous signs were savored by the ears and eyes of everyone, such as five rays of light shining from the heart of the Fivefold Naturally Arisen Jowo[834] and dissolving into the image of the Noble One, a rain of flowers falling from a pavilion of five-colored rainbows in the sky, and the sound of cymbals that was pleasant to the ears. Several disciples with pure karma actually beheld the great adept [219] as noble Avalokiteśvara.

His retinue asked, "What were the causes and conditions for this to happen?"

The great adept replied, "Seven hundred and thirty lifetimes before this life, I was born in the brahmin caste in a great city in Kashmir.[835] I became dissatisfied with saṃsāra, which appears although it does not exist, and with a firm attitude of renunciation I became the fully ordained monk Padmākara. On the wall of a naturally arisen rock cave known as Karita there is a naturally arisen image of the Noble One. Until the age of eighty, I was supported there by patrons with yogurt, milk, butter, and so forth from a water buffalo, and I propitiated and meditated on the Noble One by means of the rite of ritual fasting. Reciting the mantra of pure awareness, I beheld the face of the Noble One with eleven heads, a thousand arms, and a thousand eyes, and was blessed. He prophesied, 'Son of good family, you will display inconceivable emanations of enlightened body, speech, and mind. During the age when fivefold degeneracy is rampant, you will deliver infinite living beings from the sea of saṃsāra by means of various methods, such as constructing ferries, boats, and stable iron bridges.'

"Through the blessings of imploring the Noble One, and the force of my prayers, the people who brought food to the cave of Karita became these craftsmen who have constructed the image of the Noble One. The water buffalo that was milked to provide me with the three white foods is now this person from Kham who offered the conch shells. The sentient beings such as insects and flies that heard the sound of the *dhāraṇī* from me at that time [220] are these disciples of mine now. Karma is very powerful and prayer is dependable in the end, so it is important to make prayers."

11: Five-Peaked Mount Wutai

Deciding to travel from Lhasa to Dokham by way of Kongpo, the great adept went on the circuit of the great sacred place of Tsari. He took the "authentic skull-cup"[836] in his hands and declared, "One no different from this will come to my monastery of Tsagong Palgyi Nesar."

Thus he made this prophecy of the placement of the skull-cup [made from the cranium] of the venerable lady Chökyi Drönmé at Tsagong.[837]

Then the great adept was invited by a treasure-owner. From a treasure trove in the Tsari Serchen Cave, he withdrew the *Bright Lamp* that prophesied himself, and *A Method for Accomplishment of Kṣetrapāla*.[838]

~

The great adept traveled to the Golden Temple of Buchu.[839] He sat for five days before the Noble One with Eleven Faces, and gave the practice of ritual fasting to those gathered there. A prophecy came from the mouth of the Jowo: "You are a holy man who has awakened the thought of enlightenment for the sake of others in many lifetimes. At the gathering place where there are thirteen palaces of Yama,[840] known as Gyala Badong, the Great Teacher of Uḍḍiyāna concealed the deed to the life essence of all yama spirits in a treasure trove that has still not deteriorated. If it does deteriorate, great people will be possessed by demons and warfare will occur in Central Tibet and Tsang. Especially, in the future the vital essence of the earth even in this hidden land will deteriorate due to contaminating turmoil. And extreme misery will occur because the four elements will rise up as enemies. If you construct a stūpa above Badong Dunpa as a method to avert this, it will bring benefit and happiness. So build it quickly!" [221]

Then he tamed beings in Kongpo, throughout upper and lower Chabkar, Chabnak, and so forth. One patron offered a large turquoise. Furthermore, huge offerings of about three measures of fine turquoise, and tea, cloth, silk, grain, and so forth were made. Especially, from the force of the great Iron-Bridge Man's prayers, many different deposits of iron emerged in all the regions of Kongpo, so that boundless offerings of iron occurred.

He took these and traveled to Tsagong Nesar. He told the people of Drak, "To manufacture iron links, I need iron, charcoal, and laborers with provisions."

Many different individual offerings and promises were made. He established factories for forging links at eight smitheries. The lord, the great adept, knew with clairvoyance that Drakpa the blacksmith's life was finished and that he would agree to give up this life. He went repeatedly to the smitheries and asked, "Will anyone give up this life?"

Drakpa the blacksmith replied, "I will give it up if you can promise my rebirth as the son of a rich man from Central Tibet."

"Well, you should assume the vajra position and sit with an undistracted mind!"

The great adept sat on the blacksmith's mat and performed the visualization for transference of consciousness three times. On the first, the body of the blacksmith shuddered. The second time, he stopped breathing. The third time, his body and pure awareness separated. When the great adept made prayers, the blacksmith was reborn as the son of a rich man in Yarlung who clearly remembered his past life.

During that time, [222] the great adept worked in the smitheries pounding with a hammer and so forth while praying to noble Avalokiteśvara:

Homage to you, Mahākaruṇika,
who compassionately loves
countless living beings,
who has assumed the role
of a mighty spiritual son of the conquerors
on the tenth spiritual level,
and who shows the path
of liberation to all embodied beings.

If absolutely all the sufferings
of the lower realms are removed
by remembering just your name,
why, O compassionate one,
would you not specially

see a person who single-mindedly
offers prayers?

Sublime deity,
I pray that you quickly
protect living beings who are
experiencing inescapable suffering,
bound by the tight iron chains
of subject and object
in the horrible dungeon
of the terrifying three worlds.[841]

Oṃ maṇi padme hūṃ

After offering these prayers, he traveled to Kongpo Gyala. A Dharma throne was built in the shape of three stacked tetrahedrons on top of a rock shaped like a tetrahedron. For twenty-one days he rested evenly in the meditative concentration known as "overcoming perversion," with his body naked, his spine held straight, his legs in the vajra position, one hand pointing and one resting in his lap, and his eyes in a fierce wide stare.

During that period he saw many curses that three renunciants from Central Tibet and Tsang had placed at Dongkha. If Dharma were performed properly at this sacred place, the practice would reach perfection, but malevolent people of the degenerate age were achieving the lower realms. The great adept built a Kūṭāgāra Stūpa, so that if there were legitimate cause, curses would be effective, but if lies were used against truth, placing curses would not be effective. [223]

When he performed the consecration, music and the pleasant aroma of incense arose. He looked in the sky and saw Brahmā and Indra surrounded by many sons and daughters of the gods scattering flowers. At that moment a yogin with a tiger-skin skirt instantly appeared. His hair was bound upon his head and he was adorned with flowers. He held in his hands a human thighbone and a small skull-drum and was surrounded by a retinue of beautiful, ferocious women. The yogin said this:[842]

In the palace of the light
of apparent existence,
you've been a true buddha forever.

Confusing appearances
and thoughts are forever pure.

The nonconceptual primordial awareness
of enlightenment
and the dharmakāya reality body
are clear of the obscuring veil
of conceptual marks.

The sambhogakāya enjoyment body
is free of conceptual awareness.

The nirmāṇakāya emanated body
tames living beings
and adorns Jambudvīpa.

Obstacles are naturally liberated
and the four māras vanquished.[843]

To make our meeting meaningful,
I, the adept,
and you, the yogin,
should hold a ritual feast today.

When the yogin raised the human thighbone and blew it, from out of space a figure of Mahottara Heruka[844] about the size of a mustard seed appeared, with twenty-one heads, forty-two arms and hand implements, and endowed with the nine dance moods. Again, when the yogin with the tiger-skin skirt lowered the skull-drum toward the earth and rattled it strongly three times, a large glistening corpse appeared in front of him. Again, when he stared directly at the women of his retinue, the women cleaned, purified, and blessed the corpse, and chopped it into pieces. [224] Using the lotus-round gesture of the hands, they served the heart and entrails of the corpse to Mahottara Heruka, the divine assembly of chosen deities, the yogin with the tiger-skin skirt, and the great adept.

When they had finished enjoying the feast, the yogin said, "I am the Indian adept Hūṃkara.[845] Since I am no different from the Buddha, you have beheld the face of a buddha, which accomplishes great benefit. The

70. **Mahottara Heruka.**

emanated wrathful assembly of yogins and yoginīs are also indivisible from me. By enjoying this ritual feast you will remember many lifetimes."

The wrathful beings dissolved into the teacher with the tiger-skin skirt. The yogin himself also faded away like a rainbow. The awakening of the thought of enlightenment and the prayers made by the great adept for a hundred thousand lifetimes appeared unobscured in the mirror of his reflexive primordial awareness. Especially, he told many stories of his birth as King Drakpa Öser, five lifetimes before this life in which he benefited living beings here in Tibet during the age when fivefold degeneracy is rampant.[846]

Then he asked his attendants, "Is anyone a practitioner of Severance?"

"Lotsāwa and a half-blind nun practice Severance," they responded.[847]

When it was night, he told the two of them, "Go!"

Lotsāwa said, "The environment is a celestial palace and the inhabiting sentient beings have the nature of gods and goddesses. There is nothing to sever."

He did not want to go. The nun went.

The next day the great adept commented, "Half of Tibet will see me as an actual buddha. Half will see me as a demon. This is because no more than one practitioner of Severance came from among this many people, and even that one had but one eye."[848] [225]

~

The great adept then traveled to the region of Dokham. He walked through Gangdruk,[849] Shödruk, Rongdruk, Shongdruk, Chudruk, Tildruk and so forth in Dokham. He built iron bridges on the rivers Dzachu, Drichu, Nyakchu, and so forth, and brought into alignment the auspicious connections for constructing representations of enlightened body, speech, and mind in Salmogang and Litang.[850]

He traveled to Ling.[851] "Show me the spirit-turquoise of Lhalung Palgyi Dorjé that is known as Flat Blue Sky,[852] which is here and repels Mongol armies," he said.

"This turquoise is a jewel," he was told, "so it is not placed in human hands. But it can be shown."

When it was shown through a window, he remarked, "Now they won't place it in my hands. But in the future they will say they offer the spirit-turquoise of Flat Blue Sky to me, and it will arrive at glorious Riwoché."

~

By the gate to a large town in Minyak, the great adept leaned his back against a wooden house and rested evenly in the meditative concentration of infinite fire. From another area, he was seen as a blazing bonfire and the cry rang out, "A wooden house has caught fire! Quick, bring water!"

Many people gathered and said, "It hasn't caught fire. The yogin is meditating on the vital wind of fire." [226]

Everyone left.

The next day, he saw with primordial awareness that sentient beings were experiencing the sufferings of a minor hell inside a large boulder about twice the size of a yak-hair tent behind the monastery of Dechen in Minyak Ga. When he sat on top of the boulder for twenty-one days in meditation to purify the remainder of their karma, the great boulder split into three pieces. Inside was a snake about the size of a wooden yoke, with many thousands of thumb-sized frogs clinging to its body with their mouths and four claws.

He showed it to everyone gathered there and said, "Look at these people who ate and gave the food of rituals for the dead without having faith and compassion themselves! Don't crave the food of the dead!"

When the great adept urinated over the snake and all the frogs, the creatures instantly disappeared.

~

The great adept traveled toward Dartsedo,[853] but just as he was about to arrive he dismounted from his mule, assumed the sevenfold posture of Vairocana, and sat for a moment without speaking. When his meditation was finished, the monks asked, "Why did you dismount and sit down just as we were about to arrive?"

He replied, "I escorted my elder brother, Lopön Paltsul in Rinchen Ding, on his trip to the land of the next life. Let's go now."

He arrived in Dartsedo. Ten men of the same clan in that region had joined together and were killing one man. The great adept said, "If an equal number of men fight, the difference in their courage can be known. It doesn't take courage for ten men to kill one."

When he saved the man's life, they said, "Tibetan renunciant, [227] your idea to save a criminal who can't take care of himself is a mistake."

They attacked the great adept and that man with their swords, but he made the man disappear. The great adept sat in midair. When he pointed down at them, the ten men helplessly dropped the weapons from their hands.

From faith in the magical ability of the great adept, the people of Dartsedo said, "This region of ours is at the border of Tibet and China. It is a gathering place for wealth and valuables and a meeting place for all the powerful and the meek people. We have great merit that an adept such as this has come to this place, where compassionate people work for the benefit of living beings."

Inconceivable offerings of hybrid yak-cows, clothing, silk, horses, mules, and so forth occurred.

The people of Dartsedo said, "We need you to create an auspicious connection for earthquakes not to come."

71. Five-Peaked Mount Wutai.

"A geomantic focal-point is necessary here," he replied.

At a place with special geographical features he performed the ground preparation ceremony and gave instructions for the construction of a Stūpa of Enlightenment.[854]

∾

Then the great adept left the monks, men, women, horses, and mules at Dartsedo and traveled into China.[855] When he arrived at the Five-Peaked Mount Wutai,[856] he met many meditators living in that sacred place. From among them, the fully ordained monk Behodharma spoke: "Yogin, you are from Tibet, the Land of Snows. This sacred place is an isolated mountain surrounded by rivers. Many vicious carnivores and so forth will cause obstacles to your body and life. On a road so difficult to travel, it is amazing that you have arrived here alone without companions. What area are you from? By what name are you called? [228] What type of masters have you served? What type of Dharma do you know? What meditation practices have you done? For what reason have you come to this sacred place?"

The great adept replied:

Listen, fortunate meditators gathered here!
By the force of your previous prayers
and accumulated merit,
you have the complete freedoms
and endowments and have taken ordination.

Energetic in the excellent Dharma
and resorting to seclusion,
your ascetic practice is amazing.

Listen with your ears
to what this man has to say!

I'm a Tibetan, the Iron-Bridge Man.

For many hundreds of thousands of lifetimes,
I've prayed for the benefit of sentient beings.

I've done what was to be done
for the Buddhist doctrine.

With constant devotion,
I serve five hundred perfect masters
on the crown of my head.

I understand the intentions
of the conquerors without error.

The darkness of ignorance
and unawareness has cleared.

The chosen deities even give me prophecies.

Refining the vital winds of consciousness,[857]
I gained self-control of the four elements.

I've completely integrated
the four means of attraction.[858]

I instantly arrive at sacred places
that are difficult to reach.

I work impartially for the sake
of living beings.

I came to this sacred place
for the benefit of sentient beings.

I have explanations such as this
about how this mountain is not isolated,
but connected.[859]

Glacial Mount Kailash,
the source of four rivers,[860]
is a mountain like a crystal stūpa,
a sacred place where many arhats live,
a gathering spot for spiritual heroes and ḍākinīs.

The mountain range extending from it
is known as glorious Chuwori.

It has inconceivable qualities.

Learned and realized masters
continually appear at that sacred place.

The ḍākinīs remove obstacles.

Experiential realization
expands like the waxing moon. [229]

Deposits of various
precious substances are there.

There are a hundred types of herbs,
and medicinal waters.

No types of earth and stone are absent.

Just the sight of it is delightful.

From there, the range arrives at Tsari.

In lower Kongpo, its mountain range
is called Gyala Tsering.

This mountain known as Drangsong Sinpori[861]
is called Püri in the region of Central Tibet.

To the right is glorious Samyé.[862]
To the left is the Lhasa Dharmacakra.

Following its mountain range,
I arrived at Gyala Tsedum
and Shinjé Dongkha in lower Kongpo.

Continuing from there
through Salmögang[863] in Dokham,
I reached this famous Five-Peaked
Mount Wutai.

Books and scriptures are important,
but to take up the practice is crucial.

The meditators were overjoyed at his words and said, "Yogin, you must stay. We'll serve you ourselves."

The great Iron-Bridge Man replied, "I can't stay in one place. It's more beneficial for me to travel around the country."

"Well, we need a Dharma connection."

When they arranged a ritual feast and offered whatever gifts they had, he gave the reading transmission of the *Litany of the Names of Mañjuśrī*[864] and a direct introduction to Mahāmudrā that benefited their minds.

Then five [forms of] noble Mañjuśrī with different colors and hand implements, whom the great adept saw to be the essence of the five types of primordial awareness, spoke this prophecy: "To tame savage Tibet,

[230] you must gradually construct geomantic focal-points to suppress the four elements."[865]

He also taught the *Saṃdhinirmocana Sūtra* and the *Kūṭāgāra Sūtra.*[866]

~

Then the great adept traveled to the Chinese Palace. He sat on a flat stone at the base of a large tree in front of the main outer gate. The emperor[867] came out from the palace with many of his retinue. All the people rose and were prostrating and offering their respects to the emperor. An officer of the law came before the great adept and demanded, "Prostrate and offer respect to the emperor!"

He glared at the emperor and his retinue and spoke this:

By the force of practicing
a little generosity in a former life,
you were born on the throne of China,
but the leader of many people
is a cause of suffering.

You sinful kings will quickly be fuel for hell.

The wealth collected from your subjects
is the nature of future retribution.

This attractive, beautiful palace
will be discarded,
and you will leave friendless and alone.

You are arrogant in your greatness,
but still a sentient being.

I'm alone, but I'm not your subject.

I'm a king—prostrate to me!

A minister that could translate said, "You're alone. How could you be a king of this world? If you are a king in harmony with Dharma, how do you subdue enemies and protect friends?"

He responded with this:

I'm alone—the dharmakāya reality body. [231]

I rule the kingdom of Dharma like this.

In the palace of naturally arisen spontaneity,
I'm the king of five bodies of enlightenment,
with five types of primordial awareness.[868]

Those queens of naturally arisen
primordial awareness embrace my body,
never apart for even an instant.

My son, that young child
of pure awareness,
is the play of the naturally dawning
dharmakāya reality body.

My provincial rulers,
the four styles of enlightened action,[869]
work for the benefit of living beings
in whatever way will tame them.

My ministers,
the four immeasurables,[870]
negotiate agreeably without grasping
at lucidity or emptiness.

My governors,
the prayers between meditation sessions,
lead the work of dredging
the pit of saṃsāra.

The wealth deities, ḍākinīs,
and protectors of Dharma
are the lay officials
constantly surrounding me.

The food of the four sessions
of yoga guards the narrow entrance
of laziness and distraction.

The taxpaying serfs of the four pledges[871]
greet and accompany the compulsory
labor of virtuous work.

With wisdom realizing the nature of space,
and without mistaking rejection and acceptance
concerning dependent arising,
I dispatch the enforcers
of the ripened results of actions
among the citizens of everything knowable.

Concerning what is permitted
and prohibited in the Dharma
of the Greater and Lesser Vehicles,
I always beat the drum of the law
of the four summations of Dharma[872]
in a way suitable for my own
and others' mindstreams.

I constantly act in a cordial way
that connects me with close friends,
the ten virtues that bring happiness.

The troops of my army,
the antidote of alertness,
take up the weapons of love
and compassion, and, [232]
on the battlefield of suffering in saṃsāra,
defeat the enemy,
the five poisons that rob one's happiness.

Therefore, I am a Dharma king.

At these words, the emperor and his retinue left without saying anything. The great adept remarked, "Not much of a positive or negative karma connection was made with the emperor and his retinue, but in the future he will honor even my name, and offerings will be delivered. That is the difference between the early and later connection of prayers."[873]

Then he went to the Dadu Palace. He gave the reading transmission of the *Litany of the Names of Mañjuśrī* to about ten thousand people.[874] There were great offerings and honors.

The great adept then returned to Dartsedo. The construction of the Stūpa of Enlightenment was finished, and he performed the consecration. He freed the people of Dartsedo from fear of earthquakes. The Dartsedo people offered many gifts of gold, silver, clothing, silk, and so forth. A Minyak man offered a horse with a harelip, together with a saddle. The great adept took it for his mount and gave the order, "Whoever mounts this horse and encourages virtue should be honored the same as me!"

Three thieves from Shiribum in Minyak had stolen many hybrid yak-cows and a huge amount of valuables. The three thieves were discovered and seized. Their arms were bound with rope behind their backs and their legs were put in irons. They were in agony, being given food only once every three days. When no one came with wealth to ransom them or to intercede with others on their behalf, the three prisoners were certain that they would be killed.

During this terrifying time, they heard about the fame of the Adept of Iron Bridges, who saved lives through his magical abilities. The three thieves placed their mouths against the wall in the direction of Dartsedo, where the great adept was staying, [233] and pleaded, "Iron-Bridge Master, please save the lives of three men whose lives are at an end."

The great adept heard with his divine hearing. By his speech of Brahmā,[875] the three prisoners were blessed to hear, and heard him say, "Pray to me! Whatever attainments you desire will come."

When they intensely offered the prayer, "Master, great adept, see us with your compassion!" the bonds and irons on the three prisoners fell off by themselves. Even the doors of the prison and the castle opened by themselves. They went out as they pleased and fled. He had liberated them from the sufferings of death.

~

From Dartsedo, the older monks, men, and women, and the many Kham people who were following the great adept as attendants, loaded whatever loads could be carried on horses, mules, hybrid yak-cows, yaks, and so forth. For what could not be carried, they encouraged huge numbers of volunteers at stages along the way, and the great adept traveled to Kharling in the region of Minyak.

Many Minyak people were engaging in archery contests and various kinds of recreation, with an inconceivable consumption of tea and beer. They shouted, "The master, the Adept of Iron Bridges, has come!"

They offered a vast ritual feast and requested a Dharma connection. One offered a sword. Others each offered a token gift when requesting a dedication. The great adept performed dedications in which he recited the names of the deceased fathers, grandfathers, and great-grandfathers of those who had requested the dedication.

Furthermore, to those gathered there he spoke with clairvoyance, perceiving the three times without obscuration: "Your paternal ancestors were called this, they had this kind of wealth, and in the future this kind of happiness and suffering and this kind of good and bad will come." [234]

When the people requested protection cords, he also knotted the sword in front of him into a vajra. They cried, "Since he ties swords into knots and speaks with unimpeded clairvoyance, he is an indisputable adept!"

There were boundless offerings of horses, mules, hybrid yak-cows, tea, cloth, silk, gold, silver, and so forth.

~

Then the great adept went to Amdar Shong and was given fine offerings and honors. He gave the entrustment of pure awareness for Avalokiteśvara in the market. He told the parents of three mute children in the rows of the initiation, "Bring your three sons here!"

When they arrived before him, he pointed the index finger of his left hand at the three mutes. With his right hand he threw leftovers from his meal at the three of them. The demon binding their speech fled far away. The three mutes were able to say, "The mountain at the root of our tongues, which seemed not to fit into our mouths, has been cleared away."

~

The great adept then stayed making prayers in the vast Minyak region, where there was continual fighting and, especially, many blood feuds. He gave a Dharma connection to many men and women who gathered. He said, "In this area of yours, the conflicts in general and, especially, the killings within the same clan, are harmful to the happiness and joy of the land of Tibet in general and Dokham in particular. Offer me your swords, and this area will have happiness and joy."

But no one offered.

Then he told a terrifying man, "Amdruk, offer me that polluted sword you have in your house."

"If I move it, the great demon of the sword will arise!" [235]

"That sword killed eighteen men of the same clan in a single day. It should not be left in this area. Scatter this barley and then bring it!"

He scattered the barley, took the sword, and offered it into the great adept's hands.

"It is a fine auspicious connection," the great adept declared. "The stream of conflicts and blood feuds in this area is broken."

He conveyed the men killed by that sword to Sukhāvatī. He performed a burnt offering ritual for the demon, who was reborn in the higher realms. He kept that polluted sword constantly on his person.

Furthermore, he worked for the benefit of living beings impartially in the Dokham region by means of constructing iron bridges, building representations of enlightened body, speech, and mind, and with infinite clairvoyance and magical abilities.

~

When the master and disciples traveled into the northern wilderness with the loads and a large number of bundles carried by volunteers, they arrived in a great empty valley without even Tibetan nomads. The monks said, "We probably won't find porters for the bundles."

"Porters for the bundles are coming. Everyone search!" the great adept ordered.

The monks thought, "Are some nomads coming?"

They looked far into the distance and saw many sentient beings gathered in rows. When they went closer, they saw many brown bears digging wild sweet potatoes. The monks quickly fled and arrived in the presence of the master.

"What is it?" he asked.

"Wondering whether there were some nomads, we looked," they replied. "But we met many brown bears. Here we'll be eaten by the bears, so it would be best to leave the valuables and flee."

"You each carry what valuables you can, and the pack animals will follow. I'll wait here [236] until the nomads come. The bundles will arrive."

"If we don't die, we can search for the valuables. By all means, you should come."

"Nothing will happen to me. We will be together in five days," he replied, and sent off the monks with the pack animals.

An inconceivable number of brown bears arrived before the great adept, offered various foods, and made circumambulations. He gave the remaining bundles to the bears and left.

When he arrived in advance of the monks, they asked, "You were coming after us. How did you arrive before us? Who transported the bundles?"

"I arrived yesterday," he replied. "The bears transported the bundles. It is foolish humans, who disregard actions and results, that are difficult to tame. It is easier to tame these animals and the gods and demons. It is very important to understand that these appearances are unreal."

~

Then the great adept traveled to the place known as Taklung Matang Kham Riwoché, where a Sangha of about a thousand were gathered.[876] Without dismounting from his horse, he circumambulated three times and went in to visit the offering chapel.

"It isn't right to ride a horse inside a monastery," they yelled, and many monks cast a great rain of stones at him, but no injury occurred to either man or horse. The Sangha became filled with faith and respectful, and invited him onto the Dharma throne of former great masters in the temple. He remained for seven days and taught much Dharma. They offered inconceivable gifts of sixty bricks of tea, forty horses and mules, ten hybrid yak-cows and yaks, clothing, silk, precious substances, and so forth. Many people arrived to go as his attendants.

At that time, the Kham man [237] Delek Pal felt undivided faith. With respectful posture, he joined his palms together and said this:

Spiritual father,
precious, authentic master,
Iron-Bridge Man whose name
is known everywhere,
emanated body of all the buddhas,
amazing person named by the ḍākinīs.

I've met many masters,
but never felt uncontrived faith before.

As I am meeting a master who is a buddha,
please give an instruction containing the key points.

He made a fine offering of nine bolts of cloth, nine rolls of silk, nine hybrid yak-cows, nine horses, nine mules, nine bricks of tea, and so forth.

With great intensity he said, "I have spent my life in the Dharma, but wander in saṃsāra without having severed the root of clinging to a self. I request a profound instruction with which to sever clinging to the five aggregates as a self,[877] realize the fundamental nature of the mind, and see the nature of the dharmakāya reality body."

The great adept spoke this oral instruction to the learned and venerable Delek Pal:

Listen, my son,
learned and venerable Delek Pal!

Obscured before
by the darkness of ignorance,
thoughts to practice Dharma
were mixed with the eight worldly concerns.

To achieve the aims of future lives,
trust in these thoughts of practice.

Completely drop the aims of this life!

Serenely release attachment
to the eight worldly concerns!

Totally part from fixation and vanity!

Chop off ties to those near and far!

Tear out the stake of existence,
clinging to a self!

Relax thoughts of hope and fear!

Cut the craving for both food and clothing! [238]

Don't be ambitious, be humble!

Willingly accept the sufferings
of renunciation!

Throw away desire, hatred, and rivalry!

Banish evil thoughts
of deception and deceit!

Leave greed and hypocrisy alone!

Strictly guard the three vows[878]
and the sacred commitments!

Dig out pride, conceit, and anger!

Even though abused by everyone,
cultivate patience!

Let ordinary enemies go!

Tame the hatred inside
your own mindstream!

Reject greedy thoughts of hoarding!

Rely on love and compassion
in your mindstream!

Establish this mind of yours
as a witness to all the Dharma
of the gods and the Dharma of men.[879]

If your aims are not achieved this time,
although hoped for later,
hope will be gone.

Relax in the genuine nature!

Cut away the ground or root of confusion!

Watch your own mind without distraction!

Hold fast with mindfulness
that never forgets!

If your very essence
isn't recognized,
you can apply this relentlessly,
but just remain afflicted.

If clear light isn't apprehended
during sleep,
you may have been introduced
to the nature of mind,
but it wasn't very beneficial.

If clear light isn't apprehended
during the intermediate state,
the torment and suffering is hideous.

If self-control of your own
mind isn't gained,

you can meditate for an aeon,
but you'll just get tired.

After one thought has ceased
and the next hasn't arisen—open space!

A lucid yet nonconceptual state,
an unsupported place
without ground or root,
this fresh awareness of the present
is your own mind,
the dharmakāya reality body
free from conceptual elaboration.

Everything that appears
is your own mind.

Your own mind
free from conceptual elaboration
is the dharmakāya reality body.

So thoughts
are the dynamic energy
of the dharmakāya reality body. [239]

Unceasing in appearance,
yet established as empty.

Whatever arises, whatever appears,
apprehend it with mindfulness!

Relax and let go!

If your very essence has been recognized,
repeatedly prolong that.

Uncontrived, undistracted,
rest in the natural state!

Free from coming and going,
and from arising, ceasing, and remaining—
this is Mahāmudrā.

To carry it on the path
without distraction is crucial.

Effortless ease is crucial.

Practice like that!

I circulate through the country
without destination.

A yogin free of attachment,
and the sun orbiting the four continents,[880]
both have no time to pause in leisure!

At those words, Geshé Delek Pal and many other spiritual friends upholding the traditions of explication and practice shed tears, prostrated, placed the great adept's feet upon their heads, and again offered boundless goods.

~

Then the great adept traveled to Tsagong Palgyi Nesar, the great sacred place in the eastern region of Kongpo.[881] Before his return from Dokham, the resident monks had prepared three hundred bundles with fifteen iron links in each bundle. The construction of a Stūpa of Great Enlightenment[882] to subdue Lo had been finished, and he performed the consecration. He established a meditation center at Menmogang.

He made the people agree and pledge to serve the meditation centers of Tsagong Nesar and Menmogang, saying, "I have appointed master Riksum Gönpo[883] to the monastic seat of Tsagong Nesar. [240] I have arranged to send someone to offer sacrificial cakes every year in front of the naturally arisen crystal stūpa at the border of Lo and Tibet. Without my advice, resident or visiting men and women must not take over land and assume authority. This kind of careful management is necessary. Follow the example of each person who is appointed at Tsagong Nesar by the

Iron-Bridge Man. If you offer service at this sacred place, happiness and joy will come to the eastern region of Kongpo in general and Gormo in the area of Drak in particular."

The hybrid yak-cows were loaded with the bundles of iron and so forth and the monks were sent on ahead. The great adept went to Waru Namtsel.[884] A master's residence had been built, and he gave instructions for the survey marking of a great stūpa and the construction of a temple. He appointed the master Tokden Nyakpo to maintain the place.

The great adept met the monks in Dakpo.[885] At terrifying places where the rivers smashed against the cliffs in Dakpo, he commanded, "Force the hybrid yak-cows, horses, and mules in without hesitation!"

When they were forced in the southern and northern rivers several times and no injuries or damage occurred, everyone knew it was proof his attainment.

12: A Geomantic Focal-Point to Suppress the Mongol Armies

The great adept and his disciples, with a huge encampment of horses, mules, hybrid yak-cows, yaks, and so forth arrived at the great bridge of Nedong in front of Mount Sodang Gongpori.[886] Many people of Nedong, Tsetang, and so forth gathered, and for seven days he gave whatever Dharma connections anyone wished. He decided to construct an iron bridge at the Nyago ferry landing, but when he urged acceptance from the crowds, the auspicious connections were not in alignment.

He met [241] the sovereign Drakpa Jungné and gave much Dharma and many initiations. Because the ruler Drakpa Gyaltsen had broken the promises he had offered, the great adept thought, "I don't know what the lifespans and power of the hereditary line of Nedong will be like."[887]

When the sovereign urgently requested an auspicious connection for long life and great power, he replied, "If an iron bridge were at this ferry landing of Nyago, it would be an auspicious connection of great benefit to living beings, and both Yarlung and Ön would always come under your rule. You should pull on one of the iron chains yourself."

"I cannot agree right now, but I will do what I can to be of service later."

"Will you offer this ferry landing at Nyago?"

"We will offer it," the people of Tsedang replied with one voice.

"If I launch a ferry at Gyerpaling, will you be helpful?"

The sovereign agreed to do so, and, to support the construction of the ferry, he offered Gyerpaling.

The great adept appointed a ferry keeper and said, "The kings of Tibet were the Ngaripa, but they have no power.[888] Then the lords of Tibet were the Sakyapa, but the same thing has happened.[889] The doctrine of the Pakmodrupa has spread. There will be happiness during the period in which Central Tibet and Tsang are kept under the rule of the Nedongpa.[890]

Offer a pregnant horse, enlarged with foal.[891] I will reply upon observing the length of that horse's lifespan and the size of the area traveled."

The great sovereign offered a mare with a full set of saddle and bridle. The great adept mounted the horse and observed how much of the area of Central Tibet and Tsang they traveled, but the mare died at the end of the Nedong bridge.

He sent a messenger, saying, "Now offer a horse!" [242]

The horse that was sent collapsed at Chasa.

"Send another horse!" he said. It collapsed at Ngamshö.

He prophesied the future: "The omens are not good for the lifespan of the great sovereign and for his subjects. I cannot benefit you greatly in this life, but in the next life you will be born as a great Dharma king in India, southwest of here, and be a patron of the precious doctrine who will honor a number of temples and many establishments of explication and practice. I will benefit you at that time."

The biography of Mahāpaṇḍita Vanaratna[892] says that when a messenger was sent to Nepal with a request for dedication prayers[893] at the passing away of the sovereign Drakpa Jungné, the mahāpaṇḍita replied with a letter saying, "The great sovereign[894] has a good rebirth in the next life. So don't be unhappy."[895]

Later, when Lochen Trukhangpa[896] went to visit the mahāpaṇḍita in Nepal, he asked in detail what had happened. The mahāpaṇḍita replied:

> "Near the Vajrāsana [of Bodhgayā], in the region known as Uruvāsa, in a town called Akṣasūra, he was born in the lineage of a Dharma king known as Caṅgala Rāja. His family line is the solar family line, his father's name is Lakṣmasena, and his own name is Rāgavaḥ. He has not taken ordination and has a great kingdom. He rules and performs great service for the doctrine."
>
> In all lifetimes, this excellent being did not let his promises expire, and so even sent a letter, together with a gift, [243] when that prince reached about four or five years of age.[897]

It seems miraculous that the statements of both the paṇḍita and the adept were in agreement.

Then the great adept practiced for several days at Samyé Chimpu.[898] He was blessed by lord Amitāyus, and held a ritual feast with the ḍākinīs.

He traveled to Lhasa and stayed before the Jowo during the day and on Chakpori Hill at night. He sent the monks to construct the iron bridges of Drigung Chökhor Gang and Shuna.

During that time, he realized that Lady Kalsang,[899] who had undivided faith in him, would soon die from a grave illness. As he was going to see about the lady's health, he met on the road the Nepa patron, master and servants, weeping and coming to offer a request for him to make divinations after the lady had died.[900]

"She hasn't died,[901] has she?" he asked.

He went to the lady's bedside and struck his hand-cymbals. The lady raised her head from the pillow and said, "Son, the Dharma lord has come. Bring a gift!"

The son placed a golden myrobalan plum in her hand. She offered it to the lord, saying, "Essence of the buddhas of the three times, it is kind of you to come here. When I was young, I fell under the power of sons, husband, and arrogance, and did not remember the excellent Dharma. After meeting you, O lord, O great adept, I used illusory food, wealth, and possessions for what is essential. [244] I engaged in spiritual practices of body and voice and investigated my mind, so that I am at least unafraid at death. Master, this is your kindness. Now the time of death has come. Please perform the transference of consciousness and make a great compassionate prayer for me to be born in the land of Uḍḍiyāna after this body is discarded."

The great adept made this prayer:

As soon as this illusory body
of faithful Kalden Rinchen Sangmo
has been discarded,
may she be magically born in an instant
in the paradise of Uḍḍiyāna,
where the ḍākinīs gather!

At that time, after being graced
by the Master of Uḍḍiyāna,

may she fully meditate
on the profound nature of phenomena
together with an assembly
of the ḍākinīs of primordial awareness,
and directly perceive the truth of reality!

When he made the prayer and performed the transference of consciousness, several of the Iron-Bridge Man's monks with good channels and essential constituents had experiential visions in which they actually saw the patroness Kalsang welcomed by an assembly of ḍākinīs and going into the presence of the Great Teacher of Uḍḍiyāna.

Then the Adept of Iron Bridges gave extensive advice to the Nepa patrons, father and sons,[902] to benefit them in this and future lives. Especially, he said, "If you do not perform rituals, you will have internal discord."

[The younger brother] responded, "Why do we need rituals for that? While your leaders, the Latö Jang rulers[903] in western Tsang, have internal discord, among we brothers, it is whatever elder brother says."

The elder brother said, "It is whatever he, the boy says, so nothing will happen to cause internal discord."

The great adept insisted, "If the Nepa patrons do not perform rituals, [245] great unhappiness will occur."

It was a prophecy of the future.[904]

~

Many Tselpa people such as Önpo Namgyal Sangpo came to request blessings from the great adept. The Lord of Iron Bridges asked, "Among you who have gathered here, will anyone give up this life?"

A hundred people such as the Tselpa man Önpo Namgyal Sangpo replied, "We will do whatever the Master of Iron Bridges says."

"Take this image of Avalokiteśvara and this horse with the harelip and go tame living beings in Dokham Gangsum.[905] Those of you who are leaders should be leaders and those who are servants should be servants. Stay harmonious among yourselves!"

When he was sending them off to tame living beings in Dokham, traders from Mön Paro offered a bearskin, complete with the four claws.

"Because the Dharma protectors will adhere to you," he said, "you will accomplish great benefit."

He gave the bear skin and a full leg of meat to the people and sent them off to build the stūpa of Salmogang and to construct iron bridges on the three rivers of the Dzachu, Drichu, and Nyakchu.[906]

⁓

The blessed Amoghasiddhi that had been created from turquoise[907] was installed on Chakpori Hill as the great adept's representative. The great adept gave orders that there would be no place for men, but only for women, to spend the night at this sacred site. He made Dharma regulations for the women practitioners: the tenth day was to be observed year round; the fasting rituals were to be observed on the eighth, fifteen, and thirtieth of the month; the unbroken recitation of *maṇis* was to be the continual practice; the recitation of one hundred million *maṇis* was to be done during the excellent time of the month of miracles; [246] and so forth.

⁓

The great adept traveled to glorious Chuwori and appointed three groups of five major disciples: the earlier, the later, and those in between. He gave them each a written edict, a link of iron, a banner of the Dharma protectors, and an image of the chosen deity Avalokiteśvara, and sent them off to collect offerings.[908]

He appointed Gyaltsen Sangpo, who was a scholar of the ten fundamental subjects, to the monastic seat and issued this edict:

> The scholar of the ten fundamental subjects will do what he can to support and finish the remaining work necessary on the partially completed virtuous projects at glorious Chuwori!
>
> There are representations of enlightened body, speech, and mind. Created from precious substances, there is Dīpaṃkara, the King of the Śākyas[909] in the nirmāṇakāya form beautified by the saffron victory banner, and the future conqueror Maitreya with inlaid ornaments of various jewels. There is a complete set of the immaculate Words of the Conqueror and the Translated Treatises of the paṇḍitas and adepts of the noble land [of India] that are commentaries on the intention of the Conqueror. The representation of enlightened mind is a stūpa ten armspans in length on each side above the lotus base. It is adorned with temples, and inside is an image of the chosen

deity Avalokiteśvara created from conch shell, which is eight handspans tall. And there is the ironclad ferry and so forth.

Furthermore, I have appointed Gyaltsen Sangpo, a scholar of the ten fundamental subjects, to be in charge of the images on Chakpori Hill, such as the golden Mañjuśrī in the Gar style and the silver Vajrapāṇi in the Gar style that are each eighteen inches tall; the Mahākaruṇika of conch shell; the buddha Vajradhara, the Medicine Buddha, and the Amoghasiddhi created from old turquoise; the ḍākinīs of the five families from gold, turquoise, lapis lazuli, amber, and conch shell; the large and small monastic establishments such as the temple and stūpa of Drakralkha, the large ferry and small house of Gyerpaling, the geomantic focal-point of Tonga; [247] and, furthermore, the numerous iron bridges and large ferries on the great rivers of sunlit Central Tibet.[910]

Therefore, if the monks I have appointed as keepers of the ironclad ferries and as managers of the monastic establishments and land would not go against my commands and the sacred commitments, they should not go against the words of the scholar of the ten fundamental subjects.[911]

⁓

Then he traveled to the large lake of Yamdrok, where he saw fishermen killing many fish and tearing out their entrails. He felt great compassion for the fish that were experiencing suffering and the fishermen who were accumulating the causes for unbearable suffering. When he offered prayers to noble Avalokiteśvara, by the compassion of the Noble One and the blessings of the great adept the feet of some fishermen became numb and their hands stiffened, some became depressed about their own sinful work, and some began to feel nauseous. The fishermen put aside the remainder of their sinful work and gathered together in one spot.

"During this momentary time when we have obtained human bodies, we have only accumulated sins," they said. "Birth in the lower realms in the next life will be terrifying. Better that we abandon sin and do virtue, as the master says."

The great adept spoke this oral instruction to further inspire the fishermen toward Dharma.

Listen, sinful fishermen!

No other sin is greater
than that of taking a life. [248]

Among the ten nonvirtues,
wrong view is the worst.

Renouncing sin and cultivating virtue
are called the actions of a clever person.

It is action that benefits you.

Fishermen, a person who has eyes
doesn't jump over an abyss!

If you want to be content in this life
and happy in the next,
keep in mind these words I say.

A home is Māra's dungeon.
Don't be so attached, leave it behind!

A spouse is saṃsāra's leash.
Don't be so lustful, meditate alone!

Children are upholders of a lineage of sins.
If you don't have the suffering of raising them,
you'll be happy.

Food and wealth are illusory temptations.
If you don't hoard,
body and mind become calm.

A renunciant goes around the country.
If he acts according to Dharma,
he'll accomplish a great goal.

In rags and tatters, he has no enemies.
If without shame and hypocrisy,
he'll be happy.

The illusory body is a bubble
of flesh and blood.
Use it for virtue while you have
the self-control.

Praise and blame are echoes in space.
Look at the essence of unreal appearances.[912]

Meditate that the world
of apparent existence is a celestial palace,
without impure mountains and rivers.

Meditate that sentient beings and creatures
are the chosen deity,
and that the ordinary six types
of living beings are deities.

Meditate that each and every
specific sound and voice
is the sound of mantra,
resonant yet empty.

I have nothing more profound
than that to say.

Confess today with cleansing remorse!

At those words, the fishermen became devoted and filled with faith. They offered fish traps and fish knives, and requested dedication prayers. Seven fishermen followed the great adept as attendants. Those who stayed in the area offered promises to not kill fish and to offer respect to the clergy.[913]

~

The great adept then went to Nyemo.[914] [249] An earth spirit, short but very stout, displayed various magical abilities, offered seven man-loads of ground azurite, and said, "This is my first offering toward the vast and lofty virtuous work you are doing on glorious Riwoché in Latö in western Tsang."

He made prostrations and circumambulations and disappeared.

~

Then the great adept gave the vows of ritual fasting to about a hundred people at Yakdé in Rong.[915] Three strict monks said, "You lay people are idiots. You may prostrate to that fake renunciant, but he has no Dharma to teach."

One person responded, "If the master Tangtong Gyalpo, famous in India and famous in Tibet, has no Dharma to teach, what master of India, Tibet, or Mongolia can we venerate?"

The great adept said, "You worldly people, respect all who enter the door of the doctrine! Especially, respect those who uphold the tradition of Mahāpaṇḍita Śākyaśrī!"[916]

An elder strict monk said, "Please give a versified Dharma connection to those gathered here, led by we four close friends."

He gave this:

Homage to Lokeśvara

If you fortunate men and women
gathered here sincerely want
to practice the excellent Dharma
while you've gained a precious human body
with the freedoms and endowments that are
difficult to find, as shown by example and cause,[917]
be energetic in learning, reflection, and meditation,
fortunate people!

Without wasting this unique find
of the freedoms and endowments
that are difficult to find later,

think about impermanence and death,
that everything composite
is like lightning and clouds, [250]
without even the slightest possibility of lasting,
fortunate people!

Close relatives, agreeable friends,
and so forth,
the tempting companions of this life,
are teachers who educate you
in the eight worldly concerns
and guides who lead you
into the three realms of saṃsāra.
Meditate alone, without companions,
fortunate people!

Built castles, accumulated wealth,
and so forth, these foods, valuables,
possessions, and things
are the roots for the growth
of the three poisonous afflictions
and are the weapons
that cut the vital artery of liberation.
So don't hoard wealth,
fortunate people!

Towns, monasteries, bustling places,
and so forth,
all these residences of careless behavior,
produce envy, desire, and hatred,
and are nooses that bind you
in the three realms of saṃsāra.
Resort to an isolated hermitage,
fortunate people!

Our kind parents
from beginningless time
are constantly burned by blazing hellfire
and tortured by the diseases

of intense suffering such as hunger,
thirst, murder, birth, old age,
sickness, and death.
Think about the sufferings of saṃsāra,
fortunate people!

The result of great, medium,
and small nonvirtuous actions
is birth in the three lower realms,
and the result of great, medium,
and small tainted virtue
is birth in the three pleasant realms.
So think about the infallibility of cause and result,
fortunate people!

The result from great, medium,
and small untainted actions [251]
is attainment of the three nirvāṇas,[918]
and after liberation from the sufferings
of the three realms of saṃsāra,
the final attainment of omniscient buddhahood.
So pay special attention to virtue,
fortunate people!

Because these sentient beings
wandering in saṃsāra
have acted for their own benefit
and accumulated bad karma
for themselves
through beginningless time,
they have fallen into saṃsāra
and experience suffering.
Awaken the sublime thought of enlightenment,
fortunate people!

This selfish desire of cherishing yourself
has put you in saṃsāra's chains
through beginningless time
and tortured you with the intense sufferings

of karma and the afflictions.
Release now the cherishing of self,
and cherish others,
fortunate people!

If someone else has injured you wrongly,
don't repay the injury in an angry way,
but know him to be a friend
for cultivating patience,
and repay injury in a polite way
with beneficial offerings, praise, and so forth,
fortunate people!

By constantly meditating
on both sending and taking,
with yourself taking the illness
and suffering of all sentient beings
who have been our kind parents,
sending your virtue and happiness
to your mother, and so forth,
constantly develop motive and application,
fortunate people![919]

To protect the six types of living beings
from the fears of saṃsāra, without
hoping for worldly gods to be protectors,
take refuge with respectful body, speech,
and mind in the infallible sources of refuge,
the precious Three Jewels, [252]
and enter under the protection of those Jewels,
fortunate people!

Any virtuous learning, reflection,
and meditation you do,
never do it for your own benefit,
but for all living beings to obtain
the bliss of liberation.
Realize that they appear but have no self-nature,

and awaken the two enlightenment minds,[920]
fortunate people!

These four continents and Mount Meru
adorned with the sun and moon;
the five sensory objects,
the seven jewels,[921] and so forth;
and your body, possessions,
and whatever basic virtues you have—
offer with faith, longing, and devotion
to the precious Three Jewels
for the sake of living beings,
fortunate people!

Before the abbot and the teacher
you promised to accept
the pratimokṣa and bodhisattva vows
and the root and branch
sacred commitments of secret mantra,
but you should confess with purifying remorse
infractions of the three vows[922]
due to the power of the afflictions,
fortunate people!

After meditating that your body
has become the clear form
of a chosen deity such as Saṃvara,
and after realizing through the constant
practice of the three carry-overs[923]
that whatever appears is the deity,
abandon ordinary thoughts,
fortunate people!

The clear form of the glorious master
who embodies all masters, chosen deities,
buddhas, bodhisattvas, and so forth
constantly dwells in the palace
of the cakra of great bliss

at the crown of your head.
Pray to him single-mindedly,
fortunate people!

Because the root from which all faults arise
is this [253] root of clinging to a self,
and because the "self"
is a totally imagined fiction
that is not established as real,
subdue the demon of clinging to a self,
fortunate people!

Whatever appearances arise as objects
to the six types of consciousness[924]
are the confusing appearances
of your own mind,
just like the appearance of objects in a dream.
Thus, after realizing that they appear
but are without self-nature,
quit clinging to their essence as real,
fortunate people!

Whatever appears is your own mind,
and the nature of mind is forever unborn,
so rest in just that state,
the groundless, rootless state of Mahāmudrā,
the path of Great Madhyamaka
beyond eternalism and nihilism,
fortunate people!

Whatever happiness and suffering,
benefit and harm,
and praise and blame occur,
they are the confusing apparitions
of your mind.
Therefore, after realizing
that they appear but are unreal,
and without clinging to them as real

and to be denied or affirmed,
rejected or accepted,
relate to whatever happens as a friend,
fortunate people!

The basic virtue that comes
from practicing in that way,
and whatever virtues you and others have,
you should dedicate
with the wisdom of threefold purity[925]
to the multitude of all sentient beings.
Understand in that way,
fortunate people!

If you haven't practiced these virtues
at this time when you understand
rejection and acceptance
concerning cause and result,
and if you fall into the bottomless, boundless,
fiery pit of saṃsāra for many aeons,
achieving benefit for both yourself
and others will be very difficult. [254]
Consider this well,
fortunate people!

If you have practiced these now,
after liberation from the sufferings
of the three realms of saṃsāra,
you will go to the isle of great bliss
and liberation, and,
finally reaching the citadel of the conquerors,
achieve benefit for both yourself and others,
fortunate people!

It is rare for another to teach you
words from the heart.
If you don't advise yourselves,
it will be difficult to gain a human body

with the freedoms and endowments later.
Therefore, advise yourselves right now
and take advantage of what you have gained,
all you fortunate people![926]

At those words, the strict monks and so forth gathered in that marketplace felt great faith and respect and offered prayers.

He traveled to Panam[927] in Tsang and left the hybrid yak-cows, horses, mules, and so forth there.

~

When the great adept rode through the main gate of Pal Khorlo Dechen[928] without dismounting from his horse, people complained: "It isn't right to ride a horse inside a monastery."

They attacked him with stones, but he was not at all injured. He dismounted from the horse in front of the temple and visited the Auspicious Stūpa of Many Doors. He consecrated it everywhere, inside and out, with the *Essence of Dependent Origination*.[929]

When he went to visit the temple, the steward pushed him away at the threshold and shut the doors.

The great adept spoke a prophecy of the future: "For me, it is a fine auspicious connection. But his own family line will be broken and some will have to roam from place to place."

Lord Rabtenpa[930] heard, [255] and said the great adept had to come to the palace.

"Since I have renounced thresholds, I won't come," he replied. But many people lifted up his body and he went to the Tsegyal.[931] Some offerings and honors were made.

"You must act as a patron for my virtuous work," the great adept said.

Lord Rabtenpa replied, "I have already finished my own temple, stūpa, and monastery," and gave an account of work still remaining to be done. The auspicious connections for a patron-priest relationship with the great adept were not in alignment.[932]

The great adept flew down from the Tsegyal [castle] to the meadow. He had the fine offerings by many people there delivered as offerings to the Jonang great adept Palden Lekpa[933] and his disciples at the Ganden Hermitage. This brought the auspicious connections into alignment for many offerings to be delivered later.

72. The monastic complex of Pal Khorlo Dechen, Gyantsé.

The great adept went to Tsechen and met Lord Dusi,[934] who said, "I need an auspicious connection for me to have a son and to bring Jé Bodong under my rule."

"A son will not come to Lady Kharkama," he replied. "A son will come to Lady Shaluma. Jé Bodong will soon come under your rule. Great changes will later occur."[935]

The great adept traveled to Chumik and gave many profound key points of Dharma to Sakya Dagchen Lodrö Wangchuk.[936] Ten thousand loads of barley were offered, and the great adept made dedications and prayers. He also gave much Dharma and many initiations and oral instructions to Delek Tashi,[937] the nephew of Tekchen Chöjé,[938] who came to Chung Chokar in Yeru Jang.

From Nartang the great adept went to Urgyen Dzong in Tanak.[939] When he arrived at the bank of the Tsangpo River, [256] a dark-red woman with bone ornaments and a dress of white clouds hemmed with five-colored rainbows invited him on a path of white silk across the surface of the

Tsangpo. He went to the meditation cave of Tsenden Bima[940] and held a ritual feast. When lamps were lit on the extra sacrificial cakes that were taken in the four directions, everyone gathered there saw them carried away by four nonhumans adorned with terrible ornaments.

At that moment, an eighteen-year old woman of Tanak who had jewelry and clothing valuable enough to provide a livelihood said this:

> O great adept, emanated body.
>
> I offer supplications
> to your emanated body.
>
> I wander in saṃsāra;
> look on me with compassion.
>
> Please cut these locks of hair
> from a woman who desires Dharma.
>
> This is not an expensive offering,
> but the faith of desire for Dharma has arisen.

When she offered a headdress with intermingled turquoise, coral, and pearls, the great adept spoke this:[941]

> Intelligent girl,
> your desire for Dharma is marvelous,
> but isn't this an angry threat
> to frustrate your parents,
> friends, relatives, and so forth?
>
> I never said there was no share
> of Dharma for disciples without offerings.
>
> With your lower birth
> in a common woman's body,[942]
> that momentary faith of desire
> for Dharma now arises,
> but may now fade away.

Just now you hastily offered
the token gift of a headdress,
but since attachment
has not receded from within,
I fear regret may later arise.

Although your hair is cut
and you enter the door of Dharma,
with little determination and courage, [257]
I fear the vows may be transgressed.

Although you've left your home behind,
you're not able to experience the equal taste
of the eight worldly concerns,
so there is danger that craving for wealth may arise.

There are many faults in a woman's body
that appear as impediments
to the practice of divine Dharma.

The independence of a woman,
and lifting a mountain onto your lap,
are both very difficult and of little point.

Think and examine
whether these three are true or false:
a woman's independence in Dharma,
a donkey catching up to a horse,
and relics appearing from a dog!

The self-sufficiency of a woman
is like a dragon landing on a plain.

I wonder if it's possible;
it would be marvelous!

When practicing
the divine Dharma from the heart,
strive to roam throughout the mountain ranges.

For friends, there are the eight tribes
of gods and demons.

Without distraction,
observe your own mind!

Buddha will be found in the mind.

Meditate on the master
constantly at the top of your head.

Blessings will fall like rain.

If you don't transgress
the master's word,
his mind and your mind
will blend together.

Meditate with disdain
for body and life!

The nature of confusion
will be utterly resolved.

Draw the thoughts
through a narrow swage![943]

The sun of the dharmakāya reality body
will dawn.

When the girl practiced the great adept's instructions, she became endowed with experiential realization and entered the path.

~

Then the great adept traveled to the Bön monastery of Darding. They said he was an emanation of Tsewang Rikzin. [258] All the teachers and disciples such as master Shenpa became deeply faithful and respectful.[944]

barley, materials for sacrificial cakes, and so forth. Using these as the basis, the work was begun on the first day of the month of miracles in the Fire Female Rabbit Year [1447], when the great adept was eighty-seven years old.[949] The iron bridge was completely finished within three months. He performed the consecration and did the ground preparation ceremonies and the survey markings for a stūpa.

He prophesied the accomplishing of vast works of virtue and left his nephew and spiritual son, Jampa Nyendrak, to carry the virtuous work to completion. He spoke this advice: "Quickly finish the stūpa to benefit the many people who die from weapons because of the widespread fighting here, where the rivers of Tsang make a triangle! Building it early will make a big difference, so be diligent! It is the decree of the Great Teacher of Uḍḍiyāna that from the blessings of this stūpa, people who are killed within the area from Tasur up to Jonang, and as far away as Sakya, will not be reborn in the lower realms."

When the Chözong patron invited him to the top of the fortress, he replied, "I won't come because I have renounced thresholds."[950]

He gave extensive Dharma and worldly advice, stood up, and went in the direction of the rear of the fortress. [260] The Chözong leader and servants thought, "Except for birds, there is no passage to the rear of the fortress. He is seeing whether or not the fortress is secure."

"We will await your return," they said.

He circled the fortress and returned to say, "The fortress of the Chözong patron is secure."

They were certain he had flown, and made some further offerings with great devotion.

~

From Chözong, the great adept went to visit Lekhawa Sherab Sangpo and made offerings of the five kinds of precious substances.[951] Lekhawa said, "In the three regions of Central Tibet, Tsang, and Kham, you are famed as an indisputable adept. You have completed vast virtuous work, which is amazing. If you would stay in one place now and please teach the guiding instructions of the profound path of the Vajrayoga[952] to the faithfully gathered monks, men, and women, many would benefit."

"I don't know the explanations of the creation and completion stages and the negation and affirmation of the philosophical tenets," he replied. "So the monks also, burdened with wood, iron, and stone work, are only a

"We request an auspicious connection for long life and great prosperity," they said.

He bestowed the initiation of the Destroyer of the Lord of Death.[945] He placed master Shenpa on the throne and made offerings of tea, clothing, and silk, thereby aligning the auspicious connections for an unceasing delivery of offerings by people from Kham.

~

At Tashi Tsé, the great adept met the horses, mules, and monks who had come from Panam.[946] Many people of Jé Bodong came to meet him, and he gave a detailed Dharma teaching about karma, the law of cause and effect.

"I will provide ink and paper," he said. "You people of Jé Bodong must provide the food and offerings for the scribes."

Many people agreed to be patrons. The scribes were gathered, wrote out the Dharma, and when two sets of the Translated Scriptures were finished, he performed the consecration. On a mountain with the shapes of the three poisonous afflictions—a bird, a snake, and a pig,[947] he established a stūpa containing the two sets of the Translated Scriptures as a geomantic focal-point.

He gave detailed directions: "If you honor the iron bridge and the sets of the Translated Scriptures no differently than when I am here, happiness and contentment will arise in snowy Tibet in general and, if linked by this iron bridge, for Jé Bodong in particular under the rule of the Dharma king of Yeru Jang.[948] If the iron is harmed and the benefit to living beings broken, there will be internal turmoil in Jé Bodong and short lives and changes among the aristocracy. Ruled by different leaders, you will have a great burden of military tax. So think about this. Everyone should be careful."

~

The great adept traveled to Yongru in upper Tsang. [259] He decided to build an iron bridge on the river where he had crossed before on the surface of the ice that was like an unrolled woolen cloth. He told the patrons of Chözong, Lhatsé, and so forth, "Compulsory labor and supplies will be necessary to build an iron bridge."

When he urged all the people toward virtue, many came to make offerings. Especially, the Lhatsé patron Wangdrak offered a hundred loads of sluggish bunch who don't know anything. Nevertheless, I think that those involved in the virtuous work will be born in the three pleasant realms in the next life. In any case, I will not break the master's word, so you please teach the profound path [of the Vajrayoga] to those striving for the citadel of sublime bliss."

Then he made farewell prostrations.

~

At Lhadong, the great adept offered gifts to the master Sönam Chokpa, such as a rosary of one hundred crystal beads as an auspicious connection for his longevity, and said, "The great anchorite master lived to be one hundred years old. [261] If you are also able to reach one hundred, disciples who follow will have long lives and the treasure teachings of the great upholder of pure awareness, Gökyi Demtruchen, will be regarded as reliable sources."[953]

~

Then the great adept traveled to Ngamring. This was during the period that he had renounced thresholds, except for those of temples and the residences of masters. So he met the great Kalkī Namgyal Draksang in front of the Great Maitreya of Ngamring.[954] From the Dharma king of Jang, ruler of heaven and earth, he requested a message with the official seal addressed to the three regions of Lho, Jang, and Ngari, stating, "When the people I have urged to virtue travel from place to place in the land, whatever loads they have that are chiefly religious offerings must be conveyed along the stages of the route."

With eyes of vast wisdom, the great Kalkī saw that because the great adept had gained control of the key points of auspicious connections, this would bring auspicious connections into alignment for the Kalkī to draw the three regions of Lho, Jang, and Ngari under his rule. When he offered the official seal to the great adept, that is exactly what later happened. This is direct proof of the incomparable qualities of this great ruler.

~

During that time, Mongolian armies had repeatedly raided Mangyul and Gugé, the gold prospectors of Yeru Jang, and victims among the Jang nomads. Frightened and terrified, everyone was saying, "Now the Mongols are coming to Tibet!"[955]

73. The great Kalkī Namgyal Draksang (1395–1475).

When the great adept had traveled to Cāmara Island,[956] the Teacher of Uḍḍiyāna, who knows the three times, had said, "Complete the restoration of a stūpa, [262] a geomantic focal-point at the border of Mongolia and Tibet, by the tenth day of the first month of summer in the Earth Dragon Year [1448]."

Realizing that the time had come, the great adept sat with his body immobile for eight months on top of the Dharma throne of Ngamring Bumtang. During that period, a huge crowd of the eight tribes [of gods and demons] came at night and a crowd of many people came during the day.

He asked them, "Will anyone give up this life for the benefit of sentient beings?"

Sangyé Sangmo, a noble nun from Jisur Puk, who was a mantra-born ḍākinī[957] blessed by the Great Teacher of Uḍḍiyāna, said, "If it benefits sentient beings, I will give up this life."

"A fine auspicious connection," he replied. However, to see how determined she was, he said, "In that case, jump into the lake over there!"

With no hesitation, she went to the shore of the lake.

He realized that she was determined and called her before him. To bless her so that she would be unaffected by obstacles, he gave her a skull-cup filled with beer and said, "You don't need to commit suicide. You must go to restore a stūpa made by Guru Padmasambhava as a geomantic focal-point to suppress the Mongol armies."[958]

"Alone, without companions and with no knowledge of the route to that distant place, how will I get to where the stūpa was built?"

"While you are rebuilding the stūpa, do not lead your companion there. Do it with your own body. A guide and a companion will come. On the return trip, a companion of similar birth will come."

That night, [263] the noble nun's relatives and friends tried but were unable to dissuade her. The great adept had said, "Come tomorrow morning," so she went.

He gave her a scroll, saying, "This is for protection. Wrap it in your blouse. If you open and look at this, you will die."

While he was giving her advice, a nomad from Böru named Düdül Samdrup asked him to consecrate a new painting of the Great Teacher of Uḍḍiyāna.

He did so and commented, "The auspicious connections have come into alignment naturally."

The great adept gave her that painting and some of his hair as auspicious substances that were to be the inner contents of the stūpa, and a white cloth with the fringe uncut, which was for a prayer flag.

"I will come myself for the consecration," he said.

As the sun rose, an emanated nomad arrived, carrying a bow and arrows and leading a hunting dog.

The great adept said, "You should be this nun's companion. The female dog will serve as a guide. By following the dog wherever she goes, you won't mistake the route. Load the dog with just a token load. Nomad, don't part with your bow and arrows! You should both take whatever roasted barley flour you can carry. The dog will not harm sentient beings until the roasted barley flour runs out. On the morning after the roasted barley flour runs out, the dog will kill a wild animal. Then for three days there will be an empty valley with no water, and you will have to carry water in the belly of the wild animal."

The two of them followed the dog, and when about seven months had passed, they came to a great plain where they did not know east from west, [264] and the swishing sound of the grass made them depressed. Sentient beings were very scarce, and they had to travel for three days without water. Then there was a forbidding mountain with a snowcapped peak to the southwest. At a place with scattered forest on the mountain slope, the dog went to sleep at about midday and stayed with no wish to leave.

The nomad was exhausted from hunger and thirst and said, "That man called 'great adept' has sent us into the endless north. We will probably die from starvation before we find the stūpa. If we killed this dog, there would be no one to catch wild animals. We would both die. If I died, the two of you wouldn't be able to kill wild animals and would probably die of starvation. Now, if I killed you, nun, both of us could eat your flesh. Killing some wild animals, we could do whatever we must to get home."

The noble nun thought, "It is better for me alone to die than for all three of us to die. Now the time has come to look at this protection the master gave me, saying that I would die if I looked at it."

When she looked, there were written directions inside, with a blessed *dhāraṇī* to be placed inside the stūpa. When she looked closely, she realized that they had arrived at a place near the stūpa, from which it was not far to water.

"Don't kill me today," the nun said. "You should kill some wild animal. I'll search for water. If I don't find it today, kill me and you can eat. We'll meet at this place tonight."

He went after wild animals. The nun looked at the scroll [265] and then searched for the stūpa. On a ridge jutting out from a great cliff on the east face of the mountain, she arrived in front of the stūpa. She made prostrations and circumambulations, collected rocks and water, and partially completed the restoration of the lotus-base. In the evening she returned, carrying water to where they were staying. The nomad had also arrived, carrying the meat of a sentient being he had killed.

[The next day] he said, "The two of us have collected meat and water. But we don't know where the stūpa is. Let's go back."

The nun replied, "We've probably arrived near the stūpa. This pass is the pass at the border of Mongolia and Tibet that was mentioned by the Dharma lord. I'll search for the stūpa today. You both go see whether you can find something to eat!"

The nomad left, leading the dog. The noble nun went to build the stūpa. The previous day, the noble nun had not finished more than just the restoration of the lotus-base of the stūpa, but during the night, the building of the lower foundation had been completed. Two-thirds of the podium[959] had also been built, and a marvelous tree with excellent fragrance and branches had been set up as the central pole. She wondered who had done it, but when she looked in all directions, there was no one, human or otherwise. To the central pole, she attached the blessed *dhāraṇī* and the substances for an auspicious connection that the lord, the great adept, had given her,

Again she gathered earth and stone, and finished most of the building. When she returned to their sleeping place, the nomad had also arrived, after killing a sentient being. [266]

[The next day] the nomad asked, "Did you find the stūpa? If you didn't find it, we had better go back."

"We've both come a great distance," she replied. "We would be ashamed if we returned without accomplishing our goal. Persistence is needed to accomplish a great goal. If I search today and don't find it, there is nothing to do but go back. You two rest. I'll search again today!"

That evening, she applied plaster to the stūpa and whitewashed the foundation. Whitewash had been prepared in a hole in the ground, so she whitewashed the upper levels and then went back.

The nomad asked, "Did you find the stūpa?"

"The stūpa is found," she replied. "Tomorrow the three of us will go to perform the consecration."

He did not think it was true. Early the next day, when they were preparing to go, the nomad said, "The dog isn't here. Where has she gone? This nomad will search for the dog."

"The dog hasn't gone anywhere," the nun replied. "She'll arrive later."

As they left, the sun rose on the morning of the tenth day of the first month of summer. The dog had arrived in front of the stūpa before them. They fastened the prayer flag on the central pole of the stūpa and arranged a small ritual feast with their remaining provisions.

When the nun offered single-minded prayers to Urgyen Tangtong Gyalpo, from high in the sky a vulture descended to the tip of the tree. There was an inconceivable rain of flowers, sounds of music, an aroma of incense, and so forth. She scattered barley given to her by the lord, the great adept, made prayers, and spoke auspicious words. [267] At that time, a joy like the attainment of the first spiritual level, and many varieties of meditative concentration, arose in the mindstream of the noble nun Sangyé Sangmo.

The nomad performed prostrations and circumambulations and made what prayers he knew. They slept in front of the stūpa that night. In an experiential vision at the break of dawn, the noble nun saw the great adept sitting in the center of a mass of light on top of the stūpa, teaching Dharma to a gathering of spiritual heroes and ḍākinīs, performing a ritual feast, and many sons and daughters of the gods presenting offerings. When she offered single-minded prayers, the great adept said, "Noble nun, if you have no selfish desire, in the next life you will become a powerful female who can travel through space in the land of Uḍḍiyāna. It is difficult to calculate the blessings of this stūpa. No one is able to realize the extent and benefits of this."

When she looked at the stūpa, she saw that it was created from various precious substances, was fascinating to gaze upon, and so vast that its size could not be estimated. She saw countless figures of buddhas, bodhisattvas, spiritual heroes, and ḍākinīs residing inside.

When they rose in the morning, she asked the nomad, "What kind of dreams did you have?"

"Because the stūpa has been finished," he replied, "my mind is content and I fell deep asleep during the middle of the night. In the last part of the night, I dreamed that this dog chased many sentient beings said to be the spirits of the Mongols. When I shot arrows, they all died. [268] It was said, 'Now the Mongols won't come to Tibet.'"

The written directions[960] said, "Many Mongolian things are at the peak of the Mongolian-Tibetan pass. Bring back some trophies."

The three of them went to the top of the pass. When they saw the land of Mongolia, the dog barked five times and the two of their bodies shivered each time. When they had taken Mongolian clothing, bows, and arrows, and were coming back, the three of them saw a person coming from far away. Wondering, "Is it a Mongol?" they watched. When they realized it was a Tibetan woman, they waited. When she reached them, they talked.

"When the Mongol armies came to Maryul,"[961] the woman said, "many men and women of Maryul were taken prisoner. I have been left in Mongolia until now. Today I was sent to collect wood. In a dream last night I was told, 'You should flee to this pass. Companions, Tibetan people, are coming. Escape at sunrise!' I wondered how it could be true, and came to the top of the pass to look. When I saw you, I was happy and came."

They came back with Tashi Sangmo of Maryul. From that evening, snow fell for many days and nights, down as far as the stūpa. The pass became a glacial mountain and the Mongol route was cut off.

On the return trip, they traveled with contented minds and plenty of food. On the first month of the Horse Year [1450], they arrived before the master at glorious Riwoché. When they offered the trophies and told the story of the trip and so forth, he replied, "I know more about the route than you. The trophies must be pressed under the Auspicious Stūpa of Many Doors.[962] [269] The Mongols will not come into Tibet until the stūpa at the Mongolian-Tibetan border has crumbled. It is excellent that you have made meaningful use of a human body."

• • •

When the Mongol hordes swept in,
malevolent, vicious,
and hungry for the kill,
keeping the custom of the demigods
who eat flesh,
but only flesh they kill themselves,
the people of Tibet were terrified.

With inconceivable wisdom,
love, and ability,
this great, accomplished lord
bound the hordes of Māra
immobile in their own place
by means of a geomantic focal-point
eulogized everywhere.

The barbarian incursions
had not covered the whole earth,
but I wonder,
from special love for the Land of Snows,
did Mañjughoṣa return quickly
as Raudra, the angry Cakravartī?[963]

• • •

13: The Auspicious Stūpa of Many Doors

While the noble nun had been sent to establish the geomantic focal-point for suppression of the Mongols, the great adept had remained at Bumtang in Jang Ngamring. During that time, the eight tribes of gods and demons all came before him and each offered their life essence, saying this: "You have given the name Glorious Riwoché to Dongshur Mountain up in Chung. You will do vast virtuous work there, such as the construction of representations of enlightened body, speech, and mind intended to be a geomantic focal-point for the suppression of the four elements. At that time, we will each offer the earth and stone from where we live. Furthermore, master, great adept, we agree to provide protection from obstacles and to create favorable conditions for those you have sent impartially throughout the country to inspire virtue, those doing virtuous work in their own places, and those delivering offerings." [270]

During that time, the masters and strict monks of the Ngamring Monastery came before him and said, "We who are gathered here request a prophecy of what will later happen here."

He replied, "Sangyé Sengé, a scholar of the ten fundamental subjects, will act as abbot of the monastery. The chant master Trom Yönpa will act as abbot of Gendun Gang. From among these young monks, eight will be fit for teaching and study."

He went to the stable of the Ngamring ruler and said, "If you rulers, father and son, will grant exemption from military tax and compulsory labor to the estates of my parents, the two estates that I have in Rinchen Ding in general,[964] and give tax-free earth, water, and straw for construction, I will begin the virtuous work on glorious Riwoché."

"The taxes that applied to your father and mother are lifted," they replied, "and we will offer the construction materials. By all means, you must begin the virtuous work."

"If I had artisans and volunteers," he said, "I could do the virtuous work."

They gave an official seal sending artisans and volunteers from the ten thousand households of the district until the virtuous works were completed. On the basis of that, he agreed to do the virtuous work.

~

The great adept traveled from Ngamring to the upper valley of Drolung. After making prostrations, offerings, and prayers at the residence of Choksang Lekpai Lodrö, he traveled to Shelkar in Lho.[965] Tai Situ Lhatsen Kyab,[966] with many chieftains and attendants, pitched several white and black tents at the end of the bridge and offered a fine ritual feast.

Tai Situ remarked, "It's said that no matter how much food the Adept of Iron Bridges consumes, he [271] will pass no excrement. Let's see whether it's true."

Many patrons surrounded the great adept and offered various kinds of food. When he did not move his body for a month and eighteen days, they believed that his excretions had ceased.[967]

"I have been considering whether to begin virtuous work here in Latö Lho," the great adept said. "Will you not defend your place and be helpful?"

Lhatsen Kyab replied, "There are great obstacles to doing this huge virtuous work. So please don't do it. Honorable sir, you have already constructed an iron bridge at Dongshur,[968] a gathering place for the three regions of Lho, Jang, and Ngari. Perform virtuous work there, and I will offer from my district of ten thousand households any necessary artisans, a labor tax upon my subjects, and any necessary wooden materials."

While the actual body of the great adept accepted the fine honors of Tai Situ Lhatsen Kyab in a tent at the end of the Shelkar bridge, another body stayed at Shrī Götsong, another body acted as the group leader for many persons observing the fasting rituals in front of the Kyirong Jowo, another body urged the recitation of *maṇis* in the area of Nyeshang, another body meditated on clear light in the upper residence of glorious Chuwori, another body stayed in front of the Jowo of Lhasa, another body observed the tenth day in Sabulung, another body stayed in the Kongpo region, another body gave instructions for constructing the iron bridge in Tölung, and another body stayed in glorious Sakya. He acted for the benefit of living beings by turning the wheel of Dharma in each place. [272]

Lhatsen Kyab, the lord of the Lho people, requested a prophecy about his lifespan and how his family line would flourish. The great adept replied, "Tai Situ himself will have a good lifespan. The son will have just a medium lifespan.[969] His son will have just a minimal lifespan. At that time, the public must hold discussions. A change of leadership will occur."[970]

The lord of the Lho people made lavish offerings.

~

The great adept traveled to glorious Riwoché. In the Earth Female Snake Year [1449], many of the Jang district governor's compulsory laborers had gathered to lay the foundation of the Auspicious Stūpa of Many Doors. When the teacher and disciples did the earth and stone work, a great quantity of earth and stone came forth effortlessly, but three times the stūpa collapsed when it had been completed up to the dome.[971]

When they laid a foundation even more marvelous and vast than before, a scattering of grain constantly appeared on the tops of the walls. All the resident monks and workers had become depressed and discouraged.

The great adept said, "We figure on the individual person dying and figure on the community lasting. Even if this virtuous work being done for the benefit of the doctrine and sentient beings isn't finished in this life, I will make prayers and do it in the next life. But it must be completed before I die. If this isn't finished, untimely winds will arise here in snowy Tibet, and sometimes the blazing fire of drought, or else great rains. With the four elements out of balance, bad harvests and disturbances will occur. Many people will die from unknown diseases. For those events not to happen, all thoughtful and thoughtless people must concentrate. All the sentient beings who have been involved in the causes, conditions, and work of this stūpa will be born in Sukhāvatī."[972] [273]

Everyone became filled with faith and dedicated to the work.

At that time, a man from Ngari came before him and said, "My father and mother have already passed away and the wealth is gone as though blown by the wind. Since I have no possessions, my paternal relatives despise me and I'm depressed. I request a Dharma for liberation from saṃsāra."

He replied, "If you want to permanently break with saṃsāra, practice this!" and gave him the method for accomplishment of Avalokiteśvara. "Here is the way to practice," he said, and spoke this oral instruction:

You may have no power, attendants, and servants,
but you can stand it.

Live alone and meditate on the chosen deity!

You may have no home or place to live,
but you can stand it.

Wander the mountain ranges and practice!

You may have no busy distractions,
but you can stand it.

Stop doing things and recite *maṇis*!

You may have no fame in this life,
but you can stand it.

Resort to solitude
and meditate on the chosen deity!

You may not be in harmony with everyone,
but you can stand it.

Reject the eight worldly concerns
and meditate on the chosen deity!

Enemies may become obstinate,
but you can stand it.

Abandon your home
and meditate on the chosen deity!

You may have nothing nice to wear,
but you can stand it.

Wear a patched blanket
and meditate on the chosen deity!

You may have nothing tasty to eat,
but you can stand it.

Eat what there is
and meditate on the chosen deity!

You may have nothing much to eat,
but you can stand it.

Drink soup
and meditate on the chosen deity!

You may have no soup to drink,
but you can stand it. [274]

Cut the stream[973]
and meditate on the chosen deity!

You may starve to death
for the sake of Dharma,
but you can stand it.

Don't hunt for food;
meditate on the chosen deity!

The phenomena of saṃsāra
are not repulsive or reliable.

Parting from hope and fear,
you'll realize nirvāṇa.

If you act courageously,
you'll reach attainment.[974]

At those words, the man from Ngari felt extreme faith. When he practiced the method for the realization of Mahākaruṇika, he became a courageous man able to wander the mountain ranges, a person who beheld the face of Mahākaruṇika.

~

The great adept was working during the day and retiring to his meditation hut at night. Foolish men who were unable to work had a discussion, saying, "Let's wait for him and throw him off the cliff."[975]

Many men came wearing armor, and the great adept said, "Go do the required stone work!"[976]

They stabbed his body with spears, which they thought went in one side of his body and out the other. But he snatched away the spears and broke them over his knee.

"If I died every time I was struck with a sword or a spear," he observed, "it would have happened many times."

~

While the great adept was digging stone in the stone quarry, the monk Dramré took a stone as large as he could lift and heaved it against a boulder. It struck the head of the great adept.

"I've killed the master," he sobbed.

But the great adept just said, "Nothing has happened."

~

Then, in the form of an obstacle to getting the remaining quantity of earth and stone, they were unable to quarry stone for three days, which caused a shortage for the masons. The great adept took an iron chisel that was an armspan in length and stuck it into a gap in the stone. When he leaned on it, a landslide occurred, and he was covered for three days and nights.

The compulsory laborers were happy and said, [275] "The adept has died. Now we don't have to work!"[977]

"We can't finish the stūpa," the disciples said. "We'd better search for the body."

When they went there, offering prayers and carrying tools, the great adept was sitting on top of a large stone, even more majestic than before.

"Those on the side of the māras are causing obstacles," he declared. "If the obstacles are effective, the māras win. If they are not effective, I, Tangtong Gyalpo, win. If I, Tangtong Gyalpo win, the living beings of southern Jambudvīpa win.[978] The evil omens have been transformed into good. The landslide has opened the door to a deposit of stone. Now there

74. Amitāyus.

will be no shortage of stone. Now, instead of me traveling around the country, if people are sent out to encourage virtue, a greater increase of disciples will occur."

From that time on, without moving for even an instant, he sat in the meditation hut of Dzamling Gyen that is like the tip of a victory banner on the peak of glorious Riwoché. When he performed life-sustaining practices for twenty-one days, he beheld the faces of the assembled deities of lord Amitāyus,[979] father and mother, who gave him five pills for immortal life, saying, "Upholder of pure awareness, by giving longevity pills like these to increase the lifespan and merit of living beings, you will free them from the fear of untimely death and increase the assemblies of merit and primordial awareness."

Thereafter, the longevity pills of the great adept have prevented the untimely deaths of infinite living beings.[980] [276]

~

A large gate was on the road in front of glorious Riwoché. When a road toll was imposed, people detoured to other roads without understanding it was a way to engage in the virtuous work. The strong made war and others condemned the toll, thinking the remaining work might be postponed and compulsory labor would not be necessary.

The great adept declared, "Those who establish a link of positive or even negative karma with me and this virtuous work will quickly be freed from saṃsāra and take the path to liberation."

Indifferent to praise or blame, he continued to work without break on the virtuous projects.

At that time, a fight broke out between many monks of the Ngamring Monastery and the road-toll collectors of glorious Riwoché. On the basis of that, the clergy of the [Ngamring] Monastery made war. More than a thousand geshés encircled the boundaries of glorious Riwoché. The forty or so monks at glorious Riwoché came before the great adept and said, "If we don't fight the army of the clergy, they will rob the personal possessions of the teacher and the disciples and probably beat us."

He replied, "You need patience at times like these. We are doing service for the doctrine, but it won't work if you harm the Sangha. If you fight, you won't meet me again in this life or the next."

While his monks cultivated patience, the monks of the [Ngamring] Monastery prepared to harm the iron bridge and the stūpa. On all the slopes of glorious Riwoché, the great adept magically emanated [277] many frightening men carrying weapons, who could not be caught. The actual body of the great adept acted like he was surrounding the monks.[981]

The teachers and Sangha of the [Ngamring] Monastery said, "The Iron-Bridge Man has a powerful army. We can't beat them and had better flee." They retreated.[982]

During the construction of the dome of the stūpa, the availability of gravel and mud decreased. But the walls still to be built grew higher, and various grains appeared scattered on the tops of the walls. When they told the great adept, he replied, "At Ngamring, in the Dragon Year [1448], I decided to construct this stūpa. When I urged the trio of gods, demons, and humans toward virtue, the Jang governor[983] said that he would provide whatever service was necessary. The Lho patron[984] took responsibility for any necessary wooden materials and for the golden spire. The lord of Menkhab[985] said he would build the podium, the gods of the four races of the great kings[986] said they would build the dome, and the gods and demons of apparent existence said they would create whatever favorable conditions were necessary. If it were necessary to complete this much work on a virtuous project with only the compulsory labor of humans, it would be extremely difficult. The walls are growing higher during the night because they are being built by the deities of the four great races.[987] The sprinkling of grain is the consecration by the conquerors and their spiritual children."

At about that time, one monk was working faithfully with great energy. Sufferings that would have had to be experienced in the lower realms struck him as an intensely painful illness while he still had a human body, and he screamed from the excruciating pain. The great adept heard with his divine hearing and said [278] to call the sick man to him. When the man had been summoned, the great adept told him, "You don't need to be unhappy about illness. Practice like this!"

He gave this oral instruction:[988]

> Illness is a purification of obscurations,
> so be happy!
>
> The unwanted is an attainment,
> so accept it!
>
> Bad circumstances inspire you to virtue,
> so accept them!
>
> Death is on the list,
> so don't regard it as a fault.

Demons and obstructing spirits are the master,
so offer prayers![989]

Demons and obstructing spirits are the chosen deity,
so meditate and recite!

Demons and obstructing spirits are our parents,
so meditate on compassion!

Demons and obstructing spirits are retribution,
so practice generosity!

Demons and obstructing spirits are coemergence,
so rest in the natural state!

In general, the appearance of a demon,
the apprehension of a demon,
and the thought of a demon
are confusing thoughts
of subject and object.

Watch your own mind
without distraction!

The roots of saṃsāra and nirvāṇa
meet in the mind.

No falling into extremes
is the view.

Resting undistracted
is the meditation.

No negation and affirmation
are the conduct.

No gain or loss
is the result.

No expectation
is the yoga.

No self-clinging
is the destruction of confusion.

Unceasing lucidity
is the sambhogakāya enjoyment body.

Appearance in various forms
is the nirmāṇakāya emanated body.

Empty clear light
is the dharmakāya reality body.

The purity of your own mind
is buddha.

Appearances are the ephemeral
images of a dream.

When phenomena are understood in that way,
there are no karma and no result of karma.
There are no ripening of karma
and no cause and result.
There is no experiencing individual.

The reason for [279] that is no self-clinging.

There is no result of positive and negative karma.
The reason for that is no confusion.

In the relative, confused perception
of a person with no realization,
there is karma and there are results of karma.
There is ripening of karma
and there are pleasure and suffering.
There is an experiencing individual.

The reason for that is self-clinging.

There are positive and negative karma,
and there are results.

In conventional, relative,
confused perception,
accept cause, result, and karma as true!

Act with the thought of enlightenment
and great compassion!

Cultivate care, mindfulness,
and attention!

Strictly guard the three vows
and the sacred commitments!

Act with great modesty and shame!

Faithfully observe the rules of society!

Act with little greed and attachment!

Throw away obsessive self-clinging!

Reject anger, bad thoughts,
and harsh words!

Dress the mind
in the armor of patience!

Develop diligence
in virtuous work!

Cultivate meditation
in an isolated place!

Develop the wisdom
that realizes selflessness!

Dedicate the merit
for the benefit of sentient beings!

At those words, the disciple was instantly freed from illness.[990]

⁓

In the past, the great adept had been extremely strict about giving initiations and blessings, but from then on he gave an initiation on every tenth day [of the month] and at the time of the twenty-ninth-day offering of sacrificial cakes. On one tenth day, when he gave the initiation of Opening the Door to the Sky,[991] everyone saw the five deities of Vajravārāhī brilliantly present in the sky in front.

A powerful monk who was a dialectician said, [280] "The initiation was a great blessing. How many years old are you?"

"From when I was born to my mother, up until now," the great adept replied. "I can be old, and I can be young. To display emanations that are old, young, or in the prime of life, it doesn't matter how many years have passed."

During one twenty-ninth-day offering of sacrificial cakes, he bestowed the ritual permission for a Dharma protector. The disciples saw him as the Six-armed Protector. The patrons saw him as Pañjaranātha. A practitioner who had done the recitation retreat of the Four-armed Protector saw him as the Four-armed Protector.

The next day, a monk thought, "I will ask for an explanation of whether it was a single figure of a Dharma protector, but individual visual manifestations, or whether the great adept emanated as different Dharma protectors."

When he went in front of the residence, a brilliant Avalokiteśvara with a thousand arms and a thousand eyes was in the residence. The monk thought, "Where did the great adept go?"

When he circumambulated once and looked, the great adept was sitting and observing silence. Then the great adept said, "A disciple who has faith sees the master, the chosen deity, and the Dharma protectors as indivisible."

~

On another occasion, many men from Kham came to meet the great adept. One man who constantly propitiated Amitāyus said, "This is Amitāyus."

One said, "A heap of roasted barley flour, and boiling milk with steam rising is in here."

One man said, "The residence is empty."

One said, "No one except the master, the great adept himself, is inside the residence."

The great adept displayed [281] bodies in a variety of forms according to each of their good fortune.

~

The great adept spoke to the emanated wrathful conqueror, Namkha Leksang,[992] who was a scholar of the ten fundamental subjects: "There is danger of an epidemic occurring here, throughout Tibet. If the plastering of the inside and outside of the great stūpa, the geomantic focal-point, is quickly completed, it will serve as the necessary ritual for the epidemic not to occur. Great effort is necessary."

"We have gathered the other kinds of earth to make plaster," he replied, "but if we must get limestone from Sumtön, which is far away, it will be quite difficult."

"There is a deposit of limestone down there," he told him, and threw out a leather bag full of roasted barley flour that was in front of him. It landed far from the residence and rolled down. When they dug at the spot where the roasted barley flour had spilled out as a white patch, they got whatever limestone was necessary.

Just when the plastering of the outside and inside of the great stūpa was finished, 118 painters and sculptors[993] gathered from the three regions of Lho, Jang, and Ngari. Without delay, the great adept gave them the azurite that had been offered by the earth spirit of Nyemo.[994]

"A large quantity of vermilion and gold will be necessary," they said.

He told seven monks, "Go extract vermilion in the upper valley of Nyamkhar!"

"We have no information about where vermilion is," the monks replied. "We've never heard it said before that vermilion exists. It may, but the earth spirit is dangerous, so we won't be able to extract it, will we?"

"Where the upper valley is shaped like a frying pan, two small streams come together in front of a rock that is shaped like a turtle. [282] To the right of that, there is as much vermilion and gold as we want. When this letter is given to the earth spirit, he will be friendly. The earth spirit will do it."

He gave them this edict:

Homage to Lokeśvara

This is to Yamar, the earth spirit of the upper valley of Nyam-khar.

In the meditation hut of Tarpa Ling you offered a promise not to go against my orders, and at Ngamring in the Dragon Year [1448] you agreed to create whatever favorable conditions were necessary.

Remember that, and send seven ounces of gold and as much vermilion as you can!

Don't disobey this letter. If you do disobey, the clouds of a host of wrathful emanations will gather in the sky of primordial awareness, and when they make the thunder of fierce mantras roar and a rain of vajra lightning fall, won't you be afraid?

This was written from the victorious peak of glorious Riwoché.

Virtue!

The monks offered a large quantity of gold and vermilion into the hands of the sovereign master.

~

One sculptor who was very devoted to the sovereign master offered each meal to him, and performed unbroken sessions of prostrations, offerings, and circumambulations. In a visual manifestation, he saw the great adept seated in the midst of rainbow light, while many women who were fascinating to gaze upon presented offerings in front of him with songs and dances.

On the tenth day [of the month], many people saw the great adept to actually be the Teacher of Uḍḍiyāna.

~

Once, when an artist went before the great adept, a white vulture flew out of the residence. In the residence was a Vajrabhairava [283] with complete faces and arms, radiating light. The artist thought, "Is it a constructed image or a naturally arisen one? What kind of faces does it have?" When he looked, it had stacked faces.[995]

The vulture arrived back inside the residence. Although the artist had watched undistracted, without knowing where the Vajrabhairava and the vulture had gone, he saw the great adept making a drawing.

~

The assembled deities of the four classes of tantra were painted on the levels of the stūpa, and the stages of the four enlightened bodies of the master were painted up through the two-level dome, like the Auspicious Stūpa of Many Doors in Tāmradvīpa.[996]

The venerable lady Chökyi Drönmé arrived at that time. She was Vajravārāhī working for the benefit of living beings through taking the guise of a human being in a series of lifetimes. She was the third rebirth of the ḍākinī Sönam Drenma and had been born as a daughter of the lord of Tibet.[997] She offered rosaries of precious jewels and so forth. The great adept gave her much Dharma and instructions.[998]

That occasion coincided with the raising of the central pole of the great stūpa.[999] The great adept gave the order: "Today we are raising the central pole. So, madame teacher, please come with your disciples and make prayers. Everyone chant the 'Mothers Infinite As Space,'[1000] and raise it!"

The venerable lady and her disciples came. The Iron-Bridge Man's monks tied many ropes to the intimidating, great central pole, and finished the preparations in about the time it takes to have tea. The main work was quite brief, and during a single chanting of [284] the "Mothers Infinite As Space," the pole was raised with a roar. Wherever huge stones, slate, and so forth fell from each of the levels of the stūpa, the people did not appear to selfishly worry about their cherished lives. The venerable lady also especially rejoiced, and with great pure perception, said that the master was astounding and the monks were also not ordinary.

Then the venerable lady decided to travel to one of the hidden lands of Guru [Padmasambhava] with her disciples, and requested a prophecy.

"Madame teacher Chödrön," the great adept replied, "if you stay in

75. The venerable lady Chökyi Drönmé (1422–55).

the western direction, your lifespan will be long, but the benefit will be uncertain for disciples. If you go in the eastern direction, it will be great for disciples, but your lifespan will be uncertain."[1001]

"I must benefit sentient beings," she said.

"In the Kongpo region to the east, my monastery known as Tsagong Palgyi Nesar is a place where the hosts of mother ḍākinīs gather like clouds and mist. Go there! It will benefit sentient beings. When you arrive in

Central Tibet, Riksum Gönpo, the holder of my monastic seat, will come from Tsagong to welcome you."

~

Then, as the venerable lady Chökyi Drönmé was about to arrive in Central Tibet, a black man with braids wrapped upon his head, and with conch-shell earrings, appeared at the place of master Riksum Gönpo in Kongpo.[1002]

"Where have you come from?" he asked. "Whom do you seek?"

"I came this morning from glorious Riwoché," the man replied.[1003] [285] "I was sent by the great adept to summon you."

"What do I do after I'm summoned?"

"He said that someone from the lineage of the gods of clear light[1004] is coming to this sacred place. So you must come to Central Tibet with me to welcome her. Let's go quickly."

"This man is an emanation," Riksum Gönpo thought, and followed him. When they arrived in Central Tibet, the man vanished.

He met the venerable lady and told her stories of what had happened. He welcomed her, and she traveled to Tsagong Nesar.

The venerable lady expanded the meditation center of Menmogang.[1005] There was a pile, almost a small mountain, of links for the iron bridge that had been ordered by the great adept. She gave great gifts to the Kongpo people because they had fulfilled the master's order, and she went in person to deliver the loads of iron as far as Orsho. When the iron arrived at the Nyago ferry landing, the great adept was delighted.[1006]

Not long after that, the venerable lady passed away into Khecara, her true home. Her authentic skull-cup remained as the wish-fulfilling gem of the great practice center of Tsagong. Because the great adept had said, "An authentic skull-cup and the mountain man of Ngari will come to this sacred place," and the prophecy of the future had come true, the faith and devotion of the Kongpo people greatly increased.[1007]

~

Then, in the Fire Male Mouse Year [1456], when the great adept had reached the age of ninety-six,[1008] the structural work such as the golden parasol and the golden spire of the great stūpa was completely finished. He empowered as his heir the spiritual son of the conquerors Nyima Sangpo, who was born from the three vajras of the great adept,[1009] [286] and at the

76. The great stūpa of Chung Riwoché before recent repairs.

same time scattered flowers to consecrate the great stūpa. At that time, in the sky above the great stūpa and Tenzin Nyima Sangpo, disciples with pure karma saw inconceivable buddhas and bodhisattvas; the eighty-four great adepts, such as the glorious lord Śavaripa; the preservers of good, such as the mighty gods Indra, Brahmā, Īśvara, and Viṣṇu; and many sons and daughters of the gods, who were carrying various offering articles, such as parasols, victory banners, pendants, incense burners, and canopies.

The barley scattered by the great adept from his meditation hut of Dzamling Gyen covered all the inside and outside of the great stūpa, and there was a rain of flowers and a sweet fragrance of the incense of the gods. This was perceived by the sense organs of all the Iron-Bridge Man's monks and artisans who were gathered there.

On that occasion, when the spiritual son of the conquerors Tenzin Nyima Sangpo ascended to the monastic seat, offerings were delivered from the emperor of China.[1010] There was a silk brocade ceremonial hat with a golden crossed vajra and a crown ornament of a wish-fulfilling gem of fire-crystal in the shape of the sun and the moon; thirteen silk brocade robes; and a great measure of gold and a measure of silver, each wrapped in sixteen layers of iron mesh. Furthermore, there were various precious substances; porcelain cups, bowls, and plates; eighty bricks of tea; and fifty bolts of satin and silk. [287] The spiritual son Namgyal Sangpo offered many precious substances such as the Flat Blue Sky spirit-turquoise of Lhalung Palgyi Dorjé, together with clothing, silk, horses, mules, and two hundred bricks of tea.[1011]

Furthermore, a wish-fulfilling gem that had come from the stomach of a fish in the region of Central Tibet was offered. The price of a hundred hybrid yak-cows together with their loads had been paid for this, and it had been passed down from the hands of Drogön Pakpa.[1012] At the same time, inconceivable gems and special valuables were offered from all directions, so that the auspicious connections came naturally into alignment.

~

Then an expert named Lodrö Gyaltsen, a scholar of the ten fundamental subjects who had studied the sūtras and tantras, came to the great adept with the intention to practice the profound path of the Dharmas of Niguma. He received detailed experiential guidance in Niguma's teachings.[1013] While he meditated for seven months in the Sanyalma Cave, he had good experiences of the blissful warmth of the inner fire and the illusory [body]. By means of emanation and transformation in dreams, he reached a decisive conclusion about the appearance of things such as the Vajrāsana in India, and vast visions of clear light arose. When the guiding instructions were finished, he looked at the guidance manuals.[1014] He had been taught many visualizations that were not there, and he wondered what they were. He came before the great adept, who immediately told him, "Many of the visualizations are not in the guidance manuals, but they should not be discarded. They are instructions actually given by the ḍākinī of primordial awareness."

"Well, could I make summarizing notes?"

"No, I haven't received the ḍākinī's permission." [288]

When Lodrö Gyaltsen then practiced energetically even while carrying out the responsibilities of being the teacher of the monastery, his meditation was even more effective in the middle of the monastery assembly and so forth than when he had meditated in solitude.

Then he went again before the great adept, who said, "Scholar of the ten fundamental subjects, you haven't forgotten Niguma's visualizations?"

"I haven't forgotten."

"In that case, explain the visualizations!"

When he told the stages of visualization, the great adept replied, "Yes. Get paper and write!"

"Well, why did you say they could not be written last year?"

"Now I have received the permission of the ḍākinī."

Then Lodrö Gyaltsen wrote them down precisely and offered them for him to see.

"Exactly," he said. "Call Nyima Sangpo[1015] and the others."

He gave the reading transmission to a few fortunate people, with Tenzin Rinpoché foremost. This is a very great teaching for this Dharma transmission.[1016]

~

To the east of the great stūpa, the foundations were then laid for a temple with four pillars, in which would reside a twenty-five-handspan Great Sage [Śākyamuni] made from precious substances; for a temple with six pillars, in which would reside a thirty-one-handspan Amitābha made from precious substances as the main image, together with the eight close bodhisattva sons, the four guardian kings,[1017] and two wrathful deities, made from clay; for a temple with four pillars in which would be a fifteen-handspan Maitreya image made from precious substances; and for a temple with four pillars, in which would be a twenty-seven-handspan Medicine Buddha image made from precious substances. [289] In front of these temples would be a verandah with forty pillars.

To the east of that would be a temple with four pillars, in which would be a thirty-three-handspan Mahākaruṇika image made from precious substances. To the east of that would be a temple with four pillars for a thirty-seven-handspan Vajrasattva made from precious substances. In front of these two temples would be a verandah area with thirty pillars.

To the west of the great stūpa would be a temple with four pillars, in which would be a twenty-five-handspan Prajñāpāramitā made from precious substances; a temple with four pillars, in which would be a twenty-one-handspan eleven-faced Avalokiteśvara made from clay; and temples with four pillars each, in which would reside a thirty-five-handspan Vajrabhairava, a twenty-one-handspan Hevajra, and a twenty-one-handspan Cakrasaṃvara. In front of these temples would be a verandah area with fifty pillars.

To the right of that would be a temple with two pillars for a thirteen-handspan Kālacakra made from precious substances. To the right of that would be a temple with two pillars, in which would be an eleven-handspan Vajradhara cast from precious substances. In front of these two temples would be a verandah with ten pillars.[1018]

~

The great adept constantly worked on the virtuous projects, and the time came to put on the roofs. The Iron-Bridge Man's monks cut and trimmed juniper and willow trees that grew in Central Tibet and were owned by the gods and demons, and appealed in different areas for compulsory laborers to deliver them to Riwoché.

But people said, "We can't bring them because we would have to pay a tax of military service to our leaders." [290]

The trees were left where they were. This was bad for the roofing, but by the magical ability of the great adept, the trees arrived at Riwoché without anyone knowing. The people in the different areas thought that the Iron-Bridge Man's monks had taken them. The monks thought that the area people had delivered them. The carpenters asked, "Who delivered these trees last night?" But no one had any information.

When they asked the great adept, he said, "It is sufficient that the trees arrived. Of course someone delivered them."

The emanated wrathful conqueror, who was the work leader,[1019] said, "If we get the roofing slate from Serlung in the upper valley of Yulpoché, we'll have to carry it over the iron bridge, which will risk lives. Please see us with your compassion."

"Don't do work that risks lives," the great adept replied. "Get it from the place where this goes."

He threw out a copper dish, which landed on the mountainside just above the great stūpa. When they dug, a deposit of slate was there.

~

Then the Great Sage [Śākyamuni] was completed. When it was time to gild the image of Amitābha, the great adept said, "Nyima Sangpo, holder of the monastic seat, get the vase full of gold that is inside the cliff of Gyasakhu, the mountain behind Sunglung. The earth spirits will help you with the work of breaking open the cliff."

Nyima Sangpo went there, and the yakṣa spirit Gyaltang appealed to the nine demon sisters of Chung and so forth. When many earth spirits of different appearances broke open the cliff, much rock tumbled down, cutting off travel on the road to the north. From the south of the Tsangpo River, shepherds from Lhadrang [291] saw the yakṣa spirit Gyaltang, surrounded by many figures of different appearances, give a vase to a monk. Then all the workers disappeared in a single instant.

When it was time to gild the Maitreya and the Medicine Buddha, the artisans requested gold. The great adept gave them a leather bag full of gold, saying, "See whether it's enough."

"It is more than five thousand ounces of gold," they replied.

Many people were in his presence, and he realized that several were thinking to steal the gold. When the people dispersed, he told Nyima Sangpo, the holder of the monastic seat, "If the gold is left here, thieves will come. Take it to the master's residence," and gave him the gold.

At about midnight that evening, ten thieves appeared. One said, "I'll kill the adept and throw him out of the residence. You roll him off the cliff."

He stabbed the great adept with a knife and demanded, "Where is the bag full of gold?"

Even when he stabbed him ten times with the knife, the great adept didn't say anything. "Now I've killed him," he thought. "I'll throw him outside."

He tried to lift him onto his lap, but couldn't move the body. "This great corpse won't budge," he said, and left.

The next day, the supplies of meat and butter being offered by a patron for a ritual feast were getting warm in the sun.

"Cover them with this cloak," the great adept said, and gave it to the man.

"What are the many knife holes in the cloak?" the patron asked.

"Those are the handiwork of evil men who came to rob the gold that is to be offered to the buddha images."

"You recognized the men. It would be best for us to tell the governor, and they will be punished by law." [292]

"Of course I recognized the men. But what can come from one person breaking a knife in ignorance, and one breaking a plate in ignorance?"[1020]

"Was there no harm to your body?"

"If I could be harmed by weapons, there would be little point in having gained self-control over the elements."

At that time, the great adept realized that among the many geshés who were there to listen to Dharma during that ritual feast, one from Jamchen

Gyedé would accomplish whatever he requested.[1021]

"Is anyone among you capable of taking my edict and going to the Chinese Palace?" he asked.

Gendun Gyaltsen from Gyedé replied, "If it pleases the master, I can go to China."

"In that case," he said, "take this small but marvelous gift to accompany the letter," and gave him some steaming cooked white rice and this edict.

Homage to Lokeśvara

> This is to the Emperor, Source of Glory.[1022]
>
> Emperor, when I came in that direction, I just barely met you. I stayed for eight months on the Five-Peaked Mount Wutai. I received a prophecy from Mañjughoṣa and came back to Tibet. I have completed huge virtuous works.
>
> Emperor, your offerings were delivered. I received a great measure of gold, a great measure of silver, a hat with crown-ornaments of fire crystal, thirteen embroidered robes, fifty bolts of satin and silk, and eighty bricks of tea, for which I performed a dedication.
>
> The auspicious connections have come into alignment. My disciples and I are thinking of the happiness of Jambudvīpa. The many images of the buddhas and bodhisattvas that had been completed had been left naked. When I sent out my major disciples, teachers and students, to collect offerings, [293] a large quantity of satin and silk robes were offered [to the images] to protect all sentient beings from the sufferings of cold.
>
> The emperor himself should eat this marvelous food as an auspicious connection.
>
> From the victorious peak of glorious Riwoché in Tibet.
>
> May virtue and goodness flourish!

~

Once a woman practitioner in a charnel ground near the great adept's residence saw a white vulture fly out of his residence and go in the north-east direction. When the woman practitioner went to look in the residence, Dorjé Drakpotsel was standing there, endowed with the nine dance moods.[1023] She made extensive prostrations and offerings before him. When she had finished receiving the four initiations, two white vultures appeared and went into the residence. When she looked inside the residence, she heard the great adept speak:

> Padmasambhava,
> the embodiment of all the conquerors,
> resides in the mighty palace
> of Uḍḍiyāna to the southwest.
>
> Son, you must join the ranks
> of the heroic upholders of pure awareness,
> and practice the Dharma
> of the Mahāyāna and Secret Mantra!

"Who is the fortunate person to whom he is giving a prophecy?" she wondered. "No human being is there."

Three days passed, and a messenger arrived with word that the major disciple Chökyi Gyaltsen from Tsang had died in Mü. Three days had passed since the master from Tsang had been escorted into the ranks of the upholders of pure awareness in the presence of Padmasambhava of Uḍḍiyāna. Later, the nun realized that the great adept had been giving a prophecy to his major disciple from Tsang.

~

During that time, a man who had been constantly reciting *maṇis* in retreat said, "O great adept. [294] This unawareness has great power in the mindstreams of fools like us. We have not seen this essence of the nature of mind, clear light, vivid and stark. Please give an instruction with which to see it."

The great adept gave this edict:

Homage to Lokeśvara

The word of Vajradhara.
The transmission of Mahākaruṇika.
The writing of Tangtong Gyalpo.

This is to the coemergent unawareness in those who wish to attain enlightenment.

This *maṇi* devotee[1024] says you have forcibly concealed the [universal] ground, the forever spontaneous nature of the mind that fulfills all needs and desires like a [wish-fulfilling] gem. Because the fundamental nature of the mind has not been recognized, he has been used as a servant of desire, bound with the tight rope of self-clinging, saddled with a great burden of evil karma, flailed with the whip of the three poisons on the plain of saṃsāra, and tortured for a long time with harsh loads of suffering difficult to bear in the locations of the lower realms.[1025] This is unacceptable.

Now, let the *maṇi* devotee himself, while reciting[1026] the six syllables, saying *Oṃ maṇi padme hūṃ hrīḥ*, have the greatest power over the *maṇi* devotee's own [universal] ground, the forever spontaneous nature of the mind that fulfills all needs and desires like a [wish-fulfilling] gem!

Without tormenting him by using him as a servant of desire and so forth, which is unwanted, you must let him comfortably remain in a transcendent state free from attachment!

Know that if you disobey, I will dispatch the enforcer of mindfulness, and with the harsh punishment of truthlessness, you will be sent into the state of the true nature of phenomena without a trace!

Until you reach a decisive conclusion, I have told him to [295] recite many thousands of *maṇi*s every day.

Written from the peak of glorious Riwoché.[1027]

~

On one occasion, the great adept told those who had come before him, "Take refuge by chanting the 'Mothers Infinite As Space'!"

He sat in reflection without saying anything. When he had finished meditating, they asked, "Why did you tell us to take refuge for a long time today?"

"A large area of Mön known as Sarahata[1028] was about to be lost under a landslide. We took refuge to save it."

"Did harm not come to the large area in Mön?"

"Because the compassion of the masters, chosen deities, and Three Jewels is infallible, the people of Sarahata just barely avoided being swept beneath the landslide."

~

Once a man in Lhasa killed his mother. Feeling intense guilt, he came to the great adept to work on the virtuous projects. Because of that inexpiable act,[1029] he could not see the great adept's body at all. According to the master's words, he sincerely dug stone for building the stūpa and temples. For seven years without interruption, he confessed every day in front of the great adept's residence, and made thirteen circumambulations.

Then he saw the radiant body of the great adept, who gave an edict: "I guarantee that those who have offered food, wealth, and possessions, and who have endured the difficult work of the illusory body for the sake of this virtuous project, will drink the nectar of the Mahāyāna Dharma in Sukhāvatī[1030] in the next life."

~

During that time, the coppersmiths who had constructed the large images of the deities came to the great adept to request a blessing. [296] He gave a gift to the coppersmith Samten Paljor, and said, "Bring that stolen copper!"

"I did not steal copper," he replied. "If I stole, you would see it with your clairvoyance, so please tell the time of theft."

"You stole the copper three days ago. You intend to take it when you go home. It is hidden in the water at the end of the iron bridge."

Since the great adept spoke with unimpeded clairvoyance, the coppersmiths were unable to take even a workcloth.

14: To the Palace of the King of Kāmata in India

The actual body of the great adept sat without moving from a single cushion in the Dzamling Gyen meditation hut at glorious Riwoché. The apparent images of his emanated bodies, in whatever forms necessary to tame everyone, continued to arise in the clear mirrors of the minds of disciples in India, China, the three regions of Central Tibet, Tsang, and Kham, and in Dakpo and Kongpo.

During that period, the laborers at the stūpa and temples were artisans and workers from the three regions of Lho, Jang, and Ngari. These workers on the virtuous projects had gathered from all directions without distinction because of their faith in the Great Adept of Iron Bridges. The great adept gave the Dharma that each of them wanted: the various methods of guidance according to the Mahāmudrā, the Great Perfection, the Six Dharmas of Nāropa, the Six Dharmas of Niguma, the Guiding Instructions of Severance, Mind Training, and so forth. He gave as general Dharma the *Karmaśataka Sūtra*, the *Saṃdhinirmocana Sūtra*, the *Kūṭāgāra Sūtra*,[1031] and so forth.

Monks in whom no understanding and experience of the guiding instructions had arisen, and who were possessed by the māras, gathered together in one place. [297] "We are sick and tired of this work that never ends," they complained. "If we did this much work in trading and farming at home, we would get very rich. If we had wealth, we could get rid of our enemies and care for our relatives."

Some said, "If we meditated at Tsari, Kailash, and Chuwar,[1032] a great enhancement would occur due to the special qualities of the sacred places."

Some said, "If we sometimes visited the representations of blessed, sacred places, and made circumambulations and prayers, and sometimes practiced Severance in the charnel grounds, our bodies and minds would be at ease and the Dharma would flourish."

Some said, "If we studied as much as we do this work, we would reach the ranks of masters and teachers. If that happened, we would be happy and the Dharma would flourish."

The great adept knew with clairvoyance that such things were being said, and announced, "Gather the monks, artisans, and laborers in front of the residence tomorrow to listen to Dharma."

He held a ritual feast and gave this commanding oral instruction in verse:

> All workers dependent on me,
> the time has come
> to engage in spiritual practice.
>
> There's no end of things to do.
>
> The time has come
> to postpone activities.
>
> There's more you must tame
> than the enemies you've tamed.
>
> The time has come
> to tame your own mindstream.
>
> There're more who are angry
> than the relatives you've pleased.
>
> The time has come
> to postpone placation.
>
> There's more you must assemble
> than assembled wealth.
>
> The time has come
> for unattached action.
>
> There's more you must be concerned about
> than what has concerned you.

The time has come
to postpone flattery.

There's more you must learn
than the Dharma you've learned. [298]

The time has come
to put it into practice.

There's more you must do
than wishful thinking.

Rest in the unborn state
of the dharmakāya reality body.

There's more you must do
than the benefit you've done.

The time has come
to achieve what benefits you.

Even if you die while forming
good propensities,
it isn't an obstacle.

When creating benefit and happiness
for yourself and others,
depression and laziness are obstacles.

The time has come
to clear away obstacles.[1033]

At these words, a comprehension and great enhancement compatible with each individual method of guidance arose for those who had listened to the guiding instructions, and all became enthusiastic toward the virtuous work.

~

There are five dialectical schools[1034] outside the doctrine of the Conqueror, the source of benefit and happiness. From among these, the evil tenets of the Cārvāka[1035] maintain that since no past or future lives exist, when a human being dies it is like dust being carried away by the wind. A sinful king accepted this and was occupied only with the sacrifice of the lives of various sentient beings merely as a method to prolong his own life, and the holder of this wrong view sacrificed the flesh and blood of a hundred pregnant women every year. To subdue him, the emanated great adept went from the Samdrup Temple in Pari, by way of Paro, to the palace of the king of Kāmata in India,[1036] unimpeded by a series of seven moats, fences, and gates, with ten masters and servants to guard each gate. He rested evenly in vajralike meditative concentration on the right of the two golden thrones of the king, which was smeared with camphor and sandalwood [299] and had a soft cushion of flowers spread upon it. Food and drink was served to the king, and when the great adept partook of it together with him, the king became angry and demanded, "Why was this man let into the palace?"

The guards of the gates were frightened and said, "No one like him came to our gates."

The king told his retinue, "Dig a hole in the ground eighteen armspans deep, put him in it, and make the earth level!"

When they did so and returned, the great adept arrived at the gate together with those who had enforced the order. When he came inside like before, the king was furious and ordered, "You will all be harshly punished!"

The men who had thrown him out were terrified and said, "O great king, we acted according to the king's orders, but the man arrived here. Now we will put his limbs in iron chains, and his body in an iron net, and throw him into the river. We beg the king to also observe this."

The king did as they requested, but again the great adept appeared in the king's palace as before. The king declared, "This man is not harmed by water. Cut him into pieces with sickles."

They cut him up in that way, but the pieces reassembled and he appeared inside the palace as before.

"Burn him with fire!" the king commanded.

So the king's retinue put the great adept in the middle of a large box of sandalwood logs and other wood. When the fire was lit, a mass of smoke filled the sky. The flames reached for about a league in all directions. When the fierce sounds of *hūṃ* and *phaṭ* roared in the center of the mass of flames, the king and his retinue [300] fainted and stiffened.

When three days had passed, everyone saw the Iron-Bridge Master on top of a great pile of charcoal, his body fascinating to gaze upon, with his right hand in the gesture of granting the sublime attainment, and holding a white utpala flower in his left. They all heard him say, "*Oṃ maṇi padme hūṃ.*"

The king and ministers talked. "This is a man who cannot be harmed by anything," they said. "We must ask him what he is."

They came before the Iron-Bridge Master and asked, "Where are you from? By what name are you known? For what reason have you come?"

"I come from snowy Tibet," he replied. "I am called the Iron-Bridge Man, Tangtong Gyalpo. I am establishing a sinful kingdom in the Dharma."

The king, the ministers, and the retinue became filled with faith, offered much gold and silver, and cried, "Please hold us with your compassion!"

Corresponding to each person's devotion, the sovereign master spoke in the Kāmata language to the king, the ministers, and the retinue, teaching the taking of refuge by means of the "Mothers Infinite As Space," the awakening of the thought of enlightenment, and the meditative recitation of Avalokiteśvara, together with the benefits of *maṇis*.

At a major crossroads, the great adept constructed a Stūpa of Enlightenment with a temple inside. It contained images of the conquerors of the three times created from gold and silver and surrounded by murals of the infinite buddhas and bodhisattvas of the ten directions. As the doorkeeper, a figure of the sovereign master was painted, surrounded by venerable Tārā and the ten wrathful deities. [301] A copy of the five royal sūtras[1037] written in gold was made as the representation of enlightened speech.

When he performed the consecration, the surface of the earth was filled from the ten directions with light of various colors and the incense of the gods, and a pleasant sound of music was heard. The king and his retinue became filled with faith. "Tangtong Gyalpo," they declared, "we will do whatever you say, so give us advice!"

"To these representations," he replied, "continually make offerings of water scented with camphor and sandalwood, rows of lamps with mustard seed oil and butter, foods such as fruit and rice, and pure water, flowers, fragrant incense and so forth! As soon as you get up on the fifteenth, thirtieth, and eighth days of the month, you should bathe, dress in new clothing, and keep the eight-branch vow of renewal and purification[1038] for the entire day and night. If you make good prayers before the representations of the precious Three Jewels in this stūpa, happiness and contentment will arise. Furthermore, under your rule as king, it is the local custom to take the lives of many sentient beings and perform the sacrifice of their flesh and blood, saying that it is a religious ceremony for you. O king, this killing of one hundred pregnant women every year serves as a cause for shortening your life. You will have an evil reputation at the present time and have to experience suffering difficult to bear in the hell of supreme torture[1039] in the next life. Therefore, from today on, do not take the lives of sentient beings, and to purify the sin of your previous killings, make prints with this mold every day without break!"

He gave the king a mold of one hundred stūpas. The king also offered a vow to do as the great adept had ordered. [302]

The Kāmata king applied sandalwood paste to the body of the Adept of Iron Bridges, and beautified him with a tiara and necklace of gold, and also with rings on all his fingers and toes. He honored him with a complete set of fine silken clothing, a headdress of flowers, and with rice, brown sugar, and various fruits.

The great adept dedicated the gold, silver, silks, and so forth that were heaped up like a mountain, and furthermore, the measureless silver coins and so on from the ministers and people of Kāmata, and then returned them to the different individuals who had offered them.

The Kāmata king had hoped that the great adept would stay as his priest. But when the great adept showed no pleasure at the honors and services that had been rendered, nor any anger at the attacks made upon his person, and instantly returned by magic to glorious Riwoché,[1040] the Kāmata king became very depressed. For several years, he abandoned the sacrifices of flesh and blood from killing a hundred pregnant women and other living beings, and he was physically and mentally healthy. But then the soothsayers and astrologers subject to the king deceived him by saying that if offerings of flesh and blood were not made to Maheśvara, the king's prosperity would decline. When the king of Kāmata broke his vow, he became afflicted with a severe disease that was difficult to endure.

Hoping to cure the disease, the king assembled the physicians of the realm. The 270 physicians who came thought that if the previous rites of local custom were not imposed, the king's disease could not be cured. [303] To the evil non-Buddhist gods such as Īśvara, offerings were made with the flesh and blood of a hundred men in the prime of life and a hundred pregnant women, a hundred each of animals such as water buffalo, goats, sheep, and oxen, a hundred each of wild animals such as elk and deer, a hundred each of fish and frogs who lived in the water, and a hundred each of countless types of birds, such as domestic fowl. The physicians tried various medical treatments, but due to the truth of the great adept's command, the disease of the king became more painful.

When nothing was left to do, the king assembled the soothsayers and astrologers of the realm. More than two hundred came. They performed divinations and calculations as to what would relieve the king's disease and, in agreement, they told the king, "The disease is the result of having broken the vow you offered to Tangtong Gyalpo of Tibet, and of having harmed his body with earth, water, fire, and sickles. If you enter under his protection and complete a thousand fulfillment and healing rituals for the protectors who guard the Dharma, O king, you will be released from this disease. Whatever other rituals you perform will be useless."

The king then asked people from Mön who had come to India to trade, "In Tibet, is someone known as the Iron-Bridge Man, Tangtong Gyalpo?"

The traders replied with one voice, "An emanation of the Guru of Uḍḍiyāna, known as the Adept of Iron Bridges, Tangtong Gyalpo, lives in Tibet. His monks and people who do virtuous work come to our region."

When the king heard this, he sent his minister Malik, who was from a Tibetan region, together with a large retinue, to deliver the offerings of a flower with a thousand petals beaten from pure gold, a white conch shell with a clockwise spiral, [304] necklaces of gold, many sets of clothing made from the fine silken cloth of India, various kinds of food such as rice, sugar, and grapes, countless types of medicines such as sandalwood, camphor, and aloe, various kinds of precious substances such as silver and rubylike stones, and various kinds of musical instruments such as bowl-drums and many-stringed instruments.

At the same time as their arrival with the urgent request for the great adept to make the necessary trip to cure the king's disease, invitations arrived from the king of Yatsé, the king of Kashmir, and from Kongpo in the east.[1041] The great adept sent back the envoy of the Yatsé king, telling him that if the auspicious connections came into alignment, he would send a representative later. He told the envoy from Kashmir, "This year you must go back. Next year I will send Geshé Dharmashrī with an image of Avalokiteśvara with a thousand arms and a thousand eyes."

He gave a turquoise Vajradhara to his physical son Kyabpa Sangpo,[1042] and sent him to the Kongpo region as his representative.

When the Indians looked at the body of the sovereign master, they saw that he was indistinguishable from the person who had come to India before. They made countless prostrations, and each offered their own clothing, jewelry, and so forth.

The great adept sent as his representatives thirteen masters and disciples such as Mupa Shenyen from Mangar and Dewa Sangpo from Paro in Bhutan, led by his spiritual son Könchok Palsang, to be the master of the Kāmata king.[1043] He gave them an edict and prophecy that clearly presented the subtle details of actions and results, together with the gifts of a crystal rosary and a hundred life-sustaining pills. [305]

He told them, "The king must not split open the bellies of pregnant women, tear out the infants, and use them as offerings to the demon. As a substitute for the human beings, he must make the full number of human effigies from food and use those. He must not burn women alive whose husbands have died. He must not kill prisoners in the prisons, nor take ransom payments. If he is able to keep these vows, the king will have a long life and quickly be released from the disease."[1044]

Minister Malik said, "The king can heed the order of the great adept and put aside the giving of flesh and blood to the demon, but the demon is more powerful than the king and will not listen. What is best?"[1045]

"Proclaim this letter of mine to Īśvara and his consort," the great adept replied, and gave him an edict that said such things as this:

> As long as relative, confusing appearance occurs, the causes and results of actions are true. Therefore, as a substitute for the flesh and blood of a hundred pregnant women, you will be given a full count of effigies that have been blessed by mantra and meditative concentration.
>
> Be satisfied with that! Do not eat the flesh and blood of those who have gained human bodies, led by the king who lives in Köntso.[1046] Do not take lives.

> If you disobey this, I will drag you into the vast furnace of emptiness with the iron hook of naked, empty lucidity. If the illusory body of habitual propensities for clinging to things is burned in the fire of unattachment and emptiness, won't you be afraid?[1047]

The bhuta demon was satisfied with the effigies of food as substitutes for the hundred pregnant women. The king was cured of the disease and accepted the vows from the spiritual son Könchok Palsang and the others. The great adept had cut the stream of sin.

~

People on a great pilgrimage from Paro in Bhutan then came to meet the great adept. [306] "When the Dharma had not spread in our country," they said, "you kindly spread the Dharma. Now the Dharma has spread even more than it had when you came. Master, we are about to die from missing you so much. Please, by all means, come to Paro."

The great adept replied, "If you are devoted to me, meditate that I am on the top of your head, and offer prayers."

"If we meditate on you, blessings come, but since we have little pure perception in regard to Dharma, and great attachment and hatred, we will die competing with our paternal relatives about which of us is best. So we request an oral instruction that will benefit our minds."

"Keep this warning about impermanence in mind and think about it!" he said, and spoke this:

> The lord, the Dharma lord
> whose kindness can never be repaid,
> rests as an ornament
> on the top of my devoted head.
>
> In general, sentient beings
> wandering in saṃsāra,
> and in particular,
> all who know that those beings
> have been your mother,
> spead your fingers on your chests
> and think about this!

When you think about death
and the impermanence of life,
sadness and renunciation arise.

Don't be attached
to this saṃsāra as a home!

Rely on the antidote for this enemy,
the afflictions!

Don't carry a load
of sins and obscurations!

Don't accumulate ripening
evil karma!

This precipitous path
of the intermediate state
is difficult to travel.

This road to the next life
leads to a distant place.

Everyone falls into the hands
of the Lord of Death.

This life is dwindling right now,
moment by moment.

Like cattle being led to the slaughter ground,
it's uncertain whether death
will be tomorrow or the day after.

The circulation of breath
is about to stop
at the entrance to your nostrils.

All the soothsayers, Bönpos,
and doctors give up. [307]

A soft mat is laid out,
but you hurt from below.

A soft pillow is placed,
but the flesh of your jaw stiffens.

You wear many clothes,
but can't get warm.

The odor of the dying
clings to your body.

The filth of a corpse
attaches to your face.

The sublime taste
of many delicious foods is lost.

You drink a sip of water,
but it catches in the throat.

Your tongue can't speak
a single word of speech.

Your nose, the organ of scent,
is blocked with mucus.

The clear lamps of your eyes
shrink inward.

Unable to move the body,
your physical strength is gone.

The mere thread of your breath
makes a rasping sound.

Anguished relatives
cry and hold you.

You have no idea where you will go,
but they hope for the dying
to fulfill the aims of the living,
crying, "Give us advice, leave a will!"

And as you are thinking,
sadness arises.

You want to stay,
but have no self-control.

You're lost to the power
of the māra of the Lord of Death.[1048]

Loving relatives
are depressed and grieving.

Hateful enemies praise the gods,
singing and dancing.

Some hide your food and valuables
in secret.

Some make arrangements
for the corpse.

You have no self-control
over the mode of birth[1049]
or where you will be reborn.

Even if you know what to do,
the force of karma is too strong.

Valuable things
won't turn the face
of the Lord of Death.

The wealthy leave
empty-handed and naked.

There are no eloquent,
fine words to say.

A fine, clever man
is stricken mute.

There is nowhere
for heroes to join swords.

The bravery of virile men
ends here.

The radiant complexion
of a stunning woman fades.

The face of a charming girl
is no use here.

Even with many subjects, attendants,
and servants who bear suffering
for you in many ways, [308]
you will go alone.

Even though your sons
and daughters have gathered,
you will go alone.

Anguished people can't bear to part.

Grasping people
are attached to their valuables.

They remember Dharma at that moment,
but it's too late.

All people who have
committed nonvirtuous acts
are welcomed in advance

by the agents of Yama,
driven from behind
by the winds of their evil deeds,
and crushed from above
by the burden of ripened karma.

The various fears
of a confused mind appear.

Unbearable punishments
torment the mind.

Guilt arises about actions
done before.

You think, "From now on,
I must practice Dharma!"

But if you die right now,
what can you do?

It's time to think it over again.

Everyone eats a mouthful of food.

Everyone wears clothes on the body.

Food and wealth other than that
are extra.

It's better if you resort
to the jewel of contentment.

Everyone keep these words in mind!

Ask the experts, "Is this true?"

When people
with renunciation and faith

hear and think about these words,
weariness of saṃsāra
will certainly arise.[1050]

~

On another occasion, many wolves approached the huge group of animals whose lives had been spared when patrons offered them to the great adept. The herdsmen of the yaks and sheep came to him and said, "We request a blessing for the wolves not to kill the animals whose lives have been spared."

"Shout this message of mine into the ears of the wolves," he replied, and gave them this edict.

Homage to Lokeśvara

This is to the carnivores, the gray wolves. [309]

None of the yaks and sheep owned by the Iron-Bridge Man, and you gray wolves, are not connected as parents and children in past and future lives. Therefore, if you eat their flesh, you will not be able to bear the retribution.

Think about the difficulty of purifying the sin of taking life, and don't kill the animals whose lives have been spared!

When you can't stand being hungry, eat grass!

If you gray wolves disobey, I will bind your mouths with the vajra-lasso of emptiness, and a great lion endowed with the ten powers will spread his four clawed-feet of the four immeasurables,[1051] and frighten and terrify you with his immutable vajra gaze.

So don't take life and don't eat flesh!

When they shouted the edict into the ears of the wolves, from then on the wolves ate grass with the herd of yaks and sheep and they lived together peacefully.

Also at that time, the Mendong Ringmo field, which was the field that provided barley for the soup of the workers on the Iron-Bridge Man's virtuous projects, was greatly damaged by insects at the roots of the plants and birds at their tips.

[The workers] said, "We need you to establish an auspicious connection with a blessing for no damage to occur."

"Chödrak Palsang[1052] must read this letter at the edge of the Mendong Ringmo field," he replied, and gave this edict.

Homage to Lokeśvara

> This is to the insects and birds in the Mendong Ringmo field.
>
> This field is the field of barley for the soup of the workers on the virtuous projects, so it will be a great sacrilege if you eat it. You creatures would not be liberated from the suffering of stupidity in the lower realms that you are experiencing now [310] and would have no opportunity of gaining the higher realms.
>
> Think about the consequences of that, and go to a place with unplanted crops, grains, and so forth, where no sacrilege will occur!

The edict was used, and the next day no birds and insects were in the field.

~

Then the noble nun Delek Chödren,[1053] who was a disciple of the venerable lady Chökyi Drönmé, arrived before the great adept to offer a request for him to make divinations because the venerable lady had passed away in Kongpo.

"Will a rebirth appear?" she asked.

"You keep quiet, girl. She won't deceive us," he replied, prophesying that a new female incarnation would soon appear.

In the Earth Female Rabbit Year [1459], the venerable lady Kunga Sangmo[1054] was born in the region of Kongpo to the east. Delek Chödren arrived again before the great adept and said, "You must give from here a verification of whether or not she is the rebirth."

He gave a prophecy verifying that she was. He declared, "Her own statement will come in the Snake Year [1461]." He gave her a mirror that became bright when wiped, hand cymbals for renown, and flowers of white barley to be scattered for her long life.

Then, when the venerable lady became five years old, the great adept took charge. He gave her much Dharma of the new and old secret mantra traditions, and told her to go to the three regions of Ngari[1055] to tame living beings. Her servants urgently requested that she be excused because of her youth, but he responded, "You must go to Gungtang to perform the transference of consciousness for Dodé, your mother in the last life.[1056] Then I will gradually advise you."

The venerable lady traveled to Ngari Dzongkar.[1057] She told stories of her previous lifetime as if she were awakening from sleep, saying such things as, "At my departure for Kongpo, when you came to escort me, mother, [311] I said, 'Mother, I will definitely arrive at your bedside when you are dying.' You haven't forgotten, have you?"

As a result, there was excitement among disciples, and she realized that vast benefit to living beings would come. In the edict of the great adept, he had told her, "Tame living beings in the three regions of Ngari. Even though you servants don't wish to go, ask her."

"It is the command of the master," she said. "Even if I die, I will not disobey his word."

The young queen of ḍākinīs reached a decisive conclusion.

Just as she had finished collecting offerings in the three regions of Ngari, an edict from the great adept arrived, saying that she must go again to suppress the Mongols. Everyone said that the Mongols would kill her, but she replied, "Even if others don't go, Pal[1058] and I will go."

Furthermore, the venerable lady and nineteen disciples willing to give up this life traveled to Maryul.[1059] With clairvoyance and magical ability, she stopped the conflict between the two kings of upper and lower Maryul. In about sixty villages where the Western Mongols[1060] had settled in Maryul, she gave the oral transmission of *maṇi*s and taught about the ethics of abandoning sin and cultivating virtue. To fulfill the intentions of the great adept, she performed meditations to overwhelm the Mongol armies. She made a rain of mice fall in Mongolia and destroy the grain, and due to a severe famine and pestilence, no opportunity arose for the hordes of the Western Mongol armies to enter the Land of Snows.

Then the venerable lady offered to the Iron-Bridge Man's virtuous projects all the various things that she had been offered in the three regions of Ngari, [312] such as gold, copper, coral and amber. The great adept made her elegant with various pieces of precious jewelry and, with a well-equipped encampment that seemed overwhelming to others, the queen of ḍākinīs was sent to Kham to collect offerings for the Iron-Bridge Man.

Infinite disciples also appeared in Central Tibet and Tsang, and she immediately had their offerings delivered.

The venerable lady later took up residence at glorious Riwoché. She adorned the great adept's residence with a copper gilt pagoda roof, and the north side of the podium of the great stūpa with copper gilt. Furthermore, she remained unrivaled in supporting[1061] the Iron-Bridge Man's enlightened activities for as long as she lived.[1062]

~

Then the great adept sealed his one-armspan circular residence down to the gaps around the door where air circulated.[1063] When his body was not seen and his speech was not heard, it was no different from when he was not present. Many hundreds of faithful men and women, disciples, artisans, and patrons, gathered in front of the residence, which was built like [a one-armspan circular structure].[1064] Arranging an inconceivable ritual feast and offering of sacrificial cakes, they prayed to him, raising their voices high, calling out, "If you won't show your body, please speak! If you won't speak, please give us [teachings on] a writing slate."[1065]

But for three months he did not even accept food, and his body and speech were not perceived through the senses of the people.

After three months, he taught on a writing slate, "If you admire me, be willing to give up this life! Be kind-hearted!"

Then he gave writing slates to everyone who needed advice, [313] and wrote various scripts such as *lañcana, vartula,*[1066] and the symbolic script of the ḍākinīs. For the great adept's writing, day and night were no different, but those staying near him had to read by a lamp when there was no sunlight. When they saw his body, he was even more stout and tough than before, and his majestic radiance was nectar to their eyes. All the people were now happy, and when eighty persons came in a single day to offer meals, he ate everything.

During that time, the artisans gathered before him said, "O great adept. Unless it is some special auspicious connection, please do not keep silent, and please give a teaching without hiding the meaning or making it crooked."

He gave them this on a writing slate:

Faithful workers on the projects of virtue!

Listen to whether this is crooked or straight!

All straight isn't straight.
A fool's straight is crooked.

All crooked isn't crooked.
A wise man's crooked is straight.

All benefit isn't benefit.
A fool's benefit is harm.

All harm isn't harm.
A wise man's harm is benefit.

All pleasure isn't pleasure.
A fool's pleasure is suffering.

All suffering isn't suffering.
A wise man's suffering is pleasure.[1067]

At those words, the artisans concentrated on their individual work and became filled with faith.

That day, three monks from Kham came from Jang Taklung[1068] to meet the great adept. One Kham man saw him to be a man with youthful skin, who was about twenty-five years old. [314] One Kham man saw him to be about forty years old, with a fleshy body radiating light rays. One saw him as an extremely old man leaning on a cane.

The three of them returned to Jang Taklung and spoke to many geshés about what they had each seen. One old monk remarked, "It's true to say that the great adept is old. He was old when I was a young monk!"

Other geshés said, "All three of you are correct. Since he is an emanation of the Teacher of Uḍḍiyāna, he manifests as old, young, and in the prime of life."

~

While the great adept did not stray from vajralike meditative concentration on the peak of glorious Riwoché, the ornamental wheel of his inexhaustible enlightened body, speech, and mind manifested in three great regions of Kham.

At Gyalmorong, a person who had received the Path with the Result at Sakya, and who meditated single-mindedly on the Time of the Path during four sessions and on the Profound Path Guruyoga,[1069] saw the great adept to be Vajradhara, the lord of all spiritual families, and made countless prostrations.

A person who recited thirty thousand *maṇis* without break every day declared, "This isn't Vajradhara. I'm happy to meet Avalokiteśvara," confessed his sins, and offered prostrations.

A person who recited a thousand of the heart-mantra of Tārā every day, declared, "This isn't Avalokiteśvara. It's Tārā."

Also, a person said, "This is the Great Adept of Iron Bridges. O great adept, why do different visual manifestations appear to us?"

The great adept replied:

> By bringing the vital winds
> and mind under control, [315]
> taking control of how things appear to myself,
> overwhelming how things appear to others,
> and positioning magical bodies,
> I display whatever
> will tame sentient beings
> according to their various inclinations.

~

Once the great adept stayed at a large crossroads in Boborgang, intending to benefit living beings through sight, hearing, awareness, and touch. When he recited the six-syllable mantra himself and urged others to do so, one person said, "Many people have urged us to recite the six syllables, but this man's speech is beautiful and benefits our minds."

Another person said, "Are you speaking of the *Litany of the Names of Mañjuśrī*[1070] as *maṇis*?"

Another said, "This man is reciting the longevity *dhāraṇī*."

Another said, "This man is reciting the Medicine Buddha [mantra]."

Another said, "He is reciting the *Two-Part [Hevajra] Tantra.*"

When the great adept's single voice was understood differently by five people, they asked, "Why do we separately understand the great adept's recitation of *maṇis*?"

He replied, "An attribute of a perfect buddha is said to be, 'While he speaks with only one voice, it is separately understood as many.'"[1071]

The great adept also went to the Markham[1072] area, and a great crowd gathered before him. When he spoke with unimpeded clairvoyance, knowing the individual minds of others, they exclaimed, "Your knowledge of our individual thoughts is incredible."

"With the mind resting evenly, like the all-encompassing sky, I know the three times clearly," he replied. "So concentrate and offer prayers with the attitude that I am an actual buddha!" [316]

During that time he realized that the river was spilling over the top of the Lhasa levees and that the circumambulation path would be flooded.[1073] When he merely sat on top of the levees, the overflowing water instantly receded. The chief steward came to look at the levees, and when he met the great adept sitting there, he said, "Yesterday the precious Jowo was almost lost in the water, but by the compassion of the Jowo, the great adept was invited. Now, please come before the Jowo and teach, turning the wheel of Dharma for the residents and visitors."

The steward called the people of Lhasa. But when they came to invite him with parasols, victory banners, incense, and music, the wings of a vulture extended from his body and he flew away in the direction of Latö in western Tsang.

During that time, the subjects of the Kāmata king had made large offerings to him and asked to be allowed to perform the [sacrifices of] burning and chopping that were forbidden by his vows. The great adept knew with clairvoyance when the king had given permission, and a physical emanation sat in the sandalwood market of Kāmata.

"Summon that greedy king who has broken his vows!" he ordered.

The merchants attacked him from behind with knives, but his back turned to stone. They shot him from in front with many poisonous arrows, but the front of his body turned to iron and he was not injured at all. The great adept appeared sitting in the sky in front of the king. The king and his son recognized the great adept, prostrated, and vowed to not [317] burn women alive.

At that time a villager in the Kāmata marketplace had a poisonous potion that could overcome about a thousand people. The great adept magically robbed him and hid it in a hole. The woman who had prepared the poisonous potion was stopped by a strict vow according to the custom of her region. Then the emanation returned to the peak of glorious Riwoché.

~

The major disciples who had gone to collect offerings in Central Tibet and Tsang, Mön, and Kongpo arrived at the peak of glorious Riwoché.[1074] The great adept was staying in retreat.

The major disciples said, "When you sometimes don't even speak like this, all the people say that you have passed away. We tell them that you are alive, but they say that if they calculate from the time of their ancestors who met the great adept, many generations have passed, and that you aren't alive now. They don't believe it."

He replied, "I'm not a yogin who gets old and hasn't gained self-control over death. Those who want to meet me, will meet me."[1075]

~

Then, at the great monastic seat of glorious Sakya, the people were struck down in various ways by fatal combinations of the Indian disease of jaundice, the Nepalese disease of dysentery, unconscious convulsions,[1076] tetanus, and so forth. They were dying while still eating and drinking and while still working. Losing their senses, they died leaping and racing about, shouting various cries, and so forth. No spirit traps, sacrificial-cake rituals for repulsion, Bönpo rites, protective remedies of physicians and mantra practitioners, and so on were of any benefit. The great monastic seat was nearly emptied.[1077]

In that situation, the great adept gave an image of himself, an Auspicious Stūpa of Many Doors, and an edict to his major disciple Shākya Palsang [318] and seven disciples. He told them, "After arriving early, progressively arrange a ritual feast at absolutely every door. Take refuge by means of the 'Mothers Infinite As Space'! Recite *maṇi*s! Make this prayer!"

1. The great adept Tangtong Gyalpo (1361?–1485).
Fifteenth-century copper alloy image consecrated by the great adept himself.
He holds a medicinal pill and a longevity vase.
Published in Weldon and Singer (1999), p. 185.

3. Tangtong Gyalpo holding an iron chain. Detail of a tangka of the fifteenth-century Taklung Kagyü master Sangyé Drakpa.

Photograph courtesy of Ulrich von Schroeder.

Opposite:

2. Tangtong Gyalpo's great stūpa at Chung Riwoché after repairs.

Photograph by Maria Antonia Sironi. Courtesy of Hildegard Diemberger.

Below:

4. The iron bridge over the Tsangpo River at Puntsok Ling.

Photograph by Maria Antonia Sironi. Courtesy of Hildegard Diemberger.

5. Image of Tangtong Gyalpo holding a longevity vase.
Fifteenth-century bronze image.
After Christie's Indian and Southeast Asian Art catalogue, New York, September 17, 1999, p. 61.

Above:
6. Chung Riwoché.
After Vitali (1990), plate 75.

Right:
7. Tangka of Tangtong Gyalpo in the tradition of the Heartdrop of the Great Adept.
Photograph courtesy of Ani Lodrö Palmo.

8. Tangtong Gyalpo's iron bridge and great stūpa at Chung Riwoché.
Photograph by Maria Antonia Sironi. Courtesy of Hildegard Diemberger.

9. Image of Tangtong Gyalpo holding a medicinal pill and longevity vase.
Fifteenth-century image in the Potala collection.

Photograph courtesy of Ulrich von Schroeder.
Published in von Schroeder (2001), plate 276-D.

10. Iron suspension bridge near Shang, in Tsang.
Photograph courtesy of Moke Mokotoff.

77. **The Great Temple of Sakya.**

May all the illnesses
that bring misery
to sentient beings,
such as the harm of bhuta demons,
disease, and evil demons,
which come from karma
and sudden circumstances,
not appear in this world!

May all the sufferings
of the illnesses that rob life
and separate body and mind
in a single instant,
just like an executioner and his victims,
not appear in this world!

May all embodied beings
remain unharmed by epidemics
such as those of a single day
and those that are constant,
even the names of which illnesses
are frightening to hear

and are like being sucked
into the mouth of Yama,
the Lord of Death!

May all embodied beings
not be hurt by the eighty thousand types
of harmful obstructions,
the 360 sudden obstacles caused by nonhumans,
the 404 illnesses, and so forth!

May each and every suffering
from the disruption of the four elements,
which rob absolutely all
physical and mental comfort, be pacified,
and may everyone have vitality, long lives,
no illness, and be happy and content!

By the compassion of the masters
and the precious Three Jewels,
by the power of the ḍākinīs
and the protecting guardians of Dharma,
and by the force of the infallible truth
of karma and its results,
may the dedication and prayers
be fully realized!

"Make this [319] prayer along with all the crowds you urge to recite *maṇis*!" the great adept ordered. "Pañjaranātha[1078] has been entrusted with the enlightened activities that will soon end the diseases. Give a longevity pill to every person you meet. As each disease gradually ends, chant auspicious verses."

He sent them to Sakya, and when they had done everything according to the sovereign master's instructions, the epidemic diseases came to an end and the people were happy and content.

~

One day a boy came from Dangra[1079] to offer half an ounce of gold, three tails from wild yaks, and fifteen boiled tongues for the sake of his father who had died. "Please don't let my father be reborn in the lower realms," he pleaded.

The great adept replied, "If you are devoted to me and want your father to be born in Sukhāvatī, do seven days of virtuous work!"

"I can't come from Dangra again and again," the boy thought. "It won't benefit father if I disobey the order."

He did seven days of hard, virtuous work. Then he went before the great adept and announced that he was leaving.

"Your father met Amitābha three days ago. Tens of thousands have offered me ritual tablets, but I have never dispatched one aimlessly. I extracted my father Önpo Dorgyal[1080] from hell, and he is now happy. Dangra boy, you should distribute this mantra-blessed barley of mine to all the area people," he said and gave him a small parcel.

The boy distributed a grain of the barley from the great adept's hand to each of all the area people, without excess or shortage. After they ate the barley, they refrained from sins.

"Even I don't know how many people are in the area," the boy commented, "but the great adept knew through clairvoyance."

Everyone became devoted.

~

By that time the lives of many thousands of hybrid yak-cows and yaks had been spared when they had been offered to the great adept. He left them at his birthplace, Rinchen Ding, [320] saying, "They are all my parents."

He cared for the animals whose lives had been spared, without giving them away or letting them be sold. But three treacherous men stole a ram. When they stabbed the ram with a knife, the great adept heard its scream with his divine hearing.

"Thieves have killed an animal whose life had been spared," he said, and told those in his presence, "Recite the *Prayer of Maitreya* three times!" The great adept looked up into space, snapped his fingers three times, and declared, "The ram has been born in Tuṣita as a son of the gods named Drimé Rabga."[1081]

Although the great adept had not invoked the Dharma protectors against the men who had stolen the ram, one thief lost consciousness when he killed the ram and was left for five days without recognizing day and night. When one thief ate the ram's flesh, he was stricken with a parasitic disease and died. One fell into a rocky gorge and broke his foot.

The great adept knew through clairvoyance and said, "These Dharma protectors of ours have sharp eyes and quick feet. They should not harm others without being invoked."

He threw a writing slate at a banner of the Dharma protectors that was in front of his residence. The Dharma protectors became less touchy after that.

~

On one occasion an evil demoness arrived in Jé Bodong and Sakya. For six weeks, many people died from a deadly disease. The great adept glared with his eyes, pointed with the index finger of his left hand, and made the gesture of brandishing a vajra with his right hand in the direction of the deadly disease. He sent several major disciples, masters and students, into the country to [321] perform rites for the people, cattle, and fields, saying, "I have been able to increase the life spans of people in Latö Lho, Latö Jang, and Ngari."

~

On a tenth day, five women with fine faces who were singing sonorous songs of *hūṃ* appeared before the great adept. They served him various kinds of food, offered full-length prostrations, made circumambulations, and flew off into space like birds.

People who were listening to Dharma asked, "Who were those women who honored you?"

"Did you see the ḍākinīs who appeared just now?" he asked.

"We saw five beautiful women, but we don't know who they were."

"They were the five classes of sorceress ḍākinīs, sent to deliver a share of the ritual feast being held by the upholders of pure awareness, the spiritual heroes and ḍākinīs in Uḍḍiyāna, the Land of Ḍākinīs."

~

During that period the great adept did not even come with his actual body to direct the construction of the representations of enlightened body, speech, and mind at the foot of Riwoché. But in front of the door to the temple of the protectors, he sat for seven days on top of the rock shaped like a Dharma throne that is at the base of the present Ewaṃ Gakyil meditation hut.[1082] He blessed five lumps of clay, identical in size, which had been prepared from precious substances, silken cloth, and medicines to be the material for five images of the protectors. When the sculptors were also drawn under the influence of the blessing, from a natural state free of mental activity they immediately finished images of the seven siblings[1083] that appeared naturally after the innate energy of the images had come to fruition in the unimpeded radiance of the unborn state of reality. [322]

Then the great adept told the compulsory laborers who had come to the virtuous work from the three regions of Lho, Jang, and Ngari, and all the artisans and monks, to gather at the door to the temple of the protectors. The gathering was like a sea of human beings. The great adept, in a form that seemed very old, performed the initiation of meditative concentration, or the ultimate consecration, from within the Circular Residence of the Sleeping Dog.[1084] However, because he did not recite even the words of the *Essence of Dependent Origination*[1085] and auspicious verses, everyone said, "There's nothing to connect with in the Iron-Bridge Man's consecration," and dispersed.

Then he asked, "What was the crowd saying?"

When he was told what was being said, he ordered, "In that case, prepare a lavish ritual feast for tomorrow also, and tell the crowd to come for the spectacle of a consecration!"

They did as he said, and when all the people from the three regions of Lho, Jang, and Ngari had been satisfied by the ritual feast, the great adept lifted his head up from the pillow and commanded, "You protectors of the excellent Dharma, put on a spectacle so this crowd will believe!"

The images of the seven siblings transformed to display flirtatiousness, bravery, ugliness, ferocity, and so forth.[1086] When the people heard voices laughing and making the sounds of *hūṃ* and *phaṭ*, everyone was astonished, and the Dharma protectors became known as fierce. The temple of the protectors in which those images reside has an area of ten pillars and has three stories.

⁓

The majority [323] of the structural work was completed for a temple with an area of four pillars, containing an eight-handspan-high image of venerable Tārā created from precious substances, together with murals, and for [a temple] containing a fifteen-handspan-high cast-image of Samantabhadra.[1087] On the day the sanctified contents were being inserted into the Samantabhadra, a man from Dangra offered the great adept an ounce of gold, a large copper kettle, and a goat horn with a naturally arisen Stūpa of Enlightenment at the tip.[1088]

The great adept asked, "Do you have any information about this naturally arisen image?"

"I was told that my ancestors have had this naturally arisen image for about ten generations," the man replied.

"I once took birth as a white goat to benefit the many people and livestock of Dangra Chuktso," the great adept said. "That goat had two straight horns. This is the Stūpa of Enlightenment that was on the tip of the right horn. A Victory Stūpa was on the tip of the left horn. In the third generation of the goat's owner, Samdrup Dar, it was worn for protection on the throat of a boy and lost on the shore of Yumtso Lake. The lake goddess[1089] of Dangra recovered it. By the kindness of that bodhisattva ram, people and wealth were attracted to the owner. He commissioned a volume made from gems and gold. In competition with that model, volumes were written in gold, priests were supported, and so forth, so that the doctrine spread. The people who enjoyed that goat's hair, flesh, bones and so forth gained the higher realms and liberation. Put this naturally arisen image in the heart of the dharmakāya reality body, Samantabhadra." [324]

The inner contents of the temples at the summit and foot [of Riwoché], and the arrangement of the murals and images above and below, should be known from *An Ocean of Marvels*,[1090] where they are clear!

From the Earth Female Snake Year [1449], up until the Wood Male Dragon Year [1484], countless murals and images of the buddhas and bodhisattvas were created in the great stūpa and so forth of glorious Riwoché from precious substances and clay, and four complete sets of all the Words of the Conqueror that had been translated to become the lamp of the snowy land of Tibet were completed as representations of enlightened speech.

On the occasion when the great adept scattered the flowers for the consecration, a rain of flowers fell from the cloudless sky and a sweet aroma of incense and the pleasant sound of the music of the gods arose. From the blessing of the Three Jewels, the glory of happiness and contentment was perfect, because foreign armies had been repelled, the crops were good, and the people and livestock were free from disease.

• • •

The countless figures of the conquerors
with their spiritual children,
created from various blazing,
precious substances like a series
of golden mountains,
were a field producing a crop
of merit for living beings.

The saliva of the translators and paṇḍitas,
those dragons of the sky,
produced a gentle rain of the complete
Translated Scriptures and Treatises,
so that even the vastness of the earth
became too cramped
for those innumerable volumes.

He created a massive,
sublime representation
of the marvelous dharmakāya reality body,
with many doors symbolizing
the countless articles of Dharma,
whose soaring glory I think
blocked the expanse of the sky
and whose light rays blinded the sun.

• • •

15: A Yogin Departs into the Basic Space of Phenomena

One day the great adept ordered, "Arrange all kinds [325] of offerings in the Auspicious Stūpa of Many Doors and in the temples. Renew the sacrificial cakes in the temple of the protectors. Gather here, arrange a fine ritual feast, recite the 'Mothers Infinite As Space,' and intensely make prayers with single-minded fervor!"

He sat with the vajra-gaze and strongly clapped his hands three times. When he finished meditating, the people asked, "Why did you suddenly make offerings and meditate today?"

"The non-Buddhist teacher Karma Goraṇa sent an army against the Vajrāsana in India. The Vajrāsana Temple was about to be lost, and I was offering prayers to repel the army."

"The Vajrāsana Temple wasn't lost to the non-Buddhists?" they asked. "Did the armies disperse?"

"If the blessing of praying to the masters and chosen deities was given a form, it would be as massive as Mount Meru, the king of mountains. The Buddhists around the Vajrāsana were unable to oppose the non-Buddhists, but because we prayed to the Three Jewels, they decided to make war. They assembled a greater army than the non-Buddhists, and killed the non-Buddhist Karma Goraṇa and many others. When the troops who did not die fled into the jungle, they encountered poisonous snakes. For a battle celebration of the defeat of the non-Buddhist armies, repeat the offerings that were presented at the shrines and place sacrificial cakes in the temple of the protectors! Also arrange a lavish ritual feast for us." [326]

Then he sent off the major disciple Kunga Palden to collect the offerings of nomads to the far north. He got male and female yaks, goats, sheep, horses, and so forth. The *maṇi* devotee Lekpa Gyaltsen, who had beheld the face of Mahākaruṇika after the great adept had given him the entrustment of pure awareness for Avalokiteśvara, the *Karaṇḍavyūha Sūtra,*[1091] and so forth, sent offerings such as a tenth of an ounce of gold, eighteen bricks of tea, and a large bronze kettle, together with a written message. The major disciple Kunga Palden and his disciples burned the written message in a fire from guilt at having boiled up the tea.

When they presented the offerings before the great adept, he said, "Kunga Palden, this is the gold and the bronze kettle sent by the *maṇi* devotee Lekpa Gyaltsen. You drank the eighteen bricks of tea. And you were petty enough to burn the written message in a fire. To purify your obscurations, work constantly on the virtuous projects during the day and make three thousand circumambulations around my residence at night!"

Since the great adept was clearly aware of the three times, all of the *maṇi* devotees he sent to collect offerings were unable to lie. Wherever he sent them in India, China, the three regions of Central Tibet, Tsang, and Kham, and in Mön Khashi, they accomplished whatever he had told them to do and were all courageous renunciants who offered whatever they had with great devotion and respect.

~

During that time, a master craftsman of clay images was with the great adept.[1092] Six faithful and wealthy men who were listening to Dharma offered the sculptor the best food and gifts, saying, "You stay in the presence of the great adept. Observe the shape of his body, [327] and please make each of us an image just like his actual body."

In a single day, the sculptor crafted central poles of identical length for the six statues. For the faces, the hands, the postures, and the folds of the clothing, he looked at the actual body of the great adept and made exact portraits painted with precisely the same flesh-colored paint. After the sculptor had completed the structural work, the six patrons and the sculptor asked the great adept for a consecration, and the colors and postures of the six statues changed.[1093]

One statue had a brilliant white and gleaming face, loose hair, and elongated eyes gazing with a peaceful, compassionate expression. The hands were held in the gestures of meditation and giving protection.

One statue had a color like refined gold, smooth[1094] yellow hair, and both eyes gazing straight ahead with a delighted expression. The right hand was in the gesture of granting the sublime attainment and the left held a jewel bliss-whorl.

One statue had become red and bright like coral, with dark reddish hair, and with round bloodshot eyes looking to the side. Both hands were in the meditation gesture, holding a vase.

One statue was young and burly,[1095] with light blue hair hanging down, and both eyes slightly wrathful with an expression that was half calm and half fierce. The smiling face was extremely beautiful, and the two hands held a vajra and a bell.

One statue was the color of sapphire, with greenish-red hair wrapped on the top of the head, and the eyes looking at the sky with the vajra-gaze. Both hands were making the sky-treasury mudrā gesture. [328]

One statue was a wrathful figure, maroon in color, and haughty with dark red braids plaited into a topknot. The eyes were triangular and flashed like lightning. The right hand was waving a vajra and the left was pointing with the index finger.

The patrons said to the sculptor, "These statues were to have been identical. Why do they have individual colors, hand implements, and postures?"

The sculptor replied, "The great adept magically transformed them. I can't figure it out. Are they benefiting living beings by way of the four styles of enlightened action?[1096] Let's ask the great adept himself."

When they asked, he said, "As for the meaning of my portraits becoming different, it is a sign that I benefit living beings in whatever way necessary to tame them, while being in essence Vajradhara, the buddha of the sixth race, who is the pure nature of the five poisons."[1097]

~

During that time, the great adept manifested an emanated body in the region of Dakpo to the east. He sat on top of a large rock behind a mountain shaped like a rising vulture. A woman who acted like she was a mute lived in that area. She went to search for wood and was frightened when she saw him.[1098] "I take refuge in the adept Tangtong Gyalpo!" she cried.

"I am the adept Tangtong Gyalpo," he said.

She heard him and told the local people, "I met Tangtong Gyalpo."

"Where did you meet him?" they asked.

"I met him at the top of the mountain."

"Let's go."

Many people of the Dakpo district came and looked. When they saw a vulture flying in the sky and many footprints left in that rock, they offered prayers and arranged a ritual feast. [329] They agreed to make a rule that said such things as this: "Tangtong Gyalpo came to our region. It is great merit that footprints appeared. He will come again to this place, so we should observe the tenth day here every month without break. We should give supplies to people who stay here, and not take revenge at this place even though you meet the person who killed your father."

A vast meditation center and temple were constructed there. That place was known as Shabjé Tarling, "Footprint Sanctuary of Liberation."

⁓

A patron who had gained undivided faith in the great adept had much wealth, but no son. When he offered prayers, he received a prophecy in a dream: "If you construct an image of the great adept, you will have a son." So he built an image of the great adept as a child about eight years old, and a son and wealth came to him. By the blessing of the primordial-awareness aspect residing within it, the image had inconceivable magical powers, such as curing a large number of lepers of their disease when they made prostrations, offerings, and circumambulations. When the image grew like the waxing moon into the prime of life, the roof of the temple apparently had to be raised several times.

⁓

During that period, the major disciple Gendun Gyaltsen,[1099] who had been willing to give up this life, offered the great adept many sets of silken robes and, for the stūpa and the temples, canopies of multicolored brocade, red brocade, pale white satin, embroidered satin, and so forth, countless offering articles such as parasols, victory banners, pendants, and incense burners, and furthermore, satins and silks, special fabrics, parasols and fans of peacock feathers, and various other tail-hair fans from India, China, Kashmir, Mongolia, and Nepal. These rivaled the abundance of qualities in the pure land of the bodhisattva Mañjuśrī. [330]

Furthermore, the great adept stated, "As a way to benefit Jambudvīpa in general and the people of snowy Tibet in particular, I have constructed fifty-eight precious iron bridges, a total of 118 large ferries and boats, and sixty wooden bridges. I have built 120 assembly halls and temples with many hundreds of representations of enlightened body created from the precious substances of gold, silver, coral, lapis lazuli, amber, and conch shell, the largest measuring thirty-seven handspans tall and the smallest measuring about five finger-widths; five thousand created from clay, from between fifty-five handspans and three handspans tall; and inconceivable murals and canvas paintings. As representations of enlightened speech, I have made eighteen sets of the Translated Scriptures and fifteen sets of the Translated Treatises, with the foremost being a set of the Translated Scriptures written in gold. As representations of enlightened mind, I have constructed 111 stūpas, the largest being the great stūpa of glorious Riwoché, measuring forty armspans on each side, and the smallest measuring eight armspans on each side. I have established many meditation centers such as the isolated site of Tarpa Ling, and, to save the lives of sentient beings, I have opened the gates and so forth to hidden lands and to sacred places in barbarian borderlands. According to the command of the Great Teacher of Uḍḍiyāna, I have established geomantic focal-points throughout Tibet. Therefore, this happiness and contentment, like the sun between clouds, is due to the kindness of me, Tangtong Gyalpo."[1100]

At that time, eight spiritual friends who maintained the pure conduct of the Kadampa tradition came from the monastery of Nartang[1101] to meet the great adept. "Many adepts, translators, and paṇḍitas have appeared in India and Tibet," they said, [331] "but no legacy of impartial work for the benefit of living beings and work on virtuous projects in India, China, the barbarian borderlands of Mön and Kongpo, and so forth, has been more vast and enduring than yours, O adept. This is the fruition of your past prayers. Holy man, just as you have made prayers, so we would also make them. Please give us a prayer."

He gave them this:

> I prostrate with devotion to the conquerors
> and their spiritual children in the ten directions,
> and to the masters, chosen deities, and ḍākinīs.
> Bless me to be able to benefit living beings!
>
> After accepting my vast offerings,
> both actually arranged and mentally emanated,
> please fulfill these prayers
> for the benefit of living beings.
>
> To the conquerors and their spiritual children
> I confess whatever sinful acts

I have committed due to an ignorant
unawareness.
Please save me from the abyss
of the lower realms.

With deep sincerity,
I rejoice in all the virtue
of the conquerors and their spiritual children,
the śrāvakas, the pratyekabuddhas,
and people in the ten directions.

I urge the lords in the ten directions
to turn the wheel of the excellent Dharma
for the benefit of living beings.
I pray for them to remain
and not pass into nirvāṇa
for as long as saṃsāra has not been emptied.

Until I reach the heart of enlightenment,[1102]
I take full refuge in the Buddha,
Dharma, and Sangha,
and in the masters, chosen deities, and ḍākinīs.

Just as past conquerors
and their spiritual children [332]
awakened the thought of enlightenment
and gradually performed those topics
of training for bodhisattvas,
so will I awaken the thought of enlightenment
for the benefit of living beings
and gradually perfect the topics
of training for bodhisattvas.

By the virtue accumulated in the three times
with my body, speech, and mind,
may I gain unexcelled, sublime enlightenment,
and liberate all beings from the sea of existence.

Until I reach enlightenment,
may I have no obstacles on the path
and have perfect favorable conditions,
and may I gain ordination
until I reach the spiritual level of Delight.[1103]

May I be an ordained person
endowed with Dharma,
always of the noble spiritual family,
and have perfect moral discipline.

Without concern for body and life,
may I resort to excellent spiritual friends,
and endowed with the seven riches of a Noble One,[1104]
always uphold the excellent Dharma.

May I fully keep the three vows,
and combine method and wisdom.

May I always make offerings
to the Three Jewels,
and always please the masters.

Without hoping for return and result,
may I practice impartial generosity.[1105]

Without hypocritical aims,
may I guard immaculate moral discipline.

May I always remain patiently able
to bear disagreeable things.

May I have firm diligence,
which is the armor of enthusiasm
for the benefit of sentient beings. [333]

May I gain the power
of a sharply focused mind,
unharmed by outer and inner disturbances.

May I gain the sublime wisdom
of penetrating insight
into all phenomena
as empty and without self-nature.

May a sudden realization
of the unborn nature of my mind arise.

Until I have gained stability of mind,
may I live alone in the mountain ranges,
fearless like a wild beast,
and gain control over all
appearances and the mind.

After gaining control over all
appearances and the mind,
may my body, speech, and mind be unharmed,
and by means of nonreferential
primordial awareness unstained
by conceptual elaborations,
may I tame all living beings
in whatever way necessary,
thereby bringing perfect benefit to others.

May everyone who commits nonvirtuous sins
in the ten directions of this world
turn to virtuous merit instead.

May everyone suffering in the lower realms
because of the maturation of their evil karma
gain the happiness of the higher realms through my merit.

In the ten directions of this world,
may all sentient beings who are sick
gain the joy of freedom from illness through my merit.

In the ten directions of this world,
may the blind see forms, the deaf hear sounds,
and the insane regain their senses.

May the hungry and thirsty find food and drink,
those without clothing find clothing, [334]
and the poor gain wealth.

May the frightened become fearless
and the bound become free.

May any sentient being who is dying
be free from the pains of death.

May sentient beings
in the intermediate state between existences
gain fearless self-control.

May all sentient beings
tame their angry minds.

May no mutual conflict arise
between those with the awareness
of being parents and children.

May everyone who is filled with faith and devoted to me,
and who gives food and drink
and offerings and praise,
gain virtue and reach excellent enlightenment.

May unimpeded blessings come to anyone
who makes fervent prayers to me.

May anyone who has abused me,
been angry with me, beaten me,
taken my life, and so forth
quickly feel regret
and become foremost in my retinue.

Whatever use I have made of the bodies
and possessions of sentient beings,
and whatever use others
have made of my body and possessions,

may each of those sentient beings
all gain vast happiness.

May every sentient being
whom I have given Dharma
and material goods,
and every sentient being
who has seen or touched my body
or heard my speech,
be purified of physical and vocal obscurations.

May the physical and mental illnesses
and sufferings of everyone
who has heard my name [335]
be fully removed,
and may they gain excellent happiness.

For as far as the sky reaches,
may my body also reach,
bringing benefit by appearing
in the form wished by each and every living being.

May the sound of my voice
also reach that far
and proclaim the sound of Dharma.

May my mind enter the minds
of sentient beings who are as infinite as space,
and may they be endowed
with the enlightenment mind
of indivisible emptiness and compassion.

May I also become whatever
nurtures sentient beings,
such as the major elements of earth and so forth,
and such as a precious wish-fulfilling gem,
a heavenly tree, a fine vase, an unplanted crop,
a wish-fulfilling cow,

an accomplishing mantra of pure awareness,
great medicine, and the sun and moon.

By the force of my prayers,
the force of the generosity
of the conquerors and their spiritual children,
and the force of the basic space of phenomena,
may the benefit of living beings
be accomplished effortlessly and spontaneously,
just as I pray,
for as long as saṃsāra has not been emptied.

On that occasion, the great adept gave this edict to the boundless humans and nonhumans of different languages and races who were listening to Dharma from Urgyen Tangtong Gyalpo:

> As my legacy, there are vast representations of enlightened body, speech, and mind, and bridges, ferries, and so forth. It is very important who the person to maintain these will be, so I have consulted the trio of gods, demons, and human beings. [336]
>
> The people of Mön and Kongpo said to appoint a descendant. Others said to appoint a disciple. The Nepa of Lhasa[1106] said to appoint a descendant and a very knowledgeable disciple. When I requested an opinion from the Jowo Śākyamuni, he said it would be good when upheld by a descendant.
>
> I have appointed venerable Nyima Sangpo as my heir. You must all understand this.[1107]

At that time, offerings came from the Yarlung sovereign Chen Nga Ngawang Drakpa,[1108] Tsokyé Dorjé of Rinpung,[1109] and the Ja governor Tashi Dargyé,[1110] and from the eastern regions of Mön, Dakpo, Kongpo, the three ridges of Dokham, and so forth. Tens and hundreds of thousands of arable fields were offered, and gold, turquoise, silk brocade, a hundred bricks of tea, and a superb stallion with jeweled saddle and head stall.

The requests unanimously said, "Lord, great adept, please regard our defenders and supporters with compassion. By all means, you must come, and we will accomplish whatever virtuous work you command. We will offer our own retinues, together with our possessions."

The great adept replied, "I traveled extensively around the country before, and also completed some virtuous works. I traveled around in all directions, so my body is now decrepit. Tricking people, I tricked myself.[1111] The escorts of karma and its results have arrived from in front. The agents of Yama pursue from behind. I am about to reach the common destination. So it is difficult for me to come myself. I previously had the wish to construct an iron bridge at the boat crossing of Nyago, but the auspicious connections were not in alignment until now. [337] The gods and demons of glacial Tibet went to the virtuous work a month ago. Stone will be scarce, but you will uncover a stone deposit. Your disciples will be equal to those of Tangtong Gyalpo. Venerable Nyima Sangpo, it is time for you to go."

He sent Nyima Sangpo off with the envoys, and as soon as the Snake Year [1485] dawned, the virtuous work at Nyago in Yarlung began.[1112] The spiritual son of the conquerors Tenzin Nyima Sangpo and about three hundred masters and disciples gathered at the Nyago boat crossing. To search for the spot to pile up the bridge pier in the middle of the river, the precious spiritual son of the conquerors, and several masters and disciples, held a very long pole beautified with a flag, and went out in the ferry. When he secured the large Dharma flag in the middle of the Tsangpo River, all the teachers of scripture and reasoning at Tsetang[1113] accepted him as an indisputable adept. They demonstrated their respect by spreading out their hats on all the path that the gems of his toenails touched, making prostrations from afar by touching the five points of their bodies to the earth, and so forth.

Stone was extremely scarce to both the south and the north, but a large stone deposit was uncovered in the midst of the sands. They put the stones into the ferries and coracle boats, and when they arrived at the great flag, they readily threw the stones into the great river. The eight tribes of gods, tsen demons, nāgas, and so forth piled up the walls of different colors, better and more stable than we humans could have done. When the water of the Tsangpo River is clear, they can be seen very clearly, because even nowadays the walls are undamaged.

The bridge abutments were properly completed. [338] When the connecting of the iron chains was finished and they were to be pulled up with great ropes, Tenzin Rinpoché urged everyone in the crowd to chant the "Mothers Infinite As Space." As the words were murmured, many people with pure karma, led by the precious spiritual son of the conquerors, saw the great adept—the essence of Vajradhara, who is the embodiment of the masters and chosen deities—up in the sky adorned with charnel-ground garments. A great assembly of the gods and demons of apparent existence gathered. When the iron chains were pulled, the two long and short spans of the iron bridge, a pathway to enlightenment, were properly raised. The rope nets, the flat boards for the walkway, and so forth, were completed. Since the waters of all Central Tibet and Tsang collect on the vast plain of Yarlung, like a brimming sea, there were thirty-two [stone] piers on the northern side.[1114] Everything was properly completed by the fifteenth day of the seventh month of the Wood Female Snake Year [1485].[1115]

On the occasion of the consecration, both the Desi Rinpoché[1116] and the great master of Tsetang came from Nedong Peak with teachers and members of the Sangha and so forth, and countless laypersons and clergy of Yarlung and Ön were present. In their midst, the spiritual son of the conquerors Tenzin Nyima Sangpo, the lord of yogins who had gained stability in the creation and completion stages, urged the crowd of gods, demons, and human beings to take refuge by chanting the "Mothers Infinite As Space," and scattered the flowers of consecration. The gods who delight in goodness caused miraculous signs to appear, such as parasols and victory banners of rainbow light, and a rain of flowers.

That great spiritual son of the conquerors then repaired the slightly damaged iron bridge at Urtö Chökhor Gang. [339] He constructed new iron bridges at Drakralkha in Penyul and at the ferry crossing of Shar Drukha, and became an excellent heir who maintained the great adept's tradition without decline.[1117]

Moreover, the great adept's nephew and spiritual son Jampa Nyendrak was appointed to be his heir as priest to the country, thus receiving the order to tame living beings. The great adept focused his attention on the hereditary lineage continuing through his physical son Döndrup Sangpo. And his son Kyabpa Sangpo[1118] performed benefit for living beings equal to that of the great adept himself at the monastic seat of Tsagong, and in Sharmön, Lo Khatra, and so forth.

Furthermore, the best of the great adept's six sublime spiritual sons and the nine upholders of pure awareness, governors of men who wore Mongol dress, was the Dharma king Namkha Dorjé,[1119] whom the Teacher of Uḍḍiyāna, who knows the three times, had prophesied as an emanation of Vajrapāṇi. Namkha Dorjé saw the master, the great adept, to be the Buddha. In order for the custom of the road tax urged upon all living beings who traveled in front of the great vital mountain [of Riwoché] not to decline for as long as the doctrine remained, every time Namkha Dorjé came to this place of practice he would carry seven loads of stone on his fine robes and do whatever pleased the master. Furthermore, he instituted the custom of the Chung Valley residents offering wood and rope at glorious Riwoché every year.[1120]

The fifty-eight people with the karma, the sixteen hidden ḍākinīs, and the one million human and nonhuman beings capable of benefiting others, who are counted among the disciples of the great adept, performed infinite actual and invisible benefit for living beings. [340] The *Prophecy* of the Teacher of Uḍḍiyāna, who knows the three times, says:

> Actual and invisible benefit for living beings
> will be accomplished by a retinue of emanations
> and an assembly of disciples:
> spiritual sons who practice
> the transmission of the true meaning
> while maintaining worldly conduct;
> nine governors of men, who wear Mongol costume;
> fifty-cight with thc karma,
> who have different dress and behavior;
> and sixteen hidden ḍākinīs.
>
> Furthermore, those with the karma
> and good fortune,
> and who are emanations
> of spiritual heroes and ḍākinīs,
> will constantly gather as his retinue.[1121]

This is just a general statement. The special places for this great accomplished lord are mentioned in the *Prophecy*:

> The place of practice is Potala.
> The place of blessings is Kharchu Drak.
> The place of prophecy is Takdrö Rong.
> The place of benefit to living beings is Tsari Tsa.
> The place of disciples is the land of Tibet.
> The place of attainment is Sukhata.[1122]

The [last line] means, "The place where he reached attainment is Sukhāvatī."[1123] "Sukhata" is a corruption of Sukhāvatī, the equivalent of Dewachen [in Tibetan].

Furthermore, [the *Prophecy*] says:

> The place of truth is the basic space of phenomena.
> Pure awareness is present unmoved.[1124]

Resting evenly with the same vision that a buddha has of the fundamental nature of the [universal] ground just as it is, the great adept replied to all questions and continually worked for the benefit of sentient beings.

~

One day the great adept had also informed the venerable lady Chökyi Drönmé, [341] "The way I will die has never happened before to any human being. Now it will be said that such a thing is impossible for anyone."

Delek Chödren[1125] had asked the venerable lady, "What was that?"

She had replied, "He said that he will certainly die in a special way that has not happened to anyone before."[1126]

~

The great adept's lifespan is mentioned in the *Prophecy*:

> His lifespan will be eighty-one,
> but if he practices the elixir
> of the life-sustaining goddess,
> he will be able to live longer than that.[1127]

Since he had vanquished the four māras,[1128] he was completely victorious in battle over the Lord of Death, the same as the perfect Buddha. The *Sūtra of Excellent Golden Light* says:

> Buddhas do not completely pass into nirvāṇa,
> nor does the Dharma disappear.[1129]

As it says, because this peerless great Iron-Bridge Man had also obtained the glory of eternal and indestructible life, he could have remained for an aeon or more without falling under the control of the Lord of Death. However, to urge toward the Dharma those people who cling to permanence, the perfect Buddha displayed the manner of passing away, because the act of passing into nirvāṇa is much more marvelous than the other eleven acts.[1130] In a similar way, the *Prophecy* of the Great Teacher of Uḍḍiyāna says:

> At some point, when he displays
> the manner of passing away,
> among sounds and lights
> and with an assembly
> of spiritual heroes and ḍākinīs,
> he will attain enlightenment in Sukhāvatī.[1131]

No sign of any physical illness occurred. [342] When calculated by adding the extra days to two sixty-year cycles and five single years, the great adept was 128 years old.[1132] On the fourth day of the month of miracles in the Wood Female Snake Year [1485] of the eighth sixty-year cycle, he spoke these words:

> The dynamic energy of ceaseless [thoughts]
> is consummated in the unborn state.
>
> That ineffable mind is unawareness
> and pure awareness.
>
> All conceptual elaborations vanish
> in utter simplicity.
>
> If conceptual mind is transcended,
> saṃsāra is laughable.[1133]

As he spoke, streaks of light flashed, much symbolic language of the ḍākinīs buzzed, various sounds roared, and Sanskrit words rang out. At that moment, his body became a mass of light radiating light rays in a hundred directions, and rose into the sky above his meditation hut. At that time, many spiritual heroes and ḍākinīs greeted him with multicolored parasols, victory banners, incense burners, tail-hair fans, and so forth of rainbow light, and with various sounds of music. All the earth was covered with the sweet fragrance of incense.

As the great adept rose higher and higher, the spiritual son [Sherab Palden][1134] offered prayers with intense feeling, beginning with this:

> O great adept, though here just now,
> your body has disappeared,
> fading into light!

So the body of the great adept, just eighteen inches tall, appeared in the sky in front of him and said this:

> Mourner, grieving and wailing aloud,
> a yogin departs into the basic space of phenomena,
> but "death" pains the mind of a child.
>
> If you don't know it's your own mind,
> there's no chance for the suffering
> of confusion to wear out.
>
> So, like waking from a dream,
> know that all the appearances
> of external and internal things
> are your mind!
>
> If you practice according to my words,
> it will be beneficial in all of this life and the next.

The spiritual son [343] cried, "O great adept, you have gained self-control over birth and death, so please remain for the benefit of infinite sentient beings, without passing into nirvāṇa!"

"I have gained self-control over birth and death, so I'm leaving right now."

"Even though you don't remain in your body for an aeon, please stay until Tenzin Rinpoché arrives. If you definitely won't stay, and if no body can be shown as an object of merit for the people of snowy Tibet, how will I face them? What will I say? You really must leave a body. Please give complete advice for positioning your body, and for Tenzin Rinpoché and me to benefit living beings and care for disciples."

The great adept replied, "Venerable Nyima Sangpo should not stay in one place, but perform the benefit of living beings impartially and concentrate on ways to spread my legacy. Although for me there is no cause for the separation of matter and awareness known as 'death,' you should leave this mere form of a body here in the meditation hut in the posture of a king at leisure with the pointing index finger aimed at the Mongols and the smiling face turned toward the governor of Jang. For the Mongols not to come to Tibet, it is necessary just to say that I, Tangtong Gyalpo, am in Tibet. So keep this secret for one hundred years at best, fifty as medium, and at least for about thirty! As for the way to tame living beings in the external world, think that you are me, and take control of the gods, demons, and human beings! Continually benefit living beings!"

Accordingly, the spiritual son of the conquerors Tenzin Nyima Sangpo and the spiritual son Sherab Palden both put that into practice. [344] By the compassion and blessing of the great adept, they both came to have unimpeded clairvoyance and magical abilities, and all the human beings[1135] on the surface of the earth believed that the great adept was actually still living.

Because of pristine prayers in the past, when this spiritual son Sherab Palden was twenty-six years old, he had come before the great adept. Special blessings had entered him when they met. He acted as the great adept's close personal attendant for sixteen years. He received countless oral instructions. Then he acted as the great adept's regent for thirty-two years, which brought vast benefit to sentient beings, such as no harm from the Western Mongols occurring in Tibet.

⁓

In the Fire Female Ox Year [1517], [the great adept's] precious body was invited into a silver stūpa. The Dharma king Namkha Lekpa,[1136] whom the Great Teacher [of Uḍḍiyāna] had prophesied to be an emanation of Songtsen Gampo, came on the occasion of the consecration. He established many ritual objects of worship and rows of offering lamps. Jedrung Sangpo Palrin was installed on the monastic seat.

Colophon

THIS BIOGRAPHY of the great accomplished lord, the Iron-Bridge Man Tangtong Gyalpo, is known as *A New Jewel Mirror in Which All the Marvels Are Clear.*[1137] When the auspicious cakras on the soles of the feet of the Kalkī Dharma king Namkha Tsewang Puntsok Wangi Gyalpo,[1138] the lord of all regions, touched this great site of practice, I was urged by his command, "Compile together in one place the fine actions the great adept accomplished!" Again later, as an excellent ornament to beautify this site of practice, he kindly bestowed a mural of the events in [345] the great adept's life, and made a sincere request. As a result, [this biography was written] by the bilingual monk Gyurmé Dechen, who was born from the stream of the vajra-moon[1139] that was the support for the immutable great bliss of the sublime lord of adepts, and which melted due to his impartial affection for sentient beings. Since his hereditary line was blessed for the benefit of the doctrine, my comprehension is somewhat broad, and I am able to utilize the volumes of the noble land [of India] and Tibet in conjunction and teach the unerring significance of the scriptures.

I made Könchok Dewé Jungné of the Samdrup Temple, who is a paternal descendant of the great Iron-Bridge Man[1140] and an upholder of his Dharma tradition, repeatedly read the ancient biographical writings. I once again examined and made many additions and deletions to the hasty compilation of new biographical writings done by the Buddhist monk Ngagi Wangchuk, who was endowed with the same maternal ancestry as me. This was properly completed on the fifteenth day of the tenth month of the Earth Female Bird Year [1609] in the Ewaṃ Gakyil,[1141] the home of the sublime adept on the slope of the great mountain of glory, 125 years after the great adept passed away.

On the basis of the biography done by Gyalwang Könchok Jungné, [this new edition] was written down by the scribe, the beggar whose home is in the region of Latö in western Tsang, in the Earth Female Sheep Year.[1142]

May this bring excellent virtue to living beings!

The Final Story Concerning the Nirvāṇa of the Great Adept

by Kunga Sönam Drakpa Palsang

ན་མོ་གུ་རུ།

སྟོན་པ་སངས་རྒྱས་འཕགས་པ་རབ་འབྱོར་དང་།
སྤྱན་རས་གཟིགས་དབང་ཨོ་རྒྱན་པདྨ་དང་།
ཀུ་ཀུ་རི་པ་རྗེ་བཙུན་ཏི་ལླི་པ།
གང་འདུལ་སྒྱུར་སྟོན་སྤྲུལ་སྐུ་ལྷུགས་ཟམ་པ།
ཐང་སྟོང་རྒྱལ་པོའི་ཞབས་ལ་ཕྱག་འཚལ་ལོ།

དེ་ཡང་མཉམ་མེད་ལྷུགས་ཟམ་པ་ཆེན་པོ། ཐང་སྟོང་རྒྱལ་པོ་ཞེས་ཁམས་གསུམ་ན་འགྲན་ཟླ་བྲལ་བའི་སྐྱེས་བུ་དེ་ཉིད་ཀྱི། གདུལ་བྱའི་ཐ་མ་མྱ་ངན་ལས་འདས་ཏེ་དགོངས་པ་ཟབ་མོ་ཆོས་ཀྱི་དབྱིངས་སུ་ཐིམ་པར་མཛད་པའི་རྣམ་ཐར་ནི། སྐྱེས་བུ་དམ་པ་དེ་ལྟ་བུ་ལ་སྐྱེ་འཆི་མི་མངའ་ཡང་། རྟག་པར་བལྟ་བའི་སྐྱེ་བོ་འགོག་པ་དང་། མི་རྟག་པ་རྒྱུད་ལ་སྐྱེས་ཏེ་རྫོགས་པའི་བྱང་ཆུབ་ཐོབ་པར་བྱ་བའི་ཕྱིར་དང་། ཞིང་ཁམས་གཞན་གདུལ་བྱ་རྒྱ་ཆེ་བ་ལ་དགོངས་པས་སོ།
འོ་ན་སྐྱེ་འཆི་མི་མངའ་བའི་རྒྱུ་མཚན་ནི། མྱང་འདས་ཀྱི་ཐོབ་པའི་གང་ཟག་ཡིན་པའི་ཕྱིར་རོ། དེ་བཞིན་གཤེགས་པའི་ལུང་བསྟན་པ་འམ། གཉིས་སུ་མེད་པ་ལྟ་བུ་སྟེ། འདུལ་བ་ལུང་ལས།

ད་ལྟའི་དུས་ཀྱི་དགེ་སློང་རབ་འབྱོར་འདི་ཉིད། མ་འོངས་པའི་དུས་ན། བྱང་ཕྱོགས་ཁ་བ་ཅན་དུ་དགེ་སློང་བརྩོན་འགྲུས་ཞེས་བྱ་བར་འགྱུར་རོ།

ཅེས་དང་། ཨོ་རྒྱན་ཆེན་པོ་པདྨ་འབྱུང་གནས་ཀྱི་ལུང་བསྟན་གསལ་བའི་སྒྲོན་མེ་ལས་ཀྱང་།

ཞི་བ་ཐུགས་རྗེ་ཆེན་པོ་དང་།
དྲག་པོ་ཁྲོ་བོ་དབང་ཆེན་གཉིས།
གཉིས་མེད་གཅིག་ཏུ་སྲེས་པ་ལས།
སྐུའི་ཆ་ལུགས་ཞི་མ་ཁྲོ།

Namo Guru

I prostrate at the feet
of the Iron-Bridge Man Tangtong Gyalpo,
the emanated body who manifests
in any form that tames living beings,
such as that of our Teacher the Buddha,
noble Subhūti,[1143] powerful Avalokiteśvara,
Padmasambhava of Uḍḍiyāna, Kukkuripa,
and the venerable lord Tilopa.

This is the story of the last act performed for disciples by the peerless, great Iron-Bridge Man Tangtong Gyalpo, that person unrivaled in the three realms, which was to pass into nirvāṇa and dissolve his awareness into the profound basic space of phenomena. Although such a holy person is not subject to birth and death, he performed this act to refute people who held the view of permanence, to cause a recognition of impermanence to arise in their mindstreams so that they would achieve perfect enlightenment, and because he was concerned for the vast number of living beings who were to be tamed in other realms.

In that case, for what reason was the great adept not subject to birth and death? Because he was an individual who had achieved nirvāṇa. He had been prophesied by the Tathāgata or was seemingly indivisible from him. The *Scriptures of the Monastic Code* say:

This monk Subhūti at the present time will, in a future time,
be known in the snowy north as the monk Tsöndru.[1144]

The great teacher of Uḍḍiyāna, Padmasambhava, also says in the *Bright Lamp of Prophecy*:

Combining indivisibly as one
both calm Mahākaruṇika
and the terrible Great Wrathful Lord,
his physical appearance will be semiwrathful.

མདོག་ནག་དྲི་ཞིམ་སྣི་བས་རྒྱན།
སྐད་རིགས་མི་ཅིག་འཕོར་གྱིས་བསྐོར།

ཅེས་དང༌། སྤྲུལ་སྐུ་པདྨ་གླིང་པའི་ལུང་བསྟན་ལས།

པདྨའི་སྤྲུལ་པ་ཐང་སྟོང་པ་ཞེས་འབྱུང༌།
དེ་དུས་བོད་འབངས་སེམས་ཅན་ཅུང་ཟད་བདེ།

ཅེས་གསུངས་པས་ན། སྐྱེ་འཆི་མེད་པའི་རྒྱ་མཚན་ནོ།

ད་ནི་དད་པའི་སྨུ་གུ་སྨྱུང་འདས་ཀྱི་རྣམ་ཐར་ཆེད་དུ་བརྗོད་པ་ནི། ཞིང་འདིའི་གདུལ་བྱ་རྫོགས་ནས། འགྲོ་བའི་དོན་གཞན་དུ་མཛད་པའི་རྒྱ་མཚན། ཨོ་རྒྱན་ཆེན་པོས།

སྐྱེས་བུ་ལྕགས་ཟམ་གླང་པོ་པ། [162a]
བརྒྱད་བརྒྱ་ཕྲག་གཅིག་ཚོའི་ཚད།
ཚེ་འཛིན་ལྷ་མོའི་ཚེ་གྲུབ་ན།
དེ་བས་རིང་བ་ཐུབ་པའང་སྲིད།
ཚེ་ལ་བར་ཆད་ལན་བདུན་འབྱུང༌།

Dark in color, with a pleasant fragrance,
and adorned with moles,
he will be surrounded by a retinue
who speak different languages.[1145]

A prophecy of the emanated body Pema Lingpa says:

An emanation of Padmasambhava
called Tangtongpa will appear.

At that time some comfort will come
to the citizens and sentient beings of Tibet.[1146]

These statements express the reason the great adept was free from birth and death.

~

Now, as a seedling for faith, the specific story of the great adept's nirvāṇa will be told. The reason he acted for the benefit of living beings elsewhere after completing his work for those to be trained in this world is stated by the Great Teacher of Uḍḍiyāna:

The Iron-Bridge Man, born in an Ox Year,
will have a lifespan of eighty-one.

If he perfects the longevity [techniques]
of the life-sustaining goddess,
it is also possible that he will
live longer than that.

If a māra who has broken
the sacred commitments appears,
it is also possible that he will
pass away at twenty-five.

Obstacles to his life will occur seven times.[1147]

འགྲོ་དོན་ཁ་བ་ཅན་ལ་བྱེད།
དགོངས་པ་སྨྲས་པའི་ཡུལ་དུ་ཕེབས་བཏའ།

ཅེས་གསུངས་པ་བཞིན་དུ། ཕྱིར་ཡང་ལྷ་བ་བཀའ་རྟགས་ཀྱི་ཆོས་བཞི་ནང་ནས་ཀྱང་།
འདུས་བྱས་མི་རྟག་པར་གསུངས། སྐོས་འོ་བསྐོལ་རྣམས་བསོད་ནམས་དམན་པའི་སྐལ་
བ་རན་པར། གཟུགས་ཆོས་དབྱིངས་སུ་ཐིམ་པའམ། འཇིག་རྟེན་གྱི་ཁམས་གཞན་དུ་
འགྲོ་བ་མཐའ་ཡས་པ་སྨིན་གྲོལ་གྱི་ལམ་ལ་འགོད་པར་བྱ་ཕྱིར་མྱ་ངན་ལས་འདའ་བར་
མངོན་ཏེ། གྲུབ་ཐོབ་ཆེན་པོའི་ཞལ་ནས།

སྐྱེ་མེད་ངང་ལ་འགག་མེད་རྩལ་རྫོགས་ཏེ།
བརྗོད་མེད་སེམས་དེ་མ་རིག་རིག་པ་ཡིན།
སྤྲོས་པ་ཐམས་ཅད་སྤྲོས་མེད་ངང་དུ་ཐལ།
བློ་འདས་ཡིན་ན་འཁོར་བ་རྐོད་རེ་བྲོ།

ཅེས་གསུངས་ཤིང་། གྲུབ་ཐོབ་ཆེན་པོས་དགུང་ལོ་བརྒྱ་དང་ཉེར་བརྒྱད་བཞེས་ཚེ། སྤྲུལ་
ལོ་ཟླ་བ་དང་པོ་ཡང་དག་པར་རྫོགས་པའི་སངས་རྒྱས་དཔལ་རྒྱལ་བ་ཤཱཀྱ་ཐུབ་པའི་
ཆོ་འཕྲུལ་ཆེན་པོའི་དུས་ཆེན་བསྟན་པའི་ཚེས་བཞིའི་ཉིན། སྐུ་འོད་ཀྱི་ཕུང་པོར་བྱས་ཏེ།
བསྒྲུབ་ཁང་གི་སྟེང་དཔག་ཚད་བདུན་ཙམ་གྱི་ནམ་མཁར་འཕགས་སོ།
དེའི་ཚེ་ནམ་མཁའ་ལ་འཇའི་དྲ་བ་དང་། ལྷའི་བུ་མོ་རྣམས་ཀྱི་མེ་ཏོག་གི་ཆར་ཆེན་པོ་དང་།
ལྷ་རྫས་ཀྱི་བདུག་སྤོས་དང་། འོད་ཀྱི་གློག་ཁྱུག སྒྲའི་སྐད་ཅེམ་ཅེམ་ཙུར་ཙུར་འཁྲུག་པ་
དང་། སམ་སྙི་ཏའི་སྐད་ལྷང་ལྷང་པའི་ཆོམས་སྒྲ། མཁའ་འགྲོ་མ་རྣམས་བརྡའི་སྐད་དིར་
དིར་བ་དང་བཅས་ཏེ་སྐབས་ཅིག་ནས་མི་སྣང་བར་གྱུར་ཏོ།
དེ་ནས་ཐུགས་སྲས་པ་ཐུགས་དྲན་མེད་ལ་སོང་སྟེ་ཡུན་རིང་དུ་བརྒྱལ་ལོ།
དེ་ནས་མདུན་གྱི་ནམ་མཁའ་ནས། བུ་ཞེས་པའི་སྒྲ་ཅིག་བྱུང་བས་ཐུགས་དྲན་པ་བསྐྱེད་དེ།
གྲུབ་ཐོབ་ཆེན་པོ་དམིགས་པའི་ཡུལ་དུ་ལམ་ལམ་དང་། དྲིན་ཆེ་བས་ [162b] མིག་

He will work for the benefit
of living beings in the Snowy Land.

His awareness will travel to a hidden land.

In accordance with this statement, in general, from among the four topics that summarize the view and teachings,[1148] it is taught that composite things are impermanent. In particular, due to our share of inferior merit, the great adept dissolved his form into the basic space of phenomena, or, to place infinite living beings in other worldly realms upon the path of maturation and liberation, he actualized nirvāṇa. The great adept said:

The dynamic energy of ceaseless [thoughts]
is consummated in the unborn state.

That ineffable mind is unawareness
and pure awareness.

All conceptual elaborations vanish
in utter simplicity.

If conceptual mind is transcended,
saṃsāra is laughable.

When the great adept had reached the age of 128 years, in the first month of a Snake Year [1485],[1149] on the fourth day of the observance of the great occasion of the major miracles of the perfectly complete Buddha, the glorious conqueror Śākyamuni, he transformed his body into a mass of light and rose into the sky about seven leagues above his meditation hut.

At that point, with lattices of rainbows in the sky, a great rain of flowers from the daughters of the gods, incense of divine substances, flashing streaks of light, rumbling, roaring, thundering noises, the resounding sounds of distinctly clear Sanskrit, and the reverberating symbolic language of the ḍākinīs, after a moment the great adept disappeared.

The spiritual son [Sherab Palden] then fainted and lost consciousness for a long time. Then a sound—"Son!"—came from the sky in front, and he regained consciousness. Because the great adept was vividly clear in his mind, and had been so very kind, the spiritual son was instantly aware of

ལམ་དུ་ཡུད་ཡུད་དྲན་པ་དང་། དབང་མེད་ཆིལ་མའི་ཆུ་རྒྱུན་ཉིལ་ཉིལ་འཆོར་བ་དང་། རྩེ་གཅིག་ཏུ་དད་པའི་ཤུགས་ཀྱིས་དུང་དུངས་པར་ཡོང་བ་དང་། སྐབས་སུ་གཞན་སྟོབས་མ་ཐོན་པས་གྲུས་པའི་འོ་དོད་ལྷང་ལྷང་འཆོར་བ་དང་། ཧུ་ཞེས་པའི་ཤུགས་རིང་ཡང་ཡང་དུ་ནོར་བ་དང་། ཨ་ཕ་ཕ། ཨ་མ་མ་ཞེས་གང་གྲག་ལ་སོང་ངོ་།
དེའི་ནང་ལ་རྩེ་གཅིག་གྲུས་པའི་བློ་ནས་འདི་སྐད་དུ་གསོལ་བ་བཏབ་བོ།

ཨེ་མ་ཧོ།

ཕ་དྲིན་པའི་གདུངས་སེལ་ཆོས་ཀྱི་རྗེ།
དད་ལྡན་འདྲེན་མཛད་སྐུ་དྲིན་ཅན།
ཐང་སྟོང་རྒྱལ་པོར་མཚན་གསོལ་བའི།
བཀའ་དྲིན་ཅན་ལ་གསོལ་བ་འདེབས།

བདག་དང་འགྲོ་དྲུག་སེམས་ཅན་ལ།
ཐུགས་རྗེའི་སྤྱན་གྱིས་གཟིགས་སུ་གསོལ།
ཀྱི་ཧུད་འདི་འདྲའི་དུས་བྱུང་ངོ་།
བསོད་ནམས་འདི་འདྲའི་དམན་པའོ།

ཕ་མཉམ་མེད་ད་ལྟ་བཞུགས་བཞིན་དུ།
སྐུ་ནི་འོད་དུ་ཡལ་ལ་ལ།
མེ་ཏོག་ཆར་པ་ཐིབས་སེ་ཐིབ།
སྤོས་ཀྱི་དྲི་ངད་ཐུ་ལུ་ལུ།
འོད་དང་གློག་ཆེན་ཁྱུགས་སེ་ཁྱུག
སྒྲ་དང་ཅུར་སྒྲ་དི་རི་རི།
མཁའ་འགྲོའི་བརྡའ་སྐད་ཁྲོལ་ལོ་ལོ།
འཇའི་དྲ་བ་ཁྲིགས་སེ་ཁྲིག

འདི་འདྲའི་བྱ་བ་ཅི་ཞིག་ཡིན།
རྨི་ལམ་ཡིན་ནམ་མངོན་སུམ་ཡིན།

him before his eyes, and helplessly shed a flowing stream of tears and was filled with yearning from the power of his single-minded faith. Sometimes, unable to bear the intensity, loud wails of devotion burst from him and he cried out over and over, "Oh, no!" and, "Oh, father! Oh, mother!" not knowing what was best.

In that state, the spiritual son offered this prayer with single-minded devotion:

> Oh my!
>
> Father, memory of whom removes anguish,
> Dharma lord, who kindly leads the faithful,
> I offer this prayer to the kind one
> given the name Tangtong Gyalpo.
>
> With compassionate eyes,
> please gaze upon me
> and the sentient beings of the six realms.
>
> Alas! That such a time as this has come.
> That we have such inferior merit as this.
>
> Peerless father, though here just now,
> your body faded and vanished in light,
> a rain of flowers grew thick and dense,
> the fragrance of incense swirled and curled,
> great lights and lightning flickered and flashed,
> sounds and noises rumbled and roared,
> the ḍākinī's symbolic language echoed and rang,
> and rainbow lattices formed into patterns.
>
> What is a deed such as this?
> Is it a dream or is it real?
>
> Great adept, where are you now?
> Is this true or is it pointless?
>
> Your body disappeared and faded in light.
> This heart of mine grew cold.

གྲུབ་ཆེན་ད་ལྟ་གང་ན་བཞུགས།
དོན་དམ་ལགས་སམ་གྱི་ན་ལགས།

སྐུ་ནི་མི་སྣང་འོད་དུ་ཡལ།
བདག་གི་སྙིང་འདི་གྲང་ཆོད་དེ།

འདི་འདྲ་ངེས་པར་བདེན་གྱུར་ན།
སྔ་རབས་བདག་གིས་ལས་བྱས་པ།
དོན་མེད་‥‥ན་དུ་མ་སོང་ངམ།
ཕྱི་རབས་མི་ཚེ་ཇི་ལྟར་འབྱིད།

སྲས་མཆོག་བསྟན་འཛིན་ཆོས་རྗེ་ལ།
གྲུབ་ཆེན་གང་ན་བཞུགས་ཡོད་ཟེར།

ཡོན་བདག་བུ་སློབ་གྲྭ་པ་ལ།
ས་ཕྱོགས་གང་ན་བཞུགས་ཡོད་ཟེར།

དེ་ཁྱེད་ཀྱི་ཐུགས་རྗེས་མི་གཟིགས་ན།
གཞན་གྱི་བྱ་བའི་ཐབས་མ་མཆིས།

བྲག་གཙོང་འདི་ལ་ལྟེབ་པར་ཞུ།

ཅེས་མཆི་མ་འཁྲུག་བཞིན་དུ་རམ་འདའ་རྒྱང་འབོད་བྱས་པས། དུས་རིང་པོ་ཞིག་ནས། འོད་ཆེན་པོ་ཅིག་གིས་ས་ཕྱོགས་ཀུན་བཀང་སྟེ། དྲི་ཞིམ་པོ་གཅིག་གིས་ཁྱབ་པར་བྱུང་ངོ། [163a] དེ་ནས་ཡུན་རིང་པོ་ཞིག་ནས། རྗེ་གྲུབ་ཐོབ་ཆེན་པོ་སྐུའི་བོངས་ཁྲུ་གང་ཙམ་བྱས་པ་གཅིག་མདུན་གྱི་ནམ་མཁར་བྱོན་ཏེ། འདི་སྐད་ཅེས་གསུངས་སོ།

འོད་དོད་འབོད་པའི་ལྷང་ལྷང་ཆེར་ཆེར་པོ།
རྣལ་འབྱོར་ཆོས་ཀྱི་དབྱིངས་སུ་འགྲོ་བ་ལ།

If such as this is really true,
then don't the deeds that I have done
in this first generation become worthless?[1150]
How will people of future generations
live their lives?

Where will I tell the sublime son,
the Dharma lord Tenzin,[1151]
that the great adept is?

Where on earth will I tell the patrons,
disciples, and monks
that you are?

If you don't see me
with your compassion,
I can do nothing else.

I'll commit suicide
from this rocky cliff.

When the spiritual son had spoken, bursting with tears and crying for help, after a long time a great light filled all directions and a pleasant fragrance spread.

Then, after a long time, the lord, the great adept, with a body about eighteen inches tall, appeared in front in the sky and said this:

Mourner, grieving and wailing aloud,
a yogin departs into the basic space of phenomena,
but "death" pains the mind of a child.

If you don't know it's your own mind,
there's no chance for the suffering
of confusion to wear out.

So, like waking from a dream,
know that all appearances
as external and internal things
are your mind!

འཆི་བ་ཞེས་བྱ་བྱིས་པ་སེམས་སྡུག་བྱེད།
དེ་ཉིད་རང་གི་སེམས་སུ་ཤེས་ན།
འཁྲུལ་པའི་སྡུག་བསྔལ་མཛད་པའི་གནས་སྐབས་མེད།

དེས་ན་ཕྱི་ནང་དངོས་པོར་སྣང་བ་ཀུན།
རྨི་ལམ་སད་པ་བཞིན་དུ་རང་གི་སེམས།
ཡིན་པར་ཤེས་པར་གྱིས་ལ་ང་ཉིད་ཀྱི།
བཀའ་བཞིན་བསྒྲུབ་ན་འདི་ཕྱི་ཀུན་དུ་ཕན།

ཅེས་གསུང་ཞིང་མདུན་གྱི་ནམ་མཁར་བཞུགས་པ་གཟིགས་སོ།

དེ་ནས་ཡང་འདི་སྐད་ཅེས་ཞུས་པ། རྗེ་གྲུབ་ཐོབ་ཆེན་པོ་ལགས། ཁྱེད་སྐྱེ་འཆི་ལ་རང་དབང་ཐོབ་པའི་གང་ཟག་ལགས་པས། བསྟན་པ་དང་སེམས་ཅན་གྱི་དོན་དུ་བཞུགས་པར་ཞུ་ལགས། བརྟན་པར་བཞུགས་སུ་གསོལ་ཞུས་པས།

རྗེའི་ཞལ་ནས། ང་སྐྱེ་འཆི་ལ་རང་དབང་ཐོབ་པས། ད་ལན་འགྲོ་བ་ཡིན་གསུངས།

ཡང་ཐུགས་སྲས་པས་ཞུས་པ། ཅི་སྟེ་ད་ལན་འགྲོན་པར་ཐག་ཆོད་ན་བསྟན་འཛིན་རིན་པོ་ཆེ་ཕེབས་ཕེབས་བཞུགས་པ་མཁྱེན་མཁྱེན། དེ་ཡང་མ་བྱུང་ན་བདག་ལ་གདུང་གཅིག་སྟོན་རྒྱུ་མ་བྱུང་ན། ངོ་གང་གིས་འདེགས། གཏམ་དུ་ཅི་ལབ།

གདུང་ཅེས་ཀྱང་འཇོག་དགོས་ཞེས་ཞུ་བ་ནན་གྱིས་ཕུལ་བས།

གྲུབ་ཐོབ་ཆེན་པོའི་ཞལ་ནས། ལར་ང་ལ་འཆི་བ་ཞེས་བེམ་རིག་འབྲལ་རྒྱུ་མེད་དེ། ད་ལན་བེམ་པོར་སྣང་བ་འདི་འཇོགས་སོ་གསུང་ནས། སྒྲུབ་ཁང་གི་ནང་དུ་ཆུང་ངུའི་སྐུ་དེ་ཉིད་ཕེབས་སོ།

དེ་ནས་ཐུགས་སྲས་པས་ཕྱག་གྲངས་མེད་པ་འཚལ། བསམ་པ་ལ་ད་ནང་དུ་བྱོན་ཕྱིན་ཞབས་ནས་བཟུང་དགོས་དགོངས་པ་དང་། གྲུབ་ཆེན་གྱིས་མཁྱེན་ཏེ། བུ་མཁའ་ལ་ལྡིང་བའི་བྱ། [163b] ཁྱེ་ཞེ་སྡང་ཆེ་ཡང་མི་ཟིན་གསུང་།

དེས་ཀྱང་ཤིན་ཏུ་མོས་ཏེ། ཐུགས་སྲས་པས་ཞུས་པ། འོ་ན་ཞལ་ཆེམས་གལ་ཆེ་བ་སྦྱར་ཀྱི་བྱ་བ་གང་ལྟར་བྱེད། ཕྱི་རོལ་དུ་འགྲོ་བ་འདུལ་ལུགས་ཅི་ཞིག་བགྱིད། བདག་ཆོས་རྣམས་ཀྱི་ནང་ནས་གང་ཉམས་སུ་ལེན་ཞུས་པས།

If you practice according to my words,
it will be beneficial in all of this life and the next.

The spiritual son saw the great adept in front of him in the sky as he spoke this.

Then the spiritual son again said this: "Lord, great adept. You are an individual who has gained self-control over birth and death. So, for the benefit of the doctrine and sentient beings, please remain! Please remain firm!"

The lord replied, "I have gained self-control over birth and death, so I'm leaving right now."

Again the spiritual son offered a fervent appeal: "If you have decided to leave right now, please, please stay just until Tenzin Rinpoché arrives. If even that doesn't happen, and there is not even a body for me to show, how will I face him? What can I tell him? By all means, you must leave a body!"

The great adept replied, "In general, for me there is no cause for the separation of matter and awareness known as 'death,' but right now I will leave this material manifestation," and that small body came inside the meditation hut.

Then the spiritual son offered countless prostrations and thought, "Now that he has come inside, I must grab his feet!"

The great adept knew and remarked, "Son, even a furious dog cannot catch a bird soaring in the sky."

That filled the spiritual son with devotion and he asked, "In that case, as an important last testament, how should your corpse be treated? What is the way to tame living beings in the external world? From among the Dharma teachings, what should I practice?"

The great adept replied, "Leave my bones in this posture of a king at leisure. Make an earthen stūpa. The way to tame living beings in the external world is to take control of the gods, demons, and human beings as though I were present, and to continually do virtuous work! If you want to be no different from me, do not indulge your desires! If you want whatever you do to be beneficial to others, discard self-clinging! If you want to quickly reach the citadel of buddhahood, closely investigate the nature of the mind! Without carelessly living in leisure, maintain the lifestyle of a master! I have appointed Nyima Sangpo as my heir, so he must impartially benefit living beings and think of what will spread the doctrine! Do not use

གྲུབ་ཐོབ་ཆེན་པོའི་ཞལ་ནས། ངའི་རུས་པ་རྒྱལ་པོ་རོལ་པའི་འདུག་སྐྱངས་འདི་ལ་ཞོག སའི་བུམ་སྐུ་བྱས་པས་ཡོང་། ཕྱི་རོལ་དུ་འགྲོ་བ་འདུལ་ལུགས་ང་ཡོད་པ་བཞིན། ལྷ་འདྲེ་མི་གསུམ་ལ་ལུང་བསྟུར་ལ་དགེ་ལས་རྒྱུན་མ་ཆག་པ་གྱིས། ང་དང་ཁྱད་མེད་པ་འདོད་ན་འདོད་པ་ཡོགས་སུ་མ་བསྒྲུབ། ཅི་བྱས་གཞན་དོན་དུ་འགྲོ་བར་འདོད་ན་བདག་ཏུ་འཛིན་པ་སྤོངས། མྱུར་དུ་སངས་རྒྱས་ཀྱི་གོ་འཕང་ཐོབ་པར་འདོད་ན་སེམས་ཀྱི་རྩ་བཙར་ཆོད། བག་མེད་དལ་བར་མ་སྡོད་པར་བླ་མའི་རྣམ་ཐར་སྒྲིངས། ཉི་མ་བཟང་པོ་ངའི་ཚབ་ལ་བཀོད་པ་ཡིན་པས། འགྲོ་དོན་ཕྱོགས་མེད་སྒྲིངས་ལ་བསྟན་པ་གང་དར་སོམས། ནག་ཆང་དང་ཉེ་རིང་མ་བྱེད་བཟོ་དང་སོ་ནམས་སློབས། ཡོན་ཏན་སློབ་མི་དགོས་སྤྱང་ལ་རྒྱུ་རྫོལ་བ་དང་འདྲ། དམ་ཆ་དེ་རྣམས་ཐུབ་ན་ང་དང་ཁྱད་མེད། གང་ཤར་རང་གྲོལ་དུ་ཐོང་། དམ་ཆ་དེ་རྣམས་མ་ཐུབ་ན་ཚེ་བཞུག་ཀོད་མ་སྡོན་མོ་ལ་སྒྲོན་ནོ། ཟེར་བ་གྱིས། ཆོས་གང་ཉམས་སུ་ལེན་ན། སྤྱིར་བཅོམ་ལྡན་འདས་ཀྱིས་ཉོན་མོངས་པ་རེ་རེའི་གཉེན་པོར་ཆོས་རེ་རེ་གསུངས། ལར་ཆོས་དེ་དག་ལ་བཟང་ངན་གྱི་ཁྱད་པར་མེད། སྣང་བ་ལ་གདོང་འདེད་རིག་པ་ཅེར་གྱིས་བཟུང་། སྣང་ཙམ་ན་སྟོང་པ་ལགས་སོ། སྟོང་ཙམ་ན་སྣང་བ་ཡིན་པའི་དོན་ཆེན་པོ་འཕྲུལ་གྲུབ། གཏད་མེད་པོ་ཐང་སྟོང་རྒྱལ་པོའི་མདུན་མ་ལེགས་སོ། [164a] རབ་ང་ཤི་བ་ལོ་བརྒྱ། འབྲིང་ལྔ་བཅུ་དྲུག་བཅུ། ཐ་མའང་སུམ་ཅུ་ཙམ་བསྒོང་ཐུབ་པར་གྱིས། དོན་ཆེན་པོ་ཡོད་དོ་གསུངས། ཡང་ཐུགས་སྲས་ཞུས་པ། གྲུབ་ཐོབ་ཆེན་པོ་ལགས། ཁྱེད་ལྷ་བུའི་གང་ཟག་ལ་ལ་ནི་ཨོ་རྒྱན་ཆེན་པོའི་སྤྲུལ་པ་ཡིན་ནམ་ཟེར། ལ་ལ་ཏི་ལློ་པའི་སྤྲུལ་པ་ཡིན་ནམ་ཟེར། ལ་ལ་གྲུབ་ཆེན་ཀུ་ཀུ་རི་པའི་སྤྲུལ་པ་ཡིན་ནམ་ཟེར། ལ་ལ་ཀུན་དགའ་བཤེས་གཉེན་ཡིན་ནམ་ཟེར་བ་འདུག་པ་ཅི་ལགས་ཞུས་པས།

གྲུབ་ཐོབ་ཆེན་པོའི་ཞལ་ནས།

ཨོ་རྒྱན་པདྨ་ཏི་ལློ་ཤེས་བཟང་སོགས།
ཐ་དད་སྣང་ཡང་ངོ་བོ་གཅིག་ལས་མེད།

དཔེར་ན་ཆུ་ལ་འགྲོ་བའི་མཐོང་སྣང་ལྟར།
ངོ་བོ་གཅིག་ལ་རྣམ་པ་དུ་མར་སྣང་།

strong liquor and do not be prejudiced! Study the crafts and agriculture! It is not necessary to cultivate the qualities; they are like water that bursts forth in a pasture. If you are able to keep those pledges, you will be no different from me. Let whatever arises be naturally liberated! If you are not able to keep those pledges, say, "I was put upon the old gray mare!"[1152] As for what Dharma you should practice, in general, the Blessed One taught a Dharma as an antidote for each of the afflictions. Basically, there is no difference of good and bad among those Dharma teachings. When confronting appearances, hold fast to pure awareness. Because they are merely apparent yet empty and empty yet apparent, a great truth is immediately realized. Those are the good concerns of the aimless Tangtong Gyalpo. Keep my death a secret for one hundred years at best, fifty or sixty as medium, and at least for about thirty! Great benefit will come."

Again, the spiritual son said, "O great adept. Some people ask whether a person like you is an emanation of the Great Teacher of Uḍḍiyāna. Some wonder whether you are an emanation of Tilopa. Some ask whether you are an emanation of the great adept Kukkuripa. Some wonder whether you are Ānandamitra.[1153] Which are you?"

The great adept replied:

Padmasambhava of Uḍḍiyāna,
Tilo Prajñābhadra, and so forth
may appear as different,
but are no more than one in essence.

As, for example,
with the visual appearance
to living beings of water,
which has one essence,
but appears in many forms.

Furthermore, understand
those phenomena
such as the appearance
of the sun and moon in the sky,
son of good family!

གཞན་ཡང་མཁའ་ལ་ཉི་ཟླ་ཤར་བ་སོགས།
དེ་དག་ཤེས་པར་གྱིས་ཤིག་རིགས་ཀྱི་བུ།

ཅེས་གསུངས་སོ།

ཡང་ཐུགས་སྲས་པས་ཞུས་པ། བསྟན་འཛིན་རིན་པོ་ཆེ་མ་བྱོན་པར་རྡོ་ཐེབས་པའི་རྒྱུ་ཅི་ལགས།

རྐྱེན་གང་ལགས་ཞུས་པས།

གྲུབ་ཐོབ་ཆེན་པོའི་ཞལ་ནས། ཁ་སང་ངའི་རྨི་ལམ་དུ། མཁའ་སྤྱོད་ནས་ཡོངས་ཟེར་བའི་བུད་མེད་དཀར་མོ་ཕག་གི་གདོང་པ་ཅན་ཅིག་བྱུང་ནས། ཀྱེ། གྲུབ་ཐོབ་ཆེན་པོ་རྒྱལ་བའི་སྲས་པོ་ལགས།

ད་ཡང་ཞིང་གཞན་ན། སངས་རྒྱས་དང་། ཆོས་དང་། དགེ་འདུན་གྱི་སྒྲ་མི་གྲག་པའི་ཞིང་འདུག་པས། དེ་རྣམས་འདུལ་བ་ལ་འབྱོན་དགོས་ཟེར་བ་བྱུང་བས་འགྲོ་གསུང་། རྐྱེན་སྤྱིར་འདུས་བྱས་ཐམས་ཅད་མི་རྟག་པ་ཁོ་ན་ཡིན་པས་ཀྱང་། ངེས་པར་འགྲོ་གསུང་།

དེ་དུས་ཐུགས་སྲས་པ་ལ་རྡོ་རྗེ་འཆང་ལ་དངོས་སུ་གྲུབ་ཆེན་རང་གིས་གསན་པའི་བླ་མའི་རྣལ་འབྱོར་ཐུན་མོང་མ་ཡིན་པ་ཚིག་བརྒྱད་དུ་གནང་ངོ་།

དེ་ནས་གྲུབ་ཐོབ་ཆེན་པོ་ཕྱིའི་རྒྱུ་བ་བཅད་དེ། འོད་གསལ་འགྲོ་འོང་དང་བྲལ་བའི་ངང་ལ་ཞག་བདུན་བཞུགས་སོ། [164b]

དེ་ནས་ཐུགས་སྲས་པས་ཀྱང་། བཀའ་ལུང་དང་། གདམས་པས་ཆོམ་སྐམ་པའི་ངོར་ནས། དུ་བྲོ་ལ་ཡིད་ཆེས་པའི་རྣམ་པས། མཆོད་པ་ཅི་འབྱོར་པ་ཉིན་མཚན་དུ་ཕུལ། གདུང་ཤུགས་རྩེ་གཅིག་གི་སྒོ་ནས། གསོལ་བ་རྒྱུན་མ་ཆད་པར་བཏབ། དེའི་དུས་ལྷའི་རྫས་ཀྱི་མཆོད་པ་བསམ་གྱིས་མི་ཁྱབ་པ་ཡང་འདུག་གོ

དེ་ནས་དགོངས་པ་ཟབ་མོ་ཆོས་ཀྱི་དབྱིངས་སུ་ཐིམ་པར་མཛད་དེ། དབུའི་གཙུག་ཆེར་འཕར་བ་དང་། ཤངས་གཉིས་ནས་བྱང་སེམས་དཀར་དམར་གྱི་རྒྱུན་འབབ་པ་དང་། ཐུགས་ཁར་རྡོ་རྗེ་རྩེ་ལྔ་པའི་རྣམ་པ་འབུར་དུ་དོད་པ་དང་གཞན་ཡང་ཡ་མཚན་ཆེ་བའི་ལྟས་མང་དུ་བྱུང་ངོ་།

དེ་ནས་ཐུགས་སྲས་པས། སྔར་གྲུབ་ཆེན་རང་ཉིད་ཇི་ལྟར་གསུང་བ་བཞིན། རྒྱལ་པོ་རོལ་པའི་འདུག་སྟངས་དེ་ལ། ཚ་དང་གོས་དར་ལ་སོགས་པས་ཚགས་ལེགས་པར་བྱས་ཏེ། སའི་བུམ་སྐུ་བྱས་ཏེ་བཞུགས་སུ་གསོལ། མཆོད་པ་རྒྱུན་མ་ཆད་པར་ཕུལ། དེའི་ཚེ་ཕྱི་རོལ་དུ་ཡང་མི་རྣམས་སྐྱིད་ལྷུག་པ་དང་། ཉི་ཟླ་རྣམས་སྒྲ་གཅན་གྱིས་ཟིན་པ་དང་། དད་ལྡན་གྱི་སྐྱེ་བོ་ཀུན་གྱིས་ཀྱང་སེམས་ཀྱི་ཚོར་ཏེ་སེམས་མི་བདེ་བའི་རྣམ་པ་ཤིན་ཏུ་ཆེ་བ་དང་། ལོ་ཐོག་རྣམས་ཀྱང་སའི་བཅུད་ཉམས་པ་ལྟ་བུ་སྐམ་པ་དང་། ནག་པོར་སོང་བ་ལ་སོགས་པ་བྱུང་ངོ་།

Again, the spiritual son asked, "Lord, what is the main cause for you to leave before Tenzin Rinpoché arrives? What is the secondary cause?"

The great adept replied, "In my dream last night, a white woman with the face of a sow appeared, saying that she had come from Khecara.[1154] 'Hey! Great adept, spiritual son of the conquerors!' she called. 'Even now, in a realm in another world the names of the Buddha, Dharma, and Sangha are unknown. You must go to tame those beings!' So I'm going. As for the secondary cause, in general, all composite things are only impermanent, so I'm definitely going."

At that time, the great adept gave to the spiritual son, in a unique transmission, the uncommon guruyoga that he had actually received from Vajradhara.[1155]

Then the great adept's external breathing ceased and he rested in clear light without fluctuation for seven days.

The spiritual son, feeling satisfied with the commands and the instructions, and despondent yet filled with confidence, then presented day and night whatever offerings he could find. With single-minded intense longing, he continually offered prayers. Inconceivable offerings of divine substances also occurred at that time.

Then the great adept dissolved his awareness into the profound, basic space of phenomena. His cranial dome greatly protruded upward, streams of the white and red enlightenment mind flowed from his two nostrils, the form of a vajra with five prongs bulged out in the center of his chest, and many other miraculous signs also occurred.

Just as the great adept himself had commanded, the spiritual son then took the corpse that was in the posture of a king at leisure, carefully packed it with salt, silk cloth, and so forth, made an earthen stūpa, and placed it inside. He continually made offerings. At that time, even in the external world, human beings became lethargic, the sun and moon were eclipsed by Rāhu,[1156] all faithful people felt it in their minds and experienced severe forms of mental distress, and the crops also dried up, became blackened, and so forth, as though the vitality of the soil had diminished.

In particular, the spiritual son himself also lost consciousness for a short while, and even when he had somewhat regained consciousness, it had become dark and gloomy in all directions, and he lost physical strength for a moment and his eyes also became blind. He cried out, "Oh, no!" and his tongue became black, dry, and prickly.

Then the Dharma lord Tenzin Rinpoché, who had constructed the iron

ཁྱད་པར་ཐུགས་སྲས་པ་རང་ཀྱང་། ཐུགས་དྲན་མེད་ལ་སོང་སྟེ་དུམ་ཙམ་ལུས་པ་ཅུང་ཟད་དྲན་པས་ཟིན་ཡང་། སའི་ཕྱོགས་ཀུན་ནག་མུན་མུན་པར་གྱུར་པ་དང་། ལུས་ཀྱི་བཟུངས་ཀྱང་ཡུད་ཙམ་ལ་འཚེར་ཞིང་མིག་ཀྱང་ཡོང་མོར་སོང་བ་དང་། ཧུ་ཞེས་པའི་ཤུགས་རིངས་འཚེར་བ་དང་། ལྟོགས་ཀྱང་ནག་པོར་སོང་། སྐམ་ཞིང་ཚབ་ཚབ་པར་གྱུར་ཏོ།

དེ་ནས་ཆོས་རྗེ་བསྟན་འཛིན་རིན་པོ་ཆེ་ཉང་པོའི་ལྕགས་ཟམ་ཚུགས་ཏེ་རི་བོ་ཆེར་ཕེབས་སོ།

གྲུབ་ཆེན་པ་མཇལ་དགོངས། བསྒྲུབ་ཁང་གི་སྒོར་བྱོན་པས། ཐུགས་སྲས་པས་ཡུས་ཀྱི་མ་ཐུབ་པར་སྤྱན་ཆབ་བཤིལ་ཞིང་ཐུགས་ཁ་ལ་གཡུགས་པས། བསྟན་འཛིན་རིན་པོ་ཆེ་ [165a] བརྒྱལ་ཏེ་གཉིས་ཀ་ཡུན་རིང་གི་བར་དུ་ཐུགས་རྣམས་དྲན་མེད་ལ་སོང་ངོ་།

དེ་ནས་ཐུགས་རྣམས་དྲན་པས་ཟིན། ཐུགས་སྲས་པས་ཞལ་ཆེམ་ལུང་བསྟན་རྣམས་ཞིབ་ཏུ་བསྐྱད་པས། བསྟན་འཛིན་རིན་པོ་ཆེ་ཡང་ལྷབ་སེ་ཕྱོད་དེ་བ་ཅིག་ཏུ་འདུག་གོ

དེ་ནས་གདུང་ཡིད་བཞིན་ནོར་བུ་ལ་བྱིན་བརླབས་ཞུས་མཆོད་པ་ཕུལ། གྲུབ་ཐོབ་ཆེན་པོ་མྱ་ངན་ལས་འདས་པ་གོང་དུ་ཞལ་ལྟ་ཇི་ལྟར་ཡོད་པ་བཞིན། ཕྱི་རོལ་གྱི་དད་ལྡན་བུ་སློབ་ཡོན་བདག་དང་བཅས་པ་སེམས་མྱ་ངན་གྱིས་ནོན་པའི་དོགས་དང་། ཧོར་ལ་སོགས་པའི་མཐའ་དམག་མི་འབྱུང་བའི་ཕྱིར་གྱི་རྟེན་འབྲེལ་དང་། གདུལ་བྱ་མཐའ་དབུས་ཀུན་ཏུ་སྟོར་ཇི་ལྟར་ཡོད་པའི་ཁྱུད་བཞིན་དུ་ཡོང་པར་བྱ་ཕྱིར། མྱ་ངན་ལས་འདས་པ། བསྟན་འཛིན་རིན་པོ་ཆེ་དང་ཐུགས་སྲས་པ་རང་མ་གཏོགས་ལྷ་འདྲེ་མི་གསུམ་ཐམས་ཅད་ལ་གསང་ནས། གྲུབ་ཆེན་བཞུགས་བཞིན་པའི་ལུགས་སུ་མཛད་དེ། སྐུ་གསུང་ཐུགས་ཀྱི་རྟེན་བཞེངས་པ། སའི་མེ་ཚ་རྒྱབ་པ། དགྲ་བགེགས་ཟིལ་གྱིས་གནོན་པ། ཁམས་གསུམ་དབང་དུ་བསྡུད་པ། ཕྱི་ནང་ཀུན་ཏུ་བཀའ་ཤོག་བྱིན་བརླབས་ཀྱིས་འགྲོ་དོན་སོགས་བཀའ་སྩོལ་ཇི་ལྟ་བ་བཞིན་དུ་མཛད་དོ།

དེ་ལྟར་བྱས་པས་གྲུབ་ཆེན་རང་གིས་ཐུགས་རྗེའི་མངོན་ཤེས་དང་རྫུ་འཕྲུལ་ཐོགས་མེད་དུ་བསྟན་འཛིན་རིན་པོ་ཆེ་དང་། ཐུགས་སྲས་པ་རང་ལ་བྱུང་ངོ་།

དེ་ནས་གྲུབ་ཐོབ་ཆེན་པོའི་དགོངས་པ་རྫོགས་ཕྱིར། མཆོད་རྟེན་བཀྲ་ཤིས་སྒོ་མངས་ཀྱི་ཆོས་འཁོར་རིམ་པ་བཅུ་གསུམ་ཡན་རྗེ་རང་བཞུགས་དུས་ན་བཟའ་ཕུལ་གྲུབ། དེ་ནས་ཆོས་འཁོར་རིམ་པ་བཅུ་གསུམ་གྱི་པདྨ་ནས་བཟུང་སྟེ། བུམ་པ་ཡན་གྱི་ན་བཟའ་གསེར་ཟངས་འབའ་ཞིག་གིས་གསོལ། དཔལ་རི་བོ་ཆེའི་རྩེར། གོང་དུ་ཆ་ཙམ་གསལ་བ་བཞིན་བགྱིས། དཔལ་ཀུན་ཏུ་བཟང་པོའི་ཕོ་བྲང་དུ། གསེར་ཟངས་ལུགས་མ་ལས་གྲུབ་[165b]པ་ཆོས་སྐུ་ཀུན་ཏུ་བཟང་པོའི་སྐུ་རྒྱབ་མཐོ་བཅོ་ལྔ་པ་གཅིག་བཞེངས། བླ་མ་ལྷ་ཁང་དུ་གྲགས་པའི་གཙུག་ལག་ཁང་ཀ་བ་བཞིའི་ས་ན། རྗེ་གྲུབ་ཐོབ་ཆེན་པོའི་སྐུ་ལུགས་མ་རྒྱབ་མཐོ་བཅུ་གཅིག་པ་གཅིག་དང་། དེའི་གཡས་སུ་དཔལ་རྣལ་འབྱོར་དབང་ཕྱུག་འབིར་ཝ་པའི་སྐུ་གྲུབ་ཆེན་རང་གི་ཞལ་གཟིགས་ལུགས་མ་རྒྱབ་མཐོ་བཅུ་གཉིས་བྱས་པ་གཅིག་དང་། གཡོན་དུ་ཨོ་རྒྱན་ཆེན་པོ་པདྨ

bridge of Nyangpo,[1157] arrived at Riwoché. Intending to meet the great adept, he came to the door of the meditation hut. When the spiritual son, unable to speak, gestured at his heart with tears glistening in his eyes, Tenzin Rinpoché fainted, and they both lost consciousness for a long time.

Then they regained consciousness. When the spiritual son told Tenzin Rinpoché the last testament and prophecies in detail, he also became determined.[1158]

They then requested blessings from the wish-fulfilling physical remains and presented offerings. Precisely in accordance with the great adept's advice before he passed into nirvāṇa, the nirvāṇa was kept secret from all gods, demons, and human beings, except for Tenzin Rinpoché and the spiritual son, from fear that faithful disciples and patrons in the outside world would be oppressed by grief, and as an auspicious connection for foreign armies such as the Mongols not to appear, and for the total number of disciples everywhere in the center and borderlands of the country to remain just as it was before. [Tenzin Rinpoché and Sherab Palden] acted as though the great adept were alive, and built representations of enlightened body, speech, and mind, established geomantic focal-points, overcame obstructing enemies, brought the three realms under control, benefited living beings with edicts and blessings everywhere inside and out, and so forth, precisely according to the great adept's custom.

Because they acted in that way, the great adept himself caused unimpeded compassionate clairvoyance and miraculous abilities to come to Tenzin Rinpoché and the spiritual son.

To fulfill the intentions of the great adept, the offering of a [gilt] coating had been completed down through the thirteen levels of the Dharma wheels of the Auspicious Stūpa of Many Doors during the lifetime of the lord himself. Then a coating of gilt copper alone was applied from the lotus of the thirteen levels of the Dharma wheels down through the dome. At the peak of glorious Riwoché, [the work] had been done as partially explained above.[1159] There in the palace of glorious Samantabhadra, a fifteen-handspan-tall cast image of the dharmakāya reality body, Samantabhadra, had been constructed from gilt copper.[1160] At the place of the temple with four pillars that was known as the Master's Temple, they [now] made a cast image of the lord, the great adept, which was eleven handspans tall. To its right, according to the great adept's own vision, they made a cast image of the glorious lord of yogins, Virūpa, which was twelve handspans tall. To the left, they made a cast image of the Great Teacher of

འབྱུང་གནས་ལུགས་མ་རྒྱབ་མགོ་བཅུ་གཉིས་བྱས་པ་གཅིག་རྣམས་དང་། གཙུག་ལག་ཁང་ཀ་བ་བཞིའི་ས་བྱས་པ་གཅིག་ན། རྣམ་པར་སྣང་མཛད་ཀྱི་སྐུ་ལུགས་མ་རྒྱབ་མགོ་བཅུ་བདུན་བྱས་པ་གཅིག དཔལ་རི་བོ་ཆེའི་སྙེད་པར་གཙུག་ལག་ཁང་ཀ་བ་བརྒྱད་ཀྱི་ས་ན། དཔལ་ཤ་ཝ་རི་དབང་ཕྱུག་གི་སྐུ་ལུགས་མ་རྒྱབ་མགོ་གཅིག་རྣམས་བཞེངས། གཟུངས་རྫོགས་རབ་གནས་ལེགས་པར་གྲུབ་རྗེས། རབ་སྟོན་ལ་སྒྲི་བོ་འབུམ་ཚོ་ཙམ་ལ་རིན་པོ་ཆེའི་ཡོ་བྱད་མན་ཤེལ་དང་། བྱི་རུ་དང་། མ་ནི་ཧོ་དང་། མུ་མེན་ལ་སོགས་པ་དང་། གཞན་ཡང་ཚོགས་ཀྱི་འཁོར་ལོ་བསམ་གྱིས་མི་ཁྱབ་པ་སྒྲུབ་ཞིང་ཡིད་ཆེས་པར་བྱས་སོ། རྒྱལ་ཁམས་ཀུན་ཏུ་མ་ཎི་བསྐུལ་བ་དང་། འབུལ་བ་སྣ་ཚོགས་སྤྱད་པ། ལྕགས་ཟམ་འཛུགས་པ། གྲུ་བཤན། མི་འཛངའ་འདུམ་པ། སྲོག་སྐྱོབ་པ་ལ་སོགས་བསམ་གྱིས་མི་ཁྱབ་པ་སྒྲུབ་ཅིང་། མཛད་པ་དེ་དག་ནི་འབད་བཙོལ་མེད་པར་མྱུར་དུ་གྲུབ་པ་དེ་ནི། གྲུབ་ཆེན་རང་གི་ཐུགས་རྗེ་དང་ནུས་མཐུ་ལས་བྱུང་ཞེས་པ་ནི། ཐུགས་སྲས་པའི་ཞལ་ནས་གསུངས་པའོ།

གཞན་ཡང་དུས་མཆོད། ཟླ་མཆོད་སོགས་འབད་པ་ཆེན་པོས་དུས་ཀུན་ཏུ་བསྒྲུབས་སོ། དེ་དག་གི་སྐབས་སུ་དྲི་བཟང་དང་། མེ་ཏོག་གི་ཆར་དང་། སེམས་བདེ་བ་ལ་སོགས་པ་དཔག་ཏུ་མེད་པ་བྱུང་ཞིང་ [166a] ད་དུང་ཡང་ཡོད་དོ།

དེ་ལྟར་ལོ་སུམ་ཅུ་སོ་གཉིས་ཀྱི་བར་ལ། བསྟན་འཛིན་རིན་པོ་ཆེས་རྒྱལ་ཁམས་ལ་གདུལ་བྱ་དང་འབུལ་བསྡུད་ལ་ཕེབས། ཐུགས་སྲས་ཤེས་རབ་དཔལ་ལྡན་གྱིས། རྗེ་གྲུབ་ཐོབ་ཆེན་པོའི་ཚབ་མཛད། ཁོང་གཉིས་ཀྱིས་དགེ་བསྐུལ་ལ་སོགས་རྒྱུན་མ་ཆད་པར་མཛད་པ་དེ་དག་ནི་ངོ་མཚར་བའི་གཏམ་དུ་ཆེའོ། དེའི་བར་ལ་ཕྱོགས་ཀུན་ཏུ་ལོ་ལེགས་པ་དང་། ཆར་དུས་སུ་འབབ་པ་དང་། བཀྲ་ཤིས་པ་དང་། ཆོས་ལྡན་བདེ་བའི་རང་བཞིན་དུ་གནས་པ་དང་། ཁྱད་པར་ཧོར་ལ་སོགས་པ་མཐའ་དམག་གི་གནོད་པ་མི་འབྱུང་ཞིང་། ཆོས་ཁྲིམས་རྒྱལ་ཁྲིམས་རྣམས་ཀྱང་བསྟན་པ་རིན་པོ་ཆེ་དང་མཐུན་པ་སོགས་བསམ་གྱིས་མི་ཁྱབ་པ་བྱུང་ངོ་།

དེ་ནས་ལོ་སུམ་ཅུ་སོ་གཉིས་སོང་ནས། བསྟན་པའི་འཕེལ་འགྲིབ་ཀྱི་སྟོབས་ཀྱིས། འགའ་ཞིག་གིས། གྲུབ་ཆེན་མི་བཞུགས་པར་འདུག་པ་གསང་ཐོལ་བ་གྲག་ཟེར། གདུང་གི་ཞལ་ཕྱེ། གཙང་ཁང་ཀ་བ་གཉིས་བྱས་པ་གཅིག་གི་མདུན་ན། ཁྲམས་ཀ་བ་བཅུ་དྲུག་གིས། བསྐོར་ལམ་ཕྱི་ནང་དང་བཅས་པའི་གཟིམས་ཁང་གི་རྩེ་ལ་གསེར་ཟངས་ཀྱི་ཆར་ཁེབས་ཏོག་དང་བཅས་པའི་ནང་ན། དངུལ་ལས་གྲུབ་པའི་མྱང་འདས་མཆོད་རྟེན་གྱི་ནང་ན་བཞུགས་སུ་གསོལ། རྒྱལ་ཁམས་ཀྱི་གནས་བསྐོར་བ་དད་པ་ཅན་རྣམས། བྱིན་བརླབ་ཞུ་བ་སོགས་བྱས་པ་ནི་ད་ལྟ་ཡོད།

Uḍḍiyāna, Padmasambhava, which was twelve handspans tall. At a place in a temple with four pillars, they made a cast image of Vairocana that was seventeen handspans tall. At the place of a temple with eight pillars on the middle of glorious Riwoché, they constructed a cast image of the glorious lord Śavaripa that was eleven[1161] handspans tall. After the sanctified contents had been completely inserted and the consecrations carefully finished, during the celebration feast they pleased[1162] and satisfied about one hundred thousand people with precious objects, quartz, coral, agate, lapis lazuli, and so forth, as well as an inconceivable ritual feast.

They urged the recitation of *maṇis* throughout the land, and accomplished inconceivable deeds, such as gathering various offerings, constructing iron bridges, boats, and ferries, resolving violent conflicts, and saving lives. As for the effortless and rapid accomplishment of those deeds, the spiritual son told me, "It came from the compassion and ability of the great adept himself."[1163]

Furthermore, they carried out the specifically timed offerings, monthly offerings, and so forth with great energy at all times. On those occasions, infinite sweet aromas, rains of flowers, mental bliss, and so forth occurred and are present even now.

In that way, for thirty-two years, Tenzin Rinpoché traveled the land to tame living beings and gather offerings. The spiritual son Sherab Palden acted as the regent of the lord, the great adept. The ceaseless deeds these two performed, such as urging people toward virtue, is a great and marvelous story.

During that period fine harvests occurred in all directions, the rains fell on time, auspicious signs arose, and people were religious and lived happily. In particular, no harm came from foreign armies such as the Mongols, the Dharma regulations and government regulations were also observed in accordance with the precious doctrine, and so forth, to an inconceivable extent.

Then, after thirty-two years had passed, due to the fluctuation of the doctrine some people said it would be best to reveal the secret that the great adept was not alive. The tomb was opened. A sanctuary with two pillars was made at the residence, which has a verandah with sixteen pillars in front, and outer and inner circumambulation paths. At the peak of the residence is a gilt copper rain shield and pinnacle. A Stūpa of Nirvāṇa made from silver is inside, within which [the body] was placed. It is here now for faithful pilgrims of the land to request blessings and so forth.

གྲུབ་ཐོབ་ཆེན་པོའི་རྣམ་ཐར་ཕྱི་མ་མྱ་ངན་ལས་འདས་པའི་སྐོར་འདི་ཉིད་གྲུབ་ཐོབ་ཆེན་པོའི་ཐུགས་སྲས་དམ་པ་རྗེ་བླ་མ་ཤེས་རབ་དཔལ་ལྡན་གྱིས་མཛད་པའི་རྣམ་ཐར་ངོ་མཚར་རྒྱ་མཚོའི་ཁ་སྐོང་དུ། དེ་ཉིད་ཀྱི་སྲས་སྔགས་རམ་པ་ཀུན་དགའ་བསོད་ནམས་གྲགས་པ་དཔལ་བཟང་ལ། གྲུབ་ཐོབ་ཆེན་པོའི་གདུང་བརྒྱུད་དྲི་མ་མེད་པ། བློ་གྲོས་རྒྱལ་མཚན་པའི་བཀས་བསྐུལ་ནས་མཛད་པ་འདི་ནི་ལས་བདག་རྟ་མགྲིན་གྱིས་རྣམ་ཐར་ཆེན་མོའི་ཁ་སྐོངས་སུ་ཞལ་ཤུས་ནས་བྲིས་པའོ།

~

Urged by the command of Lodrö Gyaltsen, a member of the stainless family line of the great adept, to write a supplement to the *Ocean of Marvels*, the biography written by the holy spiritual son of the great adept, the lord and master Sherab Palden,[1164] this *Final Story Concerning the Nirvāṇa of the Great Adept* was written by his [Sherab Palden's] own son, the mantra master Kunga Sönam Drakpa Palsang. I, Tamdrin, copied and wrote it out as a supplement to the great biography.

Notes

1 Dezhung Rinpoché quoted from memory the entire series of extraordinary verses in which this quatrain is found. I have always felt that he was thus pointing me to the heart of the biography. See Gyurmé Dechen, *Jewel Mirror in Which All Is Clear*, 205–7 (293–97 of the translation).

2 Radzinsky (1992), 238.

3 According to Tibetan tradition a person is one year old at birth. This custom has been preserved in the following essay and in the translations from Tibetan texts.

4 The *Bright Lamp of Prophecy (Lung bstan gsal ba'i sgron me)* is a biographical prophecy *(lung bstan rnam thar)* said to have been hidden by Guru Padmasambhava in the Mansion of Secret Mantra at Tsari (Tsa ri) in an Ox Year during the reign of King Mutri Tsenpo (Mu khri btsan po) and translated into Tibetan by Kawa Paltsek (Dka' ba dpal brtsegs). It is one of the hidden treasure teachings mentioned by Padmasambhava when Tangtong Gyalpo actually met him in Uḍḍiyāna. Tangtong himself retrieved the text from its place of concealment. The most extensive excerpts from these prophetic verses are found in the biography by Könchok Palsang and Dewa Sangpo, *Bright Lamp*, 100–103, and, although not identified as such, 161–67.

5 See the biography by Könchok Palsang and Dewa Sangpo, *Bright Lamp*, 161–73. The biography by Sherab Palden, *Ocean of Marvels*, 158–70, says Tangtong's retreat began in the Wood Male Tiger Year (1422) and lasted for six years. Sherab Palden also reproduces the complete text of a long and important edict *(bka' shog)* that Tangtong wrote at the end of the retreat in the Monkey Year (1428), but ordered not to be opened until after his death.

6 See Könchok Palsang and Dewa Sangpo, *Bright Lamp*, 98–103, and 161–67. Individual lines from the *Bright Lamp* are also quoted and explained throughout their work.

7 See Könchok Palsang and Dewa Sangpo, *Bright Lamp*, 466–67, 589. Tangtong Gyalpo specifically told Dewa Sangpo to write down his prophecies concerning Chökyi Drönmé later at Wang Partsam (Dbang Spar/Pa 'tshams), which is apparently at Tachok Norbugang (Rta mchog Nor bu sgang) in Bhutan.

8 See Sherab Palden, *Ocean of Marvels*, 159–70, 257–72, 491–505, 521–28, and Könchok Palsang and Dewa Sangpo, *Bright Lamp*, 254–58, 276–79, 288–90, 389–94, 405–9, 436–39, 440–42, 459–61, 493–527, and 527–32. I hope to translate a selection of these edicts in the future.

9 See Author Unknown, *Biography of the Venerable Lady Chökyi Drönma*, 127a–28a. I am grateful to Leonard van der Kuijp for a copy of this rare text. Although the spelling Chökyi Drönma (Chos kyi sgron ma) is found in the title of this biography, I have used the more common form of Chökyi Drönmé (Chos kyi sgron me) when discussing this great yoginī. Diemberger et al. (1997), 111, and Dorjé Phagmo Dechen Chödrön and Dra Tupten Namgyal, *Past Lives of the Samding Dorjé Phagmo Incarnations*, 35, both say Chökyi Drönmé died at the age of thirty-four (thirty-three according to Western calculation). Author Unknown, *Biography of the Venerable Lady Chökyi Drönma*, 2b, says she was born in a Tiger *(stag)* Year, which must correspond to 1422 since her rebirth appeared in 1459. Chökyi Drönmé met Tangtong Gyalpo in 1455, so she was his consort for less than a year. For a fascinating study of Chökyi Drönmé's biography and the Dorjé Phagmo incarnation line, see Diemberger (forthcoming 2007). I am grateful to Hildegard Diemberger for an unpublished copy of her work, which was received after the completion of this book.

10 Tangtong Gyalpo's statement to Chökyi Drönmé is recorded in Author Unknown, *Biography of the Venerable Lady Chökyi Drönma*, 128a: *lcags zam gyi thag pa'i khyud mo gcig gnang nas/ 'di khab 'bo gang la tho rgyag nga rang gis byas nas brdungs pa'i rab gnas chags pa lags/ 'dis rkong po lan gnyis bskor da lan lag rtags la 'bul ba lags.* Sherab Palden, *Ocean of Marvels*, 331, also mentions that Tangtong was known to have said that he had begged for needles throughout the land, made iron links, and, by connecting the links, built iron bridges over the great rivers of Tibet.

11 See Könchok Palsang and Dewa Sangpo, *Bright Lamp*, 288–90, 436–39.

12 The first of these works was perhaps the brief biographical supplication *(rnam thar gsol 'debs)* to Tangtong Gyalpo written at Tsagong in 1455 by the venerable lady Chökyi Drönmé. See Chökyi Drönmé, *Untitled*, which is also known simply as *A Biography of Master Tangtong Gyalpo (Bla ma thang stong rgyal po'i rnam thar)* and is quoted in Könchok Palsang and Dewa Sangpo, *Bright Lamp*, 5, 75–76, 87–88, 112–13, 155, 167–68, 184, 193, 212, 229–30, 311–12, 347–48, and 586–88. Chökyi Drönmé also composed a biography of her teacher Bodong Panchen Cholé Namgyal (Bo dong paṇ chen Phyogs las rnam rgyal, 1376–1451), a verse from which is found in Author Unknown, *Biography of the Venerable Lady Chökyi Drönma*, 83b. Another short biographical prayer to Tangtong was written by the hermit Namkha Lekpa, the sole heir to his special visionary transmission of Chöd (Gcod), or Severance. See Namkha Lekpa, *Practicing Severance*. Various other similar works by Tangtong's disciples and heirs are gathered together in the *Supplemental Texts to the Collected Works of Thang stong rgyal po Series (Grub chen thang stong bka' 'bum gyi rgyab chos)*, vol. 2: 31–86, 225–86.

13 See Könchok Palsang and Dewa Sangpo, *Bright Lamp*, 588.

14 See Könchok Palsang and Dewa Sangpo, *Bright Lamp*, 436. The name Kāmata, or Kāmarūpa, stands for the northeastern part of Bengal and the western district of Assam. See Nölle (1965) concerning the bloody Śakti cults and ancient human sacrifice in this area. The Kāmata kingdom was apparently destroyed during the period of 1501–1505 by Husayan Shāh, the Moslem Sultan of Bengal. See Aris (1980), 104–7, concerning the Hindu kingdom of Kāmata and the Bhutanese

treasure revealer Pema Lingpa's (Padma gling pa, 1450–1521) meeting with the last Kāmata king in 1507. Kāmarūpa is also a famous tantric pilgrimage site. In this context, see Wallace (2001), 78, and the many entries in White (1996).

15 Gendun Rinchen, *Ear Ornament for Students*, 76a. Dewa Sangpo (Bde ba bzang po) was the first Tachok Chöjé (Rta mchog Chos rje). According to Bhutanese tradition, he was born from the droppings of a bird-emanation of his master.

16 See Könchok Palsang and Dewa Sangpo, *Bright Lamp*, 378–80.

17 Könchok Palsang and Dewa Sangpo, *Bright Lamp*, 588–89. Chökyi Drönmé is referred to here as Adrön Chödrön (A sgron Chos sgron) because she was recognized as a rebirth of the great yoginī Machik Labdrön (Ma gcig Lab sgron, eleventh–twelfth centuries), who was sometimes called Adrön. According to Sarah Harding, Machik originally received the nickname because she had a hair-thin white *āḥ* in the middle of her third eye.

18 Many examples could be given, among which see Könchok Palsang and Dewa Sangpo, *Bright Lamp*, 147, where the first person "I" *(bdag)* is used by Tangtong Gyalpo when relating a story to one of the authors, and 151–52, where Tangtong's comments about his experiences are closed with the honorific "said" *(gsung)*. Clear first-person statements by the co-author Dewa Sangpo about conversations he had with Tangtong are found in Könchok Palsang and Dewa Sangpo, *Bright Lamp*, 410, 411 *(kho bo bde ba bzang po)*, 415, 466–67, etc.

19 See Anonymous, *All-Illuminating Lamp*, 160b: *rnam thar bcos ma rnams 'bud pa'i rlung chen.* Tsering (2001), 42, attributes this anonymous work to Kunga Sönam Drakpa Palsang (Kun dga' bsod nams grags pa dpal bzang), the son of Tangtong Gyalpo's disciple Sherab Palden (Shes rab dpal ldan). I believe this identification is based on a mistaken reading of the colophon to Kunga Sönam Drakpa Palsang's *Final Story*, which is appended to the anonymous biography. Also see note 28.

20 Compare Anonymous, *All-Illuminating Lamp*, 16b–17a, to Könchok Palsang and Dewa Sangpo, *Bright Lamp*, 130–31, and Anonymous, *All-Illuminating Lamp*, 147a, to Könchok Palsang and Dewa Sangpo, *Bright Lamp*, 464–67.

21 For example, the description of Tangtong's birth found in Anonymous, *All-Illuminating Lamp*, 6b, is somewhat different than in any other source. Anonymous, *All-Illuminating Lamp*, 11a, also mentions Tangtong was fifteen years old at a certain point, but his age is not mentioned in the corresponding passage of Könchok Palsang and Dewa Sangpo, *Bright Lamp*, 114, or in any other source.

22 See Sherab Palden, *Ocean of Marvels*. Sherab Palden's son, Kunga Sönam Drakpa Palsang, later wrote a versified biographical supplication to Tangtong Gyalpo in 1528 summarizing the main events in the biography written by his father. See Kunga Sönam Drakpa Palsang, *Untitled*. An otherwise unknown biography of Tangtong entitled *Dredging the Pit of Saṃsāra ('Khor ba dong sprug)*, written by a certain Tuksé Rinpoché (Thugs sras Rin po che, Precious Spiritual Son), is also mentioned by Shuchen Tsultrim Rinchen (Zhu chen Tshul khrims rin chen, 1697–1774). See Tsultrim Rinchen, *Shuchen Tsultrim Rinchen's Record of Teachings Received*, vol. 1: 392.

23 See Sangyé Gyatso, *Banquet to Delight the Seers*, 310–32, for information on the Jang medical lineage. Previously in the Jang medical line, Lhatsun Tashi Palsang (Lha btsun Bkra shis dpal bzang) had also been a disciple of Tangtong Gyalpo. Sherab Palden's father, Lekdrup Pal (Legs grub dpal), had met the treasure revealer Gökyi Demtruchen (Rgod kyi ldem 'phru can, 1337–1408) and was a respected physician and a disciple of Namgyal Draksang (Rnam rgyal grags bzang, 1395–1475). Before going to stay with Tangtong, Sherab Palden had a son with the unusual name Lhunding Gema (Lhun sdings dge ma) who continued the family medical tradition and became the royal physician at the Ngamring court. See Sangyé Gyatso, *Banquet to Delight the Seers*, 323, 326–27.

24 See the definitive text by Kunga Sönam Drakpa Palsang translated at the end of this book. Also see Gyurmé Dechen, *Jewel Mirror in Which All Is Clear*, 344, and Sangyé Gyatso, *Banquet to Delight the Seers*, 327. It is interesting that Sangyé Gyatso was later responsible for concealing the death of the Fifth Dalai Lama from 1682–95. See Snellgrove and Richardson (1968), 204.

25 This date is mentioned twice in Sherab Palden, *Ocean of Marvels*, 561.

26 For example, see Sherab Palden, *Ocean of Marvels*, 12, 13, 16, 23, 29, 31, 79, 93, etc., where the honorific "said" *(gsungs)* is used at the end of passages to indicate that Tangtong Gyalpo himself gave the information to the author.

27 See Sherab Palden, *Ocean of Marvels*, 291, 538, 564–65.

28 See Kunga Sönam Drakpa Palsang, *Final Story Concerning the Nirvāṇa of the Great Adept*. I am grateful to Roberto Vitali for sending me a photocopy of this text. The colophon to Kunga Sönam's work clearly says it was written as a supplement to his father's biography of Tangtong Gyalpo. However, the sole surviving manuscript of the *Final Story* is appended to the text of the anonymous *All-Illuminating Lamp*. As discussed above, the *All-Illuminating Lamp* is almost certainly by Könchok Palsang and was used by Dewa Sangpo as the basis for the *Bright Lamp*. The *All-Illuminating Lamp* cannot be the work of Kunga Sönam, because it clearly has no relation to his father Sherab Palden's *Ocean of Marvels*.

29 See Kunga Sönam Drakpa Palsang, *Untitled*.

30 Gyurmé Dechen, *Jewel Mirror in Which All Is Clear*, 5. Gyurmé Dechen's work apparently became famous as the biography of Tangtong Gyalpo that was an "abridgement of five biographies" *(rnam thar lnga bsdus)*. See Kunga Lodrö, *Boundless Miracles*, 166. This is also emphasized in the long versified title of what is probably an early Riwoché edition of the biography. See Gyurmé Dechen, *Beautiful Forms of Pure Faith*.

31 Gyurmé Dechen, *Beautiful Forms of Pure Faith*, is probably an example of the original Riwoché edition of the biography. This edition was used by Giuseppe Tucci, although he mistakenly identified the author as Ngagi Wangchuk (Ngag gi dbang phyug). See Tucci (1949), vol. 1: 163. In Gyurmé Dechen, *Jewel Mirror in Which All Is Clear*, 347, the Dergé editor Tenzin Gyaltsen (Bstan 'dzin rgyal mtshan) says the Riwoché print was used as the basis for the new Dergé edition.

32 Also see Zangpo (2003), 168–69, for a translation of a spiritual song by Gyurmé Dechen.

33 See Gyurmé Dechen, *Rosary of Utpala Flowers.*

34 See note 1138 and Dradul Wangpo, *Jewel Rosary of Elegant Explications,* 320. It is also interesting that some ten volumes of Sanskrit manuscripts that may have belonged to Lochen Gyurmé Dechen came from Riwoché into the hands of the Jonang master Tāranātha (1575–1635) soon after Gyurmé Dechen's death. See Tāranātha, *Extremely Detailed, Unpretentious, and Candid Narrative,* 489, 499.

35 According to Sönam Gyaltsen, *Rainfall of Blessings to Expand the Summer Lake of Faith,* 358, Ngawang Chödrak (Ngag dbang chos grags) traveled to Riwoché in 1614, the year before Gyurmé Dechen's death, and received from him the transmission of all the Shangpa Kagyü (Shangs pa Bka' brgyud) teachings. Ngawang Chödrak's writings on the Shangpa teachings are found in volume 1 of the *Supplemental Texts to the Collected Works of Thang stong rgyal po Series (Grub chen thang stong bka' 'bum gyi rgyab chos).* This volume also includes Tangtong Gyalpo's Shangpa texts, as well as two short works by Gyurmé Dechen.

36 The young Yölmo Tulku (Yol mo sprul sku) writes in his autobiography about his meetings with Gyurmé Dechen and his experiences with the practice of the Six-branch Yoga under his guidance. See Tenzin Norbu, *Lute of Vajra Sound,* 90, 96–98. On page 48 a marvelous drawing by Yölmo Tulku himself shows Gyurmé Dechen teaching and Yölmo Tulku bound with straps into the strict yoga posture required for the Kālacakra practice. The drawing is reproduced on page 10 of this book.

37 See Dradul Wangpo, *Jewel Rosary of Elegant Explications,* 320.

38 In the ninteenth century, Jamgön Kongtrul wrote a biographical supplication to Tangtong Gyalpo summarizing his accomplishments, and Jamyang Khyentsé Wangpo composed a eulogy of Tangtong's inner spiritual biography *(nang gi rnam thar)* focused on his practice of the Six Dharmas of Niguma and the six perfections. Khyentsé also received a series of biographical verses related to the Heartdrop of the Great Adept (Grub thob thugs thig) from Tangtong in the form of a mental treasure *(dgongs gter).* See Jamgön Kongtrul, *Melody of Accomplishment,* and Jamyang Khyentsé Wangpo, *Flower of the Upholders of Pure Awareness,* and *Cycle of Five Essential Methods for Accomplishment,* 450–53. Kongtrul's work is translated in Zangpo (2003), 307–11. Also see Jamyang Khyentsé Wangpo, *Net of the Three Bodies of Enlightenment,* which is an ecstatic song of supplication addressed to Tangtong Gyalpo.

39 See Könchok Palsang and Dewa Sangpo, *Bright Lamp,* 358.

40 See Kunga Sönam Drakpa Palsang, *Final Story Concerning the Nirvāṇa of the Great Adept,* 162a.

41 Sangyé Puntsok, *Source of Wish-fulfilling Good Qualities,* 231.

42 See Tsultrim Rinchen, *Catalogue of the Dergé Edition of the Translated Treatises,* vol. 1: 327.

43 The Nyingma historian Guru Tashi, writing in the early ninteenth century, follows the dates of 1361–1485 and the age of 128 years (as will be explained below) that is also mentioned in the biography by Gyurmé Dechen. See Guru Tashi, *Musical Sea of Amazing Stories*, 507–11. Jamgön Kongtrul (1813–1900), *Rosary of Precious Beryl*, 125a, gives the age of 125 years, but no dates. Most recently, Dudjom Rinpoché (1904–87) places Tangtong Gyalpo's birth in the Wood Ox Year (1385) of the sixth cycle of the Tibetan calendar and says he lived for 125 years. See Dudjom (1991), 802–3. Dudjom Rinpoché follows Kongtrul's account, but with the added birth date and mention of Tangtong's invention of the Aché Lhamo (A lce lha mo) opera.

44 See Stein (1959), 32, 238, and Tucci (1949), vol. 1: 163. Smith (2001), 283–84, prefers the dates 1361–1464. Smith and Tucci have both calculated the date for Tangtong Gyalpo's death based on the date *Earth Mouse (sa byi*, 1588) for the composition of the biography, which is found in the colophon of what is probably the original Riwoché edition of the work. See Gyurmé Dechen, *Beautiful Forms of Pure Faith*, 181a. This biography was written 125 years after Tangtong's death. The date of composition given in the Dergé edition of the same biography, which is the edition translated here and used by Stein, is *Earth Bird (sa bya*, 1609). Since Tangtong's birth is specifically dated to the *Iron Ox (lcags glang)* Year (1361) in all editions, which also say he lived for 125 years (=1485, *sa bya*), the *sa byi* in the old edition must be a mistake for *sa bya*, which was corrected in the later Dergé edition. Stein also says the dates 1385–1464 are found in the *Neckace of White Beryl* composed by Desi Sangyé Gyatso (1653–1705) and the chronological study of Sumpa Khenpo Yeshé Paljor (1704–88). The birth date of 1385 is found in both works, but there does not seem to be any mention of Tangtong in the entries for 1464. Stein (1959), 238. In Yeshé Paljor, *Fine Tree of Noble Aspiration*, 41, the entry for the Wood Ox *(shing glang)* Year of the sixth cycle (1385) reads: *sman pa thang stong rgyal po skyes*, "The physician Tangtong Gyalpo was born." Sangyé Gyatso, *Necklace of White Beryl*, 49, reads: *shing glang tshe yi rig 'dzin mchog/ thang stong rgyal po'i 'khrung lo yin*, "The Wood Ox (1385) was the birth year of Tangtong Gyalpo, the sublime upholder of longevity."

45 Gyurmé Dechen, *Jewel Mirror in Which All Is Clear*, 342. According to Dhongthog Rinpoché, the term *gshol rtsis* refers to the calculation of the extra months *(zla lhag)* sometimes found in the Tibetan year. It seems that every third year contains an extra month, making it a thirteen-month year, which is not usually counted when stating someone's age. Because of Tangtong Gyalpo's longevity it is stated here for extra emphasis. This explains why the age of 128 years is sometimes encountered instead of the more common 125.

46 See Sherab Palden, *Ocean of Marvels*, 561.

47 Gyurmé Dechen, *Jewel Mirror in Which All Is Clear*, 324, 336.

48 Gyurmé Dechen, *Jewel Mirror in Which All Is Clear*, 337–38, 342. Smith, who wrote that the last date in the biography is the Earth Female Rabbit Year *(sa mo yos)* of 1459, apparently overlooked these last two dates. See Smith (2001), 283.

49 See Ngödrup Palbar, *Lion of Faith at Play on a Glacial Peak of Good Qualities*, 10b; Rinchen Namgyal, *Making the Body Hairs of the Faithful Flutter*, 41–42; and

Natsok Rangdrol, *Heart of the Sun Illuminating the Vajrayāna*, 46–47. I am grateful to Kurtis Schaeffer for a copy of Ngödrup Palbar's work.

50 See Kunga Sönam Drakpa Palsang, *Final Story Concerning the Nirvāṇa of the Great Adept*, 162a.

51 See Kunga Sönam Drakpa Palsang, *Final Story Concerning the Nirvāṇa of the Great Adept*, 164b.

52 See Könchok Palsang and Dewa Sangpo, *Bright Lamp*, 478–80.

53 See Sönam Drakpa, *Magical Key to Royal Genealogies*, 95.

54 See Losang Trinlé, *Clarification of Knowledge*, 1180.

55 Ngagi Wangpo (Ngag gi dbang po) was enthroned as the abbot of Densatel (Gdan sa thel) Monastery in 1454, but did not became the eighth ruler of the Pakmodru dynasty until 1481. See Sönam Drakpa, *Magical Key to Royal Genealogies*, 92–95, and Losang Trinlé, *Clarification of Knowledge*, 1180.

56 Quoted in Gyurmé Dechen, *Jewel Mirror in Which All Is Clear*, 19 and 341. Tangtong's birth in an Ox *(glang)* Year is also mentioned in the verse biography of him composed by his disciple Namkha Lekpa. See Namkha Lekpa, *Practicing Severance*, 44.

57 See Sherab Palden, *Ocean of Marvels*, 167, and Könchok Palsang and Dewa Sangpo, *Bright Lamp*, 175. The latter has the name Tangtong Gyalpo instead of Crazy Tsöndru (Brtson 'grus smyon pa). These biographies place this statement at two different times in his life. The same lines are quoted in Gyurmé Dechen, *Jewel Mirror in Which All Is Clear*, 12. Tsöndru Sangpo was the name Tangtong received upon ordination.

58 See Guru Tashi, *Musical Sea of Amazing Stories to Delight Experts*, 511. He also names some disciples of Tangtong Gyalpo who lived to be very old, three of them older than Tangtong himself. Also see Jamgön Kongtrul, *Rosary of Precious Beryl*, 126a, who says the great adept of Ngari named Tsultrim Sangpo (Mnga' ris grub chen Tshul khrims bzang po) lived to the age of 130.

59 This is the most famous verse in praise of Tangtong Gyalpo, composed by the yoginī Jetsun Chökyi Drönmé (Rje btsun Chos kyi sgron me, 1422–55), who was also one of his consorts. Quoted in Yeshé Lhundrup, *Golden Rosary*, 58. The original version in Chökyi Drönmé, *Untitled*, 241, is slightly different.

60 For a detailed description of Chaksam Chuwori (Lcags zam Chu bo ri) Monastery, see Chökyi Gyatso, *Necklace of Moon Crystals*, 151–55.

61 See Gyurmé Dechen, *Jewel Mirror in Which All Is Clear*, 72, for Rendawa's prophecy. Also see Könchok Palsang and Dewa Sangpo, *Bright Lamp*, 125.

62 The one exception is the transmission of Tangtong Gyalpo's white and red medicinal pills, where Tenzin Nyima Sangpo is listed after Tangtong and before Shākya Shenyen. See the *Collected Works of Grub chen Thang stong rgyal po*, vol. 3: 346.

63 See Könchok Palsang and Dewa Sangpo, *Bright Lamp*, 356.

64 See Könchok Palsang and Dewa Sangpo, *Bright Lamp*, 130–31.

65 See Ngawang Losang Gyatso, *Crystal Mirror*, 46. This identification assumes the spelling Bstan 'dzin Nyi 'brang is a corruption of the spelling Bstan 'dzin Nyi (ma) bzang (po).

66 Jamyang Khyentsé Wangpo, *Pleasure Grove of Amazing Lotus Flowers*, 12: *lcags zam chu bo ri'i tshe chu sgrub sde ni thang stong pas btab/ thugs sras skyob pa bzang po'i yang srid lcags zam sprul sku rim byon gyi gdan sa mdzad cing/ bstan 'dzin ye shes lhun grub sogs mkhas grub chen po mang du byon.*

67 Chökyi Gyatso, *Necklace of Moon Crystals*, 153: *thugs sras bstan 'dzin rin po che'i sku phreng dgu.*

68 See Yeshé Lhundrup, *Seedling of Faith*, 21.4. This text is a versified autobiography.

69 But see note 186 concerning an unavailable manuscript biography of the Chaksam master Losang Tobden Paljor (Blo bzang stobs ldan dpal 'byor).

70 For example, following Nyida Sangpo, the Iron-Bridge Man (Lcags zam pa) Tenzin Kunga Sönam Wangchuk (Bstan 'dzin Kun dga' bsod nams dbang phyug) gave Tangtong Gyalpo's descendant Ngawang Puntsok (Ngag dbang phun tshogs, 1648–1714) novice vows in 1660. Another hierarch at Chuwori *(lcags zam chu bo ri'i mchog sprul)* was Ngawang Losel Nyida Öbar (Ngag dbang blo gsal nyi zla 'od 'bar), who was active at the beginning of the eighteenth century. The Iron-Bridge Man Losang Paldrup (Lcags zam pa Blo bzang dpal 'grub) was a teacher of the Sakya master Kunga Lekpai Jungné (Kun dga' legs pa'i 'byung gnas, 1704–60). See Jamyang Khyentsé Wangpo, *Words of the Mahāpaṇḍita Śīlaratna*, 279, 342, and 353–54.

71 See Guru Tashi, *Musical Sea of Amazing Stories to Delight Experts*, 664. Also see Jamyang Khyentsé Wangpo, *Pleasure Grove of Amazing Lotus Flowers*, 9, where similar information about Yölmo Tulku and his brother is given. I have used the spelling Gam (Sgam), found in Yölmo Tulku's autobiography, instead of Gom (Sgom), found in Guru Tashi and Khyentsé Wangpo, because the brother is referred to in the autobiography as "Chakdor Norbu, [emanation of] Gampopa, the Spiritual Son of the Conquers" (Rgyal sras Sgam po pa Phyag rdor nor bu). Note that the Nyön *(smyon)* in the name Gam Nyön (Sgam smyon) means "mad," "crazy."

72 See Kunga Lodrö, *Boundless Miracles*, in particular 165–69, 238, 261. Much information about Tangtong Gyalpo's descendants, teachings, and legacy is found in this biography.

73 See Sherab Palden, *Ocean of Marvels*, 89–95, and Gyurmé Dechen, *Jewel Mirror in Which All Is Clear*, 63. The "Seven Jewels" of the Shangpa tradition are: Vajradhara, Niguma, Khyungpo Naljor, Mokchokpa Rinchen Tsöndru, Kyergangpa Chökyi Sengé, Rigongpa Sangyé Nyentön, and Sangyé Tönpa. For a translation of the collected spiritual songs of these and other masters of the Shangpa tradition, and information about their lives, see Zangpo (2003). Also see Smith (2001),

53–57, and Kapstein (1980) for brief information on the lineages and teachings of the Shangpa Kagyü tradition.

74 Tangtong's meeting with Namkhai Naljor (Nam mkha'i rnal 'byor) is described by Könchok Palsang and Dewa Sangpo, *Bright Lamp*, 176–77, and Gyurmé Dechen, *Jewel Mirror in Which All Is Clear*, 77–78. Jamgön Kongtrul, *Rosary of Precious Beryl*, 125a, mentions that Tangtong studied with Dorjé Shönu (Rdo rje gzhon nu).

75 The *Vajra Lines (Rdo rje'i tshig rkang)* are succinct verse summaries of the crucial teachings of the Shangpa transmission. For a translation of one of these texts, the *Vajra Lines* for the Amulet Mahāmudrā, see Zangpo (2003), 45–46. Also see Kapstein (1980). Khecarī (Mkha' spyod ma) is a form of Vajrayoginī.

76 This vision of Niguma is recorded in spectacular detail in Sherab Palden, *Ocean of Marvels*, 95–100.

77 Sherab Palden, *Ocean of Marvels*, 103–5, does not identify the girl as Niguma, but Gyurmé Dechen, *Jewel Mirror in Which All Is Clear*, 102–3, makes the identification.

78 The blessing of the illusory body *(sgyu lus byin brlabs)* is a particular blessing or initiation connected with the Six Dharmas of Niguma in the Shangpa tradition.

79 Tangtong Gyalpo's texts on the Niguma teachings are found in *Supplemental Texts to the Collected Works of Thang stong rgyal po Series (Grub chen thang stong bka' 'bum gyi rgyab chos)*, vol. 1: 241–386, and in Jamgön Kongtrul, *Treasury of Oral Instructions (Gdams ngag mdzod)*, vol. 8: 147–205. These works are signed "Madman of the Empty Valley" (Lung stong smyon pa), one of the names the ḍākinīs gave Tangtong. Also see Gyatso (1981), 186–202, for more information about Tangtong's Niguma texts and his role in the Shangpa tradition.

80 See Jamgön Kongtrul, *Pleasure Grove of Amazing Udumvara Flowers*, 507.

81 For Machik Labdrön (Ma gcig Lab sgron) and the Severance (Gcod) tradition in general, see Harding (2003), Edou (1996), Gyatso (1985), and the other works listed in their bibliographies. For Gökyi Demtruchen's (Rgod kyi ldem 'phru can) life and teachings, see Herweg (1994) and Dudjom (1991), 780–83.

82 These teachings are presently available in two editions: *Tangtong's Oral Transmission (Thang stong snyan brgyud)*, and the *Oral Transmission of Machik's Secret Behavior (Ma gcig gsang spyod snyan brgyud)* that is included in vols. 1–4 of the *Collected Works of Thang stong rgyal po*. Some works of the tradition are also found in vol. 3 of the *Collected Works of Grub chen Thang stong rgyal po*. Also see Gyatso (1981), 160–85, for a discussion of Tangtong Gyalpo's system of Severance and the various texts of the collection.

83 Gyurmé Dechen, *Jewel Mirror in Which All Is Clear*, 72–73.

84 See Khetsun Tenpai Gyaltsen, *Extensive Initiation for the Blessing of Opening the Door to the Sky*, 89.5–90.1. For a short biography of Namkha Lekpa, see Shākya Shenyen, *Biography of Jamyang Namkha Lekpa*.

85 See Khetsun Tenpai Gyaltsen, *Extensive Initiation for the Blessing of Opening the Door to the Sky*, 90.1.

86 See Tangtong Gyalpo, *Infinite Benefit for Living Beings*. Jamgön Kongtrul, *Infinite Benefit for Others* and Khakyap Dorjé, *Rainfall to Benefit Living Beings* explain Tangtong's work. The Tibetan texts and English translations of all three texts (with later additions to Tangtong's original work) are found in Dewar (2004). Jamgön Kongrul, *Essence of All Sūtra and Tantra* is an expanded form of Tangtong's famous text that is commonly used today.

87 Khakhyap Dorjé, *Rainfall to Benefit Living Beings*, 2a. This text has been translated in McLeod (n.d.) and Dewar (2004). For a detailed discussion of Tangtong Gyalpo's Avalokiteśvara teachings, see Gyatso (1981), 100–142.

88 The *Compendium of Maṇis (Ma ṇi bka' 'bum)* is a large collection of Avalokiteśvara literature attributed to the seventh-century Tibetan king Songtsen Gampo (Srong btsan sgam po). This popular treasure text has been discussed by Vostrikov (1970), 52–57, and Kapstein (1992). Information concerning the various systems of practical instructions *(dmar khrid)* for meditation on Avalokiteśvara can be found in the *Jonang Collection of One Hundred and Eight Profound Guiding Instructions (Jo nang zab khrid brgya rtsa brgyad)*, a collection compiled by Kunga Drolchok (Kun dga' grol mchog, 1507–66) and included in Jamgön Kongtrul's *Treasury of Oral Instructions (Gdams ngag mdzod)*, vol. 12. The history of some of these traditions is recorded in Roerich (1976), 1006–42.

89 The refuge formula given by Avalokiteśvara to Ka Ngapa for Tangtong Gyalpo is known as "Mothers Infinite As Space" (Ma nam mkha' ma'i skyabs 'gro) and is a distinguishing characteristic of Tangtong's meditation practices. It is also used in some Shangpa and Severance traditions. See note 389 for a translation of these lines. Jamgön Kongtrul, *Infinite Benefit for Others*, 23, says *Infinite Benefit for Living Beings* is the quintessence of all the teachings Tangtong received from Avalokiteśvara.

90 See Gyatso (1979), 113.

91 See Kunga Drolchok, *Basic Text and Clarification of the Practice of the Essential Six Syllables*, 17–21.

92 For example, while staying in retreat on Chakpori Hill in Lhasa, Tangtong Gyalpo had a vision of Avalokiteśvara that caused him to write down a method for meditation on Avalokiteśvara in conjunction with the practice of ritual fasting *(snyung gnas)*. This entire text is reproduced in Könchok Palsang and Dewa Sangpo, *Bright Lamp*, 533–78. See Tangtong Gyalpo, *Combined Practice of Both the Palmo Tradition and the King's Tradition*.

93 Gyurmé Dechen, *Jewel Mirror in Which All Is Clear*, 294. The same phrases are also found in Tangtong Gyalpo's edicts *(bka' shog)*. For example, see Könchok Palsang and Dewa Sangpo, *Bright Lamp*, 389. Mahākaruṇika is one of the epithets of Avalokiteśvara.

94 The most famous originators of the tradition of *maṇi* devotees were the Nyingma masters Guru Chökyi Wangchuk (Chos kyi dbang phyug, 1212–70) and Nyang Nyima Öser (Nyang Nyi ma 'od zer, 1136–1204).

95 See the fine collection of research on Tibetan opera in *Lungta 15* (Winter 2001): *The Singing Mask: Echoes of Tibetan Opera.* See also Stein (1956), Stein (1959), 513–18, and Gyatso (1986).

96 See Tangtong Gyalpo and Jamyang Khyentsé Wangpo, *Basic Texts and a Clarification of the White and Red Pills.* This work is composed of two short texts by Tangtong himself for making white and red medicinal pills, together with an explanation by Jamyang Khyentsé Wangpo. On page 336 Tangtong refers to himself in the first person as "Old Father Tangtong Gyalpo" (Pha rgan Thang stong rgyal po), and on page 339 as "Madman of the Iron Bridges" (Lcags zam smyon pa). These writings are of special interest because they are the only solid evidence of Tangtong's involvement in medicine and contain his own version of the vision that served as the basis for the development of the red and white medicinal pills. Gyurmé Dechen, *Jewel Mirror in Which All Is Clear*, 176, connects the origin of these pills with a different vision following an attempted assassination of Tangtong during a visit to Ngari Dzongkha (Mnga' ris Rdzong kha). Also see Yeshé Paljor, *Fine Tree of Noble Aspiration*, 41, where Tangtong is referred to as a physician *(sman pa).* Some traditions also say he founded the Chakpori Medical College in Lhasa.

97 These ceremonies were probably formulated after the time of Tangtong Gyalpo, but seem to be based on episodes in his life. Also see Stein (1959), 514–15, Roerich (1932), H.R.H. Prince Peter of Greece and Denmark (1962), and Hummel (1968). For more recent photographs of the ritual, see Kahlen (1993).

98 See Jamgön Kongtrul, *Rosary of Precious Beryl*, 125a.

99 See Könchok Palsang and Dewa Sangpo, *Bright Lamp*, 493.

100 Gyurmé Dechen, *Jewel Mirror in Which All Is Clear*, 66–67.

101 When receiving the initiations of Jamyang Khyentsé Wangpo's Heartdrop of the Great Adept (Grub thob thugs thig) from Dilgo Khyentsé Rinpoché, I asked what had happened to Tangtong Gyalpo's original treasures. Khyentsé Rinpoché told me that the Heartdrop of the Great Adept were in fact them.

102 See Könchok Palsang and Dewa Sangpo, *Bright Lamp*, 144, 149–50, and Gyurmé Dechen, *Jewel Mirror in Which All Is Clear*, 57, 62. Tangtong received the three yogas *(yo ga rnam gsum)* from Kunga Nyingpo (Kun dga' snying po) and heard all the Nyingma teachings from Dorjé Drakpa (Rdo rje grags pa). The three yogas are the anuyoga, mahāyoga, and atiyoga teachings of the Nyingma tradition.

103 The Indian adept Hūṃkara is a major figure in the transmission of the mahāyoga of the Nyingma tradition, in particular the teachings of Yangdak Heruka. He was one of the eight great adepts, or holders of pure awareness, through whom the lineage of the Eight Transmissions of Great Attainment is traced according to the Nyingma tradition. See Dudjom (1991), 475–77. Tangtong Gyalpo had a vision of Hūṃkara that caused him to remember one hundred thousand of his past lives, and he told many stories from one of them to his disciples. See Könchok Palsang and Dewa Sangpo, *Bright Lamp*, 232–40, and Gyurmé Dechen, *Jewel Mirror in Which All Is Clear*, 223–24.

104 See in particular Könchok Palsang and Dewa Sangpo, *Bright Lamp*, 411–15, where Tangtong Gyalpo's responses to a series of questions from the co-author Dewa Sangpo are recorded. Tangtong's comments emphasize the Great Perfection teachings in style and content, after which he bestowed the Northern Treasure teachings of the *Naturally Arising and Naturally Dawning Great Perfection (Rdzogs pa chen po Rang 'byung rang shar)* and the *Penetration of the Intention (Dgongs pa zang thal)*, the initiation of the dynamic energy of pure awareness *(rig pa rtsal gyi dbang)*, and the general initiation as a regent *(rgyal 'tshabs spyi lugs kyi dbang)*. The Fifth Dalai Lama, Ngawang Losang Gyatso (1617–82), mentions that he also received several Northern Treasure transmissions that had passed through Tangtong, among them the Heart Practice of Drakpotsel *(thugs sgrub drag po rtsal)*. See Ngawang Losang Gyatso, *Current of the Ganges River*, vol. 3: 287. The Sakya master Kunpang Doringpa (1449–1524) received Nyingma transmissions directly from Tangtong himself. See Jamyang Khyentsé Wangpo, *Words of the Mahāpaṇḍita Śīlaratna*, 401.

105 For information on Kunkyong Lingpa (Kun skyong gling pa), see Guru Tashi, *Musical Sea of Amazing Stories*, 416–21, and Kunsang Ngedön Longyang, *Jewel Necklace*, 207–16.

106 The Ten Royal Sūtras *(rgyal po'i mdo bcu)* are listed in Losang Trinlé, *Clarification of Knowledge*, 660. The Six Dharmas of Niguma (*Ni gu chos drug*) are mainly practiced in the Shangpa Kagyü. They are inner fire, illusory body, dream, clear light, transference of consciousness, and intermediate state. The Heart Practice (Thugs sgrub) and the *Penetration (Zang thal)* are treasure teachings of Gökyi Demtruchen (Rgod kyi ldem 'phru can, 1337–1408). The *Penetration* is the same as the *Penetration of the Intention (Dgongs pa zang thal)*.

107 See Pema Trinlé, *Biographies of the Masters*, 295–96.

108 See Könchok Palsang and Dewa Sangpo, *Bright Lamp*, 441–42.

109 Gyurmé Dechen, *Jewel Mirror in Which All Is Clear*, 49.

110 See Gökyi Demtruchen, *Longevity Practice of the Iron Tree*.

111 Gökyi Demtruchen, *Longevity Practice of the Iron Tree*, 250. According to Könchok Palsang and Dewa Sangpo, *Bright Lamp*, 50, the goddess of longevity named Caṇḍālī *(tshe'i lha mo tsan dha li)* is the consort of the buddha Amitābha.

112 See Ngawang Kunga Tashi, *Seed for Attaining Immortality*, 294. This author also wrote on the *Glorious Giver of Immortality ('Chi med dpal ster)*, Tangtong's own system of life-sustaining practices.

113 Ngawang Kunga Tashi, *Seed for Attaining Immortality*, 278–79.

114 Quoted in Gyurmé Dechen, *Jewel Mirror in Which All Is Clear*, 240. On the basis of readings in older texts, I understand the spelling *brgya bcu phrag gcig* (110) to be a mistake for *brgyad bcu phrag gcig* (81). In the oldest source, Kunga Sönam Drakpa Palsang, *Final Story Concerning the Nirvāṇa of the Great Adept*, 162a, the same verse says Tangtong's lifespan will be eighty-one *(brgyad bcu phrag gcig)*. The same line quoted in Könchok Palsang and Dewa Sangpo, *Bright Lamp*, 102, predicts a lifespan of eighty-three *(brgyad bcu phrag gsum)* years.

115 Oral communication from Dezhung Rinpoché. A notable exception was the treasure revealer Jatsön Nyingpo ('Ja' tshon snying po, 1585–1656), who was a fully ordained monk.

116 Many versions of the teachings of the *Glorious Giver of Immortality ('Chi med dpal ster)* have been preserved. The most important works are Yeshé Lhundrup, *Precepts for Achieving Immortality* and *Stream of Nectar*, and Ngawang Kunga Tashi, *Method for Accomplishment, Rite of Initiation, and Esoteric Instructions.* This latter text reflects the form in which the *Glorious Giver of Immortality* has been transmitted in the Sakya tradition. Key texts are found in the *Collected Works of Grub chen Thang stong rgyal po*, vol. 3: 739–56, and in the *Supplemental Texts to the Collected Works of Thang stong rgyal po Series*, vol. 4: 449–603. Also see Gyatso (1981), 142–59, for a discussion of Tangtong Gyalpo's longevity practices and the various texts concerning them.

117 For this journey, see Könchok Palsang and Dewa Sangpo, *Bright Lamp*, 338–41, Gyurmé Dechen, *Jewel Mirror in Which All Is Clear*, 95–102, and, in particular, Sherab Palden, *Ocean of Marvels*, 123–52. Sherab Palden, page 152, also mentions that the details of Tangtong's journey would be too lengthy to describe in his text and are clear elsewhere. This reference indicates that another more detailed account was available to Sherab Palden, but has presumably now been lost.

118 The Nyingma master Terdak Lingpa (Gter bdag gling pa, 1646–1714) says this in his treatise concerning the longevity practices. See Terdak Lingpa and Lochen Dharmashrī, *Fine Wish-fulfilling Vase of Methods for Accomplishment*, 189–90. Tangtong Gyalpo's biographies do not mention the *Glorious Giver of Immortality* by name among the treasure texts extracted from the wall of the cave in Chimpu (Mchims phu). But the appearance of the treasure trove was heralded by the shape of a glowing red shield in the rock interior of the cave, encircled in a clockwise fashion by the long *dhāraṇī-mantra* of Amitāyus that is said to vanquish the Lord of Death. Especially see Könchok Palsang and Dewa Sangpo, *Bright Lamp*, 194–95, where the episode is told in the first person, apparently related by Tangtong himself. The version in the translated biography is based on this account.

119 A longevity practice *(srog sgrub)* written by a later author based on the *Glorious Giver of Immortality* does contain verbatim sections from *A Single Syllable Hrī (Hrī gcig ma)*, the secret third section of Gökyi Demtruchen's *Iron Tree.* This at least shows a liturgical link between the two traditions later in their history, although no similarity whatever is found in the actual techniques of the *Iron Tree* and the *Glorious Giver of Immortality.* See Khardo Chökyi Dorjé, *Secret Treasury of the Ḍākinīs*, 325–26. The original source of these quotes is found in Gökyi Demtruchen, *Longevity Practice of the Iron Tree*, 260.

120 Yeshé Lhundrup, *Stream of Nectar*, 613. For Tangtong's original words, see Tangtong Gyalpo, *Untitled.*

121 Yeshé Lhundrup, *Stream of Nectar*, 613–14. For brief descriptions of the Dalai Lama's marvelous visions of Tangtong Gyalpo, see Karmay (1988), 32, 38, 46–48. Also see Dzamling Dorjé, *Method of Accomplishment and Ritual of Initiation.* Dzamling Dorjé, *Uncontrived, Naturally Arisen Vajra Words*, is a eulogy addressed to Tangtong in connection with his life-sustaining practices.

122 See Gyatso (1998), 290 n. 45, for references to the Nyingma master Jikmé Lingpa's ('Jigs med gling pa, 1730–98) visions of Tangtong Gyalpo. Kunsang Pema Tsewang of Tangtong's Severance (Gcod) lineage is said to have met Tangtong face to face. See Chökyi Gyatso, *A Necklace of Utpala Flowers of Elegant Explication*, 126.2. Mental treasure teachings *(dgongs gter)* inspired by visions of Tangtong have occurred even in modern times to teachers such as Tülshuk Lingpa (Brtul zhugs gling pa, 1916–65?). See the *Collected Revelations (gTer chos) and Writings of brTul-zhugs-gling-pa*, 183–227.

123 See Kunga Lodrö, *Boundless Miracles*, 242.

124 Tsultrim Rinchen, *Annual Account of the Leaves and Petals of Happiness and Suffering*, 559. Also see Tsultrim Rinchen, *Ocean of Pure Realms to Delight Everyone*, 273, where the same dream is briefly described in verse. I first learned of this episode from my teacher Dezhung Rinpoché, who also noted that the urine of great adepts—such as his own teacher Gatön Ngawang Lekpa (Sga ston Ngag dbang legs pa, 1864–1941)—was sometimes drunk by faithful disciples to receive blessings.

125 Jamgön Kongtrul, *Pleasure Grove of Amazing Udumvara Flowers*, 351, 439.

126 Jamgön Kongtrul, *Heart of Elegant Explication*, 190–91.

127 Jamyang Khyentsé Wangpo, *Essence of Primordial Awareness in Action*, 180, and Jamgön Kongtrul, *Heart of Elegant Explication*, 191.

128 See Barron (2003), 98, for Kongtrul's vision of Tangtong Gyalpo. See also Gyatso (1981), 131–53, for more about the Heartdrop of the Great Adept and the different texts of the cycle.

129 Jamyang Khyentsé Wangpo, *Cycle of Five Essential Methods for Accomplishment*, 451.

130 Gyurmé Dechen, *Jewel Mirror in Which All Is Clear*, 66.

131 Jamyang Khyentsé Wangpo, *Essence of Primordial Awareness in Action*, 167–80.

132 Jamyang Khyentsé Wangpo, *Cycle of Five Essential Methods for Accomplishment*, 449–580.

133 Jamyang Khyentsé Wangpo's basic text is found in vol. 24 of the *Precious Treasury of Treasure Teachings (Rin chen gter mdzod)*, 261–365. Further explanations were composed by Jamgön Kongtrul and are included in vols. 24–25 of the same collection. These works are also found in vols 4–5 of the *Supplemental Texts to the Collected Works of Thang stong rgyal po Series.*

134 The longevity practices and the *Vajra Lines* are found in Jamgön Kongtrul's *Treasury of Precious Treasure Teachings (Rin chen gter mdzod)*, vol. 17: 181–86 and 229–31. Kongtrul also composed texts concerning the longevity practices, which are included in the same volume. These works are also found in vols. 3 and 4 of the *Supplemental Texts to the Collected Works of Thang stong rgyal po Series.*

135 Kunga Sönam Drakpa Palsang, *Untitled*, 382. Kunga Sönam Drakpa Palsang wrote these lines at Riwoché in 1528, just eleven years after the announcement that Tangtong Gyalpo had actually passed away in 1485.

136 Lo (Klo) or Loyul (Klo yul) is the Tibetan name for a portion of the tribal areas on the Tibeto-Assamese border now included in Arunachal Pradesh. See Ardussi (1977), 49 n. 38.

137 Könchok Palsang and Dewa Sangpo, *Bright Lamp*, 407–8, 495.

138 See Pawo Tsuklak Trengwa, *Banquet for Experts*, vol. 1: 164. Also see Sørensen (1994), 144, etc., concerning Pudé Gungyal (Pu de gung rgyal).

139 See Losang Trinlé, *Clarification of Knowledge*, 794–95.

140 See Sönam Gyaltsen, *Bright Mirror of Royal Genealogies*, 95–6, and Sørensen (1994), 210–11.

141 See Losang Trinlé, *Clarification of Knowledge*, 795.

142 See Nyang Nyima Öser, *Nectar of Honey from the Hearts of Flowers*, 424.

143 See Tsering (2001), 59.

144 *khyud mo*. The usual word for an iron *link* in Tangtong Gyalpo's biographies is *rkang bu*, and, more rarely, *a long*. But the term *khyud mo* is also used in Author Unknown, *Biography of the Venerable Lady Chökyi Drönma*, 128b: *lcags zam gyi thag pa'i mkhyud mo*.

145 See Chödrak Palsang, *Jewel Rosary of Great Excellence*, 326–28. Tāranātha, *Necessary Discussion of the Origins of the Dharma Cycles of Glorious Kālacakra*, 30, tells the same story with some slight differences, and specifies that the bridge was located at Rinchen Ding (Rin chen sdings). Also see Lhai Gyaltsen, *Biography of the Great Omniscient Jonangpa Dharma Lord*, 13a, 14b, and 19a. In his eulogy of the Jonang stūpa, Dolpopa himself mentions the pulling of the iron chains by a vast assembly of nonhuman and human beings during the construction work. See Dolpopa Sherab Gyaltsen, *Dredging the Pit of Saṃsāra*, 456.

146 See Könchok Palsang and Dewa Sangpo, *Bright Lamp*, 317–18. This bridge is not mentioned in the biography by Gyurmé Dechen.

147 See Gyurmé Dechen, *Jewel Mirror in Which All Is Clear*, 174–78, and Vitali (1996), 81, 503.

148 Oral communication from Dezhung Rinpoché on August 23, 1978. According to Dezhung Rinpoché and also Chökyi Gyatso, *Necklace of Moon Crystals*, 476–77, the iron bridge in front of Puntsok Ling (Phun tshogs gling) was built by Tangtong Gyalpo. Several nice pictures of this iron bridge are found in Hedin (1917), vol. 2: 302, one of which is reproduced on page 36 of this book.

149 Sönam Drakpa, *Magical Key to Royal Genealogies*, 76.

150 See Jikmé Drakpa, *Rain of Attainments for a Crop of Faith*, 50–51, and Tāranātha, *Entryway for Experts*, 51–52. The supervisor of the work *(las rgyab gnyer chen po)* on the bridge, who was named Amoghavajra (A mo gha badzra), was perhaps Nepalese.

151 Jamyang Khyentsé Wangchuk, *Summarizing Notes on the Path Presented as the Three Appearances*, 341. This text is translated in Stearns (2006).

152 Könchok Palsang and Dewa Sangpo, *Bright Lamp*, 515–16, and Sherab Palden, *Ocean of Marvels*, 501, 525.

153 See Könchok Palsang and Dewa Sangpo, *Bright Lamp*, 143, and Gyurmé Dechen, *Jewel Mirror in Which All Is Clear*, 55–56.

154 For example, see Könchok Palsang and Dewa Sangpo, *Bright Lamp*, 263, 266, and Gyurmé Dechen, *Jewel Mirror in Which All Is Clear*, 186, 191.

155 See Chökyi Drönmé, *Untitled*, 243, which is also quoted in Könchok Palsang and Dewa Sangpo, *Bright Lamp*, 167.

156 See Mingyur Dorjé, *Examination of the Legacy of Tangtong Gyalpo's Iron-Bridge Building Activities*, 325.

157 These numbers are according to Tangtong Gyalpo's statement in Könchok Palsang and Dewa Sangpo, *Bright Lamp*, 485, and in Gyurmé Dechen, *Jewel Mirror in Which All Is Clear*, 230. However, in one of his edicts Tangtong also mentions having built thirty-four iron bridges, twenty ferries, and fifty wooden bridges. See Könchok Palsang and Dewa Sangpo, *Bright Lamp*, 523. When summing up Tangtong's accomplishments during the fifty-six years from the Earth Bird Year (1429) until the Wood Dragon Year (1484), Sherab Palden, *Ocean of Marvels*, 561, says he had built forty-eight iron bridges, eighteen ferries, and many wooden bridges.

158 See Mingyur Dorjé, *Examination of the Legacy of Tangtong Gyalpo's Iron-Bridge Building Activities*, 326–28, for a detailed discussion and list of the various iron bridges that still exist in Tibet.

159 The discussion of Tangtong Gyalpo's activities in this section follows the narrative sequence in the translated biography.

160 See Könchok Palsang and Dewa Sangpo, *Bright Lamp*, 125–26, and Gyurmé Dechen, *Jewel Mirror in Which All Is Clear*, 73. Different lists of the eight tribes of gods and demons *(lha srin sde brgyad)* can be found. One of the more general lists according to the tantras is: *klu*, *gnod sbyin*, *lto 'phye*, *mkha' lding*, *lha min*, *brul bum*, and *mi'am ci*. For an extremely detailed listing of these groups according to the Nyingma tradition, see Dorje and Kapstein (1991), 158–59. Also see Harding (2003), 320 n. 2.

161 Kongtsun Demo (Kong btsun de mo) is one of twelve great goddesses bound to an oath of protection by Padmasambhava during his visit to Tibet. For the various lists and descriptions of these twelve *tenma* goddesses *(brtan ma bcu gnyis)*, see Nebesky-Wojkowitz (1956), 181–98. An account of Kongtsun Demo's past lives and history was rediscovered by the treasure revealer Urgyen Ledro Lingpa (U rgyan las 'phro gling pa), which is one of the names of Jatsön Nyingpo ('Ja' tshon snying po, 1585–1656). See Tselé Götsangpa Natsok Rangdrol, *Fragmentary Account of Kongtsun Demo*.

162 Varuṇa (Wa ru ṇa) is one of the eight great nāga kings. According to Dezhung Rinpoché, Varuṇa is the king of all the nāgas and travels to different subterranean locations in much the same way that a worldly king might travel to make contact

with his subjects. Tangtong bound Varuṇa to a vow of cooperation, and later left the realized yogin Tokden Nyakpo (Rtogs ldan Nyag po) to supervise the building of a temple and stūpa. Another account of this event is found in Sangyé Gyatso, *Mirror of Yellow Beryl*, 229. The monastery at Waru Namtsel in later years apparently followed the tantric traditions of the Geluk monasteries of Sera and Drepung.

163 See note 658 for information on Lady Kalsang, who was the wife of the governor of the Lhasa area.

164 See Ngawang Losang Gyatso, *Crystal Mirror*, 46. Could the Chakpori image of Tangtong Gyalpo blessed with barley from his own hand *(phyag nas ma)* be the one now in the Nyingjei Lam collection that bears the inscription "This image of the adept Tangtong Gyalpo contains barley from the lord's own hand" *(grub thob thang stong rgyal po'i sku rje rang nyid gyi phyag nas bzhugs so)*? The term *phyag nas* is either an honorific term for barley *(nas)* or refers to barley tossed from the hand *(phyag)* during consecration of the image, and does not indicate that the image was made "from his own hand." See Weldon and Singer (1999), 184–86. The image is also reproduced as illustration 1 and plate 1 in this book.

165 See Ngawang Losang Gyatso, *Crystal Mirror*, 46.

166 Ferrari (1958), 41.

167 Chökyi Gyatso, *Necklace of Moon Crystals*, 133.

168 Oral communication from Dezhung Rinpoché.

169 Gendun Rinchen, *Ear Ornament for Students*, 76a.

170 See Turner (1971), 54–55, for fine drawings of the Chukha bridge, one of which is reproduced on page 43 of this book. Michael Aris informed me that the bridge at Norbugang (Nor bu sgang) stood until 1969.

171 Communication from Michael Aris.

172 Also see Tucci (1949), 662–70, for the text of an edict issued by Rabten Kunsang Pak (Rab brtan kun bzang 'phags) in 1440 that refers to the Pari (Phag ri) workers transporting loads under the orders of the Gyantsé (Rgyal rtse) government.

173 See Sherab Palden, *Ocean of Marvels*, 343–44, 358, and Gyurmé Dechen, *Jewel Mirror in Which All Is Clear*, 203, 212.

174 See Tāranātha, *Extremely Detailed, Unpretentious, and Candid Narrative*, 202.

175 See Waddell (1906), 312–14, who says no toll was taken for crossing the bridge because the villagers kept it in free repair.

176 *Condensed Verses on the Perfection of Wisdom (Āryaprajñāpāramitāsañcayagātha. 'Phags pa shes rab kyi pha rol tu phyin pa sdud pa tshigs su bcad pa)*, Toh 13, sher phyin, *ka*, 1b–19b. The eight sugatas *(bde bar bshegs pa brgyad)* or buddhas are probably the same as the eight sugata siblings *(bde bshegs mched brgyad)* connected with practices of the Medicine Buddha. Several different lists of these eight are found. According to Losang Trinlé, *Clarification of Knowledge*, 1641–42, the eight are: Mtshan legs, Rin chen zla ba, Gser bzang dri med, Mya ngan med mchog

dpal, Chos grags rgya mtsho, Mngon mkhyen rgyal po, Sman gyi bla ma, and Shākya thub pa.

177 See Könchok Palsang and Dewa Sangpo, *Bright Lamp*, 249–50, and Gyurmé Dechen, *Jewel Mirror in Which All Is Clear*, 217.

178 See Ngawang Losang Gyatso, *Crystal Mirror*, 46. The Dalai Lama also lists several other images made by Tangtong Gyalpo that were enshrined on Chakpori Hill, and says the ḍākinīs offered the precious substances to him while he was staying at the Kaṃṇi Goshi (Kaṃ ṇi sgo bzhi) in Lhasa, not during his travels as described in the biography.

179 See Ngawang Losang Gyatso, *Crystal Mirror*, 12.

180 Dokham (Mdo khams) is the general name for a large region in eastern Tibet, including the areas of Amdo and Kham. Minyak (Mi nyag) is a region in Kham, stretching west from Dartsedo. Kongpo is a wilderness area in southeast Tibet. See Dorje (1999), 227–42, for a modern description of the region.

181 See Sherab Palden, *Ocean of Marvels*, 385–86, and Gyurmé Dechen, *Jewel Mirror in Which All Is Clear*, 221–22, where the prayer that Tangtong Gyalpo made is also reproduced. The following information follows Gyurmé Dechen's account.

182 The construction of this bridge is described in some detail in the translated biography. See also Mingyur Dorjé, *Examination of the Legacy of Tangtong Gyalpo's Iron-Bridge Building Activities*, 338, and Dorje (1999), 186, who notes that five large stone bridge piers are all that now remain of the Nyago bridge.

183 See Kunga Sönam Drakpa Palsang, *Final Story Concerning the Nirvāṇa of the Great Adept*, 165b.

184 See Ngawang Namgyal, *Ocean of Marvels*, 659.

185 See Yeshé Lhundrup, *Biographical Supplication to the Lord of Realization*, for a short biography of Ngawang Yongdrak (Ngag dbang yongs grags). Also see Kunga Lodrö, *Boundless Miracles*, 261.

186 See Mingyur Dorjé, *Examination of the Legacy of Tangtong Gyalpo's Iron-Bridge Building Activities*, 329. A manuscript biography of Losang Tobden Paljor was used by Mingyur Dorjé for his article, but this work is not available to me. It would probably shed much light on the Chaksam tradition and the later descendants of Tangtong Gyalpo.

187 See Kunga Lodrö, *Boundless Miracles*, 172, 242.

188 See Ricard et al. (1994), 457.

189 For photographs of the iron bridge at Riwoché in 1988, see Vitali (1990), pl. 75; Kahlen (1990), 92 and 94; and Kahlen (1993), 141. Some of these photographs are also reproduced in this book,

190 Mingyur Dorjé, *Examination of the Legacy of Tangtong Gyalpo's Iron-Bridge Building Activities*, 327.

191 Hauri and Peters (1979), 14–15.

192 Oral communication from Dezhung Rinpoché on June 22, 1978.

193 Mingyur Dorjé, *Examination of the Legacy of Tangtong Gyalpo's Iron-Bridge Building Activities*, 336–37. This source also contains further details about anchoring techniques, the quality and size of the links, and so forth.

194 Songtsen Gampo, *Compendium of Maṇis*, vol. 1: 394–98. Also see Aris (1980), 8–33, Gyatso (1989), and Sørensen (1994).

195 Ferrari (1958), 66, 154. Also see Gyatso (1989) and Sørensen (1994).

196 Some of this information is from Michael Aris. The restoration is mentioned by Sherab Gyaltsen, *Chariot for Realization of the Two Truths*, 27b, 63a–b. Also see Aris (1980), 188.

197 The four mountains are Chakpori (Lcags po ri) in Lhasa, Hepori (Has po ri) in Samyé (Bsam yas), Gongpori (Gong po ri) at Tsetang (Rtses thang), and Palchen Chuwori (Dpal chen Chu bo ri). See Kunga Tenpai Nyima, *Seed of Speech*, 10. The number of Tangtong's stūpas is given in Sherab Palden, *Ocean of Marvels*, 562, and Gyurmé Dechen, *Jewel Mirror in Which All Is Clear*, 330.

198 Songtsen Gampo, *Compendium of Maṇis*, vol. 1: 394. Also see Gyatso (1989) and Sørensen (1994).

199 See Sherab Palden, *Ocean of Marvels*, 177–78, 180. The episode at Jonang is translated in the next section, "Madman of the Empty Valley." For the story of Dolpopa's construction of the huge stūpa at Jonang, see Stearns (1999), 19–23.

200 See Könchok Palsang and Dewa Sangpo, *Bright Lamp*, 104–6, and Gyurmé Dechen, *Jewel Mirror in Which All Is Clear*, 35.

201 See Sherab Palden, *Ocean of Marvels*, 117, Könchok Palsang and Dewa Sangpo, *Bright Lamp*, 148, and Gyurmé Dechen, *Jewel Mirror in Which All Is Clear*, 59–60. The Auspicious Stūpa of Many Doors (Bkra shis sgo mang mchod ldan) is one of the eight types of stūpas that symbolize eight significant events in the life of the Buddha, in this case the Buddha's teaching of the Dharma *(chos kyi 'khor lo bskor ba)*.

202 Sherab Palden, *Ocean of Marvels*, 119. The name Tāmradvīpa, or Copper Island (Zangs gling), was used at different times for a number of islands (such as Ceylon) and other locations in Southeast Asia. See von Schroeder (1990) for what little is known about the Vajrayāna tradition in ancient Ceylon.

203 Sherab Palden, *Ocean of Marvels*, 57, and Gyurmé Dechen, *Jewel Mirror in Which All Is Clear*, 85. Pal Riwoché (Dpal Ri bo che) is perhaps named after Śrīparvata (Dpal kyi ri bo), a famous tantric pilgrimage site in ancient India that Tangtong visited during his travels. See Könchok Palsang and Dewa Sangpo, *Bright Lamp*, 288–90, where Tangtong mentions in one of his edicts that he visited Śrīparvata (which is probably another name for Śrīśailam).

204 See Sherab Palden, *Ocean of Marvels*, 539–60, for a detailed description of the various temples at Riwoché and the sculptures and paintings in them. Ngawang Tenzin Norbu, *Meaningful to Behold*, is a description of the sculptures and

paintings in the stūpa itself. The building of the various temples of the monastic complex around the Riwoché stūpa continued for some years. Although the artists who worked on the temples are not named in Tangtong Gyalpo's biographies, a famous sculptor *(lha bzo ba)* of the Jang district during this time was the master Tashi Rinchen (Byang pa'i dpon Bkra shis rin chen), whose work was even preferred by some over that of the renowned Leu Chungpa (Sle'u chung pa). In 1460 the First Dalai Lama, Gendun Drupa (Dge 'dun grub pa, 1391–1475), tried to get Tashi Rinchen to work on the large Maitreya image he wished to build at his monastery of Tashi Lhunpo. Tangtong apparently prevented Tashi Rinchen's departure, probably because the Riwoché work was not yet complete. See Yeshé Tsemo, *Rosary of Amazing and Marvelous Gems*, 266–67. Also see Stearns (1980), 145 n. 71; Vitali (1990), 133; and Jackson (1996), 96–98, 135 n. 266.

205 See Gyurmé Dechen, *Jewel Mirror in Which All Is Clear*, 84: *mtha' dmag gi bla ri bla chu*, and Ngawang Tenzin Norbu, *Meaningful to Behold*, 4b, 7a.

206 See Sherab Palden, *Ocean of Marvels*, 483, and Gyurmé Dechen, *Jewel Mirror in Which All Is Clear*, 283.

207 For a discussion of the stylistic relationship between the stūpas at Jonang, Gyang, and Riwoché, see Vitali (1990), 126–33.

208 Chökyi Drönmé's stay at Riwoché with Tangtong Gyalpo is described in Author Unknown, *Biography of the Venerable Lady Chökyi Drönma*, 112b–28b. Also see Könchok Palsang and Dewa Sangpo, *Bright Lamp*, 464–66; Sherab Palden, *Ocean of Marvels*, 485–88; and Gyurmé Dechen, *Jewel Mirror in Which All Is Clear*, 283–85.

209 See Author Unknown, *Biography of the Venerable Lady Chökyi Drönma*, 10b–17b, for the story of Chökyi Drönmé's engagement and marriage, and 26a for the birth of her daughter. Tsewang Tashi's death is mentioned on 114b.

210 By covering his mouth with his cloak, Tangtong Gyalpo is showing his deep respect for Chökyi Drönmé.

211 See *Author Unknown, Biography of the Venerable Lady Chökyi Drönma*, 112b–13b. A brief passage near the end of this episode has been omitted in the translation.

212 For brief information about Chökyi Drönmé and her successors in the Samding Dorjé Phagmo incarnation line, see Dorjé Phagmo Dechen Chödrön and Dra Tupten Namgyal, *Past Lives of the Samding Dorjé Phagmo Incarnations*, 33–46, and Diemberger et al. (1997), 111–14. For a complete study, see Diemberger (forthcoming 2007). Samding Monastery was founded by Bodong Panchen. In the nearby Bodong monastery of Drokgang Ding, Situ Chökyi Gyatso (1880–1925) saw a Nepalese-style painting of the white Cakrasaṃvara maṇḍala that had been the special meditation object of Chökyi Drönmé, whom he identifies as Tangtong Gyalpo's consort. See Chökyi Gyatso, *Necklace of Moon Crystals*, 371.

213 The translated biography and other texts also say that the skull-cup of Chökyi Drönmé's cranium was enshrined at the retreat site of Menmogang, which would

seem to be included in the area of Tsagong. Also see Sherab Palden, *Ocean of Marvels*, 488, and Könchok Palsang and Dewa Sangpo, *Bright Lamp*, 466.

214 See Ratnabhadra, *Brief Clarification of My Life*, 413.

215 See Ricard et al. (1994), 456-57. Shabkar also wrote a separate detailed account of the restoration, which is not available to me.

216 Ngawang Tenzin Norbu, *Meaningful to Behold*, 7a. The work was begun in the sixth month of the Water Bird Year (1933). The previous damage to the stūpa had apparently been caused by a severe earthquake. See Jackson (1996), 368 n. 828.

217 Kunga Tenpai Nyima, *Music of an Auspicious Conch Shell*, 91.

218 See Anonymous (1979). The man who returned to Riwoché after a twenty-year absence was named Ngawang Gelek.

219 See Vitali (1990), 123–36, for a detailed discussion of the art and style of the Riwoché stūpa and splendid photographs taken in 1988. In the caption to pl. 78 and elsewhere Vitali mentions that "the altars in the Ri.bo.che stūpa did not have statues as main images but painted deities." Actually, according to Könchok Palsang and Dewa Sangpo, *Bright Lamp*, 353–54, the main images were sculptures, some made from mixtures of special medicinal substances *(sman sku)* and others from gilt copper *(gser zangs las grub pa)*. The description by Dzatrul Ngawang Tenzin Norbu during his restorations of the stūpa beginning in 1933 also specifically lists statues *('bur sku)* as the main figures in each chapel. The walls were painted with the various maṇḍalas. See Ngawang Tenzin Norbu, *Meaningful to Behold*, 7b–12a. My copy of this text is incomplete. Also see Kahlen (1990), for an excellent photograph of the stūpa in 1988 and of a painting at Riwoché that shows the original complex before its destruction. Jackson (1996), 97, also reproduces a modern drawing of the stūpa. Several of Kahlen and Vitali's photographs are also in the present book.

220 Chökyi Gyatso, *Necklace of Moon Crystals*, 151–55.

221 Tucci (1965), 67. At the time of Tucci's visit the monastery was Nyingma.

222 The later history of Tangtong Gyalpo's hermitage at Tsagong is completely unknown. The only mention of it that I have seen is in the autobiography of the Drukpa Kagyü master Pema Karpo ('Brug chen Padma dkar po, 1527–92), who spent the summer retreat of 1547 in Kongpo at the "hermitage of Tsagong (Rtsa gong), the place of the great adept Tangtong Gyalpo." While there, Pema Karpo sent the yogin known as Drong Nyön ('Brong smyon), the Madman of Drong, off to engage in secret conduct *(gsang spyod)*. See Pema Karpo, *Opera of Great Compassion*, 418–19.

223 Gendun Rinchen, *Ear Ornament for Students*, 76b.

224 Gendun Rinchen, *Ear Ornament for Students*, 76a. The first Tachok Chöjé (Rta mchog Chos rje) was Mönpa Dewa Sangpo (Mon pa Bde ba bzang po), Tangtong's disciple and the co-author of one of his biographies, which was completed at Tachok Norbugang (Rta mchog nor bu sgang). The knowledge that no community of monks remained at Tachok Norbugang in 1980 I owe to Michael Aris.

225 Tsultrim Rinchen, *Catalogue of the Dergé Edition of the Translated Treatises*, vol. 1: 327–28.

226 Ngawang Damchö Gyatso, *Key to Open a Hundred Doors of Profound Meaning*, 47a. The meeting of Tangtong and Ngorchen is described in Könchok Palsang and Dewa Sangpo, *Bright Lamp*, 334, and Gyurmé Dechen, *Jewel Mirror in Which All Is Clear*, 289–90.

227 Oral communication from Dezhung Rinpoché on August 26, 1978. According to my notes, the place name was spelled Yid lhung gzhi.

228 This verse is from a eulogy to Tangtong Gyalpo written by his disciple Gyaltsen Sangpo, whom Tangtong Gyalpo appointed as the first abbot of his monastery at Chuwori. See Gyaltsen Sangpo, *Untitled*, 251.

229 In a letter requesting Tangtong Gyalpo to return to southeast Tibet, the Drukpa Kagyü master Gyalwang Kunga Paljor (Rgyal dbang Kun dga' dpal 'byor, 1428–76) praised Tangtong using the name Madman of the Empty Valley (Lung stong smyon pa) and the other names given to him by the ḍākinīs. This is one of several independent testimonies that Tangtong was famed by this name even during his lifetime. See Kunga Paljor, *Letter Offered to Dharma Lord Tangtong Gyalpo*, 445. Some mention of Drukpa Kunlek, Tangtong Gyalpo, and mad yogins is also found in Stein (1959). The most detailed discussion in English of Drukpa Kunlek ('Brug pa Kun legs) is Ardussi (1972), and Stein (1972b) contains a French translation of the first of the four volumes of his autobiography. For information on Tsang Nyön Heruka (Gtsang smyon He ru ka) and religious madness in Tibet, also see Stearns (1985) and Smith (2001), 59–79. For the Tibetan biographies of Ü Nyön (Dbus smyon), see Ngawang Drakpa, *Making the Body Hairs of Those with Impartial Faith Flutter*, and Shenyen Namgyal, *Drumbeat of Ornamental Deeds*. Franz-Karl Ehrhard has recently written about Ü Nyön in an unpublished paper entitled "'The Madman of dBus' and His Relationships with Tibetan Rulers of the 15th and 16th Centuries."

230 See Ngawang Losang Gyatso, *Current of the Ganges River*, vol. 3: 255.

231 An excellent summary of many topics associated with deliberate behavior according to the tantras is found in Jamgön Kongtrul, *Encompassment of All Knowledge*, 935–52. Also see Namgyal (1986), 330–50.

232 Dezhung Rinpoché's words were: *'jig rten gyi spyod pa brtul/ sangs rgyas kyi spyod pa la zhugs/ yang na spyod pa ma rung ba brtul/ spyod pa yang dag pa la zhugs*. See Stearns (1985), 18.

233 The following brief comments about the essence, timing, motives, and practice of deliberate behavior are based on Jamgön Kongtrul, *Encompassment of All Knowledge*, 938–44.

234 The eight worldly concerns *('jig rten chos brgyad)* are gain *(rnyed pa)* and loss *(ma rnyed pa)*, reputation *(snyen pa)* and notoriety *(mi snyen pa)*, slander *(smad pa)* and praise *(bstod pa)*, and pleasure *(bde ba)* and suffering *(sdug bsngal)*.

235 See Gyaltsen Sangpo, *Untitled*, 251.

236 See Jamgön Kongtrul, *Rosary of Precious Beryl*, 48a. Holy madness is frequently mentioned in the lineage of Nyang Nyima Öser.

237 See Kunsang Ngedön Longyang, *Jewel Necklace*, 208, and Guru Tashi, *Musical Sea of Amazing Stories*, 417. Kunkyong Lingpa later sent his disciple Jamyang Rinchen Gyaltsen to receive teachings from Tangtong Gyalpo.

238 Stein (1972a), 276. Also see 153–56 for a short discussion of mad yogins in Tibet.

239 See Padma gling pa, *Illuminating Lamp of Prophecy*, 561: *padma gling pa gter ston smyon pa nga.*

240 See Aris (1988), 23, who notes that Ashi Drubtob Sangmo's remains are still enshrined in a stūpa at Sombrang, Bhutan.

241 See Ngawang Losang Gyatso, *Ocean of Marvelous Deeds*, 443: *rnal 'byor smyon pa skra rgod can zhig byung.*

242 See Herweg (1994), 64–65.

243 Ngawang Tenzin Norbu, *Ocean of Blessings*, 110: *gcod pa'i brtul zhugs sam smyo spyod lta bu bzhes.*

244 See Anonymous, *Extensive Explication of the Practice of the Six Perfections*, 53.3–4.

245 Smith (2001), 59–61.

246 See Milarepa, *Some Miscellaneous Teachings, Such as Vajra Songs, of the Venerable Lord Milarepa*, 106b–7a. For another translation, see Kunga Rinpoche and Brian Cutillo (1978), 86–7.

247 See the quotation from Padmasambhava's *Bright Lamp of Prophecy (Lung bstan gsal ba'i sgron me)* in an annotation in Gyurmé Dechen, *Jewel Mirror in Which All Is Clear*, 4, and also in Könchok Palsang and Dewa Sangpo, *Bright Lamp*, 100, 101.

248 See Könchok Palsang and Dewa Sangpo, *Bright Lamp*, 115–17, and Gyurmé Dechen, *Jewel Mirror in Which All Is Clear*, 33–34.

249 See Gyurmé Dechen, *Jewel Mirror in Which All Is Clear*, 75.

250 Gyurmé Dechen, *Jewel Mirror in Which All Is Clear*, 51. The four defeating acts *(pham pa bzhi)* are: 1) to kill, 2) to engage in sexual activity, 3) to lie about possessing supernormal powers or attainments that you do not have, 4) to steal. According to the monastic code of the vinaya, these acts destroy the vows of a fully ordained monk, and for this reason are called "defeating" *(pham pa)*. Sakya Paṇḍita (Sa skya Paṇḍi ta, 1182–1251) also wrote, "Even the four defeating acts, if performed with a mind firmly set on benefiting others, are taught to be virtues for a bodhisattva and sins for śrāvakas." See Sakya Paṇḍita, *Treatise Distinguishing the Three Vows*, 9b.

251 Sakya Paṇḍita, *Treatise Distinguishing the Three Vows*, 12a, points out that if it were simply the garments of ordination that indicated the possession of a state of

mind disciplined by vows, then the bodhisattvas who wear jewel ornaments and fine attire forbidden to monks would be open to criticism. He also mentions that the great adepts Virūpa, Tilopa, and Nāropa discarded the outer costume of the fully ordained monk, but can hardly be considered sinners because of it.

252 The famous Jonangpa master Dolpopa Sherab Gyaltsen (1292–1361). Tangtong Gyalpo claimed to be his rebirth. Also see note 304.

253 Tangtong Gyalpo sometimes observed vows of silence. During those periods he wrote messages and teachings on a writing slate *(sa 'bor ra)*. Ashes or dust would be scattered upon a wooden board, and then letters could be drawn in the ashes or dust. For a photograph of such a writing slate, see Goldstein (1989), 169.

254 Sherab Palden, *Ocean of Marvels*, 175–79. The episode in Jonang is also partially described in the translated biography, but with much less detail.

255 Gyurmé Dechen, *Jewel Mirror in Which All Is Clear*, 75. For the eight worldly concerns, see note 234.

256 Gyurmé Dechen, *Jewel Mirror in Which All Is Clear*, 206. I have translated this line according to the suggestion of Dezhung Rinpoché, who corrected the reading *spyod pa byed pa*, which is found in the Dergé edition, to *spyod pa byed sa*.

257 Tölung (Stod lung) is a valley to the west of Lhasa in Central Tibet. The Tölung area contained several of the major monasteries of the Karma Kagyü tradition, such as Tsurpu (Mtshur phu), the main monastery of the Karmapa.

258 Gyurmé Dechen, *Jewel Mirror in Which All Is Clear*, 162. Also see Könchok Palsang and Dewa Sangpo, *Bright Lamp*, 254.

259 See Könchok Palsang and Dewa Sangpo, *Bright Lamp*, 284, and Gyurmé Dechen, *Jewel Mirror in Which All Is Clear*, 201.

260 See Ngödrup Palbar, *Lion of Faith at Play on a Glacial Peak of Good Qualities*, 10a–b, and Natsok Rangdrol, *Heart of the Sun Illuminating the Vajrayāna*, 43–45. Tsang Nyön continued to Lhasa and was invited to the palace of the governor, Depa Neu Dzongpa Paljor Gyalpo (Sde pa Sne'u rdzong pa Dpal 'byor rgyal po, d. 1490), the son of Drungchen Drakpa Palsang (Drung chen Grags pa dpal bzang) and his wife Kalden Rinchen Sangmo, who had previously been Tangtong Gyalpo's main patron in Lhasa. Also see note 539 for information about the Kaṃṇi Goshi stūpa.

261 Könchok Palsang and Dewa Sangpo, *Bright Lamp*, 322, and Gyurmé Dechen, *Jewel Mirror in Which All Is Clear*, 212–13.

262 Tangtong Gyalpo would travel through eastern Tibet in 1445–46, visit the famous Five-Peaked Mount Wutai in China, and build many iron bridges, including one over the Nyakchu River.

263 Tangtong Gyalpo built the iron bridge over the Kyichu River in Lhasa in 1430. The translated biography does not mention Tangtong and Rongtön meeting at Sangpu (Gsang phu), but Sherab Palden, *Ocean of Marvels*, 193–95, describes a very interesting meeting of the two masters there. Before he was recognized by

Rongtön, who then asked him for teachings, Tangtong slept for three days at the foot of the stūpa of Chapa Chökyi Sengé (Phya pa Chos kyi seng ge, 1109–69), and people thought he was a corpse.

264 As often mentioned in his biographies, Tangtong Gyalpo made a vow at a certain point not to go inside buildings, except for temples, stūpas, and so forth.

265 Shākya Chokden, *Enjoyable Ocean of Amazing Faith*, 354–55. Also see Shākya Chokden, *Letter to the Great Adept Tangtong Gyalpo*, which is a letter he sent to Tangtong along with a rosary of fifty coral beads and the prayer that Tangtong live for another fifty years.

266 See Natsok Rangdrol, *Heart of the Sun Illuminating the Vajrayāna*, 34–35, 37–39.

267 See Sherab Palden, *Ocean of Marvels*, 199–200.

268 See Ngawang Drakpa, *Making the Body Hairs of Those with Impartial Faith Flutter*, 494–95.

269 Oral communication from Dezhung Rinpoché.

270 Rinchen Namgyal, *Making the Body Hairs of the Faithful Flutter*, 47–48.

271 Kham, Amdo, and Minyak are all areas in eastern Tibet.

272 Gyurmé Dechen, *Jewel Mirror in Which All Is Clear*, 158. The Jowo in Lhasa is the most holy statue in Tibet. It is a likeness of the Buddha Śākyamuni at age twelve and is said to have been brought to Tibet in the seventh century by the Chinese wife of the Tibetan king Songtsen Gampo.

273 Sherab Palden, *Ocean of Marvels*, 214–15, and Gyurmé Dechen, *Jewel Mirror in Which All Is Clear*, 224.

274 Gyurmé Dechen, *Jewel Mirror in Which All Is Clear*, 313. In Könchok Palsang and Dewa Sangpo, *Bright Lamp*, 396–97, this teaching is much longer and seems to be a record of everything Tangtong Gyalpo wrote on the slate.

275 *Hevajra Tantra (Hevajratantrarājanāma. Kye rdo rje zhes bya ba rgyud kyi rgyal po/ Kye'i rdo rje mkha' 'gro ma dra ba'i sdom pa'i rgyud kyi rgyal po)*, Toh 418, Kangyur, rgyud 'bum, *nga*, 16a. According to the commentary translated in Farrow and Menon (1992), 173, "Buddhists and non-Buddhists" *(sangs rgyas mu stegs)* refers to śrāvakas and others whose practices are in conflict with the essence of the Vajrayāna teachings.

276 Anonymous, *Rejection of Confusion about Virtue and Sin*, 40.4–41.1.

277 Gyurmé Dechen, *Jewel Mirror in Which All Is Clear*, 278–79. The three vows *(sdom gsum)* are the vows of individual liberation, the bodhisattva vow, and the vows of secret mantra.

278 This episode is translated from Rinchen Namgyal, *Making the Body Hairs of the Faithful Flutter*, 41–42, except for the phrase "I don't need you and you don't need me," which is found only in Natsok Rangdrol, *Heart of the Sun Illuminating the Vajrayāna*, 46–47. This phrase is an echo of the same words spoken by the Indian

master Padampa Sangyé to Milarepa at their parting nearly four hundred years earlier. See Chang (1962), vol. 2: 609. With minor omissions and additions, both Rinchen Namgyal and Natsok Rangdrol have copied the episode from Ngödrup Palbar, *Lion of Faith at Play on a Glacial Peak of Good Qualities*, 10b, which is the earliest of the biographies, written in 1508, the year after Tsang Nyön's death.

279 See Tangtong Gyalpo's various works in the bibliography concerning the practices of the Shangpa teachings of Niguma and the fasting ritual of Avalokiteśvara. In most of his edicts he also uses the name Madman of the Empty Valley (Lung stong smyon pa), along with the other names he received from the ḍākinīs.

280 Dickinson (1961), 209.

281 An annotation in the Tibetan text says, "This is from the Great Teacher's *Bright Lamp of Prophecy*: 'The place of truth is the basic space of phenomena. Pure awareness is present unmoved.' The basic space of phenomena and pure awareness are precisely *evaṃ*. These are employed as poetical figure metaphors *[gzugs can gyi rgyan]*." The *Bright Lamp of Prophecy (Lung bstan gsal ba'i sgron me)* is the biographical prophecy of Tangtong Gyalpo concealed by Guru Padmasambhava as a treasure teaching to be recovered centuries later by Tangtong himself. The verse quoted in this annotation is also preserved in the fragment of the *Bright Lamp* found in Könchok Palsang and Dewa Sangpo, *Bright Lamp*, 161. The Sanskrit term *evaṃ* refers to a state of fusion or unity. The opening lines here describe the unity of the basic space of phenomena and introspective awareness *(nang rig)*.

282 An annotation in the Tibetan text says, "This is also a poetical figure metaphor." Padmapāṇi, "Lotus in Hand," is a name of the bodhisattva Avalokiteśvara. Hayagrīva is a wrathful form of Avalokiteśvara.

283 An annotation in the Tibetan text says, "It is said, 'As a sign of emanating indivisibly as one, both calm Mahākaruṇika and wrathful, glorious Hayagrīva, his physical appearance will be semiwrathful.'" The verse quoted here is also preserved in the fragment of the *Bright Lamp* found in Könchok Palsang and Dewa Sangpo, *Bright Lamp*, 102. Mahākaruṇika, "The Great Compassionate One," is another name for Avalokiteśvara.

284 Lord Padmākara is Guru Padmasambhava. An annotation in the Tibetan text says, "It has been said, 'To the east in front of Owa, one with the name Tsöndru will appear.' And from a treasure text of Pema Lingpa: 'An emanation of Padmasambhava called Tangtongpa will appear. At that time some comfort will come to the citizens and sentient beings of Tibet.'" Pema Lingpa (Padma gling pa, 1450–1521) was a famous Bhutanese treasure revealer. The first of these quotations would seem to be from the *Bright Lamp*, but is not found in the fragments in Könchok Palsang and Dewa Sangpo, *Bright Lamp*.

285 An annotation in the Tibetan text says, "This is a poetical figure simile *[dpe rgyan]*. As for those particular characteristics, it is said, 'Maroon in color, with a pleasant fragrance, and adorned with moles, he will have an easy disposition, dynamic pure awareness, and care for various [living beings] through unpredictable behavior. He is my mental emanation.'" The first portion of this quote from Padmasam-

bhava's *Bright Lamp of Prophecy* is found in Könchok Palsang and Dewa Sangpo, *Bright Lamp*, 101, and another similar quote mentioning Tangtong Gyalpo as a mental emanation is found on page 100.

286 In Buddhist tantra, usually in the context of the practice of the third and fourth of the four initiations, four levels of joy are cultivated. These are joy, sublime joy, beyond joy, and coemergent joy. Each of these can be further divided into four levels with the same names, such as the joy of joy, the joy of sublime joy, and so on, for a total of sixteen facets of joy.

287 An annotation in the Tibetan text says, "It is said, 'As a sign of the great joy of unity, he will be embraced from the basic space [of phenomena] by great secret consorts, and actually resort to sixteen female embodiments of pure awareness. Furthermore, whether apparent or not apparent, they are definitely emanations of the ḍākinīs of primordial awareness. Many ḍākinīs of sacred commitment will gather.'" This quote from the *Bright Lamp* is also found in Könchok Palsang and Dewa Sangpo, *Bright Lamp*, 102. The nine dance moods *(gar dgu'i nyams)* are manifested by the semiwrathful tantric deities and consist of three of enlightened body: flirtatiousness, bravery, and ugliness; three of enlightened speech: laughter, ferocity, and fearsomeness; and three of enlightened mind: compassion, majesty, and calm.

288 It is often traditionally calculated that the teachings of Śākyamuni Buddha will last for five thousand years. Briefly, the first period of fifteen hundred years is the time of fruition, the second fifteen hundred years is the period of realization, the third fifteen hundred years is the period of scripture, and the final five hundred years is the period of mere semblance to the authentic teachings. For a more detailed explantion, see Dorje and Kapstein (1991), 94 n. 1349. Fivefold degeneracy is the degeneracy of lifespan to a maximum of one hundred years, degeneracy of the age to an age of strife *(kaliyuga)* and turmoil, degeneracy of the afflictions into extreme perversion and coarseness of long duration, degeneracy of sentient beings so that their character and sense faculties are very difficult to tame, and degeneracy of the view in regard to the nature of reality.

289 Jambudvīpa *('dzam bu gling)* is the southern of the four continents that surround Mount Meru in Buddhist cosmology. See note 160 for information on the eight tribes of gods and demons.

290 The six syllables are the famous six-syllable mantra of Avalokiteśvara: *Oṃ maṇi padme hūṃ.*

291 See page 9 of the Introduction.

292 This verse occurs later in the biography (with the last two lines reversed) in a song Tangtong Gyalpo sings during his visit to the famous Five-Peaked Mount Wutai in China.

293 The following story is based on Könchok Palsang and Dewa Sangpo, *Bright Lamp*, 233–40, where it is told as one of the one hundred thousand past lives that Tangtong Gyalpo remembered following a vision of the great adept Hūṃkara and then told to his disciples. Gyurmé Dechen also mentions this later in the

biography when describing the vision, but he chose to remove the story from its original context and tell it here.

294 The Tripiṭaka *(sde snod gsum)*, or Three Baskets, are the fundamental canonical teachings of sūtra, vinaya, and abhidharma.

295 In the Mahāyāna and Vajrayāna traditions it is believed that all the one thousand buddhas of this aeon reach enlightenment at Bodhgayā seated in meditation beneath the Bodhi tree. The site of their enlightenment is referred to as the "vajra seat" *(vajrāsana)*. The Mahābodhi at the Vajrāsana is the holy temple and image of Śākyamuni Buddha at Bodhgayā, marking the place where the Buddha achieved complete enlightenment. It is believed to have been built by the son of a woman who had actually met Śākyamuni Buddha.

296 The seven-branch offering *(yan lag bdun pa)* is to offer prostrations, offerings, confession and repentance, sympathetic joy, prayer that the wheel of the doctrine be turned, prayer that buddhas and bodhisattvas remain active in the world, and dedication of merit. The seven types of precious substances *(rin po che sna bdun)* are gold, silver, turquoise, coral, pearl, emerald, and sapphire. See Dorje and Kapstein (1991), 154, 156.

297 What is traditionally known as *a precious human existence* is composed of eighteen *freedoms and endowments (dal 'byor)*. The eight freedoms are freedom from birth as a hell being, as a hungry ghost, as an animal, as a god, as a barbarian, as someone with wrong view, as someone living in an age when no buddha has appeared, and as someone who is mute. The first five endowments, which refer to yourself, are to be born as a human being, to be born in a central land, to have complete sense faculties, to have faith in the Dharma, and not to commit the worst crimes. The second five endowments, which refer to others, are for a buddha to appear, for that buddha to teach the Dharma, for the doctrine to endure, for there to be followers, and for there to be compassion for others.

298 See the text of the *Bright Lamp of Prophecy* in Könchok Palsang and Dewa Sangpo, *Bright Lamp*, 100.

299 See the text of the *Bright Lamp of Prophecy* in Könchok Palsang and Dewa Sangpo, *Bright Lamp*, 100–101.

300 This master Rongtön (Rong ston) has not been identified. Gomtsul (Sgom tshul) is probably the Kagyü master Dakgom Tsultrim Nyingpo (Dwags sgom Tshul khrims snying po, 1116–69), who was the son of Gampopa's elder brother and also one of Gampopa's main disciples. See Kunga Dorjé, *Red Annals*, 447.

301 Jayul (Bya yul), also called Ja (Bya), is an area south of the Dakpo and Yarlung regions of southcentral Tibet.

302 See the text of the *Bright Lamp of Prophecy* in Könchok Palsang and Dewa Sangpo, *Bright Lamp*, 101.

303 Könchok Palsang and Dewa Sangpo, *Bright Lamp*, 175, say Tangtong Gyalpo made this statement (with some variations) when he visited the stūpa built by Dolpopa at Jonang. Sherab Palden, *Ocean of Marvels*, 167, places it among his pro-

nouncements and prophecies after his early retreat at Tarpa Ling (Thar pa gling), where he prefaces it by yelling, "Listen up everyone, and I'll tell you another lie!" *(yang rdzun gcig labs kyis nyon cig mi 'ong kun).*

304 The Omnisicient Dolpopa Sherab Gyaltsen (Kun mkhyen Dol po pa Shes rab rgyal mtshan, 1292–1361) was one of the most controversial and important masters in Tibetan history. He built his great stūpa at Jonang from 1330 to 1333. At the time of its construction it was the largest such structure in all of Tibet. Dolpopa's own description of the construction of the Jonang stūpa contains fascinating similarities to the description of Tangtong Gyalpo's later construction of a great stūpa at Chung Riwoché, completed in 1456. Both stūpas are said to have been constructed by human beings during the day and by nonhuman beings during the night. See Dolpopa Sherab Gyaltsen, *Dredging the Pit of Saṃsāra*, 455–57. For a study of Dolpopa's life and teachings, see Stearns (1999).

305 Jang (Byang) was one of the thirteen districts of ancient Tibet, with its capital at Ngamring. Tangtong Gyalpo's monastery of Riwoché is in this district.

306 See also Könchok Palsang and Dewa Sangpo, *Bright Lamp*, 166. With some variations, these lines are found in a series of verses spoken to Tangtong Gyalpo by Guru Padmasambhava during one of Tangtong's long meditation retreats. Although not specifically identified as the *Bright Lamp of Prophecy*, some verses match those identified as such elsewhere, and the text is identified as a treasure. See Könchok Palsang and Dewa Sangpo, *Bright Lamp*, 161–67.

307 Tachok Khabab (Rta mchog kha bab) is the name used for the western portion of the Tsangpo River, which originates from the southern side of Mount Kailash in western Tibet.

308 Both secular and religious traditions.

309 An adoptive bridegroom *(go mag)* is a man who goes to live with his wife's family after marriage.

310 See also Könchok Palsang and Dewa Sangpo, *Bright Lamp*, 51. Dong (Ldong) is an abbreviation for Lhadong Karpo (Lha ldong dkar po), one of the six original clans *(rus)* in ancient Tibet. It was one of the most important and ancient clans of the Minyak (Mi nyag) area in East Tibet and also figures in the Gesar epics. See Stein (1959), 217 and 219. It is interesting to note that the governors of Jang Ngamring (Byang Ngam ring) also traced their lineage back to a Minyak clan, perhaps the Lhadong Karpo. See Palden Chökyi Sangpo, *Series of Jewels*, 167.

311 This description basically follows Könchok Palsang and Dewa Sangpo, *Bright Lamp*, 79. In contrast, Sherab Palden, *Ocean of Marvels*, 7–8, describes Tangtong Gyalpo's father in only negative terms as a very bad person, saying that he was a great sinner, dishonest, had no faith in people who practiced Dharma or in masters from whom he had received Dharma, and deceived other people of the area. This negative version is perhaps closer to the truth, since Tangtong himself mentions later in the translated biography that he saved his father from being reborn in the hell realms as a result of his evil deeds.

312 Sherab Palden, *Ocean of Marvels*, 8, seems to say that Trowo Palden was the third child.

313 See Könchok Palsang and Dewa Sangpo, *Bright Lamp*, 99–100. Tsari in Kongpo is one of the major holy mountains in Tibet and is believed to be the home of Cakrasaṃvara and his consort Vajravārāhī. The area was first opened up for pilgrims through the efforts of Tsangpa Gyaré Yeshé Dorjé (Gtsang pa rgya ras Ye shes rdo rje, 1161–1211), the founder of the Drukpa Kagyü sect who was a disciple of Lama Shang (Bla ma Zhang, 1123–93) and Lingrepa (Gling ras pa, 1128–88), and Drigung Kyopa Jikten Gönpo ('Bri gung skyob pa 'Jig rten mgon po, 1143–1217) and other disciples of Pakmodrupa Dorjé Gyalpo (Phag mo gru pa Rdo rje rgyal po, 1110–70). It is thus a special holy area for the Kagyü traditions, especially the Drukpa. The mountain is a glacial peak, but is believed to be a crystal Auspicious Stūpa of Many Doors inside. See Kunsik Chökyi Nangwa, *Detailed Explanation of the Sacred Site of Tsari*, 19, 29, and Toni Huber, *The Cult of the Pure Crystal Mountain: Popular Pilgrimage and Visionary Landscape in Southeast Tibet* (New York: Oxford University Press, 1999).

314 Part of this quotation is found in the fragment of the *Bright Lamp of Prophecy* in Könchok Palsang and Dewa Sangpo, *Bright Lamp*, 100.

315 The substance of the preceding paragraph, and portions of this quote from the *Bright Lamp of Prophecy*, are found in Könchok Palsang and Dewa Sangpo, *Bright Lamp*, 100.

316 See the text in Könchok Palsang and Dewa Sangpo, *Bright Lamp*, 101.

317 The four initiations are the vase initiation, secret initiation, initiation of primordial awareness dependent on an embodiment of wisdom, and the fourth initiation.

318 See the text in Könchok Palsang and Dewa Sangpo, *Bright Lamp*, 101.

319 See the text in Könchok Palsang and Dewa Sangpo, *Bright Lamp*, 101, which is somewhat different.

320 All the dreams are related in detail in Könchok Palsang and Dewa Sangpo, *Bright Lamp*, 80–87, where Tangtong is said to have remained in his mother's womb for *twelve* months!

321 Amitābha (Snang ba mtha' yas), the buddha of infinite light, is associated with the paradise of Sukhāvatī, the realm of bliss, in the western direction. The five precious substances *(rin po che sna lnga)* are usually listed as gold, silver, turquoise, coral, and pearl. See also Dorje and Kapstein (1991), 147.

322 The Glorious Copper-Colored Mountain (Zangs mdog dpal ri) is the paradise of Guru Padmasambhava, traditionally located to the southwest of Tibet.

323 A paradise associated with the goddess Vajrayoginī or Vajravārāhī.

324 The anchorite Dönyö Gyaltsen (Kun spangs Don yod rgyal mtshan) was a master of the Northern Treasure (Byang gter) lineage of the Nyingma tradition. He was a disciple of the Gökyi Demtruchen (Rgod kyi ldem 'phru can, 1337–1408), the original revealer of the treasure texts of this lineage. Dönyö Gyaltsen would later

become Tangtong Gyalpo's first important teacher, from whom he received the complete transmission of Gökyi Demtruchen's Northern Treasures. According to an episode later in the translated biography, Dönyö Gyaltsen apparently lived to be one hundred years old.

325 The Guru Calm and Wrathful *(gu ru zhi drag)* refers to Guru Padmasambhava in both calm and wrathful forms.

326 This quote would seem to be from Padmasambhava's *Bright Lamp of Prophecy*, but is not found in the fragments of the text reproduced in Könchok Palsang and Dewa Sangpo, *Bright Lamp*.

327 This section seems to have been quoted from an earlier source recording a first-person statement by Tangtong Gyalpo's mother, Gyagar Lhamo (Rgya dkar lha mo).

328 See the text in Könchok Palsang and Dewa Sangpo, *Bright Lamp*, 101, which is very different.

329 The month of miracles is the first month of the year in the Tibetan lunar calendar.

330 According to Könchok Palsang and Dewa Sangpo, *Bright Lamp*, 88, the newborn child exclaimed, "*A a a*," while resting his mind in the intended meaning of the vinaya, sūtra, and abhidharma; again "*A a a*," while resting in the meaning of the śrāvaka, pratyekabuddha, and bodhisattva vehicles; again "*A a a*" for the three tantra sets of action tantra, performance tantra, and yoga tantra; again "*A a a*," for the mahāyoga, anuyoga, and atiyoga; and finally a single "*Āḥ*," while resting in the natural lucidity of the primordial awareness of the birthless dharmakāya reality body. The syllable *a* or *āḥ* is often considered an expression of birthless reality.

331 The sevenfold posture of Vairocana is to sit with legs crossed in the vajra-position, hands in the lap in meditation gesture, spine straight, shoulders back, chin tucked in toward the esophagus, tip of the tongue touching the palate, and eyes focused in front of the tip of the nose.

332 According to Könchok Palsang and Dewa Sangpo, *Bright Lamp*, 92, the vulture flew the child so high that he saw a heavenly realm and received profound teachings directly from Vajrasattva.

333 Sherab Palden, *Ocean of Marvels*, 12–13, says Tangtong was fifteen years old (*bco lnga*, which must be a scribal mistake for "five," *lnga*) at this time, and gives a long list of the various teachings he received, such as the *Penetration of the Intention of the Great Perfection (Rdzogs chen dgongs pa zang thal)*, the Heartdrop of the Ḍākinī (Mkha' 'gro snying thig), and the cycle of Severance teachings (Gcod skor). Tangtong's disciple Namkha Lekpa gives the age of five for this event and also says Tangtong received Severance teachings (the spelling *spyod* is a scribal mistake for *gcod*) at this time. See Namkha Lekpa, *Practicing Severance*, 44–45.

334 Ka Ngapa Paljor Sherab (Bka' lnga pa Dpal 'byor shes rab) would become one of Tangtong Gyalpo's most important teachers. He is known to have studied under the Shangpa master Müchen Namkhai Naljor (Mus chen Nam mkha'i rnal

'byor). The title *Ka Ngapa (bka' lnga pa)* means Paljor Sherab had mastered the five fundamental subjects of epistemology *(tshad ma)*, the perfection of wisdom literature *(phar phyin)*, madhyamaka or middle-way philosophy *(dbu ma)*, abhidharma according to the *Abhidharmakośa (mdzod)*, and the monastic code *('dul ba)*. Mangtö Ludrup Gyatso, *Bright Sun of Pure Altruism*, 247, says that, according to Ka Ngapa's biography, he became abbot of Dzong Chödé (Rdzong chos sde) when he was thirty-two and became the ninth abbot of the monastery at Ngamring when he was thirty-seven. Ka Ngapa was a teacher of many notable figures of the fifteenth century, including Namgyal Draksang (1395–1475), the physician and realized scholar who was the governor of Jang Ngamring. See Sangyé Gyatso, *Banquet to Delight the Seers*, 307. Mangtö Ludrup Gyatso, *Bright Sun of Pure Altruism*, 219, says the Sakya master Müchen Könchok Gyaltsen (Mus chen Dkon mchog rgyal mtshan, 1388–1469) received the transmission of Rendawa's madhyamaka teachings from Ka Ngapa in Jang when he was thirty-four years old (1421).

335 According to Könchok Palsang and Dewa Sangpo, *Bright Lamp*, 93, Tangtong was eight (seven according to Western calculation) years old at this time.

336 That is, taking refuge in the Masters, the Buddha, the Dharma, and the Sangha.

337 *Lañcana* and *vartula* are two scripts used to write Sanskrit, with *vartula* being a rounded form of *lañcana.*

338 Könchok Palsang and Dewa Sangpo, *Bright Lamp*, 94, say Tangtong was ten years old at this point.

339 According to Dezhung Rinpoché, a nāga-māra *(klu bdud)* is a malicious type of spirit whose parents are a nāga *(klu)* and a māra *(bdud)*. This kind of spirit is believed to cause leprosy and other similar diseases.

340 This is probably because the family lived in her ancestral home.

341 In Könchok Palsang and Dewa Sangpo, *Bright Lamp*, 528, Tangtong Gyalpo himself says he went twenty-five times in place of his father and older brothers.

342 According to Anonymous, *All-Illuminating Lamp*, 11a, Tangtong Gyalpo was fifteen years old at this time. His age at this point is not mentioned in Könchok Palsang and Dewa Sangpo, *Bright Lamp*, 114, or any other source.

343 Gugum Rinchen Gyaltsen (Gus gum Rin chen rgyal mtshan) was the governor at Ngamring (Ngam ring), the capital of the district of Jang (Byang). The title *gus gum* or *gu'i gung* is the Tibetan rendering of the Chinese title *guogung* ("Duke") that was given during the Yuan Dynasty to rulers who were of royal descent. Rinchen Gyaltsen was a benign ruler famed as an emanation of Avalokiteśvara. He was a practitioner of the Six-branch Yoga of Kālacakra and was said to have actualized all of the signs of this practice and to have performed miracles such as leaving footprints in stone. For a sketch of his life, see Palden Chökyi Sangpo, *Series of Jewels*, 179–81. Rinchen Gyaltsen was the grandfather of the Jang governor Namgyal Draksang (1395–1475), who later became one of Tangtong Gyalpo's main supporters.

344 These verses are found in the story of the Indian master Śāntideva's life. For example, see Obermiller (1932), vol. 2: 162, and Yeshé Gyaltsen, *Biographies of the Lineal Masters of the Stages of the Path*, 137. As a result of the dream, Śāntideva realized that it was wrong for him to assume his father's throne, and he fled to Nālandā Monastery and took ordination.

345 Amoghapaśa (Don yod zhags pa) is a form of Avalokiteśvara.

346 Ngamring (Ngam ring) was the capital of the district of Jang (Byang), one of the thirteen districts of ancient Tibet. About 1225, the Ngamring ruler Drakpa Dar (Grags pa dar), also known as Yöntsun (Yon btsun), invited the Sakya master Shākya Sengé (Shākya seng ge) to Ngamring and founded the monastery there. It was later expanded by the governor Tai En Namkha Tenpa (Ta'i dben Nam mkha' brtan pa, b. 1316) in 1354, with the assistance of his teacher, the Omniscient Dolpopa Sherab Gyaltsen (Dol po pa Shes rab rgyal mtshan, 1292–1361). The monastery was originally Sakya, but also followed the Jonang and Bodong traditions, and Geluk colleges formed there later as well. Tangtong Gyalpo's teacher Ka Ngapa Paljor Sherab (Bka' lnga pa Dpal 'byor shes rab) was the ninth abbot at Ngamring.

347 The *Pramāṇavārttika* is the first of a set of seven treatises on epistemology by the Indian master Dharmakīrti. The Five Dharmas of Maitreya *(Byams chos sde lnga)* are important Mahāyāna treatises traditionally believed to have been spoken by the future buddha Maitreya to the Indian master Asaṅga. These five are the *Ratnagotravibhāga* (or *Uttaratantra*), the *Abhisamayālaṃkāra*, *Dharmadharmatāvibhāga*, *Mahāyāna-sūtrālaṃkāra*, and *Madhyāntavibhāga*.

348 The famous monastery of Sakya has been one of the most important centers of learning and practice in Tibet for almost a thousand years. It was founded by Khön Könchok Gyalpo ('Khon Dkon mchog rgyal po, 1034–1102) in 1073 and has been the main center for the Sakya tradition ever since. The four fundamental subjects *(bka' bzhi* in the text, but often spelled *dka' bzhi)* are the five academic subjects of epistemology *(tshad ma)*, the perfection of wisdom literature *(phar phyin)*, madhyamaka or middle way philosophy *(dbu ma)*, and either abhidharma or the monastic code *('dul ba)*. See Losang Trinlé, *Clarification of Knowledge*, 128, under the entry for *dka' bzhi*. According to Sherab Palden, Ocean of Marvels, 23, Tangtong also received many tantric teachings at Sakya, such as those of the Kālacakra and Vajradhātu traditions.

349 Śāntideva. *Engaging in the Conduct of a Bodhisattva (Bodhisattvacaryāvatāra. Byang chub sems dpa'i spyod pa la 'jug pa)*, 14b. Toh 3871, Tengyur, dbu ma, *la*, 1b–40a. P 5272, *la*.

350 The eight worldly concerns (*'jig rten chos brgyad*) are gain and loss, reputation and notoriety, slander and praise, and happiness and suffering.

351 Maitreya, *Mahāyānottaratantraśāstra. Theg pa chen po rgyud bla ma'i bstan bcos*, 61b. Toh 4024, Tengyur, sems tsam, *phi*, 54b–73a.

352 According to Könchok Palsang and Dewa Sangpo, *Bright Lamp*, 116, Tangtong had experienced a brilliant vision of Mañjuśrī and the lineage masters, who dissolved into his heart and caused a meditative concentration in which all

phenomena were like dream and illusion to arise in his mind. Thus he had nothing to say.

353 This verse is from Yoginī Cinṭa's *Realization of Reality*, perhaps from a different Tibetan translation than what is now available. See Yoginī Cinṭa, *Realization of Reality That Subsequently Clarifies Entities. Vyaktabhāvānugatatattvasiddhi. Dngos po gsal ba'i rjes su 'gro ba'i de kho na nyid grub pa*, Toh 2222, Tengyur, rgyud, *wi*, 63a7.

354 These lines are from the Indian adept Saraha's *Treasury of Dohā in a Song* (also known as *People's Dohā*), 73b–74a. *(Dohākoṣagīti. Do hā mdzod kyi glu)*, Toh 2224, Tengyur, rgyud, *wi*, 70b–77a. P 3068, *mi*. The text in the canon varies from the quotation here. Cf. Guenther (1993), 103, v. 62.

355 Quotation not located.

356 Most of this verse is a very close rendering of a famous verse from the Indian master Rāhulabhadra's *Eulogy to the Perfection of Wisdom (Prajñāpāramitāstotra. Sher phyin bstod pa)*, Toh 1127, Tengyur, bstod tshogs, *ka*, 76a–b. The text is attributed to Nāgārjuna in the canon. Rāhulabhadra is often identified with Saraha.

357 Dakpo Sönam Tashi (Bdag po Bsod nams bkra shis, 1352–1407) was born into the Lhakang Palace (Lha khang bla brang) branch of the Khön ('Khon) family of Sakya. He was a master of the *Pramāṇavārttika* of Dharmakīrti and had very widespread activities, including the construction of the Great Stūpa of Gyang (Rgyang 'bum mo che). See Jamgön Ameshap, *Fulfillment of All Needs and Wishes*, 357–58, for a brief sketch of the life of Sönam Tashi. The construction of the Great Stūpa of Gyang was the first such project that Tangtong Gyalpo participated in and perhaps served as an early inspiration for his own later work.

358 According to Natsok Rangdrol, *Heart of the Sun Illuminating the Vajrayāna*, 62, this line is from the *Hevajra Tantra*. However, I have not been able to locate it in the tantra itself.

359 One *zho* is a tenth of an *ounce (srang)*. Tangtong Gyalpo offered ten *zho*. A *load (khal)* is a unit of measure equivalent to about twenty-five to thirty pounds or twelve to fourteen kilos.

360 The great adept Darma Palwa (Sgrub chen Dar ma dpal ba) may be identical to the dedicated meditator Darma Pal (Sgom chen pa Dar ma dpal) whose vision at the death of the Sakya master Khenchen Gyalwa Chokyang (Mkhan chen Rgyal ba mchog dbyangs, 1360–1433) is described in Jamgön Ameshap, *Sun Illuminating All the Teachings of the Doctrine Protectors*, vol. 2: 82.

361 Mind Training *(blo sbyong)* is a general term used to refer to many different techniques for training the mind, most of which originate from the Kadampa tradition.

362 Mahākaruṇika Who Tames Living Beings *(Thugs rje chen po 'gro 'dul)* is a treasure teaching of the Nyingma master Nyang Nyima Öser (Nyang Nyi ma 'od zer, 1136–1204).

363 The *Compendium of Maṇis (Ma ṇi bka' 'bum)* is an important treasure teaching composed of texts discovered by the adept Ngödrup (Dngos grub), his contemporary Nyang Nyima Öser, and Shākya Sangpo. This collection focuses on the teachings and meditation practices of the bodhisattva Avalokiteśvara and the life and activities of the Tibetan emperor Songtsen Gampo, who is said to have composed the texts in the seventh century and then concealed them for later rediscovery. The *Compendium of Maṇis* is the basic source for the account of the geomantic subduing of the terrestrial forces in the land of Tibet. The story of Songtsen Gampo and his two queens from Nepal and China contains the narrative of the construction of the Jokhang in Lhasa and the various other temples for gaining control of the land on the basis of geomantic principles. Tangtong Gyalpo's establishment of many terrestrial focal-points *(sa'i me btsa')* is clearly based on the scheme presented in this collection. Also see Aris (1980), 8–33. For the various systems of practical instruction *(dmar khrid)* for meditation on Avalokiteśvara, see the *Jonang Collection of One Hundred and Eight Profound Guiding Instructions (Jo nang zab khrid brgya rtsa brgyad)* compiled by Kunga Drolchok (Kun dga' grol mchog, 1507–66) and included in Jamgön Kongtrul's *Treasury of Oral Instructions (Gdams ngag mdzod)*, vol. 12. The history of some of these traditions is recorded in Roerich (1976), 1006–42.

364 Mön (Mon) is a general term for the eastern Himalayan regions. See Aris (1980), xvi, who says the term came to mean little more than "southern or western mountain-dwelling non-Indian non-Tibetan barbarian." Kongpo is in southwest Tibet, and includes the holy mountain of Tsari. See Dorje (1999), 227–42, for a description of the region. According to Ardussi (1977), 49 n. 38, Lo Khatra (Klo Kha khra) is one of the three divisions of the region of Lo (Klo yul), the Tibetan name for a portion of the tribal areas on the Tibeto-Assamese border now included in Arunachal Pradesh. Aris (1980), 105–6, says Khatra *(kha khra)*, literally "striped mouths," may refer to the eastern Bhutanese Aka tribesmen.

365 Kyirong (Skyid grong) is a major point on the trade route from southwest Tibet into Nepal.

366 Ngari Dzongka (Mnga' ris Rdzong kha) is the royal palace and monastic complex at Gungtang (Gung thang), the capital of the Ngari region in far western Tibet.

367 See note 331 for the sevenfold posture of Vairocana.

368 An annotation in the Tibetan text glosses the term *ca ga che* ("very sharp") as "the name of a tool for cutting grass" (?): *rtswa shing nyo spyad kyi bca' lag gi ming.* Sherab Palden, *Ocean of Marvels*, 59, uses the spelling *ca kha tsha.*

369 This famous Jowo (Jo bo) image of Avalokiteśvara in the two-armed form known as Khasarpaṇa was one of the most holy images in Tibet. Also known as the Noble Wati ('Phags pa Wa ti), it is one of the four sandalwood images called the four Avalokiteśvara siblings. Tradition says the seventh-century Tibetan emperor Songtsen Gampo emanated to Nepal in the form of a monk and took four sandalwood images of Avalokiteśvara that had naturally arisen from within the trunk of a single sandalwood tree. He left one image in Nepal, brought one to the Nepalese-Tibetan border, one to Kyirong, and one to Lhasa. See Kunga Dorjé, *Red Annals*, 415. The

Kyirong image was removed from the temple at the time of the Chinese invasion of Tibet and taken to Dharamsala, India, where it is now kept in the private chapel of H. H. the Dalai Lama. See also Wylie (1970), 14–15. The definitive work on the subject is now Franz-Karl Ehrhard, *Die Statue und der Tempel des Arya Va-ti bzang-po: Ein Beitrag zu Geschichte und Geographie des tibetischen Buddhismus* (Wiesbaden: Ludwig Reichert Vlg., 2004).

370 The four enlightened actions are peaceful, enriching, powerful, and terrible.

371 Tangtong Gyalpo is believed to have been a dual emanation of the peaceful aspect of Avalokiteśvara, or Mahākaruṇika, and the terrible aspect known as Hayagrīva.

372 The three carry-over practices *('khyer so gsum)* are the means for carrying the state of meditative concentration over into daily activities. Tangtong Gyalpo's method for accomplishment of Avalokiteśvara, known as *Infinite Benefit for Living Beings ('Gro don mkha' khyab ma),* says, "My apparent body and those of others are the enlightened body of the Noble One. Sounds are the melody of the six syllables. Memory and thoughts are the expanse of great primordial awareness." The entire text (with later additions) is translated in Dewar (2004), 29–45.

373 According to Sherab Palden, *Ocean of Marvels*, 63, it was during this time that Tangtong Gyalpo went to the forest hermitage of Metok Dangchen (Me tog mdangs can) and met the Sakya master Rendawa Shönu Lodrö (Red mda' ba Gzhon nu blo gros, 1349–1412), from whom he received Dharma teachings for seven days. However, in the translated biography Tangtong does not meet Rendawa until much later.

374 The six kinds of living beings are gods, demigods, humans, animals, hungry spirits, and hell beings.

375 Mangyul (Mang yul) is the old name for the region of West Tibet, north of Nepal, stretching from the western area of Purang in Ngari east to Ngamring in the north and Kyirong to the south.

376 The seven riches of a Noble One *('phags pa'i nor bdun)* are faith, moral discipline, learning, generosity, shame, modesty, and wisdom.

377 The five poisons are desire, hatred, ignorance, pride, and envy.

378 The ten virtues are not to kill, not to steal, not to engage in sexual misconduct, not to lie, not to slander, not to speak harshly, not to engage in idle speech, not to covet, not to be malicious, and not to have wrong views. The first three are physical, the next four vocal, and the final three mental.

379 The five types of primordial awareness are mirrorlike primordial awareness, the primordial awareness of equality, discriminating primordial awareness, all-accomplishing primordial awareness, and the primordial awareness of the basic space of phenomena.

380 The three poisons are desire, hatred, and ignorance. The three bodies of enlightenment (*sku gsum*) are the dharmakāya reality body *(chos sku),* the sambhogakāya

enjoyment body *(longs spyod rdzogs pa'i sku)*, and the nirmāṇakāya emanated body *(sprul sku)*.

381 According to Sherab Palden, *Ocean of Marvels*, 68, Tangtong's companions also say he has gone crazy.

382 According to Sherab Palden, *Ocean of Marvels*, 70, Tangtong Gyalpo prefaced his final statement with the following comment: "This madman has gained control of his own mind, so he can change external appearances into anything."

383 Könchok Palsang and Dewa Sangpo, *Bright Lamp*, 111–12, describe how the harsh and abusive reactions of the local people, Tangtong's own family, and even the household servants caused him to finally give up on them and leave home for good, vowing to practice in a way that combined all of the Buddhist traditions into one.

384 This quote is from the *Kālacakra Tantra*. See Kalkī Puṇḍarīka, *Immaculate Light (Vimalaprabhā. Dri med 'od). Vimalaprabhānāma mūlatantrānusāriṇīdvādaśasāh asrikā lagukālacakratantrarājaṭīkā. Bsdus pa'i rgyud kyi rgyal po dus kyi 'khor lo'i 'grel bshad/ rtsa ba'i gyud kyi rjes su 'jug pa stong phrag bcu gnyis pa dri ma med pa'i 'od)*, 353b. Toh 845, dus 'khor 'grel bshad (in the Kangyur), *shrī*, 1b–469a. For some explanation of this topic, see Khedrup Norsang Gyatso (2004), 213–14.

385 See note 334.

386 Kukkuripa (Ku ku ri pa) was one of the eighty-four great adepts of ancient India. He is said to have introduced the *Mahāmāyā Tantra* from Uḍḍiyāna into India. If he is the same as Kukkurājā (Khyi'i rgyal po), he is also very important for the Nyingma lineages of the eighteen mahāyoga tantras, which he is said to have transmitted to King Dza. Tangtong Gyalpo is sometimes referred to as an emanation of Kukkuripa.

387 The three representations of enlightened body, speech, and mind, such as statues, texts, and stūpas, respectively.

388 The Fivefold Mahāmudrā *(phyag rgya chen po lnga ldan)* is a special Drigung Kagyü Mahāmudrā system structured around five topics: meditation on bodhicitta, meditation on the chosen deity, guruyoga meditation, Mahāmudrā meditation, and dedication. The Coemergent Union *(lhan cig skyes sbyor)* is a Mahāmudrā teaching of Gampopa Sönam Rinchen (Sgam po pa Bsod nams rin chen, 1079–1153). The *Ganges Mahāmudrā (Gang gā ma)* is a fundamental instruction on Mahāmudrā given by Tilopa to Nāropa that was bestowed on the banks of the Ganges (Gangā) River. The text is found in many collections, such as the *Phyag chen rgya gzhung*, 85–90 (Kangra: D. Tsondu Senghe, 1985). The Six Dharmas of Nāropa are mostly practiced in the various Kagyü lineages that spread from the students of Gampopa. The Six Dharmas of Niguma are mainly practiced in the Shangpa Kagyü. The practical instructions *(dmar khrid)* are special transmissions of Avalokiteśvara meditation. The history of some of these transmissions is recorded in Roerich (1976), 1006–42. The Six-branch Yoga *(sbyor drug)* is the completion stage of meditation in the Kālacakra tradition. See Wallace (2001) and Khedrup Norsang Gyatso (2003) for details. Sherab Palden, *Ocean of Marvels*, 24, 29–30, describes

two trips to meet Ka Ngapa. During the first of these Tangtong received initiations such as Guhyasamāja, Red Yamāri, Black Yamāri, and Vajrabhairava, as well as many other teachings such as madhyamaka philosophy, Mind Training, and Severance (Gcod yul). During the second meeting he took full ordination and received many more teachings, including most of those listed in the translated biography, as well as the Mind Training and Severance again.

389 The lines known as "Mothers Infinite As Space" *(ma nam mkha' ma'i skyabs 'gro)* are a special set of phrases for taking refuge: "All mother sentient beings as infinite as space take refuge in the Master, the precious Buddha. We take refuge in the Buddha, the Dharma, and the Sangha. We take refuge in the assembly of masters, chosen deities, and ḍākinīs. We take refuge in our own minds, empty yet lucid, the dharmakāya reality body "*(Ma nam mkha' dang mnyam pa'i sems can thams cad bla ma sangs rgyas rin po che la skyabs su mchi'o/ sangs rgyas chos dang dge 'dun rnams la skyabs su mchi'o/ bla ma yi dam mkha' 'gro'i tshogs la skyabs su mchi'o/ rang sems stong gsal chos kyi sku la skyabs su mchi'o)*. According to Dezhung Rinpoché, this refuge formula is also known as the "nine-point taking of refuge" *(skyabs 'gro dgu skor)*: (1–2) the Master and the Buddha, who may appear different but are actually indivisible; (3–5) the Three Jewels of Buddha, Dharma, and Sangha; (6–8) the Three Roots of masters, chosen deities, and ḍākinīs; and (9) the dharmakāya reality body inherent in every living being.

390 During this time Tangtong Gyalpo was engaging in the deliberate behavior *(brtul zhugs kyi spyod pa)* of a yogin and was very candid and open in his conduct and frankly spoke the truth with no shame and hypocrisy. Because of their own wrong points of view *(log lta)*, this caused everyone to hate him. He also had an extraordinary consort during this period, who was in essence Yigé Drugma (Yi ge drug ma), the consort of Avalokiteśvara. This woman, known as Khandroma Sengé (Mkha' 'gro ma Seng ge), prophesied that she would later give birth to a son named Nyima Sangpo (Nyi ma bzang po, b. 1436) who would uphold and spread Tangtong's tradition. See Könchok Palsang and Dewa Sangpo, *Bright Lamp*, 130–31.

391 Gökyi Demtruchen, whose personal name was Ngödrup Gyaltsen (Rgod kyi ldem 'phru can Dngos grub rgyal mtshan, 1337–1408) was one of the major discoverers of hidden treasures *(gter ma)* in the Nyingma tradition. His discoveries came to be known as the Northern Treasures (Byang gter). See Herweg (1994) and Dudjom (1991), 780–83.

392 The Heartdrop of the Ḍākinī (Mkha' 'gro snying thig) is the Great Perfection teachings given by Padmasambhava to Yeshé Tsogyal in the Great Gathering Cave of the Ḍākinīs at Tidro (Ti sgro) in Drigung. It was hidden there as a treasure teaching and later revealed by Pema Lendreltsal (1231–59). The lineage came down to Longchen Rabjampa (1308–63), who incorporated the teachings in his Nyingtik Yashi. Also see Aris (1988), 27–31, for detailed stories about this cycle of teachings.

393 The Cycle of the Great Perfection of Aro (Rdzogs chen a ro'i skor) is a tradition of the Mental Class *(sems sde)* section of the Great Perfection. It takes its name

from the eleventh-century master Aro Yeshé Jungné (A ro Ye shes 'byung gnas). Brief information on Aro is found in Roerich (1976), 999–1001.

394 The eight yakṣa horsemen *(gnod sbyin rta bdag brgyad)* are the entourage of the wealth deity and guardian Vaiśravaṇa. The eight are 'Dzam bha la, Gang ba bzang po, Nor bu bzang po, Yang dag shes, 'Brog gnas nag po, Lnga rtsen ser skya, Tsi pi, and Kun dha li. See Losang Trinlé, *Clarification of Knowledge*, 1229.

395 Riwo Drasang (Ri bo bkra bzang) is a mountain in the Jang district of northern Latö. The first monastery at Riwo Drasang was founded by the upholder of pure awareness Gökyi Demtruchen and maintained by teachers of his tradition. Gökyi Demtruchen discovered the treasure texts of the Northern Treasure tradition at Riwo Drasang, and Tangtong Gyalpo would spend three years there meditating on these teachings in retreat.

396 Ekajaṭī (E ka dza ti) is the main protectress of the Great Perfection teachings and is considered to be an emanation of Samantabhadrī (Kun tu bzang mo). A *treasure-owner (gter bdag)* is a deity who has been entrusted with a hidden treasure *(gter ma)*.

397 Ṛṣī Rāhula (Drang srong Rā hu la) is another major guardian deity of the Nyingma tradition.

398 The *Iron Tree (Lcags kyi sdong po)* is the text in the Heart Practice (Thugs sgrub) cycle of Gökyi Demtruchen's treasures for achieving longevity through meditation on Amitābha, Amitāyus, and Hayagrīva. See Gökyi Demtruchen, *Longevity Practice of the Iron Tree.*

399 In the Nyingma tradition, the *canonical lineage (bka' ma)* is the teachings and texts transmitted from India to Tibet and translated into the Tibetan language, while the *treasures (gter ma)* are the esoteric instructions and so forth concealed in Tibet by Guru Padmasambhava and rediscovered later and spread by treasure revealers.

400 *Magical Net (Sgyu 'phrul).* The text in this case is probably *Śrīguhyagarbhatattvaviniścaya. Dpal gsang ba'i snying po de kho na nyid rnam par nges pa*, Toh 832, Kangyur, rnying rgyud, *ka*, 110b–132a. This tantra is known by various names. See Dorje and Kapstein (1991), 275. Gödrochen is an abbreviated form of Gökyi Demtruchen's name.

401 For the four defeating acts *(pham pa bzhi)*, see note 250.

402 The twenty-ninth-day offering of sacrificial cakes *(dgu gtor)* is a ritual often performed on the twenty-ninth day of the last month of the year to destroy negativity built up during the previous year.

403 The Newar Buddhist master Paṇḍita Mahābodhi was the son of Paṇḍita Jagadānandajīvabhadra. See Roerich (1976), 1045. According to an annotation in Kunga Drolchok, *Record of Precious Beautiful Ornaments*, 540, who refers to him as *nai pā la'i paṇḍi ta* Mahābodhi, this master's personal name was actually Manobodhi (Yid kyi byang chub). Mahābodhi was succeeded by his nephew, Paṇḍita Jīvabodhi (Mdze ba 'bu ti), to whom Tangtong Gyalpo later sent a letter and some nectar pills

for longevity. In the letter Tangtong says the essence of Paṇḍita Mahābodhi, Tangtong Gyalpo, and Cakrasaṃvara had blended together indivisibly. Tangtong also mentions his 512 masters, and says he has gained control of his lifespan *(tshe la rang dbang 'dus pa byung)* due to their kindness. See Könchok Palsang and Dewa Sangpo, *Bright Lamp*, 399–400. Paṇḍita Mahābodhi was a master of the Cakrasaṃvara tradition, and in particular the source of the transmission of a rare completion-stage practice of the donkey-faced *(bong zhal)* form of Cakrasaṃvara that has been passed down in the Sakya tradition to the present day.

404 The great stūpas of Svayambhūnāth (Shing kun) and Bodhnāth (Bya rung kha shor) are two of the most important Buddhist holy sites in the Kathmandu Valley of Nepal.

405 The Asura Cave (A su ra'i brag phug) is a famous cave in present-day Pharping in the Kathmandu Valley. It is said that Guru Padmasambhava meditated in this cave on his way to Tibet, destroyed all spiritual obstacles through the meditations of Vajrakīla and Yangdak Heruka, and displayed the sublime attainment of Mahāmudrā.

406 The term *'dra min* is obscure. Könchok Palsang and Dewa Sangpo, *Bright Lamp*, 137, have *'bra men*. Perhaps the meaning is similar to the term *'bra go*, which is used for a mango or a persimmon.

407 The oldest biographies of Tangtong Gyalpo describe his visit to the Charnel Ground of Ramadoli at this point. See Sherab Palden, *Ocean of Marvels*, 37–40, and Könchok Palsang and Dewa Sangpo, *Bright Lamp*, 137–38. The translated biography places the visit much later in his life.

408 The city of Bhaktapur (Kho khom) lies about seven miles east of Kathmandu and Patan in the Kathmandu Valley of Nepal. It was the capital of the Tripura dynasty that ruled Nepal from the middle of the twelfth century until the end of the fifteenth century. The king of Bhaktapur at the time of Tangtong Gyalpo's visit was probably Sthitimalla (reign: 1382–95) or Dharmamalla (reign: 1396–1408). See Slusser (1982), 101, 126, 399.

409 Magadha (Ma ga dha) was an ancient central Indian state that roughly corresponds to the modern district of Bihar.

410 *ku mu da*. A type of lily said to blossom in the moonlight.

411 Mitrayogin (Mi tra dzo ki) was an Indian adept who was a disciple of Lalitavajra, a direct disciple of Tilopa. Mitrayogin gained realization after meditating on Avalokiteśvara for twelve years. He was invited to Tibet by Tropu Lotsāwa Jampa Pal (Khro phu Lo tsā wa Byams pa dpal, 1172–1236), and taught for about eighteen months. Different lineages of initiations and teachings from Mitrayogin survive, most notably a collection of one hundred methods for accomplishment. See Roerich (1976), 1030–42.

412 According to Könchok Palsang and Dewa Sangpo, *Bright Lamp*, 140, during this first month Tangtong also had a vision of Guru Saroruhavajra (Guru Mtsho skye rdo rje) and the eight great adepts who are upholders of pure awareness (Rig 'dzin grub thob brgyad). Guru Saroruhavajra is the name of an emanation of Guru

Padmasambhava, but could also indicate Guru Padmavajra, who is included in one list of the eight great adepts. For the two lists of eight great Indian adepts, see note 564.

413 According to Könchok Palsang and Dewa Sangpo, *Bright Lamp*, 141, Tangtong also had visions of Vajradhara, Vajravārāhī, Guhyasamāja, Cakrasaṃvara, and Kālacakra during this second month of retreat.

414 Könchok Palsang and Dewa Sangpo, *Bright Lamp*, 141, mention that Tangtong also had a vision of the buddhas of the five spiritual families and their consorts during this third month.

415 According to Könchok Palsang and Dewa Sangpo, *Bright Lamp*, 141–42, Tangtong also had a vision of Śākyamuni Buddha and various buddhas, bodhisattvas, and sthaviras during this fifth month.

416 *hor sog po.* This Tibetan term is used several times in the biography, as is the term *hor.* Both have been understood in the translation as terms used to designate the various Mongol peoples. The word *hor* was used at different times during Tibetan history to refer to the Mongols *(sog po)*, the nomads to the north of Tibet, and the *gru gu* (Turkmen or Uigur?) people of a kingdom to the north of Tibet and in the Xinjiang and Lake Kokonor regions. See Losang Trinlé, *Clarification of Knowledge*, 2137.

417 In Könchok Palsang and Dewa Sangpo, *Bright Lamp*, 142–43, Dharmaratna's detailed interpretation of the visions during Tangtong Gyalpo's retreat is in prose, not verse. It would seem to have been rendered into verse by Lochen Gyurmé Dechen for the present biography, or perhaps taken from another unknown source.

418 The name Ratnakāra (Ratna kā ra) refers to Tangtong Gyalpo's teacher Dharmaratna, whose full name name was perhaps Dharmaratnakāra.

419 The Stūpa of Descent from the Gods *(lha babs mchod rten)* was built to mark the spot where Śākyamuni Buddha is said to have descended to earth in Śrāvastī (modern Sahet Hahet, Uttar Pradesh) after having traveled to a heavenly realm to teach his mother who had been reborn there. This particular style of stūpa is also one of the eight main types of stūpas. Ushuri (U shu ri) has not been identified.

420 The visual manifestation of fire was a result of focusing on the vital wind of fire *(me rlung)*. Many types of vital winds exist in the body, some of the basic categories of which are earth, water, fire, wind, and space.

421 The term "unique transmission" *(chig brgyud)* can mean transmitted to only one person at a time or to only one person and no one else. According to Könchok Palsang and Dewa Sangpo, *Bright Lamp*, 144, Tangtong Gyalpo studied with Siddhiratna and his consort at the Vajrāsana for three years.

422 According to an annotation in Tāranātha, *Entryway for Experts*, 139, Mount Kukkuṭakapāda (Ri rkang can) is the mountain where the master Asaṅga practiced meditation on Maitreya for twelve years. The three yogas *(yo ga rnam gsum)* are the anuyoga, mahāyoga, and atiyoga teachings of the Nyingma tradition. It is

extraordinary to find mention of these teachings being given in fifteenth-century India, at least two centuries after the final obliteration of organized Buddhism by the Muslim invasions. The renunciant Kunga Nyingpo (Ku sa li Kun dga' snying po) is otherwise unknown. He and Kalden Dorjé Drakpa (Skal ldan Rdo rje grags pa) were the only Nyingma teachers that Tangtong Gyalpo met in India. Since the names of these two are in Tibetan, whereas the names of all the other masters Tangtong met in Nepal and India are given in Sanskrit, they were perhaps two Tibetan masters living in India. According to Könchok Palsang and Dewa Sangpo, *Bright Lamp*, 144, Tangtong practiced the three yogas there for one year.

423 The huge monastic complex of Nālandā was probably the most famous Buddhist institution in India after the Gupta period. The first monastery was founded at Nālandā in the early fifth century, and it was destroyed by Moslem invaders at the end of the twelfth century. By the time Tangtong Gyalpo visited the area, the monastic buildings at Nālandā would have been in ruins. According to Könchok Palsang and Dewa Sangpo, *Bright Lamp*, 145, Tangtong stayed at Nālandā for one year.

424 The phrase *zhabs kyi mdo bzhi* should be corrected to *phyag zhabs kyi mdo bzhi*, as found in Könchok Palsang and Dewa Sangpo, *Bright Lamp*, 145.

425 See note 287 for the nine dance moods *(gar dgu'i nyams)*.

426 Tāmradvīpa, or Copper Island (Zangs gling), is one of the ancient names for the island of Ceylon, although it was also used for other locations. For the earliest descriptions of Tangtong Gyalpo's trip, see Sherab Palden, *Ocean of Marvels*, 109–19, and Könchok Palsang and Dewa Sangpo, *Bright Lamp*, 145–49. Also see von Schroeder (1990) for what little is known about the Vajrayāna tradition in Ceylon.

427 No mention of magical travel is found in the original biographies of Sherab Palden, *Ocean of Marvels*, 110, and Könchok Palsang and Dewa Sangpo, *Bright Lamp*, 145.

428 The Indian adept Śavaripa was one of the most important medieval masters of tantra. He is especially associated with the Mahāmudrā teachings, the Dohā tradition of the great adept Saraha, and the practice of the Six-branch Yoga of Kālacakra. For the story of his life according to the Six-branch Yoga tradition, see Stearns (1996), 139–41, and in connection with his student Maitrīpa, see Tatz (1987).

429 See Könchok Palsang and Dewa Sangpo, *Bright Lamp*, 147, for details about Śavaripa's displays and their meaning.

430 Qualities such as the liberation of sentient beings who are touched by the shadow of the stūpa, or by the wind that has also touched the stūpa, or even by water that has been touched by the shadow of the stūpa, were also attributed to the great stūpa of Jonang by its creator, Dolpopa Sherab Gyaltsen, of whom Tangtong Gyalpo was the rebirth. See Dolpopa Sherab Gyaltsen, *Dredging the Pit of Saṃsāra*, 459, and *Prayer Made at the Completion of the Great Stūpa*, 465.

431 See note 386 for information on the Indian master Kukkuripa.

432 Sukhāvatī (Bde ba can), the realm of bliss, in the western direction, is the heavenly paradise of Amitābha (Snang ba mtha' yas), the buddha of infinite light.

433 Sherab Palden, *Ocean of Marvels*, 119, just says Tangtong Gyalpo returned in the trader's boat, but Könchok Palsang and Dewa Sangpo, *Bright Lamp*, 149, say he traveled magically without sinking into the water.

434 Kalden Dorjé Drakpa (Skal ldan Rdo rje grags pa) is otherwise unknown. Since Dorjé Drakpa and Kunga Nyingpo were the only two teachers from whom Tangtong Gyalpo received Nyingma transmissions in India, and the only masters in India and Nepal whose names are not given in Sanskrit instead of Tibetan, they were perhaps Tibetan masters of the Nyingma tradition who were living in India. As with the previous mention of Tangtong studying the anuyoga, mahāyoga, and atiyoga teachings with the renunciant Kunga Nyingpo (see note 422), it is extraordinary to find the Nyingma tradition of secret mantra being taught in fifteenth-century India.

435 The "general initiation as a regent" *(rgyal tshab spyi lugs kyi dbang)* is an essential form of bestowing the four initiations condensed into one by means of giving the blessing with the vase and transferring the totality of the blessing as if emptying completely one vase into another. I am grateful to Matthieu Ricard for this information.

436 The three wheels *('khor lo rnam gsum)* are the three turnings of the Dharma wheel. According to Dolpopa Sherab Gyaltsen (Dol po pa Shes rab rgyal mtshan, 1292–1361), whom Tangtong Gyalpo claimed to have been in his previous lifetime, the first two turnings of the Dharma wheel, concerned respectively with the Four Noble Truths and the presentation of emptiness as a lack of all defining characteristics, do not emphasize the definitive teachings on ultimate truth. The second turning primarily presented relative phenomena as empty of self-nature and not transcending the chain of dependent origination. The third turning of the Dharma wheel presented the teachings on the Buddha-nature, which are the final definitive statements on the nature of ultimate reality, the primordial ground or substratum beyond the chain of dependent origination, which is only empty of other relative phenomena. For further information on these points, see Stearns (1999).

437 Sherab Palden, *Ocean of Marvels*, 89–100, provides fascinating information about Tangtong Gyalpo's study and practice of the Six Dharmas of Niguma with the master Jangsem Jinpa Sangpo (Byang sems Sbyin pa bzang po) at the monastery of Dorjéden. Tangtong was with a small group of more important and wealthy people who ridiculed and continued to call him Crazy Tsöndru. After having to sit outside during a Cakrasaṃvara initiation, while the others sat inside, Tangtong vowed to always teach Dharma in the future to everyone regardless of their social position. Then he went and slept in the monastery's spring for the night. When the others found him sitting in the water the next day they cried, "Crazy Tsöndru has spoiled our spring!" After trying unsuccessfully to pull him out by the hair and by his hands and feet, they heaped stones, boulders, and pieces of wood on top

of him, but he did not even speak. While they were complaining to the master about his deranged behavior, Tangtong crossed over to the other side of the river without a boat or anyone to help him, and was seen wandering off reciting the refuge verses of "Mothers Infinite As Space." After this event Tangtong practiced the teachings of Niguma in isolated retreat spots and had the vision of her that is described in the translated biography, although in Sherab Palden, *Ocean of Marvels*, 95–100, the vision is described in much more detail. Curiously, Könchok Palsang and Dewa Sangpo, *Bright Lamp*, 121, say Tangtong received only madhyamaka from Jangsem Jinpa Sangpo, and received all the Niguma teachings and those of the Six-armed Protector from the adept Sangpo Palwa (Bzang po dpal ba).

438 Except for the practices of the White and Red Khecarīs, Tangtong Gyalpo later wrote special texts for all these teachings, which are listed individually in the bibliography.

439 For the "Seven Jewels," see note 73. For more information on this lineage and the Shangpa tradition in general, see Zangpo (2003), Kapstein (1980), and Smith (2001), 53–57. Jagchungpa Tsangma Shangtön ('Jag chung pa Gtsang ma Shangs ston, 1234–1309) was the main disciple of Sangyé Tönpa (Sangs rgyas ston pa), the last of the Seven Jewels, or first seven figures in the Shangpa lineage.

440 Niguma's *Vajra Lines (Rdo rje'i tshig rkang)* are succinct verse summaries of the crucial teachings of the Shangpa transmission. For a translation of one of these texts, the *Vajra Lines* for the Amulet Mahāmudrā, see Zangpo (2003), 45–46. Khecarī (Mkha' spyod ma) is a form of Vajrayoginī.

441 This vision of Niguma is described with incredible detail in Sherab Palden, *Ocean of Marvels*, 95–100.

442 The *Collection of the Essentials (Snying po kun 'dus)* and the other texts that Tangtong Gyalpo wrote are listed in the bibliography. The events surrounding the composition of these texts are described later in the translated biography.

443 The Sanskrit term *nāda* means *sound (sgra)* and is used here to indicate that Tangtong Gyalpo taught the Khecarī practices orally and did not write down the instructions. In the oldest biographies several of his other teachers and what he received from each of them are listed. Many of these masters are not mentioned in the translated biography. According to Sherab Palden, *Ocean of Marvels*, 100–102, Tangtong received teachings such as the Path with the Result (Lam 'bras) from the Sakya Dharma lord Kunga Gyaltsen (Chos rje Kun dga' rgyal mtshan). He received the *Litany of the Names of Mañjuśrī*, the huge commentary on the *Kālacakra Tantra*, and so forth, from the Jonang Dharma lord Chöpal Gönpo (Chos dpal mgon po), who was a disciple of Nya Ön Kunga Pal (Nya dbon Kun dga' dpal, 1285?–1379?), and the complete Kālacakra initiation and Six-branch Yoga of the Jonang tradition from the Dharma lord Sherab Sangpo (=Sle kha ba Shes rab bzang po). Chöpal Gönpo was the twelfth abbot of Jonang Monastery and Sherab Sangpo was the thirteenth abbot. From the meditation master Sangpo Pal (Sgrub pa po Bzang po dpal) he received thirteen different initiations of the Six-armed Protector, and then received the Cakrasaṃvara ('Khor lo sdom chen)

initiation and teachings from the great adept Gyalwang (Sgrub chen Rgyal dbang). From the great adept Sangpo Kyong (Grub chen Bzang po skyong) Tangtong received many Kadampa teachings, such as the six fundamental treatises of the Kadampa tradition (Bka' gdams gzhung drug), the *Kadam Volumes* (*Bka' gdams glegs bam*, concerning which see note 821), the Mind Training instructions (Blo sbyong), and the reading transmission for the collected works of Gyalsé Tokmé (Rgyal sras Thogs med, 1295–1369). Then he received the Uḍḍiyāna Practices of Approach and Accomplishment (U rgyan snyen sgrub) from the Omniscient Nütrawa (Kun mkhyen Snud kra ba), and Mahamudra teachings from Kashipa Namkha Öser (Bka' bzhi pa Nam mkha' 'od zer). Könchok Palsang and Dewa Sangpo, *Bright Lamp*, 121–24, list many of the same masters and teachings, with some variations in what Tangtong received. This source also mentions that he received the Six-branch Yoga of Kālacakra from the master Könchok Dorjé (Bla ma Dkon mchog rdo rje), and practiced the dark retreat with special results. He also received Tārā teachings at the famous mountain of Gyalgyi Tsiri in Latö (Las stod Rgyal gyi Rtsi ri) from the great adept Kunga Gyaltsen (Sgrubs chen Kun dga' rgyal mtshan) and practiced retreat there, which resulted in a vision of Tārā and prophecies. And from the Dharma lord Samdrup Gyaltsen (Bsam 'grub rgyal mtshan) Tangtong received various teachings of the vinaya monastic code, the abhidharma, and so forth. Further teachings are also noted.

444 See note 331 for the sevenfold posture of Vairocana.

445 The five long mantras, or *dhāraṇīs (gzungs chen lnga)*, are listed in Losang Trinlé, *Clarification of Knowledge*, 1826.

446 See note 176 for the eight sugatas or buddhas. *Condensed Verses on the Perfection of Wisdom (Prajñāpāramitāsañcayagātha. 'Phags pa shes rab kyi pha rol tu phyin pa sdud pa tshigs su bcad pa)*, Toh 13, Kangyur, sher phyin, *ka*, 1b–19b. The stūpa is the representation of enlightened mind.

447 According to Sherab Palden, *Ocean of Marvels*, 32, and Könchok Palsang and Dewa Sangpo, *Bright Lamp*, 528, Tangtong brought lawsuits against his two elder brothers, twenty-five paternal relatives, and sixty-four maternal relatives.

448 The clay grotto *(rdza khrod)* was perhaps a natural overhanging rock around which Tangtong Gyalpo built clay walls. According to Könchok Palsang and Dewa Sangpo, *Bright Lamp*, 151, 155, Tangtong built a shelter for meditation in which he could just barely fit, and directed a small trickle of water from a little stream to flow through the grotto beside him. He meditated for six and a half years with just six measures *(bre)* of barley for provisions, and had one measure left over at the end of the retreat. A *measure (bre)* is equivalent to about 1.35 pounds or 650 grams.

449 The genyen *(dge bsnyen)* are an ancient class of spirits, usually mountain deities, who were subdued by Guru Padmasambhava. See Nebesky-Wojkowitz (1956), 304–5.

450 Sherab Palden, *Ocean of Marvels*, 72–76, places the vision of the lord of yogins, Virūpa, during this retreat, saying Tangtong Gyalpo flew out from his retreat to go to the charnel ground where they met. In the translated biography by

Gyurmé Dechen, the meeting with Virūpa occurs later, during another retreat. By separating the events into two distinct retreats, Gyurmé Dechen is following the sequence of events in Könchok Palsang and Dewa Sangpo, *Bright Lamp*, 151–60.

451 Könchok Palsang and Dewa Sangpo, *Bright Lamp*, 151–54, quote Tangtong Gyalpo's comments about the effects of his austere meditation during this retreat and also describe important visions and prophecies from Avalokiteśvara, Hayagrīva, and Śākyamuni Buddha.

452 Könchok Palsang and Dewa Sangpo, *Bright Lamp*, 154, say the retreat ended after six years and six months.

453 The spelling *yi drag* is a mistake for *mi drag*.

454 Sherab Palden, *Ocean of Marvels*, 78–79, notes that Tangtong Gyalpo said that after this experience he vowed to never give blessings with his hands or feet to anyone again.

455 The winter month of miracles is the first month of the Tibetan calendar, usually beginning sometime in February or March of the Western calendar.

456 See note 296 for the seven branches *(yan lag bdun pa)*.

457 The two assemblies of merit and primordial awareness, which are necessary to attain enlightenment.

458 The Jowo Śākyamuni (Jo bo Shāk ya mu ni) is the most holy image in Tibet. It is an ancient image of the Buddha at the age of twelve that was brought to Tibet in the seventh century by the Chinese princess Kongjo when she came to be the bride of the Tibetan king Songtsen Gampo. It is kept in the Lhasa Jokhang, also known as the Tsuklakhang (Gtsug lag khang) or Trulnang ('Phrul snang). Also see Sørensen (1994).

459 For lists and descriptions of the twelve tenma goddesses *(brtan ma bcu gnyis)* who were bound to an oath of protection by Guru Padmasambhava, see Nebesky-Wojkowitz (1956), 181–98. See note 160 for the eight tribes of gods and demons *(lha srin sde brgyad)*.

460 In this context, Lho indicates the approximate area of present-day Bhutan. The word *lho* (Lho) means "south" in Tibetan. It has a wide range of use in the biography. It may be used to designate the district of Lho, to the south of the Tsangpo River in West Tibet, which was the frequent foe and sometimes ally of the district of Jang (Byang, meaning "north") to the north of the river. On the other hand, the term Lho is often used to indicate the country of Bhutan, which is south of Tibet, another name for which is Lhomön (Lho mon).

461 The master Choksang Lekpai Lodrö (Mchog bzang legs pa'i blo gros) was a disciple of the famous Sakya teacher Rendawa Shönu Lodrö (Red mda' ba Gzhon nu blo gros, 1349–1412), in whose biography he is described as being extremely learned but living the lifestyle of a renunciant *(ku su lu)*. See Sangyé Tsemo, *Amazing and Marvelous Biography of the Glorious Great Rendawa*, 302. Choksang Lekpai Lodrö seems to have also been called Chokden Lekpai Lodrö (Mchog ldan legs

pa'i blo gros). Tangtong Gyalpo refers to him by this name in Author Unknown, *Biography of the Venerable Lady Chökyi Drönma*, 116b, saying that he received the Fivefold Mahāmudrā (Phyag chen lnga ldan) instructions from Chokden Lekpai Lodrö, who had received it from Kashipa Namkha Öser (Bka' bzhi pa Nam mkha' 'od zer). The Fivefold Mahāmudrā is one of the instructions Tangtong receives from Choksang Lekpai Lodrö in the translated biography. According to Sherab Palden, *Ocean of Marvels*, 102, Tangtong himself also received Mahāmudrā teachings from Gyampa Kashipa Namkha Öser (Gyam pa Bka' bzhi pa Nam mkha' 'od zer). Könchok Palsang and Dewa Sangpo, *Bright Lamp*, 121–24, list many of the same masters and teachings.

462 See note 388 for an identification of the Mahāmudrā teachings of the *Ganges Mahāmudrā (Gang gā ma)*, the Amulet, the Coemergent Union, and the Fivefold, which are all from different Kagyü traditions. The *Unwritten Mahāmudrā (Phyag rgya chen po yi ge med pa)* of the Indian master Vāgīśvarakīrti is from the Sakya tradition, and is one of the so-called Eight Cycles of the Path (Lam skor brgyad) that are connected with the teachings of the Path with the Result (Lam 'bras). See Stearns (2001), 210–11, and Davidson (2005), 198–99. Sherab Palden, *Ocean of Marvels*, 86, lists more of the teachings Tangtong received at this time, such as the symbolic cycle of Mahāmudrā *(Phyag rgya chen po'i brda'i skor*, which is connected with Padampa Sangyé), the cycle of Dohā songs *(Mdo ha skor*, probably meaning those of Saraha), the cycle of equal taste *(Ro snyoms skor)*, the cycle of Nāropa *(Na ro skor*, i.e., the Six Dharmas), and the cycle of immortality *('Chi med skor)*. According to Könchok Palsang and Dewa Sangpo, *Bright Lamp*, 121, Tangtong also received complete ordination from the Dharma lord Choksang Lekpai Lodrö (Chos rje Mchog bzang legs pa'i blo gros), wore the saffron robes, and was known as the fully ordained venerable monk Tsöndru Sangpo (Dge slong Brtson 'grus bzang po). But in the translated biography, Lochen Gyurmé Dechen follows Sherab Palden, *Ocean of Marvels*, 29–30, who says Tangtong received ordination and the name Tsöndru Sangpo (Brtson 'grus bzang po) from Ka Ngapa Paljor Sherab (Bka' lnga pa Dpal 'byor shes rab), as described earlier. Sherab Palden, *Ocean of Marvels*, 86–87, also says that after leaving Choksang Lekpai Lodrö, Tangtong received various teachings at Jangding (Byang sdings) from Jangsem Nyima Sengé (Byang sems Nyi ma seng ge); different yogatantras and so forth from the Dharma lord Samdrup Gyaltsen (Chos rje Bsam grub rgyal mtshan); and many teachings such as the textual transmission of the Translated Scriptures *(Bka' 'gyur)* and the Collected Works of the Great Sakya Masters *(Sa skya bka' 'bum)* from Tekchen Chökyi Gyalpo (Theg chen Chos kyi rgyal po Kun dga' bkra shis, 1349–1425). This teacher was from the Lhakang Palace (Lha khang bla brang) branch of the Khön family of Sakya.

463 The Sakya master Rendawa Shönu Lodrö (Red mda' ba Gzhon nu blo gros, 1349–1412) is most famous for establishing the teachings of the prāsaṅgika madhyamaka in Tibet. He was also a master of the *Guhyasamāja Tantra* and one of the most important teachers of Jé Tsongkhapa Losang Drakpa (Rje Tsong kha pa Blo bzang grags pa, 1357–1419). The meeting of Tangtong Gyalpo and Rendawa is also mentioned in a late and short biography of Rendawa. See Yeshé Gyaltsen,

Biographies of the Lineal Masters of the Stages of the Path, 897–98. I have not located any mention of the meeting in Rendawa's earlier and longer biographies.

464 In the Sakya tradition, the transmission of the special instructions of Red Yamāri (Gshin rje gshed dmar) is traced back to the Indian master Virūpa. Various transmission lines exist for Vajrabhairava (Rdo rje 'jigs byed) and Black Yamāri (Gshin rje gshed nag), but the most famous are those connected with the Tibetan master Ra Lotsāwa Dorjé Drak (Rwa Lo tsā ba Rdo rje grags, eleventh century). The episode in the translated biography is based on Könchok Palsang and Dewa Sangpo, *Bright Lamp*, 124–26. Sherab Palden, *Ocean of Marvels*, 88, only specifically mentions that Tangtong received from Rendawa the initiation and textual transmission of Guhyasamāja, instructions on the view *(lta khrid)*, and a Mind Training instruction *(blo sbyong sems dpa'i rim pa)* called *Taking Happiness and Suffering as the Path (Skyid sdug lam khyer)*. On this last teaching, see note 798.

465 The master Lekhawa Sherab Sangpo (Sle kha ba Shes rab bzang po) was the thirteenth abbot of Jonang Monastery. The *Kālacakra Tantra*, and in particular its profound completion-stage practices of the Six-branch Yoga *(sbyor drug)*, are specialties of the Jonang tradition.

466 The term *secret behavior (gsang spyod)* here and in the next paragraph is a synonym for *deliberate behavior (brtul zhugs spyod pa)*. See the fourth part of the Introduction for clarification of these terms.

467 Sherab Palden, *Ocean of Marvels*, 172–75, describes the following events in an understated way, without direct reference to ḍākinīs or supernatural events. Nevertheless, he signals that the action is taking place in an interior landscape by prefacing the episode with the statement that Tangtong's breath stopped *(rlung 'gags byung pa)* in the center of the plain, and so he stayed there. Then he was approached by five girls of Gyedé, the foremost of whom had a harelip. Although the girls are not called ḍākinīs, the reader would assume in this context that they are. The girls sang the same song as in the translated biography, each singing a verse and giving Tangtong a name. They held a ritual feast together, and after repeated requests from the girls and other people who came, Tangtong taught the Mind Training (Blo sbyong) and many other instructions. Then he became known by the name Tangtong Gyalpo, King of the Empty Plain. This same episode is described in a very different way in Könchok Palsang and Dewa Sangpo, *Bright Lamp*, 117–21. According to this source, the plain is vast and triangular in shape, in the middle of which Tangtong builds a triangular throne where he sits in meditation. A dark, dense fog fills the plain, thunder roars, lightning flashes, and hail crashes down. When he is not disturbed by these events, the five ḍākinīs and their retinues appear in space and give him five names and explain their meanings, but not in verse. Finally they each dissolve into a different part of his body. A man in a nearby town sends his two sons to see what all the flashing lights and so forth are on the plain. The elder son reports back that it is just the monk from Jang called Crazy Tsöndru, sitting on a triangular throne, but the younger son sees the spectacular deity Hayagrīva in the middle of a bonfire.

468 The five ḍākinīs of primordial awareness are associated with the five spiritual families.

469 The three worlds *(sa gsum)* are the realms above, upon, and below the earth.

470 The temple at Drampa Gyang (Gram pa Rgyang) is near Lhatsé (Lha rtse), where Tangtong helped the Sakya master Sönam Tashi during the construction of the Gyang Stūpa many years before. This temple was also the site for treasure discoveries by other masters, and one of Padmasambhava's meditation caves is nearby. See Ferrari (1958), 66.

471 Jonang (Jo nang) is a famous monastery in Tsang founded by Shang Tukjé Tsöndru (Zhang Thugs rje brtson 'grus, 1243–1313). The monastery originally followed the Sakya tradition, but during the time of the Omniscient Dolpopa (Kun mkhyen Dol po pa, 1292–1361) it became the seat of an independent tradition. Jonang was a major center of learning and practice for many centuries, with a special emphasis on the teachings of the *Kālacakra Tantra* and the practice of the Six-branch Yoga of Kālacakra. The view known as "emptiness of other" *(gzhan stong)* was first spread by Dolpopa and set the Jonangpa apart from the Sakya School. For more about the Jonang tradition, see Stearns (1999).

472 According to Könchok Palsang and Dewa Sangpo, *Bright Lamp*, 175, when Tangtong visited the Jonang stūpa built by Dolpopa, he spoke the verses quoted earlier in the translated biography, declaring that he had been known as the Omniscient Dolpopa in his previous lifetime.

473 A note in Tibetan text glosses the term *gu pa* to mean *lkugs pa'i ming* ("a term for a stupid person").

474 The words "[in retreat]" are added from Könchok Palsang and Dewa Sangpo, *Bright Lamp*, 176.

475 Jagö Shong (Bya rgod gshongs) was a Sakya monastery in the Bodong region of Tsang. Some sources say it was built for the conversion of barbarians during the reign of King Songtsen Gampo. See Ferrari (1958), 67. The image of Vaiśravaṇa with a Red Lance (Rnam sras mdung dmar can) was a special object of worship at Jagö Shong Monastery.

476 The five precious substances are usually listed as gold, silver, turquoise, coral, and pearl.

477 The master called the adept Japurwa (Grub thob Bya 'phur ba) or Tsenden Namkhai Naljor (Mtsan ldan Nam mkha'i rnal 'byor) is also known as Müchen (Mus chen) Namkhai Naljor. His actual name was Namkha Gyaltsen (Nam mkha' rgyal mtshan). He received the Niguma teachings of the Shangpa tradition from Müchen Gyaltsen Palsang (Mus chen Rgyal mtshan dpal bzang, d. 1347), and then spent most of his life in meditation retreat. Namkhai Naljor was one of the teachers of Tangtong Gyalpo's master Ka Ngapa Paljor Sherab, and so he is referred to in Tangtong's biography as "his master's master."

478 The great pilgrimages *(skor chen)* from Sakya to Lhasa during the fifteenth century were organized historical events that can be verified from other sources. For example, Dharma lord Sangyé Gyaltsen (Chos rje Sangs rgyas rgyal mtshan), who was the paternal uncle of the Sakya and Jonang master Gorumpa Kunga Lekpa (Sgo rum pa Kun dga' legs pa, 1477–1544), was the leader *(skor dpon)* of a number

of these pilgrimages. He led his first pilgrimage at thirteen years of age, and on the way to Lhasa actually met Tangtong Gyalpo at Chuwori. Tangtong gave him a small cup full of beer, and although Sangyé Gyaltsen had never even smelled beer before, he drank it without hesitation. Tangtong said, "A fine auspicious connection. Keep drinking!" When Sangyé Gyaltsen had drunk thirteen cups of beer, Tangtong prophesied, "You will be pilgrimage leader thirteen times." And sure enough, Sangyé Gyaltsen led the pilgrimage from Sakya to Lhasa thirteen times. Gorumpa himself later led the pilgrimage in 1498, and crossed the Tsangpo River at Chuwori in the great ferry *(gru bo che)*. See Jamyang Khyentsé Wangchuk, *Rippling Ocean of Wish-fulfilling Marvels*, 257–58, 325–31.

479 Aṅgaja (Yan lag 'byung) is one of the Sixteen Arhats. He is said to reside on Mount Kailash.

480 *Perfection of Wisdom in Eight Thousand Lines (Āryāṣṭasāhasrikāprajñāpāramitā. 'Phags pa shes rab kyi pha rol tu phyin pa brgyad stong pa)*, Toh 12, Kangyur, shes phyin, *ka*, 1b–286a. For a translation of this text, see Conze (1973). The reading transmission *(lung)* of the *Perfection of Wisdom in Eight Thousand Lines* that Tangtong Gyalpo received on this occasion was passed down for centuries. For example, the Sakya master Mangtö Ludrup Gyatso (Mang thos klu sgrub rgya mtsho, 1523–96) says Tangtong received the explanation at Nartang (Snar thang) from two arhats: Bakula (Ba ku la) and Aṅgaja (Yan lag 'byung). Mangtö Ludrup received the transmission from the leader of Tangtong's tradition, Tenzin Nyida Sangpo (Bstan 'dzin Nyi zla bzang po), in 1583, and the Sakya master Kunga Lekpai Jungné (Kun dga' legs pa'i 'byung gnas, 1704–60) received it from the abbot of Riwoché in 1745. See Mangtö Ludrup Gyatso, *Coquette's Mirror*, 619, and Kunga Lodrö, *Boundless Miracles*, 168.

481 According to Sherab Palden, *Ocean of Marvels*, 48–49, Tangtong Gyalpo traveled from Nartang to Samdrup Tsé (Bsam grub rtse), not Tsongdu Gurmo. He sat there reciting the *Hevajra Tantra* and a crowd of children gathered. Then an old man came up and asked the children what they were doing. When they said they were listening to Dharma from the renunciant, the old man told them Tangtong was a rākṣasa demon *(srin po)*, and all the children fled in terror.

482 The main temple in Shalu Monastery was founded by Chetsun Sherab Jungné (Lce btsun Shes rab 'byung gnas) in 1040. The monastery was most closely associated with the Sakya tradition, and a Shalu subsect developed following the time of Butön Rinchen Drup (Bu ston Rin chen grub, 1290–1364).

483 This is probably the image of Avalokiteśvara, also known as the Mahākaruṇika of Shalu (Zhwa lu'i thugs rje chen po), which is considered the main image at Shalu. It is a black stone image of Avalokiteśvara Khasarpaṇa brought to Tibet in the eleventh century from Bodhgayā by Chetsun Sherab Jungné (Lce btsun Shes rab 'byung gnas), who had gone to India and become a disciple of the famous master Abhayākaragupta. In another chapel in Shalu is an image of Mahākaruṇika that had belonged to Paṇḍita Smṛtijñāna. See Tucci (1989), 71. The seven branches are: offering prostrations, making offerings, confessing sins, delighting in virtue, urging teachers to teach the Dharma, urging the buddhas not to pass into nirvāṇa, and dedicating merit toward the enlightenment of all beings.

484 The crystal-colored youth is an emanation of Avalokiteśvara.

485 Obkha ('Ob kha) is part of the Shalu monastic complex.

486 The five kinds of flesh *(sha sna lnga)* are elephant, human, horse, dog, and cow or peacock. It must have been a very special horse!

487 The five bone ornaments (*phyag rgya lnga*) worn by female deities are a tiara, earrings, necklace, bracelets and anklets, and apron.

488 The Tantra Trilogy of Hevajra *(Kye rdo rje'i rgyud gsum)*: the root tantra of the two-part *Hevajra Tantra (Hevajratantrarājanāma. Kye'i rdo rje zhes bya ba rgyud kyi rgyal po)*, Toh 417–18, Kangyur, rgyud 'bum, *nga*, 1b–30a; the uncommon explanatory tantra of the *Vajrapañjara Tantra (Āryaḍākinīvajrapañjaramahātantrarājakalpanāma. 'Phags pa mkha' 'gro ma rdo rje gur zhes bya ba'i rgyud kyi rgyal po chen po'i brtag pa)*, Toh 419, Kangyur, rgyud 'bum, *nga*, 30a–65b; and the common explanatory tantra of the *Sampuṭa Tantra (Sampuṭanāmamahātantra. Yang dag par sbyor ba zhes bya ba'i rgyud chen po)*, Toh 381, Kangyur, rgyud 'bum, *ga*, 73b–158b. For translations of the *Hevajra Tantra*, see Snellgrove (1959) and Farrow and Menon (1992).

489 *Tantra of the Direct Emergence of Vajravārāhī (Phag mo mngon byung gi rgyud). (Ḍākinīsarvacittādvayācintyajñānavajravarāhyabhibhavatantrarājanāma. Mkha' 'gro ma thams cad kyi thugs gnyis su med pa bsam gyis mi khyab pa'i ye shes rdo rje phag mo mngon par 'byung ba'i rgyud kyi rgyal po shes bya ba)*, Toh 378, Kangyur, rgyud 'bum, *ga*, 60b–71a.

490 Nairātmyā is the consort of Hevajra. Avalokiteśvara as the One Who Dredges the Pit of Saṃsāra ('Khor ba dong sprugs) is a treasure teaching of the Nyingma master Guru Chökyi Wangchuk (Gu ru Chos kyi dbang phyug, 1217–70). Avalokiteśvara as the Wish-fulfilling Gem (Yid bzhin nor bu) is probably the treasure teaching of the adept Ngödrup (Grub thob Dngos grub) and Nyang Nyima Öser (Nyang Nyi ma 'od zer, 1136–1204). I am grateful to Chökyi Nyima for this information. The other two forms of Avalokiteśvara have not been identified.

491 The Jonang master Kunga Drolchok (1507–66) visited the famous statue of Tārā at Ngurmik (Ngur mig) in the year 1533 and recorded his observations: "The Venerable Lady is made from precious alloyed *[zi khyim]* material. Her size, from the hairline down to the soles of her feet, is four handspans; the hair gathered on the back of the head is four fingerwidths; and the small crown is about one and a half fingerwidths. The arms and legs are each wrapped with bracelets. Her two legs are extended in the standing position, and she is moving forward with the right foot shifted ahead about one-half fingerwidth and the left about that much to the rear. The right arm is fully extended and making the gesture of charity, but there does not appear to be any hand implement. On the left side, the stem of an utpala flower, which grows from the lotus base and comes forward in the form of a branch just at the hand, is held with the thumb and ring finger of the hand just at the side of the left breast. She has three eyes and her face is elongated. She has a calm and sensuous demeanor. In brief, the workmanship is like that of the old alloyed *[li ma]* images of West India." See Kunga Drolchok, *Travelogue to Dispel Darkness from Discerning Hearts*, 6b–7b.

492 The places in this list are mostly in present-day Bhutan, except for Kāmata, which refers to the north-eastern part of Bengal and the western district of Assam. See Aris (1980), 105–106, for Khatra (Kha khra), literally "striped mouths," which may refer to the eastern Bhutanese Aka tribesmen. According to Ardussi (1977), 49 n. 38, Lo Khatra (Klo Kha khra) is one of the three divisions of Loyul (Klo yul), the Tibetan name for a portion of the tribal areas on the Tibeto-Assamese border now included in Arunachal Pradesh.

493 The palace is the Potala and the Malchak (Smal lcags) is the base of Chakpori (Lcags po ri), the mountain where Tangtong Gyalpo later built a temple and where the Medical College of Lhasa is located. Lhasa Dharmacakra (Lha sa chos 'khor) is another name for the Jokhang Temple.

494 The temples of the Rasa Trulnang (Ra sa 'phrul snang), the original name of the Jokhang, form the most holy building in Tibet, housing the precious Jowo image of Śākyamuni Buddha and many other ancient and sacred objects. See Dorje (1999), 78–88, for a detailed description.

495 According to Aris (1980), xxiv, 119, Lhorong (Lho rong) is another name for Bhutan (Lho). Later in the biography, when referring to the goods Tangtong had brought back from this trip, the term Lho is used.

496 Dongshur (Gdong zhur) is perhaps the name of the place before Tangtong renamed it Riwoché. The governor of Jang (Dpon po Byang pa) is the ruler at Ngamring, the capital of Jang district. The governor at this time was probably Gugung Chödrak Pal Sangpo (Gu'i gung Chos grags dpal bzang po), or perhaps his son Namgyal Draksang (Rnam rgyal grags bzang, 1395–1475), who later became one of Tangtong's main patrons.

497 The text has only *forehead (spyi bo)*, but Ngawang Tenzin Norbu, *Meaningful to Behold*, 4b, specifically says *forehead of the scorpion (sdig rwa'i spyi bo)* when repeating this passage in his account of the 1933 renovation of the stūpa.

498 The author Gyurmé Dechen's teacher, Lochen Ratnabhadra (1489–1563), built two practice centers and carried out renovations at Riwoché when he was seventy years old (1558). See Ratnabhadra, *Brief Clarification of My Life*, 413. Ratnabhadra was a lineage holder of the Kālacakra teachings in the Jonang tradition, which he transmitted to Gyurmé Dechen and Jonang Kunga Drolchok (1507–66). Ratnabhadra was one of the most important teachers of Kunga Drolchok, and he founded many monasteries, such as Mending (Sman sdings) close to Ngamring, where he seems to have spent most of his time

499 That is, from the trip to Lhorong mentioned just above.

500 Sherab Palden, *Ocean of Marvels*, 298, says the meditation hut *(sgrub khang)* of Shalkar Lhadong (Zhal dkar lha gdong) was at Rinchen Ding (Rin chen sdings), which was Tangtong Gyalpo's birthplace. The isolated site of Tarpa Ling (Thar pa gling) at Rinchen Ding was probably the ancestral retreat of Tangtong's clan, the Lhadong Karpo (Lha gdong dkar po), as also indicated by the name of the meditation hut. Sherab Palden, *Ocean of Marvels*, 158, says Tangtong entered this retreat in the Water Male Tiger Year (1422) and stayed for six years (1428). Tang-

tong wrote an edict *(bka' shog)* at the end of the retreat dated in the Monkey Year (1428). See Sherab Palden, *Ocean of Marvels*, 161–70. Curiously, Lochen Gyurmé Dechen chose not to use these dates in the present biography.

501 The Charnel Ground of Blazing Skeletons (Dur khrod Keng rus me 'bar) is probably the same as the Charnel Ground Endowed with Skeletons (Keng rus can), which is one of the eight great charnel grounds in ancient India. For a list of these eight, see Dorje and Kapstein (1991), 157. Könchok Palsang and Dewa Sangpo, *Bright Lamp*, 159, say this event occurred after two years had passed in retreat, and that a formless voice spoke from the sky. This source places Virūpa in the Most Fierce Charnel Ground (Gtum brag [>drag] gi dur khrod), which is another of the eight major charnel grounds.

502 Virūpa, the lord of yogins (Rnal 'byor dbang phyug Bi rū pa) was one of the eighty-four great adepts of ancient India. His ordination name was Śrī Dharmapāla, and he became a consummate scholar and abbot of the monastic university of Nālandā. Virūpa meditated on Cakrasaṃvara until he was about seventy years old, at which point he despaired of ever attaining success in Vajrayāna practice, and threw his rosary into the toilet. Early the next morning the goddess Vajra Nairātmyā, the consort of Hevajra, appeared to him, gave him advice, and initiated him into an emanated maṇḍala. Within six days he reached the sixth spiritual level of realization. He soon left the monastery and, engaging in deliberate behavior *(brtul zhugs spyod pa)*, wandered through India forcefully subduing and converting followers of savage religious traditions. Virūpa is most important for Tibetan Buddhism as the source of the teachings of the Path with the Result (Lam 'bras), which is the fundamental tantric system of the Sakya tradition. Tangtong Gyalpo received the Path with the Result instructions in a direct transmission from Virūpa himself and also from Ngorchen Kunga Sangpo (Ngor chen Kun dga' bzang po, 1382–1456). The full biography of Virūpa is translated in Stearns (2006).

503 The secret initiation is the second of the four initiations. Sherab Palden, *Ocean of Marvels*, 76, says Virūpa gave Tangtong Gyalpo five nectar pills of secret behavior *(gsang spyod kyi bdud rtsi ril bu lnga)*. When he ate one of the pills, his excretions gradually ceased. Könchok Palsang and Dewa Sangpo, *Bright Lamp*, 160, say Virūpa placed seven pills on Tangtong's tongue after referring to them as pills of pure behavior *(tshangs spyod kyi ril bu)*, and prophesied that Tangtong would become a yogin for whom the three excretions ceased. After that time, no matter what food Tangtong ate, he did not have to expel feces. He later explained in some detail his freedom from the three excretions when this attainment was tested by the Latö Lho governor Tai Situ Lhatsen Kyab (Ta'i si tu Lha btsan skyabs). See Könchok Palsang and Dewa Sangpo, *Bright Lamp*, 315.

504 Several different explanations of the six limits *(mtha' drug)* are found. See Losang Trinlé, *Clarification of Knowledge*, 1063. One common explanation is that the six limits are guidelines for the interpretation of Vajrayāna texts or scriptures according to provisional meaning and definitive meaning *(drang don nges don gnyis)*, according to whether the meaning is literal or not *(sgra ji bzhin pa dang ji bzhin ma yin pa gnyis)*, and according to whether the intended meaning is concealed or not *(dgongs pa can dang dgongs pa can ma yin pa gnyis)*. Also see Dorje and

Kapstein (1991), 151. According to Losang Trinlé, *Clarification of Knowledge*, 1703, several explanations of the four styles *(tshul bzhi)* are also found. One of these, as explained in Dorje and Kapstein (1991), 138, is the lexical *(yi ge)*, general *(spyi)*, concealed *(sbas pa)*, and conclusive *(mthar thug)* styles for the interpretation of secret mantra texts. See Stearns (2001) and (2006) for information on the early history of the Path with the Result in Tibet and for translations of fundamental texts from this tradition, including Virūpa's *Vajra Lines*. Also see Davidson (2005).

505 The *rasanā (rkyang ma)* is the right channel, the *lalanā (ro ma)* is the left channel, and the *dhūtī* or *avadhūtī* is the central channel. In concealed tantric symbology, Vairocana is feces and Akṣobhya is urine.

506 Texts on this guruyoga practice are found in the *Collected Works of Grub chen Thang stong rgyal po*, vol. 3: 275–317, and in Jamyang Khyentsé Wangpo and Loter Wangpo, *Compendium of Methods for Accomplishment (Sgrub thabs kun btus)*, vol. 10: 33–53. See also Gyatso (1981), 210–18, for information about this practice and the various related texts.

507 See note 288.

508 Paro (Pa gro) is in Bhutan. Mön (Mon) is a vague term referring to non-Tibetan non-Indian mountain regions to the south of Tibet.

509 The *Prophecy* is the *Bright Lamp of Prophecy*, the biographical prophecy of Tangtong Gyalpo concealed by Guru Padmasambhava. These lines are found in a portion of the text reproduced in Könchok Palsang and Dewa Sangpo, *Bright Lamp*, 165.

510 Although not grouped together, these lines are mostly found in a portion of the *Bright Lamp of Prophecy*, the biographical prophecy of Tangtong Gyalpo that is reproduced in Könchok Palsang and Dewa Sangpo, *Bright Lamp*, 165–66.

511 The Jowo of Kyirong (Skyid grong gi jo bo) is one of the most holy images of ancient Tibet. See note 369 for more information about this sandalwood image of Avalokiteśvara Khasarpaṇa.

512 Sherab Palden, *Ocean of Marvels*, 158, dates the beginning of this retreat to the Water Male Tiger Year (1422) and says it lasted for six years (1428). Some spectacular events happened after this retreat, when Tangtong Gyalpo read out a long scroll in which he had written the prophecies and so forth he had received in visions, and people laughed at him, insulted him, and said he had just gone crazy. See Könchok Palsang and Dewa Sangpo, *Bright Lamp*, 171–75.

513 The Charnel Ground of Ramadoli (Dur khrod Ra ma do le) is one of the main charnel grounds in the Kathmandu Valley of Nepal. For the possible location of this charnel ground between Kathmandu and Patan, see Macdonald and Dvags-po rin-po-che (1987), 104, 116. According to the Sixth Shamarpa, Garwang Chökyi Wangchuk (Zhwa dmar pa Gar dbang Chos kyi dbang phyug, 1584–1630), who actually visited the charnel ground in 1629–30, its Sanskrit name was Ramadoli, but it was known in Newari as Bājambu. See Decleer (n.d.), 26. In the old biographies, this visit to Ramadoli is described much earlier in Tangtong Gyalpo's travels, when he first went to Nepal to meet Paṇḍita Mahābodhi. The old biographies simply say

that Tangtong went to the charnel ground, with no mention of magical travel. See Sherab Palden, *Ocean of Marvels*, 37–40, and Könchok Palsang and Dewa Sangpo, *Bright Lamp*, 137–38. The term *secret behavior (gsang spyod)*, which occurs several times in the biography, is another name for *deliberate behavior (brtul zhugs spyod pa)*, indicating that Tangtong was engaging in special behavior dictated by the tantras for heightening his realization.

514 In Könchok Palsang and Dewa Sangpo, *Bright Lamp*, 300–303, the woman is said to be eighty years old, and Tangtong Gyalpo gives her a wonderful teaching that is not in the translated biography.

515 That is, the holy golden image of Jowo (Lord) Śākyamuni at the Jokhang in Lhasa.

516 That is, Guru Padmasambhava, who was from the region of Uḍḍiyāna, the Swat Valley of present-day Pakistan.

517 See note 506. Sherab Palden, *Ocean of Marvels*, 46–47, also says the guruyoga was from Vajradhara, but makes no mention of Śākyamuni during the following events and says the old woman saw Tangtong Gyalpo as Vajradhara after meditating. Könchok Palsang and Dewa Sangpo, *Bright Lamp*, 302, say the guruyoga was passed down from Nāropa.

518 The Jowo's prayer of *Fivefold Benefit for Living Beings (Jo bo'i gsol 'debs 'gro don lnga ma)* has not been identified.

519 *Hevajra Tantra*, 10a2. *(Hevajratantrarājanāma. Kye'i rdo rje zhes bya ba rgyud kyi rgyal po)*, Toh 417–18, Kangyur, rgyud 'bum, *nga*, 1b–30a

520 These lines are from the Indian master Saraha's *Treasury of Dohā in a Song* (also known as *People's Dohā*), 76a. *(Dohākoṣagīti. Do hā mdzod kyi glu)*, Toh 2224, Tengyur, rgyud, *wi*, 70b–77a. P 3068, *mi*. The text quoted here varies from that in the Dergé edition of the canon. Cf. Guenther (1993), 117.

521 That is, the deity Cakrasaṃvara.

522 The Charnel Ground of the Grove of Terrifying Darkness ('Jigs byed mun pa tshal) has not been identified. It is perhaps the same as the Charnel Ground of Śītavana (Bsil bu tshal), which is one of the eight great charnel grounds.

523 Brahmin Vararuci (Bram ze Mchog sred) was from eastern India. He studied under the master Kāṇha, the disciple of the great adept Virūpa, and received the initiations and instructions of Hevajra and Cakrasaṃvara. Then he meditated for twelve years near the Charnel Ground of Śītavana. When obstacles arose to his practice, he requested help from his teacher Kāṇha, who gave him the initiations and instructions of Mahākāla Pañjaranātha in the temple of the protectors at the north gate of the Vajrāsana of Bodhgayā. Then he meditated on Cakrasaṃvara for twelve years and again encountered obstacles. When he prayed for assistance, Pañjaranātha actually appeared to him and gave him instructions. From that time Pañjaranātha was always with him, and Vararuci placed in writing the instructions he had been given. See Jamgön Ameshap, *Sun Illuminating All the Teachings of the Doctrine Protectors*, vol. 1: 123–34.

524 Pañjaranātha (Gur gyi mgon po) is the form of Mahākāla with one face and two arms, standing upright, holding a curved knife and skull-cup. The transmissions of this form of Mahākāla exist in Tibet both in the treasure tradition of the Nyingma and in other lineages. Pañjaranātha is most important as the special protector of the Sakya tradition, specifically of the Path with the Result (Lam 'bras) system connected with the deity Hevajra. For information on the texts and practice of Pañjaranātha according to Tangtong Gyalpo's vision, see Gyatso (1981), 203–9.

525 The Land of Demonesses (Srin mo'i gling) is below the Copper-Colored Mountain (Zangs mdog dpal ri) of Guru Padmasambhava. In the fifteenth century the externally located Uḍḍiyāna, which corresponds to the Swat region in present-day Pakistan, was an Islamic area. The following description of the Uḍḍiyāna visited by Tangtong Gyalpo has a different meaning in the context of the inner spiritual topography of the twenty-four sacred sites of tantric pilgrimage *(gnas chen)*. According to Dezhung Rinpoché, when Tangtong traveled to sacred sites such as Uḍḍiyāna and the Charnel Ground of Rāmeśvara, he did so in a single instant because of his high realization. The barriers in the subtle vajra body had been transcended, so that he actually went *(dngos su phebs)*, which is equivalent to going in a pure vision *(dag snang su phebs)*. I like the statement in Herman Melville's *Moby Dick*: "It is not down in any map; true places never are."

526 A league *(yojana, dpag tshad)* is equivalent to about eight thousand yards or 7.4 km. See Kongtrul (2003), 425 n. 91.

527 Different identifications of these eight great nāga kings *(klu chen po brgyad)* are found. According to one list, their names are Vāsuki, Śaṅkhapāla, Nanda, Takṣaka, Padma, Varuṇa, Karkoṭaka, and Kulika. Also see Harding (2003), 314 n. 49.

528 The eight qualities of pure water *(yan lag brgyad dang ldan pa'i chu)* are coolness, sweetness, lightness, softness, clearness, soothing quality, pleasantness, and wholesomeness. See Dorje and Kapstein (1991), 160–61.

529 Könchok Palsang and Dewa Sangpo, *Bright Lamp*, 339, say the heart-shaped *(rtsi ta'i dbyibs can)* mountain is the Copper-Colored Mountain (Zangs mdog dpal ri).

530 The Eight Transmissions of Great Attainment *(sgrub pa chen po bka' brgyad)* were received by Guru Padmasambhava from the eight great adepts. These teachings concern the practices of the eight great herukas of the mahāyoga class in the Nyingma tradition: Yamāntaka, Hayagrīva, Śrīheruka, Vajrāmṛta, Vajrakīla, Mātaraḥ, Mundane Praise, and Malign Mantra. See Dorje and Kapstein (1991), 157. When Guru Padmasambhava gave the first initiations in Tibet, he gave the initiations of these eight deities, and according to where the flowers cast by each of his eight main disciples fell within the maṇḍala, each one of them meditated upon one of the eight deities and gained realization.

531 The eight close sons *(nye ba'i sras brgyad)* are the bodhisattvas Mañjuśrī, Vajrapāṇi, Avalokiteśvara, Kṣitigarbha, Sarvanivāranaviṣkambhin, Ākāśagarbha, Maitreya, and Samantabhadra. See Dorje and Kapstein (1991), 157.

532 Könchok Palsang and Dewa Sangpo, *Bright Lamp*, 340, have the date Water Male Dragon *(chu pho 'brug)*, which would be 1412 or 1472.

533 The four elements are earth, water, fire, and air. Stūpas are the main representations of the Buddha's dharmakāya reality body.

534 The Indian teacher Niguma was the sister of the master Nāropa. See Zangpo (2003), 227–34, for information about her life and teachings. In this context, the term *khecarī* is a synonym for *ḍākinī*. The blessing of the illusory body *(sgyu lus kyi byin rlabs)* is an initiation or blessing given in connection with the Six Dharmas of Niguma. Sherab Palden, *Ocean of Marvels*, 103–5, does not identify the girl as Niguma or list the teachings from her.

535 *Mañjuśrījñānasattvasyaparamārthanāmasaṃgīti, 'Jam dpal ye shes sems dpa'i don dam pa'i mtshan yang dag par brjod pa*, Toh 360, rgyud 'bum, *ka*, 1b–13b. For a translation and study of this fundamental tantric scripture, see Davidson (1981). The two words *mtshan brjod* from the abbreviated title of this work have been omitted in the text. Sherab Palden, *Ocean of Marvels*, 107, from which this episode has been taken, has the complete spelling: *'Jam dpal mtshan brjod*.

536 Sherab Palden, *Ocean of Marvels*, 183, says this trip to Lhasa occurred in the Earth Female Bird Year (1429).

537 An annotation in the Tibetan text notes that the meaning of the term *'gor ba* ("lumpy") is unclear.

538 The Jowo (Jo bo) is the famous figure of Śākyamuni Buddha at the age of twelve in the Jokhang Temple of Lhasa. The Mikyö Dorjé (Akṣobhyavajra, Mi bskyod rdo rje) is an image of the Buddha at the age of eight, brought to Tibet by the Nepalese princess Bhrikuti, who was the second wife of Songtsen Gampo, and kept in the Ramoché Temple of Lhasa. The Fivefold Naturally Arisen One (Rang byon lnga ldan) is a holy image of the eleven-faced Avalokiteśvara kept in the Jokhang in Lhasa. Several different explanations are given for its name. According to Losang Trinlé, *Clarification of Knowledge*, 1888, the image is known by this name because it has the five naturally arisen blessings of itself, a naturally arisen smaller image of the eleven-faced Avalokiteśvara that dissolved into the larger image's heart, and those of King Songtsen Gampo, the Chinese princess Wencheng Kongjo, and the Nepalese princess Bhrikuti, all of whom are said to have dissolved into the image at the time of their deaths. Also see Gyurme Dorje (1999), 82–83, and Ricard et al. (1994), 238–39.

539 Könchok Palsang and Dewa Sangpo, *Bright Lamp*, 182–83, place this episode much earlier, when Tangtong was in Lhasa with the pilgrims from Sakya. During his year at Kaṃṇi Goshi some said that he was a demon *('dre)* and some accused him of being a non-Buddhist. The Kaṃṇi Goshi (spelled *kaṃ ṇi sgo bzhi*, *ka ka ṇi sgo bzhi*, or *kakṇi sgo bzhi*) was a large and famous square stūpa in Lhasa with gateways through each of its four sides below the terraced steps. See Losang Trinlé, *Clarification of Knowledge*, 19–20. Nearly a century after Tangtong's visit, Tsang Nyön Heruka spent time at the Kaṃṇi Goshi and some people said he was a rākṣasa demon *(srin po)* and others said he was Tangtong Gyalpo. See Ngödrup Palbar, *Lion of Faith at Play on a Glacial Peak of Good Qualities*, 10a–b.

540 The Mahāmudrā master Shang Yudrakpa Tsöndru Drakpa (Zhang G.yu brag pa Brtson 'grus grags pa, 1123–93), also known as Lama Shang, founded the Tselpa Kagyü (Tshal pa bka' brgyud) tradition, building the hermitage of Tsel in 1175 and the main monastery at Gungtang in 1187. According to Sherab Palden, *Ocean of Marvels*, 184, when Tangtong Gyalpo arrived, he took off his cloak, put it down, and walked naked around the marketplace three times. Then he performed the thirty-two yogic exercises for immortality while taking only three breaths. Unfortunately, when he returned to pick up his clothes, they were gone. See note 593 concerning these thirty-two yogic exercises.

541 Shang Yudrakpa Tsöndru Drakpa, known as Lama Shang, constructed the large Lhachen Palbar (Lha chen dpal 'bar) image of Śākyamuni Buddha at Gungtang in 1187.

542 For the fascinating Shang Yudrakpa Tsöndru Drakpa, or Lama Shang, see Martin (1992) and Jackson (1994). Lama Shang was a disciple of Dakpo Gomtsul (Dwags po Sgom tshul), the nephew of Gampopa. Among Lama Shang's many works is an important verse treatise on Mahāmudrā, translated in Martin (1992).

543 Tangtong Gyalpo was given the name Tsöndru Sangpo when he first took ordination. Tsöndru means "diligence," "energy."

544 According to Sherab Palden, *Ocean of Marvels*, 186–87, much blood poured from Tangtong Gyalpo's nose after he was beaten. When people later came to ask him for blessings after he miraculously crossed the river, his hair was thickly matted with blood, and they thought his skull had been crushed.

545 In the old biography by Sherab Palden these verses are not mentioned during this episode, but are found at the end of a long prayer Tangtong made in Uḍḍiyāna. See Sherab Palden, *Ocean of Marvels*, 144–45. In Könchok Palsang and Dewa Sangpo, *Bright Lamp*, 187, Tangtong speaks the verses after floating over the river, and many of the same lines are also repeated in a prayer given much later in his life at the request of a group of artisans. See Könchok Palsang and Dewa Sangpo, *Bright Lamp*, 584–86.

546 Sherab Palden, *Ocean of Marvels*, 187, mentions that some people said Tangtong walked straight across the water, while some said that he went across seated on the dog skin. A similar incident also occurred in the life of Ga Lotsāwa Namgyal Dorjé (Rga Lo tsā ba Rnam rgyal rdo rje, eleventh–twelfth centuries). Ga Lotsāwa came to the banks of a river and asked the ferryman to take him across. When the ferryman would not take him because he did not have the fare, Ga Lotsāwa scolded him, and the ferryman beat him with his oar. Ga Lotsāwa then crossed the river by floating above the water seated in the meditation posture. This story comes from the biography of Ga Lotsāwa written by none other than his disciple Lama Shang, who founded the monastery of Tsel Gungtang that Tangtong Gyalpo had just visited. See Shang Yudrakpa, *Biography of Pal*, 378.

547 The adept Samten Palwa (1291–1366) was a famous yogin and teacher of the Kagyü and Shijé traditions. See Roerich (1976), 884–86.

548 Sherab Palden, *Ocean of Marvels*, 187–88, mentions that Tangtong sat in the hole for seven days. Because it became known that he was the renunciant who had magically crossed the Kyichu River recently, everyone came to him at night in respect. But they still called him an idiot during the day. When nobody asked for any Dharma teachings, Tangtong thought he had no connection with Tibet and decided to go to India the next day. Then three nuns came to ask for teachings. He wrote instructions to them on a writing slate *(sa 'bo ra)*, and when they returned with their offerings, he gave many teachings.

549 For the three turnings of the Dharma wheel, see note 436.

550 The vows of ritual fasting involve meditation on Avalokiteśvara, and the *maṇi* transmission *(ma ṇi lung)* is the transmission from teacher to student of Avalokiteśvara's mantra, *Oṃ maṇi padme hūṃ.*

551 The Naturally Arisen Eleven-faced Avalokiteśvara (Rang byon bcu gcig zhal) is a famous image of Avalokiteśvara in the Jokhang Temple in Lhasa. It is also known as the Fivefold Naturally Arisen Lord (Jo bo Rang byon lnga ldan). See note 538.

552 Machik Palha (Ma gcig Dpal lha) is the same as Machik Palden Lhamo (Ma gcig Dpal ldan lha mo), an emanation of the guardian goddess Palden Lhamo (Śrī Devī, Dpal ldan lha mo). Machik Palha is the main guardian goddess of Lhasa, and is also the chief *ma mo*. See Nebesky-Wojkowitz (1956), 23–24.

553 Dorjé Drolö (Rdo rje gro lod) is one of the eight aspects of Guru Padmasambhava. In this form the Indian master is said to have subdued all evil forces and concealed countless treasures at Paro Taktsang in Bhutan.

554 Yeshé Dorjé (Ye shes rdo rje) is Tsangpa Gyaré Yeshé Dorjé (Gtsang pa rgya ras Ye shes rdo rje, 1161–1211), the founder of the Drukpa Kagyü sect. He was a disciple of Lama Shang (1123–93) and Lingrepa (Gling ras pa, 1128–88), and is one of the masters responsible for first opening up the area of Tsari. Nyö (Snyos) is Nyö Gyalwa Lhanangpa (Gnyos Rgyal ba Lha nang pa), also known as Chökyi Siji (Chos kyi gzi brjid, 1164–1224). He was an important disciple of the Kagyü master Jikten Gönpo ('Jig rten mgon po, 1143–1217) and also a teacher of the Path with the Result (Lam 'bras). See Roerich (1976), 601–2, and Stearns (2000), 24 n. 26. Gar ('Gar) is Gardampa Chödingpa ('Gar dam pa Chos sdings pa, b. 1180), another main disciple of Jikten Gönpo. See Roerich (1976), 602–3). Gyaré (Rgya ras) is perhaps Palchen Chöyé (Dpal chen chos ye), another of Jikten Gönpo's disciples who accompanied Nyö and Gar when they went to Tsari. Nyö, Gar, and Chöyé are often referred to as a trio. See Roerich (1976), 603.

555 This line is from Padmasambhava's *Bright Lamp of Prophecy (Lung bstan gsal sgron)*. See the fragment of the text in Könchok Palsang and Dewa Sangpo, *Bright Lamp*, 103.

556 Kongtsun Demo (Kong btsun de mo) is one of the twelve indigenous goddesses of Tibet *(brtan ma bcu gnyis)* whom Guru Padmasambhava subdued and made into guardians of Buddhism. See note 161.

557 *lha 'dre mi gsum.* In instances such as this it is clear that the terms *lha (god)* and *'dre (demon)* indicate separate categories, but sometimes the term *lha 'dre (god-demon)* is also used to designate a specific type of divine being.

558 Drepung ('Bras spungs) is one of the three main Geluk monasteries in the Lhasa area. It was founded in 1416 by Jamyang Chöjé Tashi Palden ('Jam dbyangs chos rje Bkra shis dpal ldan, 1397–1449), who was also the first abbot. A scholar of the ten fundamental subjects *(bka' bcu pa)* has mastered and passed academic exams in epistemology *(tshad ma)*, the perfection of wisdom literature *(phar phyin)*, madhyamaka or middle-way philosophy *(dbu ma)*, abhidharma, and the monastic code *('dul ba)*, as well as another five suitable topics. See Mangtö Ludrup Gyatso, *Bright Sun of Pure Altruism*, 197. The following episode in the translated biography is mainly based on Könchok Palsang and Dewa Sangpo, *Bright Lamp*, 188–92, which has much more detail and some extra teachings. Sherab Palden, *Ocean of Marvels*, 189–90, says Tangtong was questioned by a disciple of the Sakya master Rongtön (Rong ston Shes bya kun rig, 1367–1449), not a Drepung scholar.

559 Perhaps a reference to monk's vows that prohibit external activities at night.

560 That is, the eight tribes of gods and demons. See note 160.

561 In Sherab Palden, *Ocean of Marvels*, 193–95, Tangtong Gyalpo spoke the last half of this teaching (with some variations), beginning with the first phrase "Whatever appears," not in Lhasa to a scholar from Drepung, but in Sangpu (Gsang phu) to the Sakya master Rongtön Sheja Kunrik (1367–1449). Before Rongtön recognized him and asked for teachings, Tangtong had been sleeping for three days at the foot of the stūpa of the famous scholar Chapa Chökyi Sengé (Phya pa Chos kyi seng ge, 1109–69), and people thought he was a corpse. In this older version of the teaching, Tangtong's verses are all in the past tense, explaining how these qualities had arisen due to his own practice. In the translated biography, which follows Könchok Palsang and Dewa Sangpo, *Bright Lamp*, 191–92, the verbs are in the imperative, urging the recipient to act.

562 This couplet is from the *Condensed Verses on the Perfection of Wisdom (Prajñāpāramitāsañcayagātha. 'Phags pa shes rab kyi pha rol tu phyin pa sdud pa tshigs su bcad pa)*, 6b. Toh 13, Kangyur, sher phyin, *ka*, 1b–19b.

563 Yerpa (Yer pa) is the famous Drak Yerpa (Brag Yer pa), an important early site of hermitages and meditation caves since at least the seventh century. See Ferrari (1958), 103–4.

564 The eight great adepts *(grub chen brgyad)*, or mahāsiddhas, of ancient India are usually identified as Indrabhūti, Kukkuripa, Padmavajra, Nāgārjuna, Ḍombi Heruka, Lūipa, Ghaṇṭāpa, and Saraha. Another set of eight great Indian adepts is also recognized in the Nyingma tradition: Vimalamitra, Hūṃkara, Mañjuśrīmitra, Nāgārjuna, Padmasambhava, Dhanasaṃskṛta, Rambuguhya-Devacandra, and Śāntigrabha. See Dorje and Kapstein (1991), 159. The stories of these eight masters are told in Dudjom (1991), 75–83.

565 Dawa Puk (Zla ba phug), the Cave of the Moon, is a famous cave in the Yerpa Valley near Lhasa, where Guru Padmasambhava meditated and concealed treasures. Ferrari (1958), 43 and 104.

566 The name Ngaripa (Snga ris pa) presents a problem. In Sherab Palden, *Ocean of Marvels*, 191, the name is spelled Mnga' ris pa, which would indicate that this man was from the Ngari (Mnga' ris) region in far western Tibet. The words *snga ris* and *mnga' ris* are pronounced exactly the same. However, it is clearly said that this first disciple was from Latö (La stod), not Ngari (Mnga' ris). In the translated biography Gyurmé Dechen has changed the spelling so that it makes sense in the present context. As such, it would seem that this Ngaripa (Snga ris pa) is not the same as the disciple mentioned several times elsewhere in the biography as the mountain man of Ngari (Mnga' ris pa'i ri pa).

567 The Drom ('Brom) is a nomad clan in the upper Tölung (Stod lung) Valley. Könchok Palsang and Dewa Sangpo, *Bright Lamp*, 255, specify Lama Lotsāwa (Bla ma lo tsā ba) was from the Tölung Valley, which is a short distance west of Lhasa. His appointment as spokesman of the writing slate *(sa 'bo ra sgrog mi la bskos)* means that when Tangtong wrote on a writing slate during periods of silence, Lama Lotsāwa read out his words. Lama Lotsāwa figures in several episodes later in the biography, and seems to have accompanied Tangtong much of the time. Könchok Palsang and Dewa Sangpo, *Bright Lamp*, 209–10, tell of an episode in Tsari that is not in the other biographies. Tangtong discovered a special cave with many miraculous contents, including a treasure text, which he recovered from its place of concealment. After making many prayers and ecstatically dancing about, he gave a cup full of beer to Lama Lotsāwa and said, "Pray to me!" Lotsāwa repeated verses of prayer to the master, taking a gulp of beer after each verse, and experienced tremendous blessing.

568 According to Könchok Palsang and Dewa Sangpo, *Bright Lamp*, 255, Sanawa (Sa sna ba) was from the Yarlung Valley.

569 Könchok Palsang and Dewa Sangpo, *Bright Lamp*, 255, call Lama Dülwapa (Bla ma 'Dul ba pa) by the name Dülwa Sangpo ('Dul ba bzang po), and say he was from Shu Nemo (Bzhu sne mo).

570 The valley of Penyul ('Phan yul) northeast of Lhasa is a region where many of the early teachers of the Kadampa tradition settled. Tangtong Gyalpo later built a temple and a stūpa in Drakral (Brag ral), and his son Tenzin Nyima Sangpo built an iron bridge.

571 Chimpu (Mchims phu) is the retreat place above Samyé where Guru Padmasambhava gave the first tantric initiations in Tibet. He bestowed the initiations of the Deities of the Eight Transmissions of Great Attainment to the Tibetan king Trisong Detsen and seven other disciples who each reached attainment through the practice of one of the eight herukas. King Trisong Detsen was born at Drakmar Drinsang (Brag dmar mgrin bzang).

572 The main temple of Samyé Monastery was built by Guru Padmasambhava and King Trisong Detsen (Khri srong lde btsan) in the late eighth century.

573 Sheldrak (Shel brag) is the rock cavern in Yarlung related to the heruka of enlightened qualities, Vajrāmṛta, and is where Guru Padmasambhava's disciple Karchen Yeshé Shönu reached attainment. It is also where the treasure revealer Orgyen Lingpa (O rgyan gling pa, 1323–ca. 1360) discovered the treasure of

Padmasambhava's Chronicles (Padma thang yig). See Ferrari (1958), 128. Also see Dorje (1999), 164.

574 Nedong Peak (Sne gdong rtse) was the palace of the rulers of Tibet during the Pakmodru (Phag mo gru) dynasty, which had been founded by Tai Situ Jangchup Gyaltsen (Ta'i si tu Byang chub rgyal mtshan, 1302–64). The sovereign *(gong ma)* Drakpa Gyaltsen (Grags pa rgyal mtshan, 1374–1432) was the fifth ruler *(sde srid)* of the dynasty, reigning over all of Tibet from 1385 until his death in 1432. For the life and reign of Drakpa Gyaltsen, see Sönam Drakpa, *Magical Key to Royal Genealogies*, 83–86. For a sketch of his life focusing more on his religious activities as a Dharma teacher and patron, see Tsewang Gyal, *Lhorong History of the Dharma*, 387–89.

575 Tangtong Gyalpo's comments may be seen to foreshadow the internal revolt that erupted in the Pakmodru dynasty following Drakpa Gyaltsen's death in 1432 and the enthronement of his successor Drakpa Jungné (Grags pa 'byung gnas, 1414–45), which signaled the beginning of the dynasty's decline.

576 According to Sherab Palden, *Ocean of Marvels*, 415, Tangtong gave the Avalokiteśvara initiation consisting of the entrustment of pure awareness *(rig gtad kyi dbang)* to the ruler Drakpa Gyaltsen alone, and the initiation of Opening the Door to the Sky (Nam mkha' sgo 'byed), the transmission of the *maṇi* mantra *(ma ṇi'i lung)*, and other teachings to the ruler and his followers in common.

577 Nyakpuwa Sönam Sangpo (Snyag phu ba Bsod nams bzang po, 1341–1433) was an important master of the Jonang tradition. He was first the close attendant *(nye gnas)* of the Omniscient Dolpopa Sherab Gyaltsen (1292–1361), from whom he received many Dharma teachings. After Dolpopa passed away, Sönam Sangpo studied with the master's major disciples such as Nya Ön Kunga Pal (Nya dbon Kun dga' dpal, 1285?–1379?), Sasang Mati Panchen (Sa bzang Ma ti Paṇ chen, 1294–1376), and Jonang Cholé Namgyal (Jo nang Phyogs las rnam rgyal, 1306–86). Sönam Sangpo became Jonang Cholé Namgyal's main disciple, and was particularly expert in the explanation and practice of the Kālacakra. He was later offered the monastery at Tselmin (Mtshal min), where he took up residence, and so he is also known as Tselmin Sönam Sangpo (Mtshal min Bsod nams bzang po). He was a teacher of many masters during the fifteenth century and taught actively into old age, explaining the huge *Kālacakra Tantra* commentary of the *Vimalaprabhā* when he was ninety-two years old. See Ngawang Lodrö Drakpa, *Moon Lamp to Clarify the Teachings of the Conqueror*, 38–39, and Mangtö Ludrup Gyatso, *Bright Sun of Pure Altruism*, 190–93.

578 The Vajrayoga *(rdo rje rnal 'byor)* is the Six-branch Yoga of Kālacakra, which Tangtong Gyalpo had received and practiced under the guidance of several teachers, such as Ka Ngapa Paljor Sherab (Bka' lnga pa Dpal 'byor shes rab), the Jonang abbot Lekhawa Sherab Sangpo (Sle kha ba Shes rab bzang po), and Könchok Dorjé (Dkon mchog rdo rje). Jomonang (Jo mo nang) is the full form of the name of the Jonang (Jo nang) tradition.

579 According to Sherab Palden, *Ocean of Marvels*, 196, Tangtong also said, "If one is an adept, one must have reached the Path of Seeing, but I wouldn't even recognize the Path of Seeing!"

580 The point in this exchange is that Tangtong Gyalpo is a monk, but dresses like a yogin. Guru Padmasambhava had told him in an earlier vision, "Tilopa and Nāropa had the dress of yogins."

581 Sherab Palden, *Ocean of Marvels*, 198, reproduces the first four lines of the prayer and says it was three verses long.

582 According to Könchok Palsang and Dewa Sangpo, *Bright Lamp*, 255, Lama Riksum Gönpo (Bla ma Rigs gsum mgon po) was from the Central Tibetan area of Kyishö (Skyi bshod>Skyid shod). Tangtong would later appoint Riksum Gönpo to the monastic seat of his monastery of Tsagong Nesar (Tsa gong gnas gsar) in Kongpo.

583 For the many religious sites in the Dra (Gra) or Dranang (Grwa nang) region to the south of the Tsangpo River in Lhokha (Lho kha), see Ferrari (1958), 54–55, 132–33. Sherab Palden, *Ocean of Marvels*, 199–200, says Tangtong Gyalpo searched for the heart of the dead horse to use for the feast, but could not find it. So he used the pus-filled lungs, which he blessed and ate during the ritual feast. People said, "This man is a rākṣasa demon!" and fled. That night the rest of the horse's corpse disappeared.

584 According to Sherab Palden, *Ocean of Marvels*, 200, Tangtong said, "I thought the ritual feast the day before (with the rotten, pus-filled lungs of the horse) was perfect, but nobody was able to eat it. Today's wasn't like that." None of Tangtong's biographies identify the Yargyab governor (Yar rgyab dpon chen pa). He may have been Rinchen Sangpo (Rin chen bzang po), who was the governor of Yargyab for many years during the middle of the fifteenth century. See Ehrhard (2002), 77, etc.

585 The monastery of Densatel (Gdan sa thel) was founded by Pakmodrupa Dorjé Gyalpo (Phag mo gru pa Rdo rje rgyal po, 1110–70) in 1158. During the Pakmodru dynasty, this monastery was the religious center of the rulers. The abbots of the monastery came from the Pakmodru family line.

586 The Pakmodru abbot at Densatel, Chen Nga Sönam Gyaltsen (Spyan snga Bsod rnams rgyal mtshan, 1386–1434), was the brother of the previously mentioned Pakmodru ruler, Drakpa Gyaltsen (Grags pa rgyal mtshan, 1374–1432). Although a member of the Pakmodru ruling family, and thus a teacher of the Kagyü tradition, Sönam Gyaltsen also became a disciple of lord Tsongkhapa (Tsong kha pa Blo bzang grags pa, 1357–1419), from whom he received many teachings. He even composed an instruction manual combining the ancient Kagyü instructions of the Six Dharmas of Nāropa with the new instructions of the Six Dharmas taught by Tsongkhapa, using the Dohā songs of Saraha and the *Five Stages (Pañcakrama, Rim lnga)* as sources for authenticating these teachings. This text was highly regarded in the Geluk tradition. See Losang Chökyi Nyima, *Tukwan's Philosophical Tenets*, 124.

587 Translated according to the reading *phyag mchod byas nas na bun sangs pa*, found in the original Dergé print, not the mistaken *phyag mchod byas na phan kun spangs pa* in the Indian reprint.

588 The Fivefold Mahāmudrā is a special teaching of the Drigung Kagyü tradition. See note 388 for more information.

589 The cave hermitage of Sangri Khangmar (Zangs ri khang dmar) was the main residence of Machik Labdrön (Ma gcig Lab sgron, eleventh–twelfth centuries), the originator of the tradition of Severance, or Chöd (Gcod). See Edou (1996), 164, for a picture of an image of Machik at Sangri Khangmar. See also Ferrari (1958), 47–48, 121, and Dorje (1999), 218–19.

590 In Sherab Palden, *Ocean of Marvels*, 206, the girl does not say, "I blessed this place," but says, "The emanated body Machik and others also blessed this place in the past." The text here certainly implies that this girl is an emanation of Machik Labdrön. Tangtong Gyalpo was a practitioner and teacher of Machik's tradition of Severance, or Chöd (Gcod).

591 For Ölkha Taktsé ('Ol kha stag rtse), see Ferrari (1958), 48, 121, and Dorje (1999), 219. Sherab Palden, *Ocean of Marvels*, 206, gives the nun's name as Ané Rinchen Tsomo.

592 The Sixth Karmapa, Tongwa Dönden (Mthong ba don ldan, 1416–1453), was the leader of the Karma Kagyü tradition in particular and all Kagyü traditions in general. He spent time in the Tsari and Kongpo region and was especially famous for spreading the teachings of tantra. For references to sources about Tongwa Dönden's life, see Losang Trinlé, *Clarification of Knowledge*, 35–36. According to Könchok Palsang and Dewa Sangpo, *Bright Lamp*, 197, about five hundred people were in the Karmapa's encampment, which contained about one hundred black and white tents.

593 The thirty-two yogic exercises for immortality *('chi med 'khrul 'khor gsum cu rtsa gnyis)* are based on the Indian master Virūpa's *Root Text for the Attainment of Immortality (Amṛtasiddhimūla)*. These exercises are used during the practice of the fruition stage of the Shangpa Kagyü teachings, the Immortality of Body and Mind, specifically for achieving physical immortality. This Virūpa, who taught the ḍākinī Sukhasiddhī, formulated the practices associated with Vajravārāhī of the Severed Head (Phag mo dbu bcad ma), and authored the *Amṛtasiddhimūla*, is *not* the same as the Virūpa who was the source of the teachings of the Path with the Result (Lam 'bras) practiced in the Sakya tradition of Tibetan Buddhism. Also see Schaeffer (2002) for discussion of the *Amṛtasiddhi* teachings and their relation to the Indian Nātha tradition.

594 Mahākaruṇika Who Tames Living Beings (Thugs rje chen po 'gro 'dul) is a treasure teaching of the Nyingma master Nyang Nyima Öser (Nyang Nyi ma 'od zer, 1136–1204), and Mahākaruṇika Who Dredges the Pit of Saṃsāra ('Khor ba dong sprugs) is a treasure teaching of the Nyingma master Guru Chökyi Wangchuk (Gu ru Chos kyi dbang phyug, 1217–70).

595 Könchok Palsang and Dewa Sangpo, *Bright Lamp*, 200, say the woman was possessed by a malignant "wealth demon" *(nor 'dre)*.

596 The monastery of Daklha Gampo (Dwags lha sgam po) was founded in 1121 by Gampopa Sönam Rinchen (Sgam po pa Bsod nams rin chen, 1079–1153), also

known as Dakpo Lhajé (Dwags po lha rje). Gampopa was one of the two main disciples of the peerless Milarepa, and his monastery of Daklha Gampo became the principal monastery of the Dakpo Kagyü (Dwags po Bka' brgyud) tradition. See also Dorje (1999), 222.

597 See note 288.

598 These verses are quite different in Könchok Palsang and Dewa Sangpo, *Bright Lamp*, 200, where it is said that Tangtong would live for either ten decades or seventeen decades.

599 See note 161 for information about the goddess Kongtsun Demon (Kong btsun de mo), one of the twelve goddesses bound to an oath of protection by Guru Padmasambhava during his visit to Tibet. Sodruk (So drug) is unidentified, but see also Könchok Palsang and Dewa Sangpo, *Bright Lamp*, 201 and 287, where the name of this place is given as Podruk (spelled Po drug and Spo drug).

600 For the holy Tsari (Tsa ri) area and its pilgrimage circuits, see Dorje (1999), 224–27. The sacred Lake Yutso (G.yu mtsho), Turquoise Lake, is the most important maṇḍala lake of the Tsari sanctuary. During the fifteenth century this lake was a main pilgrimage destination for many Tibetan yogins. See Ehrhard (2002), 80–81. See note 287 for the nine dance moods *(gar dgu)*.

601 Waru Namtsel (Ba ru gnam tshal). The spellings *ba ru gnam tshal* and *wa ru gnam tshal* are both found in this text and others. It is the same place as the Waru Namtsul in Dorje (1999), 240.

602 See note 162 concerning the nāga king Varuṇa (Wa ru ṇa).

603 Translated according to reading *lung bstan* in the original Dergé edition, not *'dul bstan* in the Indian reprint.

604 Waru Seso (Wa ru se so) would seem to be the name of the local mountain, the earth spirit of the place *(gzhi bdag)*, and another name for Varuṇa.

605 The three vows *(sdom gsum)* are the vows of individual liberation, the bodhisattva vow, and the vows of secret mantra.

606 That is, emanation and transformation *(sprul sgyur)* of one's body in dreams.

607 A lumen *(klu sman)* spirit is a being whose parents are a nāga *(klu)* and a men *(sman)* goddess. See Nebesky-Wojkowitz (1956), 198–202, for details about the *sman* goddesses.

608 That is, take her as a consort.

609 The eight tribes of gods and nāgas *(lha klu sde brgyad)* is basically the same as the eight tribes of gods and demons, for which see note 160. The eight tribes of gods and nāgas are listed in Losang Trinlé, *Clarification of Knowledge*, 2146.

610 These lines are not found in the fragments of the *Bright Lamp of Prophecy* preserved in Könchok Palsang and Dewa Sangpo, *Bright Lamp*, 100–103, 161–67.

611 The earth spirit Waru Seso (*gzhi bdag* Wa ru se so) is the same as the nāga king Varuṇa.

612 The actual construction of the stūpa and temple is described later in the biography.

613 This female nāga *(klu mo)* is the same as the lumen *(klu sman)* spirit mentioned above.

614 The celestial planetary demons *(steng gdon gza')* are thought to cause diseases such as epilepsy *(gza' nad)*. For the various kind of planetary demons *(gza')*, see Nebesky-Wojkowitz (1956), 259–62. The gyalgong *(rgyal gong)* demons often infest monasteries and temples. The nyen *(gnyan)* demons are an ancient race of evil spirits that make people lame. They live in space between the earth and the sky, but also in many terrestial locations such as stones, trees, water, and so forth. See Nebesky-Wojkowitz (1956), 288–89.

615 Various garudas *(khyung)* are sometimes associated with certain forms of Vajrapāṇi and emanate from him. In one example, the green karma-garuda *(las khyung)* emanates from his genitals. See Nebesky-Wojkowitz (1956), 257–58.

616 Rāhu (Sgra gcan) is the chief of all the planetary gods *(gza')*. He is believed to be responsible for eclipses. See also Nebesky-Wojkowitz (1956), 259–63.

617 Bhakha (Bha kha) is probably the same as the valley of Bhaga. See Dorje (1999), 228.

618 According to Buddhist cosmology, Mount Meru is surrounded by four continents: Jambudvīpa in the south, Pūrvavideha in the east, Aparagodanīya in the west, and Uttarakuru in the north.

619 The offering of united *evaṃ (e waṃ zung 'jug)* probably means the secret offering of sexual union, the unity of bliss and emptiness, symbolized by the Sanskrit syllables *e* (emptiness) and *vaṃ* (bliss).

620 Dorjé Nangzema (Rdo rje snang mdzad ma) would seem to be another name for the goddess Vajrayoginī, perhaps designating a particular form.

621 The three realms *(khams gsum)* are the desire realm, form realm, and formless realm.

622 This is a prophecy that the "authentic skull-cup" *(mtshan ldan dbu thod)* made from the cranium of Jetsun Chökyi Drönmé (1422–55) would be enshrined there in the future. She was believed to be an incarnation of the goddess Vajravārāhī.

623 Dorjé Drakpotsel (Rdo rje drag po rtsal) is a wrathful aspect of Guru Padmasambhava who manifests in blue or red color, usually carrying a meteorite vajra in the right hand and a nine-headed scorpion in the left hand.

624 Trapa Ngönshé (Gra pa Mngon shes, 1012–90) is an important figure in the Nyingma, Pacification (Zhi byed), and medical lineages. He studied with many Indian and Tibetan masters, such as Padampa Sangyé (Pha Dam pa sangs rgyas), Somanātha, Atiśa, and Marpa Lotsāwa. The famous yoginī Machik Labdrön studied the Perfection of Wisdom, or Prajñāpāramitā, literature and other topics under his direction for seven years. Trapa Ngönshé also discovered many treasures texts, the most important of which were the Four Medical Tantras *(Rgyud bzhi)* that he

extracted from a pillar in the Samyé (Bsam yas) temple in 1038. For the story of his life focusing on his Nyingma and medical contributions, see Dudjom (1991), 753–54.

625 Dzagom Jodar (Rdza sgom Jo dar) and the renunciant Ngönpo Yöndar (Bya gtang Sngon po yon dar) have not been identified.

626 Lama Dampa of Sakya (Bla ma dam pa Bsod nams rgyal mtshan, 1312–75) was born into the Rinchen Gang Palace (Rin chen sgang bla brang) branch of the Khön family of Sakya. He was the fifteenth patriarch of Sakya and the greatest master to appear at Sakya after the time of the five great founding masters. Lama Dampa is particulary known as an expert in the Sakya teachings of the Path with the Result (Lam 'bras) that are based on the *Hevajra Tantra.* He was also a practitioner and teacher of the *Kālacakra Tantra* and the Six-branch Yoga. See Jangchup Tsemo, *Virtuous at the Beginning, End, and Middle*, 42b–43b, for Lama Dampa's activities in the Kongpo region.

627 The Mu *(rmu>dmu)* and Tsan *(btsan)* are two ancient classes of demons. See the multiple entries in Nebesky-Wojkowitz (1956).

628 The field-protector Kunga Shönu (Zhing skyong Kun dga' gzhon nu) is one of the names of a green four-armed form of Mahākāla. For a description of him, see Nebesky-Wojkowitz (1956), 65.

629 Sangri Bawachen (Zangs ri Lba ba can), whose name indicates that he was afflicted with a goiter, is listed as one of Tangtong Gyalpo's "thirteen heroic disciples who were devoted to virtue and acted in ways that concealed their good qualities." See Könchok Palsang and Dewa Sangpo, *Bright Lamp*, 388. See note 582 for information about Riksum Gönpo (Rigs gsum mgon po), to whom Tangtong gave ordination earlier in the biography. Khandro Sangpuk (Mkha' 'gro gsang phug) is the cave of stone mentioned just above in the text.

630 These are three forms of Mahākāla. The Six-armed Protector is specially connected to the teachings of the Shangpa tradition. Tangtong Gyalpo wrote a text for the special Shangpa practice of the six-armed Mahākāla, known as "Master and Protector Indivisible" *(Bla ma mgon po dbyer med).* See Tangtong Gyalpo, *Guiding Instructions on the Six-armed Primordial-Awareness Protector.* For a description of the various forms of the Four-armed Protector, which is mostly practiced in the Kagyü traditions, see Nebesky-Wojkowitz (1956), 44–47. See note 524 for information about Pañjaranātha, the most important protector of the Sakya tradition.

631 For a description of the form of Mahākāla known as the Raven-faced Karmanātha (Las mgon Bya rog gdong can), see Nebesky-Wojkowitz (1956), 48–49.

632 This prophecy concerns a skull-cup that would later be made from the cranium of Jetsun Chökyi Drönmé (1422–55), who became Tangtong Gyalpo's consort for a brief period and then traveled to Tsari. The skull-cup of her cranium was enshrined in a stūpa at Menmogang. Also see Diemberger et al. (1997), 111, and Diemberger (forthcoming 2007). The mountain man of Ngari (Mnga' ris pa'i ri pa) would seem to be a different disciple than the man known as Ngaripa (Snga ris pa). See note 566. According to Könchok Palsang and Dewa Sangpo, *Bright*

Lamp, 255, this disciple from Ngari was named Palden Gyaltsen (Bla ma Mnga' ris pa Dpal ldan rgyal mtshan).

633 The Kongpo people do not believe Tangtong Gyalpo's statement because of a misunderstanding. They think he is referring to another "authentic skull-cup" that was enshrined at the main monastery of Tsari and was perhaps the most holy relic there at the time. They do not realize that he is prophesying that an "authentic skull-cup" made from the cranium of Jetsun Chökyi Drönmé will later be enshrined at Menmogang, not that the famous skull-cup at Tsari would be moved to Menmogang. In Sherab Palden, *Ocean of Marvels*, 227, the comments of the Kongpo people begin with the exclamation, "That's a huge lie!" and end with, "He's tricking us!" The author also mentions that detailed information is to be found in a "great guidebook" *(gnas yig chen mo)*.

634 Dülwapa ('Dul ba pa) was one of Tangtong Gyalpo's earliest disciples. See note 569. The nun Kalden Rinchen Tsomo (Skal ldan Rin chen mtsho mo) was previously mentioned as an attendant of Tangtong, and just called Ané Tsomo.

635 See notes 582 and 629 concerning these two disciples.

636 This prophecy probably refers to the venerable lady Chökyi Drönmé (Rje btsun Chos kyi sgron me), who would come to Kongpo and live briefly at Menmogang in 1455, the year of her death.

637 The term translated here as *single man (pho reng po)* usually means *bachelor*, but the prayers this man made as he grabbed each chain are given in Sherab Palden, *Ocean of Marvels*, 234–35, and they concern his pregnant wife and the safe birth of a son.

638 Sherab Palden, *Ocean of Marvels*, 235–36, gives a more detailed and entertaining version of this part of the story: The great adept ordered the blacksmith Kunga, "Bring oil and clay!" He smeared the oil on his hand and pressed it into the clay.

"There's a handprint for you!"

"That won't do," the people replied. "It has to be in stone."

The great adept smeared oil on his foot and placed it on a flat stone. "There's a footprint for you!" he said.

"That won't do," they replied. "It has to be like it's been carved."

The great adept told the blacksmith Kunga, "Bring a little hammer!" Holding the hammer in his right hand, he spread his left hand on the stone and chipped around it with the little hammer.

"That won't do!" they cried. "If you don't have any proof of attainment to show, you can't take the iron to Central Tibet. We'll collect arrows and stones, and each person will fire an arrow and throw a stone. Then, if you haven't died, all will be well. And you can take the iron to Central Tibet."

The lord replied, "I'm not a bird that flies in the sky! I'm not a mouse that burrows into the ground! I'm not a fish that swims in the water!"

639 Karmapa Rangjung Dorjé (Kar ma pa Rang byung rdo rje, 1284–1339) was the third and perhaps greatest of the Karmapas, the leaders of the Karma Kamtsang Kagyü tradition in particular and the entire Kagyü tradition in general. The activities of

Rangjung Dorjé were extremely widespread. He founded many monasteries, and composed some of the most important texts of theory and practice in the Kagyü tradition. Pawo Tsuklak Trengwa, *Banquet for Experts*, vol. 2: 933–35, describes the year or more that Rangjung Dorjé spent in the Kongpo and Tsari area.

640 Sherab Palden, *Ocean of Marvels*, 239, says Tangtong Gyalpo was attended by the young monk *(btsun chung)* Chözom (Chos 'dzom), Kongpo Pöntruk (Kong po Dpon sprug), and Lama Gyalgyal (Bla ma Rgyal rgyal).

641 Hevajra (Kye rdo rje) is one of the major deities of the highest yoga tantra classification, particularly practiced in the Sakya tradition, and to a lesser degree among the Kagyü. For translations of the primary scripture of the *Hevajra Tantra*, see Snellgrove (1959) and Farrow and Menon (1992).

642 Amoghapaśa (Don yod zhags pa) is a form of Avalokiteśvara.

643 The lion-faced ḍākinī Siṃhamukha (Seng ge'i gdong pa can) and the wrathful black ḍākinī Tröma Nakmo (Khros ma nag mo).

644 The meaning of the term *sha banhe* remains obscure. Könchok Palsang and Dewa Sangpo, *Bright Lamp*, 204, have the spelling *sha ban dhe*. The term *bande/bandhe* usually means "monk," which would not seem to be applicable here because these people have no knowledge of Buddhism.

645 This is the same man who earlier grabbed the four chains and made prayers in Kongpo. According to Sherab Palden, *Ocean of Marvels*, 240, when Tangtong Gyalpo first traveled to Lo, he arrived in the area where the man from Lo lived. The man recognized Tangtong, honored him, and warned him of the dangers in Lo. Perhaps the man then accompanied Tangtong during his travels in Lo.

646 The ten virtues are to refrain from engaging in the ten nonvirtues, which are killing, stealing, sexual misconduct, lying, slander, harsh words, idle speech, covetousness, malice, and wrong view.

647 Sherab Palden, *Ocean of Marvels*, 246, emphasizes that Tangtong Gyalpo taught many Dharma cycles of Avalokiteśvara, such as Mahākaruṇika Who Dredges the Pit of Saṃsāra (Thugs rje chen po 'khor ba dong sprugs) and the fasting rituals.

648 The lords of the three spiritual families *(rigs gsum mgon po)* are Avalokiteśvara, Mañjuśrī, and Vajrapāṇi.

649 The seventh century Tibetan emperor Songtsen Gampo is traditionally credited with introducing the royal code of the ten virtues *(dge ba bcu)* throughout the Tibetan cultural regions.

650 Cakravartī ('Khor lo can) is Raudra Cakrī (Drag po 'khor lo can), the emperor of the legendary land of Shambhala. It is prophesied that Raudra Cakrī will appear at a future time and destroy the barbarian teachings that will have spread over the earth.

651 These are the shepherds from Drakyul in Kongpo who warned Tangtong before that he would be killed if he went to Lo, and who then guided him there when he insisted on going.

652 This is the same cave in Kongpo where Tangtong had previously retrieved the guidebooks and keys to the sacred places of Kongpo and Lo before he went to Lo. Sherab Palden, *Ocean of Marvels*, 257–72, records a long and important teaching that Tangtong Gyalpo gave to the Kongpo people at this place.

653 The Sixth Karmapa, Tongwa Dönden (Mthong ba don ldan, 1416–53), was the head of the Kagyü tradition. Tangtong Gyalpo had previously met him in Gampo and offered him several teachings. The five inexpiable acts *(mtshams med kyi las)* are to kill your father, to kill your mother, to kill an arhat, to cause a schism in the Sangha, and to maliciously cause a buddha to bleed.

654 This date has been taken from Sherab Palden, *Ocean of Marvels*, 275, who does not mention how old Tangtong Gyalpo was at the time.

655 The Nepa governor (Sne pa Dpon) in 1430 was Drungchen Drakpa Palsang (Drung chen Grags pa dpal bzang), who had received his grant to rule the regions around Lhasa and beyond from the Pakmodru sovereign Drakpa Jungné (Grags pa 'byung gnas, 1414–45). See Ngawang Losang Gyatso, *Song of the Lark*, 175. Kyishö (Skyid shod) is the general name for the area along the lower course of the Kyichu River below Lhasa.

656 Among the various opinions expressed by the people, Sherab Palden, *Ocean of Marvels*, 276, mentions that everyone said, "This renunciant is crazy. We've never heard that bridges of iron exist. He's really babbling when he says he's going to build an iron bridge on the Kyichu River." According to the Fifth Dalai Lama, the ancient stone levees of Lhasa are said to have been first constructed during the reign of the seventh-century king Songtsen Gampo. See Dorje and Kapstein (1991), 59 n. 802. Könchok Palsang and Dewa Sangpo, *Bright Lamp*, 213, specifically mention that Tangtong built the bridge over the Kyichu River at Drib (Grib) for the purpose of preventing the river from flooding into Lhasa. After Tangtong's time, the Bhutanese treasure revealer Pema Lingpa (Padma gling pa, 1450–1521) referred to rumors of the Jowo image being in danger of being swept away by floods in 1521. See Aris (1988), 94. Jonang Tāranātha gives an eyewitness description of flooding in Lhasa in the 1580s. For several days it was necessary to take a boat between Lhasa and the Ramoché Temple. All the circumambulation paths were flooded, and everyone was in despair because the waters destroyed the temporary levees as soon as they were built. The Jokhang Temple was in severe danger. Despite the situation, Tāranātha visited the Jokhang and the Ramoché daily and made a few circumambulations while sloshing through the water. See Tāranātha, *Extremely Detailed, Unpretentious, and Candid Narrative*, 79. For much interesting information about the continuing struggle to combat flooding in the Lhasa area, see Akester (2001) and Sørensen (2003).

657 That is, the southern ends of the two chains were attached to the spikes.

658 The patroness Kalsang, whose full name was Kalden Rinchen Sangmo (Skal ldan Rin chen bzang mo), became the most important patron for Tangtong Gyalpo's activities in Central Tibet. She was born into the ruling family of the Sharkhapa (Shar kha pa) at Gyantsé (Rgyal rtse) and married the Neu (Sne'u) governor Drungchen Drakpa Palsang (Drung chen Grags pa dpal bzang), who had received his grant to

rule the Lhasa area and beyond from the Pakmodru sovereign Drakpa Jungné (Grags pa 'byung gnas, 1414–45). Their son was Drungchen Paljor Gyalpo (Drung chen Dpal 'byor rgyal po, d. 1490), who succeeded his father as governor *(rdzong dpon)*. See Ngawang Losang Gyatso, *Song of the Lark*, 175.

659 See note 389 concerning these refuge verses.

660 According to Sherab Palden, *Ocean of Marvels*, 280, the bridge was pulled up by five monks, such as the Lo man Gyalgyal. This original source contains no mention of any help from spirits or gods.

661 Kharnak (Mkhar nag) is said to be the son of the nāga king Dungkyong (Śaṅkhapāla; Dung skyong), one of the eight nāga kings, and his domain is about twenty miles west of Lhasa, at the confluence of the Tölung (Stod lung) and Kyichu (Skyid chu) Rivers. See Epstein (1968), 71.

662 See Ferrarri (1958), 161–62, for information on the Shu Nyemo (Zhu Snye mo) area. See note 478 concerning the pilgrimages from Sakya to Lhasa.

663 Chakpori Hill (Lcags po ri), one of the four important mountains of central Tibet, is southwest of the Potala Palace in Lhasa. This mountain is believed to be the "spirit-mountain" *(bla ri)* of the bodhisattva Vajrapāṇi. Marpori Hill (Dmar po ri), on which the Potala is built, is believed to be the spirit-mountain of Avalokiteśvara. Tangtong Gyalpo stayed for some time on Chakpori and founded a nunnery there. Many of the images he made from semiprecious stones were kept in the Chakpori temple into the 1950s, along with various other relics associated with his treasure discoveries. See Ngawang Losang Gyatso, *Crystal Mirror*, 45–47.

664 See note 570 for Penyul ('Phan yul), a valley north of Lhasa.

665 Kham (Khams), Minyak (Mi nyag), and Amdo (A mdo) are regions in eastern Tibet. The people of the different areas did not always have cordial relations.

666 See note 658 for information about the lady Kalsang (Skal bzang), who was Tangtong Gyalpo's main supporter in Central Tibet. The building of this residence on Chakpori Hill was previously predicted when an arrow that Tangtong had shot landed on Chakpori, which he understood to be an auspicious omen for building a residence and center for practice there.

667 The term *naraka* is a Sanskrit word for hell *(na rag dmyal ba)*.

668 Lady Kalsang's son was Drungchen Paljor Gyalpo (d. 1490), who would seem to have been the governor at this point. According to the Fifth Dalai Lama, Lady Kalsang's husband, the governor Drungchen Drakpa Palsang, took monastic vows for a period of time, and then again became a layman and ruled. Either the son ruled during the period the father was a monk, or the father had already passed away by this time. See Ngawang Losang Gyatso, *Song of the Lark*, 175. The date for Paljor Gyalpo's death is found in Sönam Drakpa, *Magical Key to Royal Genealogies*, 95.

669 Lady Shakhama (Dpon mo Shag kha ma) is an epithet of Kalden Rinchen Sangmo, referring to the fact that she was from the Shakhapa line of rulers from Gyantsé in Tsang.

670 Jamyang Tashi Palden ('Jam dbyangs bkra shis dpal ldan, 1379–1449), also mentioned in the next sentence as Jamyang Chöjé ('Jam dbyangs Chos rje), studied with lord Tsongkhapa at Ganden Monastery. He founded the Geluk monastery of Drepung in 1416, and served as its first abbot. He could explain 130 volumes of scripture and had achieved a level of meditative concentration in which he could see the colors of the five vital winds. For a sketch of his life and activities, see Losang Trinlé, *Clarification of Knowledge*, 884–85.

671 An annotation in the Tibetan text mentions a problem in this sentence, but whether it is a problem of spelling or information is unclear to me. The sentence structure is odd. Sherab Palden, *Ocean of Marvels*, 285, says only that it was a Pig Year, without supplying the second element that makes the date certain.

672 Sherab Palden, *Ocean of Marvels*, 285, only mentions that it was a Mouse Year *(byi lo)*, not giving the second element that would make the date certain.

673 Tölung (Stod lung) is a valley to the west of Lhasa that is an ancient stronghold of the Karma Kagyü tradition. See Ferrari (1958), 69, 73–74, 78, 167, 169, and Dorje (1999), 134–38.

674 Vaiśravaṇa (Rnam sras) is a wealth deity and the protector of the northern direction.

675 Sherab Palden, *Ocean of Marvels*, 286, only gives the date as an Ox Year *(glang lo)*, without a second element or Tangtong Gyalpo's age.

676 Chuwori (Chu bo ri) is one of the four main mountains in Tibet. It is located on the southern bank of the Tsangpo River in Central Tibet near Gongkar. Regarded as a holy mountain for many centuries, the first hermitage was founded there by the Tibetan king Trisong Detsen in the eighth century.

677 Tachok Khabab (Rta mchog kha bab) is the name of the western portion of the Tsangpo River (Gtsang po), which originates from the southern side of Mount Kailash.

678 The ancient palace at Nakartsé (Sna dkar rtse) in Lhokha was the residence of the governors of the Yamdrok (Yar 'brog) district. The governor, or "ruler of ten thousand households" *(khri dpon)*, at this time was probably Namkha Sangpo (Nam mkha' bzang po). Namkha Sangpo and his nephews Kunga Gyaltsen (Kun dga' rgyal mtshan) and Amoghasiddhi were dedicated disciples and supporters of Bodong Panchen Cholé Namgyal (Bo dong paṇ chen Phyogs las rnam rgyal, 1376–1451). Amoghasiddhi was the author of the main biography of Bodong Panchen. See Ehrhard (2002), 59–61. Cf. Lozang Trinlé, *Clarification of Knowledge*, 1242–43. See also Diemberger (1997), 33, where it is noted that the Nakartsé governor Namkha Gyaltsen (Nam mkha' rgyal mtshan) helped the venerable lady Chökyi Drönmé (1422–55) establish a small meditation site at Samding in 1440. Dorje (1999), 214–17, contains information on the area of Nakartsé.

679 Ralung (Ra lung) Monastery was founded in 1180 by the Kagyü master Tsangpa Gyaré (Gtsang pa rgya ras Ye shes rdo rje, 1161–1211) and became the main monastery of the Drukpa Kagyü tradition. The Pökya residence (Spos skya gzims khang) mentioned in the next sentence has not been identified, but is probably

the official residence of the Drukpa Kagyü throne-holders at Ralung. Gyalwang Kunga Paljor (1428–76) was the leader of the Drukpa Kagyü tradition at the time of Tangtong Gyalpo's visit. See note 229 concerning a letter Kunga Paljor sent to Tangtong. See also Dorje (1999), 253–54, for the present situation at Ralung.

680 The yakṣa Gangwa Sangpo (*gnod byin* Gang ba bzang po), or Gangsang, is one of the eight yakṣa horsemen in the entourage of the wealth deity Vaiśravaṇa. Gangwa Sangpo makes his residence on the high glacial mountain of the same name (Gnod byin Gang bzang) that is between Nakartsé and Gyantsé in eastern Tsang.

681 Nénying (Gnas rnying) is an ancient monastery south of Gyantsé that was founded in the eleventh century. It has had Nyingma, Gelukpa, Bodongpa, and Shangpa affiliations over the centuries. See Losang Trinlé, *Clarification of Knowledge*, 1225–26, and Dorje (1999), 290. The Six-armed Protector (Mgon po Phyag drug pa) is the form of Mahākāla most associated with the Shangpa Kagyü tradition.

682 Pari (Phag ri) is near the Tibetan border, on the trading route south to Paro, Bhutan.

683 The Kaṃṇi (Kaṃ ṇi) is unidentified. The unusual term *kaṃ ṇi* is also in the name of a famous stūpa in Lhasa. Perhaps it is a general name for the type of stūpa with gates through it? See note 539 for information about the Kaṃṇi Goshi stūpa in Lhasa.

684 Jomo Lhari (Jo mo lha ri) is the mountain known as Mount Everest and the name of the goddess who resides there. The other figures are spirits associated with the Paro (Pa gro) and Ha (Has) Valleys in Bhutan. Lhokha Shi (Lho Kha bzhi) is a name for the area of Bhutan, literally meaning "the southern country of four approaches." These four geographical areas are Khaling (Kha gling) in the east, Ghatakha (Gha ta kha) or Paksamkha (Dpag bsam kha), that is, Cooch Bihar or Buxa Duar, in the south, Dalingkha (Brda gling kha) near Kalimpong in the west, and Taktsekha (Stag rtse kha) on the northern border. See Aris (1980), xxv.

685 See note 530 for the Deities of the Eight Transmissions of Great Attainment (Sgrub chen bka' brgyad kyi lha). Vajrakīla is one of these eight herukas, corresponding to the aspect of enlightened activity, and is one of the main deities of the Nyingma tradition. Vajrakīla is said to be the best deity for dispelling inner and outer obstacles on the spiritual path. Taktsang (Stag tshang) is a famous holy place in the Paro Valley of Bhutan where Guru Padmasambhava manifested as Dorjé Drolö (Rdo rje gro lod) and concealed many treasure teachings.

686 The mountain of Singri (Shi gi ri) is a famous Assamese pilgrimage site. See Aris (1980), 113 and 188. As mentioned in the next paragraph, the Viśuddha Stūpa (Mchod rten rnam dag) at Singri was thought to be where Śākyamuni Buddha, who was the son of King Śuddhodana, had renounced the life of a householder. This must be an apocryphal tradition, since Śākyamuni never traveled to the eastern regions of Assam. Vijayā (Rnam rgyal) is the goddess of longevity, Uṣṇiṣavijayā (Gtsug tor rnam rgyal).

687 Mahāvairocana (Rnam snang chen po) is a form of the buddha Vairocana. Tringyi Shukchen (Sprin gyi shugs can) is one of the names of the Indian master

Gayadhara (d. 1103), who brought the teachings of the Path with the Result (Lam 'bras) to Tibet. It may also refer to an earlier Indian adept. See Stearns (2001), 53–54, 191–92.

688 The Charnel Ground of Tumdrak (Gtum drag), the "Most Fierce," is one of the eight major charnel grounds of ancient India. See Dorje and Kapstein (1991), 157.

689 Vajrabhairava (Rdo rje 'jigs byed), one of the major deities of the class of unexcelled yoga tantra, is a wrathful form of Mañjuśrī.

690 According to Michael Aris, the throne built at that time for Tangtong on a rock shaped like a heap of turtles was still visible in the 1980s.

691 The name Kāmata, or Kāmarūpa, stands for the northeastern part of Bengal and the western district of Assam. See note 14 for more information.

692 Lholingka (Lho Gling kha) is identical to the Khaling (Kha gling) at the eastern border region of Bhutan, the first of the "four approaches" to that country. See note 684.

693 Referring to an unknown source, Sherab Palden, *Ocean of Marvels*, 291, mentions that the signs of attainment and miracles that Tangtong Gyalpo displayed are clearly explained in detail elsewhere.

694 Wam Tengchen (Waṃ Steng chen) is in western Bhutan. See Aris (1980), under the entry for Wang. A *ṭaṃga (ṭaṃ ga)* is a silver coin minted in Nepal or in Chooh Behar in India. See Rhodes (1980). Könchok Palsang and Dewa Sangpo, *Bright Lamp*, 263, say seventeen loads of coins were offered, and Sherab Palden, *Ocean of Marvels*, 292 and 518, specifies that the coins were silver. A load *(khal)* is a unit of measure equivalent to about twenty-five to thirty pounds or twelve to fifteen kilos.

695 Shambhala is a legendary kingdom to the north ruled by enlightened Buddhist kings who are masters of the *Kālacakra Tantra.*

696 According to Aris (1980), xxiv, 119, Lhorong (Lho rong) is another name for Bhutan.

697 Gyaldung (Rgyal gdungs), is mentioned in Aris (1980), 121, 123. Ha (Has) is a valley in western Bhutan.

698 Kyewang Pakné (Skye dbang 'phags gnas) is the place in the Paro Valley where Tangtong Gyalpo had previously sat immobile on a throne for three months.

699 Tachok Gang (Rta mchog sgang), also known as Tachok Norbugang (Rta mchog nor bu sgang), is the monastery Tangtong Gyalpo founded in Bhutan that later became the main center for his tradition in that country. He also built an iron suspension bridge there, which remained until it was washed away in a flood in 1969. The monastery was the seat of the hereditary line known as the Tachok Chöjé (Rta mchog Chos rje), who claim descent from Dewa Sangpo, the disciple of Tangtong and co-author of one of his biographies. Also see Aris (1980), 186, 188.

700 These numbers are taken from Könchok Palsang and Dewa Sangpo, *Bright Lamp*, 270. Sherab Palden, *Ocean of Marvels*, 296, mentions only three hundred loads of iron and one thousand loads of other Bhutanese goods.

701 The meaning of the terms *rdo dung kha can* ("fossil shells") and *gyeng sa nyan pa* ("special type of soil") remains uncertain.

702 Pari (Phag ri) is near the Tibetan border with Bhutan, and Nénying (Gnas rnying) is fifteen kilometers south of Gyantsé. This trip would usually take several days, not the half-day journey mentioned here. Könchok Palsang and Dewa Sangpo, *Bright Lamp*, 271, make no mention of an emanation, simply saying that Tangtong Gyalpo carried seventy iron links to Chuwori.

703 As above, the speed of the journey would be recognized by the reader as a supernatural feat. Könchok Palsang and Dewa Sangpo, *Bright Lamp*, 271, mention that Tangtong then set the monks to work gathering stones for the bridge abutment *(zam phung)* at Chuwori.

704 The Gampa Pass (Gam pa la) is the main pass on the road between Chuwori and Yamdrok Lake in Central Tibet. The yakṣa Gangwa Sangpo (*gnod byin* Gang ba bzang po) or Gangsang is one of the eight yakṣa horsemen in the entourage of the wealth deity Vaiśravaṇa. As described previously in the biography, and mentioned in the next paragraph, Gangsang had come to meet Tangtong Gyalpo when he was at the Pökya residence at Ralung.

705 The spirit Gangsang is referring to his previous meeting with Tangtong Gyalpo at Ralung. Some spirits are said to be offended and injured by the smell of scorching or burning materials.

706 That is, Tangtong himself was the source of the emanation *(sprul gzhi'i grub thob chen po)* whose activities have just been described.

707 The Samdrup Temple that Tangtong Gyalpo built at Pari was visited in 1820 by the twenty-fifth Head-abbot of Bhutan, Sherab Gyaltsen (1772–1847), who made offerings and recited prayers in front of a blessed image of Tangtong that was kept there. See Sherab Gyaltsen, *Chariot for Realization of the Two Truths*, 29a. Giuseppe Tucci also passed through Pari twice during his twentieth-century expeditions, noted the art work in the temple, and mentioned that by his second trip it had been largely painted over with lesser quality new work in the guise of restoration. See Tucci (1965), 36. The Dharma king Kunsang Pak (Chos rgyal Kun bzang 'phags, 1389–1442), who is referred to as lord Rabtenpa (Bdag po Rab brtan pa) just below, was the ruler of Gyantsé (Rgyal rtse), which is in upper Nyang (Nyang stod). Kunsang Pak founded the monastery of Palkhor Chödé (Dpal 'khor chos sde) at Gyantsé in 1418 and constructed the famous stūpa there in 1427. Könchok Palsang was one of Tangtong's important disciples and was the author of one of the earliest biographies.

708 Drogön Pakpa ('Gro mgon 'Phags pa Blo gros rgyal mtshan, 1235–80) was the fifth Early Patriarch of the Sakya tradition. He became the spiritual master of the Mongolian conqueror Kubilai Khan (1215–94), who was the first emperor of the Yuan dynasty (1279–1368) in China.

709 Latö Jang (La stod Byang) was Tangtong Gyalpo's home district, where he built the monastery of Riwoché. Sherab Palden, *Ocean of Marvels*, 298, agrees that two hundred loads of iron links were sent to Chuwori, but says Tangtong took only one hundred loads to Latö Jang.

710 Sherab Palden, *Ocean of Marvels*, 298, says the meditation hut *(sgrub khang)* of Shalkar Lhadong (Zhal dkar lha gdong) was at Tangtong Gyalpo's birthplace of Rinchen Ding (Rin chen sdings). The isolated site of Tarpa Ling (Thar pa gling) at Rinchen Ding was probably the ancestral retreat of Tangtong's clan, the Lhadong Karpo (Lha gdong dkar po), as also indicated by the name of the meditation hut. Sherab Palden, *Ocean of Marvels*, 298–99, says only that the iron bridge was built in front of the Shalkar Lhadong meditation hut of Rinchen Ding in a Tiger Year *(stag lo)* and does not mention Tangtong's age.

711 The Dharma king of Jang (Chos rgyal Byang pa) was Namgyal Draksang (Rnam rgyal grags bzang, 1395–1475). See note 763 for more information about this Buddhist master and ruler who became one of Tangtong Gyalpo's main patrons.

712 Sherab Palden, *Ocean of Marvels*, 299, gives only the single element for the Rabbit Year *(yos lo)*. I take the term "western regions" *(stod phyogs)* in this context to be a general reference to the Latö and Ngari areas.

713 The iron bridge at Gangla Longka (Gangs la klong kha) is perhaps the same as the iron bridge of Longka (Klong kha) built in the upper Chung Valley (Bcung stod) mentioned in Sherab Palden, *Ocean of Marvels*, 472. However, according to Sherab Palden's description, the bridge was built much later, during Tangtong Gyalpo's eight-month stay in Ngamring, when he left his close attendant *(nye gnas)* Chözom (Chos 'dzom) as the bridge keeper. Chözom is also listed as one of Tangtong's "thirteen heroic disciples who were devoted to virtue and acted in ways that concealed their good qualities." See Könchok Palsang and Dewa Sangpo, *Bright Lamp*, 388. The young monk Chözom (Btsun chung Chos 'dzom) had earlier accompanied Tangtong as an attendant when he went to the savage borderlands of Lo. See Sherab Palden, *Ocean of Marvels*, 239.

714 The famous Jowo (Jo bo) image of Avalokiteśvara in the two-armed form known as Khasarpaṇa. Enshrined in the Kyirong Temple, this statue was also known as the Noble Wati ('Phags pa Wa ti). See note 369 for more information.

715 Sherab Palden, *Ocean of Marvels*, 300, makes the meaning clear by saying *sku khrus gsol ba*, instead of just *khrus gsol ba*, which is found in the translated biography.

716 The name of this type of stūpa (Lhung bzed kha sbub mchod rten) indicates that it was shaped like a begging bowl turned upside down.

717 Ngari Dzongka (Mnga' ris Rdzong kha) is the royal palace and monastic complex at Gungtang (Gung thang), the capital of the Ngari region in far western Tibet. The Ngadak king (Mnga' bdag rgyal po) at this time was either Tri Lhawang Gyaltsen (Khri Lha dbang rgyal mtshan, 1404–64), the father of Jetsun Chökyi Drönmé (1422–55), or his son Tri Namgyal Dé (Khri Rnam rgyal sde,), who succeeded his father on the throne in 1436. The Dzongka Monastery (Rdzong kha

chos sde) was founded in 1394 by the Bodong master Drakpa Gyaltsen (Grags pa rgyal mtshan, 1352–1405).

718 Könchok Palsang and Dewa Sangpo, *Bright Lamp*, 303–6, and in particular Sherab Palden, *Ocean of Marvels*, 302–11, tell the following story in much more detail, but do not mention the name of the king's teacher. Lochen Gyurmé Dechen has specifically identified the teacher as Chöpal Sangpo (Chos dpal bzang po, 1371–1439), who was the half-brother of the Ngari king Tri Chokdrup Dé (Khri mchog grub lde, 1371–1404). Chöpal Sangpo was born in Sakya and studied Dharma there as well as in Bodong. He became an important Sakya master and was one of the main teachers of Müsepa Dorjé Gyaltsen (Mus srad pa Rdo rje rgyal mtshan, 1424–98). In 1420 he was appointed as the royal chaplain of the Ngari king Tri Lhawang Gyaltsen (Khri lha dbang rgyal mtshan, 1404–64), who had ascended the throne in 1419. See Tsewang Norbu, *Magical Mirror of Clear Crystal*, 122–23. I have found no mention of Tangtong Gyalpo or this alleged assassination attempt in the two available biographies of Chöpal Sangpo.

719 Könchok Palsang and Dewa Sangpo, *Bright Lamp*, 304, specifically give the name of the consort here as Semo Remo (*phyag rgya ma* Sras mo re mo), who is also mentioned by this name later in the translated biography. According to his biography, Chöpal Sangpo had two consorts, named Ané Chösang (A ne Chos bzang) and Ané Jinsangma (A ne Sbyin bzang ma). See Mañjuśrījñāna, *Biography of the Great Master Chöpal Sangpo*, 32a–35a. Semo Remo is either another consort or perhaps a nickname for Ané Chösang or Ané Jinsangma.

720 Chöpal Sangpo is often referred to as the "great master" (Bla chen) Chöpal Sangpo.

721 I understand the spelling *brten tshig* to be a mistake for *bden tshig*.

722 Peacocks are said to be able to eat poison without suffering any harm.

723 See Tangtong Gyalpo and Jamyang Khyentsé Wangpo, *Basic Texts and a Clarification of the White and Red Pills*, which contains two short texts by Tangtong for making the white and red medicinal pills, together with an explanation by Khyentsé Wangpo. The text for the red pills mentions that it was given by Avalokiteśvara when Tangtong was feigning illness and the text for the white pills is connected to a vision of the five ḍākinīs at Riwoché. According to Sherab Palden, *Ocean of Marvels*, 309–10, at the end of Tangtong's seven-day retreat after the attempted assassination, he announced, "It's true to say Tangtong Gyalpo has died. The five poisons and three poisons of the afflictions have died. It's also true to say I didn't die. The enlightenment mind doesn't die. Those who would be glad if I had died, say I died! Those who would be glad if I didn't die, say I didn't die! I'm a yogin who has achieved self-control. Whatever I do, I'm happy." Then a woman comes forward, tells of the many previous evil deeds of the master who tried to assassinate Tangtong, and asks him to "liberate" (kill by means of magical ritual) the master. Könchok Palsang and Dewa Sangpo, *Bright Lamp*, 306, specifically mention the type of magic *(mthu)* that Tangtong directed back toward Dzongka after his departure and note that it was said the master died the next day. It is known that the master Chöpal Sangpo died in 1439. However,

according to the dates and chronology in the translated biography, Tangtong's visit to Dzongka would seem to have been earlier than 1439.

724 Mount Kailash (Ti se, Gangs Ti se) is a famous mountain in far western Tibet, sacred to both Buddhists and Hindus. The Great Cave of Miracles (Rdzu 'phrul phug mo che) is where Milarepa and the Bönpo teacher Naro Bönchung (Na ro Bon chung) dueled by displaying signs of attainment.

725 The nun Ané Paldren (A ne Dpal 'dren) was from Kyirong and had become an attendant of Tangtong Gyalpo when he visited that region before going to Ngari Dzongka.

726 The Drukpa Kagyü master Tsangpa Gyaré (Gtsang pa rgya ras Ye shes rdo rje, 1161–1211).

727 Lake Mapam Yutso (Ma pham g.yu mtsho) is the Tibetan name for Lake Manasarovar, 4,600 meters above sea level at the foot of Mount Kailash.

728 For an exhaustive investigation of the ancient kingdoms of Gugé and Purang (Gu ge pu rang) in far western Tibet, see Vitali (1996). Some confusion exists in the Tibetan sources concerning the exact identity of the Three Silver Brothers (Dngul sku mched gsum) of the Khachar (Kha char) Temple, which is also known as Khojarnāth. These famous images seem to have been of the three bodhisattvas Mañjuśrī, Avalokiteśvara, and Vajrapāṇi. Although the biography of Tangtong Gyalpo clearly states that Avalokiteśvara was the central image, it is more common to find the Mañjuśrī image described as the main figure of the triad. Some sources also mention Maitreya as the central image. The most detailed discussion of these images and the Khachar Temple, which was founded in 996, is Vitali (1996), 258–65. See also Heller (2003), which contains photographs of the images in the temple before their destruction, and of an exceptional thirteenth-century set of images that may have been copied from the Khachar originals.

729 Gyalti (Rgyal ti) was for centuries the capital of the kingdom of Purang. For a discussion of Gyalti and the other major castles of Purang, see Vitali (1996), 390–93.

730 Mangyul (Mang yul) is one of the three regions of Ngari in western Tibet.

731 Samdrup Tsé (Bsam grub rtse) was the fortress at Shigatsé (Gzhis ka rtse).

732 The Charnel Ground of Rāmeśvara (Dur khrod Ra me shwa ra) is one of the twenty-four holy pilgrimage sites according to the tantric tradition. See Wallace (2001), 78, for the conflicting opinions of where Rāmeśvara was located. Also see note 525 for Dezhung Rinpoché's comments about Tangtong's travels to various sacred sites such as Rāmeśvara. See the second part of the Introduction for more about the Severance (Gcod) teachings that Tangtong received from Vajravārāhī at Rāmeśvara.

733 The three white milk products are yogurt, milk, and butter.

734 The term *falling transmigration ('pho ltung)* refers to the eventual rebirth of gods in a lower realm, which entails severe suffering.

735 This prayer has been taken from Sherab Palden, *Ocean of Marvels*, 373–77, where it is not placed here in the story, but included later when Tangtong again tells the tale of this past life as the monk Padmākara. This second telling of the tale is also found in the translated biography, but without the prayer. The prayer is not found in Könchok Palsang and Dewa Sangpo, *Bright Lamp*.

736 The jasmine flower *(kun da)* is used as a metaphor for bodhicitta, or enlightenment mind *(kunda lta bu'i byang chub kyi sems)*.

737 The spelling *dbu logs* has been corrected in the translation to *dbu legs* as in Könchok Palsang and Dewa Sangpo, *Bright Lamp*, 312, where it is said to be the name of a monastery.

738 The Dradun Temple (Pra dun lha khang) is the same as Draduntsé (Spra dun rtse), one of the four ancient temples to "subdue the extremity" *(mtha' 'dul)* that were built by King Songtsen Gampo in the seventh century. This temple was built to pin down the right knee of the gigantic prone demoness whose body is said to cover the Tibetan plateau and beyond. Dradun is located west of Saga Dzong (Sa dga' rdzong) in the Ngari province of western Tibet. See Aris (1980), 23, etc.

739 The Bön monastery of Yungdrung Ling, founded by the master Nyima Gyaltsen, was one of the two main Bön monasteries in Central Tibet and Tsang during the later spread of the doctrine. See Losang Tsering, *Discussion of the History of Philosophical Tenets*, 28. According to Könchok Palsang and Dewa Sangpo, *Bright Lamp*, 317, the stūpa contained *dhāraṇī-mantra*s praying for the Buddhist teachings to decline and for the Bönpo teachings to spread.

740 In Sherab Palden, *Ocean of Marvels*, 319, when Tangtong Gyalpo said, "*Oṃ maṇi padme hūṃ*," the Bönpos became angry, shouted, "Recite your demon-language in heaven!" *(lha yul du 'dre skad labs)*, and threw him down from the stūpa.

741 Tsanda (Tsha mda') is about twelve kilometers west of Dingri Langkor. See the map in Dorje (1999), 296. This Tsanda chieftain (Tsha mda' ba'i dpon po) was probably the patron of Tsang Nyön Heruka who is mentioned in Natsok Rangdrol, *Heart of the Sun Illuminating the Vajrayāna*, 52. A very similar event is also recorded on page 30 of the same text, where Tsang Nyön meets a ruler called Governor Horshakpa (Nang so Hor shag pa) at a ferry crossing. When questioned, Tsang Nyön replies with almost the exact words used by Tangtong Gyalpo in this episode. However, the meeting has a more auspicious ending than that in this biography.

742 According to Könchok Palsang and Dewa Sangpo, *Bright Lamp*, 296, when Tangtong Gyalpo said, "There's nothing to do about it" *(bya sa med)*, the chieftain and his attendants replied, "Oh, yes there is!" *(bya sa yod)*, and attacked him.

743 The White Mausoleum (Sku gdung dkar po) is the shrine where the remains of the Indian master Dampa or Padampa Sangyé (Pha Dam pa sang rgyas, d. 1105) were kept at Dingri Langkor, 182 kilometers from the Tibetan border with Nepal. Sherab Palden, *Ocean of Marvels*, 320–21, and Könchok Palsang and Dewa Sangpo, *Bright Lamp*, 296–97, describe Tangtong Gyalpo's vision of buddhas

and wealth deities at Padampa's mausoleum or reliquary that was in the form of a Stūpa of Great Enlightenment with three levels.

744 Lapchi (La phyi) is a valley south of Dingri Langkor in the Mount Everest region, where the great yogin Milarepa spent much time in meditation. Many Kagyü hermitages were later developed in the region. Also see Dorje (1999), 303. The Kagyü master Lapchiwa Namkha Gyaltsen (La phyi ba Nam mkha' rgyal mtshan, 1382–1447) was the main disciple of the Drigung hierarch Nyernyipa Chökyi Gyalpo (Nyer gnyis pa Chos kyi rgyal po, 1395–1467). Namkha Gyaltsen lived for thirty-one years practicing meditation at Lapchi. For a short biography of Namkha Gyaltsen, see Tenzin Pemai Gyaltsen, *Golden Rosary*, 137–39. Guru Drakpotsel (Gu ru Drag po rtsal), or Dorjé Drakpotsel, is a wrathful aspect of Guru Padmasambhava who manifests in blue or red color, usually carrying a meteorite vajra in the right hand and a nine-headed scorpion in the left hand.

745 Drin Chuwar (Brin Chu dbar) is where Milarepa passed away. Also see Könchok Palsang and Dewa Sangpo, *Bright Lamp*, 297. The goddess Tashi Tseringma (Bkra shis tshe ring ma) is the leader of the Five Sisters of Long Life. See the following note.

746 The Five Sisters of Long Life (Tshe ring mched lnga) are goddesses who became disciples and consorts of Milarepa and have been guardians of his lineage of the Kagyü tradition ever since. The leading goddess is Tashi Tseringma (Bkra shis tshe ring ma), and her four sisters are Tingi Shalsangma (Mthing gi zhal bzang ma), Miyo Losangma (Mi g.yo blo bzang ma), Chöpan Drinsangma (Cod pan mgrin bzang ma), and Tekar Drosangma (Gtad dkar 'gro bzang ma).

747 Sherab Palden, *Ocean of Marvels*, 322, says it was the first month of a Dragon Year *('brug lo zla ba dang po)*, but mentions no age for Tangtong Gyalpo.

748 See note 334 concerning Tangtong Gyalpo's teacher Ka Ngapa Paljor Sherab.

749 Potala is the paradise of Avalokiteśvara.

750 The Jangpa brothers (Byang pa sku mched) were the Jang governor Namgyal Draksang (1395–1475) and his brother Könchok Lekpai Gyaltsen Pal Sangpo (Dkon mchog legs pa'i rgyal mtshan dpal bzang po, d. 1468). See note 763 for information about Namgyal Sangpo. Yeru Jang (G.yas ru Byang) is another name for the region of Latö Jang. Tangtong's monastery of Riwoché was in the Chung (Gcung) Valley of the Jang district, and the Chungpa patron was probably the local chieftain or a rich patron of the area.

751 Tsenden Ridröma (Mtshan ldan ri khrod ma) was a hermitess in the lineage of the Fivefold Mahāmudrā (Phyag chen lnga ldan) of the Drigung Kagyü tradition. In Author Unknown, *Biography of the Venerable Lady Chökyi Drönma*, 116b–18a, Tangtong Gyalpo himself tells the wonderful story of Kashipa Namkha Öser (Bka' bzhi pa Nam mkha' 'od zer) and his meeting with the old yoginī in retreat. Tangtong received the Fivefold Mahāmudrā teachings from Chokden Lekpai Lodrö (Mchog ldan legs pa'i blo gros or Mchog bzang legs pa'i blo gros), who had received them from Kashipa Namkha Öser.

752 The Teacher Śākyamuni Buddha and his two disciples Śāriputra and Maudgalyāyana.

753 Some of these tales are given in Sherab Palden, *Ocean of Marvels*, 328–29. When Tangtong left the retreat place and came into town, many weavers and others said that he had come from hell, that he was a hungry ghost, and that he was a demon. He did not speak to them, but crossed the Dok River seated on a dogskin. Some children saw him and, because he had gone straight across the water, said he was a demon.

754 Ngorchen Kunga Sangpo (Ngor chen Kun dga' bzang po, 1382–1456) was one of the most influential masters of the Sakya tradition. He founded the monastery of Ngor Gönsar (Ngor dgon gsar) in 1429, which became the main monastery of the Ngor subsect of the Sakya tradition. Ngorchen was particularly expert in the Sakya teachings of the Path with the Result (Lam 'bras), which he gave eighty times.

755 According to Sherab Palden, *Ocean of Marvels*, 101–2, Tangtong received all the teachings of the Path with the Result (Lam 'bras) from Ngorchen.

756 The oath-bound Dorjé Lekpa (Dam can Rdo rje legs pa) is one of the four main Dharma protectors of the Nyingma tradition. The other three are Gönpo Maning, Ekajaṭī, and Rāhula.

757 Shang Sambulung (Shangs Zam bu lung) is considered the principal pilgrimage site in all of the Tsang region. It is especially associated with Guru Padmasambhava and the Nyingma treasure tradition. See Ferrari (1958), 69, and Dorje (1999), 251. The genyen *(dge bsnyen)* are a tribe of mountain-gods that were bound to oaths by Guru Padmasambhava. Genyen Dölpo (Dge bsnyen gdol pa) would seem to be the leader of the twenty-one genyen spirits. See the many entries under *dge bsnyen* in Nebesky-Wojkowitz (1956), especially 222–23, which deals with the twenty-one.

758 The term *sku 'khyos* is glossed in the Tibetan text as a polite term for *gift (phyag 'bab kyi ming).*

759 Sherab Palden, *Ocean of Marvels*, 329, only says it was a Dragon Year *('brug lo).*

760 The text actually says Nyida Sangpo (Nyi zla bzang po), which is an obvious spelling mistake for Nyima Sangpo (Nyi ma bzang po), Tangtong Gyalpo's son and main Dharma heir. Very little is known of Nyima Sangpo except what is mentioned in the various biographies of his father. Nyima Sangpo's mother was one of Tangtong's consorts known as Khandroma Sengé (Mkha' 'gro ma Seng ge). She had prophesied that she would give birth to a son named Nyima Sangpo (Nyi ma bzang po) who would uphold and spread Tangtong's tradition. This woman was said to have been in essence Yigé Drugma (Yi ge drug ma), the consort of Avalokiteśvara. See Könchok Palsang and Dewa Sangpo, *Bright Lamp*, 130–31.

761 This complete date was taken from Sherab Palden, *Ocean of Marvels*, 331.

762 This attack was described above. Also see note 741.

763 The Kalkī Namgyal Drakpa Sangpo (Rigs ldan Rnam rgyal grags pa bzang po, 1395–1475) was the grandson of Gugum Rinchen Gyaltsen (Gus gum Rin chen rgyal mtshan), the governor of the Jang district who had advised Tangtong Gyalpo's parents to send him to the monastery when he was a boy. Namgyal Draksang also ruled the Jang district and was a master of the Kālacakra tradition and one of the most important physicians in Tibetan history. He received the title Tai Situ (Ta'i si tu) from the Ming emperor of China, and was also known by the epithets Kalkī Puṇḍarīka (Rigs ldan Padma dkar po) and Mahākalkī (Rigs ldan chen po), allusions to his identity with the Kalkī emperor of Shambhala known as Puṇḍarīka. From a young age Namgyal Drakpa engaged in intensive studies under masters such as Tangtong's teacher Ka Ngapa Paljor Sherab, the Indian Mahāpaṇḍita Vanaratna (1384–1468), and Bodong Panchen Cholé Namgyal (Bo dong paṇ chen Phyogs las rnam rgyal, 1376–1451). From about 1435, he began ambitious projects at the Jang capital of Ngamring, such as the construction of a large three-dimensional Kālacakra maṇḍala created from gold and silver and adorned with jewels. Together with his brother Könchok Lekpai Gyaltsen Pal Sangpo (Dkon mchog legs pa'i rgyal mtshan dpal bzang po, d. 1468), he completed a huge image of the future buddha Maitreya at Ngamring in 1466. Namgyal Draksang composed many treatises, especially concerning the Kālacakra tradition of meditation and astrology, and also wrote many medical texts. For the main biography of Namgyal Draksang, see Kunga Drolchok, *Melodious Dragon Roar of Highest Praise.* Also see Palden Chökyi Sangpo, *Series of Jewels*, 184–86, and Sangyé Gyatso, *Banquet to Delight the Seers*, 306–12.

764 The translation of the term *kar gzugs* as *porcelain cups* is somewhat uncertain. Sherab Palden, *Ocean of Marvels*, 343, has the spelling *dkar gzugs*. Shelkar Gyantsé (Shel dkar rgyal rtse) was the capital of the district of Latö Lho (La stod Lho), ruled at this time by Tai Situ Sönam Pak (Ta'i si tu Bsod nams 'phags).

765 Governor Norsangpa (Nang so Nor bzang pa, 1403–66) was at this time still a minister at the court of the Pakmodru rulers of Tibet. His Rinpung family would later overthrow the Pakmodru dynasty and rule Tibet. For a sketch of Norsangpa's life, see Losang Trinlé, *Clarification of Knowledge*, 1915–16.

766 A *load (khal)* is a unit of measure equivalent to about twenty-five to thirty pounds or twelve to fourteen kilos. In Sherab Palden, *Ocean of Marvels*, 331–32, Tangtong explains at length the causes and symptoms of the famine, linking it to the degenerate behavior of people at the time.

767 According to Sherab Palden, *Ocean of Marvels*, 333, although the Jowo image had many other golden offering items, it had no alms bowl at that time. Could the alms bowl that Tangtong Gyalpo offered be the one that continued to be held by the Jowo for centuries thereafter?

768 See note 658 for information about the patroness Kalsang, wife of the Lhasa ruler.

769 Twenty *measures (bre)* are equivalent to one *load (khal)*, which is equivalent to about twenty-five to thirty pounds or twelve to fourteen kilos.

770 Sherab Palden, *Ocean of Marvels*, 336, adds the fascinating detail that during that time Tangtong Gyalpo dressed as a monk in the mornings and as a yogin in the afternoons. This would be considered very eccentric behavior.

771 Gangādevī (Gang gā'i lha mo) is the Ganges River of India personified as a goddess.

772 See note 478 about the pilgrimages from Sakya to Lhasa, one of which Tangtong Gyalpo had joined as described earlier in the biography. Sherab Palden, *Ocean of Marvels*, 340, just says "many" thousands of pilgrims *(stong phrag du ma)*.

773 These three texts are indicated by the extremely abbreviated expression *'Jam sdud bzang*, mentioning only one word from each title. *Litany of the Names of Mañjuśrī (Mañjuśrījñānasattvasyaparamārthanāmasaṃgīti. 'Jam dpal ye shes sems dpa'i don dam pa'i mtshan yang dag par brjod pa)*, Toh 360, Kangyur, rgyud 'bum, *ka*, 1b–13b. *Condensed Verses on the Perfection of Wisdom (Prajñāpāramitāsañcayagātha. 'Phags pa shes rab kyi pha rol tu phyin pa sdud pa tshigs su bcad pa)*, Toh 13, Kangyur, sher phyin, *ka*, 1b–19b. *Prayer of Good Conduct (Āryabhadracaryāpraṇidhāna. 'Phags pa bzang po spyod pa'i smon lam gyi rgyal po)*, Toh 1095, Kangyur, gzungs 'dus, *waṃ*, 262b–266a. The lords of the three spiritual families *(rigs gsum mgon po)* are the bodhisattvas Avalokiteśvara, Mañjuśrī, and Vajrapāṇi.

774 Governor Drakwang of Neu Dzong (Sne'u rdzong pa Grags dbang) is the same as Drungchen Drakpa Palsang, who had received his grant to rule the Lhasa area from the Pakmodru sovereign Drakpa Jungné (1414–45). For more information about this ruler, his wife Kalsang, and their family, see note 658.

775 Guru Lhakhang (Gu ru lha khang) is a temple in western Lhodrak (Lho brag) where the famous treasure revealer Guru Chökyi Wanchuk (1212–70) lived. See Ferrari (1958), 58. Layak in Lho (Lho La yag) is an area of nomadic communities northeast of Mount Everest who have a distinct language and dress of their own. See Aris (1980), xiii.

776 The mountain of the local spirit Kulahari (Gzhi bdag Sku la ha ri) is mentioned in Aris (1988), 58, with a somewhat different spelling. For more detailed information on this specific deity, who is one of the four main mountain-spirits *(sku la)*, see Nebesky-Wojkowitz (1956), 203–4. Pemaling (Padma gling) is a famous lake in the Lhodrak region, said to be one of the four great lakes. The other three lakes are Kyem (Skyems), Yamdrok (Yar 'brog), and Namtso (Gnam mtsho). See Ferrari (1958), 57–58, 139. Könchok Palsang and Dewa Sangpo, *Bright Lamp*, 280, say Guru Padmasambhava's handprint was in a stone in the lake.

777 This is one of Tangtong Gyalpo's treasure texts that seem to have been lost centuries ago.

778 Sekhar Gutok (Sras mkhar dgu thog) is the famous nine-storied tower built by Milarepa for his teacher Marpa Lotsāwa (Mar pa Lo tsā ba, 1012–93?). Marpa was one of the most important translators and masters during the later spread of Buddhism in Tibet and is revered as the forefather of the Kagyü tradition in Tibet. The building of the tower is described in Milarepa's biography. For a translation of Tsang Nyön Heruka's biography of Milarepa, see Lhalungpa (1977). See Tsang Nyön

Heruka (1982) for a translation of the biography of Marpa Lotsāwa. Mahāmāyā is a deity of the unexcelled yoga tantra class.

779 Mön Bumtang (Mon Bum thang) is the location of an ancient temple built in Bhutan during the reign of the Tibetan king Songtsen Gampo. It was constructed according to geomantic principles, specifically to pin down the left knee of the gigantic demoness whose prone body is believed to cover the Tibetan plateau.

780 Lhodrak (Lho brag) is a large province south of the Chongyé ('Phyongs rgyas) Valley and bordering on Bhutan. Kharchu (Mkhar chu) is an important site in Lhodrak on the Tibetan border with Bhutan. Guru Padmasambhava meditated in a cave at Kharchu and the eighth-century master Namkhai Nyingpo (Nam mkha'i snying po) was exiled and meditated in another cave there. Chakpurchen (Lcags phur can), "Iron Dagger Cave," is a cave at Kharchu where the treasure master Guru Chökyi Wangchuk (1212–70) is said to have extracted a ritual dagger of meteorite iron from the stone.

781 The eight-branch vow of renewal and purification *(bsnyen gnas yan lag brgyad=gso sbyong yan lag brgyad)* is abstinence from killing, theft, lying, and sexual misconduct, as well as abstinence from alcohol, dancing and decoration, high expensive seats or beds, and food in the afternoon. See Dorje and Kapstein (1991), 162.

782 Nyal (Dmyal or Gnyal) is the Nyal river valley in southeastern Lhokha (Lho kha) near the border of Bhutan. The stūpa of Serché in lower Nyal (Dmyal smad gser phye 'bum pa) was apparently a famous holy site. See Jangchup Tsemo, *Virtuous at the Beginning, End, and Middle*, 44a, where the Sakya master Lama Dampa Sönam Gyaltsen (Bla ma dam pa Bsod nams rgyal mtshan, 1312–75) is described as making extensive offerings and prayers at the monument in 1367 and commenting upon how remarkable it was.

783 See note 558 concerning the ten fundamental subjects.

784 Könchok Palsang and Dewa Sangpo, *Bright Lamp*, 283, say Tangtong Gyalpo had pulled his cloak over his head and was resting in a state free from conceptual elaborations *(spros med)*. Then the monks unwrapped the cloak from his head, called him a fake *(zog po)*, and made the other abusive comments in the translated biography.

785 Tangtong Gyalpo used "any trick in the book" to get people to be good. He once told Delek Chödren, who was the attendant of his consort Chökyi Drönmé, "I have never tricked and lied to people who practice Dharma. I have done whatever was necessary to tame those who don't practice Dharma." See Author Unknown. *Biography of the Venerable Lady Chökyi Drönma*, 118b: *nga chos byed pa'i mi la mgo skor dang brdzun byed ma myong/ chos mi byed pa rnams la gang la gang 'dul byas pa lags.* In one of his edicts, Tangtong also says, "I've tricked those who have no faith, urging them toward virtue." See Könchok Palsang and Dewa Sangpo, *Bright Lamp*, 288: *dad med rnams la mgo bskor byas dge ba skul.*

786 The four styles of enlightened action are peaceful, enriching, powerful, and terrible.

787 These lines are from the Mind Training instructions (Blo sbyong) of Sumpa Lotsāwa Darma Yönten (Sum pa Lo tsā ba Dar ma yon tan, twelfth–thirteenth

centuries). When he was about to return from India to Tibet, Sumpa Lotsāwa was suddenly overwhelmed by anxiety about what to do at the point of death. After all other remedies failed, he went to make offerings at the Mahābodhi temple of Bodhgayā. In the sky above the temple he saw a blue woman and a red woman. The blue woman prostrated to the red woman and said, "I'm unhappy day and night. My mind doesn't stay where it's put. In general, it would be better if there were no death. This death is terrifying." The red woman then looked directly at Sumpa Lotsāwa and spoke the lines repeated in our text by Tangtong Gyalpo. Upon hearing her words, an exceptional realization arose in Sumpa Lotsāwa's mind. The red woman was Vajravārāhī and the blue woman was Tārā. See Kunga Drolchok, *Lineage History of the One Hundred Guiding Instructions*, 315–16, and *Text of the One Hundred and Eight Profound Guiding Instructions*, 379–80. For a translation of Sumpa Lotsāwa's Mind Training, see Gyalchok and Gyaltsen (2006), 215–16.

788 For the Jar (Byar) Valley north of Nyal (Gnyal), see Ferrari (1958), 51, 127. Rechungpa (Ras chung pa Rdo rje grags, 1083–1161) was a chief disciple of Milarepa. Amitāyus (Tshe dpag med) is the buddha of infinite life.

789 Loro (Lo ro) is in the same general area as Nyal and Jar in southeast Tibet. See Ferrari (1958), 51, 127.

790 Drakyang Dzong (Sgrag yang rdzong) is a famous meditation cave of Guru Padmasambhava in the upper Drak Valley on the north side of the Tsangpo River west of Samyé. Two of Padmasambhava's major disciples, Nubchen Sangyé Yeshé (Gnubs chen Sangs rgyas ye shes) and Dorjé Dujom (Rdo rje bdud 'joms), practiced meditation there. This cave was a site of many discoveries of hidden Dharma treasures and has continued to be an important meditation place. Also see Dorje (1999), 190–91.

791 Pañjaranātha and the Six-armed Protector are two forms of Mahākāla. Lekden (Legs ldan) is the protector Dorjé Lekpa, one of the main protectors of the Nyingma tradition. See Nebesky-Wojkowitz (1956), 154–59. Vaiśravaṇa is a wealth deity and also a protector of the nothern quarter of the world. The eight yakṣa horsemen (Snod sbyin rta bdag brgyad) are the entourage of Vaiśravaṇa. See Nebesky-Wojkowitz (1956), 68–81, for information on the various forms and functions of Vaiśravaṇa.

792 Gongkar (Gong dkar) is the district immediately to the east of Chuwori on the south side of the Tsangpo River in Central Tibet. It was one of the thirteen ancient districts in Tibet.

793 The complete date is originally from Sherab Palden, *Ocean of Marvels*, 344.

794 The man was a follower of the Jonang tradition of Tibetan Buddhism.

795 Opening the Door to the Sky (Nam mkha' sgo 'byed) is a special practice for the transference of consciousness *('pho ba)* according to the Severance, or Chöd (Gcod), tradition. It is considered to be the most profound essence of the Severance teachings, and one hundred times superior to ordinary transference practices. See Harding (2003), 50. Tangtong Gyalpo received an extraordinary version

of this practice from Machik Labdrön herself in a vision at the Charnel Ground of Rāmeśvara in Kashmir. See Khetsun Tenpai Gyaltsen, *Extensive Initiation for the Blessing of Opening the Door to the Sky.*

796 See note 567 for information about Lama Lotsāwa, who was one of Tangtong Gyalpo's earliest disciples. Sherab Palden, *Ocean of Marvels*, 347, says (Lama) Lotsāwa and the Lo man Gyalgyal (Blo>Klo Rgyal rgyal) conferred and then gathered the others. Lama Gyalgyal had been one of Tangtong's attendants when he traveled from Kongpo into the barbarian regions of Lo. See Sherab Palden, *Ocean of Marvels*, 239.

797 The three representations *(rten gsum)* are of the enlightened body, speech, and mind of the buddhas.

798 The basic instruction of *Taking Happiness and Suffering as the Path* (*Skyid sdug lam khyer)* is a set of couplets spoken by the Kashmiri mahāpaṇḍita Śākyaśrī (1127–1225) on his way to Tibet: "If I'm happy, I will dedicate the joy to the assembly. May benefit and joy fill the sky! If I'm suffering, I will take on the suffering of everyone. May the ocean of suffering dry up!" For the story of this Mind Training instruction, see Kunga Drolchok, *Lineage History of the One Hundred Guiding Instructions*, 315. For the instruction itself, see Gyalchok and Gyaltsen (2006), 213–14.

799 See note 297 for the eighteen freedoms and endowments.

800 It is taught that prosperity in the present life comes only from generosity practiced in a past life.

801 Tangtong Gyalpo poetically refers to the dharmakāya reality body as the famous Mahābodhi (Great Enlightenment) image of Buddha Śākyamuni at the Vajrāsana of Bodhgayā in India. This is more explicit in Könchok Palsang and Dewa Sangpo, *Bright Lamp*, 375, where the lines are somewhat different: "Before the Vajrāsana of immutable mind, sits the Mahābodhi of the dharmakāya reality body." Dezhung Rinpoché noted that the phrase *immutable universal ground (kun gzhi 'gyur med)* was an indication of the *shentong (gzhan stong)* view that reality is empty only of other relative, changing phenomena.

802 I have translated this line according to the suggestion of Dezhung Rinpoché, who corrected the reading *spyod pa byed pa*, which is found in the Dergé edition, to *spyod pa byed sa.*

803 The importance of the human body is emphasized in the unexcelled yoga tantras because it is the indispensable basis for the attainment of enlightenment. If the inherent potential of a human being is actualized, the result is a transformation of the ordinary illusory body *(sgyu lus)* into an indestructible vajra body *(rdo rje lus).* The spiritual heroes and ḍākinīs *(dpa' bo mkha' 'gro)* reside in external locations and are also present in the human body in the form of the essential constituents and vital winds. In an external sense, the twenty-four sacred places are located at specific sites in India, Tibet, and the Himalayan regions. In the esoteric sense, they exist in each human body. For these sacred sites and their locations, see Snellgrove (1959), vol. 1: 68–70, Tsuda (1974), 260–63, Wallace (2001), 76–85, and Zangpo (2001) 63–73.

804 That is, a singer can be eloquent without understanding a single word of his song.

805 Also see Namkha, *Twenty-five Points to Carry on the Path.* According to this text in *Tangtong's Oral Transmission,* demons *('dre)* should be seen as the master, because just as the master first causes you to begin a religious life by urging you toward Dharma, so also as a result of the harm or illness caused by a demon you practice deity meditation, recitation of mantra, devotion, and other virtuous activities. In this way, demons lead you along the spiritual path, as does the master. Demons are also to be seen as the chosen deity, because just as you are granted attainments as a result of offering prayers to the chosen deity, so also as a result of illness brought upon your body by a demon, your obscurations are purified. Furthermore, when obstacles and problems occur, by instantly pursuing them you realize that they are empty of any true nature. Thus your problems are actually agents that bring about self-transformation.

806 Ja (Bya) or Jayul (Bya yul) is an area south of the Dakpo (Dwags po) and Yarlung (Yar lung) regions of southcentral Tibet.

807 Könchok Palsang and Dewa Sangpo, *Bright Lamp,* 287–91, give the names of six disciples who were designated "major disciples" *(bu chen)* at this time, and reproduces the complete text of the edict *(bka' shog)* given to each of them. Three of the major disciples were sent to gather offerings. Chödrak Palsang was sent to Tangtong Gyalpo's birthplace to commission a copy of the Translated Scriptures (not the Translated Treatises as mentioned in the translated biography), Namgyal Sangpo was sent to build a stūpa at Salmogang in Dokham and iron bridges on the Dzachu (Rdza chu) and Drichu ('Bri chu) Rivers, and Kachupa Gyaltsen Sangpo was appointed to the monastic seat at Chuwori.

808 The Shiga Neupa (Gzhis ka Sne'u pa) ruler Drungchen Drakpa Palsang was the governor of the Lhasa area at this time. See note 658 for more information about this ruler and his family. The demon *(gnyan)* Kharnak (Mkhar nag) is said to be the son of the nāga king Dungkyong (Śaṅkhapāla; Dung skyong), one of the eight nāga kings. His domain is about twenty miles west of Lhasa, at the confluence of the Tölung and Kyichu Rivers. See Epstein (1968), 71.

809 Drak Lhadong (Brag Lha gdong) is the place where a ferryman had hit Tangtong Gyalpo over the head with an oar and thrown him into the river when he was returning from Tsel Gungtang earlier in his life.

810 Könchok Palsang and Dewa Sangpo, *Bright Lamp,* 272, also mention that one blacksmith fell into the river and drowned during the attempt to raise the chains.

811 After saying that the eight tribes of gods and spirits raised the bridge, Könchok Palsang and Dewa Sangpo, *Bright Lamp,* 273, note that the monks and craftsmen present at the time could not explain how the bridge had been raised.

812 Sherab Palden, *Ocean of Marvels,* 358, just says that the iron bridge was completed on the tenth day of the second month of a Mouse Year *(byi lo)* after six years, one month, and ten days of work.

813 Könchok Palsang and Dewa Sangpo, *Bright Lamp*, 273, describe the miraculous consecration in some detail, even noting that deities were clearly visible on each stone of the bridge abutment *(zam phung)* and that the river stopped flowing.

814 Lake Namtso Chukmo (Gnam mtsho phyug mo) is a huge lake to the northwest of Lhasa. See Dorje (1999), 139.

815 As mentioned above, Tangtong Gyalpo had vowed in 1438 to remain in retreat at Chuwori until the completion of the bridge, which was accomplished in 1444.

816 A *phul* is a measurement of volume equivalent to about one cupped handful or one sixth of a "measure" *(bre)*, which is equivalent to about 1.35 pounds or 650 grams.

817 As mentioned above in the biography, in about 1437 the people of Gongkar had stolen most of the iron that Tangtong Gyalpo had shipped back from Bhutan to build the iron bridge at Chuwori. According to Kunga Dorjé, *Red Annals*, 94, the Gongkar governor Lhawang Kunga (Lha dbang kun dga') was present at the new year festivities at Nedong (Sne gdong) in the Iron Ox Year *(lcags mo glang)* of 1481. The Gongkar governor Lhawang Paljor mentioned in the biography could be this same ruler or one of his predecessors. Also see Könchok Palsang and Dewa Sangpo, *Bright Lamp*, 338, for the same event.

818 Tölung (Stod lung) is a valley to the west of Lhasa.

819 Rongtön Sheja Kunrik (Rong ston Shes bya kun rig, 1367–1449) was one of the most important masters of the Sakya tradition. He was famed as an emanation of the future buddha Maitreya. In 1436, Rongtön founded the monastery of Nālendra in Penyul ('Phan yul), north of Lhasa. He composed more than three hundred works and is said to have reached the sixth spiritual level *(bhūmi)*. A much more detailed version of his meeting with Tangtong Gyalpo has been translated in the fourth part of the Introduction. An earlier meeting between the two masters at the monastery of Sangpu (Gsang phu) is recorded in Sherab Palden, *Ocean of Marvels*, 173–75, where Tangtong gives a verse teaching to Rongtön that is identical to many of the verses in the teaching he gives on pages 112–13 of the translated biography, where it is presented as an instruction given to a scholar of Drepung Monastery.

820 Ratreng (Rwa sgreng) Monastery was founded in 1056 by Dromtön ('Brom ston Rgyal ba'i 'byung gnas, 1005–64), and became the main seat of the Kadampa tradition.

821 The *Kadam Volumes (Bka' gdams glegs bam)* are a two-volume collection of the fundamental instructions of the Kadampa tradition. The first volume, known as the Father's Dharma *(pha chos)*, is mainly the questions of Dromtön, who was the founder of the Kadampa tradition, and his teacher Atiśa's (982–1054) replies. The second volume, known as the Son's Dharma *(bu chos)*, is basically the questions of Ngog Lekpai Sherab (Rngog Legs pa'i shes rab) and Kutön Tsöndru Yungdrung (Khu ston Brtson 'grus g.yung drung, 1011–75), and their teacher Atiśa's replies. See Losang Trinlé, *Clarification of Knowledge*, 164, 167–68.

822 *Prayer of Good Conduct (Āryabhadracaryāpraṇidhāna. 'Phags pa bzang po spyod pa'i smon lam gyi rgyal po)*, Toh 1095, Kangyur, gzungs 'dus, *waṃ*, 262b–266a. Atiśa

(982–1054) was a great Indian master from Bengal who came to Tibet in 1042 and was the most important figure in the revival of Tibetan Buddhism. The Kadampa tradition in particular followed his teachings. Dromtön (’Brom ston Rgyal ba’i ’byung gnas, 1005–64) was the most important of Atiśa’s Tibetan disciples. Kutön (Khu ston Brtson ’grus g.yung drung, 1011–75) was another of Atiśa’s three main Tibetan disciples.

823 The monastery of Taklung (Stag lung) was founded north of Lhasa in 1180 by Tashi Pal (Bkra shis dpal, 1142–1210), a disciple of Pakmodrupa Dorjé Gyalpo (1110–70). The Taklung Kagyü tradition is one of the eight minor branches of the Kagyü School.

824 The Drigung (’Bri gung) monastery of Drigung Til, northeast of Lhasa, is the main center of the Drigung Kagyü tradition. A small hermitage was first established here in 1167 by Minyak Gomring, and the monastery itself was founded in 1179 by Kyopa Jikten Gönpo (Skyob pa ’Jig rten mgon po, 1143–1217), who was a disciple of Pakmodrupa Dorjé Gyalpo.

825 The *śāsana* mantra is the long mantra of Mahākāla. Tangtong Gyalpo manifested in the form of the four-armed Mahākāla, which is mostly practiced in the various Kagyü traditions.

826 The Drigung hierarch that Tangtong Gyalpo met was probably Nyernyipa Chökyi Gyalpo (Nyer gnyis pa Chos kyi rgyal po, 1395–1467), the teacher of Lapchiwa Namkha Gyaltsen (La phyi ba Nam mkha’ rgyal mtshan), whom Tangtong had met earlier when visiting the Lapchi area. At this time the leadership of the Drigung tradition was still a hereditary role passed down in the Kyura (Skyu ra) family line of Jikten Gönpo.

827 See Tenzin Pemai Gyaltsen, *Golden Rosary*, 140–41, 144–45, 158–59, for reference to the future disasters that occurred at Drigung. Many of the teaching lineages of the Drigungpa were later broken at Drigung itself, and had to be sought elsewhere and revived.

828 Drigung Jikten Gönpo (’Bri gung ’Jig rten mgon po, Rin chen dpal, 1143–1217), also known as Kyopa Jikten Gönpo, was the founder of Drigung Monastery and the Drigung Kagyü tradition.

829 A *measure (bre)* is equivalent to about 1.35 pounds or 650 grams.

830 Vajradhara is called the sixth buddha because he is the pure essence of the five afflicting poisons of desire, hatred, ignorance, pride, and envy.

831 Also see Könchok Palsang and Dewa Sangpo, *Bright Lamp*, 249–50: “The sculptors replied, ‘O great adept. We can’t melt turquoise. We can’t beat turquoise. There’s no precedent in Tibet for making images by arranging pieces of turquoise. Please don’t *(’i>mi?)* show off the many turquoises you have.’

“The great adept said, ‘I have the oral instructions for making images from turquoise.’ He arranged and ground the turquoise, saying, ‘This is the way to make images by arranging pieces of turquoise according to the prophecy of the chosen deity.’”

832 The Gar style *(gar lugs)* is unknown. It cannot be the same as the Encampment style *(sgar lugs)*, which did not emerge until the sixteenth century.

833 According to the Fifth Dalai Lama, writing in 1645, the load of conch shells was offered by a woman from Minyak in Kham *(khams mo mi nyag ma)*, and the Avalokiteśvara image made from her conch shells was still enshrined in the inner sanctuary of the temple on Chakpori Hill, along with other relics and many images made from precious substances at this time. See Ngawang Losang Gyatso, *Crystal Mirror*, 45.

834 The Fivefold Naturally Arisen Jowo (Jo bo Rang byon lnga ldan) is a holy image of the eleven-faced Avalokiteśvara kept in the Jokhang in Lhasa. See note 538 for more information.

835 This story was told in more detail earlier in the biography. The prayer given in the text before was originally placed at this point in Sherab Palden, *Ocean of Marvels*, 373–77.

836 The "authentic skull-cup" *(thod pa mtshan ldan)* that Tangtong Gyalpo held in his hands during this visit to Tsari was a famous and mysterious holy object. It is particularly mentioned in the biographies of many Kagyü masters of the time, such as Trimkhang Lotsāwa Sönam Gyatso (Khrims khang Lo tsā ba Bsod nams rgya mtsho, 1424–82), Gö Lotsāwa Shönu Pal ('Gos Lo tsā ba Gzhon nu dpal, 1392–1481), and the Madman of Central Tibet, Ü Nyön Kunga Sangpo (Dbus smyon Kun dga' bzang po, 1458–1532). It is most often referred to as the "authentic small maroon skull-cup" *(mtshan ldan thod pa smug chung)*, but also as the "miraculous little vermilion skull-cup" *(ya mtshan thod pa 'tshal chung)*. For example, see Sherab Palden, *Ocean of Marvels*, 223, and Könchok Palsang and Dewa Sangpo, *Bright Lamp*, 247. Trimkhang Lotsāwa's biography contains detailed and fascinating descriptions of the relic and how it was venerated at the time. In Roerich (1976), 824, a note says this relic was the skull-cup made from the cranium of Milarepa. This is probably incorrect. None of the old Tibetan sources are clear about where the skull-cup came from, and at least one mentions that its origin was a mystery. See Chökyi Drakpa, *Ocean of Marvels*, 85a.

837 The venerable lady Chökyi Drönmé (Rje btsun Chos kyi sgron me, 1422–55) was the consort of Bodong Panchen and then Tangtong Gyalpo.

838 A *treasure-owner (gter bdag)* is a deity who has been entrusted with a hidden treasure *(gter ma)*. The *Bright Lamp (Gsal ba'i sgron me)* is the prophetic biography of Tangtong Gyalpo hidden as a treasure text by Guru Padmasambhava. The other text is one of Tangtong's lost treasures.

839 The Golden Temple of Buchu (Sbu chu gser gyi lha khang) is an ancient temple in the Kongpo region. It was built according to geomantic principles during the reign of King Songtsen Gampo specifically for the purpose of pinning down the right elbow of the gigantic demoness whose prone body is believed to cover the entire Tibetan plateau and beyond. The treasure revealer Jatsön Nyingpo ('Ja' tshon snying po, 1585–1656), who was born at Waru Namtsel in Kongpo, referred to Tangtong Gyalpo's visit to Buchu and quoted the prophecy given by the Jowo (which must be the image of the Eleven-faced Avalokiteśvara), but

in verse and considerably different than what is found in Tangtong's known biographies. Included in the prophecy is information about a future emanation of Tangtong, which Jatsön Nyingpo says prophesied his own appearance. The verses he quotes may have come from another unknown biography of Tangtong, since Jatsön Nyingpo refers to three short, medium, and long biographies. Several other unique points about Tangtong are mentioned in this text. See Jatsön Nyingpo, *Pavilion of Rainbow Light*, 29–33.

840 Yama (Gshin rje) is the Lord of Death. The yama are also a class of spirits.

841 The *three worlds (srid gsum)* are the realms above, upon, and below the earth.

842 In Könchok Palsang and Dewa Sangpo, *Bright Lamp*, 232–40, this entire episode, which includes the complete account of Tangtong Gyalpo's past life as King Drakpa Öser that Lochen Gyurmé Dechen moved from here to the beginning of the translated biography, was apparently spoken directly by Tangtong to the author. For example, the first person pronoun *(bdag)* is used here, saying the yogin and his retinue of women "said this to me." Dewa Sangpo specifically mentions at the end of the biography that he supplemented the earlier work of Könchok Palsang by adding the accounts of previous lifetimes that Tangtong had told him. See Könchok Palsang and Dewa Sangpo, *Bright Lamp*, 589.

843 The four māras *(bdud bzhi)* are of the afflictions, the Lord of Death, the aggregates, and the child of the gods. For some explanation of these, see Harding (2003) 34–38.

844 Mahottara Heruka (Che mchog Heruka) is the essential embodiment of the eight great herukas of the mahāyoga class of the Nyingma tantras. See Dudjom (1991), 475–83.

845 See note 103 concerning the adept Hūṃkara, who was one of the eight great adepts of India according to the Nyingma tradition.

846 The story of Tangtong Gyalpo's previous life in India as King Drakpa Öser was moved by Lochen Gyurmé Dechen from this context to the beginning of the translated biography. Tangtong originally told the story at this point as one of the one hundred thousand previous lifetimes he remembered. See Könchok Palsang and Dewa Sangpo, *Bright Lamp*, 233–40.

847 Lotsāwa is Lama Lotsāwa, one of Tangtong Gyalpo's earliest disciples. For more about this disciple, who seems to have been troublesome on several occasions, see notes 567 and 796. Also see Sherab Palden, *Ocean of Marvels*, 214.

848 The spelling *mi gcig* ("one person") is a mistake for *mig gcig* ("one eye").

849 The Gangdruk *(sgang drug)* are six main ridges and the regions between them in eastern Tibet.

850 The Dzachu (Rdza chu) is one of the major rivers in East Tibet, known as the Mekong River in China. The Drichu ('Bri chu) is another of the great rivers in East Tibet, known as the Yangtse River in China. See the following note for information about Salmogang (Zal mo sgang), and Dorje (1999), 432–37, for details about the Litang (Li thang) area.

851 An annotation was added here to the Dergé edition of the Tibetan text: "The Ling [Gling] mentioned here refers to the period when this fortress of Chakra [Lcags ra], a subject of Dergé in Dokham, was seized by Ling. This was approximately the period in which the 'Lingpa colleges' were formed in the Central Tibetan monasteries such as Ngor and Nālendra. The statement that the great adept constructed representations of enlightened body, speech, and mind at Salmogang [Zal mo sgang] specifically refers to this presently famous Dzadri Salmogang [Rdza 'bri Zal mo sgang] in the Sibgön [Srib dgon] of Dergé Lhundrup Teng [Sde dge Lhun grub steng] that is known as the Tangtong Temple. The great adept was eighty-six years old in this year. This annotation was written by the chief editor Tenzin Gyaltsen during the proofreading of this biography."

852 Lhalung Palgyi Dorjé (Lha lung Dpal gyi rdo rje) was the monk who assassinated the anti-Buddhist Tibetan king Langdarma in 842 and then fled to eastern Tibet. His special talisman, or spirit-turquoise *(bla g.yu)*, probably worn at the throat, was apparently given the name Flat Blue Sky (Gnam sngo leb).

853 Dartsedo (Dar rtse mdo) is a major center on the eastern border of Tibet and China. See Dorje (1999), 447–50.

854 This is the stūpa mentioned in the third part of the Introduction. It was later repaired by Gangkar Rinpoché Chökyi Sengé (1891–1957) after it had been destroyed by an earthquake.

855 For the following episode and verse instruction, also see Sherab Palden, *Ocean of Marvels*, 387–91. In Könchok Palsang and Dewa Sangpo, *Bright Lamp*, 218–20, the verse instruction is extremely different, and the substance of some verses is also found in the same text in one of Tangtong Gyalpo's edicts *(bka' shog)*, 520–21.

856 The Five-Peaked Mount Wutai (Ri bo rtse lnga, Wutaishan) is a famous mountain in China that is traditionally believed to be the home of the bodhisattva Mañjuśrī and is an important pilgrimage site.

857 According to Chogye Trichen Rinpoché, *vital winds of consciousness (rnam shes rlung)* is another term for *vital action winds (las rlung)*.

858 The four means of attraction *('du ba rnam bzhi)* are used by a teacher to attract others to the Dharma. These four are generosity, pleasant speech, helpfulness, and being agreeable.

859 My translation of these lines is influenced by the very different readings in Sherab Palden, *Ocean of Marvels*, 390, and Könchok Palsang and Dewa Sangpo, *Bright Lamp*, 219.

860 In Könchok Palsang and Dewa Sangpo, *Bright Lamp*, 520–21, detailed information is found about these four rivers and their courses in one of Tangtong Gyalpo's edicts. The four rivers are the Langpo Khabab (Glang po kha 'babs), Tachok Khabab (Rta mchog kha 'babs), Sengé Khabab (Seng ge kha 'babs), and Maja Khabab (Rma bya kha 'babs). See also Dorje (1999), 336–50.

861 For Drangsong Sinpori (Drang srong Srin po ri), see Ferrari (1958), 47, and Dorje (1999), 156. This mountain was famous because of a temple founded in the thir-

teenth century by the Indian master Vibhūticandra, who also fashioned a holy image of Cakrasaṃvara there. See Stearns (1996).

862 Samyé (Bsam yas) was the first Buddhist monastery in Tibet. It was built by King Trisong Detsen (Khri srong lde btsan) and Guru Padmasambhava in the late eighth century. For detailed information see Dorje (1999), 172–80.

863 Salmögang (Zal mo'i sgang) is the same as Salmogang. See note 851.

864 *Litany of the Names of Mañjuśrī (Mañjuśrījñānasattvasyaparamārthanāmasaṃgīti. 'Jam dpal ye shes sems dpa'i don dam pa'i mtshan yang dag par brjod pa)*, Toh 360, Kangyur, rgyud 'bum, *ka*, 1b–13b.

865 Könchok Palsang and Dewa Sangpo, *Bright Lamp*, 220, mention that Tangtong stayed in meditation at Mount Wutai for eight months, during which the vision of the different forms of Mañjuśrī occurred.

866 *Āryasaṃdhinirmocananāmamahāyānasūtra, 'Phags pa dgongs pa nges par 'grel pa zhes bya ba theg pa chen po'i mdo*, Toh 106, Kangyur, mdo sde, *ca*, 1b–55b. *Kūṭāgāra Sūtra, Khang bu brtsegs pa'i mdo*, Toh 332, Kangyur, mdo sde, *sa*, 260a–263b.

867 The emperor of China during this period was Chu Ch'i-chen (1427–64). He was the only Ming emperor to reign over two periods, Chen-t'ung (1436–49) and T'ien-shun (1457–64). Between these two reigns Chu Ch'i-chen was a captive of the Oirat Mongols for about a year and then kept in confinement while his brother ruled in his place. He regained the throne in 1457. His temple name was Ying-tsung. See Goodrich and Fang (1976), 289–94. Tangtong Gyalpo later sends a letter to the emperor, in which he refers to him by the epithet Source of Glory (Dpal gyi 'byung gnas). In Könchok Palsang and Dewa Sangpo, *Bright Lamp*, 416, Tangtong addresses the emperor as Chinese Emperor Piwang Kotra, Leonine Source of Glory (Rgya nag rgyal po Pi wang ko tra dpal gyi 'byung gnas seng ge).

868 Tangtong is probably referring to the five bodies of enlightenment *(sku lnga)* or buddhas that are at the heart of the maṇḍala of the one hundred peaceful and wrathful deities in the tradition of the Great Perfection. These are the forms of the sambhogakāya enjoyment body that emerge from the dharmakāya reality body mentioned in the previous verse, each of which are the lord of one of the five spiritual families.

869 The four styles of enlightened action are peaceful, enriching, powerful, and terrible.

870 The four immeasurables (*tshad med bzhi*) are love, compassion, joy, and equanimity.

871 The four pledges *(dam bca' bzhi)* have not been identified.

872 The Greater and Lesser Vehicles are the Mahāyāna and Hinayāna. The four summations of Dharma *(chos sdom bzhi)* teach that all composite things are impermanent, all afflictions cause suffering, all phenomena are empty and lack self-nature, and nirvāṇa is peace.

873 In Könchok Palsang and Dewa Sangpo, *Bright Lamp*, 223, Tangtong Gyalpo's comments contain much further prophetic information.

874 Construction of the imperial capital of Dadu (Tib: Ta'i tu) was ordered in 1266 by the Mongol emperor Kubilai Khan (1215–94). His new capital was located near the modern city of Beijing and came to be known as Dadu (Great Capital) in Chinese, Khanbalikh (City of the Khan) to the Turks, and Daidu to the Mongols. See Rossabi (1988), 131–35. *Litany of the Names of Mañjuśrī (Mañjuśrījñānasattvasya-paramārthanāmasaṃgīti. 'Jam dpal ye shes sems dpa'i don dam pa'i mtshan yang dag par brjod pa)*, Toh 360, Kangyur, rgyud 'bum, *ka*, 1b–13b.

875 This is one of the thirty-two marks of a buddha.

876 Könchok Palsang and Dewa Sangpo, *Bright Lamp*, 223, say the Sangha numbered about three thousand. The monastery of Riwoché (Ri bo che) in Kham was founded by Sangyé Ön (Sangs rgyas dbon, 1251–96) in 1276. It became the main monastery of the Taklung (Stag lung) tradition in Kham. See Smith (2001), 44. This monastery should not be confused with Tangtong Gyalpo's monastery of Riwoché in Latö Jang.

877 The five aggregates (*phung po lnga*) are form, feeling, discernment, conditioning factors, and consciousness.

878 The three vows *(sdom gsum)* are the vows of individual liberation, the bodhisattva vow, and the vows of secret mantra.

879 "Dharma of the gods" (*lha chos*) is an ancient term originally applied to the Bön (Bon) religion and then later to Buddhism. The term "Dharma of men" (*mi chos*) refers to the sixteen-point moral code established by King Songtsen Gampo in the seventh century, and was also applied to the indigenous popular traditions of Tibet. See Stein (1972a), 100, 192–97.

880 According to Buddhist cosmology, Mount Meru is surrounded by four continents: Jambudvīpa in the south, Pūrvavideha in the east, Aparagodanīya in the west, and Uttarakuru in the north.

881 Tsagong Palgyi Nesar was Tangtong Gyalpo's monastery at Tsagong in Kongpo.

882 The Stūpa of Great Enlightenment (Byang chub chen po'i mchod rten) is one of the eight styles of Buddhist stūpa monuments. It commemorates Śākyamuni Buddha's enlightenment and has a square base with four steps.

883 Riksum Gönpo (Rigs gsum mgon po) was one of Tangtong Gyalpo's earliest disciples.

884 As described earlier in the biography, Tangtong Gyalpo had previously visited Waru Namtsel and subdued the nāga king Varuṇa. The Drukpa Kagyü master Gyalwang Kunga Paljor (Rgyal dbang Kun dga' dpal 'byor, 1428–76) visited Waru Namtsel in about 1470, and made camp near the Auspicious Stūpa of Many Doors that Tangtong had built there. See *Dpal ldan bla ma dam pa'i mdzad pa rmad du byung ba ngo mtshar bdud rtsi'i thigs pa*, 25a, in volume 1 of the *Collected Works (gSung-'bum) of rGyal-dbang Kun-dga' dpal-'byor.* Thimphu: Kunzang Topgey,

1976. I cannot identify the author of this text because the book is no longer available to me.

885 See Ferrari (1958), 48, and Dorje (1999), 220–22, for descriptions of the region of Dakpo (Dwags po), south of the Tsangpo River.

886 Mount Sodang Gongpori (Zo dang gong po ri) is one of the four sacred mountains of Central Tibet, and is linked to the legendary origins of the Tibetan people. See Dorje (1999), 186. The first Pakmodru ruler, Tai Situ Jangchup Gyaltsen (Ta'i Si tu Byang chub rgyal mtshan, 1302–64), built the bridge of Nedong in the mid-fourteenth century.

887 The sixth Pakmodru sovereign, Drakpa Jungné (Gong ma Grags pa 'byung gnas, 1414–45), came to power in 1432 following the death of his predecessor Drakpa Gyaltsen. Soon after Drakpa Jungné's ascension to the throne, internal disputes and power struggles erupted within the dynasty, but he continued to rule until his death in 1445. For details about Drakpa Jungné's life and reign, see Sönam Drakpa, *Magical Key to Royal Genealogies*, 87–90, and Losang Trinlé, *Clarification of Knowledge*, 1524. The sovereign Drakpa Gyaltsen (Gong ma Grags pa rgyal mtshan, 1374–1432) was the fifth ruler of the Pakmodru dynasty, reigning over Tibet from 1385 until his death in 1432. Tangtong Gyalpo's meeting with Drakpa Gyaltsen and the promises the ruler made to him were described earlier in the biography. According to the sequence of events in the translated biography, the meeting with the ruler Drakpa Jungné occurred after Tangtong founded the monastery of Lhundrup Teng (Lhun grub steng) at Dergé in the eastern Kham region of Tibet in 1446. However, the Drakpa Jungné is known to have died in 1445. See also Könchok Palsang and Dewa Sangpo, *Bright Lamp*, 323–24. Sherab Palden, *Ocean of Marvels*, 413–18, places the meeting with the previous ruler Drakpa Gyaltsen at this point, including much of the following episode that is here connected with his successor, Drakpa Jungné.

888 The rulers of Ngari (Mnga' ris) in western Tibet were the descendants of the ancient kings of Tibet, but no longer held power except in their own district.

889 The Sakyapa masters of the Khön ('Khon) family held power in Tibet during the Yuan dynasty in China, but were overthrown by Tai Situ Jangchup Gyaltsen (1302–64), who founded the Pakmodru dynasty in Tibet.

890 Nedongpa (Sne gdong pa) is another name for the Pakmodrupa, based on the name of the ruler's residence at Nedong.

891 Könchok Palsang and Dewa Sangpo, *Bright Lamp*, 323, also say the horse was pregnant. In Sherab Palden, *Ocean of Marvels*, 416, Tangtong Gyalpo's statement is not given, but the horse offered to him is only described as "good" *(rta bzang pa)*, and not as a mare or as pregnant.

892 Mahāpaṇḍita Vanaratna (Pan chen Nags kyi rin chen, 1384–1468) was one of the last Indian masters to travel to Tibet. He was a major teacher of the Kālacakra tradition, and visited Tibet on four different occasions. Beginning in 1436 Vanaratna gave many teachings to the Pakmodru ruler Drakpa Jungné at the monastery of Tsetang (Rtse thang) and became one of his most important spiritual masters. A

sketch of Vanaratna's life can be found in Roerich (1976), 797–805. For details on Vanaratna's three trips to Tibet, see Ehrhard (2004). While Vanaratna was stranded in Nepal at the end of his life, Tangtong Gyalpo sent him a letter in which he refers to a previous meeting between himself, the paṇḍita, and the Gyantsé ruler Rabten Kunsang Pak at Pari. Tangtong also mentions that the King of Bhaktapur (Kho khom) was preventing Vanaratna from leaving Nepal for India, and prophesies the death of the paṇḍita in Nepal. See Könchok Palsang and Dewa Sangpo, *Bright Lamp*, 397–99.

893 The spelling *sngon zhus* should be corrected to *bsngo zhus* as found in the original episode in Vanaratna's biography. See Shönu Pal and Sönam Gyatso, *Biography of the Dharma Lord*, 39b.

894 The Tibetan text has the Sanskrit term *mahādhipati*, indicating the word that Vanaratna actually used.

895 Vanaratna's reply is quoted from the biography written by his disciple Trimkhang Lotsāwa Sönam Gyatso (Khrims khang Lo tsā ba Bsod nams rgya mtsho, 1424–82), which is a supplement to the biography written by Gö Lotsāwa Shönu Pal ('Gos Lo tsā ba Gzhon nu dpal, 1392–1481). See Shönu Pal and Sönam Gyatso, *Biography of the Dharma Lord*, 39b.

896 Lochen Trukhangpa (Lo chen Khrus khang pa) is another name for Trimkhang Lotsāwa Sönam Gyatso (Khrims khang Lo tsā ba Bsod nams rgya mtsho, 1424–82), the translator and teacher who often interpreted for Vanaratna during the Indian master's travels in Tibet. For Trimkhang Lotsāwa's life and activities, see Ehrhard (2002) and Roerich (1976), 805–38.

897 This entire quote is taken from Trimkhang Lotsāwa's biography of Vanaratna. See Shönu Pal and Sönam Gyatso, *Biography of the Dharma Lord*, 39b.

898 See note 571 for Samyé Chimpu (Bsam yas Mchims phu).

899 Lady Kalsang (Dpon mo Skal bzang) was the wife of the ruler of the Lhasa region and was one of Tangtong Gyalpo's main patrons.

900 The Nepa patron (*yon bdag* Sne pa) was the governor of the Lhasa region. As mentioned in note 658, Lady Kalsang's son was Drungchen Paljor Gyalpo (d. 1490), who received his position as governor *(rdzong dpon)* from the Pakmodru sovereign Drakpa Jungné (1414–45) and his brother, the seventh Pakmodru ruler, Kunga Lekpa (Kun dga' legs pa, 1433–83). See Ngawang Losang Gyatso, *Song of the Lark*, 175.

901 The spelling *gi* in the Tibetan text should be corrected to *shi*.

902 Also see Sherab Palden, *Ocean of Marvels*, 422. Lady Kalsang's son, the Nepa patron and governor Paljor Gyalpo, had three sons, one of whom died young. The two remaining sons were Ngawang Sönam Lhunpo (Ngag dbang bsod nams lhun po) and Ngawang Sönam Namgyal (Ngag dbang bsod nams rnam rgyal). See Ngawang Losang Gyatso, *Song of the Lark*, 175.

903 The governors of Latö Jang (La stod Byang) ruled the area where Tangtong Gyalpo had been born and where his monastery of Riwoché was located. The

Jang governor at this time was Namgyal Draksang (1395–1475), whose brother was Könchok Lekpai Gyaltsen Pal Sangpo (Dkon mchog legs pa'i rgyal mtshan dpal bzang po, d. 1468). Internecine quarrels between the Jangpa brothers were also mentioned previously in the biography.

904 Tangtong Gyalpo's comments can be understood as a prophecy of the future loss of the Nepa domain by Paljor Gyalpo's sons, Ngawang Sönam Lhunpo and Ngawang Sönam Namgyal. This occurred when the Rinpung (Rin spungs) prince Dönyö Dorjé (Don yod rdo rje, 1462–1512) invaded Central Tibet. See Ngawang Losang Gyatso, *Song of the Lark*, 175, and Losang Trinlé, *Clarification of Knowledge*, 1915.

905 Dokham Gangsum (Mdo khams sgang gsum) is a term used to refer to three of the six regions making up the Dokham area of East Tibet. The horse with the harelip had been offered to Tangtong when he was in Dokham before, and he had given instructions that anyone who rode it should be obeyed the same as himself.

906 See note 851 for Salmogang. The Dzachu (Rdza chu) is known in China as the Mekong River and the Drichu ('Bri chu) is known as the Yangtse River.

907 This is one of the images Tangtong Gyalpo created before from precious substances in Lhasa.

908 Also see Könchok Palsang and Dewa Sangpo, *Bright Lamp*, 288–90, for another edict given to disciples at this time. Tangtong specifically mentions in the edict that he had previously made twenty-eight distant journeys, ranging from Mount Wutai in China to the east, Tāmradvīpa (Zangs gling=Ceylon?) and the famous pilgrimage site of Śrīparvata (Dpal gyi ri bo) to the south in India, Kashmir (Kha che) to the west, and the four border regions to the north *(byang mtha' bzhi).*

909 Dīpaṃkara (Mar me mdzad) is the buddha Kāśyapa, third of the one thousand buddhas said to appear in this aeon. The King of the Śākyas is the historical Buddha Śākyamuni, who was born as a prince in the Śākya clan.

910 Sunlit Central Tibet (Nyi ma Dbus) would seem to be an archaic expression for Central Tibet (Dbus). The expression Sunlit Latö Jang (Nyi ma La stod byang) is also found in old biographies when referring to Latö Jang (La stod byang). For example, see Sherab Palden, *Ocean of Marvels*, 470.

911 Also see note 807, where these events and the investiture of Kachupa Gyaltsen Sangpo are mentioned. Compare Könchok Palsang and Dewa Sangpo, *Bright Lamp*, 324–26, where the full edict *(bka' lung)* is reproduced, but is very different. It includes a list of seventeen disciples in three groups and also mentions the completion of a Maitreya image inlaid with ten pieces of lapis lazuli, three hundred pieces of coral, five hundred pieces of medium turquoise, five hundred pieces of old turquoise, and so on, and fifty wooden bridges, ten ferries, twenty-eight iron bridges, and so forth.

912 My translation follows the reading *bden med snang ba'i ngo bo ltos* in Könchok Palsang and Dewa Sangpo, *Bright Lamp*, 292, instead of the *bden med snang ba'i ngo bos stong* in Gyurmé Dechen's text.

913 The spelling *ser chag* should be corrected to *ser phyag* as in Könchok Palsang and Dewa Sangpo, *Bright Lamp*, 292.

914 See Dorje (1999), 246–47, for information about the Nyemo (Snye mo) region.

915 See Dorje (1999), 253, for the location of Yakdé (G.yag sde) in Rong (Rong).

916 Mahāpaṇḍita Śākyaśrī (Pan chen Shākya shrī, 1127–1225) was a famous Kashmiri master who traveled to Tibet in 1204 and gave many teachings for a period of ten years. See Roerich (1976), 1063–71, for a discussion of Śākyaśrī's life and activities. In particular, Śākyaśrī granted monastic ordination to a large number of people, and the vinaya transmissions from him continue to the present day. This is why Tangtong Gyalpo emphasizes the connection between Śākyaśrī and the strict monks *(jo gdan)* following his tradition. This connection is made explicit in Sherab Palden, *Ocean of Marvels*, 426.

917 The difficulty of being born as a human being with the complete freedoms and endowments is traditionally illustrated by various examples. For instance, when many mustard seeds are dumped onto a needle held with the point up, most will strike the ground. It is barely possible that a mustard seed will stick on the point of the needle. When beans are thrown at the side of a wall, almost all will fall to the ground. In these examples, the number that strike the ground represent beings born in the lower realms and the number that stick to the point of the needle or to the wall represent those that obtain human bodies. In general, it is explained that the cause for birth as a human being with all the freedoms and endowments is virtue and, in particular, that a human body is obtained if moral discipline has been perfectly maintained.

918 The three nirvāṇas *(myang 'das gsum po)* are nirvāṇa in which a residue of the aggregates still remains, nirvāṇa in which no residue of the aggregates remains, and nonabiding nirvāṇa.

919 *Motive and application (bsam sbyor)* are two aspects of the relative enlightenment mind, cultivated by means of the practice of *sending and taking (gtong len)*, which is a technique from the tradition of Mind Training (Blo sbyong).

920 The two enlightenment minds are the relative altruistic attitude and the absolute nature of reality.

921 The seven jewels *(rin chen bdun)* are seven possessions of a Universal Ruler: the precious wheel, precious wish-fulfilling gem, precious queen, precious minister, precious elephant, precious horse, and precious general.

922 The three vows *(sdom gsum)* are the vows of individual liberation, the bodhisattva vow, and the vows of secret mantra.

923 Saṃvara (Bde mchog) is the deity Cakrasaṃvara, one of the major deities of unexcelled tantra. The three carry-over practices *('khyer so gsum)* are the means for carrying the state of meditative concentration over into daily activities. A yogin cultivates awareness of his ordinary body as the body of the deity, ordinary speech as the deity's mantra, and the ordinary state of mind as the enlightened state of primordial awareness.

924 The six types of consciousness *(tshogs drug)* are consciousness by means of the eyes, ears, nose, tongue, body, and mind.

925 The phrase *threefold purity ('khor gsum yongs su dag pa)* refers to performing an act with full awareness of the nonsubstantiality of the person doing the action, the action itself, and the object of the action.

926 In Sherab Palden, *Ocean of Marvels*, 438, this teaching is referred to as the *Twenty-three Verses for Fortunate People (Skal ldan nyer gsum ma).*

927 Panam (Pa rnam) is on the route from Shigatsé to Gyantsé. See Dorje (1999), 262.

928 Pal Khorlo Dechen (Dpal 'Khor lo bde chen) is the monastic complex in Gyantsé (Rgyal rtse) founded in 1418 by the governor Rabten Kunsang Pak (1389–1442), who also built a massive bridge over the Nyangchu River in 1414 and the Auspicious Stūpa of Many Doors in 1427. See Ricca and Lo Bue (1995) and Dorje (1999), 256–60.

929 *Essence of Dependent Origination (Āryapratītyasamutpādahṛdayanāma. 'Phags pa rten cing 'brel bar 'byung ba'i snying po zhes bya ba)*, Toh 521, Kangyur, rgyud 'bum, *na*, 59a. A famous summation of the Buddhist doctrine of dependent origination.

930 Lord Rabtenpa (Bdag po Rab brtan pa) is the governor Rabten Kunsang Pak (1389–1442), whom Tangtong Gyalpo had previously met at Pari. At that time the ruler had provided workers for transporting Tangtong's iron into Tibet. According to the sequence of events in the translated biography, the present meeting at Gyantsé occurred between 1444 and 1447. Rabten Kunsang Pak is known to have died in 1442.

931 The Tsegyal (Rtse rgyal) is the castle of the governor, on a peak above the monastic complex and stūpa.

932 According to the genealogy of the Sharkapa family line, the princess Jangsem Urgyen Gema (Byang sems U rgyan dge ma), wife of another governor in the Shakhapa family line of Rabten Kunsang Pak, met Tangtong Gyalpo on the road as she was traveling to her wedding. Tangtong was riding bareback on a red mule, and prophesied that the princess would have eight sons that would benefit sentient beings. Urgyen Gema later had eleven children: eight sons and three daughters. See Author Unknown, *Rosary of Ornaments*, 74–75.

933 The Jonang great adept Palden Lekpa (Jo nang Sgrub chen Dpal ldan legs pa) was a disciple of the Sakya master Tekchen Chojé (1349–1425). He later became one of the teachers of the Sakya master Dakchen Lodrö Gyaltsen (Bdag chen Blo gros rgyal mtshan, 1444–95), to whom he transmitted the complete Kālacakra initiations and many other teachings in 1474. See Losel Gyatso, *Necklace of Enchanting Utpala Flowers*, 90–91.

934 The monastery of Tsechen (Rtse chen) was founded by the Gyantsé governor Pakpa Palsang ('Phags pa dpal bzang, 1318–70) and the master Nya Ön Kunga Pal (Nya dbon Kun dga' dpal, 1285?–1379?). It is located five kilometers west of Gyantsé on the Shambu Tsegu (Sham bu rtse dgu) ridge. Lord Dusi (Bdag po

Dus si) was the ruler at Tsechen. *Dusi (dus si)* is the Tibetan transliteration of the Chinese title *tusi,* meaning *local chieftain* or *headman.*

935 Lord Dusi had two wives, one from the Kharka (Mkhar kha) family line and one from the aristocratic Che (Lce) line of Shalu (Zhwa lu). The Shalu wife was Dagmo Tenzin Gyalmo (Bdag mo Bstan 'dzin rgyal mo), the only child of the ruler Namgyal Palsang (Rnam rgyal dpal bzang). Tenzin Gyalmo's son, prophesied by Tangtong Gyalpo, was known as Lord Pagö Khyungyal (Bdag po Pha rgod khyung rgyal). See Amoghasiddhi, *Genealogy of the Che Lords,* 41a–b.

936 Sakya Dagchen Lodrö Wangchuk (Sa skya Bdag chen Blo gros dbang phyug, 1402–81) was the last member of the Zhitok Palace (Bzhi thog bla brang) branch of the Khön family of Sakya. He was a monk who spent many years at Ngor Monastery and later made his residence at Chumik (Chu mig).

937 Delek Tashi (Bde legs bkra shis, b. 1408) was the son of the Sakya master Dakchen Sönam Tashi (Bdag chen Bsod nams bkra shis, 1352–1407) of the Lhakhang Palace (Lha khang bla brang) branch of the Khön family of Sakya, whom Tangtong Gyalpo had assisted in the building of the stūpa at Gyang. Also see Könchok Palsang and Dewa Sangpo, *Bright Lamp,* 483–85, where Delek Tashi asks Tangtong how many iron bridges, wooden bridges, ferries, temples, images, and so forth he had built. Tangtong's detailed reply matches in content, but not exact wording, a statement that is found much later in the translated biography.

938 Tekchen Chojé Kunga Tashi (Theg chen chos rje Kun dga' bkra shis, 1349–1425) was a master from the Lhakhang Palace (Lha khang bla brang) branch of the Khön family of Sakya. The Ming emperor Che'ng Tsu gave him the title of Tekchen Chökyi Gyalpo (Theg chen chos kyi rgyal po), "King of Mahāyāna Dharma."

939 The important Kadampa monastery of Nartang (Snar thang) was founded in 1153 by Tumtön Lodrö Drakpa (Gtum ston Blo gros grags pa, 1106–66). See Ferrari (1958), 61–62, 145–48, and Dorje (1999), 275–76. For the Tanak (Rta nag) region, see Ferrari (1958), 68, 157, and Dorje (1999), 277–78.

940 Tsenden Bima (Mtshan ldan Bi ma) is perhap the Indian master Vimalamitra, from whom many of the Great Perfection teachings were passed down. Vimalamitra was a disciple of Śri Siṃha and came to Tibet in the eighth century and taught the king Trisong Detsen. See Dudjom (1991), 497–501, 555, etc.

941 The following song is very different in Könchok Palsang and Dewa Sangpo, *Bright Lamp,* 426–27.

942 See also Chang (1962), vol. 1: 408–20, for the encounter between the great yogin Milarepa and a young woman who became his disciple. In the present episode, as in the earlier Milarepa story, Tangtong Gyalpo will test the young girl to see if she is sincere in her renunciation and wish to practice meditation. Tangtong's deliberately insulting comments about the inferiority of women are made to see if the girl is really ready to give up an ordinary lifestyle.

943 Here Tangtong Gyalpo uses an example from his personal experience of working with iron. A *swage ('jur mig)* is a piece of iron with a narrow hole through which a blacksmith draws red hot iron to make wire.

944 See Martin (2001), 79 n. 35, concerning Darding (Dar sdings) Monastery, which was founded in 1173 or 1233 and became the main seat of the Shen (Gshen) clan of the Bönpo tradition. According to some Bönpo teachings, Tsewang Rikzin (Tshe dbang rig 'dzin) and Padmasambhava were the sons of the ancient Bön sage Dranpa Namkha (Dran pa nam mkha'). Könchok Palsang and Dewa Sangpo, *Bright Lamp*, 335, mention that the Bönpos said Tangtong was the rebirth of an adept of the Bön teachings named Tsewang Rangdrol (Bon gyi grub thob Tshes dbang rang grol).

945 The Destroyer of the Lord of Death ('Chi bdag 'joms pa) is Amitāyus, the buddha of infinite life. Könchok Palsang and Dewa Sangpo, *Bright Lamp*, 335, say Tangtong Gyalpo bestowed the reading transmission *(lung)* for Amitāyus as the Destroyer of the Lord of Death (Tshe dpag med 'Chi bdag 'joms pa).

946 The horses, mules, and monks had been sent ahead when Tangtong Gyalpo was previously in Panam.

947 Desire is symbolized by a bird, hatred by a snake, and ignorance by a pig.

948 The Dharma king of Yeru Jang (Chos rgyal G.yas ru Byang pa) was Namgyal Drakpa (1395–1475), who was one of Tangtong Gyalpo's patrons.

949 Sherab Palden, *Ocean of Marvels*, 447, gives basically the same information, but does not specify the year or Tangtong Gyalpo's age at the time.

950 According to Sherab Palden, *Ocean of Marvels*, 448, Tangtong Gyalpo sat outside the door while teaching.

951 Tangtong Gyalpo's studies with the Jonang master Lekhawa Sherab Sangpo, who was the thirteenth abbot of Jonang Monastery, were described earlier in the biography. During his previous visit, Tangtong had received from Lekhawa the higher initiations of Kālacakra and the teachings of the Six-branch Yoga according to the Jonang tradition. Also see Sherab Palden, *Ocean of Marvels*, 449–51, for extra details of this episode. The five precious substances *(rin po che sna lnga)* are usually listed as gold, silver, turquoise, coral, and pearl. See also Dorje and Kapstein (1991), 147.

952 The Vajrayoga (Rdo rje'i rnal 'byor) is the Six-branch Yoga of Kālacakra that Tangtong Gyalpo had received from Lekhawa earlier.

953 Lhadongpa Sönam Chokpa (Lha gdong pa Bsod nams mchog pa) was one of the main teachers from whom Tangtong Gyalpo received many of the Nyingma and Great Perfection teachings earlier in his life. Gökyi Demtruchen (Rgod kyi ldem 'phru can Dngos grub rgyal mtshan, 1337–1408) was one of the major discoverers of hidden treasures *(gter ma)* in the Nyingma tradition. His tradition is known as the Northern Treasure *(byang gter)* tradition. Also see Sherab Palden, *Ocean of Marvels*, 451.

954 Ngamring was the capital of the Jang district. See also Könchok Palsang and Dewa Sangpo, *Bright Lamp*, 342, where the correct spelling of *byams pa* is given for Maitreya, instead of the *byang pa* in the text of the translated biography. Namgyal Draksang (1395–1475), the governor of the Jang district, and his brother

Könchok Lekpai Gyaltsen Pal Sangpo (Dkon mchog legs pa'i rgyal mtshan dpal bzang po, d. 1468) completed construction of the Great Maitreya of Ngamring (Ngam ring Byams pa chen po) in 1466. Namgyal Draksang is referred to by the epithet Kalkī (Rigs ldan) because of his identification with the Kalkī emperors of the legendary kingdom of Shambhala, especially Kalkī Puṇḍarīka. See note 763 for detailed information about Namgyal Draksang.

955 Sherab Palden, *Ocean of Marvels*, 452, says the Mongols had come once to Mangyul and had once carried away many gold prospectors of Gugé and Latö Jang. This is also mentioned in Könchok Palsang and Dewa Sangpo, *Bright Lamp*, 343.

956 Tangtong Gyalpo's trip to Cāmara Island (Rnga yag gling) and his meeting with Guru Padmasambhava in the Palace of Lotus Light were described earlier in the biography.

957 A *mantra-born ḍākinī (sngags skyes kyi mkha' 'gro ma)* is a woman who meditates on herself in the form of a female deity such as Vajrayoginī.

958 In Könchok Palsang and Dewa Sangpo, *Bright Lamp*, 345, Tangtong's comments are considerably longer. Among other things, he explains to the nun that as long as the stūpa on the Tibetan border with Mongolia remained, the pass would be blocked by glacial snow. When the stūpa decayed, the glacial snow would melt and the Mongols would be able to invade Tibet through the opened pass.

959 The podium *(bre)* is the section between the main dome *(bum pa)* and the Dharma wheels *(chos 'khor)* of a stūpa.

960 This is the scroll that Tangtong Gyalpo had given to the nun. In Könchok Palsang and Dewa Sangpo, *Bright Lamp*, 345, the statement quoted from these written directions *(lam yig)* is in the advice he gave the nun before her departure.

961 Maryul (Mar yul) seems to be a term for the far southwestern regions of Ngari, including Ladakh.

962 Tangtong Gyalpo's Auspicious Stūpa of Many Doors at Riwoché.

963 Lochen Gyurmé Dechen, the author of this text, is expressing his astonishment at Tangtong Gyalpo's protection of Tibet against barbarian invasion, and wondering if he could have been an emanation of the Shambhala emperor Raudra Cakrī. According the prophecies of the Kālacakra tradition, the Shambhala emperor Yaśas, an emanation of the bodhisattva Mañjuśrī, will return in the future as the militant Shambhala emperor Raudra Cakrī (Drag po 'khor lo can) and destroy the savage barbarian *(kla klo, mleccha)* armies and evil religious doctrines that will have spread over the earth. For a clear discussion of these prophecies, see Wallace (2001), 115–18.

964 The Ngamring ruler *(sde srid)* was Namgyal Draksang (1395–1475), whose son and successor was Namkha Dorjé (Nam mkha' rdo rje). Rinchen Ding was Tangtong Gyalpo's birthplace.

965 See note 461 for information about Tangtong Gyalpo's teacher Choksang Lekpai Lodrö (Mchog bzang legs pa'i blo gros). Shelkar (Shel dkar) was the capital of the district of Latö Lho (La stod Lho). See Dorje (1999), 296–97, for the location and present situation at Shelkar.

966 Tai Situ Lhatsen Kyab (Ta'i Si tu Lha btsan skyabs) was the governor of the district of Lho. He married Lady Tsencham Gyalmo (Btsan lcam rgyal mo), a sister of the Jang governor Namgyal Draksang. Their son was Drung Tsewang Tashi (Drung Tshe dbang bkra shis, d. 1454/55). See Palden Chökyi Sangpo, *Series of Jewels*, 178, 184.

967 In Könchok Palsang and Dewa Sangpo, *Bright Lamp*, 314–15, when Tai Situ Lhatsen Kyab expresses his amazement at Tangtong Gyalpo's feat, Tangtong explains how he is a yogin for whom the three excretions have ceased *(zag pa zad pa gsum dang ldan pa)*. This freedom from the three excretions was specifically prophesied by the Indian adept Virūpa earlier in Tangtong's life. See note 503. The present episode brings to mind a similar event in the life of Ga Lotsāwa Namgyal Dorjé (Rga Lo tsā ba Rnam rgyal rdo rje, eleventh–twelfth centuries), while he was living in India. After a vision of the Cakrasaṃvara maṇḍala, Ga Lotsāwa's physical excretions ceased *(lus kyi zag pa yang chad)*. To test whether this had really happened, he was sealed inside the residence of his teacher Tsami Lotsāwa at Nālandā and guarded day and night by three men who also served him food. After one month had passed it was verified that his excretions had indeed ceased. See Shang Yudrakpa, *Biography of Pal*, 368, 376.

968 Dongshur (Gdong zhur) is a name for the area of Riwoché, perhaps the name of the place before Tangtong Gyalpo renamed it Riwoché.

969 Lhatsen Kyab's son, Drung Tsewang Tashi (d. 1454/55), married Könchok Gyalmo of the royal house of Ngari. They had a daughter in 1440, who died very young. Könchok Gyalmo later became a nun and was known as the venerable lady Chökyi Drönmé (1422–55), who became the consort of Bodong Panchen and then Tangtong Gyalpo. Drung Tsewang Tashi later remarried, taking Pönmo Chögyal (Dpon mo Chos rgyal), the daughter of the Nyak chieftain (Snyag mi dpon), as his new wife. See Author Unknown, *Biography of the Venerable Lady Chökyi Drönma*, 142a.

970 Tangtong Gyalpo's prophecy to Lhatsen Kyab may be seen to herald later historical events. Wars broke out between Lho and Jang, with Lho first suffering defeat and then regaining its territory after a second conflict. Then another period of severe difficulty arose. Later the two districts seem to have merged together as a single large territory. See Sönam Drakpa, *Magical Key to Royal Genealogies*, 62.

971 The date for the laying of the foundation is taken from Sherab Palden, *Ocean of Marvels*, 473. Könchok Palsang and Dewa Sangpo, *Bright Lamp*, 348–49, mention that the foundation of the stūpa was forty armspans *('dom)* in length on each side, and also give further details about the early construction and the discovery of the necessary stone. The western side of the stūpa collapsed in the Horse Year (1450), and Tangtong considered moving the work to a different site, but signs indicated the original site was good.

972 This statement is much longer in Sherab Palden, *Ocean of Marvels*, 474–77, where Tangtong also explicitly refers to the stūpa as a geomantic focal-point *(sa'i me btsa')*.

973 According to Chogye Trichen Rinpoché, the practice of *cutting the stream (rgyun gcod)* refers to a yogic practice that enables a person to survive on nectar generated within the body.

974 See also Sherab Palden, *Ocean of Marvels*, 194–95, where this instruction is given to the Sakya master Rongtön Sheja Kunrik (Rong ston Shes bya kun rig, 1367–1449) during their meeting at Sangpu (Gsang phu).

975 Tangtong Gyalpo's residence was on the peak of Riwoché Mountain, with a high cliff nearby.

976 The *required stone work (rdo khral)* was a tax in the form of a set amount of stone work required for one person.

977 In Könchok Palsang and Dewa Sangpo, *Bright Lamp*, 351, the laborers shout, "The devil with braids has died!" *(bdud ral pa can shi).*

978 Jambudvīpa *('dzam bu gling)*, where human beings live, is the southern of the four continents that surround Mount Meru in Buddhist cosmology.

979 Lord Amitāyus (Mgon po Tshe dpag med) is the buddha of infinite life.

980 With some differences, this entire episode is based on Sherab Palden, *Ocean of Marvels*, 479–81. However, in Könchok Palsang and Dewa Sangpo, *Bright Lamp*, 351–53, a very different story is told in the first person by the author Dewa Sangpo, who was a participant in the events. The accident happened in a Sheep Year (1451), and it seems certain from this eyewitness account that Tangtong Gyalpo was seriously injured in the rockslide. Dewa Sangpo and another monk carried Tangtong from the worksite up to his residence after the accident. Then Dewa Sangpo went down and made soup, which he brought back to Tangtong and served while weeping. Tangtong reassured him, saying that he did not need to cry, and told him to post guards at the door for seven days so that he would not be disturbed. During this time Dewa Sangpo sent five physicians to Tangtong, but he said he had no need for medicines. The Jang governor (Namgyal Draksang) also sent eighty monks from Ngamring to perform rituals. However, they were really checking to see whether Tangtong had actually achieved the ability to pass no excretions. After a month of taking shifts to always have someone in his presence, they were convinced.

981 A note glosses the term *bskor ba* ("surrounding") in the Tibetan text as "a term for 'stopping'" *(bkag pa'i ming).*

982 According to Könchok Palsang and Dewa Sangpo, *Bright Lamp*, 351, apologies were made by elder monks for the attack and, led by Dolpa Sangyé Sengé (Dol pa Sangs rgyas seng ge), who was abbot of the Ngamring Monastery, the monks of the monastery contributed to the work and made large offerings. As mentioned earlier in the biography, Tangtong Gyalpo had prophesied that Sangyé Sengé would become abbot of Ngamring Monastery.

983 The Jang governor *(dpon po byang pa)* was Namgyal Draksang.

984 The Lho patron *(yod bdag lho pa)* was Tai Situ Lhatsen Kyab.

985 Diemberger et al. (1997), 97 n. 189, says Menkhab was an area to the northwest of Dingri.

986 The gods of the four races of the great kings *(rgyal chen rigs bzhi'i lha)* are one of the six types of gods in the desire realm.

987 This is very similar to events that occurred during the construction of the stūpa at Jonang by Dolpopa Sherab Gyaltsen (of whom Tangtong Gyalpo was the rebirth) from 1330 to 1333. See Dolpopa Sherab Gyaltsen, *Dredging the Pit of Saṃsāra*, 455–56, where he mentions that nonhuman beings worked on building the Jonang stūpa at night just as human beings worked on it during the day, the gods of the four races of the great kings *(rgyal chen sde bzhi)*, spiritual heroes, and ḍākinīs attached the ornaments, and so forth.

988 Many significant differences are found in this instruction in Könchok Palsang and Dewa Sangpo, *Bright Lamp*, 400–403.

989 For an explanation of the ideas behind this and the following verses as explained in Tangtong Gyalpo's tradition of Severance, or Chöd (Gcod), see note 805.

990 Könchok Palsang and Dewa Sangpo, *Bright Lamp*, 403, also say this disciple practiced what Tangtong Gyalpo taught him. When he died, a pavilion of rainbow light and a rain of flowers appeared, and he reached complete buddhahood.

991 See note 795 for information about the special Severance practice called Opening the Door to the Sky *(nam mkha' sgo 'byed)*.

992 The emanated wrathful conqueror Namkha Leksang (Sprul pa'i khro rgyal Nam mkha' legs bzang) is the same as Namkha Lekpa (Nam mkha' legs pa), the sole heir to Tangtong Gyalpo's secret teachings of Chöd, or Severance (Gcod). See also Könchok Palsang and Dewa Sangpo, *Bright Lamp*, 360–61, 365, who call him Namkha Lek (Nam mkha' legs). Namkha Lekpa's role in the transmission of this tradition was discussed in the second part of the Introduction. For his short verse biography of Tangtong, see Namkha Lekpa, *Practicing Severance*. Curiously, the brief verse biography of Namkha Lekpa himself does not mention his connection with Tangtong. See Shākya Shenyen, *Biography of Jamyang Namkha Lekpa*.

993 The term *bris 'bur ba* is an abbreviated form. Sherab Palden, *Ocean of Marvels*, 482, makes the meaning clear by saying *lha bris 'bri ba* and *lder sku bzo ba*.

994 The offering of azurite by the earth spirit of Nyemo (Snye mo) was described earlier in the biography.

995 That is, it was the form of the wrathful deity Vajrabhairava (Rdo rje 'jigs byed) with the faces stacked on top of each other. Other forms of this deity also exist.

996 Tāmradvīpa, or Copper Island (Zangs gling), is perhaps Ceylon, although the term has also been used for other locations in Southeast Asia. As described earlier in the biography, Tangtong Gyalpo had traveled to Tāmradvīpa and worshipped a large stūpa there. Sherab Palden, *Ocean of Marvels*, 119, mentions that Tangtong carefully memorized the architectural details of the Tāmradvīpa stūpa, such as its two-level dome *(bum pa gnyis rim)*. Also see Sherab Palden, *Ocean of Marvels*,

483, and Könchok Palsang and Dewa Sangpo, *Bright Lamp*, 353–54, for important information on the art work in the Riwoché stūpa.

997 Chökyi Drönmé (1422–55) was the daughter of Tri Lhawang Gyaltsen (1404–64), the King of Ngari Gungtang, and a descendant of the ancient kings of Tibet. The ḍākinī Sönam Drenma was a disciple of the Kagyü master Pakmodrupa Dorjé Gyalpo (Phag mo gru pa Rdo rje rgyal po, 1110–70). Her rebirth was named Sönam Paldren (Bsod nams dpal 'dren), whose rebirth was Chökyi Drönmé. See Dorjé Phagmo Dechen Chödrön and Dra Tupten Namgyal, *Past Lives of the Samding Dorjé Phagmo Incarnations*, 32–33, and Diemberger et al. (1997), 110–11. The relationship between Tangtong Gyalpo and Chökyi Drönmé during their brief time together at Riwoché, and the events of her trip to Central Tibet and Kongpo, are described in extraordinary detail in Author Unknown, *Biography of the Venerable Lady Chökyi Drönma*, 112b–46b. Also see Diemberger (forthcoming 2007).

998 According to Könchok Palsang and Dewa Sangpo, *Bright Lamp*, 465, Chökyi Drönmé offered Tangtong Gyalpo five rosaries with one hundred beads of conch shell, one hundred beads of pearl, one hundred beads of coral, one hundred beads of lapis lazuli, and one hundred beads of amber. She saw him to be the eleven-faced, one-thousand-armed form of Avalokiteśvara. Tangtong gave her the complete teachings of the Heart Practice *(thugs sgrub)* of the cache of treasure teachings from Trasang *(bkra bzang gter kha)*, which means the Northern Treasure teachings of Gökyi Demtruchen that were recovered at Mount Trasang (Ri bo Bkra bzang). According to Author Unknown, *Biography of the Venerable Lady Chökyi Drönma*, 116a–b, Chökyi Drönmé also received the Severance, or Chöd (Gcod), teachings of Machik Labdrön and Mahāmudrā instructions.

999 The following account of the raising of the central pole *(srog shing)* of the Riwoché stūpa is copied with very slight editing from the biography of Chökyi Drönmé. See Author Unknown, *Biography of the Venerable Lady Chökyi Drönma*, 124b–25a.

1000 See note 389 concerning the "Mothers Infinite As Space."

1001 See also Author Unknown, *Biography of the Venerable Lady Chökyi Drönma*, 128b.

1002 The following story is told with much more detail in Chökyi Dronmé's biography. See Author Unknown, *Biography of the Venerable Lady Chökyi Drönma*, 139b–42b.

1003 The trip from Riwoché in west Tibet to Kongpo in southeast Tibet would usually take many days.

1004 Chökyi Drönmé was a member of the royal family at Ngari, descendants of the ancient kings of Tibet, who were believed to belong to the lineage of the gods of clear light *('od gsal lha'i brgyud pa)*.

1005 As mentioned above in the translated biography, Tangtong Gyalpo had previously established a meditation center at Menmogang (Sman mo sgang) in the Tsagong region of Kongpo.

1006 Tangtong Gyalpo had been planning to build an iron brige at the ferry landing of Nyago (Nya mgo gru kha) on the Tsangpo River for many years. This was previously mentioned in the biography when he unsuccessfully tried to get the Pakmodru ruler Drakpa Jungné to support the project.

1007 In Könchok Palsang and Dewa Sangpo, *Bright Lamp*, 466, Dewa Sangpo records a fascinating but difficult prophecy that Tangtong Gyalpo gave to Chökyi Drönmé concerning the skull-cup of her cranium in previous lives, the present life, and future lives. Among other things, he mentions that the skull-cup from one of her past lifetimes was recovered by the treasure revealer Kunkyong Lingpa (1396–1477) from a treasure trove in Padmasambhava's White Stūpa at Samyé Monastery. See Guru Tashi, *Musical Sea of Amazing Stories to Delight Experts*, 419–20, for the story of Kunkyong Lingpa's extraction of treasures from the White Stūpa of Samyé when he was twenty-one years old (1416). Among the sacred items he retrieved was a pair (?) of blessed skull-cups described as "facing craniums bound together with iron wire" *(srin thod kha sbyar lcags thag gis bsdams pa)*. Also see note 632. The skull-cup of the cranium of Jetsun Nyendrak Sangmo (Rje btsun Snyan grags bzang mo), who was Chökyi Drönmé's third rebirth and the third Samding Dorjé Phagmo, was later kept as a relic at Nakartsé (Sna dkar rtse), where its blessing was experienced by Jonang Kunga Drolchok (1507–66). See Kunga Drolchok, *Record of Precious Beautiful Ornaments*, 659. The repeated statement about the mountain man of Ngari (Mnga' ris pa'i ri pa) coming to Tsagong is curious, because it was Tangtong's disciple Riksum Gönpo (Rigs gsum mgon po) who came to first hold the monastic seat of the Tsagong Nesar Monastery. Riksum Gönpo was from Kyishö (Skyid shod) in Central Tibet.

1008 This complete date is taken from Sherab Palden, *Ocean of Marvels*, 488, but no age for Tangtong Gyalpo is given. Könchok Palsang and Dewa Sangpo, *Bright Lamp*, 354, say Nyima Sangpo was installed on the monastic seat in a Dragon Year *('brug lo)*, which could be 1448, 1460, or 1472.

1009 Tenzin Nyima Sangpo (Bstan 'dzin Nyi ma bzang po, b. 1436) was Tangtong Gyalpo's son. *Three vajras* is an honorific euphemism for Tangtong's body, speech, and mind. Sherab Palden, *Ocean of Marvels*, 488–90, also refers to Nyima Sangpo as an emanation body *(sprul sku)*. Tangtong passed to his son all the teachings he had received from his five hundred Tibetan, Indian, and Nepalese masters, which he had gathered into Eight Great Transmissions *(bka' babs chen po brgyad)*. An extremely long and important edict *(bka' shog)* issued by Tangtong at the investiture of Nyima Sangpo is reproduced in Sherab Palden, *Ocean of Marvels*, 491–506.

1010 This is the Chinese emperor whom Tangtong Gyalpo met during his previous travels to eastern Tibet and China, perhaps to be identified as the Ming emperor Chu Ch'i-chen (1427–64). See note 867.

1011 As described earlier in the biography, Tangtong Gyalpo had sent his disciple Önpo Namgyal Sangpo (Dbon po Rnam rgyal bzang po) to the eastern Tibetan regions of Dokham (Mdo khams). Lhalung Palgyi Dorjé (Lha lung Dpal gyi rdo rje) was the monk who assassinated the anti-Buddhist Tibetan king Langdarma in 842 and then fled to eastern Tibet. When Tangtong had visited Ling (Gling) during his travels in eastern Tibet, he had seen the special spirit-turquoise *(bla g.yu)* called Flat Blue Sky (Gnam sngo leb) and prophesied that it would later be offered to him at Riwoché.

1012 Drogön Pakpa ('Gro mgon 'Phags pa Blo gros rgyal mtshan, 1235–80) was the fifth Early Patriarch of the Sakya tradition. He became the spiritual master of the Mongolian conqueror Kubilai Khan (1215–94), who was the first emperor of the Yuan dynasty (1279–1368) in China. He traveled through eastern Tibet several times.

1013 The Six Dharmas of Niguma, which are fundamental teachings of the Shangpa Kagyü tradition, are inner fire, illusory body, dream, clear light, transference of consciousness, and intermediate state. The term *experiential guidance (nyams khrid)* indicates that Lodrö Gyaltsen meditated on each practice as it was taught by Tangtong Gyalpo, not preceding to the next practice until some *experience (nyams)* of the previous one had arisen.

1014 That is, earlier guidance manuals of the tradition.

1015 Tenzin Nyima Sangpo (Bstan 'dzin Nyi ma bzang po, b. 1436), Tangtong Gyalpo's son and heir.

1016 Tangtong Gyalpo's guidance manuals on the Six Dharmas of Niguma and related teachings, written down by Lodrö Gyaltsen at Riwoché in a Tiger Year *(stag lo)*, which probably corresponds to the Earth Tiger of 1458, are listed separately in the bibliography.

1017 The eight close bodhisattva sons *(byang chub sems dpa' nye ba'i sras brgyad)* are Mañjuśrī, Vajrapāṇi, Avalokiteśvara, Kṣitigarbha, Sarvanivāraṇaviṣkambhin, Ākāśagarbha, Maitreya, and Samantabhadra. The four guardian kings *(rgyal chen sde bzhi)* are Dhṛtarāṣṭra in the east, Virūḍhaka in the south, Virūpākṣa in the west, and Vaiśravaṇa in the north. See Dorje and Kapstein (1991), 131.

1018 See Sherab Palden, *Ocean of Marvels*, 539–60, for a more detailed listing of these and other temples, images, and murals.

1019 As mentioned above, the emanated wrathful conqueror *(sprul pa'i khro rgyal)* is Namkha Lekpa (Nam mkha' legs pa), the sole heir to Tangtong Gyalpo's secret teachings of Chöd, or Severance (Gcod). Könchok Palsang and Dewa Sangpo, *Bright Lamp*, 360–61, give his full name here: *sprul pa'i khro rgyal bka' bcu pa nam mkha' legs.* I take the term *mgo lung pa* to mean *work leader* or *foreman.* See Könchok Palsang and Dewa Sangpo, *Bright Lamp*, 365: *dge las kyi mgo lung pa sprul pa'i khro rgyal bka' bcu pa nam mkha' legs.*

1020 The translation of this sentence is uncertain. See also Könchok Palsang and Dewa Sangpo, *Bright Lamp*, 363.

1021 See also Könchok Palsang and Dewa Sangpo, *Bright Lamp*, 415. Jamchen Gyedé (Byams chen brgyad sde) was at Ngamring.

1022 This is the Chinese emperor whom Tangtong Gyalpo is said to have met during his previous travels to eastern Tibet and China, perhaps to be identified as the Ming emperor Chu Ch'i-chen (1427–64). See note 867 for more information. In

Könchok Palsang and Dewa Sangpo, *Bright Lamp*, 416, Tangtong addresses the emperor as Chinese Emperor Piwang Kotra, Leonine Source of Glory (Rgya nag rgyal po Pi wang ko tra dpal gyi 'byung gnas seng ge).

1023 Dorjé Drakpotsel (Rdo rje drag po rtsal) is a wrathful aspect of Guru Padmasambhava. He usually holds a meteorite vajra in the right hand and a nine-headed scorpion in the left hand. Könchok Palsang and Dewa Sangpo, *Bright Lamp*, 364, specify that the figure was dark blue. See note 287 for the nine dance moods *(gar dgu'i nyams)*.

1024 The *maṇi* devotees *(ma ṇi pa)* are itinerant practitioners of meditation on Avalokiteśvara, who constantly recite the mantra *Oṃ maṇi padme hūṃ* and urge people wherever they go to do likewise. They often hold skits or morality plays to illustrate and teach the Buddhist doctrine and use icons, dance, and didactic stories to teach Buddhism in a popular setting.

1025 The three poisons are desire, hatred, and ignorance. The lower realms are the animal realm, the realm of hungry spirits, and the hell realm.

1026 An annotation in the Tibetan text questions the meaning of *mthong bzhin* ("while seeing"), which has been translated as "while reciting." The same doubtful spelling is also found in Könchok Palsang and Dewa Sangpo, *Bright Lamp*, 370.

1027 The text of this edict *(bka' lung)* is very difficult and corrupt. The Dergé editor also seems to have had trouble with it. The translation has been made using some readings from Könchok Palsang and Dewa Sangpo, *Bright Lamp*, 369–70.

1028 Sarahata is spelled Parahata in Könchok Palsang and Dewa Sangpo, *Bright Lamp*, 371.

1029 The five inexpiable acts *(mtshams med kyi las)* are to kill your father, to kill your mother, to kill an arhat, to cause a schism in the Sangha, and to maliciously cause a buddha to bleed.

1030 Sukhāvatī (Bde ba can) is the paradise of the buddha Amitābha.

1031 *Karmaśataka, Mdo sde las brgya pa*, Toh 340, Kangyur, mdo sde, *ha*, 1b–309a. *Saṃdhinirmocanasūtra, Dgongs pa nges par 'grel pa*, Toh 106, Kangyur, mdo sde, *ca*, 1b–55b. *Kūṭāgāra Sūtra, Khang bu brtsegs pa'i mdo*, Toh 332, Kangyur, mdo sde, *sa*, 260a–263b.

1032 Tsari is the holy mountain in Kongpo often mentioned in this biography. Mount Kailash is a famous pilgrimage site in western Tibet. Chuwar (Chu bar) is a site at Lapchi (La phyi) where the great yogin Milarepa spent time in meditation.

1033 Also see Könchok Palsang and Dewa Sangpo, *Bright Lamp*, 374–76, where this oral instruction is very different and includes lines from a previous teaching.

1034 The five dialectical schools *(rtog ge ba sde lnga)* are probably the Sāṃkhya, Aiśvara, Vaiṣṇava, Jainism, and Nihilism (=Cārvāka). See Dudjom (1991), 64-67.

1035 The Cārvāka (Tshu rol mdzes pa) were a hedonistic school of nihilism in ancient India that denied the existence of an eternal soul, the possibility of past or future lives, and the law of cause and effect. For a short summary of the Cārvāka views, see

Brunnhölzl (2004), 798–99. The following episode is similar to a common model of the lives of the Indian adepts, with several aspects very similar to the great adept Virūpa's story.

1036 Pari (Phag ri) is near the Tibetan border, on the trade route south to Paro in Bhutan. Tangtong Gyalpo built the Samdrup Temple at Pari in 1434. Sherab Palden, *Ocean of Marvels*, 508, says an emanation of Tangtong went to Kāmata. Könchok Palsang and Dewa Sangpo, *Bright Lamp*, 428, say Tangtong actually went, but used deliberate behavior so that he was not seen or harmed. They also give the name of the Kāmata king, or *rājā*, as Rājā King Doruk Naran (Ra tsa Rgyal po Rdo rug na ran). Although this is clearly some form of the common name Narayan, it is not found in extant lists of the Kāmata rulers. The ancient Hindu kingdom of Kāmata had its capital, Kāmatapur, on the west bank of the Dharla River in modern Cooch Bihar, on the plains of West Bengal bordering on western Bhutan. See Aris (1980), 104–7, for a vivid description of the Bhutanese treasure revealer Pema Lingpa's (1450–1521) meeting in 1504 with another king, of Dongkha in eastern Mön, and the horrific bloody sacrifices of human beings and cattle that this king made to Śiva. In 1507 Pema Lingpa also met Nilambhar, the last King of Kāmata, who had fled his capital after its destruction by the Moslem Sultan of Bengal, Husayn Shāh, sometime between 1501 and 1505.

1037 The five royal sūtras *(rgyal po mdo lnga)* are the *Bhadracaryāpraṇidhāna (Bzang po spyod pa'i smon lam)*, which is the sūtra of prayers; the *Vajravidāraṇadhāraṇī (Rdo rje rnam 'joms kyi gzungs)*, which is the sūtra of lustrations; the *Prajñāpāramitāhṛdaya (Shes rab snying po)*, which is the sūtra of the view; the *Atajñāna ('Da' ka ye shes)*, which is the sūtra of meditation; and the *Bodhyāpattideśana (Byang chub ltung ba)*, which is the sūtra of confession. See Losang Trinlé, *Clarification of Knowledge*, 660.

1038 See note 781 concerning the eight-branch vow of renewal and purification.

1039 The hell of supreme torture *(mnar med pa'i dmyal ba)* is described as the worst of the eight hot hells.

1040 Könchok Palsang and Dewa Sangpo, *Bright Lamp*, 433, say Tangtong Gyalpo went from Kāmata to the Vajrāsana at Bodhgayā in India and to Tāmradvīpa, or Copper Island (Ceylon?), before returning to Riwoché in Tibet.

1041 The kingdom of Yatsé (Ya tshe) in western Nepal is identical to Seṃjā, also known as Khāsa or Kasiyā in the Nepalese chronicles. See Petech (1980). Könchok Palsang and Dewa Sangpo, *Bright Lamp*, 435, say Tangtong Gyalpo had observed a vow of silence for the previous fourteen years, and began to speak again only when these invitations arrived. In Tangtong's own words, recorded in an edict sent to the Kāmata minister Malik (Ma glig), he mentions he had sat immobile on the same cushion for twenty-three years, remaining silent for the last fourteen. See Könchok Palsang and Dewa Sangpo, *Bright Lamp*, 441.

1042 The term *physical son (sku'i sras)* is used for Kyabpa Sangpo (Skyab pa bzang po) to indicate clearly that he was Tangtong Gyalpo's actual son. As discussed in the second part of the Introduction, Jamyang Khyentsé Wangpo (1820–92) stated that the Chaksam Tulkus (Lcags zam sprul sku) who have been the leaders of

Tangtong's Iron Bridge (Lcags zam) tradition since the sixteenth century are the rebirths of Kyabpa Sangpo. Könchok Palsang and Dewa Sangpo, *Bright Lamp*, 435, describe Kyabpa Sangpo as a bodhisattva learned in the four fundamental subjects, whom Tangtong had acknowledged as his son *(sras su zhal gyis bzhes pa'i/ byang chub sems dpa' kyab pa bka' bzhi pa).*

1043 Dewa Sangpo's (Bde ba bzang po) descendants became the leaders of Tangtong Gyalpo's tradition in Bhutan. Dewa Sangpo was also the co-author of one of the most important old biographies of Tangtong, *The Bright Lamp (Gsal ba'i sgron me).* Könchok Palsang (Dkon mchog dpal bzang), who was from Ngamring in Latö Jang, was the original author of *The Bright Lamp.* In about 1433, Tangtong had appointed Könchok Palsang to supervise the construction of the Samdrup Temple at Pari.

1044 This quotation paraphrases information in the actual edict *(bka' shog)* that Tangtong Gyalpo sent to the Kāmata king. The original text is fully reproduced in Könchok Palsang and Dewa Sangpo, *Bright Lamp*, 436–39. There Tangtong gives the name of the Kāmata king as Rājā Doruk Naran (Ra tsa Rdo rug na ran), mentions in some detail the events that had happened when he visited Kāmata, and also says he traveled around many regions of the Indian subcontinent, going even as far as the Turkic Qarlug (Gar log) areas, on the way home to Riwoché in Tibet. Another edict sent to the king at the same time is fully reproduced in Sherab Palden, *Ocean of Marvels*, 521–28, and is dated in a Dragon Year *('brug lo)*, perhaps corresponding to 1472 or 1484.

1045 An edict given to the minister Malik (Ma glig), who was from a Tibetan region and had acted as a translator for Tangtong Gyalpo, is fully reproduced in Könchok Palsang and Dewa Sangpo, *Bright Lamp*, 440–42. This edict is also dated in a Dragon Year *('brug lo)*, and Tangtong mentions he had sat immobile on the same cushion for twenty-three years, remaining silent for the last fourteen.

1046 The name Köntso (Kon tsho, with various spellings) seems to be another name for Kāmata. See also Könchok Palsang and Dewa Sangpo, *Bright Lamp*, 439: *ko 'tsho ka ma ta*, and also 440 and 558.

1047 The entire text of this edict addressed to Maheśvara and Uma is reproduced in Könchok Palsang and Dewa Sangpo, *Bright Lamp*, 439–40, and dated in a Dragon Year *('brug lo).*

1048 The māra of the Lord of Death is one of the four māras. See also note 843.

1049 The four modes of birth (*skyes gnas gzhi*) are birth from a womb, magical birth, birth from an egg, and birth from moisture.

1050 In Könchok Palsang and Dewa Sangpo, *Bright Lamp*, 378–81, extra lines are found at the end of this teaching.

1051 The ten powers *(stobs bcu)* of a buddha are the powers of knowing what are and are not appropriate circumstances; knowing the maturation of actions; knowing various inclinations; knowing various constituents; knowing who has supreme faculties and inferior faculties; knowing the paths going everywhere; knowing meditation, liberation, meditative concentration, absorption, and so forth; knowing previous existences; knowing the transference of consciousness at death and birth; and knowing the cessation of taints. The four immeasurables *(tshad med bzhi)* are love, compassion, joy, and equanimity.

1052 Chödrak Palsang (Chos grags dpal bzang), who was from Yarlung, was one of Tangtong Gyalpo's major disciples *(bu chen)*. See also note 807.

1053 The noble nun *(dpon btsun ma)* Delek Chödren (Bde legs chos 'dren) was the venerable lady Chökyi Drönmé's most trusted companion and attendant, and is mentioned many times in her biography. Delek Chödren was a novice nun *(dge tshul ma)* and a disciple of Bodong Panchen Cholé Namgyal.

1054 For a brief sketch of the life of the venerable lady Kunga Sangmo (Rje btsun Kun dga' bzang mo, 1459–1502), the second Samding Dorjé Phagmo incarnation, see Dorjé Phagmo Dechen Chödrön and Dra Tupten Namgyal, *Past Lives of the Samding Dorjé Phagmo Incarnations*, 36–37, and Diemberger et al. (1997), 111–12. Also see Diemberger (forthcoming 2007). See Rinchen Namgyal, *Making the Body Hairs of the Faithful Flutter*, 18–19, for a detailed description of the fascinating encounter between the mad yogin Tsang Nyön Heruka (1452–1507) and Jetsun Kunga Sangmo.

1055 Different opinions exist about the precise identification of the three regions of Ngari (Mnga' ris skor gsum). Generally, these are the upper, lower, and central regions of western Tibet. The upper is Ngari Mangyul (Mnga' ris Mang yul), surrounded by the lakes of Sangkar (Zangs dkar); the central is Ngari Takmo (Mnga' ris Stag mo), surrounded by the glacial peaks of Purang (Spu rangs); and the lower is Ngari Shangshung (Mnga' ris Zhang zhung), surrounded by the slate cliffs of Gugé (Gu ge). See Losang Trinlé, *Clarification of Knowledge*, 760. For a detailed discussion, see Vitali (1996).

1056 In her previous life as Jetsun Chökyi Drönmé, her mother had been Dodé Gyalmo (Mdo sde rgyal mo), the Queen of Ngari. See Author Unknown, *Biography of the Venerable Lady Chökyi Drönma*, 2b. Gungtang (Gung thang) is the capital of Ngari, where Chökyi Drönmé had lived as a young girl. The information provided here in Tangtong Gyalpo's biography suggests the date of 1463 for Dodé Gyalmo's death.

1057 Ngari Dzongkar (Mnga' ris Rdzong dkar) is an alternate spelling for Ngari Dzongka (Mnga' ris Rdzong kha), the royal palace and monastic complex at Gungtang (Gung thang), the capital of the Ngari region in far western Tibet.

1058 An annotation in the Tibetan text questions the word Pal (Dpal). However, it is clear now that Pal is actually an abbreviation of Palden Chimé Drubpa (Dpal ldan 'chi med grub pa), a major disciple of Bodong Panchen. He was an important teacher of the Bodong tradition and is mentioned several times in the biography of the venerable lady Chökyi Drönmé, with whom he also spent some time. For information about Chimé Drubpa, see Diemberger et al. (1997), 110–12, and Diemberger (forthcoming 2007). See also Rinchen Namgyal, *Making the Body Hairs of the Faithful Flutter*, 18–19, for the encounter of Lady Kunga Sangmo and Pal Chimé Drubpa (Dpal 'chi med grub pa) with the mad yogin Tsang Nyön Heruka in 1472.

1059 Maryul (Mar yul) is sometimes listed as one of the three regions of Ngari in western Tibet. Dorjé Phagmo Dechen Chödrön and Dra Tupten Namgyal, *Past Lives of the Samding Dorjé Phagmo Incarnations*, 36, specifically name Chimé Drubpa ('Chi med grub pa) as one of the group that accompanied the venerable lady Kunga Sangmo to Maryul.

1060 The term *Western Mongols (stod hor)* was first applied to the dominions of Hülugü Khan in Iran. But from the fourteenth century it was used to refer to the Jaghatai Khanate, the Turkestan kingdom in Central Asia ruled by descendants of Genghis Khan's son Jaghatai (ca. 1185–1242). See Petech (1990), 30 n. 113, etc.

1061 Literally, "elevating the wings" *(gshog rlabs 'degs pa).*

1062 According to Dorjé Phagmo Dechen Chödrön and Dra Tupten Namgyal, *Past Lives of the Samding Dorjé Phagmo Incarnations*, 37, and Diemberger et al. (1997), 112, the venerable lady Kunga Sangmo died at the age of forty-four (forty-three according to Western calculation) at Riwoché. Since she was born in 1459, her death can be dated to 1502. Also see Diemberger (forthcoming 2007).

1063 Tangtong Gyalpo's one-armspan circular residence *(gzims khang gzhu sgor mo)* was apparently just one armspan in diameter, as would be the case for a meditation cell. See also Könchok Palsang and Dewa Sangpo, *Bright Lamp*, 394, who say Tangtong stopped speaking and sealed his one-armspan circular residence in the sixth month of a Tiger Year *(rtag lo>stag lo)*, which could be 1474 or 1482.

1064 The text actually reads only "the residence, which was built like" *(gzims khang zo ba lta bu).* This section is based closely on Könchok Palsang and Dewa Sangpo, *Bright Lamp*, 394: *gzims khang gzhu 'gang [>gang] sgor mo zo [>bzo] ba*, "the residence, which was built like a one-armspan circular [structure]." It seems that part of the original sentence was mistakenly omitted when copied into the newer biography.

1065 Tangtong Gyalpo wrote on a writing slate *(sa 'bo ra)* during periods when he was observing vows of silence.

1066 *Lañcana* and *vartula* are two scripts used to write Sanskrit, with *vartula* being a rounded form of *lañcana.*

1067 In Könchok Palsang and Dewa Sangpo, *Bright Lamp*, 396–97, this teaching is much longer and seems to be a record of everything Tangtong Gyalpo wrote on the slate.

1068 Jang Taklung (Byang Stag lung) was the main monastery of the Taklung Kagyü tradition, founded north of Lhasa in 1180 by the master Tashi Pal (Bkra' shis dpal, 1142–1210).

1069 The Path with the Result (Lam 'bras) is the most important tantric system of the Sakya tradition. The Time of the Path (Lam dus) is the common name used for the daily Hevajra meditation practice. The Profound Path Guruyoga (Lam zab bla ma'i rnal 'byor) is the term for the Hevajra guruyoga practice used in the Path with the Result.

1070 *Litany of the Names of Mañjuśrī (Mañjuśrījñānasattvasyaparamārthanāmasaṃgīti. 'Jam dpal ye shes sems dpa'i don dam pa'i mtshan yang dag par brjod pa)*, Toh 360, Kangyur, rgyud 'bum, *ka*, 1b–13b.

1071 Quote not identified.

1072 Markham (Smar khams) is an area in far eastern Tibet. Its eastern border with the Szechuan province of China is marked by the Drichu River, its western border is marked by the Dachu River, and the province of Yunnan is to the south.

1073 According to Könchok Palsang and Dewa Sangpo, *Bright Lamp*, 423, Tangtong Gyalpo was at Riwoché in western Tibet when he realized the river was flooding over the levees in Lhasa. He magically traveled to Lhasa. The levees seem to have had specific names, one called White Smiling Levee *(chu rags dkar po 'dzum ldan)* and another called White Solid Levee *(chu rags dkar po rab brtan)*. For information about another historical threat of flooding in Lhasa, see note 656.

1074 Könchok Palsang and Dewa Sangpo, *Bright Lamp*, 476–77, tell the names of the various major disciples *(bu chen)* and where each was sent. Tangtong Gyalpo's son Kyabpa Sangpo (Skyabs pa bzang po) was among them and, as mentioned above in the biography, he was given a turquoise image of Vajradhara and sent to Kongpo.

1075 See also Könchok Palsang and Dewa Sangpo, *Bright Lamp*, 477–78. Tangtong Gyalpo was sealed in retreat with only a hole in the door *(bug sgo)* and, when speaking to his disciples, mentioned the existence of many prophecies about his long life.

1076 The translation of the term *ha la lcog 'gyel* as *unconscious convulsions* is uncertain. Sherab Palden, *Ocean of Marvels*, 529, has the spelling *rtsog sgyel ha la nag po*.

1077 In Sherab Palden, *Ocean of Marvels*, 530–31, Tangtong Gyalpo articulates many of the causes for such epidemic diseases, linking them to the degenerate behavior of people at that time.

1078 Pañjaranātha (Gur gyi mgon po) is the name of a form of the protector Mahākāla most practiced in the Sakya tradition.

1079 Dangra (Dang ra) is in the district of Jang (Byang). See Könchok Palsang and Dewa Sangpo, *Bright Lamp*, 409, 489.

1080 Tangtong Gyalpo's father, Önpo Dorjé Gyaltsen (Dbon po Rdo rje rgyal mtshan). See note 311 for descriptions of him from the different biographies.

1081 *Prayer of Maitreya (Āryamaitreyapraṇidhāna. 'Phags pa byams pa'i smon)*, Toh 1096, Kangyur, gzungs 'dus, *waṃ*, 266a–267a. Tuṣita (Dga' ldan) is the paradise of the buddha Maitreya.

1082 Ewaṃ Gakyil (E waṃ dga' 'khyil) is the name of one of Tangtong Gyalpo's residences on the mountain of Riwoché. Lochen Gyurmé Dechen wrote this biography in the same house.

1083 The seven siblings *(lcam dral bdun)* are in the retinue of Mahākāla.

1084 The Sakya master Kunga Lekpai Jungné (Kun dga' legs pa'i 'byung gnas, 1704–60) later visited "the precious great adept's Circular Residence of the Sleeping Dog" *(grub thob rin po che'i gzims chung khyi nyal sgo[r] mo)* at Riwoché in 1745. While in the room, he made intense prayers to Tangtong Gyalpo, to the point of shedding tears, and had the visionary experience of a rain of tiny figures of Tangtong, about the size of a grain of barley, falling upon him. See Kunga Lodrö, *Boundless Miracles*, 167.

1085 *Essence of Dependent Origination (Āryapratītyasamutpādahṛdayanāma. 'Phags pa rten cing 'brel bar 'byung ba'i snying po zhes bya ba)*, Toh 521, Kangyur, rgyud 'bum, *na*, 59a.

1086 See note 287 for a list of these nine dance moods *(gar dgu'i nyams)*.

1087 The Samantabhadra Temple was at the peak of Riwoché and the Tārā Temple was on the middle of the mountainside. See Sherab Palden, *An Ocean of Marvels*, 556–57.

1088 The following story is much more detailed in Könchok Palsang and Dewa Sangpo, *Bright Lamp*, 489–92, where Tangtong Gyalpo also mentions that he has already explained about some of his other past lives, such as when he took birth as a dog and as an elephant, and that those accounts have been written down *(yig cha la 'khod yod)*. These original versions do not seem to have survived.

1089 A lake goddess *(mtsho sman)* is a menmo *(sman mo)* goddess who lives in a lake. See Nebesky-Wojkowitz (1956), 198–202, for details about the men *(sman)* goddesses.

1090 *An Ocean of Marvels (Ngo mtshar rgya mtsho)* is the biography of Tangtong Gyalpo written by his disciple Sherab Palden. See Sherab Palden, *Ocean of Marvels*, 539–60, for a detailed description of the various temples at Riwoché and the sculptures and paintings in them. This text was one of the main sources used by Gyurmé Dechen when writing the translated biography. Curiously, he does not mention Sherab Palden's work in the colophon when speaking of his sources.

1091 The *Karaṇḍavyūha Sūtra* is one of the major sūtras of Avalokiteśvara, translated into Tibetan during the early period of translation in Tibet. *Āryakaraṇḍavyūhanāmamahāyānasūtra, 'Phags pa za ma tog bkod pa zhes bya ba theg pa chen po'i mdo*, Toh 116, Kangyur, mdo sde, *ja*, 200a–247b.

1092 According to Könchok Palsang and Dewa Sangpo, *Bright Lamp*, 486, this sculptor was named Palden Döndrup (Dpal ldan don grub).

1093 Könchok Palsang and Dewa Sangpo, *Bright Lamp*, 488, make the interesting comment that prior to this time Tangtong Gyalpo did not consecrate images by casting barley *(phyag nas)*, but after this he did so.

1094 The spelling *'dzum* should be corrected to *'jam*, as in the original Dergé print and in Könchok Palsang and Dewa Sangpo, *Bright Lamp*, 486, who say this image was green.

1095 Instead of *young and burly (gzhon shing rgyas pa)*, Könchok Palsang and Dewa Sangpo, *Bright Lamp*, 486–87, say *the color of a lush tree (ljon shing rgyas pa'i mdog can)*.

1096 The four styles of enlightened action are peaceful, enriching, powerful, and terrible. In Könchok Palsang and Dewa Sangpo, *Bright Lamp*, 487, the sculptor says he made all the images with the same flesh color, positions, and hand implements, and had no recollection of them changing.

1097 The five poisons are desire, hatred, ignorance, pride, and envy.

1098 According to Sherab Palden, *Ocean of Marvels*, 536, the woman was terrified and fled because she thought Tangtong Gyalpo was a rākṣasa demon *(srin po)*.

1099 As described earlier in the biography, Tangtong Gyalpo had sent his disciple Gendun Gyaltsen (Dge 'dun rgyal mtshan) to China with a message and a bowl of steaming rice for the Chinese emperor after having received gifts from him.

1100 Also see Könchok Palsang and Dewa Sangpo, *Bright Lamp*, 483–85, where the Sakya Khön master Delek Tashi (b. 1408?) asks Tangtong Gyalpo how many iron bridges, wooden bridges, ferries, temples, images, and so forth he had built. Tangtong's detailed reply matches the present statement in content, but not exact wording.

1101 The important Kadampa monastery of Nartang (Snar thang) was founded in 1153 by Tumtön Lodrö Drakpa (Gtum ston Blo gros grags pa, 1106–66).

1102 The phrase *heart of enlightenment (byang chub snying po)* has two meanings: the Vajrāsana at Bodhgayā in India, where every buddha is said to reach enlightenment, and the actual enlightenment of a buddha.

1103 The spiritual level of Delight *(sa rab dga' ba)* is the first of the ten spiritual levels *(bhūmi)* of the bodhisattva path.

1104 The seven riches of a Noble One *('phags pa'i nor bdun)* are faith, moral discipline, learning, generosity, shame, modesty, and wisdom.

1105 This and the next five couplets express the aspiration to realize the six perfections of generosity, moral discipline, patience, diligence, meditation, and wisdom.

1106 The Nepa governor of the Lhasa region (Lha sa'i sne pa) was Drungchen Paljor Gyalpo (Drung chen Dpal 'byor rgyal po, d. 1490), the son of Lady Kalsang, who had been Tangtong Gyalpo's main patron in Central Tibet.

1107 The information here is in substance, but not exact wording, only a small portion of Tangtong Gyalpo's long edict issued at the time of his son Nyima Sangpo's enthronment at Riwoché. See Sherab Palden, *Ocean of Marvels*, 491–506.

1108 The Yarlung sovereign Chen Nga Ngawang Drakpa (Yar lungs Gong ma Spyan snga Ngag dbang grags pa) is the Pakmodru ruler Ngagi Wangpo (Ngag gi dbang po, 1439–91), referred to as Depa Nedongpa Chen Nga Ngawang Chögyal (Sde pa Sne sdong pa Spyan mnga' Ngag dbang chos rgyal) in Könchok Palsang and Dewa Sangpo, *Bright Lamp*, 479. He was enthroned as the abbot of Densatel (Gdan sa thel) Monastery in 1454, but did not become the eighth ruler of the Pakmodru dynasty until 1481. As will be mentioned later in the biography, Ngagi Wangpo also helped Tangtong Gyalpo's son Tenzin Nyima Sangpo build the iron bridge of Nyago (Nya mgo) in 1485. See Sönam Drakpa, *Magical Key to Royal Genealogies*, 92–95, and Losang Trinlé, *Clarification of Knowledge*, 1180.

Since Ngagi Wangpo is called *sovereign (gong ma)* and *ruler (sde pa)* in Tangtong's biographies, this invitation from him probably took place after he came to power in 1481.

1109 The Rinpung governor *(nang so)* Tsokyé Dorjé (Mtsho skyes rdo rje, 1462–1510) was the son of the Rinpung governor Norsangpa (Nor bzang pa, 1403–66). Tsokyé Dorjé became Ngagi Wangpo's prime minister *(slon chen)*, and then ruled as a regent after the Pakmodru sovereign's death. For a short sketch of his life, see Losang Trinlé, *Clarification of Knowledge*, 1916–17.

1110 Tashi Dargyé (Bkra shis dar rgyas) was the governor, or "ruler of ten thousand households," in Ja (Byang [>Bya] pa khri dpon), also called Jayul (Bya yul), which is an area south of the Dakpo and Yarlung regions of southern Central Tibet. He was one of the most generous religious patrons of the fifteenth century.

1111 On several occasions in the biography, Tangtong Gyalpo notes that he tricked people toward virtue. In one song he said, "The reason I travel around the country/ is to trick people toward virtue/ and guide the six types of living beings/ onto the path of liberation."

1112 As mentioned several times in the biography, Tangtong Gyalpo had wished to build an iron bridge at the boat crossing of Nyago (Nya mgo gru kha) for many years. Nyago is on the Tsangpo River, linking the area of the Pakmodru capital of Nedong to the south with the Ön Valley to the north. See Dorje (1999), 182–86, for maps and the location of the ruins of the Nyago bridge.

1113 The Kagyü monastery of Tsetang (Rtsed thong>thang), which is between the Pakmodru capital of Nedong and the Tsangpo River, was founded by the first Pakmodru ruler, Tai Situ Jangchup Gyaltsen (1302–64), in 1351. See Roerich (1976), 1082–84, for the story of its construction and the series of abbots. See also Ferrari (1958), 48–50, 123, and Dorje (1999), 182–86.

1114 See Mingyur Dorjé, *Examination of the Legacy of Tangtong Gyalpo's Iron-Bridge Building Activities*, 338, for important comments about this iron bridge over the main part of the Tsangpo River and its thirty-two stone piers on the north side that allowed people and cattle to get to the bridge during flood season. The Nyago bridge was the longest bridge ever built in Tibet. See also Dorje (1999), 186, who notes that five large stone bridge piers are all that now remain of the Nyago bridge.

1115 See especially Sönam Drakpa, *Magical Key to Royal Genealogies*, 95, who says the Pakmodru ruler Ngagi Wangpo (1439–91) built the great iron bridge at the ferry crossing at Nyangpo *(nyang po gru la lcags kyi zam mo che 'dzugs pa)*. In the old biographies and elsewhere, Nyangpo (Nyang po) is a common variation of Nyago (Nya mgo). Losang Trinlé, *Clarification of Knowledge*, 1180, clarifies this important passage by saying Ngagi Wangpo provided the necessary assistance for Tangtong Gyalpo to build this iron bridge. No date is given for the Nyago bridge in the early biography of Könchok Palsang and Dewa Sangpo, *Bright Lamp*, 478–80. However, the following information proves that it was built in the Wood Snake *(shing sbrul)* Year of 1485. As discussed in the first part of the Introduction and translated at the end of this book, the first text to reveal Tangtong's death says he died in a Snake Year *(sbrul lo)* and that Tenzin Nyima Sangpo returned to Riwoché that year after completing the Nyago iron bridge, referred to here as the Nyangpo bridge *(nyang po'i lcags zam)*. See Kunga Sönam Drakpa Palsang, *Final Story Concerning the Nirvāṇa of the Great Adept*, 162a, 164b. The Pakmodru ruler Ngagi Wangpo, who was present at the completion of the bridge, did not come to power until 1481, and died in 1491. The only Snake Year *(sbrul lo)* during his reign was the Wood Snake Year *(shing sbrul)* of 1485.

1116 Könchok Palsang and Dewa Sangpo, *Bright Lamp*, 479, specify that the ruler mentioned here as the Desi Rinpoché (Sde srid Rin po che) was Depa Nedongpa Chen Nga Ngawang Chögyal (Sde pa Sne sdong pa Spyan mnga' Ngag dbang chos rgyal). As mentioned above, this is the Pakmodru sovereign Ngagi Wangpo. See also note 1108.

1117 As mentioned earlier in the biography, Tangtong Gyalpo had built a stūpa and temple at Drakralkha (Brag ral kha). Urtö Chökhor Gang (Dbur stod chos 'khor sgang) is on the Kyichu River. The ferry crossing of Shar Drukha (Shar gru kha) is at Rong in Tsang. See Könchok Palsang and Dewa Sangpo, *Bright Lamp*, 480.

1118 See note 1042 for more about Tangtong Gyalpo's son Kyabpa Sangpo (Skyabs pa bzang po).

1119 The Dharma king Namkha Dorjé (Chos rgyal Nam mkha' rdo rje) was the son of Namgyal Draksang (1395–1475) and succeeded his father as governor of the district of Jang. He is praised here as a patron and disciple of Tangtong Gyalpo. However, he is described in the biographies of Tsang Nyön Heruka (1452–1507) as an aggressive ruler who had stolen the district of Lho in addition to his own realm. See Natsok Rangdrol, *Heart of the Sun Illuminating the Vajrayāna*, 61–63, and Rinchen Namgyal, *Making the Body Hairs of the Faithful Flutter*, 51–52.

1120 The wood and rope were required to keep the iron bridge in good repair.

1121 These verses from the *Bright Lamp of Prophecy (Lung bstan gsal ba'i sgron me)* are not included in the fragment of the text by that name in Könchok Palsang and Dewa Sangpo, *Bright Lamp*, 100–103, but some are found in another series of verses that Padmasambhava spoke to Tangtong Gyalpo. See Könchok Palsang and Dewa Sangpo, *Bright Lamp*, 161–67. The names of many of Tangtong's major disciples and other followers are also listed in Könchok Palsang and Dewa Sangpo, *Bright Lamp*, 386–89, including eighteen women said to be emanations of ḍākinīs.

1122 These lines from the *Bright Lamp of Prophecy (Lung bstan gsal ba'i sgron me)* are found in the portion of the text preserved in Könchok Palsang and Dewa Sangpo, *Bright Lamp*, 102.

1123 Sukhāvatī is the paradise of the buddha Amitābha.

1124 This couplet from the *Bright Lamp of Prophecy (Lung bstan gsal ba'i sgron me)* is not included in the text by that name in Könchok Palsang and Dewa Sangpo, *Bright Lamp*, 100–103, but is found in another fragment of the text that Padmasambhava spoke to Tangtong Gyalpo. See Könchok Palsang and Dewa Sangpo, *Bright Lamp*, 161.

1125 Delek Chödren (Bde legs chos 'dren) was the venerable lady Chökyi Drönmé's most trusted companion and attendant, and is mentioned many times in the biography of Chökyi Drönmé. She was a novice nun *(dge tshul ma)* and a disciple of Bodong Panchen Cholé Namgyal.

1126 With some slight variations, these comments have all been taken from Chökyi Drönmé's biography. The conversation occurred in about 1455 at Riwoché, thirty years before Tangtong Gyalpo passed away. See Author Unknown, *Biography of the Venerable Lady Chökyi Drönma*, 122a.

1127 See note 114. According to Könchok Palsang and Dewa Sangpo, *Bright Lamp*, 50, the goddess of longevity named Caṇḍālī *(tshe'i lha mo tsan dha li)* is the consort of the buddha Amitābha.

1128 The four māras *(bdud bzhi)* are of the afflictions, the Lord of Death, the aggregates, and the child of the gods.

1129 *Sūtra of Excellent Golden Light (Āryasuvarṇaprabhāsottamasūtrendrājanāmamahāyānasūtra. 'Phags pa gser 'od dam pa mdo sde'i dbang po'i rgyal po zhes bya ba theg pa chen po'i mdo)*, 160a. Toh 556, Kangyur, rgyud 'bum, *pa*, 151b–273a.

1130 The twelve acts *(mdzad pa gcu gnyis)* of Buddha Śākyamuni were to descend from Tuṣita heaven, enter his mother's womb, take birth, gain proficiency in the arts, enjoy consorts, renounce the world, practice asceticism, meditate on the path to enlightenment at the Vajrāsana of Bodhgayā, attain perfect enlightenment, turn the wheel of Dharma, display miracles, and pass into final nirvāṇa. See Losang Trinlé, *Clarification of Knowledge*, 1739-40.

1131 These lines from the *Bright Lamp of Prophecy (Lung bstan gsal ba'i sgron me)* are found in the version of the text preserved in Könchok Palsang and Dewa Sangpo, *Bright Lamp*, 102.

1132 See note 45 for an explanation of these calculations. The following description of Tangtong Gyalpo's death is condensed from the original document, Kunga Sönam Drakpa Palsang, *Final Story Concerning the Nirvāṇa of the Great Adept.* The Tibetan text and a translation of the work are provided at the end of this book.

1133 I am grateful to Dezhung Rinpoché for his detailed explanation of these lines.

1134 The spiritual son Sherab Palden (*thugs sras* Shes rab dpal ldan) was the only witness to Tangtong Gyalpo's miraculous death and was the author of one of his earliest biographies. The full series of verses from which the following lines are quoted (with some differences) is found in the earliest description of Tangtong's death, written by Sherab Palden's son. See Kunga Sönam Drakpa Palsang, *Final Story Concerning the Nirvāṇa of the Great Adept*, fol. 162b.

1135 An annotation in the Tibetan text questions the meaning of *mi 'di.* Gyurmé Dechen, *Beautiful Forms of Pure Faith*, 180b, reads *mi'i*, which has been followed in the translation.

1136 The governor of the district of Jang, referred to here as the Dharma king Namkha Lekpa (Chos rgyal Nam mkha' legs pa), was the son of the Dharma king

Namkha Dorjé (Chos rgyal Nam mkha' rdo rje), and the grandson of Namgyal Draksang (1395–1475). In the biography of Tsang Nyön Heruka, the governor Namkha Dorjé and his two sons, Namkha Lekpa and Kunga Lekpa, are mentioned around the year 1480. See Rinchen Namgyal, *Making the Body Hairs of the Faithful Flutter*, 53.

1137 This title is somewhat different than the title on the first page of the biography.

1138 The Kalkī Dharma king Namkha Tsewang Puntsok Wangi Gyalpo (Rigs ldan Chos kyi rgyal po Nam mkha' tshe dbang phun tshogs dbang gi rgyal po) was governor of the district of Jang around the beginning of the seventeenth century. Like his ancestor Namgyal Draksang (1395–1475), this ruler is referred to as *Kalkī (Rigs ldan)* to indicate his connection with the Kālacakra tradition and his identity with the Kalkī emperors of the legendary land of Shambhala. He is also mentioned in the autobiography of the Sakya master Mangtö Ludrup Gyatso (Mang thos klu sgrub rgya mtsho, 1523–96), where he is found in strict meditation retreat at Ngamring during the year 1592. See Mangtö Ludrup Gyatso, *Coquette's Mirror*, 592. The author of the translated biography, Lochen Gyurmé Dechen, was the royal preceptor *(ti shri)* to the Jang governor. See Dradul Wangpo, *Jewel Rosary of Elegant Explications*, 320.

1139 The term *vajra-moon (rdo rje zla ba)* is a respectful euphemism for semen.

1140 Tangtong Gyalpo built the Samdrup Temple at Pari near the Tibetan border with Bhutan in 1433–34. Könchok Dewé Jungné of the Samdrup Temple (Bsam 'grub lha khang pa Dkon mchog bde ba'i 'byung gnas), who is described as a paternal descendant of the great Iron-Bridge Man *(lcags zam pa chen po'i gdung gi dbon)*, was a disciple of the author of this biography, Lochen Gyurmé Dechen. See Jamgön Ameshap, *Chariot of Amazing Faith*, 435, where one of Lochen Gyurmé Dechen's disciples is identified as "the resident of the Samdrup Temple, who is a paternal descendant of the Iron-Bridge Man *(lcags zam gdung dbon bsam grub lha khang pa)*."

1141 The Ewaṃ Gakyil (E waṃ dga' 'khyil) was one of Tangtong Gyalpo's residences on Riwoché. Also see note 44 concerning the date of composition.

1142 This final paragraph was apparently added at the time of the Dergé edition of the biography. It is not found in the original Riwoché edition, which simply says, "written down by various scribes" *(yi ge pa ni sna tshogs kyis bgyis pa)*. See Gyurmé Dechen, *Beautiful Forms of Pure Faith*, 181a, and *New Mirror in Which All the Marvels Are Clear*, 234a. The Gyalwang Könchok Jungné (Rgyal dbang Dkon mchog 'byung gnas) named in the new sentence would seem to be the same as the Könchok Dewai Jungné (Dkon mchog bde ba'i 'byung gnas) mentioned in the previous paragraph of the original colophon. However, this new sentence identifies him as the author of the biography! Another difficulty is that no Earth Female Sheep Year (*sa mo lug*, 1739, 1799, etc.) occurred during the lifetime of the Dergé king Sawang Kundrup Dega Sangpo (Sa dbang Kun grub bde dga' bzang po, 1768–90), whose long life is prayed for by the editor Shechen Drungyik Tenzin Gyaltsen (Zhe chen drung yig Bstan 'dzin rgyal mtshan, fl. 1759–71) in his closing prayer to the Dergé edition (the prayer has not been translated). See

Gyurmé Dechen, *Jewel Mirror in Which All Is Clear*, 346. I have not been able to resolve these problems.

1143 Noble Subhūti ('Phags pa Rab 'byor) is the recipient of many of the Buddha's discourses in the various sūtras on the perfection of wisdom.

1144 Quote not located. The term *Scriptures of the Monastic Code ('Dul ba lung)* is used to designate a number of basic Indian texts concerning the Buddhist monastic code, or vinaya.

1145 Mahākaruṇika is Avalokiteśvara and the Great Wrathful Lord is Hayagrīva. Portions of this quote from the *Bright Lamp of Prophecy* (although sometimes considerably different) are found in Könchok Palsang and Dewa Sangpo, *Bright Lamp*, 100.

1146 Pema Lingpa (Padma gling pa, 1450–1521) was a famous Bhutanese treasure revealer. This quotation is also found in an annotation at the beginning of the Tibetan text of the translated biography.

1147 For all the previous lines of this quotation, with some important differences, see the portion of the prophecy in Könchok Palsang and Dewa Sangpo, *Bright Lamp*, 102.

1148 These are the "four seals" of the doctrine: all composite things are impermanent *('dus byas thams cad mi rtag pa)*, all that is tainted is suffering *(zag bcas thams cad sdug bsngal ba)*, all phenomena lack self-nature *(chos thams cad bdag med pa)*, nirvāṇa is peace *(mya ngan las 'das pa zhi ba)*.

1149 The reasons for identifying this Snake Year *(sbrul lo)* as the Wood Snake Year *(shing sbrul lo)* of 1485 were presented in the introductory discussion of Tangtong Gyalpo's dates and lifespan.

1150 Part of one Tibetan word in this line is illegible in the original manuscript.

1151 The Dharma lord Tenzin (Bstan 'dzin Chos rje) is Tangtong Gyalpo's son and heir, Tenzin Nyima Sangpo (Bstan 'dzin Nyi ma bzang po, b. 1436).

1152 The meaning and translation of this phrase is uncertain.

1153 Ānandamitra (Kun dga' bshes gnyen) has not been identified.

1154 Khecara is the paradise associated with the goddess Vajrayoginī, one of whose forms bears the face of a sow.

1155 See notes 506 and 517 for information about this guruyoga, which Tangtong Gyalpo received from Vajradhara in a vision described in the biography.

1156 Rāhu (Sgra gcan) is the chief of all the planetary gods *(gza')*. He is believed to be responsible for eclipses.

1157 Nyangpo (Nyang po) is an alternate form of Nyago (Nya mgo), where Tangtong Gyalpo had planned to build a bridge for many years, which was finally accomplished by his son Tenzin Nyima Sangpo in 1485. For details about this, see note 1115.

1158 The meaning of *ldab se phyod de ba* is obscure.

1159 This would seem to be a reference to the biography of Tangtong Gyalpo written by the author's father, Sherab Palden, to which this text was originally attached as a supplement. See Sherab Palden, *Ocean of Marvels*, 556–57, where the temple at the peak of Riwoché is described in more detail.

1160 See Sherab Palden, *Ocean of Marvels*, 556–57, for a description of the Samantabhadra Temple and its contents on the peak of Riwoché.

1161 The text actually says *one (gcig)*, which I have taken to be a scribal mistake for *eleven (bcu gcig)*.

1162 The spelling *skye (to be born)* in the Tibetan text would seem to be a mistake, perhaps for another term such as *dgyes (to be pleased or happy)* or *'gyed (to distribute)*.

1163 With the phrase "the spiritual son told me" *(thugs sras pa'i zhal nas gsungs)*, Kunga Sönam Drakpa Palsang clearly says his father, the spiritual son Sherab Palden (Thugs sras Shes rab dpal ldan), personally told him this information.

1164 Tangtong Gyalpo's descendant Lodrö Gyaltsen (Blo gros rgyal mtshan) is otherwise unknown. Sherab Palden's *Ocean of Marvels (Ngo mtshar rgya mtsho)* was discussed in the first part of the Introduction.

Bibliography

Sources in Tibetan Language

Amoghasiddhi. *Genealogy of the Che Lords of the Golden Temple of the Great Monastery of Glorious Shalu. Chos grwa chen po dpal zha lu gser khang gi bdag po jo bo lce'i gdung rab. Dbu can* manuscript, 55 fols.

Anonymous. *Extensive Explication of the Practice of the Six Perfections: The Central Meaning of the Great Guidance Manual. Khrig [sic!] yig chen mo'i gzhung don phar phyin drug gi nyams len rgyas bshad.* In *Tangtong's Oral Transmission (Thang stong snyan brgyud)*, vol. 1: 53.2–63.2. New Delhi: Trayang, 1973.

Anonymous. *All-Illuminating Lamp, A Rosary of Nectar Enchanting to See: A Biography of the Great Accomplished Lord Tangtong Gyalpo, the Iron-Bridge Man. Grub pa'i dbang phyug chen po lcags zam pa thang stong rgyal po'i rnam par thar pa kun gsal sgron me bdud rtsi'i 'phreng ba mthong bas yid 'phrogs. Dbu med* manuscript, 161 fols. Nepal-German Manuscript Preservation Project, microfilm reel number AT 85/11. Another example of this work is *Biography of Lifetimes: From the Collected Works of the Great Adept (Grub thob chen po'i gsung 'bum 'khrungs rabs rnam thar)*, with the title *All-Illuminating Lamp: A Biography of the Great Adept Tangtong Gyalpo (Grub thob chen po thang stong rgyal po'i rnam thar kun gsal sgron me)* in the colophon. *Dbu can* manuscript, 273 fols. Nepal-German Manuscript Preservation Project, microfilm reel number E 3068/3–E 3069/1.

Anonymous. *Rejection of Confusion about Virtue and Sin: A Presentation of the Meaning That Clarifies Cause and Result. Dge sdig 'khrul spong rgyu 'bras gsal ba'i don ston.* In *Tangtong's Oral Transmission (Thang stong snyan brgyud)*, vol. 1: 40.3–43.3. New Delhi: Trayang, 1973.

Author Unknown. *Biography of the Venerable Lady Chökyi Drönma, the Third Rebirth of Sönam Dren, Ḍākinī of Primordial Awareness. Ye shes mkha' 'gro bsod nams 'dren gyi sku skye gsum pa rje btsun ma chos kyi sgron ma'i rnam thar.* Incomplete *dbu med* manuscript, 146 fols. Beijing: Cultural Palace of Minorities.

Author Unknown. *Rosary of Ornaments: A Genealogy of the Glorious Sharkapa. Dpal ldan shar ka pa'i gdung rabs brgyan gyi 'phreng ba.* In *Sngon gyi gtam *me tog gi phreng ba*, 51–78. Incomplete *dbu med* manuscript. Dharamsala: Library of Tibetan Works and Archives, 1985.

Chödrak Palsang, Kunpang (Chos grags dpal bzang, Kun spangs). *Jewel Rosary of Great Excellence: A Number of Bright Lamps Illuminating the Biography of the Great Omniscient Dharma Lord. Chos rje kun mkhyen chen po'i rnam thar gsal sgron gyi rnam grangs dge legs chen po nor bu'i 'phreng ba.* In *The 'Dzam-thang Edition of the Collected Works (Gsung-'bum) of Kun-mkhyen Dol-po-pa Shes-rab rgyal-mtshan*, vol. 1. Delhi: Shedrup Books, 1992.

Chökyi Drakpa, Shamarpa (Chos kyi grags pa, Zhwa dmar pa). *Ocean of Marvels: A Biography of the Omnicient Lord, the Great Translator. Rje thams cad mkhyen pa lo tsā ba chen po'i rnam par thar pa ngo mtshar rgya mtsho. Dbu can* manuscript, 130 fols.

Chökyi Drönmé, Jetsun (Chos kyi sgron me, Rje btsun). *Untitled.* In *Supplemental Texts to the Collected Works of Thang stong rgyal po Series (Grub chen thang stong bka' 'bum gyi rgyab chos)*, vol. 2: 240–48. Thimphu: National Library of Bhutan, 1984.

Chökyi Gyatso, Katok Situ (Chos kyi rgya mtsho, Kaḥ thog Si tu). *Necklace of Moon Crystals: A Travelogue of Pilgrimage in Central Tibet and Tsang. Gangs ljongs dbus gtsang gnas bskor lam yig nor bu zla shel gyi se mo do.* Tashijong: Sungrab Nyamso Gyunphel Parkhang, 1972.

———. *A Necklace of Utpala Flowers of Elegant Explication: A Supplement to the Biographies of the Great Secret Oral Transmission of Secret Behavior. Gsang chen gsang spyod snyan brgyud kyi rnam thar zhal skong legs bshad utpal do shal.* In *Tangtong's Oral Transmission (Thang stong snyan brgyud)*, vol. 2: 126.1–127.1. New Delhi: Trayang, 1973.

Dolpopa Sherab Gyaltsen (Dol po pa Shes rab rgyal mtshan). *Dredging the Pit of Saṃsāra: In Praise of the Way the Conqueror's Stūpa of Good Qualities Was Built. Rgyal ba'i mchod rten dpal yon can gyi bzhengs tshul la bstod pa 'khor ba dong sprugs.* In *The Collected Works (Gsung 'bum) of Kun-mkhyen Dol-po-pa Shes-rab rgyal-mtshan (1292–1361)*, vol. 1: 454–59. Paro/Delhi: Lama Ngodrup and Sherab Drimay, 1984.

———. *Prayer Made at the Completion of the Great Stūpa. Sku 'bum chen po grub dus btab pa'i smon lam.* In *The Collected Works (Gsung 'bum) of Kun-mkhyen Dol-po-pa Shes-rab rgyal-mtshan (1292–1361)*, vol. 1: 462–66. Paro/Delhi: Lama Ngodrup and Sherab Drimay, 1984.

Dorjé Phagmo Dechen Chödrön (Rdo rje phag mo Bde chen chos sgron) and Dra Tupten Namgyal (Grwa Thub bstan rnam rgyal). *Past Lives of the Samding Dorjé Phagmo Incarnations, Their Successive Deeds, and a Rough Guide to the Yamdrok Samding Monastery. Bsam sdings rdo rje phag mo'i 'khrungs rabs dang/ sku phreng rim byon gyi mdzad rnam/ yar 'brog bsam sdings dgon gyi dkar chag bcas rags tsam bkod pa.* In *Bod ljongs nang bstan* 2 (1994): 31–58.

Dradul Wangpo, Dartö (Dgra 'dul dbang po, 'Dar stod). *Jewel Rosary of Elegant Explications to Adorn the Throats of the Intelligent: A Clarification of the Origins of the Five Conventional Fields of Knowledge. Tha snyad rig gnas lnga ji ltar byung ba'i tshul gsal bar byed pa blo gsal mgrin rgyan legs bshad nor bu'i phreng ba.* Published with Mangtö Ludrup Gyatso, *Bright Sun of Pure Altruism: A Chronicle of the Doctrine (Bstan rtsis gsal ba'i nyin byed lhag bsam rab dkar)*, 253–322. Lhasa: Bod ljongs mi dmangs dpe skrun khang, 1987.

Dzamling Dorjé, Chöjé Lingpa ('Dzam gling rdo rje, Chos rje gling pa). *Method of Accomplishment and Ritual of Initiation for the Extremely Direct Transmission of the Longevity Practice Combining the Canonical Lineage, Treasure Teachings, and Pure Vision. Bka' gter dag snang zung du 'brel ba'i tshe sgrub shin tu nye brgyud kyi sgrub thabs dbang chog dang bcas pa.* In Jamyang Khyentsé Wangpo and Loter Wangpo, *Compendium of Methods for Accomplishment (Sgrub thabs kun btus)*, vol. 1: 471–80. Dehra Dun: G. Loday, N. Gyaltsen, and N. Lungtok, 1970.

_____. *Uncontrived, Naturally Arisen Vajra Words, the Natural Form of Ceaseless Sound Conveyed in Syllables: A Eulogy to the Great Adept Tangtong Gyalpo. Grub thob chen po thang stong rgyal po la bstod pa bcos min rang byung rdo rje'i tshig 'gags med nā da'i rang gzugs yi ger 'phos pa.* In Tangtong Gyalpo, *Supplemental Texts to the Collected Works of Thang stong rgyal po Series (Grub chen thang stong bka' 'bum gyi rgyab chos)*, vol. 4: 433–39. Thimphu: National Library of Bhutan, 1984.

Gendun Rinchen (Dge 'dun rin chen). *Ear Ornament for Students: History of the Dharma in the Southern Land of Bhutan, the Region to Be Tamed by the Glorious Drukpa. Dpal ldan 'brug pa'i gdul zhing lho phyogs nag mo'i ljongs kyi chos 'byung blo gsar rna ba'i rgyan.* Rta mgo, 1976.

Gökyi Demtruchen, Rikzin (Rgod kyi ldem 'phru can, Rig 'dzin). *Longevity Practice of the Iron Tree. Tshe sgrub lcags kyi sdong po.* In Jamgön Kongtrul, *Treasury of Precious Treasure Teachings (Rin chen gter mdzod)*, vol. 29: 249–69.

Guru Tashi (Gu ru bkra' shis). *Musical Sea of Amazing Stories to Delight Experts: An Elegant Explication Clarifying the Origins of the Teachings of Profound Definitive Meaning in the Great Secret Tradition of the Early Translations That Is the Heart of the Doctrine. Bstan pa'i snying po gsang chen snga 'gyur nges don zab mo'i chos kyi byung ba gsal bar byed pa'i legs bshad mkhas pa dga' byed ngo mtshar gtam gyi rol mtsho.* Koko Nor: Krung go'i bod kyi shes rig dpe skrun khang, 1990.

Gyaltsen Sangpo (Rgyal mtshan bzang po). *Untitled.* In *Supplemental Texts to the Collected Works of Thang stong rgyal po Series (Grub chen thang stong bka' 'bum gyi rgyab chos)*, vol. 2: 248–57. Thimphu: National Library of Bhutan, 1984.

Gyurmé Dechen, Lochen ('Gyur med bde chen, Lo chen). *Beautiful Forms of Pure Faith Appear in This New, Immaculate, Jewel Mirror in Which All the Marvels in the Five Biographies of the Peerless Accomplished Lord, the Iron-Bridge Man, Are Clear. Mtshungs med grub pa'i dbang phyug lcags zam pa'i/ rnam thar lnga yi ngo mtshar kun gsal ba/ dri med nor bu'i me long gsar pa 'dir/ rab dkar dad pa'i gzugs mdzes ci yang 'char.* Xylograph, 181 fols. Nepal-German Manuscript Preservation Project, microfilm reel number L 794/5–L 795/1. This is almost certainly an example of the original Riwoché (Ri bo che) edition. Another later reproduction of this edition is *New Mirror in Which All the Marvels Are Clear: A Biography of the Glorious Great Accomplished Lord Tangtong Gyalpo, the Iron-Bridge Man (Dpal grub pa'i dbang phyug chen po lcags zam pa thang stong rgyal po'i rnam par thar pa ngo mtshar kun gsal me long gsar pa).* Xylograph, 235 fols. Nepal-German Manuscript Preservation Project, microfilm reel number E 2958/2.

_____. *Jewel Mirror in Which All Is Clear: A Biography of the Glorious Accomplished Lord Tsöndru Sangpo. Dpal grub pa'i dbang phyug brtson 'grus bzang po'i rnam par thar pa kun gsal nor bu'i me long.* Bir: Tibetan Khampa Industrial Society, 1976. This is an Indian reprint of the revised Dergé edition. A microfilm copy of an original print is the first text on Reel C1-9 in the microfilm collection of the East Asia Library, University of Washington, Seattle. This biography has also been published in modern book format in Chengdu by Si khron mi rigs dpe skrun khang, 1982.

_____. *Rosary of Utpala Flowers: An Autobiographical Supplication. Rnam thar gsol 'debs utpa la'i phreng ba.* In Jamgön Ameshap Ngawang Kunga Sönam, *Chariot of Amazing Faith*, 431–34.

Jamgön Ameshap Ngawang Kunga Sönam ('Jam mgon A mes zhabs Ngag dbang kun dga' bsod nams). *Chariot of Amazing Faith: An Elegant Explication of the History of the Excellent Teachings of the Profound and Vast Glorious Kālacakra. Dpal dus kyi 'khor lo'i zab pa dang rgya che ba'i dam pa'i chos byung ba'i tshul legs par bshad pa ngo mtshar dad pa'i shing rta.* In *The Collected Works of A-mes-zhabs Ngag dbang kun dga' bsod nams*, vol. 19: 1–532. Kathmandu: Sa skya rgyal yongs gsung rab slob gnyer khang, 2000.

_____. *Fulfillment of All Needs and Wishes: A Treasury of Amazing Jewels, the Biographies of the Precious Hereditary Lineage of the Glorious Sakyapa, the Great Heirs of the Buddha in the Northern Regions of Jambudvīpa. 'Dzam gling byang phyogs kyi thub pa'i rgyal tshab chen po dpal ldan sa skya pa'i gdung rabs rin po che ji ltar byon pa'i tshul gyi rnam par thar pa ngo mtshar rin po che'i bang mdzod dgos 'dod kun 'byung.* Beijing: Mi rigs dpe skrun khang, 1986.

_____. *Sun Illuminating All the Teachings of Saṃvara: An Elegant Explication of the History of the Excellent Teachings of Cakrasaṃvara, the Elixir of the Ancestral Dharma of the Glorious Sakyapa. Dpal sa skya pa'i yab chos kyi nying khu 'khor lo sdom pa'i dam pa'i chos byung ba'i tshul legs par bshad pa bde mchog chos kun gsal ba'i nyin byed.* New Delhi: Ngawang Tobgay, 1974.

_____. *Sun Illuminating All the Teachings of the Doctrine Protectors: An Elegant Explication of the History of the Profound Dharma Cycles of Glorious Vajra Mahākāla. Dpal rdo rje nag po chen po'i zab mo'i chos skor rnams byung ba'i tshul legs par bshad pa bstan srung chos kun gsal ba'i nyin byed.* 2 vols. New Delhi: T. G. Dhongthog Rinpoche, 1979.

Jamgön Kongtrul Lodrö Tayé ('Jam mgon Kong sprul Blo gros mtha' yas). *Encompassment of All Knowledge: A Compendium of the Approaches of the Vehicles, A Treasury of the Jewels of the Teaching, A Treatise That Carefully Presents the Three Trainings. Theg pa'i sgo kun las btus pa gsung rab rin po che'i mdzod bslab pa gsum legs par ston pa'i bstan bcos shes bya kun khyab.* Beijing: Mi rigs dpe skrun khang, 2002.

_____. *Essence of All Sūtra and Tantra: Liturgy for the Meditation and Recitation of Mahākaruṇika According to the Direct Transmission of the Accomplished Lord Tangtong Gyalpo. Grub pa'i dbang phyug thang stong rgyal po'i nye brgyud thugs rje chen po'i sgom bzlas kyi ngag 'don mdo sngags yongs bcud.* In Jamyang Khyentsé Wangpo and Loter Wangpo, *Compendium of Methods for Accomplishment (Sgrub thabs kun btus)*, vol. 3: 31–35. Dehra Dun: G. Loday, N. Gyaltsen, and N. Lungtok, 1970. Also in Tangtong Gyalpo, *Collected Works of Grub chen Thang stong rgyal po (Grub chen thang stong rgyal po'i bka' 'bum)*, vol. 3: 705–26.

_____. *Infinite Benefit for Others: An Enhancement of the Meditation and Bestowal of the Six Syllables in the Direct Transmission of the Accomplished Lord, the Great Iron-Bridge Man. Grub pa'i dbang phyug lcags zam pa chen po'i nye brgyud yi ge drug pa'i sgom lung 'bogs tshul gzhan phan mkha' khyab.* In Jamyang Khyentsé Wangpo and Loter Wangpo, *Compendium of Methods for Accomplishment (Sgrub thabs kun btus)*, vol. 3: 21–31. Dehra Dun: G. Loday, N. Gyaltsen, and N. Lungtok, 1970. Also in Tangtong Gyalpo, *Collected Works of Grub chen Thang stong rgyal po (Grub chen thang stong rgyal po'i bka' 'bum)*, vol. 3: 585–613.

_____. *Heart of Elegant Explication: Sequential Arrangement of the Practice of the Ripening Initiation from the Heartdrop of the Great Adept. Grub thob chen po'i thugs thig las/ smin byed kyi lag len khrigs su bsdebs pa legs bshad snying po.* In Jamgön Kongtrul, *Treasury of Precious Treasure Teachings (Rin chen gter mdzod)*, vol. 17: 187–216. Paro: Ngodrup and Sherap Drimay, 1976.

_____. *Melody of Accomplishment: A Supplication to the Great Adept Tangtong Gyalpo. Grub chen thang stong rgyal po la gsol ba 'debs pa grub pa'i sgra dbyangs.* In Jamgön Kongtrul, *Treasury of Oral Instructions (Gdams ngag mdzod)*, vol. 8: 726–29. Delhi: N. Lungtok and N. Gyaltsan, 1971.

_____. *Pleasure Grove of Amazing Udumvara Flowers: A Brief Biography of the Omniscient and All-Seeing Lord and Master Jamyang Khyentsé Wangpo Kunga*

Tenpai Gyaltsen Pal Sangpo. Rje bla ma thams cad mkhyen cing gzigs pa 'jam dbyangs mkhyen brtse'i dbang po kun dga' bstan pa'i rgyal mtshan dpal bzang po'i rnam thar mdor bsdus pa ngo mtshar u dum ba ra'i dga' tshal. In *Treasury of Vast Teachings (Rgya chen bka' mdzod)*, vol. 15: 343–577. Paro: Ngodrup, 1976.

_____. *Rosary of Precious Beryl: A Brief History of the Profound Treasure Teachings and the Adepts Who Recovered Those Treasures. Zab mo'i gter dang gter ston grub thob ji ltar byon pa'i lo rgyus mdor bsdus bkod pa rin chen bai dūr ya'i phreng ba.* In Jamgön Kongtrul, *Treasury of Precious Treasure Teachings (Rin chen gter mdzod)*, vol. 1: 291–759. Paro: Ngodrup and Sherap Drimay, 1976.

_____, ed. *Treasury of Oral Instructions. Gdams ngag mdzod.* 12 vols. Delhi: N. Lungtok and N. Gyaltsan, 1971.

_____, ed. *Treasury of Precious Treasure Teachings. Rin chen gter mdzod chen mo.* 111 vols. Paro: Ngodrup and Sherap Drimay, 1976.

Jamyang Khyentsé Wangchuk ('Jam dbyangs mkhyen brtse'i dbang phyug). *Rippling Ocean of Wish-fulfilling Marvels: The Story of the Venerable Lord Vajradhara, the Great Gorumpa, Kunga Lekpai Lodrö Gyaltsen Pal Sangpo's Practice of the Mantra of Pure Awareness. Rje btsun rdo rje 'chang sgo rum pa chen po kun dga' legs pa'i blo gros rgyal mtshan dpal bzang po'i rig sngags kyi rtogs pa brjod pa'i gtam ngo mtshar yid bzhin gyi chu gter bzhad pa.* In *Saskya Lam-'bras Literature Series*, vol. 2: 249–397. Dehra Dun: Sakya Centre, 1983.

_____. *Summarizing Notes on the Path Presented as the Three Appearances. From the* Expansion of the Great Secret Doctrine, *Summarizing Notes of Guidance for the Precious Teaching of the "Path with the Result." The Infallible Version of Khau Drakzongpa. Gsung ngag rin po che lam 'bras bu dang bcas pa'i khrid kyi zin bris gsang chen bstan pa rgyas byed ces bya ba las/ snang ba gsum du bstan pa'i lam gyi zin bris kha'u brag rdzong pa'i bzhed pa ma nor ba.* In *Saskya Lam-'bras Literature Series*, vol. 14, *pha*, 1a–46a (pp. 253–343). Dehra Dun: Sakya Centre, 1983.

Jamyang Khyentsé Wangpo ('Jam dbyangs mkhyen brtse'i dbang po). *Cycle of Five Essential Methods for Accomplishment, from the Heartdrop of the Great Adept. Grub thob chen po'i thugs thig las/ sgrub thabs snying po skor lnga.* In Jamgön Kongtrul, *Treasury of Precious Treasure Teachings (Rin chen gter mdzod)*, vol. 4: 449–580. Paro: Ngodrup and Sherap Drimay, 1976. Also in Tangtong Gyalpo, *Supplemental Texts to the Collected Works of Thang stong rgyal po Series (Grub chen thang stong bka' 'bum gyi rgyab chos)*, vol. 3: 1–264.

_____. *Essence of Primordial Awareness in Action, from the Heartdrop of the Great Adept. Grub thob chen po'i thug thig las/ phrin las ye shes snying po.* In Jamgön Kongtrul, *Treasury of Precious Treasure Teachings (Rin chen gter mdzod)*, vol. 17: 167–80. Paro: Ngodrup and Sherap Drimay, 1976. Also in Tangtong Gyalpo, *Supplemental Texts to the Collected Works of Thang stong rgyal po Series (Grub chen thang stong bka' 'bum gyi rgyab chos)*, vol. 3: 265–85.

_____. *Flower of the Upholders of Pure Awareness: A Spontaneous Vajra Song in Praise of the Inner Biography of the Accomplished Lord Tsöndru Sangpo. Grub pa'i dbang phyug brtson 'grus bzang po'i nang gi rnam par thar pa la bsngags pa rdo rje'i thol glu rig pa 'dzin pa'i me tog.* In *Collected Songs of Mystical Realization*, 55–57. Dehra Dun: N. Gyaltsan, 1971.

_____. *Net of the Three Bodies of Enlightenment: A Spontaneous Vajra Song of Supplication to the Lord, the Great Adept. Rje grub thob chen po la gsol ba 'debs pa'i rdo rje'i thol glu sku gsum drwa ba.* In *The Collected Works (Gsung-'bum) of the Great 'Jam dbyangs mkhyen brtse'i dbang po*, vol. 22: 481–83. Gangtok: Gonpo Tseten, 1977.

_____. *Pleasure Grove of Amazing Lotus Flowers: A Brief Monastic History of the Old and New Traditions of Secret Mantra in the Glacial Land. Gangs can bod yul du byon pa'i gsang sngags gsar rnying gi gdan rabs mdor bsdus ngo mtshar padmo'i dga' tshal.* In *'Jam dbyangs mkhyen brtse'i dbang po'i gsung rtsom gces sgrig*, 1–216. Chengdu: Si khron mi rigs dpe skrun khang, 1989.

_____. *Words of the Mahāpaṇḍita Śīlaratna: A Rough Versified List of the Names of the Translators and Paṇḍitas Who Appeared in the Glacial Land. Gangs can gyi yul du byon pa'i lo paṇ rnams kyi mtshan tho rags rim tshigs bcad du bsdebs pa ma hā paṇḍi ta shī la rat na'i gsung.* This title apparently applies to only the first eight pages of the work. In *The Collected Works (Gsung-'bum) of the Great 'Jam dbyangs mkhyen brtse'i dbang po*, vol. 19: 1–476. Gangtok: Gonpo Tseten, 1977.

Jamyang Khyentsé Wangpo ('Jam dbyangs mkhyen brtse'i dbang po) and Loter Wangpo (Blo gter dbang po), eds. *Compendium of Methods for Accomplishment. Sgrub pa'i thabs kun las btus pa dngos grub rin po che'i 'dod 'jo.* Dehra Dun: G. Loday, N. Gyaltsen, and N. Lungtok, 1970.

Jamyang Khyentsé Wangpo ('Jam dbyangs mkhyen brtse'i dbang po) and Tangtong Gyalpo (Thang stong rgyal po). *Basic Texts and a Clarification of the White and Red Pills, the Single Medicine for a Hundred Illnesses According to the Tradition of the Great Adept Tangtong Gyalpo. Grub chen thang stong rgyal po'i lugs kyi nad brgya sman gcig ril bu dkar dmar kyi gzhung gsal byed dang bcas pa.* In Jamgön Kongtrul, *Treasury of Precious Treasure Teachings (Rin chen gter mdzod)*, vol. 73: 335–51. Paro: Ngodrup and Sherap Drimay, 1976.

Jangchup Tsemo, Lochen (Byang chub rtse mo, Lo chen). *Virtuous at the Beginning, End, and Middle: A Biography of the Dharma Lord Lama Dampa. Chos rje bla ma dam pa'i rnams thar thog mtha bar gsum du dge ba. Dbu can* manuscript, 75 fols. Beijing: Cultural Palace of Nationalities.

Jatsön Nyingpo, Rikzin ('Ja' tshon snying po, Rig 'dzin). *Pavilion of Rainbow Light: Biographies of the Lineage of the Upholders of Pure Awareness, Concerning Seven Emanations. Rig 'dzin brgyud pa'i rnam thar sprul pa bdun skor 'ja' 'od kyi gur khang.* In *The Autobiography of 'Ja'-tshon-snying-po*, 1–34. Bir: Kandro, 1974.

Jikmé Drakpa ('Jigs med grags pa). *Rain of Attainments for a Crop of Faith: A Biography of the Dharma King of Gyantsé. Rgyal rtse chos rgyal gyi rnam par thar pa dad pa'i lo thog dngos grub kyi char 'bebs.* Lhasa: Bod ljongs mi dmangs dpe skrun khang, 1987.

Khakhyap Dorjé, Karmapa (Mkha' khyab rdo rje, Karma pa). *Rainfall to Benefit Living Beings: Brief Summarizing Notes on* Infinite Benefit for Living Beings, *the Meditation and Recitation of Noble, Sublime Avalokiteśvara, the Direct Transmission of the Accomplished Lord Tangtong Gyalpo. Grub pa'i dbang phyug thang stong rgyal po'i nye brgyud 'phags mchog spyan ras gzigs kyi bsgom bzlas 'gro don mkha' khyab ma'i zin bris nyung bsdus 'gro don char rgyun. Dbu can* manuscript, 22 fols.

Khardo Chökyi Dorjé (Mkhar rdo Chos kyi rdo rje). *Secret Treasury of the Ḍākinīs: Extra Profound Longevity Practice of the Master. Yang zab bla ma'i srog sgrub mkha' 'gro'i gsang mdzod.* In Tangtong Gyalpo, *Collected Works of Thang-stong rgyal-po (Grub mchog rgyal po thang stong pa'i zab gter chos mdzod rin po che)*, vol. 4: 321–88. Thimphu: Kunsang Topgey, 1976.

Khetsun Tenpai Gyaltsen, Shongchen (Mkhas btsun bstan pa'i rgyal mtshan, Gshong chen). *Extensive Initiation for the Blessing of Opening the Door to the Sky. Byin rlabs nam mkha' sgo 'byed kyi dbang rgyas pa.* In Tangtong Gyalpo, *Tangtong's Oral Transmission (Thang stong snyan brgyud)*, vol. 1: 86.1–97.1. New Delhi: Trayang, 1973.

Könchok Palsang and Dewa Sangpo (Dkon mchog dpal bzang and Bde ba bzang po). *Bright Lamp: A Biography of Master Tangtong Gyalpo. Bla ma thang stong rgyal po'i rnam thar gsal ba'i sgron me.* In Tangtong Gyalpo, *The Collected Works of Grub chen Thang stong rgyal po (Grub chen thang stong rgyal po'i bka' 'bum)*, vol. 2. Thimphu: National Library of Bhutan, 1984.

Kunga Dorjé, Tsalpa (Kun dga' rdo rje, Tshal pa). *Red Annals. Deb ther dmar po rnams kyi dang po hu lan deb ther.* Annotated by Dung dkar Blo bzang 'phrin las. Beijing: Mi rigs dpe skrun khang, 1981.

Kunga Drolchok (Kun dga' grol mchog). *Basic Text and Clarification of the Practice of the Essential Six Syllables Actually Given by Mahākaruṇika to the Accomplished Lord Tangtong Gyalpo. Grub pa'i dbang phyug thang stong rgyal po la thugs rje chen pos dngos su gnang ba'i snying po yi ge drug pa'i nyams len gyi gzhung gsal byed dang bcas pa.* In Jamyang Khyentsé Wangpo and Loter Wangpo, *Compendium of Methods for Accomplishment (Sgrub thabs kun btus)*, vol. 3: 17–21. Dehra Dun: G. Loday, N. Gyaltsen, and N. Lungtok,

1970. Also in Tangtong Gyalpo, *Collected Works of Grub chen Thang stong rgyal po (Grub chen thang stong rgyal po'i bka' 'bum)*, vol. 3: 615–24.

_____. *Lineage History of the One Hundred Guiding Instructions. Khrid brgya'i brgyud pa'i lo rgyus.* In Jamgön Kongtrul, *Treasury of Oral Instructions (Gdams ngag mdzod)*, vol. 12: 309–340. Delhi: N. Lungtok and N. Gyaltsan, 1972.

_____. *Melodious Dragon Roar of Highest Praise: A Biography of the Kalkī Dharma King, the Lord of Jang, Namgyal Draksang. Rigs ldan chos kyi rgyal po byang bdag rnam rgyal grags bzang gi rnam par thar pa rab bsngags snyan pa'i 'brug sgra.* Kansu: Kan su'u zhing chen grangs nyung mi rigs kyi gna' dpe dag sgrib gzhung las khang and Kan lho bod sman zhib 'jug khang, 1985.

_____. *Record of Precious Beautiful Ornaments: An Autobiographical Supplement. Rnam thar zur 'debs mdzes rgyan rin po che'i lung yig.* In *The Autobiographies of Jo-nang Kun-dga' grol-mchog and His Previous Embodiments*, vol. 2: 535–84. New Delhi: Tibet House, 1982.

_____. *Text of the One Hundred and Eight Profound Guiding Instructions. Zab khrid brgya dang brgyad kyi yi ge.* In Jamgön Kongtrul, *Treasury of Oral Instructions (Gdams ngag mdzod)*, vol. 12: 369–595. Delhi: N. Lungtok and N. Gyaltsan, 1972.

_____. *Travelogue to Dispel Darkness from Discerning Hearts. Lam yig dpyod ldan snying gi mun sel. Dbu med* mansucript, 44 fols. Beijing: Cultural Palace of Nationalities.

Kunga Lodrö, Gongma (Kun dga' blo gros, Gong ma). *Boundless Miracles: A Biography of the Overlord Vajradhara Dressed in Saffron Robes, the Great Nesarwa, the Omniscient Mañjuśrīnātha Master with the Name Lekpa. Khyab bdag rdo rje 'chang ngur smrig gi bla gos 'chang ba gnas gsar ba chen po 'jam mgon bla ma thams cad mkhyen pa legs pa'i mtshan gyi zhal snga nas kyi rnam par thar pa ngo mtshar rab 'byams.* In *Sa-skya Lam-'bras Literature Series*, vol. 6: 1–299. Dehra Dun: Sakya Centre, 1983.

Kunga Paljor, Gyalwang (Kun dga' dpal 'byor, Rgyal dbang). *Letter Offered to Dharma Lord Tangtong Gyalpo. Chos rje thang stong rgyal po la phul ba'i chab shog.* In *Collected Works (gSung-'bum) of rGyal-dbang Kun-dga' dpal-'byor*, vol. 2: 445–46. Thimphu: Kunzang Tobgay, 1976.

Kunga Sönam Drakpa Palsang, Ngakrampa (Kun dga' bsod nams grags pa dpal bzang, Sngags ram pa). *Final Story Concerning the Nirvāṇa of the Great Adept. Grub thob chen po'i rnam thar phyi ma mya ngan las 'das pa'i skor.* Title taken from the colophon. *Dbu med* manuscript copied at the end of Anonymous, *All-Illuminating Lamp*, 161b–66a. See Tibetan text and English translation in the present book.

_____. *Untitled.* In Tangtong Gyalpo, *Supplemental Texts to the Collected Works of Thang stong rgyal po Series (Grub chen thang stong bka' 'bum gyi rgyab chos)*, vol. 2: 271–86. Thimphu: National Library of Bhutan, 1984.

Kunga Tenpai Nyima, Dezhung Rinpoché (Kun dga' bstan pa'i nyi ma, Sde gzhung Rin po che). *Music of an Auspicious Conch Shell: A Condensed Biography of Vajradhara Ngawang Tutob Wangchuk Drakshul Yönten Gyatso Tashi Drakpa Gyaltsen Pal Sangpo, Mantra Master and Great Throne Holder of Glorious Sakya. Shrī sa skya pa sngags 'chang bla ma khri chen rdo rje 'chang ngag dbang mthu stobs dbang phyug drag shul yon tan rgya mtsho bkra shis grags pa rgyal mtshan dpal bzang po'i rnam par thar pa mdor bsdus bkra shis skye ba lnga pa'i sgra dbyangs.* Delhi: T. G. Dhongthog Rinpoche, 1980.

_____. *Seed of Speech: A Brief History of Ga, Den, and Kyur in the Dokham Region of the Land of Tibet. Bod ljongs mdo khams sga ldan skyur gsum gyi byung tshul nyung bsdus gtam gyi sa bon. Dbu can* manuscript, 54 pages.

Kunsang Ngedön Longyang (Kun bzang nges don klong yangs). *Jewel Necklace: Biographies of the Successive Sublime Individuals Who Have Upheld the Doctrine of the Early Translations of Secret Mantra in Tibet. Bod du byung ba'i gsang sngags snga 'gyur gyi bstan 'dzin skyes mchog rim byon gyi rnam thar nor bu'i do shal.* Dalhousie: Damcho Sangpo, 1976.

Kunsik Chökyi Nangwa, Gyalwang (Kun gzigs chos kyi snang ba, Rgyal dbang). *Detailed Explanation of the Sacred Site of Tsari. Tsa ri'i gnas bshad rgyas par bshad pa'i le'u.* In *Rare Tibetan Texts from Nepal.* Dolanji: Tibetan Bonpo Monastic Centre, 1976.

Lhai Gyaltsen, Gharungwa (Lha'i rgyal mtshan, Gha rung ba). *Biography of the Great Omniscient Jonangpa Dharma Lord. Chos rje jo nang pa kun mkhyen chen po'i rnam thar. Dbu med* manuscript, 57 fols. Beijing: Cultural Palace of Nationalities.

Losel Gyatso, Tsarchen (Blo gsal rgya mtsho, Tshar chen). *Necklace of Enchanting Utpala Flowers: A Biography of Dakchen Dorjé Chang Lodrö Gyaltsen Pal Sangpo, Dharma King of the Three Realms. Khams gsum chos kyi rgyal po bdag chen rdo rje 'chang blo gros rgyal mtshan dpal bzang po'i rnam par thar pa yid 'phrog utpa la'i do shal.* In *Sa-skya Lam-'bras Literature Series,* vol. 2: 35–151. Dehra Dun: Sakya Centre, 1983.

Losang Chökyi Nyima, Tukwan (Blo bzang chos kyi nyi ma, Thu'u bkwan). *Tukwan's Philosophical Tenets. Thu'u bkwan grub mtha'.* Kansu: Mi rigs dpe skrun khang, 1984.

Losang Trinlé, Dungkar (Blo bzang 'phrin las, Dung dkar). *Clarification of Knowledge: The Great Lexicon of Tibetology Compiled by the Consummate Expert, the Honorable Dungkar Losang Trinlé. Mkhas dbang dung dkar blo bzang 'phrin las mchog gis mdzad pa'i bod rig pa'i tshig mdzod chen mo shes bya rab gsal.* Beijing: China Tibetology Publishing House, 2002.

Losang Tsering (Blo bzang tshe ring). *Discussion of the History of Philosophical Tenets. Grub mtha'i byung ba brjod pa.* Lhasa: Bod ljongs mi dmangs dpe skrun khang, 1984.

Mangtö Ludrup Gyatso (Mang thos klu sgrub rgya mtsho). *Bright Sun of Pure Altruism: A Chronicle of the Doctrine. Bstan rtsis gsal ba'i nyin byed lhag bsam rab dkar.* Lhasa: Bod ljongs mi dmangs dpe skrun khang, 1987.

_____. *Coquette's Mirror: An Autobiography Unaffected by Deceit and Falsehood, Arranged as an Account of My Experience of the Nectar of Various Objects. Rang gi rnam par thar pa yul sna tshogs kyi bdud rtsi myong ba'i gtam du byas pa zol zog rdzun gyis ma bslad pa sgeg mo'i me long.* In *Sa-skya Lam-'bras Literature Series,* vol. 3: 395–625. Dehra Dun: Sakya Centre, 1983.

Mañjuśrījñāna, Chökhor Lotsāwa (Mañjuśrījñāna, Chos 'khor lo tsā ba). *Biography of the Great Master Chöpal Sangpo. Bla chen chos dpal bzang po'i rnam thar. Dbu med* manuscript, 42 fols.

Milarepa, Jetsun (Mi la ras pa, Rje btsun). *Some Miscellaneous Teachings, Such As Vajra Songs, of the Venerable Lord Milarepa. Rje btsun mi la ras pa'i rdo rje'i mgur sogs gsung rgyun thor bu 'ba'.* Delhi: Sonam Rabten, 1985.

Mingyur Dorjé (Mi 'gyur rdo rje). *Examination of the Legacy of Tangtong Gyalpo's Iron-Bridge Building Activities. Thang stong rgyal po'i lcags zam 'dzugs skrun gyi mdzad rjes skor ched du brjod pa.* In *Bod rig pa'i gros mol tshogs 'du'i ched rtsom gces bsdus,* 316–42. Lhasa: Bod ljongs mi dmangs dpe skrun khang, 1987.

Namkha (Nam mkha'i ming can). *Twenty-five Points to Carry on the Path in Connection with Practice in One Hundred Dangerous Places. Gnyan khrod brgya rtsa'i sgrub khog dang 'brel ba'i lam khyer nyer lnga.* In Tangtong Gyalpo, *Tangtong's Oral Transmission (Thang stong snyan brgyud),* vol. 2: 25.1–29.3. New Delhi: Trayang, 1973.

Namkha Lekpa (Nam mkha' legs pa). *Practicing Severance: A Biography of the Great Adept Tangtong Gyalpo. Grub chen thang stong rgyal po'i rnam thar gcod yul nyams bzhes.* In Tangtong Gyalpo, *The Collected Works of Thang-stong rgyal-po (Grub mchog rgyal po thang stong pa'i zab gter chos mdzod rin po che),* vol. 1: 43–47. Thimphu: Kunsang Topgey, 1976.

Natsok Rangdrol, Götsangpa (Sna tshogs rang grol, Rgod tshangs ras pa). *Heart of the Sun Illuminating the Vajrayāna: A Biography of the Completely Victorious Tsang Nyön Heruka. Gtsang smyon he ru ka phyogs thams cad las rnam par rgyal ba'i rnam thar rdo rje theg pa'i gsal byed nyi ma'i snying po.* In *The Life of the Saint of gTsang.* Śatapiṭaka Series, vol. 69. New Delhi: International Academy for Indian Culture, 1969.

Ngawang Damchö Gyatso (Ngag dbang dam chos rgya mtsho). *Key to Open a Hundred Doors of Profound Meaning: A Discussion of the Origin of the* Compendium of Tantras *and How the Teachings Were Gathered. Rgyud sde rin po che kun las btus pa'i byung tshul dang bka'i bsdu ba ji ltar mdzad pa'i 'phros las brtsams te gleng ba zab don sgo brgya 'byed pa'i lde'u mig.* In Jamyang Loter Wangpo ('Jam dbyangs blo gter dbang po), *Compendium of Tantras (Rgyud sde kun btus),* vol. 30: 238–634. Delhi: N. Lungtok and N. Gyaltsen, 1972.

Ngawang Drakpa, Nyukla Panchen (Ngag dbang grags pa, Gnyug la Paṇ chen). *Making the Body Hairs of Those with Impartial Faith Flutter: A Biography of the Venerable Lord Kunga Sangpo, Glorious, Excellent, Superior Accomplished Master with Completely Victorious Behavior. Dpal ldan bla ma dam pa grub pa'i khyu mchog phyogs thams cad las rnam par rgyal ba'i spyod pa can rje btsun kun dga' bzang po'i rnam par thar pa ris med dad pa'i pu long g.yo byed.* In *Bka'-brgyud-pa Hagiographies*, vol. 2: 383–560. Tashijong: Sungrab Nyamso Gyunphel Parkhang, 1972.

Ngawang Kunga Tashi (Ngag dbang kun dga' bkra shis). *Seed for Attaining Immortality: Rite of Initiation with Many Deities for the* Iron Tree *According to the Northern Treasure Tradition. Byang gter lcags sdong ma lha mang gi dbang chog 'chi med grub pa'i sa bon.* In Jamgön Kongtrul, *Treasury of Precious Treasure Teachings (Rin chen gter mdzod)*, vol. 29: 269–94. Paro: Ngodrup and Sherap Drimay, 1976.

Ngawang Kunga Tashi (Ngag dbang kun dga' bkra shis), with later additions by Jamyang Khyentsé Wangpo ('Jam dbangs mkhyen brtse'i dbang po) and Loter Wangpo (Blo gter dbang po). *Method for Accomplishment, Rite of Initiation, and Esoteric Instructions of the* Glorious Giver of Immortality, *the Direct Transmission of Amitābha and Hayagrīva Together. Nye brgyud tshe rta zung 'brel 'chi med dpal ster gyi sgrub thabs dbang chog man ngag dang bcas pa.* In Jamyang Khyentsé Wangpo and Loter Wangpo, *Compendium of Methods for Accomplishment (Sgrub thabs kun btus)*, vol. 1: 427–70. Dehra Dun: G. Loday, N. Gyaltsen, and N. Lungtok, 1970.

Ngawang Lodrö Drakpa (Ngag dbang blo gros grags pa). *Moon Lamp to Clarify the Teachings of the Conqueror: A History of the Glorious Jonangpa Tradition. Dpal ldan jo nang pa'i chos 'byung rgyal ba'i chos tshul gsal byed zla ba'i sgron me.* Koko Nor: Krung go'i bod kyi shes rig dpe skrun khan, 1992.

Ngawang Losang Gyatso, Dalai Lama (Ngag dbang blo bzang rgya mtsho, Tā la'i bla ma). *Crystal Mirror: A Guide to the Divine Emanated Cathedral. Lha ldan sprul pa'i gtsug lag khang gi dkar chag shel dkar me long.* Lhasa: Bod ljongs mi dmangs dpe skrun khang, 1987.

_____. *Current of the Ganges River: A Record of the Profound and Vast Excellent Dharma. Zab pa dang rgya che ba'i dam pa'i chos kyi thob yig gangā'i chu rgyun (Record of Teachings Received: The gSan-yig of the Fifth Dalai Lama).* Vol. 3. Delhi: Nechung and Lhakhar, 1971.

_____. *Ocean of Marvelous Deeds: A Biography of Ngagi Wangpo, Jangpa Upholder of Pure Awareness. Byang pa rig 'dzin ngag gi dbang po'i rnam par thar pa ngo mtshar bkod pa rgya mtsho.* In *Bka' ma mdo dbang gi bla ma brgyud pa'i rnam thar*, vol. 37: 427–553. Leh: Smanrtsis Shesrig Spendzod, 1972.

_____. *Song of the Lark: A Celebration of the Young Perfect Aeon, Annals Primarily Concerned with the Exhalted Kings and Ministers Who Have Lived on Earth in the Glacial Land. Gangs can yul gyi sa la spyod pa'i mtho ris kyi rgyal blon gtso bor brjod pa'i deb ther rdzogs ldan gzhon nu'i dga' ston dpyid kyi rgyal mo'i glu dbyangs.* Beijing: Mi rigs dpe skrun khang, 1988.

Ngawang Namgyal, Taklung (Ngag dbang rnam rgyal, Stag lung). *Ocean of Marvels: Stories of the Wish-fulfilling Lineage. Brgyud pa yid bzhin nor bu'i rtogs pa brjod pa ngo mtshar rgya mtsho.* Lhasa: Bod ljongs bod yig dpe rnying dpe skrun khang, 1992.

Ngawang Tenzin Norbu, Dzatrul (Ngag dbang bstan 'dzin nor bu, Rdza sprul). *Meaningful to Behold: A Guide to the Divine Assembly of the Maṇḍala of the Nine Vehicles in the Levels and Podium of the Auspicious Stūpa of Many Doors at Glorious Riwoché. Dpal ri bo che'i mchod rten bkra shis sgo mang gi bang rim bre dang bcas par theg dgu'i dkyil 'khor lha tshogs kyi bzhugs byang dkar chag mthong ba don ldan.* My copy is an incomplete xylograph of 12 fols. Nepal-German Manuscript Preservation Project, microfilm reel number L 316/11.

_____. *Ocean of Blessings: Biographies of the Lineal Masters of the Scriptural and Treasure Traditions of Severance and Pacification of the Afflictions. Gcod yul nyon mongs zhi byed kyi bka' gter bla ma brgyud pa'i rnam thar byin rlabs gter mtsho.* Gangtok: Sonam T. Kazi, 1972.

Ngödrup Palbar (Dngos grub dpal 'bar). *Lion of Faith at Play on a Glacial Peak of Good Qualities: A Common Biography of the Venerable Lord Tsangpa Heruka. Rje btsun gtsang pa he ru ka'i thun mong gi rnam thar yon tan gyi gangs ri la dad pa'i seng ge rnam par rtse ba.* Xylograph, 31 fols. Nepal-German Manuscript Preservation Project, microfilm reel number L 834/2.

Nyang Nyima Öser (Nyang Nyi ma 'od zer). *Nectar of Honey from the Hearts of Flowers: A History of Dharma. Chos 'byung me tog snying po sbrang rtsi'i bcud.* Lhasa: Bod ljongs mi dmangs dpe skrun khang, 1988.

Palden Chökyi Sangpo (Dpal ldan chos kyi bzang po). *Series of Jewels: A Genealogy of the Rulers of Jang in Yeru. Sde pa g.yas ru byang pa'i rgyal rabs rin po che bstar ba.* In *Rare Tibetan Historical and Literary Texts from the Library of Tsepon W.D. Shakabpa*, 166–208. New Delhi: Taikhang, 1974.

Pawo Tsuklak Trengwa (Dpa' bo Gtsug lag phreng ba). *Banquet for Experts: A Clarifying History of Those Who Have Turned the Wheel of the Excellent Dharma. Dam pa'i chos kyi 'khor lo bsgyur ba rnams kyi byung ba gsal bar byed pa mkhas pa'i dga' ston.* 2 vols. Bejing: Mi rigs dpe skrun khang, 1986.

Pema Karpo, Drukchen (Padma dkar po, 'Brug chen). *Opera of Great Compassion: An Autobiography of the Great Spiritual Hero Pema Karpo. Sems dpa' chen po padma dkar po'i rnam thar thugs rje chen po'i zlos gar.* In *The Collected Works of Kun-mkhyen Padma dkar-po*, vol. 3: 330–597. Darjeeling: Kargyud Sungrab Nyamso Khang, 1973.

Pema Lingpa (Padma gling pa). *Illuminating Lamp of Prophecy. Lung bstan gsal byed sgron me.* In *The Recovered Teachings of the Great Pema Lingpa (Rig 'dzin padma gling pa yi/ zab gter chos mdzod rin po che)*, vol. 3: 555–61. Thimphu: Kunsang Tobgay, 1975.

Pema Trinlé, Rikzin (Padma 'phrin las, Rig 'dzin). *Biographies of the Masters of the Transmission of the Canonical Lineage of the Dowang. Bka' ma mdo dbang gi bla ma brgyud pa'i rnam thar,* 1–425. Leh: S.W. Tashigangpa, 1972.

Ratnabhadra, Lochen (Ratna bha dra, Lo chen). *Brief Clarification of My Life. Rtogs brjod nyung ngu rnam gsal.* In Jamgön Ameshap Ngawang Kunga Sönam, *Chariot of Amazing Faith,* 405–14.

Rinchen Namgyal, Lhatsun (Rin chen rnam rgyal, Lha btsun). *Making the Body Hairs of the Faithful Flutter: A Biography of Tsangpa Nyönpa, the Mad Adept of Tsang. Grub thob gtsang pa smyon pa'i rnam thar dad pa'i spu slong g.yo' ba.* In Gtsang-smyon He-ru-ka, *bDe-mchog mkha'-'gro snyan-brgyud,* vol. 1: 1–129. Leh: Smanrtsis Shesrig Spendzod, 1971.

Sakya Paṇḍita Kunga Gyaltsen (Sa skya Paṇḍi ta Kun dga' rgyal mtshan). *Treatise Distinguishing the Three Vows. Sdom gsum gyi rab tu dbye ba'i bstan bcos.* In *The Complete Works of the Great Masters of the Sa skya Sect of Tibetan Buddhism (Sa skya pa'i bka' 'bum),* vol. 5, *Collected Works, na,* 1a–48b. Tokyo: The Toyo Bunko, 1968.

Sangyé Gyatso, Desi (Sangs rgyas rgya mtsho, Sde srid). *Banquet to Delight the Seers: A Beryl Mirror of Elegant Explication That Is a Comprehensive Survey of the Glorious Medical Arts. Dpal ldan gso ba rig pa'i khog 'bubs legs bshad bai ḍūr ya'i me long drang srong dgyes pa'i dga' ston.* Lanzhou: Kan su'u mi rigs dpe skrun khang, 1982.

_____. *Mirror of Yellow Beryl: Clarification of the Root of All the Teachings of the Glorious and Peerless Riwo Gendenpa Doctrine, the Tradition of Those Who Wear the Yellow Crown. Dpal mnyam med ri bo dga' ldan pa'i bstan pa zhwa ser cod pan 'chang ba'i ring lugs chos thams cad kyi rtsa ba gsal bar byed pa bai ḍūr ya ser po'i me long.* Śatapiṭaka Series, vol. 12. New Delhi: International Academy for Indian Culture, 1960.

_____. *Necklace of White Beryl That Is a Treasure for the Intelligent and an Ornament for the Throats of Experts: An Elegant Explication of Astrology According to the Puk Tradition. Phug lugs rtsis kyi legs bshad mkhas pa'i mgul rgyan bai ḍūr dkar po'i do shal dpyod ldan snying nor.* In *The Vaiḍūrya dKar po of sDe-srid Sangs-rgyas-rgya-mtsho,* vol. 1: 10–635. New Delhi: T. Tsepal Taikhang, 1972.

Sangyé Puntsok, Ngorchen (Sangs rgyas phun tshogs, Ngor chen). *Source of Wish-fulfilling Good Qualities, an Ocean Collecting the Streams of Elegant Explication: A Biography of the Conqueror, Vajradhara, Kunga Sangpo. Rgyal ba rdo rje 'chang kun dga' bzang po'i rnam par thar pa legs bshad chu bo 'dus pa'i rgya mtsho yon tan yid bzhin nor bu'i 'byung gnas.* New Delhi: Trayang and Jamyang Samten, 1976.

Sangyé Tsemo, Ngaripa (Sangs rgyas rtse mo, Mnga' ris pa). *Amazing and Marvelous Biography of the Glorious Great Rendawa. Dpal ldan red mda' ba chen po'i rnam thar ngo mtshar rmad byung.* In *Sa skya pa'i bla ma kha shas kyi rnam thar*, 265–352. Kathmandu: Sa skya rgyal yongs gsung rab slob gnyer khang, 2003.

Shākya Chokden, Panchen (Shākya mchog ldan, Paṇ chen). *Enjoyable Ocean of Amazing Faith: A Biography of the Omniscient Venerable Lord, the Honorable Spiritual Friend Shākya Gyaltsen Pal Sangpo. Rje btsun thams cad mkhyen pa'i bshes gnyen shākya rgyal mtshan dpal bzang po'i zhal snga nas kyi rnam par thar pa ngo mtshar dad pa'i rol mtsho.* In *The Complete Works (Gsung-'bum) of Gser-mdog Paṇ-chen Shākya mchog-ldan*, vol. 16: 299–377. Thimphu: Kunzang Tobgey, 1975.

_____. *Letter to the Great Adept Tangtong Gyalpo, With the Gift of a Rosary of Fifty Coral Beads. Grub chen thang stong rgyal po la byu ru lnga bcu 'phreng gi rten dang bcas pa.* In *The Complete Works (Gsung-'bum) of Gser-mdog Paṇ-chen Shākya mchog-ldan*, vol. 17: 121–22. Thimphu: Kunzang Tobgey, 1975.

Shākya Shenyen (Shākya bshes gnyen). *Biography of Jamyang Namkha Lekpa. 'Jam dbyangs nam mkha' legs pa'i rnam thar.* In Tangtong Gyalpo, *Tangtong's Oral Transmission (Thang stong snyan brgyud)*, vol.1: 7.4–9.1. New Delhi: Trayang, 1973.

Shenyen Namgyal, Lhatong Lotsāwa (Bshes gnyen rnam rgyal, Lha mthong Lo tsā ba). *Drumbeat of Ornamental Deeds: Part Two of the Work Known As* Making the Body Hairs of Those with Impartial Faith Flutter: A Biography of the Venerable Lord Kunga Sangpo, Glorious, Excellent, Superior Accomplished Master with Completely Victorious Behavior. *Rje btsun kun dga' bzang po'i rnam par thar pa ris med dad pa'i spu long g.yo byed ces bya ba las/ rim par phye ba gnyis pa phrin las rgyan gyi rnga sgra.* In *Bka'-brgyud-pa Hagiographies*, vol. 2: 561–660. Tashijong: Sungrab Nyamso Gyunphel Parkhang, 1972.

Sherab Gyaltsen, Jé Khenpo (Shes rab rgyal mtshan, Rje mkhan po). *Chariot for Realization of the Two Truths: An Autobiography of the Precious Lord and Master. Rje bla ma rin po che'i rnam par thar pa zhal gsung ma bden gnyis 'grub pa'i shing rta.* In *Biographies of Three Bhutanese Prelates (rJe mkhan-po).* Thimphu: Kunzang Tobgay, 1976.

Sherab Palden (Shes rab dpal ldan). *Ocean of Marvels: A Biography of the Lord, the Great Adept of Iron Bridges. Rje grub thob chen po lcags zam pa'i rnam par thar pa ngo mtshar rgya mtsho.* In Tangtong Gyalpo, *The Collected Works of Grub chen Thang stong rgyal po (Grub chen thang stong rgyal po'i bka' 'bum)*, vol. 1. Thimphu: National Library of Bhutan, 1984.

Sönam Drakpa, Panchen (Bsod nams grags pa, Paṇ chen). *Magical Key to Royal Genealogies, or Red Annals, or New Annals. Rgyal rabs 'phrul gyi lde mig gam deb ther dmar po 'am deb gsar ma.* Lhasa: Bod ljongs mi dmangs dpe skrun khang, 1982.

Sönam Gyaltsen, Gönsarwa (Bsod nams rgyal mtshan, Dgon gsar ba). *Rainfall of Blessings to Expand the Summer Lake of Faith: A Biography of the Glorious Excellent Master, Great Vajradhara, Ngawang Chökyi Drakpa. Dpal ldan bla ma dam pa rdo rje 'chang chen po ngag dbang chos kyi grags pa'i rnam thar byin rlabs kyi char rgyun dad pa'i dbyar mtsho rgyas byed.* In *Sa-skya Lam-'bras Literature Series*, vol. 4: 337–87. Dehra Dun: Sakya Centre, 1983

Sönam Gyaltsen, Lama Dampa (Bsod nams rgyal mtshan, Bla ma dam pa). *Bright Mirror of Royal Genealogies. Rgyal rabs gsal ba'i me long.* Bejing: Mi rigs dpe skrun khang, 1981.

Songtsen Gampo (Srong btsan sgam po). *Compendium of Maṇis. Ma ṇi bka' 'bum (Punaka Redaction).* 2 vols. New Delhi: Trayang and Jamyang Samten, 1975.

Tangtong Gyalpo, Drupchen (Thang stong rgyal po, Grub chen). *Collected Works of Grub chen Thang stong rgyal po. Grub chen thang stong rgyal po'i bka' 'bum.* 3 vols. Thimphu: National Library of Bhutan, 1984.

_____. *Collected Works of Thang-stong rgyal-po. Grub mchog rgyal po thang stong pa'i zab gter chos mdzod rin po che.* 4 vols. Thimphu: Kunsang Topgey, 1976.

_____. *Collection of the Essentials: A Key Text of Guiding Instructions for the Six Dharmas of Niguma, the Ḍākinī of Primordial Awareness. Ye shes mkha' 'gro ni gu ma'i chos drug gi khrid kyi gnad yig snying po kun 'dus.* Signed by Lung stong gi smyon pa. In Jamgön Kongtrul, *Treasury of Oral Instructions (Gdams ngag mdzod)*, vol. 8: 147–79. Delhi: N. Lungtok and N. Gyaltsan, 1971. Also in Tangtong Gyalpo, *Supplemental Texts to the Collected Works of Thang stong rgyal po Series (Grub chen thang stong bka' 'bum gyi rgyab chos)*, vol. 1: 241–336.

_____. *Combined Practice of Both the Palmo Tradition and the King's Tradition: A Method for Accomplishment and a Fasting Ritual for Noble Mahākaruṇika. 'Phags pa thugs rje chen po'i sgrubs thabs snyung bar gnas pa'i cho ga dpal mo lugs dang rgyal po lugs gnyis ka sdom pa'i lag len.* Signed by Lung stong smyon pa. In Könchok Palsang and Dewa Sangpo, *Bright Lamp*, 533–78.

_____. *Guiding Instructions on Immortal Body and Mind: A Branch of Niguma's Teachings. Ni gu'i yan lag lus sems 'chi med kyi khrid.* Signed by Lung stong smyon pa. In Jamgön Kongtrul, *Treasury of Oral Instructions (Gdams ngag mdzod)*, vol. 8: 192–98. Delhi: N. Lungtok and N. Gyaltsan, 1971. Also in Tangtong Gyalpo, *Supplemental Texts to the Collected Works of Thang stong rgyal po Series (Grub chen thang stong bka' 'bum gyi rgyab chos)*, vol. 1: 369–86.

_____. *Guiding Instructions on the Amulet Mahāmudrā: A Branch of Niguma's Teachings. Ni gu'i yan lag phyag chen ga'u ma'i khrid.* Signed by Lung stong smyon pa. In Jamgön Kongtrul, *Treasury of Oral Instructions (Gdams ngag mdzod)*, vol. 8: 181–87. Delhi: N. Lungtok and N. Gyaltsan, 1971. Also in Tangtong Gyalpo, *Supplemental Texts to the Collected Works of Thang stong rgyal po Series (Grub chen thang stong bka' 'bum gyi rgyab chos)*, vol. 1: 337–52.

_____. *Guiding Instructions on the Six-armed Primordial-Awareness Protector: A Branch of Niguma's Teachings. Nying khu'i [sic!] yan lag phyag drug ye shes mgon po'i khrid.* Signed by Lung stong smyon pa. In Jamgön Kongtrul, *Treasury of Oral Instructions (Gdams ngag mdzod)*, vol. 8: 198–205. Delhi: N. Lungtok and N. Gyaltsan, 1971.

_____. *Guiding Instructions on the Three Ways to Carry the Practice on the Path: A Branch of Niguma's Teachings. Ni gu'i yan lag lam khyer gsum gyi khrid.* Signed by Lung stong smyon pa. In Jamgön Kongtrul, *Treasury of Oral Instructions (Gdams ngag mdzod)*, vol. 8: 187–92. Delhi: N. Lungtok and N. Gyaltsan, 1971. Also in Tangtong Gyalpo, *Supplemental Texts to the Collected Works of Thang stong rgyal po Series (Grub chen thang stong bka' 'bum gyi rgyab chos)*, vol. 1: 353–67.

_____. *Infinite Benefit for Living Beings. 'Gro don mkha' khyab ma.* In Tangtong Gyalpo, *Blessed Prayer Known as the Liberator of Sakya: The Vajra Speech of the Great Adept Tangtong Gyalpo (Grub chen thang stong rgyal po'i rdo rje gsung sa skya nad grol mar grags pa'i smon lam byin rlabs can)*, 6a–7a. Gangtok: Dpal ldan rgyal mtshan and Mgon po bkra shis, 1964.

_____. *Supplemental Texts to the Collected Works of Thang stong rgyal po Series. Grub chen thang stong bka' 'bum gyi rgyab chos.* 5 vols. Thimphu: National Library of Bhutan, 1984.

_____. *Tangtong's Oral Transmission. Thang stong snyan brgyud.* 2 vols. New Delhi: Trayang, 1973.

_____. *Untitled.* Original words of the *Glorious Giver of Immortality ('Chi med dpal ster).* In Ngawang Kunga Tashi (Ngag dbang kun dga' bkra shis) and Jamyang Khyentsé Wangpo ('Jam dbyangs mkhyen brtse'i dbang po), *Method for Accomplishment, Rite of Initiation, and Esoteric Instructions of the* Glorious Giver of Immortality, *the Direct Transmission of Amitābha and Hayagrīva Together*, 428.

_____. *Vajra Song About Naturally Liberated Immortal Mind. Sems 'chi med rang grol gyi rdo rje'i mgur.* In Jamgön Kongtrul, *Treasury of Oral Instructions (Gdams ngag mdzod)*, vol. 8: 814–15. Delhi: N. Lungtok and N. Gyaltsan, 1971.

Tangtong Gyalpo, Drupchen (Thang stong rgyal po, Grub chen) and Jamyang Khyentsé Wangpo ('Jam dbyangs mkhyen brtse'i dbang po). *Basic Texts and a Clarification of the White and Red Pills, the Single Medicine for a Hundred Illnesses According to the Tradition of the Great Adept Tangtong Gyalpo. Grub chen thang stong rgyal po'i lugs kyi nad brgya sman gcig ril bu dkar dmar kyi gzhung gsal byed dang bcas pa.* In Jamgön Kongtrul, *Treasury of Precious Treasure Teachings (Rin chen gter mdzod)*, vol. 73: 335–51. Paro: Ngodrup and Sherap Drimay, 1976. Also in Tangtong Gyalpo, *Collected Works of Grub chen Thang stong rgyal po (Grub chen thang stong rgyal po'i bka' 'bum)*, vol. 3: 319–43.

Tāranātha, Jonang (Tā ra nā tha, Jo nang). *Entryway for Experts: An Elegant Explication of Marvelous Tales about the Upper, Lower, and Middle Regions of Nyangyul. Myang yul stod smad bar gsum gyi ngo mtshar gtam gyi legs bshad mkhas pa'i 'jug ngogs.* Lhasa: Bod ljongs mi dmangs dpe skrun khang, 1983.

_____. *Extremely Detailed, Unpretentious, and Candid Narrative: A Book of Definite Autobiographical Statements by the Wanderer Tāranātha. Rgyal khams pa tā ra nā thas bdag nyid kyi rnam thar nges par brjod pa'i deb ther/ shin tu zhib mo ma bcos lhug pa'i rtogs brjod.* Paro: Ngodrup and Sherab Drimay, 1978.

_____. *Necessary Discussion of the Origins of the Dharma Cycles of Glorious Kālacakra. Dpal dus kyi 'khor lo'i chos bskor gyi byung khungs nyer mkho.* In *The Collected Works of Jo-nang rje-btsun Tāranātha*, vol. 2: 1–43. Leh: Smanrtsis Shesrig Dpemdzod, 1983.

Tenzin Norbu, Yölmo Tulku (Bstan 'dzin nor bu, Yol mo sprul sku). *Lute of Vajra Sound: An Autobiography. Rang gi rtogs pa brjod pa rdo rje sgra ma'i brgyud mangs.* In *The Autobiography and Collected Writings (Gsung thor bu) of the Third Rig-'dzin Yol-mo-ba sprul-sku Bstan-'dzin nor-bu*, vol. 1: 63–267. Dalhousie: Damcho Sangpo, 1977.

Tenzin Pemai Gyaltsen (Bstan 'dzin padma'i rgyal mtshan). *Golden Rosary: Monastic History of the Great Drigung Lords, Upholders of the Essence of the Doctrine of Definitive Meaning. Nges don bstan pa'i snying po mgon po 'bri gung chen po'i gdan rabs chos kyi byung tshul gser gyi phreng ba.* Gangs can rig mdzod, vol. 8. Lhasa: Bod ljongs bod yig dpe rnying dpe skrun khang, 1989.

Terdak Lingpa (Gter bdag gling pa) and Lochen Dharmashrī (Lo chen Dharma shrī). *Fine Wish-fulfilling Vase of Methods for Accomplishment. Sgrub thabs 'dod 'jo'i bum bzang.* Vol. 1. Gangtok: Sherab Gyaltsen, 1977.

Tselé Götsangpa Natsok Rangdrol (Rtse le Rgod tshangs pa Sna tshogs rang grol). *Fragmentary Account of Kongtsun Demo. Kong btsun de mo'i lo rgyus kyi 'thor bu.* In *gSung 'bum of rTse-le rgod-tshang-pa sna-tshogs rang-grol*, vol. 5: 299–302. New Delhi: Sanje Dorje, 1974.

Tsewang Gyal, Tatsak (Tshe dbang rgyal, Rta tshag). *Lhorong History of the Dharma or Tatsak History of the Dharma: An Elegant Explication of the History of the Dharma, an Exceptional Text That is Wonderful and Rare, Named for the Place of Its Composition. Dam pa'i chos kyi byung ba'i legs bshad lho rong chos 'byung ngam rta tshag chos 'byung zhes rtsom pa'i yul ming du chags pa'i ngo mtshar zhing dkon pa'i dpe khyad par can.* Lhasa: Bod ljongs bod yig dpe rnying dpe skrun khang, 1994.

Tsewang Norbu, Rikzin (Tshe dbang nor bu, Rig 'dzin). *Magical Mirror of Clear Crystal: Annals Concerning How the Hereditary Line of the Divine and Powerful Lords of Tibet Appeared at Gungtang in Lower Ngari. Bod rje lha btsad po'i gdung rabs mnga' ris smad gung thang du ji ltar byung ba'i tshul deb ther dwangs shel 'phrul gyi me long.* In *Bod kyi lo rgyus deb ther khag lnga,* 87–150. Gangs can rig mdzod, vol. 9. Lhasa: Bod ljongs bod yig dpe rnying dpe skrun khang, 1990.

Tsultrim Rinchen, Shuchen (Tshul khrims rin chen, Zhu chen). *Annual Account of the Leaves and Petals of Happiness and Suffering Grown from the Tangled Branches of the Virtues and Sins of the Tree Called the Dharma Teaching Monk Tsultrim Rinchen. Chos smra ba'i bande tshul khrims rin chen du bod pa'i rkang 'thung dge sdig 'dres ma'i las kyi yal ga phan tshun du 'dzings par bde sdug gi lo 'dab dus kyi rgyal mos res mos su bsgyur ba.* In *The Autobiography of Tshul-khrims rin-chen of Sde-dge and Other of His Selected Writings,* 278–638. Delhi: N. Lungtok and N. Gyaltsen, 1971.

_____. *Catalogue of the Dergé Edition of the Translated Treatises. Sde dge'i bstan 'gyur gyi dkar chag.* 2 vols. Delhi: Trayang and Jamyang Samten, 1974.

_____. *Ocean of Pure Realms to Delight Everyone: A Brief List of the Events in My Life for Depiction on a Tangka Painting. Rang gi rtogs brjod thang kar bkod pa'i zhal byang don bsdu kun dga' bskyed pa'i zhing khams rgya mtsho.* In *The Autobiography of Tshul-khrims rin-chen of Sde-dge and Other of His Selected Writings,* 266–77. Delhi: N. Lungtok and N. Gyaltsen, 1971.

_____. *Shuchen Tsultrim Rinchen's Record of Teachings Received. Zhu chen tshul khrims rin chen gyi gsan yig.* Dehra Dun: D. rGyal-mtshan, 1970.

Tulshuk Lingpa (Brtul zhugs gling pa). *The Collected Revelations (gTer chos) and Writings of Brtul-zhugs-gling- pa.* New Delhi: Khasdub Gyatsho Shashin, 1977.

Yeshé Gyaltsen, Tsechok Ling (Ye shes rgyal mtshan, Tshe mchog gling). *Biographies of the Lineal Masters of the Stages of the Path. Lam rim bla ma brgyud pa'i rnam thar.* Lhasa: Bod ljongs mi dmangs dpe skrun khang, 1990.

Yeshé Lhundrup, Tenzin (Ye shes lhun grub, Bstan 'dzin). *Biographical Supplication to the Lord of Realization, Ngawang Chödrak of the Hereditary Line of the Great Adept. Rtogs pa'i dbang phyug grub rigs ngag dbang chos grags kyi rnam thar gsol 'debs.* In Tangtong Gyalpo, *Tangtong's Oral Transmission (Thang stong snyan brgyud),* vol. 1 19.4–20.5. New Delhi: Trayang, 1973.

_____. *Golden Rosary: Stages of Dharma Practice That Are an Entry to the Path of Omniscience, the Liturgy of the Chaksam Bentsang Monastery. Lcags zam ban gtsang 'dus sde'i zhal 'don thams cad mkhyen pa'i lam gyi 'jug sgo chos spyod kyi rim pa gser gyi 'phreng ba.* In Tangtong Gyalpo, *Supplemental Texts to the Collected Works of Thang stong rgyal po Series (Grub chen thang stong bka' 'bum gyi rgyab chos),* vol. 2: 1–166. Thimphu: National Library of Bhutan, 1984.

______. *Precepts for Achieving Immortality: A Method of Accomplishment for the Direct Transmission of the Longevity Practice. Tshe sgrub nye brgyud kyi sgrub thabs 'chi med grub pa'i zhal lung.* In Jamyang Khyentsé Wangpo and Loter Wangpo, *Compendium of Methods for Accomplishment (Sgrub thabs kun btus),* vol. 13: 592–99. Dehra Dun: G. Loday, N. Gyaltsen, and N. Lungtok, 1970.

______. *Seedling of Faith: An Autobiographical Supplication to the Seventh Tenzin Dharma Lord Yeshé Lhundrup, Whose Other Name Is Palden Dechen Namrol Chimé Drupai Wangchuk. Bstan 'dzin chos rje bdun pa ye shes lhun grub bam mtshan gzhan dpal ldan bde chen rnam rol 'chi med grub pa'i dbang phyug gi rnam thar gsol 'debs dad pa'i myu gu.* In Tangtong Gyalpo, *Tangtong's Oral Transmission (Thang stong snyan brgyud),* vol. 1: 20.5–22.3. New Delhi: Trayang, 1972.

______. *Stream of Nectar: An Initiation Ritual for the* Glorious Giver of Immortality, *the Longevity Practice of the Direct Transmission. Nye brgyud tshe sgrub 'chi med dpal ster gyi dbang chog bdud rtsi'i chu rgyun.* In Jamyang Khyentsé Wangpo and Loter Wangpo, *Compendium of Methods for Accomplishment (Sgrub thabs kun btus),* vol. 13: 600–622. Dehra Dun: G. Loday, N. Gyaltsen, and N. Lungtok, 1970.

Yeshé Paljor, Sumpa Khenpo (Ye shes dpal 'byor, Sum pa mkhan po). *Fine Tree of Noble Aspiration. 'Phags bsam ljon bzang.* Śatapiṭaka Series, vol. 8, pt. 3. New Delhi: International Academy for Indian Culture, 1959.

Yeshé Tsemo (Ye shes rtse mo). *Rosary of Amazing and Marvelous Gems: A Biography of the Omniscient Lord Gendun Drupa Pal Sangpo. Rje thams cad mkhyen pa dge 'dun grub pa dpal bzang po'i rnam thar ngo mtshar rmad byung nor bu'i 'phreng ba.* In *'Phags pa 'jig rten dbang phyug gi rnam sprul rim byon gyi 'khrungs rabs deb ther nor bu'i 'phreng ba,* vol. 1: 207–300. Dharamsala: Sku-sger Yig-tshang, 1977.

Yoginī Cinṭa. *Realization of Reality That Subsequently Clarifies Entities. Vyaktabhāvānugatatattvasiddhi. Dngos po gsal ba'i rjes su 'gro ba'i de kho na nyid grub pa.* Toh 2222, rgyud, *wi,* 63a–68b. P 3066, *mi.*

Shang Yudrakpa (Zhang G.yu grag pa). *Biography of Pal. Dpal gyi rnam thar.* In *Writings (Bka' 'thor bu) of Zhang g.Yu-brag-pa brtson-'grus-grags-pa,* 360–92. Tashijong: Sungrab Nyamso Gyunpel Parkhang, 1972.

Shönu Pal, Gö Lotsāwa (Gzhon nu dpal, 'Gos Lo tsā ba) and Sönam Gyatso, Trimkhang Lotsāwa (Bsod nams rgya mtsho, Khrims khang Lo tsā ba). *Biography of the Dharma Lord, the Honorable Great Paṇḍita Vanaratna. Chos kyi rje paṇ chen nags kyi rin po che'i zhal snga nas kyi rnam par thar pa. Dbu med* manuscript, 60 fols.

Sources in European Languages

Akester, Matthew (2001). "The 'Vajra Temple' of gTer ston Zhig po gling pa and the Politics of Flood Control in 16th Century Lha sa." *Tibet Journal* 26 (1): 3–24.

Anonymous (1979). "Life in Chung Riwoche." *Tibetan Review* 14 (8): 5–6.

Ardussi, John A. (1972). "'Brug-pa kun-legs, the Saintly Tibetan Madman." M.A. thesis, University of Washington.

_____ (1977). "The Quest for the Brahmaputra River." *Tibet Journal* 2 (1): 35–49.

Aris, Michael (1980). *Bhutan: The Early History of a Himalayan Kingdom.* New Delhi: Vikas Publishing House.

_____ (1988). *Hidden Treasures and Secret Lives: A Study of Pemalingpa (1450–1521) and the Sixth Dalai Lama (1683–1706).* Shimla: Indian Institute of Advanced Study.

Barron, Richard (Chökyi Nyima), trans. (2003). *The Autobiography of Jamgön Kongtrul: A Gem of Many Colors.* Ithaca: Snow Lion Publications.

Batchelor, Stephen (1987). *The Tibet Guide.* London: Wisdom Publications.

Bell, Sir Charles (1968). *Tibet Past and Present.* London: Oxford University Press.

Brunnhölzl, Karl (2004). *The Center of the Sunlit Sky: Madhyamaka in the Kagyü Tradition.* Ithaca: Snow Lion Publications.

Chang, Garma C. C., trans. (1962). *The Hundred Thousand Songs of Milarepa.* 2 vols. New Hyde Park, N.Y.: University Books.

Conze, Edward (1973). *The Perfection of Wisdom in Eight Thousand Lines & Its Verse Summary.* Bolinas: Four Seasons Foundation.

Davidson, Ronald M. (1981). "The *Litany of Names of Mañjuśrī*: Text and Translation of the *Mañjuśrīnāmasaṃgīti*." In *Tantric and Taoist Studies in Honour of R. A. Stein,* edited by Michel Strickmann, vol. 1: 1–69. Brussels: Institut Belge des Hautes Études Chinoises.

_____ (2002). *Indian Esoteric Buddhism: A Social History of the Tantric Movement.* New York: Columbia University Press.

_____ (2005). *Tibetan Renaissance: Tantric Buddhism in the Rebirth of Tibetan Culture.* New York: Columbia University Press.

Decleer, Hubert (n.d.). *Garwang Chökyi Wangchug (1584–1630), the Sixth Zhwa-dmar Rinpoché's Journey to Nepal: An Investigation of the Kathmandu Valley Episode.* Unpublished booklet.

Dewar, Tyler, trans. (2004). *Trainings in Compassion: Manuals on the Meditation of Avalokiteshvara.* Ithaca: Snow Lion Publications.

Dickinson, Emily (1961). *The Complete Poems of Emily Dickinson.* Boston: Little, Brown & Company.

Diemberger, Hildegard (forthcoming 2007). *When a Woman Becomes a Religious Dynasty: The Samding Dorje Phagmo of Tibet.* New York: Columbia University Press.

Diemberger, Hildegard, Pasang Wangdu, Marlies Kornfeld, and Christian Jahoda (1997). *Feast of Miracles: The Life and the Tradition of Bodong Chole Namgyal (1375/6–1451) According to the Tibetan Texts "Feast of Miracles" and "The Lamp lluminating the History of Bodong."* Porong: Pema Chöding Editions.

Dorje, Gyurme (1999). *Tibet Handbook.* Bath: Footprint Books.

Dorje, Gyurme, and Matthew Kapstein (1991). *The Nyingma School of Tibetan Buddhism: Its Fundamentals and History.* Vol. 2. Boston: Wisdom Publications.

Dudjom Rinpoche, Jikdrel Yeshe Dorje (1991). *The Nyingma School of Tibetan Buddhism: Its Fundamentals and History.* Vol. 1. Translated by Gyurme Dorje and Matthew Kapstein. Boston: Wisdom Publications.

Edou, Jérôme (1996). *Machig Labdrön and the Foundations of Chöd.* Ithaca: Snow Lion Publications.

Ehrhard, Franz-Karl (2002). *Life and Travels of Lo-chen bSod-nams rgya-mtsho.* Lumbini: Lumbini International Research Institute.

_____ (2004). "Spiritual Relationships between Rulers and Preceptors: The Three Journeys of Vanaratna (1384–1468) to Tibet." In *The Relationship between Religion and State (chos srid zung 'brel) in Traditional Tibet,* 245–65. Lumbini: Lumbini International Research Institute.

Epstein, Lawrence (1968). "The Biography of the Second rGyal dbang Karma pa, Karma Baγsi." M.A. thesis, University of Washington.

Farrow, G.W., and I. Menon (1992). *The Concealed Essence of the Hevajra Tantra.* Delhi: Motilal Banarsidass.

Ferrari, Alfonsa (1958). *mKhyen brtse's Guide to the Holy Places of Central Tibet.* Rome: Istituto Italiano per il Medio ed Estremo Oriente.

Goldstein, Melvyn C. (1989). *A History of Modern Tibet, 1913–1951: The Demise of the Lamaist State.* Berkeley: University of California Press.

Goodrich, L. Carrington, and Chaoying Fang (1976). *Dictionary of Ming Biography (1368–1644).* 2 vols. New York: Columbia University Press.

Guenther, Herbert (1993). *Ecstatic Spontaneity: Saraha's Three Cycles of Dohā.* Berkeley: Asian Humanities Press.

Gyalchok, Shönu, and Könchok Gyaltsen (2006). *Mind Training: The Great Collection.* Translated by Thupten Jinpa. Boston: Wisdom Publications.

Gyatso, Janet (1980). "The Teachings of Thang-stong rgyal-po." In *Tibetan Studies in Honour of Hugh Richardson,* edited by Michael Aris and Aung San Suu Kyi, 111–19. New Delhi: Vikas Publishing House.

_____ (1981). "The Literary Transmission of the Traditions of Thang-stong rgyal-po: A Study of Visionary Buddhism in Tibet." Ph.D. dissertation, University of California, Berkeley.

_____ (1985). "The Development of the *Gcod* Tradition." In *Soundings in Tibetan Civilization*, edited by Barbara Nimri Aziz and Matthew Kapstein, 320–41. New Delhi: Manohar Publications.

_____ (1986). "Thang-stong rgyal-po, Father of the Tibetan Drama: The Bodhisattva As Artist." In *Zlos-gar: The Tibetan Performing Arts*, edited by Jamyang Norbu, 91–104. Dharamsala: Library of Tibetan Works and Archives.

_____ (1989). "Down with the Demoness: Reflections on a Feminine Ground in Tibet." In *Feminine Ground: Essays on Women and Tibet*, edited by Janice Willis, 33–51. Ithaca: Snow Lion Publications.

_____ (1992). "Genre, Authorship, and Transmission in Visionary Buddhism: The Literary Traditions of Thang-stong rgyal-po." In *Tibetan Buddhism: Reason and Revelation*, edited by Steven D. Goodman and Ronald M. Davidson, 95–106. Albany: State University of New York Press.

_____ (1998). *Apparitions of the Self: The Secret Autobiographies of a Tibetan Visionary.* Princeton: Princeton University Press.

Harding, Sarah, trans. (2003). *Machik's Complete Explanation: Clarifying the Meaning of Chöd.* Ithaca: Snow Lion Publications.

Hauri, H.H., and T.F. Peters (1979) *The Development of Suspension Bridge Construction from the Earliest Attempts to the Beginnings of Wire Cable Bridges.* Distributed at the ASCE Convention and Exposition, Boston, April 2–6, 1979.

Hedin, Sven (1917). *Southern Tibet.* Vol. 2. Stockholm: Lithographic Institue of the General Staff of the Swedish Army.

Heller, Amy (2003). "The Three Silver Brothers." *Orientations* 34 (4): 28–34.

Herweg, Jurgen Wilhelm (1994). "The Hagiography of Rig 'dzin Rgod kyi ldem 'phru can and Three Historical Questions Emerging from It." M.A. thesis, University of Washington.

Hummel, Siegbert (1968). "The Tibetan Ceremony of Breaking the Stone." *History of Religions* 8 (2): 139–42.

Huntington, Susan L. (1985). *The Art of Ancient India.* New York: Weatherhill.

_____ and John C. Huntington (1990). *Leaves from the* Bodhi *Tree: The Art of Pāla India (8th–12th Centuries) and Its International Legacy.* Seattle: University of Washington Press.

Jackson, David P. (1994). *Enlightenment by a Single Means.* Vienna: Verlag der Österreichischen Akademie der Wissenschaften.

_____ (1996). *A History of Tibetan Painting.* Vienna: Verlag der Österreichischen Akademie der Wissenschaften.

Kahlen, Wolf (1990). "Tibets Leonardo." *VDI Nachrichten Magazin* (November 1990): 90–100.

_____ (1993). "Thang-stong rgyal-po – A Leonardo of Tibet." In *Anthropology of Tibet and the Himalaya*, edited by Charles Ramble et al., 138–49. Zürich: Völkerkundemuseum der Universität Zürich.

_____ (1994). "The 'Renaissance' of Tibetan Architecture in the 15th Century by Thang-stong rgyal-po." *Archív Orientální* 62:300–314.

Kapstein, Matthew (1980). "The Shangs-pa bKa'-brgyud: An Unknown Tradition of Tibetan Buddhism." In *Tibetan Studies in Honour of Hugh Richardson*, edited by Michael Aris and Aung San Suu Kyi, 138–44. New Delhi: Vikas Publishing House.

_____ (1992). "Remarks on the *Maṇi bKa'-'bum* and the Cult of Āvalokiteśvara in Tibet." In *Tibetan Buddhism: Reason and Revelation*, edited by Steven D. Goodman and Ronald M. Davidson, 79–93. Albany: State University of New York Press.

Karmay, Samten (1988). *Secret Visions of the Fifth Dalai Lama*. London: Serindia Publications.

Kazi, Sonam Topgay, and Richard Bartholomew (1965). *Tibet House Museum*. Inaugural exhibition catalogue. New Delhi: Tibet House Museum.

Khedrup Norsang Gyatso (2004). *Ornament of Stainless Light: An Exposition of the Kālacakra Tantra*. Translated by Gavin Kilty. Boston: Wisdom Publications.

Kongtrul, Jamgön (2003). *The Treasury of Knowledge: Book Five: Buddhist Ethics*. Translated by the Kalu Rinpoché Translation Group. Ithaca: Snow Lion Publications.

Kossak, Steven M., and Jane Casey Singer (1998). *Sacred Visions: Early Paintings from Central Tibet*. New York: The Metropolitan Museum of Art.

Kunga Rinpoche and Brian Cutillo (1978). *Drinking the Mountain Stream*. New York: Lotsawa.

Lhalungpa, Lobsang, trans. (1977). *The Life of Milarepa*. New York: E.P. Dutton.

——— (1983). *Tibet: The Sacred Realm, Photographs 1880–1950*. New York: Aperture Foundation.

Linrothe, Rob, ed. (2006). *Holy Madness: Portraits of Tantric Siddhas*. New York: Rubin Museum of Art.

Macdonald, Alexander, and Dvags-po rin-po-che (1987). "A Little-read Guide to the Holy Places of Nepal, Part II." Translated by Vincanne Adams. In *Essays on the Ethnology of Nepal and South Asia* 2, 100–134. Kathmandu: Ratna Pustak Bhandar.

Martin, Dan (1992). "A Twelfth-Century Tibetan Classic of Mahāmudrā: *The Path of Ultimate Profundity*: The Great Seal Instructions of Zhang." *Journal of the International Association of Buddhist Studies* 15 (2): 243–319.

_____ (2001). *Unearthing Bon Treasures: Life and Contested Legacy of a Tibetan Scripture Revealer, with a General Bibliography of Bon.* Leiden: Brill.

McLeod, Ken (n.d.). *A Continuous Rain to Benefit Beings.* Vancouver: Kagyu Kunkhyab Chuling.

Namgyal, Takpo Tashi (1986). *Mahāmudrā: The Quintessence of Mind and Meditation.* Translated by Lobsang P. Lhalungpa. Boston: Shambhala Publications.

Nebesky-Wojkowitz, René de (1956). *Oracles and Demons of Tibet.* The Hague: Mouton.

Nölle, Wilfried (1965). "Kāmarupa." *Indo-Asian Studies.* Śatapiṭaka Series 37, 125–27. New Delhi: International Academy for Indian Culture.

Obermiller, E., trans. (1932). *History of Buddhism by Bu-ston.* 2 vols. Heidelberg: O. Harrassowitz.

Pal, Pratapaditya (2001). *Desire and Devotion: Art from India, Nepal, and Tibet in the John and Berthe Ford Collection.* New Delhi: Timeless Books.

Petech, Luciano (1980). "Ya-ts'e, Gu-ge, Pu-rang: A New Study." *Central Asiatic Journal* 24: 85–111.

_____ (1990). *Central Tibet and the Mongols.* Rome: Istituto Italiano per il Medio ed Estremo Oriente.

Prince Peter of Greece and Denmark, H.R.H. (1962). "The Ceremony of Breaking the Stone." *Folk* 4: 65–70.

Radzinsky, Edvard (1992). *The Last Tsar: The Life and Death of Nicholas II.* Translated by Marian Schwartz. New York: Doubleday.

Rhie, Marylin M., and Robert A. F. Thurman (1991). *Wisdom and Compassion: The Sacred Art of Tibet.* New York: Henry N. Abrams.

_____ (1999). *Worlds of Transformation: Tibetan Art of Wisdom and Compassion.* New York: Tibet House.

Rhodes, N. G. (1980). "The Development of Currency in Tibet." In *Tibetan Studies in Honour of Hugh Richardson,* edited by Michael Aris and Aung San Suu Kyi, 261–68. New Delhi: Vikas Publishing House.

Ricard, Matthieu, et al., trans. (1994). *The Life of Shabkar: The Autobiography of a Tibetan Yogin.* Albany: State University of New York Press.

Ricca, Franco, and Erberto Lo Bue (1995). *The Great Stupa of Gyantse.* London: Serindia Publications.

Richardson, Hugh (1998). *High Peaks, Pure Earth: Collected Writings on Tibetan History and Culture.* Edited by Michael Aris. London: Serindia Publications.

Roerich, George, trans. (1976). *The Blue Annals.* Delhi: Motilal Banarsidass.

_____ (1932). "The Ceremony of Breaking the Stone." *Journal of Urusvati* 2: 25–51.

Rossabi, Morris (1988). *Khubilai Khan: His Life and Times.* Berkeley: University of California Press.

Schaeffer, Kurtis R. (2002). "The Attainment of Immortality: From Nāthas in India to Buddhist in Tibet." *Journal of Indian Philosophy* 30: 515–33.

von Schroeder, Ulrich (1990). *Buddhist Sculptures of Sri Lanka.* Hong Kong: Visual Dharma Publications.

Singer, Jane Casey, and Philip Denwood (1997). *Tibetan Art: Towards a Definition of Style.* London: Lawrence King Publishing.

Slusser, Mary Shepherd (1982). *Nepal Mandala: A Cultural Study of the Kathmandu Valley.* Vol. 1. Princeton: Princeton University Press.

Smith, E. Gene (2001). *Among Tibetan Texts: History and Literature of the Himalayan Plateau.* Boston: Wisdom Publications.

Snellgrove, David (1959). *The Hevajra Tantra.* 2 vols. London: Oxford University Press.

Snellgrove, David, and Hugh Richardson (1968). *A Cultural History of Tibet.* New York: Frederick A. Praeger.

Sørensen, Per K. (1994). *The Mirror Illuminating the Royal Genealogies: Tibetan Buddhist Historiography: An Annotated Translation of the XIVth Century Tibetan Chronicle rGyal-rabs gsal-ba'i me-long.* Wiesbaden: Harrassowitz Verlag.

_____ (2003). "Lhasa Diluvium: Sacred Environment at Stake: The Birth of Flood Control Politics, the Question of Natural Disaster Management and their Importance for the Hegemony over a National Monument in Tibet." *Lungta* 16 (Spring 2003: *Cosmogony and the Origins*): 84–134.

Stearns, Cyrus (1980). "The Life and Teachings of the Tibetan Saint Thang-stong rgyal-po, 'King of the Empty Plain.'" M.A. thesis, University of Washington.

_____ (1996). "The Life and Tibetan Legacy of the Indian *Mahāpaṇḍita* Vibhūticandra." *Journal of the International Association of Buddhist Studies* 19 (1): 127–71.

_____ (1999). *The Buddha from Dolpo: A Study of the Life and Thought of the Tibetan Master Dolpopa Sherab Gyaltsen.* Albany: State University of New York Press.

_____, trans. (2000). *Hermit of Go Cliffs: Timeless Instructions from a Tibetan Mystic.* Boston: Wisdom Publications.

_____ (2001). *Luminous Lives: The Story of the Early Masters of the Lam 'bras Tradition in Tibet.* Boston: Wisdom Publications.

_____ (2003). "The Sakya School." In *Portraits of the Masters: Bronze Sculptures of the Tibetan Buddhist Lineages*, ed. Donald Dinwiddie, 204–19. Chicago and London: Serindia Publications, Inc. and Oliver Hoare, Ltd.

_____, trans. (2006). *Taking the Result As the Path: Core Teachings of the Sakya Lamdré Tradition.* Boston: Wisdom Publications.

Stearns, Ilze Maruta [Kalnins] (1985). "The Life of Gtsang-smyon Heruka: A Study in Divine Madness." M.A. thesis, University of Washington.

Stein, R. A. (1956). *L'épopée tibetaine de Gesar dans sa version lamaïque de Ling.* Paris: Presses Universitaires de France.

_____ (1959). *Recherches sur l'épopée et le barde au Tibet.* Paris: Presses Universitaires de France.

_____ (1972a). *Tibetan Civilization.* Stanford: Stanford University Press.

_____ (1972b). *Vie et chants de 'Brug-pa Kun-legs le yogin.* Paris: G. P. Maisonneuve et Larose.

Tatz, Mark (1987). "The Life of the Siddha-Philosopher Maitrīgupta." *Journal of the American Oriental Society* 107: 695–711.

Tsang Nyön Heruka (1982). *The Life of Marpa the Translator.* Translated by the Nālandā Translation Committee. Boulder: Prajñā Press.

Tsering, Tashi (2001). "Reflections on Thang stong rgyal po As the Founder of the A lce Lha mo Tradition of Tibetan Performing Arts." *Lungta* 15 (Winter 2001: *The Singing Mask: Echoes of Tibetan Opera*): 36–60.

Tsuda, Shiníchi, ed. and trans. (1974). *The Saṃvarodaya Tantra, Selected Chapters.* Tokyo: Hokuseido Press.

Tucci, Giuseppe (1949). *Tibetan Painted Scrolls.* 3 vols. Rome: La Libreria dello Stato.

_____ (1956). *To Lhasa and Beyond.* Rome: Istituto Italiano per il Medio ed Estremo Oriente.

_____ (1967). *Tibet: Land of Snows.* Translated by J. E. Stapleton Driver. New York: Stein and Day.

_____, trans. (1971). *Deb ther dmar po, The New Red Annals.* Rome: Istituto Italiano per il Medio ed Estremo Oriente.

_____ (1973). *Transhimalaya.* Geneva: Nagel Publishers.

_____ (1989). *Gyantse and Its Monasteries: Part I* [English translation of *Indo-Tibetica IV.1* by Uma Marini Vesci]. New Delhi: Aditya Prakashan.

Turner, Samuel (1971). *An Account of an Embassy to the Court of the Teshoo Lama in Tibet.* New Delhi: Mañjuśri Publishing House. Reprint of 1800 edition.

Tuttle, Gray (2006). "Tibetan Buddhism at Ri bo rtse lnga/Wutai Shan in Modern Times." *Journal of the International Association of Tibetan Studies,* no. 2 (August 2006): 1–35.

Ui, Hakuju, et al., eds. (1934). *A Complete Catalogue of the Tibetan Buddhist Canons.* Sendai: Tohoku Imperial University.

Vitali, Roberto (1990). *Early Temples of Central Tibet.* London: Serindia Publications.

_____ (1996). *The Kingdoms of Gu.ge Pu.hrang: According to the mNga'.ris rgyal.rabs by Gu.ge mkhan.chen Ngag.dbang grags.pa.* Dharamsala: Tho ling gtsug lag khang lo gcig stong 'khor ba'i rjes dran mdzad sgo'i go sgrig tshogs chung.

Vostrikov, A.I. (1970). *Tibetan Historical Literature.* Soviet Indology Series 4. Calcutta: Indian Studies: Past & Present.

Waddell, L.A. (1906). *Lhasa and Its Mysteries.* New York: E. P. Dutton.

Wallace, Vesna A. (2001). *The Inner Kālacakratantra: A Buddhist Tantric View of the Individual.* New York: Oxford University Press.

Weldon, David, and Jane Casey Singer (1999). *The Sculptural Heritage of Tibet: Buddhist Art in the Nyingjei Lam Collection.* London: Laurence King Publishing.

White, David Gordon (1996). *The Alchemical Body: Siddha Traditions in Medieval India.* Chicago: University of Chicago Press.

Wylie, Turrell V. (1970). *A Tibetan Religious Geography of Nepal.* Rome: Istituto Italiano per il Medio ed Estremo Oriente.

Zangpo, Ngawang (2001). *Sacred Ground: Jamgon Kongtrul on "Pilgrimage and Sacred Geography."* Ithaca: Snow Lion Publications.

_____ (2003). *Timeless Rapture: Inspired Verse of the Shangpa Masters.* Ithaca: Snow Lion Publications.

Index

Boldface indicates illustration

a or *āḥ* syllable, 103, 174, 495n330
Abhayākaragupta, 514n483
abhidharma, 497n347, 508–9n443, 524n558
  according to *Abhidharmakośa*, 495–96n334
  Tangtong's knowledge of, 114
Abhirati buddha field, 248
Abhisamayālaṃkāra, 114
absolute initiation, 146
abuse or nonrecognition of Tangtong, 149
  accused of impersonating adept at Ulek Monastery, 269–70
  assassination attempt on, 475n96
  attacked by merchants in Kāmata, 411–12
  attacked by Tsanda chieftain and attendants, 271
  attempt to poison at Ngari Dzongka, 261–63
  attempts to kill by king of Kāmata, 394–95
  beaten in Penyul, 246
  beating by Bönpos at Yungdrung Ling, 270–71
  and bridge over Kyichu River, 534n656
  during landslide at Riwoché, 368, 568n977
  at end of retreat at Shalkar Lhadong, 518n512
  at Jonang Stūpa, 162
  at Kaṃṇi Goshi, 521n539
  Karmapa servants attempt to kill, 243
  Kongpo and taking iron to Tibet, 240–41
  at Menmogang Monastery, 232–33
  and Minyak men, 75–76, 250
  mistaken for demon at Dok River, 545n753
  at Owa Lhatsé, 154–55
  prayer for those who have, 429
  stabbed at Riwoché when building stūpa, 368
  stabbed by gold thieves at Riwoché, 385
  stone striking head at Riwoché, 368
  stoning at Kham Riwoché Monastery, 326
  stoning when riding into Pal Khorlo Dechen, 348
  struck on head at Kyichu River, 40, 196–98, 522n544
  and ten clansmen at Dartsedo, 315
  and tying penis to rope, 69, 250
  and wearing cloak at Serché stūpa, 288–90
Aché Lhamo (A lce lha mo) opera performances, 2, 23, **24**, 470n43
adoptive bridegroom *(go mag)*, 96, 493n309
Adrön Chödrön (A sgron Chos sgron), 467n17. *See also* Chökyi Drönmé
age of strife *(kaliyuga)*, 84, 174–75, 491n288
Akaniṣṭha Khecara, paradise of, 26, 99, 494n323
Akṣobhya, 174, 518n505
Alek (A legs), 255
All-Illuminating Lamp, 6–7, 467n21, 468n28

Amdar Shong (A 'dar gshongs), 324
Amdo (A mdo), 245, 535n665
Amdruk (A 'brug) of Minyak, 325
Ami Gön (A mi mgon), 258
Amitābha, 7, 26, 507n432
  appearing in Uḍḍiyāna, 184
  dream of by Tangtong's mother, 98
  and father of Dangra boy, 415
  images of made by Tangtong, 41, 45, 306, 384
Amitāyus, 26, 27
  as Destroyer of the Lord of Death, 565n945
  dhāraṇī-mantras of, 206
  giving Tangtong longevity pills, 369–70
  and *Glorious Giver of Immortality*, 28, 477n118
  images of made by Tangtong, 45, 306
  initiation of, 105, 140
  at Samyé Chimpu, 335
  Tangtong offerings and control over lifespan, 291
Amoghapaśa, method for accomplishment of, 113, 235, 497n345
Amoghasiddhi, 41, 45, 306, 337, 536n678
Amoghavajra (A mo gha badzra), 479n150
Amulet Mahāmudrā (Phyag chen ga'u ma), 31, 150, 157
Ānandamitra, 455, 585n1153
Ané Chösang (A ne Chos bzang), 541n719
Ané Jinsangma (A ne Sbying bzang ma), 541n719
Ané Paldren (A ne Dpal 'dren), 261, 263, 542n725
Ané Tsomo, 210, 528n591, 532n634
  See also Kalden Rinchen Tsomo
Aṅgaja, arhat, 164, 514n479–80
animals
  baboons and monkeys, 235
  bears, 325–26, 336–37
  birds, 106, 116, 136, 137, 239, 405–6
  births of Tangtong as, 266
  buffalo, 266, 269, 308
  crocodiles, 136, 137
  dog's footbone relic, 288
  donkeys, 66–67, 109, 503–4n403
  eagles, 106
  easier to tame than humans, 326
  and edict to birds and insects, 406
  fish, 264–65, 338
  goats, 106–7, 172, 418
  hybrid yak-cows, 332
  jackals, 148, 149
  mice, 407
  mules, 261, 332
  peacock, 262, 541n722
  ram killed at Rinchen Ding, 415
  scorpions, 51, 170, 215, 217
  sheep, 106–7
  snakes, 321, 415
  Tangtong teaching Dharma to, 106
  tigers, 240
  whose lives were spared by Tangtong, 415
  wolves, 136, 137, 179, 405
  See also horses; vulture
arhats, 140
Aris, Michael, 254, 481n170, 483n196, 485n224, 499n364
Aro Yeshé Jungné (A ro Ye shes 'byung gnas), 502–3n393
artistic works of Tangtong, 44–46, 106, 304–7, 424–25
Asaṅga, 497n347, 505–6n422
Ashi Drubtob Sangmo (A shi [?] Grub thob bzang mo), 62, 487n240
Assam, 252–53
assemblies, two, 156, 285, 510n457
Asura Cave (A su ra'i brag phug), 133, 504n405
Atikara, 139–40
Atiśa (982–1054), 302, 530–31n624, 552n821, 552–53n822
Auspicious Stūpa of Many Doors *(bkra shis sgo mang mchod ldan)*, 301, 412, 483n201
  by Rabten Kunsang Pak in 1427 at Gyantsé, 563n928
  as a hidden treasure in Lo, 238

Tangtong's visit to in Tāmradvīpa, 51, 141–42, 144, 378, 569–70n996
and Tsari mountain, 494n313
at Waru Namtsel, 332, 558n884
See also Jonang Stūpa; Auspicious Stūpa of Many Doors at Riwoché

Auspicious Stūpa of Many Doors at Riwoché, 50, 51–52, **381**, 483–84n204
all who work on reborn in Sukhāvatī, 365
art and style of, 485n219
and attack on Vajrāsana, 421
built by nonhuman beings at night, 371, 569n987
and "Cultural Revolution," 54–55
decision to build made at Ngamring, 371
eight tribes of gods and demons offer help, 363
and geomantic suppression of forehead of scorpion, 170
as geomantic focal-point, 33, 567n972
images painted on, 378
Kukkuripa instruction to Tangtong to build, 145
landslide at, 368–69, 568n980
largest stūpa built by Tangtong, 425
laying foundation of, 365, 567n971
māras creating trouble during construction, 368
murals and images created in, 418–19
must be finished before Tangtong's death, 365
and parasol and spire, 380
raising of center pole, 378, 570n999
restorations by Shabkar Natsok Rangdrol, 54
similarities to Jonang Stūpa, 493n304
style and those Tangtong had previously seen, 51–52
Tangtong locating limestone, gold, and vermilion for, 376–77
Tangtong's address to ill man during construction, 371–75
those offering to help with, 371
and trophies from stūpa at Mongolian-Tibetan border, 361
walls built by gods of four races of kings, 371

"authentic skull-cup." *See* "skull-cup, authentic"

avadhūti, 174, 518n505

avadhūti deliberate behavior, 60–61

Avalokiteśvara, 21, **22**, 46, **113**, 124, 250, 264, 474n88
and Amoghapaśa, 497n345, 533n642
appearance on dog's footbone, 288
appearing in Uḍḍiyāna, 184
and *Compendium of Maṇis*, 499n363
as crystal-colored youth, 165, 515n484
eleven-faced statue of in Jokhang, 521n538, 554n834
and fish at Yamdrok, 338
gold image of and Tangtong and Kalsang, 249
and Gugum Rinchen Gyaltsen, 496n343
as Hayagrīva, 28, 490n282
and Heartdrop of the Great Adept, 32
image of at Chuwori, 337–38
image of at Riwoché, 383
image of at Shalu Monastery, 164, 514n483
image of to be sent to Kashmir, 398
images made under direction of Tangtong, 306, 307
initiation and entrustment of pure awareness *(rig gtad kyi dbang)* for, 206, 208, 324, 421
and instruction to people of Lo, 533n646
and Ka Ngapa, 128
and Khachar Temple, 542n728
as Mahākaruṇika, 490n283, 585n1145
and Marpori Hill, 535n663
method for accomplishment of, 365
and Mitrayogin, 504n411
as Padmapāṇi, 490n282
and rain of grain to end famine of 1437, 286
seven branches offered by Tangtong, 164, 514n483
system of meditation by Tangtong, 1, 21

Tangtong's prayer to while working as blacksmith, 310 11
Tangtong as emanation or equal of, 21, 174, 443
and Tangtong at Ramadoli Charnel Ground, 178–79
Tangtong prayer to at Karita cave, 266–67
Tangtong seen as, 263, 302, 307, 410
Tangtong visions of, 256, 510n451
and three spiritual families, 533n648
urging Tangtong to take ordination, 110–11
and vows of ritual fasting, 523n550
and Waru Namtsel, 215
and Yigé Drugma, 502n390, 545n760
See also *Infinite Benefit for Living Beings*; Jowo of Kyirong; Khasarpaṇa; Naturally Arisen Eleven-faced Avalokiteśvara
Avalokiteśvara as the Lord of the Dance (Gar gyi dbang phyug), 167
Avalokiteśvara as the One Who Dredges the Pit of Saṃsāra ('Khor ba dong sprugs), 167, 515n490
Avalokiteśvara as the Protector from the Eight Fears ('Jigs pa brgyad skyob), 166–67
Avalokiteśvara as the Wish-fulfilling Gem (Yid bzhin nor bu), 167, 515n490
awakening the thought of enlightenment, 278, 309, 313, 395, 426
azurite, 341, 376

baboons and monkeys, 235
Badong Dunpa (Rba dong bdun pa) stūpa, 309
Bājambu, 518–19n513
Bakdrong (Bag grong), 257
Bakdrong (Bag grong) iron bridge, 257
Bakula, 514n480
Bardrong bridge near Wangdü Podrang, 42
barley *(phyag nas)*
consecration with, 41, 579n1093
and Dangra, 415
and Gyang stūpa, 118
and woman from Gyalchen Tsé, 75, 76, 246
basic space of phenomena, 83, 97, 435, 451, 490n281
Basic Texts and a Clarification of the White and Red Pills (Tangtong and Khyentsé Wangpo), 475n96, 541–42n723
bears
skin of offered by Mön Paro traders, 336–37
tamed by Tangtong in northern wilderness, 325–26
Beautiful Forms of Pure Faith (Gyurmé Dechen), 468n31, 470n44
beer, attempt to kill Tangtong with poisoned, 261–63
Behodharma, Chinese monk, 316
Beijing, 558n874
benefit of sentient beings
elsewhere and death of Tangtong, 445
from images created by Tangtong, 304
prayers to accomplish made by Tangtong before Jowo, 200
and prophecy from Jowo at Jokhang Temple, 168
Tangtong achieving with sixteen ḍākinīs, 176
Tangtong prayers for at Kyirong Jowo image, 123
Tangtong's prayer for, 317, 430–31
as Tangtong's purpose, 114, 201, 297
Bhairava initiation, 158
Bhakha (Bha kha), 222, 530n617
Bhaktapur (Kho khom), 133, 504n408
Bhaktapur (Kho khom), King of, 559–60n892
bhuta demons, 252
Bhutan, 33, 42, 43, 167, 169n45, 516n492
approaches to, 537n684, 538n692
chains from bridge in Paro, 44
Chaksam tradition in, 6, 15
iron bridge at Chukha, 43

monasteries founded by Tangtong in, 56
See also Paro; Tachok Norbugang
Binang Khaché (Sbi nang kha che), 257
biographical prophecy *(lung bstan rnam thar)*, 465n4
Biography of the Venerable Lady Chökyi Drönma, 466n9, 466n12
birds, 106, 239, 405–6
eagles, 106
hawks, 136, 137
ravenlike, 239
Tangtong teaches Dharma to, 116
See also vulture
birth of Tangtong, 95–96, 97
date of, 11–14, 470n470n43–5
and dreams and omens, 103–5
inner signs of auspicious birth and dreams of mother, 97–101
and prosperity of Owa Lhatsé, 106
signs at, 103
speech of after, 103, 104–5
time in womb, 100, 101, 103–4, 494n320
Black Yamāri, 501–2n388
blacksmiths
Drakpa, 310
eight at Ochu Gadrak, 42, 254–55
and factories for forging iron links at Tsagong Nesar, 310
Kunga, 232, 532n638
Sangyé, 232
Tangtong working in smitheries, 310–11
and Tangtong's emanated body at Té Valley, 254
See also iron
blessing of the illusory body *(sgyu lus kyi byin rlabs)*, 19, 191, 473n78, 521n534
boats
ḍākinīs encouraging Tangtong to build, 40
as symbol for liberation, 38
Boborgang (Spo 'bor sgang), 410
Bodhgayā, 90, 492n295
Bodhi tree, 90
Bodhnāth stūpa, 133, 504n404
Bodong Panchen Cholé Namgyal (Bo dong paṇ chen Phyogs las rnam rgyal, 1376–1451), 52, 466n12, 484n212, 536n678
and Chökyi Drönmé, 554n837
and Delek Chödren, 576n1053
and Namgyal Drakpa Sangpo, 546n763
and Palden Chimé Drubpa, 576n1058
Bodong (Bo dong), 164
Bodong (Bo dong) tradition, 52, 484n212, 497n346
See also Ngamring Monastery
bodyprint
by Padmasambhava in rock in Mön, 287
See also footprints; handprints
Bönpos (Bon po) and Bönpo tradition, 542n724, 565n944
and "Dharma of the gods," 558n879
and monastery of Darding, 352, 565n944
and Tangtong as Tsewang Rangdrol, 565n944
and Tangtong at Yungdrung Ling, 270–71, 543n739
Brahmā, 311, 381
Breaking of the Stone (Pho bar rdo gcog) ceremony, 23
bridges
early history of, 33–34
as means to liberate beings, 174, 281
merit achieved by building, 38
number of wooden constructed by Tangtong, 40, 424, 480n157
as symbol for liberation, 38–40
See also iron bridges
Bright Lamp (Könchok Palsang and Dewa Sangpo), 5–8
compared to *All-Illuminating Lamp*, 6–7, 467n21
and Great Perfection teachings, 476n104
and teachings received by Tangtong, 508–9n443

Bright Lamp of Prophecy (Guru Padmasambhava/Tangtong), 3–4, 23, 176, 465n4, 490n281
and birth of Tangtong, 13, 103
and followers of Tangtong, 434
and inner signs of appearance of Tangtong, 97–101
and lives between Drakpa Öser and Tangtong, 92
and longevity of Tangtong, 27–28, 445–47, 476n114
and manner of passing away, 436
and mother and father of Tangtong, 95, 96
and outer and secret signs of appearance of, 96–97
and people who will meet Tangtong, 177
and physical marks of Tangtong, 103
and prophecy of appearance of, 443–45
and special places of Tangtong, 434–35
and Tangtong as mental emanation of Padmasambhava, 100
Tangtong finding in Tsari Serchen Cave, 309
Tangtong taking text of, 96
Brikuti, 521n538
brown bears, tamed by Tangtong in northern wilderness, 325–26
Buddha-nature, 507n436
Buddha Śākyamuni, 92
becomes waterfall and liberates fish, 264–65
and Bodhgayā, 492n295
eras of teachings of, 491n288
image of at Riwoché, 383, 384
and Jowo statue, 489n272
Lhachen Palbar image of at Gungtang, 522n541
and merit achieved by various acts, 38
and stūpa in Tāmradvīpa, 141
and Stūpa of Great Enlightenment, 558n882
Tangtong visions of, 113, 505n415, 510n451
and twelve acts, 436, 583n1130
and Viśuddha Stūpa in Assam, 537n686
buddha spiritual family, 229
buffalo, patron's in Karita cave in Kashmir, 266, 269, 308
"but you can stand it" refrain, 366–67
Butön Rinchen Drup (Bu ston Rin chen grub, 1290–1364), 514n482

Cakrasaṃvara, 58, 133, **135**, 345, 482n212, 505n413
blended with Tangtong and Paṇḍita Mahābodhi, 503–4n403
donkey-faced form of and Sakya tradition, 503–4n403
and home at Tsari mountain, 494n313
images of, 383, 556–57n861
initiations received from Gyalwang, 508–9n443
maṇḍala constructed by Mahābodhi, 133–34
palace in Mön, 181
and Vararuci, 519n523
and Virūpa, 517n502
Cakravartī, 239, 361, 533n650. *See also* Raudra Cakrī
Camara Island (Rnga yag gling), 28, 356, 477n117
Caṇḍālī, 26, 435, 445, 583n1127
Caṅgala Rāja, 334
canonical lineage *(bka' ma)* of Nyingma tradition, 130, 503n399
Cārvāka, 394, 573n1034–5
Catuḥpīṭha, 58
Caturmukha, 56
celestial planetary demons *(steng gdon gza')*, 219, 530n614
Ceylon, 483n202, 506n426
See also Tāmradvīpa
Chakdor Norbu (Phyag rdor nor bu). *See* Gam Nyön Chakdor Norbu
Chakpori Hill (Lcags po ri) in Lhasa, 41, **249**, 535n663
and address to Kalden Rinchen Sangmo, 247–48

arrow landing as auger of building to come, 245
images on, 338
and installation of Amoghasiddhi image, 337
and Lady Kalsang's passing, 335
and residence for Tangtong, 247, 535n666
rules regarding, 337
statues left by Tangtong on, 45–46, 482n178
Tangtong's months of meditation at, 248–49
Chakpori Medical College in Lhasa, 475n96
Chakpurchen (Lcags phur can), "Iron Dagger Cave," 288, 548n770
Chakra (Lcags ra) fortress, 556n851
Chaksam Chuwori (Lcags zam Chu bo ri) Monastery, 15, **45**, 55–56
bridge completed there, 43–44, 46, 481n175
and destruction during Cultural Revolution, 56
and Gyaltsen Sangpo, 337–38, 486n226
as "Iron-Bridge Monastery," 43
lands offered to for support, 301
practice center of Tsechu, 16
Tangtong laying foundation structures, 250
and three groups of five major disciples, 337
treasures held at, 337–38
and Tangtong's vow not to cross thresholds, 292, 301, 552n815
work on temple of, 300
Chaksam Chuwori (Lcags zam chu bo ri) stūpa, 50, 55–56, 300, 337–38
Chaksam (Lcags zam lugs) or "Iron Bridge" tradition, 6
histories of the tradition, 17
locations of practice of, 15
and Tangtong's long life, 28
Chaksam Tulkus (Lcags zam sprul sku) or Tenzin Rinpochés, 15, 16, 55, 574–75n1042
Chaktsal Gang (Phyag 'tshal sgang), 205
Changyul Rawakha (Lcang yul ra ba kha), 257
Chapa Chökyi Sengé (Phya pa Chos kyi seng ge, 1109–60), 488–89n263, 524n561
Charnel Ground Endowed with Skeletons (Dur khrod Keng rus can), 517n501
Charnel Ground of Blazing Skeletons (Dur khrod Keng rus me 'bar), 172, 517n501
Charnel Ground of Ngampa Dradrok (Dur khrod Rngam pa sgra sgrogs), 252
Charnel Ground of Ramadoli (Dur khrod Ra ma do le), 178–79
Charnel Ground of Rāmeśvara (Dur khrod Ra me shwa ra), 19, 20 266, 549–50n795
Charnel Ground of Śītavana (Dur khrod Bsil bu tshal), 519n522, 519n523
Charnel Ground of the Grove of Terrifying Darkness (Dur khrod 'Jigs byed mun pa tshal), 181–82, 519n522
Charnel Ground of Tumdrak (Gtum drag gi dur khrod), 253, 538n688
charnel grounds, 140, 159, 295, 387
Chen Nga Ngawang Drakpa (Spyan snga Ngag dbang grags pa, 1439–91), 431, 580–81n1108
See also Ngagi Wangpo
Chen Nga Sönam Gyaltsen (Spyan snga Bsod rnams rgyal mtshan, 1386–1434), 210, 527n586
Ch'eng Tsu, 564n938
Chetsun Sherab Jungné (Lce btsun Shes rab 'byung gnas), 514n482, 514n483
childhood of Tangtong
being gone three months, 108
and epidemic at Tangtong's birthplace, 109–10
infancy of, 105–6

and learning to read and write, 107–8
mad behavior, 65
and magical feats, 106–8
making figures of deities as young boy, 106
as shepherd, 106–7
and teachings from Dönyö Gyaltsen, 106, 495n333
and trading of white tails and musk pods for seven human lives, 110
and walking on water, 108
See also birth of Tangtong
Chimpu (Mchims phu), 28, 32, 206–8, 477n118, 525n571
Chinese emperor
gifts received from, 381–82, 386
prophecy of bringing under control, 137, 138
Tangtong edict to, 386, 572–73n1022
Tangtong's prophecy regarding, 323
and title Tai Situ, 546n763
See also Chu Ch'i-chen
Chöd (Gcod) tradition and practices, 19–21, 391, 466n12, 528n589
and Kongpo Gyala, 313–14
and Kunsang Pema Tsewang, 478n122
mad yogins often known in, 63
and Northern Treasure (Byang gter) tradition, 62
performed by Tangtong against demonic spirits, 41
received from Ka Ngapa, 501–2n388
reception of teachings at age five, 495n333
Rendawa and Tangtong's practice of, 158
and Tangtong's speech to ill man at Riwoché, 372
Tangtong's teachings connected with, 19–21, 528n590
See also Opening the Door to the Sky
Chöden Dzema (Chos ldan mdzes ma), 89
Chödrak Palsang (Chos grags dpal bzang), 297, 406, 551n807, 576n1052
Chöjé Lingpa Dzamling Dorjé (Chos rje gling pa 'Dzam gling rdo rje), 30
Chokden Lekpai Lodrö (Mchog ldan legs pa'i blo gros), 157, 510–11n461, 544n751
Chokgyur Lingpa (Mchog gyur gling pa, 1829–70), 31
Chökhor Gang (Chos 'khor sgang) bridge, 46, 335
Choksang Lekpai Lodrö (Mchog bzang legs pa'i blo gros), 157, 510–11n461, 511n462
Chökyi Drönmé, venerable lady (Rje btsun Chos kyi sgron me, 1422–55), 4, **379**, 466n9, 536n678, 567n969
also known as Adrön Chödrön, 467n17
arrival of at Riwoché, 378
background and story of, 52–54
biographical supplication to Tangtong, 7, 466n12
and death of Tangtong, 435, 583n1126
and Delek Chödren, 548n785
and edict by Tangtong, 4–5
father of, 540–41n717
first meeting with Tangtong, 52–53
as incarnation of Vajravārāhī, 530n622
and iron from Kongpo, 46, 53
liberating beings and net of iron, 40
and longevity practice with Tangtong, 28
member of royal family at Ngari, 380, 570n1004
and Menmogang Monastery, 53, 532n636
and Palgyi Nesar Monastery in Tsagong, 56
and prophecy from Tangtong regarding longevity and service, 378–79
rebirth of, 378, 406, 467
skull-cup enshrined at Tsagong, 54, 309, 484–85n213, 530n622
as Vajravārāhī, 378
verse in praise of Tangtong, 14, 471n59
See also "skull-cup, authentic"
Chökyi Gyaltsen from Tsang, 387
Chökyi Nyima, 515n490

Chökyi Siji (Chos kyi gzi brjid, 1164–1224), 523n544
Chökyong Palwa (Chos skyong dpal ba), 107
Chöpal Gönpo (Chos dpal mgon po), 508–9n443
Chöpal Sangpo (Chos dpal bzang po, 1371–1439), 261, 263, 541n718, 541–42n723
Chöpan Drinsangma (Cod pan mgrin bzang ma), 544n746
chosen deity, 203, 366, 367, 375
  demons equal to, 297, 551n805
Chözom (Chos 'dzom), 261, 533n640, 540n713
Chözong (Chos rdzong) patrons and fortress, 353, 354
Chu Ch'i-chen (1427–64) (Chinese emperor), 320–23, 381, 557n867, 571n1010, 572–73n1022
Chukha iron bridge, 42, **43**
Chumik (Chu mig), 349
Chung (Gcung), 544n750
Chung Riwoché (Gcung Ri bo che). *See* Riwoché
Chung Yulpoché (Cung yul po che), 169
Chuwar (Chu bar), 391, 473n1032
Chuwori (Chu bo ri) bridge, 40, 42, 43–44, **45**, 55, 481n175
  construction of, 299
  destruction during Cultural Revolution, 56
  iron sent to, 259
  logs arriving on Kyichu River, 298
  prophecy of by Vajravārāhī, 254
  pulling up of, 299–300
  speech to monks and craftsman when despondent, 293–97
  Tangtong agreeing to build, 255
Chuwori (Chu bo ri) Monastery. *See* Chaksam Chuwori Monastery
Chuwori Mountain (Chu bo ri), 55, 250, 318–19, 536n676
Chuwori (Chu bo ri) stūpa. *See* Chaksam Chuwori stūpa
Circular Residence of the Sleeping Dog (Gzims chung khyi nyal sgor mo), 417, 579n1084
clairvoyance, 150, 209, 301–2, 324
  and barley for people of Dangra, 415
  and flooding over Lhasa levees, 411, 578n1073
  given to Nyima Sangpo and Sherab Palden by Tangtong, 459
  and killed ram and Dharma protectors, 415–16
  and Kunga Palden and *maṇi* devotees, 422
  and Kunga Sangmo's work with Mongols, 407
  and stolen copper, 389
  and Tangtong addressing disgruntled workers at Riwoché, 392–93
  and Tangtong locating limestone, vermilion, and gold, 376–77
clay grotto and retreat of Tangtong at Owa Lhatsé, 153–54, 509n448
clear light, 329, 373
cliff, infant Tangtong falling from, 105
clinging to self, 328, 346, 373, 374
cloak, wearing of, 66, 70, 269, 288–90
coemergent bliss, 115, 116, 152
Coemergent Union (Lhan cig skyes sbyor), 129, 157, 501n388
Collected Works of the Great Sakya Masters, 511n462
Collection of the Essentials (Tangtong), 19, 151
colors of five spiritual families, 228–29
compassion, 125, 217, 322, 329
Compendium of Maṇis (Songtsen Gampo), 21, 51, 56, 474n88
  as influence on Tangtong, 50
  overview of, 499n363
  Tangtong's receiving of, 120
  and temples, 49
Compilation of All Chosen Deities That Is a Tool for Attainments, 206
complete stage of Vajrayāna meditation, 60
completely victorious (phyogs las rnam rgyal) deliberate behavior, 60, 61, 62

conch shells, used in various images, 304, 306–7
Condensed General Practice of the Masters of the Three Times, 206
Condensed Verses on the Perfection of Wisdom, 44, 152, 286
consorts
  and *avadhūti* deliberate behavior, 61
  and *completely victorious* deliberate behavior, 62
  of Siddhiratna and instruction to Tangtong, 139
  sixteen hidden and secret, 175
  and tantric partners and treasure revealers, 28
consorts of Tangtong
  Ashi Drubtob Sangmo, 62
  Khandroma Sengé, 502n390
  See also Chökyi Drönmé
control, bringing things under, 201–2
Copper-Colored Mountain, Glorious (Zangs mdog dpal ri), 98, **99**, 494n322
  and Land of Demonesses, 520n525
  Tangtong visit to, 185, 520n529
Copper Island (Zangs gling). *See* Tāmradvīpa
coppersmiths, 389
coracle ferries, 298–99
  See also ferries
cranial dome, 457
Crazy Tsöndru (Brtson 'grus smyon pa), 13, 92, 117, 118, 121, 471n55
  name used in mocking manner, 149, 507–8n437
  and trading merchandise for sacrificial butter lamps, 124
  See also Tangtong Gyalpo
"crazy wisdom" tradition, 2
  See also deliberate behavior; mad yogins and mad behavior; secret behavior
cremation at Gyeré Tsarpa (Gye re mtshar pa), 192
crocodiles, 136, 137
"Cultural Revolution"
  and Chaksam Chuwori Monastery and stūpa, 56
  and destruction of Chuwori bridge, 44
  and Riwoché and its stūpa, 54–55
curses, against Dongkha (Dong kha), and mediation by Tangtong, 311
cutting the stream (rgyun gcod), 367, 568n973
cycle of equal taste *(Ro snyoms skor)*, 511n462
Cycle of the Great Perfection of Aro (Rdzogs chen a ro'i skor), 129, 502–3n393

Dadu (Tib: Ta'i tu) Palace, 323, 558n874
Dagmo Tenzin Gyalmo (Bdag mo Bstan 'dzin rgyal mo), 564n935
Dakchen Jampaiyang Sönam Tashi (Bdag chen 'Jam pa'i dbyangs Bsod nams bkra shis). *See* Dakchen Sönam Tashi
Dakchen Lodrö Gyaltsen (Bdag chen Blo gros rgyal mtshan, 1444–95), 563n933
Dakchen Sönam Tashi (Bdag chen Bsod nams bkra shis, 1352–1407), 49, 118. *See also* Dakpo Sönam Tashi
Dakgom Tsultrim Nyingpo (Dwags sgom Tshul khrims snying po, 1116–69), 492n300
ḍākinīs
  appearance of in Lo, 235–36
  and attainments and secrets, 28
  and *avadhūti* deliberate behavior, 61
  and *completely victorious* deliberate behavior, 62
  and death of Tangtong, 436
  on the road from Drigung to Lhasa and statues made by Tangtong, 44–45, 46, 482n482
  five at Gyedé and names given to Tangtong, 160–61, 185, 512n467
  five at Riwoché and white medicinal pills, 541–42n723
  five classes of sorceress ḍākinīs, 416

follower of Tangtong as emanation of, 582n1121
images of made by Tangtong, 306
and Kunkyong Lingpa, 62
and *lañcana* and *vartula*, 108
mantra-born, 356, 566n957
and name "Madman of the Empty Valley," 58, 65–66, 160
and name "One for Whom Conditions Have an Equal Taste," 69, 161
remove obstacles at Chuwori, 318
reside in faultless vajra body, 295
and ritual feast for Tangtong in Uḍḍiyāna, 187–90
of sacred commitment, 491n287
"Secret Cave of" (Khandro Sangpuk), 228–30, 240
and signs on Gyagar Lhamo, 95–96
sixteen hidden, 176, 434
song at Secret Cave and each of five families, 228–30
symbolic script of, 408
Tangtong bringing under control, 97, 104
Tangtong feast with at Samyé Chimpu, 335
Tangtong meeting with at Shalu Monastery, 165–66
and Tangtong's stay at Palace of Saṃvara, 181
and *totally good* deliberate behavior, 61
in Uḍḍiyāna, 184
See also Siṃhamukha
ḍākinīs of primordial awareness, 84, 491n287
five of different colors, 160, 512n468
and guidance for Six Dharmas of Niguma, 382–83
Gyagar Lhamo as, 101
in Lo, 235
and Niguma, 150
offering ritual feast in Kongpo, 222–25
and patroness Kalsang, 336
and Secret Cave of Ḍākinīs treasures, 230
at Shalu Monastery, 165–66
Dakla Pass (Stag la'i la), 164
Daklha (Dags lha), 257
Daklha Gampo (Dwags lha sgam po), 213, 528–29n596
Dakpo (Dwags po), 214, 332, 391, 559n885
Dakpo Gomtsul (Dwags po Sgom tshul), 522n542
Dakpo Lhajé (Dwags po lha rje). *See* Gampopa Sönam Rinchen
Dakpo Sönam Tashi (Bdag po Bsod nams bkra shis, 1352–1407), 117, 498n357, 513n470. *See also* Dakchen Sönam Tashi
dance at Secret Cave of Ḍākinīs, 228–30
dance moods, nine *(gar dgu'i nyams)*, 84, 215, 387, 491n287
Dangma Dangtso (Dangs ma dangs mtsho) Lake, female nāga of, 218, 219, 221
Dangra (Dang ra), 414–15
lake goddess of, 418
man offering goat horn with Stūpa of Enlightenment, 418
Dangra Chuktso (Dang ra phyug tsho), Tangtong's lifetime as goat at, 418
Darding Monastery (Dar sdings), 352–53
Darma Kyi (Dar ma skyid), 263
Darma Pal, dedicated meditator (Sgom chen pa Dar ma dpal), 498n360
Darma Palwa, great adept (Sgrub chen Dar ma dpal ba), 119, 498n360
Dartsedo (Dar rtse mdo), 315–16
Stūpa of Great Enlightenment, 50, 58, 316, 323
Dawa Gyaltsen (Zla ba rgyal mtshan), 62–63
Dawa Puk (Zla ba phug), Cave of the Moon, 204, 206, 524n565
death
accepting of, 371
and *Glorious Giver of Immortality*, 28

of Lady Kalsang, 335–36
no regrets at, 294
Tangtong description of process of, 399–404
and Tangtong dispatching individuals and father of Dangra boy, 415
Tangtong escorting Lopön Paltsul to next life, 315
Tangtong freeing people whose boats had capsized, 155
and transmigration of dead, 109–10
See also transference of consciousness
death of Tangtong, 2, 435–38, 447–57, 470n44
and appearing eighteen inches tall, 437, 451
and body dissolving into mass of light and rising, 436–37, 447, 449
and body placed in stūpa, 7, 438, 461
care for physical body afterwards, 457
chosen, not from illness, 437
comments about his approaching, 432
date of, 11, 12, 13–14
and Delek Chödrön, 435, 583n1126
and fainting of Sherab Palden, 447
and freedom from birth and death, 443–45
kept secret, 7, 8, 438, 455, 459
manner of unique and Chökyi Dronmé, 435, 583n1126
as marvelous display, 436
miraculous physical signs at time of, 457
response to Sherab Palden during process of, 451–53
revelation that it had happened, 6, 8, 461
rumors of when in retreat, 412
Tangtong's instructions for care of corpse, 453
transcended by achieving of nirvāṇa, 443
Vajrayoginī instruction to teach in other realms, 457
words at time of, 436, 437–38, 451–57
Dechen (Bde chen) Monastery, 314
Deities of the Eight Transmissions of Great Attainment, 252, 525n571, 537n685
Dekyi (Bde skyid), 48
Delek Chödrön (Bde legs chos sgron), 52, 53, 435, 548n785, 576n1053, 583n1126
Delek Pal (Bde legs dpal), 326–31
Delek Tashi (Bde legs bkra shis, b. 1408), 349, 564n937
deliberate behavior *(vratacaryā; brtul zhugs spyod pa)*
avadhūti, 60–61
called *secret behavior*, 159
charlatans giving practice bad name, 70
Charnel Ground of Ramadoli, 178
chosen or arising spontaneously, 62
and *completely victorious* behavior, 60, 61, 62
and degrees of *warmth*, 61–62
difficulty in discerning validity of, 74
and dualistic consciousness, 78–79
at encampment of Karmapa Tongwa Dönden, 211–13
to equalize the eight worldly concerns, 117
extreme and Tsang Nyön Heruka, 72–73
extreme and Ü Nyön Kunga Sangpo, 74
forbidden until stage of *warmth* reached, 60
and *Hevajra Tantra* and example of poison, 77
Indian masters of, 59
only for liberating oneself and others, 60, 66
original range of meaning of term, 59–60
Padmasambhava instructing Tangtong to use, 66, 131
performed at foot of Gyedé Plain, 160
performing when not mature, 74
by Tangtong after ordination, 502n390
three categories of, 60–61

and *totally good* deliberate behavior, 61–62
used in Kāmata, 574n1036
virtuous or sinful and state of mind, 77–78
and Virūpa, 517n502
See also mad yogins and mad behavior; secret behavior
demons
of Amdruk's sword, 325
bhuta, 252, 413
bhuta of Kāmata, 399
and master and chosen deity, 297, 551n805
Mu and Tsan in Menmogang, 228
and mute boys at Amdar Shong, 324
nature of and practice regarding, 372
nine sisters of Chung, 384
at Ngor Gönsar liberated by Tangtong, 279
and Nyago bridge, 432
performing Chöd relative to, 41
rākṣasa, 514n481, 521n 539, 527n583, 580n1098
subduing by building projects, 41
Tangtong bringing benefit to, 281
Tangtong requiring to release victims, 220–21
various types of, 219–20, 530n614
See also earth spirits
Densatel (Gdan sa thel) Monastery, 210, 527n585, 580–81n1108
Depa Nedongpa Chen Nga Ngawang Chögyal (Sde pa Sne sdong pa Spyan mgna' Ngag dbang chos rgyal). *See* Ngagi Wangpo
Depa Neu Dzongpa Paljor Gyalpo (Sde pa Sne'u rdzong pa Dpal 'byor rgyal po, d. 1490), 335–36, 488n260, 560n900, 902
See also Drungchen Paljor Gyalpo
dependent arising, 322
Dergé (Sde dge) Monastery, 56–57
Dergé (Sde dge) printing house, 9
Desi Rinpoché (Sde srid Rin po che), 433, 582n1116
See also Ngagi Wangpo
Desi Sangyé Gyatso (Sde srid Sangs rgyas rgya mtsho, 1653–1705), 470n44
Destroyer of the Lord of Death ('Chi bdag 'joms pa), 353, 565n945
Dewa Sangpo (Bde ba bzang po), 467n15, 538n699
and accounts of previous lifetimes of Tangtong, 555n842
and biographical information from Tangtong, 6, 467n18
and biography of Tangtong, 4, 5
and *Bright Lamp of Prophecy*, 4, 6, 575n1043
expansion of *All-Illuminating Lamp* to *Bright Lamp*, 6–7
and Great Perfection teachings, 476n104
and landslide at Riwoché, 568n980
sent from Paro to king of Kāmata, 398
and Tangtong tradition in Bhutan, 575n1043
Dezhung Rinpoché (Sde gzhung Rin po che, 1906–87)), ix–x, 465n1, 488n256, 550n802, 583n1133
and bridge at Minyak and vajras embossed on iron links, 48
and bridges in Gugé and on Tsangpo, 37–38
and deliberate behavior, 60, 74
and *Infinite Benefit for Living Beings*, 21
and iron bridge at Puntsok Ling, 479n148
and "Mothers Infinite As Space" refuge, 502n389
and nāga-māra, 496n339
and *shentong* view, 550n801
and statue of Tangtong in Yilhung Shi, 57–58
and Tangtong's travel in an instant, 520n525
and urine of great adepts, 478n124
and Varuṇa and nāgas, 4 80–81n162
and visit to Chakpori Hill temple, 42

dhāraṇīs, five great *(gzungs chen lnga),* 152, 509n445
Dharma, explaining in the market, 100, 104
Dharma Cycle of the Extreme Secret and Unexcelled Realization of Mind (Tangtong), 161–62
Dharma king of Jang (Chos rgyal Byang pa). *See* Namgyal Draksang
Dharma of men *(mi chos),* 329, 558n879
Dharma of the gods *(lha chos),* 329, 558n879
Dharma protectors
  and consecration of Temple of Dharma Protectors at Riwoché, 417
  indivisible from master and chosen deity, 375
  initiations and ritual permissions of, 291, 375
  and ram killed at Rinchen Ding, 415
  Tangtong seen as various, 375
dharmakāya reality body *(chos sku),* 83, 166, 312, 330, 502n389
  and Mahābodhi image at Vajrāsana of Bodhgayā, 294
  mind seen to be, 158
  nothing but, 146
  resting in, 393
  as stūpa at Riwoché, 419
  stūpas as representations of, 189, 521n533
  Tangtong's realization of, 87, 146, 185, 194, 291, 321
Dharmamalla (reign: 1396–1408), 504n408
Dharmaratna, 38, 135–36, 137–38
Dhongthog Rinpoché (Gdong thog Rin po che), 470n45
dhūti, 174, 518n505
dialectical schools, five *(rtog ge ba sde lnga),* 573n1034
Dickinson, Emily, 80
Dilgo Khyentsé Rinpoché (Dil mgo mkhyen brtse'i Rin po che, 1910–91), ix, 475n101
diligence, 427
Dingri Langkor (Ding ri glang 'khor), 271, 544n744
Dīpaṃkara, 337, 561n909
direct transmission, 32–33
disciples of Tangtong, 434, 561n911
  edicts given to groups of, 4
  fifty-eight with karma, 434
  and lineage accomplishing great things, 123–24
  listing of names of, 582n1121
  sent to collect offerings, 412, 578n1074
  six "major disciples" *(bu chen),* 551n807
  thirteen "heroic," 540n713
  three groups of five major established at Chuwori, 337
Dodé Gyalmo (Mdo sde rgyal mo, d. 1463?), 407, 576n1056
dog's footbone relic, 288
Dohās, 115–16, 506n428
Dohās, cycle of *(Mdo ha skor),* 511n462
Dok Logkya (Mdog Klog skya), 279
Dok River (Mdog chu), 279, 545n753
Dokham Gangsum (Mdo khams sgang gsum), 336
Dokham (Mdo khams), 46, 314, 319, 325, 482n180, 571–72n1011
Dölka ('Dol kha), 110
Dölpa Nakpo (Gdol po nag po), 280
Dolpa Sangyé Sengé (Dol pa Sangs rgyas seng ge), 568n982
Dolpopa Sherab Gyaltsen (Dol po pa Shes rab rgyal mtshan, 1292–1361), 13, 14, **67**, 493n304
  and construction of stūpa at Jonang, 569n987
  and dismantling of bridge at Rinchen Ding, 36–37
  and expansion of Ngamring Monastery, 497n346
  and Nyakpuwa Sönam Sangpo, 526n577
  and stūpa at Jonang, 68, 483n199, 493n304, 506n430
  Tangtong as immediate reincarnation of, 13, 14, 36, 92, 488n252, 492–93n303, 513n472

Tangtong on throne of, 67–68, 162
Tangtong seen as, 162
and three turnings of the Dharma wheel, 507n436
Ḍombi Heruka, 59
Döndrup Gyalpo (Don grub rgyal po), and offering of iron, 232
Döndrup Sangpo (Don 'grub bzang po), 15
Dong (Ldong) clan. *See* Lhadong Karpo (Lha ldong dkar po) clan
Dongkha (Dong kha), curses placed here, 311
Dongshur (Gdong zhur) bridge, 364, 567n968
Dongshur (Gdong zhur) ferry, 169, 516n496
Dongshur (Gdong zhur) Mountain, 171, 363
donkey
and Cakrasaṃvara, 503–4n403
and healing of epidemic, 109
instruction to, 66–67
and Tsangpo River at Ngagpuk, 119
Dönyö Dorjé (Don yod rdo rje, 1462–1512), 561n904
Dönyö Gyaltsen, anchorite (Kun spangs Don yod rgyal mtshan), 100, 494–95n324
and bestowal of teachings on Tangtong, 130
and dreams regarding Tangtong's birth, 105
Dorjé Drakpa (Rdo rje grags pa). *See* Kalden Dorjé Drakpa
Dorjé Drakpotsel (Rdo rje drag po rtsal), 25, 227, 271, 387, 476n104, 530n623, 544n744, 573n1023
Dorjé Drolö (Rdo rje gro lod), 523n553, 537n685
Dorjé Dujom (Rdo rje bdud 'joms), 549n790
Dorjé Lekpa, oath-bound (Dam can Rdo rje legs pa), 545n756, 549n791
Dorjé Nangzema (Rdo rje snang mdzad ma), 530n620
Dorjé Phagmo (Rdo rje phag mo) incarnation line, 466n9
Dorjé Shingpa (Rdo rje shing pa), 243
Dorjé Shönu (Rdo rje gzhon nu), 18
Dosum bridge, eastern Bhutan, **49**
Dotö Kyara (Mdo stod skya ra) Monastery, 127
Dra (Gra) or Dranang (Grwa nang), 527n583
Dradun Temple (Pra dun lha khang), 270, 543n738
Draduntsé (Spra dun rtse), 543n738
Drak Lhadong (Brag Lha gdong), 298
Drak Yerpa (Brag Yer pa), 204–5, **205**, 524n563
Drakal (Brag ral), 206, 525n570
Drakdenma (Grags ldan ma), 87
Drakpa Dar (Grags pa dar), 497n346
Drakpa Gyaltsen (Grags pa rgyal mtshan, 1374–1432), 208, 526n574–6, 540–41n717
broken promises of, 333, 559n887
Drakpa Jungné (Grags pa 'byung gnas, 1414–45), 526n575, 534n655, 534–35n658, 559n887
and Governor Drakwang of Neu Dzong, 547n774
pregnant mare offered to Tangtong, 334
present lifespan of and future lifetime, 334
Tangtong's instruction to, 333
and Vanaratna, 334, 559–60n892
Drakpa Öser (Grags pa 'od zer), King, 88–92, 313, 555n842, 555n846
Drakpa (Grags pa) the blacksmith, 310
Drakralkha (Brag ral kha) in Penyul
bridge at, 46, 433, 582n117
stūpa and temple of, 338
Draksangpa (Grags bzang pa) (elder half-brother of Tangtong), 21, 120
Tangtong honoring and commissioning to recite *maṇis*, 155
Tangtong as attendant for retreat of, 120–21
Drakyang Dzong (Sgrag yang rdzong), 291, 549n790

Drakyé (Brag skyed) of Paro, 252
Drakyul ('Phrag yul)
shepherds from, 234, 240
thieves of, 233
Drakyong Sangpo (Grags skyong bzang po), King, 87–88
Drampa Gyang (Gram pa Rgyang) and Red Temple, 161, 513n470
Dramré ('Bram re), monk, 368
Drangsong Sinpori (Drang srong Srin po ri), 319, 556–57n861
Dranpa Namkha (Dran pa nam mkha'), 565n944
dreams
before dismantling of Rinchen Ding iron bridge, 37
by Choksang Lekpai Lodrö of Kukkuripa, 157
by Chuwori monks of Tangtong, 300
by Dönyö Gyaltsen about Tangtong, 130
by Gyagar Lhamo of Tangtong, 97–101, 103–5
by Jamyang Khyentsé Wangpo of Tangtong, 31
by Kunga Lekpai Jungné of Tangtong, 30
by lost man of Tangtong, 287
by Nyima Sengé of Tangtong, 112
prophetic to a patron, 424
by Śāntideva of Mañjuśrī, 111
by Shuchen Tsultrim Rinchen of Tangtong, 30
by Tangtong of a white woman with sow's face, 457
by Tashi Sangmo, 360
transformation of body in, 216, 529n606
Dredging the Pit of Saṃsāra (Tuksé Rinpoché), 467n22
Drepung ('Bras spungs) Monastery, 248, 524n558, 536n670
dress of adepts and monks, 66, 70, 487–88n251
only single cloak for Tangtong, 66, 70, 269, 288–90
saffron robes for Tangtong, 284
Tangtong dressed as monk in morning and as yogin in afternoon, 547n770
Tangtong dressed in dharmakāya reality body, 291
and wearing of cloak, 288–90
of yogins and Tangtong, 131
Drib (Grib), rock of, 245
Drichu ('Bri chu) River bridge, 314, 337, 555n850
Drigum Tsenpo (Gri gum btsan po), 34
Drigung ('Bri gung) Monastery of Drigung Til, 303–4, **305**, 553n824
Drigung Chökhor Gang ('Bri gung Chos 'khor sgang) iron bridge, 46, 335
Drigung Jikten Gönpo ('Bri gung 'Jig rten mgon po). *See* Kyopa Jikten Gönpo
Drigung Kagyü ('Bri gung bka' brgyud) tradition, 501n388, 544n751, 553n826
and future disasters, 304, 553n827
and Namkha Gyaltsen, 271
Drigung Kyopa Jikten Gönpo ('Bri gung skyob pa 'Jig rten mgon po, 1143–1217), 494n313
Drimé Lingpa (Dri med gling pa, d. 1775), 17
Drimé Rabga (Dri med rab dga'), 415
Drin Chuwar(Brin Chu dbar), 271, 272
Drogön Pakpa ('Gro mgon 'Phags pa, 1235–80), 259, 382, 539n708, 572n1012
Drokgang Ding Monastery, 484n212
Drolung (Gro lung), 364
Drom ('Brom) clan, 205, 525n567
Dromtön ('Brom ston Rgyal ba'i 'byung gnas, 1005–64), 302, 552n820–1, 552–53n822
Drong Nyön ('Brong smyon), Madman of Drong, 485n222
Druk Nyön Kunga Lekpa ('Brug smyon Kun dga' legs pa, Madman of Bhutan, 1455–1529), 58, 63
Drukpa Kagyü ('Brug pa bka' brgyud) tradition, 523n554
in Bhutan, 15

and Ralung Monastery, 536–37n679
and Tsari mountain area, 494n313
Drukpa Kunlek ('Brug pa Kun legs), 486n229.
See also Druk Nyön Kunga Lekpa
Drung Tsewang Tashi (Drung Tshe dbang bkra shis, d. 1454/55), 567n969
Drungchen Drakpa Palsang (Drung chen Grags pa dpal bzang), 244, 488n260, 534n655, 534–35n658, 535n668
and ferries on Kyichu River, 298, 551n808
and offering brocades for Jowo, 286, 547n774
See also Governor Drakwang of Neu Dzong; Nepa Governor
Drungchen Paljor Gyalpo (Drung chen Dpal 'byor rgyal po, d. 1490), 248, 488n260, 534–35n658, 535n668, 580n1106
and advice to Tangtong on successor, 431, 580n1106
See also Nepa governor
dualistic consciousness, 78–79
Dudjom Rinpoché (Bdud 'joms Rin po che, 1904–87), 470n43
Düdül Samdrup (Bdud 'dul bsam grub), 357–61
Dülwa Sangpo ('Dul ba bzang po), 525n569
Dülwapa ('Dul ba pa), 231, 532n634
Dumtsé Stūpa of Paro, Bhutan, 50, 254, **255**
Dungi Shalyé (Dung gi gzhal yas), 288
Dungkong (Śaṅkhapāla; Dung skyong), 551n808
Dza, King, 501n386
Dzachu (Rdza chu) River bridge, 314, 337, 555n850
Dzadri Salmogang (Rdza 'bri Zal mo sgang). *See* Salmogang
Dzagom Jodar (Rdza sgom Jo dar), 227, 531n625
Dzamling Gyen ('Dzam gling rgyan) meditation hut at Riwoché, 51, 381
Tangtong staying in, 369, 391
Dzongtsen (Rdzong btsan), 263
Dzom ('Dzom) iron bridge, 257
Dzongka Monastery (Rdzong kha chos sde), 540–41n717
Dzumdrul Pukmoché (Great Cave of Miracles), 263, 542n724

e syllable, 83, 490n281
eagles, Tangtong staying in nest of, 106
earth spirits
from Drakyul and supplies for Lo, 234
Dzongsten, 263
and gold for Amitābha image, 384–85
and invitation to secure gold in Kongpo, 41
of Lo area inviting Tangtong to come, 234
at Nyemo, 341, 376
and opening gates at Menmogang, 228
in Penyul, 206
Shalsang and Tsakhur forest, 118
of Sodruk playing instruments, 214
stūpa at Kyewang to suppress, 257
subterranean, 219–20
Tangtong dual with at Waru Seso, 215–95
Tangtong subduing at Tsozong, 219–21
at Tsagong and opening region, 227–28
at Wam Tengchen, 255
Yamar and Riwoché stūpa, 377
See also demons; genyen; hungry spirits; nāgas
earthquakes and Dartsedo, 315–16, 323
edicts *(bka' shog)* of Tangtong, 4–5, 465n5
to Chinese emperor, 386, 572–73n1022
to deities of earth and wind, 207–8
to each of six major disciples, 551n807
and folk origin of ferries and bridges, 33–34
given to groups of disciples, 4

and gold and vermilion for Riwoché stūpa, 377
to gray wolves, 405
to insects and birds, 405–6
at investiture of Nyima Sangpo, 571n1009
to Iśvara, 398–99
to Kharnak, 298
and Kunga Sangmo and Ngari, 407
and a *maṇi* devotee, 388
and Nyima Sangpo as successor, 431
to three groups of five major disciples, 337, 561n908
and travels of, 561n908
at Tsozong to eight tribes, 220–21
and visit to Śrīparvata, 483n203
and workers on Riwoché stūpa, 389
Ehrhard, Franz-Karl, 486n229
eight close bodhisattva sons *(byang chub sems dpa' nye ba'i sras brgyad)* 185, 383, 520n531, 572n1017
eight great adepts or mahāsiddhas *(grub chen brgyad)*, 524n564
Eight Great Transmissions *(bka' babs chen po brgyad)*, 571n1009
eight sugata siblings *(bde bshegs mched brgyad)*, 481n176
eight sugatas or buddhas *(bde bar bshegs pa brgyad)*, 481–82n176
Eight Transmissions of Great Attainment *(sgrub pa chen po bka' brgyad)*, 185, 520n530
eight tribes of gods and demons *(lha srin sde brgyad)*, 41, 85, 157, 158, 177, 203, 480n160. *See also* eight tribes of gods and nāgas
and address to woman of Tanak, 352
and bridge at Nyago, 432
and iron bridge of Chuwori, 300, 551n811
and iron bridge over Kyichu River, 244
pacification of at Tsozong, 220–21
and stūpa at Riwoché, 363
eight tribes of gods and nāgas *(lha klu sde brgyad)*, 218, 220–21, 529n609. *See also* eight tribes of gods and demons
eight worldly concerns *('jig rten chos brgyad)*, 60, 68–69, 114, 117, 195, 295, 327, 342, 351, 486n234
eighty-four great adepts of India, 153–54
Ekajaṭī (E ka dza ti), 130, 503n396, 545n756
elephant skull of past life of Tangtong, 266
eleven-faced Avalokiteśvara, 200, 238
and Jowo at Golden Temple of Buchu, 309
See also Avalokiteśvara; Naturally Arisen Eleven-faced Avalokiteśva
"emanated body prior to passing away" *(ma 'das sprul sku)*, 14
emanation of bodies by Tangtong
active in many distant regions, 391
appearing to Riksum Gönpo to guide him to Chökyi Dronmé, 380
and appearing to uncle, father, and Draksangpa, 120
urged to display millions of, 189
and footprint at Dakpo, 423–24
of frightening men when Riwoché attacked, 370
of great adepts at Shalkar Lhadong, 175–76
and Kāmata king and burning women, 411–12
in Mangyul, 265–66
and nāga king's proposed stūpa site, 301
and raising of Chuwori bridge, 300
shown to brother, uncle, and Yeshé Dren, 120
shown to different individuals from Kham, 376
and three bodies at Kha and Cha Passes, 121
of three bodies in Drok Megyu, 287
of three bodies in Kharchu in Lhodrak, 288
in three regions in Kham, 410
in various forms, 443

visit to Kāmata king by Tangtong, 394
as vulture at Samdrup Temple, 259
while actual body with Lhatsen Kyab at Shelkar Bridge, 364
and work with iron and blacksmiths, 254, 259, 539n704
emptiness, 125, 217, 330, 455
and mindful awareness, 213
and second turning of the Dharma wheel, 507n436
"emptiness of other," *shentong (gzhan stong)*, 513n471
Engaging in the Conduct of a Bodhisattva, 114
enlightened action, four styles of, 290, 548n786
enlightened body, speech, and mind, 85, 86, 199
Tangtong building representations of, 219
as three representations, 293, 550n797
enlightenment minds, two, 345
Enslavement of the Eight Tribes That Brings Apparent Existence Under Control, 207
environmental focal-points *(sa'i me btsa')*, 33, 49
and *Compendium of Maṇis*, 499n363
stūpas built at, 49–50
Tangtong using, 176, 199, 302, 425
See also geomantic subduing of terrestrial forces
epidemic
during childhood of Tangtong, 109–10
in Nepal and Ü Nyön Kunga Sangpo, 74
at Sakya Monastery, 412–14
Tangtong articulates causes for, 578n1077
epistemology *(tshad ma)*, 495–96n334, 497n348, 524n558
equal taste or sameness *(samarasa; ro snyoms/ro mnyam)*, 68–70, 75, 295, 351
behavior used to further realization of, 68–69
explanation given to Tangtong by ḍākinī at Shalu Monastery, 166
Essence of Dependent Origination, 348, 417, 563n929
Essential Droplet of the Enlightened Mind of the Teacher of Uḍḍiyāna, A Single Summation of the Intention of Samantabhadra, 206
eternalism, 346
evaṃ, 115, 490n281
united, 225, 530n619
Ewaṃ Gakyil (E waṃ dga' 'khyil) meditation hut, 416, 439
excretions
ceasing of three, 517n503, 567n967
and Ga Lotsāwa Namgyal Dorjé, 567n967
Tangtong's freedom from, 173, 364, 517n503
experiential guidance *(nyams khrid)*, 382, 572n1013

falling transmigration *('pho ltung)*, 268, 542n734
falsehood of appearances, 155
family of Tangtong
and inheriting family fields, 153, 155
and Tangtong leaving home, 501n383
and winning lawsuit against relatives, 153, 509n447
See also Draksangpa; Gyagar Lhamo; Löpon Paltsul; Ngadar; Önpo Dorjé Gyaltsen; Palzin Dorjema; Penpo; Sero Pal
famine
of 1437 and Tangtong's actions to alleviate, 282–86, 546n766
ending of in Penyul, 246
ferries
and charging of toll, 301
coracle, harmed by demon Kharnak, 298
of Gyerpaling, 333, 338
on Kyichu River, 298
as means to liberate beings, 174

number built by Tangtong, 40, 424, 480n157
Tangtong building at Drak Lhadong and Chuwori, 298, 300
See also boats
Fifth Dalai Lama. *See* Ngawang Losang Gyatso
Final Story Concerning the Nirvāṇa of the Great Adept (Kunga Sönam Drakpa Palsang), 8, 441–63, 468n28
Fine Tree of Noble Aspiration (Yeshé Paljor), 475n96, 476n114
fire
Tangtong meditation on vital wind of and visual manifestation of, 139, 314, 505n420
Tangtong vision of person on, 136, 138
fish
prayer for at Lake Mapam Yutso, 264–65
Tangtong's compassion for, 338
fishermen at Yamdrok, 338–40
five aggregates *(phung po lnga)*, 558n877
five bodies of enlightenment *(sku lnga)*, 321, 557n868
Five Chronicles, 62
Five Dharmas of Maitreya, 114, 497n347
five-hundred year period, final, 84, 174, 190, 491n288
five inexpiable sins, 243, 389, 534n653
five kinds of flesh *(sha sna lnga)*, 165, 515n486
Five-Peaked Mount Wutai (Ri bo rtse lnga, Wutaishan), 7, 488n262, 491n292, 556n855, 561n908
Tangtong speech at, 317–19
Tangtong visit to, 316–20, 386, 557n865
five precious substances *(rin po che sna lnga)*, 164, 354, 494n321, 513n476
five royal sūtras *(rgyal po mdo lnga)*, 574n1037
Five Sisters of Long Life (Tshe ring mched lnga), 272, 273, 544n746
five spiritual families, 140, 223–24
Fivefold Benefit for Living Beings, 180, 519n518
fivefold degeneracy, 84, 87, 177, 186, 213, 313, 491n288
Fivefold Mahāmudrā (Phyag rgya chen po lnga ldan), 129, 157, 210, 501–2n388, 510–11n461
Tangtong's receiving from Chokden Lekpai Lodrö, 544n751
and Tsenden Ridröma, 544n751
Fivefold Naturally Arisen One (Rang byon lnga ldan), 193, 521n538, 554n834
See also Naturally Arisen Eleven-faced Avalokiteśvara
Flat Blue Sky (Gnam sngo leb) spirit-turquoise, 382, 556n852, 571–72n1011
flowers, rain of at Kyirong, 261
flying by Tangtong
at fortress of Chözong, 354
from Lhasa toward Latö, 411
at Pal Khorlo Dechen, 348
food stories and miracles
and beer and buckwheat cakes at Kongpo, 240
eating whatever offered no matter how great, 408
and feeding of pilgrims during famine of 1437, 286
and meal for thirty workers, 119
no eating for three months, 408
people trapped by craving food of dead, 314–15
by Tangtong in childhood, 106, 107, 108
and Tangtong survival with only water for one year, 118–19
"Footprint Sanctuary of Liberation" (Shabjé Tarling), 424
footprints
and images at Gyalti Palace, 265
left at Dakpo, 423–24
left at Samyé, 207
left at Shalkar Lhadong, 177
left at Sipal, 287
at Menmogang, 233, 532n638

four-armed Mahākāla or Protector, 230, 291, 302–3, **303**, 375, 531n630, 553n825
four continents, 222, 331, 345, 530n618
four defeating acts *(pham pa bzhi)*, 66, 131, 487n250
four elements, 189, 317, 320, 521n533
four enlightened actions, 123, 423, 500n370
four fundamental subjects (*bka' bzhi* or *dka' bzhi*), 114, 497n348
four guardian kings *(rgyal chen sde bzhi)*, 383, 572n1017
four immeasurables *(tshad med bzhi)*, 321, 557n870, 575–76n1051
four initiations, 97, 150, 165–66, 494n317
four means of attraction, 317, 556n858
Four Medical Tantras *(Rgyud bzhi)*, 530–31n624
four modes of birth *(skyes gnas gzhi)*, 402, 575n1049
Four Noble Truths, 507n436
four races of the great kings *(rgyal chen rigs bzhi'i lha)*, gods of the, 371, 569n986, 569n987
four rivers, 318, 556n860
"four seals" of the doctrine, 447, 585n1148
four styles of enlightened action, 321, 557n869
four styles *(tshul bzhi)*, 173, 517–18n504
four summations of Dharma *(chos sdom bzhi)*, 557n772
fourfold taking of refuge, 108, 496n336
freedoms and endowments *(dal 'byor)*, 90, 293, 317, 341, 348, 492n297

Ga Lotsāwa Namgyal Dorjé (Rga Lo tsā ba Rnam rgyal rdo rje, eleventh-twelfth centuries), 522n546, 567n967
Gam Nyön Chakdor Norbu (Sgam smyon Phyag rdor nor bu), 17, 472n71
Gam Nyön Tulkus (Sgam smyon sprul sku), 17
Gamodrang bridge near Lhasa, 48
Gampa Pass (Gam pa la), 259, 539n704
Gampopa Sönam Rinchen (Sgam po pa Bsod nams rin chen, 1079–1153), 213–14, 472n71, 492n300, 501n388, 522n542, 528–29n596
Ganden (Dga' ldan) Monastery, 348, 536n670
Gangādevī, 284, 547n770
Gangdruk (Sgang drug), 314, 555n849
Ganges Mahāmudrā (Gang ga mā), 129, 157, 501–502n388, 511n462
Gangkar Rinpoché Chökyi Sengé (Gangs dkar Rin po che Chos kyi seng ge, 1891–1957), 58, 556n884
Gangla Longka (Gangs la klong kha), 261, 540n713
Gangsang (Gang bzang). *See* Gangwa Sangpo
Gangwa Sangpo (Gang ba bzang po), 250, 259, 537n680, 539n704
Gardampa Chödingpa ('Gar dam pa Chos sdings pa, b. 1180), 523n554
garlic, 107, 108
garudas *(khyung)*, 220, 530n615
Garwang Chökyi Wangchuk, Sixth Sharmapa (Zhwa dmar pa Gar dbang Chos kyi dbang phyug, 1584–1630), 518–19n513
Gatön Ngawang Lekpa (Sga ston Ngag dbang legs pa, 1864–1941), 478n124
Gayadhara (d. 1103), 537–38n687
Geluk (Dge lugs) tradition, 497n346
Gendun Drupa (Dge 'dun grub pa, 1391–1475), First Dalai Lama, 483–84n204
Gendun Gyaltsen (Dge 'dun rgyal mtshan), 385–86, 424
general initiation as a regent, 145, 507n435
generosity, 107, 126, 294, 427, 550n800
genyen *(dge bsnyen)* spirits, 153, 280–81, 509n449, 545n757
Genyen Dölpo (Dge bsnyen Gdol pa), 280–81, 545n757
geomantic subduing of terrestrial forces in Tibet, 157, 320

advice on establishing and Vajravārāhī, 228
and *Compendium of Maṇis*, 499n363
and Dartsedo, 315
and Golden Temple of Buchu, 554–55n839
and Tonga, 338
See also environmental focal-points
Gesar legends, 2, 23
Geshé Dharmashrī (Dge bshes Dharma shrī), 398
Geshé Drakpa Pal (Dge bshes Grags pa dpal), 302
Gewo Tashi Gyaltsen (Dge bo Bkra shis rgyal mtshan), 118
glacial crevasse at Sapuk (Sa phug), 287–88
Glorious Giver of Immortality ('Chi med dpal ster), 14, 28, 30, 477n118
and connection to *Iron Tree*, 477n119
most widespread and influential longevity practice, 30
text based on visionary revelation and hidden treasure teachings, 28
Gö Lotsāwa Shönu Pal ('Gos Lo tsā ba Gzhon nu dpal, 1392–1481), 554n836, 560n895
goats, 106–7, 172
Tangtong's incarnation as, 418
Gökyi Demtruchen (Rgod kyi ldem 'phru can, 1337–1408), 19, **27**, 355, 468n23, 473n81, 502n391, 565n953
crazy yogin known as "Vulture Feathered," 62
and Dönyö Gyaltsen, 494–95n324
and Dorjé Drakpotsel, 25
and Great Perfection teachings, 129, 391n502
and *Iron Tree*, 26
Penetration and the Heart Practice, 25, 476n106
teachings passed to Tangtong, 62, 66, 130
gold
alms bowl and Jowo Śākyamuni, 283–85, 546n767
collecting to end famine of 1437, 282–83
flower of a thousand petals, 397
for gilding Amitābha at Riwoché, 384
and Gyang stūpa, 118
in Kongpo, 41
and Medicine Buddha and Maitreya at Riwoché, 385
in Nyamkhar and earth spirit Yamar, 377
Tangtong offering maṇḍala of, 249
Golden Temple of Buchu (Sbu chu gser gyi lha khang), 309, 554–55n839
Goma Tsekar (Sgo ma rtse dkar) Temple, 92
Gomnak Drak (Sgom nag brag), 228, 233
Gomtsul (Sgom tshul), 92, 492n300
Gongkar (Gong dkar), 43, 292, 536n676, 549n792
Gönpo Maning (Mgon po Ma ning), 545n756
Gormo in Drak (Phrag yul Sgor mo), 332
Gorumpa Kunga Lekpa (Sgo rum pa Kun dga' legs pa, 1477–1544), 513–14n478
Governor Drakwang of Neu Dzong (Sne'u rdzong pa Grags dbang), 286, 547n774
See also Drungchen Drakpa Palsang
Governor Norsangpa (Nang so Nor bzang pa). *See* Norsangpa
Great Cave of Miracles (Rdzu 'phrul phug mo che), 263, 542n724
"great collected works" *(bka' 'bum chen mo)*, Tangtong's, 8
Great Maitreya of Ngamring (Ngam ring Byams pa chen po), 355, 565–66n954
Great Perfection teachings, 25, 129, 391, 476n104
and Cycle of the Great Perfection of Aro, 129, 502–3n393
and Heartdrop of the Ḍākinī, 502n392

taught by Tangtong to his mother, 25, 152
Great Stūpa of Gyang (Rgyang 'Bum mo che), 49, 51, 52, 117–18, **117**, 498n357
Great Temple of Sakya, **413**
Greater and Lesser Vehicles, 322, 557n872
Gugé (Gu ge), 37, 355, 566n955
Gugé and Purang (Gu ge Pu rang), 265–66, 542n728
Gugum Rinchen Gyaltsen (Gus gum Rin chen rgyal mtshan), 111, 496n343, 546n763
Gugung Chödrak Pal Sangpo (Gu'i gung Chos grags dpal bzang po), 516n496
Guhyasamāja Tantra, 58, 501–2n388, 504n413, 511–12n463, 512n464
Gungtang (Gung thang), 407, 540–41n717, 576n1056
Guru Calm and Wrathful *(gu ru zhi drag)*, 100, 495n325
See also Padmasambhava, Guru
Guru Chökyi Wangchuk (Gu ru Chos kyi dbang phyug, 1212–70), 474n94, 515n490, 528n594, 547n775
and "Iron Dagger Cave," 548n780
Guru Lhakhang (Gu ru lha khang), 287, 547n775
Guru Padmavajra, 504–5n412
Guru Saroruhavajra (Gu ru Mtsho skye rdo rje), 504–5n412
Guru Tashi (Gu ru Bkra shis), 17, 470n43
guruyoga and the Heartdrop of the Great Adept, 32
guruyoga of the profound path *(lam zam bla ma'i rnal 'byor)*, 174, 180, 410, 457, 519n517, 577n1069, 585n1155
gus gum or *gu'i gung* title, 496n343
Gyagar Lhamo (Rgya dkar lha mo), mother of Tangtong, 24–25, 44, 95–96
and approval for Tangtong to practice Dharma, 111
becomes nun, 25
and childhood of Tangtong, 105–6, 107, 108
and cutting trees in Tsakhur forest, 118
dreams before birth of Tangtong, 97–101, 103–5
entering door of Dharma as Palmo Gön, 152
faith in Tangtong, 109
and family property, 111
last days and passing of, 152, 153
and meal for thirty workers, 119
and military tax, 110
paying off debts of, 155, 169, 172
and Perfection of Wisdom teachings, 25, 152
and time Tangtong was in womb, 100, 101, 103–4, 494n320
Gyala Badong (Rgya la rba dong), 309
Gyala Tsedum (Rgya la rtse sdum), 319
Gyala Tsering (Rgya la rtse ring), 319
Gyalchen Tsé (Rgyal chen rtse), 75, 246
Gyaldung (Rgyal gdungs), 538n697
gyalgong *(rgyal gong)* demons, 219, 220, 539n614
Gyalgyi Tsiri in Latö (Las stod Rgyal gyi Rtsi ri), 508–9n443
Gyalmorong (Rgyal mo rong), 410
Gyaltang (Rgyal thang), earth spirit, 261, 384–85
Gyalti (Rgyal ti) Palace of Purang, 542n729
Gyaltsen Pal, chieftain of Tsanda (Tsha mda' ba'i dpon po Rgyal mtshan dpal), 271, 282–83
Gyaltsen Palsang (Rgyal mtshan dpal bzang), 18
Gyaltsen Sangpo (Rgyal mtshan bzang po). *See* Kachupa Gyaltsen Sangpo
Gyalwang Könchok Jungné (Rgyal dbang Dkon mchog 'byung gnas). *See* Könchok Dewé Jungné
Gyalwang Kunga Paljor (Rgyal dbang Kun dga' dpal 'byor, 1428–76), 486n229, 536–37n679, 558n884

Gyalwang, the great adept (Sgrub chen Rgyal dbang), 508–9n443
Gyang Stūpa (Rgyang 'bum mo che), 49, 51, 52, 117–18, **117**, 498n357, 564n937
  Tangtong offering gold and barley for construction of, 118
Gyantsé (Rgyal rtse), 38, 539n707
  See also Pal Khorlo Dechen
Gyaré (Rgya ras). *See* Palchen Chöyé
Gyasakhu (Rgya sa khud), mountain behind Sunglung (Zung lung), 384
Gyedé Plain (Rgyas sde thang), 160–61, 512n466
Gyeré Tsarpa (Gye re mtshar pa), 69, 192, 250
Gyerling Nyishar (Gyer gling nyi shar), 257
Gyerpaling (Gyer pa gling), 333, 338
Gyurmé Dechen, Lochen (Lo chen 'Gyur med bde chen, 1540–1615), 2, 8–11, 10
  and *A Jewel Mirror in Which All Is Clear*, 8–9, 439
  and account of King Drakpa Öser, 555n842, 846
  and birth date of Tangtong, 13–14
  and Chöpal Sangpo, 541n718
  and Ewaṃ Gakyil meditation hut, 416
  hereditary line of, 439
  and Könchok Dewé Jungné of the Samdrup Temple, 439, 584n1140
  and Lochen Ratnabhadra, 54, 516n498
  and Niguma, 473n77
  and Riwoché offered to Yölmo Tenzin Norbu, 17–18

Ha (Has) Valley, 252, 256, 537n684, 538n697
handprints, 233, 265, 532n638
  of Padmasambhava at Drultso Pemaling, 287
  of Tangtong at Tashi Tsé, 281
Harding, Sarah, 467n17
hawks, 136, 137
Hayagrīva, 23, 26, **29**, 83, 490n282–3
  and *Glorious Giver of Immortality*, 28
  and Heartdrop of the Great Adept, 32
  Tangtong as emanation of, 443, 500n371
  Tangtong seen as, 304, 512n467
  Tangtong vision of during retreat, 510n451
  vision of in India, 140
heart of enlightenment *(byang chub snying po)*, 426, 580n1102
Heart Practice (Thugs sgrub), 25, 476n106
  of the cache of treasure teachings from Trasang, 570n998
  of Drakpotsel (Thugs sgrub drag po rtsal), 476n104
Heartdrop of the Ḍākinī (Mkha' 'gro snying thig), 129, 495n333, 502n392
Heartdrop of the Great Adept (Grub thob thugs thig) (Khyentsé Wangpo), 31, 32, 475n101, 478n128
hell of supreme torture *(mnar med pa'i dmyal ba)*, 396, 574n1039
herukas, 32, 185, 520n530, 525n571
  and Mahottara Heruka, 312, 555n844
Hevajra, 167, 515n490, 520n524, 533n641
  image of at Riwoché, 383
  nine deities of, 235
Hevajra Tantra, 58, 77, 489n275, 498n358, 514n481
Hinayāna Buddhism, 74, 322, 557n882
horses
  flesh of in ritual feast, 73–74, 209, 527n583
  forced in rivers by Tangtong, 332
  with harelip offered at Dartsedo, 323, 336, 561n905
  and pregnant mare offered by Drakpa Jungné, 334
  riding inside Pal Kholo Dechen, 348
  riding inside Riwoché Monastery in Kham, 326
Horshakpa, Governor (Nang so Hor shag pa), 543n741
householder, 127
human body

difficulty of obtaining, 341, 347–48, 562n917
importance of, 550n803
Hūṃkara, 25, 311–13, 475n103, 491–92n293
hungry spirits, 247, 267
Husayan Shāh, 574n1036
hybrid yak-cows, 332

ice bridge at Umdul ('U 'dul), 256
ill monk, Tangtong's instruction to, 371–75, 569n990
illness
in Jé Bodong and Sakya cured by Tangtong, 416
prayer for freedom from, 428, 430
prayer to end at Sakya Monastery, 413–14
as purification of obscurations, 371
illusory body, blessing of *(sgyu lus byin rlabs)*, 19, 191, 473n78, 521n534
images
of deities Tangtong made as boy, 106
taken from Riwoché during Cultural Revolution, 54
images created by Tangtong from precious substances that cannot be smelted, 44–46, 304–7
at Chakpori Hill, 41–42, 45–46, 338
consecration of images, 307
different images made, 307–8
no previous tradition in India or Tibet, 304
origins of impulse to create, 306–7
past life causes of, 307–8
prophecy of Jowo requesting Tangtong to make, 305–6
recounting of numbers and types of, 424–25
relic of Buddha placed at heart of, 307
three women requesting Tangtong to make, 44–45, 304
images of Tangtong, **xx**, **3**, **35**, **59**, **71**, 97, **258**
awaiting consecration, **63**
at Chakpori Hill, 42
made by himself, 55
which grew and healed others, 424
six transformed for different individuals, 422–23
at Tangtong Temple at Dergé, 57
at Yilhung Shi in Kham, 57–58
Immortal and Infallible ('Chi med 'chug med) teachings, 150
immortality, cycle of *('Chi med skor)*, 511n462
immortality, upholder of the pure awareness of *('chi med rig 'dzin)*, 30
impermanence, 180, 439, 443
indestructible vajra body, 550n803
indestructible vajra speech, 186
Indian tantric Buddhism, 58
Indra, 311
Infinite Benefit for Living Beings (Tangtong), 21, 30, 474n86, 500n372
initiation of the words, 146
initiations
of Amitāyus, 105, 140
of Avalokiteśvara, 206, 208, 324, 421
of Bhairava, 158
of Cakrasaṃvara, 508–9n443
and Dharma protectors, 291, 375
given by Tangtong on offering days, 375
and *Mahāmāyā Tantra*, 287
and Padmasambhava, 238, 525n571
of Red Yamāri, 512n464
secret, 146, 172–74
and six-armed Protector, 291, 508–9n443
types of given by Kalden Dorjé Drakpa, 146
of Vajrapāṇi, 129
of Vajrayoginī, 165–66, 192
See also four initiations
insects, Tangtong edict to, 405–6
iron
location of in southeast Tibet, 33, 40–41
offerings of to Tangtong in Kongpo Bhakha, 222
permission to take from Kongpo to Tibet, 240–41

quantities transported to Pari, 257
robbery of at Chuwori, 292, 301, 552n817
Tangtong expedition in search of, 40, 42
Tangtong extracting at Menmogang, 232
thrown into water to be carried by nāgas, 259
and use of swage, 352, 564n943
"Iron-Bridge Man" (Lcags zam pa) epithet, 1, 15, 33, 42, 84, 269
"Iron-Bridge Monastery" (Lcags zam dgon), 43
Iron-Bridge Tradition. *See* Chaksam or Iron-Bridge tradition (Lcags zam lugs)
iron bridges, 33–58, 466n10
built by others besides Tangtong, 46–47
decision to build after being struck at Kyichu River, 40, 196
discovery bridges could be made from iron, 221–22
early by Tangtong had vajra marked in links, 48
history of prior to Tangtong, 35–38
invitation to come Lhokha Shi to build, 252
length, width, span of, 48, 483n193
number made by Tangtong, 40, 273, 424, 480n157
often attributed to Tangtong today, 46
as "pathways to enlightenment" *(byang chub kyi rgyu lam lcags zam)*, 40
rare before fifteenth century, 34
rebuilding of Tangtong's original, 47–48
Tangtong's dream of liberating people through, 174
visionary prophecy of building of, 138
See also bridges
iron bridges, by location
at Bakdrong, 257
at Bardrong near Wangdü Podrang, 42
at Drakralkha in Penyul, 46
at Chökhor Gang, 46, 335
at Chukha, 42, 43
at Chuwori completed in 1444, 40, 42, 43–44, 45, 55, 481n175
at Dosum, **49**
on Drichu River, 46, 314, 337, 551n807
on Dzachu River, 46, 314, 337, 551n807
Dzom, 257
in front of Puntsok Ling on Tsangpo, 38
in front of Tachok Norbugang, 42, 481n170
at Gamodrang in Lhasa, 48
at Gangla Longka, 261, 540n713
on Kyichu River in Lhasa, 33, 40, 72, 243–45, 298–300, 488–89n263
on Langpoché Khabap, 37–38
at Lhawang Tsé, 48
at Longka, 540n713
in Minyak, 48
at Nyago over Tsangpo River, 40, 46, 53, 333, 380, 432–33, 482n182, 571n1004, 581n1112, 1114, 581–82n1115
over Nyakchu River, 46, 72, 314, 337, 488n262
over Tsangpo River at Puntsok Ling, 5, 36, 479n148
over Yellow River in Minyak, 35
at Paro, 44
for people who visited Jowo in Lhasa, 292
at Rakdzong, 47
at Rinchen Ding, 36–37, 47, 479n145
at Riwoché built in 1436, 42–43, 55, 273, 274
at Shalkar Lhadong, 260
at Shar Drukha, 46
at Shuna, 335
at Tachok Norbugang, 538n699
at Tashi Tsé, 279, 281, 353
at Toling, 37–38, 39
in Tölung, 301
at Yongru in upper Tsang, 353–54

iron links, 466n10
Iron Tree practice for extending lifespan, 26–27, 28, 130, 477n19
Īśvara, 397, 398–99

Ja (Bya) or Jayul (Bya yul), 431, 581n1110
jackals, 178, 179
Jagchungpa Tsangma Shangtön ('Jag chung pa Gtsang ma Shangs ston, 1223–1309), 18, 150, 508n439
Jagö Shong (Bya rgod gshongs) Monastery, 163–64
Jambudvīpa, 85, 98, 105, 280, 491n289
  center of in Magadha, 134
  proclaiming Dharma and virtue to peoples of, 129, 158, 189
  as southern continent, 368, 568n978
  Tangtong suppressing by sitting in vajra position, 220
Jamgön Kongtrul ('Jam mgon Kong sprul, 1813–1900)
  and age of Tangtong, 470n43
  biographical supplication to Tangtong, 469n38
  and Heart Drop of the Great Adept, 31, 478nn133, 134
  and *Infinite Benefit for Living Beings*, 474n86
Jampa Nyendrak (Byams pa snyan grags), 14, 354, 433
Jamyang Chöjé Tashi Palden ('Jam dbyangs chos rje Bkra shis dpal ldan, 1397–1449), 248–49, 524n558, 536n670
Jamyang Khyentsé Wangpo ('Jam dbyangs mkhyen brtse'i dbang po, 1820–92), 469n38
  and Chaksam tulkus, 16, 574–75n1042
  and Heartdrop of the Great Adept, 32
  as holder of all Tangtong lineages, 31–32
  as incarnation of Tangtong, 31
  meeting with Tangtong and receiving teachings, 19, 31
  and revival and preservation of Tangtong traditions, 21, 24, 31, 475n101
  and white and red medicinal pills, 541–42n723
Jamyang Rinchen Gyaltsen ('Jam dbyangs rin chen rgyal mtshan, b. 1446?), meeting with Tangtong, 25–26, 487n237
Jang (Byang), 95, 169, 355, 493n305, 567n970
  increasing lifespan of people in, 416
  workers on Riwoché projects from, 391
Jang, Dharma king of (Chos rgyal Byang pa). *See* Namgyal Draksang
Jang medical lineage, 7, 468n23
Jang Ngamring (Byang Ngam ring) Monastery. *See* Ngamring Monastery
Jang Taklung (Byang Stag lung) Monastery, 409, 557n1068
  See also Taklung Monastery
Jangding (Byang sdings) Monastery, 107, 112
Jangpa brothers (Byang pa sku mched), 278, 336, 544n750, 560–61n903
Jangsem Jinpa Sangpo (Byang sems Sbyin pa bzang po), 18, 149–50, 511n462
Jangsem Urgyen Gema (Byang sems U rgyan dge ma), 563n932
Japurwa, adept (Grub thob Bya 'phur ba). *See* Tsenden Namkhai Naljor
Jarpo, forest monastery of (Byar po nags kyi dgon pa), 291
jasmine flower *(kun da)*, 269, 543n736
Jatsön Nyingpo ('Ja' tshon snying po, 1585–1656), 477n115, 480n161, 554–55n839
jaundice, 412
Jayul (Bya yul) or Ja (Bya), 92, 492n301
Jé Bodong ('Jad Bo dong), 281, 349, 353, 416
Jé Bodong stūpa, 50, 353
Jedrung Sangpo Palrin (Rje drung Bzang po dpal rin), 438

Jetsun Nyendrak Sangmo, venerable lady (Rje btsun Snyan grags bzang mo), 571n1007
Jetsun Tsemo (Rje btsun Rtse mo), 10
Jewel-Heap of Oral Instructions, 287, 547n777
Jewel Mirror in Which All Is Clear, (Gyurmé Dechen), 8–9, 11–13, 468n30
  date of composition of, 439, 470n44, 584n1141
  and Könchok Dewé Jungné of the Samdrup Temple, 439, 584n1140, 584–85n1142
  and Namkha Tsewang Puntsok Wangi Gyalpo, 439
  and white and red pills, 475n96
  written in Ewaṃ Gakyil, 578n1082
Jikmé Lingpa ('Jigs med gling pa, 1730–98), 478n122
Jikten Wangchuk ('Jig rten dbang phyug, 1454–1542), 46–47
Jokhang (Jo khang) Temple, 50, **168**
  and *Compendium of Maṇis,* 499n363
  and flooding in Lhasa, 244, 534n656
  and Jowo Śākyamuni, 510n458
  and statues made by Tangtong, 45, 46
Jomo Lhari (Jo mo lha ri), 252, 537n684
Jomonang (Jo mo nang). *See* Jonang tradition
Jonang Cholé Namgyal (Jo nang Phyogs las rnam rgyal, 1306–86), 526n577
Jonang (Jo nang) Monastery, 508–9n443, 513n471
Jonang Kunga Drolchok (Jo nang Kun dga' grol mchog). *See* Kunga Drolchok
Jonang Stūpa of Glorious Qualities (Jo nang gi mchod rten Dpal yon can), 37, 51, 52, **93**, **162**, 479n145, 493n304
  construction process similar to Riwoché Stūpa, 569n987
  and Dolpopa, 92
  qualities of, 506n430
  Tangtong's visit to, 68, 162–63, 488n254, 492–93n303
Jonang Tāranātha (Jo nang Tā ra nā tha, 1575–1635), 469n34, 534n656
Jonang (Jo nang) tradition, 9, 292, 508–9n443, 512n465, 513n471
  and Ngamring Monastery, 497n346
  and Nyakpuwa Sönam Sangpo, 526n577
  See also Palden Lekpa
Jowo (Jo bo) image of Avalokiteśvara. *See* Jowo of Kyirong
Jowo (Jo bo) of Golden Temple of Buchu (Sbu chu gser gyi lha khang), 309, 554–55n839
Jowo of Kyirong (Skyid grong gi jo bo), 121, **122**, 123, 364, 499–500n369
  and Tangtong retreat at Shalkar Lhadong, 177, 518n511
  Tangtong trading merchandise to worship, 121–27
  Tangtong visit to, 179–81
  Tangtong's visit in 1435, 261
Jowo Śākyamuni (Jo bo Shākya mu ni), 45, 163, **193**, 364, 489n272, 510n458, 516n494, 521n538
  alms bowl of gold, 283–85, 546n767
  barley in alms bowl of, 76, 246
  and butterlamp, 286
  and ferry tax, 299
  and flooding of levees in Lhasa, 411
  inner and outer forms of, 175
  iron bridge for, 292
  Kharnak harming people who visited, 245
  and Lady Kalsang's passing, 335–36
  and prophecy for Tangtong to make images, 305, 306
  and prophecy urging Tangtong to benefit beings, 168
  and successor for Tangtong, 431
  and Tangtong and famine of 1437, 285–86
  Tangtong offering gold maṇḍala in 1432, 249
  Tangtong seen as, 180, 286
  and Tangtong taming barbarians and building bridges, 198

Tangtong visit prior to time at Kaṃṇi Goshi, 193
Tangtong with gold for face, 156–57, 167–68
joy, sixteen facets of, 84, 491n286

Ka Ngapa Paljor Sherab (Bka' lnga pa Dpal 'byor shes rab), 16, 21, 474n89, 495–96n334
and food for scribes from child Tangtong, 107
and Jangpa brothers and Tangtong to live at Riwoché, 278
and Namgyal Drakpa Sangpo, 546n763
as ninth abbot at Ngamring, 497n346
and ordination of Tangtong, 127, 511n462
possible death mentioned by Tangtong, 278
and Six-branch Yoga of Kālacakra, 526n578
and vision of Kukkuripa, 127–28
vision predicting Tangtong's visit, 277
Kachupa Gyaltsen Sangpo (Bka' bcu pa Rgyal mtshan bzang po), 58, 551n807
and edict from Tangtong, 337–38, 561n911
as head of Chaksam Chuwori, 337
Kadam Volumes, 302, 508–9n443, 552n821
Kadampa (Bka' gdams pa) tradition, 508–9n443
and Atiśa, 552–53n822
eight spiritual friends from Nartang, 425
and Penyul, 525n570
and Ratreng Monastery, 552n820
Kagyü (Bka' brgyud) tradition
and "authentic skull-cup" of Tsari, 554n836
and four-armed Protector, 531n630, 553n825
mad yogins often known in, 63
and Marpa Lotsāwa, 547–48n778
masters of seen in vision by Tangtong at Drin Chuwar, 272
Tangtong making connection with at Densatel, 210
and Tsari mountain area in Kongpo, 494n313
and Tselpa Kagyü, 522n540
Kālacakra, 7, 9, 162, 383, 497n348, 505n413
according to Jonang tradition, 516n498, 563n933
maṇḍala of at Ngamring, 546n763
and Nyakpuwa Sönam Sangpo, 526n577
and Raudra Cakrī, 566n963
and Six-branch Yoga according to Jonang tradition, 159, 512n465
Six-branch Yoga (Sbyor drug) of, 11, 159, 496n343, 501–2n388, 508–9n443, 512n465
Tangtong's receiving of complete Jonang tradition version, 159, 508–9n443, 512n465
Kālacakra Tantra, 127, 501n384, 508–9n443
and *Vimalaprabhā* commentary, 526n577
Kalden Dorjé Drakpa (Skal ldan Rdo rje grags pa), 25, 475n102
longevity of, 146
Tangtong meeting with in India and Nyingma teachings, 145–47, 505–6n422
Kalden Rinchen Sangmo (Skal ldan Rin chen bzang mo), 41, 244, 247–48, 481n163, 488n260, 534–35n658, 560n899
and gift of reliquaries to Tangtong, 304–5
and gold Avalokiteśvara and sūtras, 249
gold given to Tangtong and precious Jowo, 249
and golden alms bowl for Jowo image, 283
and husband Drungchen Drakpa Palsang, 547n774

passing of, 335–36
Tangtong's prayer and robes dyed with saffron, 284
Kalden Rinchen Tsomo (Skal ldan Rin chen mtsho mo), 231, 532n634
See also Ané Tsomo
Kalkī *(rigs ldan)* epithet, 565–66n954
Kalkī Puṇḍarīka (Rig ldan Padma dkar po), 283, 546n763, 565–66n954
Kalsang, Lady. *See* Kalden Rinchen Sangmo
Kalu Rinpoché (Ka lu Rin po che, 1905–89), 21
Kāmata (Kāmarūpa), 6, 167, 466–67n14, 574n1036
and Dumtsé stūpa, 254, 255
prophecy regarding king of, 137–38
representatives of Tangtong sent to, 398
Tangtong's emanated visits to, 394–96, 411–12
Kāmata (Ka ma ta), King of, 394–99
and burning women, 411–12
conversion to Buddhism, 6, 252
illness of from breaking vow with Tangtong, 396–97
Kaṃṇi Goshi (Kaṃ ṇi sgo bzhi) in Lhasa, 70, 482n178, 521n539
Kāṇha, 519n523
Karaṇḍavyūha Sūtra, 421, 579n1091
Karchen Yeshé Shönu (Skar chen Ye shes gzhon nu), 525–26n573
Kharchu Drak (Mkhar chu'i brag), 434
Karita (Ka ri ta) cave, 266–69, 307–8
karma, 78, 267–68, 293, 308, 373, 434
Karma Goraṇa, 421
Karma Kagyü (Karma bka' brgyud) tradition, and Tölung Valley, 536n673
karma spiritual family, 229
Karmapa Rangjung Dorjé (Karma pa Rang byung rdo rje). *See* Rangjung Dorjé
Karmapas, 532–33n639
Karmaśataka Sūtra, 391
Kashipa Namkha Öser (Bka' bzhi pa Nam mkha' 'od zer), 508–9n443, 544n751
Kashmir (Kha che), 5, 42, 266, 307, 397–98, 561n908
See also Śākyaśrī
Kāśyapa, 561n909
Kathmandu Valley of Nepal, 74, 504n404
Katok Situ Chökyi Gyatso (Kaḥ thog Si tu Chos kyi rgya mtsho, 1880–1925), 42, 55–56
Kawa Paltsek (Dka' ba dpal brtsegs), 465n4
Khachar (Kha char) Temple, 542n728
Khakhyap Dorjé (Mkha' khyab rdo rje, 1871–1922), Fifteenth Karmapa, 21
Kham (Khams), 246, 353, 535n665
and Dergé Monastery, 57
Kunga Sangmo collecting offerings in, 407
Tangtong displays different bodies to people, 376, 409, 410
Khandro Sangpuk (Mkha' 'gro gsang phug), "Secret Cave of the Ḍākinīs," 228–30, 240
Khandroma Sengé (Mkha' 'gro ma seng ge), 16
as consort of Tangtong and mother of Tenzin Nyima Sangpo, 28, 502n390
as mother of Tenzin Nyima Sangpo, 545n760
Kharchu (Mkhar chu), 288, 548n780
Kharling (Mkhar gling) in Minyak, 324
Kharnak (Mkhar nag), 41, 245–46, 298, 551n808
edict from Tangtong to, 298
Khasarpaṇa, 179, 499–500n369
See also Jowo of Kyirong
Khatra (Kha khra), 137
Khecara (Mkha' spyod), 275, 457, 585n1154
Khecarī (Mkha' spyod ma), 18, 166, 473n75, 508n440, 521n534
See also ḍākinīs
Khedrup Shākya Shenyen (Mkhas grub Shākya bshes gnyen, d. 1549), 20–21

Khenchen Gyalwa Chokyang (Mkhan chen Rgyal ba mchog dbyangs, 1360–1433), 498n360
Khojarnāth, 542n728
Khön ('Khon) family
  Lhakhang Palace (Lha khang bla brang) branch, 506n428, 564nn937, 938
  Rinchen Gang Palace (Rin chen sgang bla brang) branch, 531n626
  Zhitok Palace (Bzhi thog bla brang) branch, 564n936
  and temporal power in Tibet, 333, 559n889
Khön Könchok Gyalpo ('Khon Dkon mchog rgyal po, 1034–1102), 497n348
Khyungpo Naljor (Khyung po rnal 'byor), 472n73
killing, 339
king-at-leisure posture, 453, 457
"King of the Empty Plain" name, 160, 512n467
kings, Tangtong discourse regarding, 320–22
Könchok Dar (Dkon mchog dar), 114
Könchok Dewé Jungné of the Samdrup Temple (Bsam 'grub lha khang pa Dkon mchog bde ba'i 'byung gnas), 439, 584n1140, 584–85n1142
Könchok Dorjé (Dkon mchog rdo rje), 508–9n433, 526n578
Könchok Gyalmo (Dkon mchog rgyal mo), 567n969
Könchok Lekpai Gyaltsen Pal Sangpo (Dkon mchog legs pa'i rgyal mtshan dpal bzang po, d. 1468), 278, 544n750, 546n763, 560–61n903
Könchok Palsang (Dkon mchog dpal bzang), 539n707
  and biographic information from Tangtong, 6, 467n18
  and *Bright Lamp* biography of Tangtong, 4, 5, 6, 575n1043
  and building of Samdrup Temple, 259, 575n1043
  sent to be master of King of Kāmata, 398, 399
Kong Lhakyab (Kong Lha skyab), 240–41
Kong Ralsum (Kong Ral gsum), 218, 232, 240
Kongjo (Kong jo), 510n458
Kongpo (Kong po), 33, 121, 431, 482n180, 499n364
  challenge of Tangtong at Menmogang Monastery, 233
  Chökyi Dronmé gifts to, 380
  Dharma throne built by Tangtong in, 227
  Kyabpa Sangpo as Tangtong's representative, 398
  meeting with five ḍākinīs, 222–25
  offerings such as iron received from people of, 309–10
  peace by following Tangtong's advice, 332
  and rocks and sacred commitments, 226–27
  shepherds from, 234, 240
  and skull-cup of Vajravārāhī, 54
  as source of iron, 33, 41, 46
  taming savages in eastern land of, 190
  treasure instructions regarding, 230
  and Tsari mountain area, 96, 494n313
Kongpo Gyala (Kong po Rgya la), 311
Kongpo Pöndruk (Kong po Dpon sprug), 234, 533n640
Kongtsun Demo (Kong btsun de mo), 41, 214, 480n161, 523n556, 529n599
Kṛṣṇacārin, 59
Kubilai Khan (1215–94), 539n708, 558n874
Kukkurājā, 501n386
Kukkuripa, 51, 128, 501n386
  Tangtong as emanation of, 129, 443, 455, 501n386
  Tangtong meeting with, 144–45
Kulahari, mountain of the local spirit (Gzhi bdag Sku la ha ri), 287
Kunga Drolchok (Kun dga' grol mchog, 1507–66), 10, 17, 21,

474n88, 499n363, 515n491, 516n498, 571n1007
and *Glorious Giver of Immortality*, 28, 30
Kunga Gyaltsen, Dharma lord (Chos rje Kun dga' rgyal mtshan), 508–9n443, 536n678
Kunga Kyi (Kun dga' skyid), 288
Kunga Lekpai Jungné (Kun dga' legs pa'i 'byung gnas, 1704–60), 472n70, 560n900
dreams and visions of Tangtong, 30
and *Perfection of Wisdom in Eight Thousand Lines*, 514n480
and visit to Circular Residence of the Sleeping Dog at Riwoché, 579n1084
and visit to Riwoché, 18
Kunga Nyingpo, the renunciant (Ku sa li Kun dga' snying po), 24, 475n102, 505–6n422, 507n434
Kunga Palden (Kun dga' dpal ldan), 421–22
Kunga Sangmo, venerable lady (Rje btsun Kun dga' bzang mo, 1459–1502), 406, 576n1054, 577n1062
at Riwoché, 407–8
and Tangtong guiding her practice, 406–7
and transference of consciousness for mother, 407
and Tsang Nyön Heruka, 576n1054, 1058
Kunga Shönu, field protector (Zhing skyong Kun dga' gzhon nu), 228, 531n628
Kunga Sönam Drakpa Palsang (Kun dga' bsod nams grags pa dpal bzang), 2, 467n19
and biographical supplication to Tangtong, 467n22
and *Final Story*, 8, 463, 467n19
and eulogy to Tangtong as Iron-Bridge builder, 33, 478n135
and Tangtong's date of death, 11, 12–13
Kunga (Kun dga') the blacksmith, 232, 532n638
Kunkyong Lingpa (Kun skyong gling pa, 1396–1477), 25, 62, 487n237, 571n1007
Kunpang Chödrak Palsang (Kun spangs Chos grags dpal bzang), 37
Kunpang Dönyö Gyaltsen (Kun spangs Don yod rgyal mtshan), 24, 62, 66
Kunpang Doringpa (Kun spangs Rdo ring pa, 1449–1524), 28, 476n104
Kunsang Pak, the Dharma king (Chos rgyal Kun bzang 'phags, 1389–1442), or lord Rabtenpa (Bdag po Rab brtan pa), 38, 259, **260**, 539n707
Kunsang Pema Tsewang (Kun bzang padma tshe dbang), 478n122
Kuntu Ö (Kun tu 'od), 88, 89
Kūtāgāra Stūpa, 152, 207, 311, 509n446
Kūtāgāra Sūtra, 320, 391
Kutön Tsöndru Yungdrung (Khu ston Brtson 'grus g.yung drung, 1011–75), 302, 552n821, 552–53n822
Kyabpa (Kyobpa) Sangpo (Skyab/Skyob pa bzang po)
activities of, 433
physical son of Tangtong, 398, 574–75n1042
reincarnations of and Chaksam Chuwori Monastery, 16
sent to Kongpo as Tangtong's representative, 398
and Tsagong Monastery, 15, 56
Kyara (Skya ra) Monastery, 277
Kyergangpa Chökyi Sengé, 472n73
Kyewang Pakné (Skye dbang 'phags gnas), 256–57
Kyichu River (Skyid chu), 535n661
building bridge on, 41, 72, 200, 488–89n263
ferry on, 298
ferryman striking Tangtong, 40, 196, 522n544
and logs floated down for ferries, 298
and preventing flooding of Lhasa, 534n656
and Tangtong's prayer for good fortune, 196–98

Kyirong (Skyid grong), 121, 499n365, 542n725
stūpa at Madun Pangka to stop fighting, 261
Tangtong visit to, 179–81
See also Jowo of Kyirong
Kyishö (Skyid shod), 244, 527n582, 534n655
Kyopa Jikten Gönpo (Skyob pa 'Jig rten mgon po, 1143–1217), 304, 553n824–5, 553n828
Kyura (Skyu ra) family line of Jikten Gönpo, 553n826

Ladakh, 42
ladders, Tangtong vision of, 38, 136, 138
Lady Kalden Rinchen Sangmo. *See* Kalden Rinchen Sangmo
Lady Kharka (Mkhar kha ma), 349, 564n935
Lady Shakhama (Dpon mo Shag kha ma). *See* Kalden Rinchen Sangmo
Lady Shaluma (Zha lu ma). *See* Dagmo Tenzin Gyalmo
lake goddess *(mtsho sman)*, 418, 579n1089
Lake Manasarovar, 264–65, 542n727
Lake Mapam Yutso (Ma pham g.yu mtsho), 264–65, 542n727
Lake Namtso Chukmo (Gnam mtsho phyug mo), 552n814
Lake Yutso (G.yu mtsho), Turquoise Lake, 529n600
lalanā *(ro ma)*, 174, 518n505
Lalitavajra, 504n411
Lama Dampa Sönam Gyaltsen (Bla ma dam pa Bsod nams rgyal mtshan, 1312–75) of Sakya, 227, 531n626, 548n782
Lama Dülwapa (Bla ma 'Dul ba pa), "Master of Monastic Discipline," 206, 525n569
Lama Gyalgyal (Bla ma Rgyal rgyal), 533n640, 550n796
Lama Lotsāwa (Bla ma Lo tsā ba), "Master Translator," 205, 293, 525n567, 550n796, 555n847
and Tangtong's request for him to practice Severance, 312–13
Lama Riksum Gönpo (Bla ma Rigs gsum mgon po), 209, 527n582
Lama Shang (Bla ma Zhang, 1123–93), 494n313, 522n546
and Yeshé Dorjé, 523n554
See also Shang Yudrakpa Tsöndru Drakpa
lañcana script, 108, 577n1066
Land of the Demonesses (Srin mo'i gling), 182, 520n525
landslide
at Riwoché stūpa, 368–69, 568n980
at Sarahata in Mön, 389
Langdarma (Glang dar ma), King, 556n852, 571–72n1011
Langpoché Khabap (Glang po che kha 'bab), 37–38
Lapchi (La phyi), 271–73, 544n744, 573n1032
Lapchiwa Namkha Gyaltsen (La phyi ba Nam mkha' rgyal mtshan). *See* Namkha Gyaltsen, Lapchiwa
Latö (La stod), 205, 525n566
Latö Jang (La stod byang), 42, 79, 259, 540n709, 544n750
collecting gold in, 282
rulers of and internecine quarrels, 278, 336, 544n750, 560–61n903
Sunlit (Nyi ma), 561n910
Latö Lho (La stod Lho), 270–71, 546n764
collecting gold in, 282
increasing life spans of people in, 416
and Tangtong at Shelkar, 364–65
Layak in Lho (Lho La yag), 287, 547n775
Lekchok (Legs mchog), 110
Lekden (Legs ldan), 291
See also Dorjé Lekpa
Lekdrup Pal (Legs grub dpal), 468n23
Lekhawa Sherab Sangpo (Sle kha ba Shes rab bzang po), 159, 354–55, 508–9n443, 512n465, 526n578, 565n951

Lekpa Gyaltsen (Legs pa rgyal mtshan), 421–22
lepers, 211
Letter to the Great Adept Tangtong Gyalpo (Shākya Chokden), 489n265
Leu Chungpa (Sle'u chung pa), 483–84n204
levees of Lhasa, 244, 534n656
levitation
  during fight in Dartsedo, 315
  Tangtong seated midair at Sheldrak, 208
  on white mule on way to Lo, 234
Lhachen Palbar (Lha chen dpal 'bar) image of Buddha at Gungtang, 194, 522n541
Lhadong (Lha gdong) ferry landing, 40
Lhadong Karpo (Lha ldong dkar po) clan, 96, 493n310, 540n710
Lhadongpa Sönam Chokpa (Lha gdong pa Bsod nams mchog pa), 19, 24, 129
Lhagyal Sangpo (Lha rgyal bzang po). *See* Shabpa Lhagyal Sangpo
Lhakang Palace (Lha khang bla brang) branch of the Khön ('Khon) family of Sakya, 498n357, 511n462
Lhalung Palgyi Dorjé (Lha lung Dpal gyi rdo rje), 314, 382, 556n852, 571–72n1011
Lhasa (Lha sa), 319
  and famine of 1437, 283–84
  flood and stone levees of, 411, 534n656, 578n1073
  as heart of prone demoness who forms land of Tibet, 50
  man who killed his wife, 389
  marketplace speech by Tangtong, 198–200
  Tangtong in hole in middle of marketplace, 198
Lhasa Dharmacakra (Lha sa chos 'khor), 100, 167
  See also Jokhang Temple
Lhatong Lotsāwa Shenyen Namgyal (Lha mthong lo tsā ba Bshes gnyen rnam rgyal, b. 1512), 10
Lhatsé (Lha rtse)
  patrons of, 353–54
  and reconcealed treasures, 32
Lhatsen Kyab (Lha btsan skyab). *See* Tai Situ Lhatsen Kyab
Lhatsun Rinchen Namgyal (Lha btsun Rin chen rnam rgyal, 1473–1557), 12, 489–90n278
Lhatsun Tashi Palsang (Lha btsun Bkra shis dpal bzang), 468n23
Lhawang Kunga (Lha dbang kun dga'), 552n817
Lhawang Paljor (Lha dbang dpal 'byor), 301, 552n817
Lhawang Tsé (Lha dbang rtse), 48
Lho (Lho), 157, 391, 510n460, 516n495, 567n970
Lhodrak (Lho brag), 288, 548n780
Lhokha Shi (Lho Kha bzhi), 252, 254, 537n684
Lhorong (Lho rong), 169, 256, 516n495, 538n696
  See also Bhutan
Lhunding Gema (Lhun sdings dge ma), 468n23
Lhundrup Teng (Lhun grub steng), 33, 57, 559n887
Lhungsé Kabub Stūpa (Lhung bzed kha sbub mchod rten) at Madun Pangka, 261
limestone, Tangtong locating for Riwoché stūpa, 376
lineage of the gods of clear light, 380, 570n1004
Ling (Gling), 314, 556n851
Lingpa colleges, 556n851
Lingrepa (Gling ras pa, 1128–88), 494n313, 523n554
Litang (Li thang) area, 555n850
Litany of the Names of Mañjuśrī, 192, 286, 319, 410, 508–9n443
  transmission of at Dadu Palace, 323
Lo Khatra (Klo Kha khra), 121, 499n364
Lo (Lko) or Loyul (Klo yul), 33, 479n136, 499n364, 516n492
  and naturally arising crystal stūpa, 240, 331

single man of, 233, 237, 240, 532n637, 533n643
Tangtong's conversion of people of, 33, 234–40
treasure instructions regarding, 230
Lo man Gyalgyal, 535n660
Lochen Gyurmé Dechen (Lo chen 'Gyur med bde chen). *See* Gyurmé Dechen
Lochen Ratnabhadra (Lo chen Ratna bha dra, 1489–1563), 9, 54, 171, 516n498
Lochen Trukhangpa (Lo chen Khrus khang pa), 334, 560n896
See also Trimkhang Lotsāwa Sönam Gyatso
Lödro Dorjé (Blo gros rdo rje), 114
Lodrö Gyaltsen (Blos gros rgyal mtshan), 8, 19, 382–83, 463, 572nn1013, 1016, 586n1164
Longchen Rabjampa (Klong chen Rab 'byams pa, 1308-63), 502n392
longevity
and adept Atikara, 139–40
dhāraṇī, 410
of disciples of Tangtong, 14, 471n58
and equal taste, 70
holder of the pure awareness of, 123
and *Iron Tree* practices, 26–27
and Kalden Dorjé Drakpa, 146
and Sönam Chokpa, 355
Tangtong increasing of peoples, 416
See also *Glorious Giver of Immortality*
longevity of Tangtong, 1, 11–14, 28, 470n43–45, 476n114
calculation of, 436, 470n45
could have remained for aeon, 435–36
and *Glorious Giver of Immortality* methods, 28
his control over, 412, 453
and making offerings to Amitāyus, 291
meditative techniques for, 1
obstacles to, 445
practices for, 26–30
prediction of by Padmasambhava, 27–28, 445–47
predictions of and elixir of Caṇḍālī, 435, 583n1127
predictions of and Gampopa, 213, 529n598
stūpa to bless, 238
and tantric methods of meditation, 28
testing by lighting butter lamp, 168
thirty-two yogic exercises for, 211, 522n540, 528n593
See also *Iron Tree*
longevity pills
Amitāyus giving Tangtong five pills, 369–70
for king of Kāmata, 398
Tangtong giving to others, 25, 370
Longka (Klong kha) iron bridge, 540n713
Löpon Paltsul (Slob dpon Dpal tshul) (brother of Tangtong), 96, 110, 111, 117–18, 496n341
lawsuit against, 153, 509n447
Lord Dusi (Bdag po Dus si), 349, 563–64nn934–35
lords of the three spiritual families *(rigs gsum mgon po)*, 238, 286, 533n648
Loro (Lo ro) stūpa, 291, 549n789
Losang Paldrup, the iron-bridge man (Lcags zam pa Blo bzang dpal 'grub), 47–48, 472n70
Losang Tobden Paljor (Blo bzang stobs ldan dpal 'byor), 18, 472n69
iron-bridge building activities of, 47, 482n186
Losang Trinlé (Blo bzang 'phrin las), 13, 521n538, 581–82n1115
lower realms, 388, 573n1025
lucid state, 330, 373
lumen *(klu sman)* spirit, 529n607
Lungtong Nyönpa (Lung stong smyon pa). *See* "Madman of the Empty Valley"

Machik Labdrön (Ma gcig Lab sgron, eleventh-twelfth century), 20, 467n17, 473n81
and mad behavior following realization, 63

not associated with Nyingma practice of Chöd, 62
and Opening the Door to the Sky, 549–50n795
and Tangtong's vision of, 19
and Tangtong's visit to Sangri Khangmar, 210, 528n589
and Trapa Ngönshé, 530–31n624
Machik Palden Lhamo (Ma gcig Dpal ldan lha mo), 200–201, 523n552
"mad" *(smyon pa)* epithet, 59
mad yogins and mad behavior, 58
acceptance of during Tangtong's life, 79–80
chosen or arising spontaneously, 62
and dualistic consciousness, 77–79
feigning of, 66
flowering in fourteenth and fifteen centuries, 63–64, 79
and Hinayāna tradition, 74
lives uncompromisingly, 75
and Nyingma, Kagyü, Shijé, and Chöd traditions, 63
ordinary people mad in eyes of, 74–75
See also deliberate behavior; secret behavior
madhyamaka or middle-way *(dbu ma)* philosophy, 346, 495–96n334, 497n348, 524n558
"Madman of the Empty Valley" (Lung stong smyon pa), 2, 58–80, 473n79
as a title, 80, 160, 486n229
"Madman of the Iron Bridges" (Lcags zam smyon pa), 475n96
"Madman of Tsang." *See* Tsang Nyön Heruka
Magadha, 134, 504n409
magical abilities of Tangtong
and appearing differently to viewer, 409, 410
and crossing Tsangpo River with point of finger, 119
and disappearance of criminal from Dartsedo, 315
during childhood, 106–8
freeing those who had died in boats at Ngampuk, 155
and goods and traders at Kyirong, 127
and illness in Jé Bodong and Sakya, 416
and image of Tangtong, 424
and Dzongka Monastery, 541–42n723
seeing three times without obscuration, 269
as sorcerer, 2
Tangtong's explanation of how he manifests, 410, 411
and trapped spirits in Minyak, 315
and tying sword into knot, 324
and what is heard depends on listener, 410–11
See also flying; food stories and miracles; levitation; walking on water
Magical Net instructions, 130, 503n400
magical travel, 140, 145, 317, 507n433
and circumambulation of Namkha Dzong, 252
from Kāmata to Riwoché, 396
to Lhasa when levees flooded, 411, 578n1073
from Pari to Nénying, 258, 539n702
to Tāmradvīpa, 140, 506n427
and travel of Tangtong, 520n525
from Yamdrok Ridge to Chuwori, 259, 539n703
Mahābodhi image of Buddha at Vajrāsana of Bodhgayā, 90, 138–39, **139**, 294, 492n295
Mahābodhi temple of Bodhgayā, 548–49n787
Mahācakra initiation, 129
Mahākāla
three forms of, 230, 531n630
See also Four-armed Mahākāla; Mahākāla Pañjaranātha; Six-armed Mahākāla
Mahākāla Pañjaranātha (Gur gyi mgon po), 182, **183**, 230, 519n523, 531n630
Mahākalkī (Rigs ldan chen po), 546n763
Mahākaruṇika, 83, 210, 388, 490n283
and appearance of Tangtong, 97, 443
image of at Riwoché, 383

image of made by Tangtong, 41, 338
and Lekpa Gyaltsen, 421
and man from Ngari, 367
Tangtong as emanation of, 500n371
and Tangtong giving refuge, 278
Tangtong's prayer to while working as smith, 310–11
Mahākaruṇika of Shalu (Zhwa lu'i thugs rje chen po), 164, 166, 514n483
Mahākaruṇika Who Dredges the Pit of Saṃsāra (Thugs rje chen po 'khor ba dong sprugs), 211, 528n594, 533n647
Mahākaruṇika Who Tames Living Beings (Thugs rje chen po 'gro 'dul), 120, 211, 498n362
Mahāmāyā Tantra and initiation, 287, 501n386, 547–48n778
Mahāmudrā, 65, 129, 331, 346, 391
and Śavaripa, 143
Tangtong teaching at Taklung Monastery, 302
Tangtong's receiving teachings of, 508–9n443
Mahāpaṇḍita Śākyaśrī (1127–1125), 46, 341, 562n916
Mahāvairocana (Rnam snang chen po), 253, 537–38n687
Mahāyāna Buddhism, 77, 322, 387, 557n882
Mahāyoga tantras, eighteen, 501n386
Mahottara Heruka, 312, **313**, 555n844
Maitreya, 114, 497n347, 505–6n422
and Rongtön Sheja Kunrik, 552n819
Maitreya images, 483–84n204
at Ngamring, 355, 546n753, 565–66n954
at Chuwori, 337, 561n911
and Khachar Temple, 542n728
at Riwoché, 383, 385
at Tropu Monastery, 50–51
Maitrīpa, 9, 506n428
Malik (Ma glig), minister of Kāmata, 397, 398, 574n1041
Mandarava, 27
Mangtö Ludrop Gyatso (Mang thos klu sgrub rgya mtsho, 1523–96), 514n480
Mangyel (Mang yel) Temple, 92
Mangyul (Mang yul) region, 265, 355
maṇi devotees *(ma ṇi pa)*, 23, 41, 422, 573n1024
edicts for, 387–88, 421
maṇi pills, 23
maṇi transmission *(ma ṇi lung)*, 198, 407, 523n550, 526n576
maṇis
benefits of, 395
and epidemic at Sakya Monastery, 412, 414
recitation required by Tangtong at Chakpori Hill, 337
recitation urged by disciples of Tangtong, 461
Tangtong recitations of in home village, 155
Tangtong vow of two hundred million, 162–63
Tangtong's heard differently by listeners, 410–11
Mañjughoṣa, 361
Mañjuśrī, 111, 424, 533n643, 556n856, 566n963
image of created by Tangtong, 307, 338
and Khachar Temple, 542n728
prophecy by and geomantic focal-points, 320, 386
Tangtong's vision of, 115, 497–98n352, 557n865
Mañjuśrībhadra, 59
Mañjuśrīmitra, 59
Manobodhi. *See* Paṇḍita Mahābodhi
Mansion of Lotus Light, 131
Mansion of Secret Mantra at Tsari, 96
mantra-born ḍākinī *(sngags skyes kyi mkha' 'gro ma)*, 356, 566n957
Manudhara, 133
māra. *See also* nāga-māra
Māra, 101, 361
māra of the Lord of Death, 402, 575n1048

māras, four *(bdud bzhi)*, 61, 312, 435, 555n843, 575n1048
Markham (Smar khams), 34, 411, 578n1072
Marpa Lotsāwa (Mar pa Lo tsā ba, 1012–93?), 64, 530–31n624, 547–48n778
  and meeting with Tangtong, 287
Marpori Hill (Dmar po ri), 50, 535n663
Maryul (Mar yul), 360, 566n961, 577n1059
master
  and chosen deity and Dharma protectors, 375
  demons and obstructing spirits as, 372
  form of at crown of head, 345–46, 399
  and judging deliberate behavior, 61, 74
  meditation that everything is, 203
  meditative concentration on, 147
Master and Protector Indivisible (Bla ma mgon po dbyer med), 150, 531n630
Maudgalyāyana, 545n752
Meaningful to Behold (Ngawang Tenzin Norbu), 483–84n204, 485n216
Medical College of Lhasa, 516n493
medical lineage, 530–31n624
medicinal pills, 23, 25, 471n62, 475n96
  See also *maṇi* pills; white and red medicinal pills
Medicine Buddha, 481n176
  image at Riwoché, 383, 385
  image of in turquoise, 306
  mantra of, 411
  sūtra ritual of, 243
  Tangtong giving blessing for creating medicinal nectar of, 263
meditation hut of Tangtong, 51, 172–77, 381, 408, 416, 439
Mekong River, 555n850
men *(sman)* goddess, 529n607
Men Valley (Sman lung), 118, 120
Mending (Sman sdings) Monastery, 516n498
Mendong Ringmo (Man gtongs ring mo) field, 405–6
Menkhab (Sman khab), 371, 569n985
menmo *(sman mo)* goddess, 579n1089
Menmogang (Sman mo sgang), 228, 331
Menmogang (Sman mo sgang) Monastery, 53, 484–85n213
  and challenging Tangtong, 232–33
  and Chökyi Drönmé, 53, 232, 380, 532n636
  meditation center at, 331
  and omens for the future, 231–32
mental treasures (*thugs gter* or *dgongs gter*), 23, 32
Method for Accomplishment of Kṣetrapāla, 309, 554n838
Methuselah, 11
Metok Dangchen (Me tog mdangs can), 500n373
mice, rain of in Mongolia, 407
Mikyö Dorjé (Akṣobhyavajra, Mi bskyod rdo rje), 193, 521n538
Milarepa (Mi la ras pa, 1040–1123), **272**, 549n788
  and "authentic skull-cup" of Tsari, 554n836
  and Chuwar, 573n1032
  and Drin Chuwar, 544n744
  and duel with Bönpo teacher at Great Cave of Miracles, 542n724
  and Lapchi, 544n744
  as perfect mad yogin, 64
  and poem upon meeting Padampa Sangyé, 64–65
  and test of young woman who became disciple, 564n942
  and tower at Sekhar Gutok, 287, 547–48n778
  and Tsang Nyön Heruka, 63, 64, 72
military service, 110–11
mind, 158, 180, 346, 372, 436, 447, 451
  fundamental nature of, 115, 201, 388
Mind Training (Blo sbyong), 120, 121, 391, 498n361, 501–2n388, 508–9n443
  given to five ḍākinīs by Tangtong, 512n467
  and sending and taking, 344, 562n919
  of Sumpa Lotsāwa Darma Yönten, 291, 548–49n787

Ming emperor, 546n763
See also Chinese emperor
Mingyur Dorjé (Mi bskyod rdo rje), 482n186
Minyak (Mi nyag), 35, 46, 48, 482n180
abuse of Tangtong in Penyul by men of, 75–76, 246
abuse of Tangtong in Tölung by men of, 69–70, 249
blood feuds and Amdruk's sword, 325
and buffalo patron, 269
and feud with people of Gyeré, 69–70, 250
and Lhadong Karpo clan, 96, 493n310
man from and horse offered at Dartsedo, 323
stūpa at Dartsedo, 50, 58, 316
Tangtong frees three thieves from, 323
and Tangtong meditation on vital fire, 314
Minyak Gomring (Mi nyag Sgom ring), 553n824
Mitrayogin, 504n411
Miyo Losangma (Mi g.yo blo bzang ma), 544n746
Moby Dick (Melville), 520n525
Mokchokpa Rinchen Tsöndru, 472n73
Mön Bumtang (Mon Bum thang), 287, 548n779
Mön (Mon), 121, 157, 175, 499n364, 518n508
and palace of Cakrasaṃvara, 181
and robbers from west at Tembu, 257
and Sarahata, 389
and successor for Tangtong, 431
and three thieves at Kyewang Pakné, 256–57
Mön Paro (Mon Pa gro), 336
monastic code *(vinaya; 'dul ba)*, 495–96n334, 497n348, 524n558
Mongolia and Mongols, 259, 407, 505n416
Kunga Sangmo taming of, 407
Padmasambhava instructions to establish geomantic focal-point, 51, 186, 356
prophecy of stūpa to counter invasion, 33, 137, 138
repelled by spirit-turquoise of Lhalung Palgyi Dorjé, 314
stopping invasion by speaking of Tangtong, 438
and stūpa on Mongolian-Tibetan border, 356–61
Tangtong's death kept secret from, 438, 459, 461
Tibetan fear of raids by, 355, 566n955
monks
confused while working at Riwoché, 391–92
and despondency building bridge at Jowo, 293
fully ordained vs. novice, 127
three strict at Yakdé in Rong, 341, 348
Mönyul (Mon yul), 252
Most Fierce Charnel Ground (Gtum drag gi dur khrod), 517n501
mother of Tangtong. *See* Gyagar Lhamo
mother tantras, 139
"Mothers Infinite As Space" (Ma nam mkha' ma'i skyabs 'gro), 277, 474n80
and attack on Vajrāsana, 421
and bridge at Nyago, 432, 433
and bridge at Riwoché, 273
and building of bridge at Kyichu, 244
explanation of by Dezhung Rinpoché, 502n389
and Ka Ngapa and Avalokiteśvara, 129
and Kāmata king and retinue, 395
and landslide at Sarahata, 389
and raising of Riwoché stūpa center pole, 378
and Sakya Monastery, 412
Tangtong giving refuge by means of, 28
motive and application *(bsam sbyor)*, 344, 562n919
Mount Everest, 537n684
Mount Kailash (Ti se, Gangs Ti se), 318, 391, 514n479, 536n677

four rivers coming from, 318
Tangtong's visit to, 263
Mount Kukkutakapāda (Ri rkang can), 139, 505–6n422
Mount Meru, 96, 275, 345, 421, 558n880
Mount Sodang Gongpori (Zo dang gong po ri), 333, 559n886
Mount Trasang (Ri bo Bkra bzang), 570n998
Mount Wutai (Wutaishan; Ri bo rtse lnga) *See* Five-Peaked Mount Wutai
mountain man of Ngari (Mnga' ris pa'i ri pa), 231, 380, 525n566, 531–32n632, 559n888, 571n1007
mountain-spirits *(sku la)*, 547n776
Mu *(dmu)* demons, 228, 531n627
Mü Sanak (Mus Sa nag), 282
Müchen Namkhai Naljor (Mus chen Nam mkha'i rnal 'byor), 18, 473n74, 513n477, 544n744
  and Ka Ngapa Paljor Sherab, 495–96n334
  and meeting with Tangtong, 164
  and Samding Monastery, 536n678
mules, 261, 332
Mupa Shenyen (Smu pa Bshes gnyen), 398
Müsepa Dorjé Gyaltsen (Mus srad pa Rdo rje rgyal mtshan, 1424–98), 541n718
mutes, Tangtong removing demon preventing speech, 324
Mutri Tsenpo (Mu khri btsan po), 96, 465n4
myrobalan plum, 157, 158

nāda or sound *(sgra)*, 508n443
nāga kings, eight great *(klu chen po brgyad)*, 184, 535n661
nāga-māra *(klu bdud)*, 109, 215, 252, 496n33
nāgas *(klu)* or water spirits, 41, 219–20, 255
  helping to carry iron, 259
  and lake in Ngu, 56
  meeting Tangtong in Penyul, 206
  single-faced water demon, 219
  and stūpa at Tashi Dung, 300–301
  and Tangtong and Waru Seso, 215, 217
  Tangtong suppressing at Tsozong, 219–21
  See also Kharnak; Varuṇa
Nāgārjuna, 498n356
Nairātmyā, 166, 167, 515n490, 517n502
Nakartsé (Sna dkar tse), 250, 536n678, 571n1007
Naktang Pang in Drakyul ('Phrag yul gyi nags thang spang), 226–28
Nālandā Monastery, 139–40, **140**, 497n344, 567n967
  history of, 506n423
  and Virūpa, 517n502
Nālendra (Nā lendra) Monastery, 70–72, 301–2
  founding of, 552n819, 556n851
names for Tangtong
  "Alchemist of Foods" (Zas rnams bcud len mkhan), 161
  Crazy Tsöndru (Brtson 'grus smyon pa), 13, 92, 117, 118, 121, 471n55
  "Free from Disgust toward or Reliance on Phenomena" (Chos rnams skyags gtad med pa), 161
  Geshé Tsöndru (Dge bshes Brtson 'grus), 127
  given by five ḍākinīs, 160–61, 185
  "Iron-Bridge Man" (Lcags zam pa), 1, 15, 33, 269
  "King of the Empty Plain" (Thang stong rgyal po), 160, 512n467
  "Madman of the Empty Valley" (Lung stong smyon pa), 2, 58, 65–66, 160
  "One for Whom Conditions Have an Equal Taste" (Rkyen rnams ro snyoms mkhan), 69
  Trowo Palden (Khro bo dpal ldan), "Wrathful Glory," 96, 105, 111, 494n312
  Tsöndru Sangpo (Brtson 'grus bzang po), "Good Diligence," 146, 195, 471n57, 511n462, 522n543

Tsöndru Sengé (Brtson 'grus seng ge), "Lion of Diligence," 113
Namgyal Drakpa Sangpo, Kalkī (Rigs ldan Rnam rgyal grags pa bzang po, 1395–1475), 283, **356**, 546n763, 565n948. *See also* Namgyal Draksang
Namgyal Draksang (Rnam rgyal grags bzang, 1395–1475), 7, 495–96n334, 496n343, 516n496, 560–61n903, 583–84n1136. *See also* Namgyal Drakpa Sangpo
incomparable qualities of, 355
and landslide at Riwoché stūpa site, 568n980
and message to Tangtong for Lho, Jang, and Ngari regions, 355
and stūpas and Latö Lho, 260, 540n711
Tangtong asked to calm quarrel between brothers, 278, 544n750
and Tangtong's request for help with Riwoché, 363–64, 371
Namgyal Palsang (Rnam rgyal dpal bzang), 564n935
Namgyal Sangpo (Rnam rgyal bzang po), 382, 551n807
Namkha Dorjé (Nam mkha' rdo rje), 433–34, 566n964, 582n1119, 583–84n1136
Namkha Dzong (Nam mkha' rdzong), 252
Namkha Gyaltsen, Lapchiwa (La phyi ba Nam mkha' rgyal mtshan, 1382–1447), 544n744, 553n826
Namkha Lekpa, Dharma king (Chos rgyal Nam mkha' legs pa), 583–84n1136
and Tangtong's body placed in stūpa, 438
Namkha Lekpa, emanated wrathful conqueror (Sprul pa'i khro rgyal Nam mkha' legs pa), 20, 466n12, 572n1019
and receiving Chöd teachings, 495n333
and slate for roofs, 384
See also Namkha Leksang
Namkha Leksang (Nam mkha' legs bzang), 376, 569n992. *See also* Namkha Lekpa, emanated wrathful conqueror
Namkha Sangpo (Nam mkha' bzang po), 536n678
Namkha Tsewang Puntsok Wangi Gyalpo, Kalkī Dharma king (Rigs ldan Chos kyi rgyal po Nam mkha' tshe dbang phun tshogs dbang gi rgyal po), 10, 584n1138
and *Jewel Mirror* to be written, 439
Namkhai Nyingpo (Nam mkha'i snying po), 548n780
naraka hell *(na rag dmyal ba)*, 247
Naro Bönchung (Na ro Bon chung), 542n724
Nāropa, 18, 64, 501n388, 521n534
dress of, 131, 209, 527n580
Nāropa, cycle of (Nā ro skor, i.e., the Six Dharmas), 511n462
Nartang (Snar thang), 164
Nartang (Snar thang) Monastery, 349, 564n939
eight spiritual friends of and prayer from Tangtong, 425–31
Nātha tradition of India, 528n593
Natsok Rangdrol (Sna tshogs rang grol), 72, 489–90n278
Naturally Arisen Eleven-faced Avalokiteśvara (Rang byon bcu gcig zhal), 200, 523n551
See also Fivefold Naturally Arisen One
Necklace of White Beryl (Sangyé Gyatso), 470
nectar pills, given by Virūpa to Tangtong, 173, 517n503
Nedong (Sne gdong) bridge, 38, 333, 559n886
Nedong Peak (Sne gdong rtse), 208, 525n574
Nedongpa (Sne gdong pa), 333, 559n890
See also Pakmodrupa

Nénying (Gnas rnying), 258–59, 539n702
Nénying (Gnas rnying) Monastery, 250–51, 537n681
Nepa governor (Sne pa Dpon), 244, 431, 534n655, 534–35n658, 580
  See also Drungchen Drakpa Palsang
Nepa patron, 335, 560n900
  See also Drungchen Drakpa Palsang
Neu (Sne'u) governor. *See* Drungchen Drakpa Palsang
New Jewel Mirror in Which All the Marvels Are Clear (Gyurmé Dechen), 439
Ngadar (Lnga dar) (brother of Tangtong), 96, 109
Ngagi Wangchuk (Ngag gi dbang phyug), 439, 468n31
Ngagi Wangpo (Ngag gi dbang po, 1439–1491), 13, 431, 471n55, 580–81n1108
  and iron bridge of Nyago, 580–81n1108–9, 581–82n1115, 582n1116
Ngamring Bumtang (Ngam ring 'bum thang), 356–57
Ngampuk (Ngam phug), 155
Ngamring (Ngam ring), 7, 36, 37, 355, 468n23, 496n343, 497n346, 516n496
  projects by Namgyal Drakpa Sangpo in, 546n763
  Tangtong's visit for collection of gold, 283
Ngamring (Ngam ring) Monastery, 114
  Tangtong prophecy regarding, 363
  and war with Riwoché over toll, 370, 568n982
Ngari (Mnga' ris), 333, 559n888
  increasing lifespans of people in, 416
  instruction to man from, 365–67
  Kunga Sangmo's visit to three regions of, 407
  royal family of, 570n1004
Ngari (Mnga' ris pa'i ri pa), mountain man of, 231, 380, 525n566, 531–32n632, 559n888, 571n1007
Ngari Dzongkha (Mnga' ris Rdzong kha), 475n96, 540–41n717, 576n1057
  attempt to poison Tangtong at, 261–63
  Kunga Sangmo's visit to, 407
Ngari Gungtang (Mnga' ris Gung thang), 570n997
Ngari Panchen Pema Wangyal (Mnga' ris paṇ chen Padma dbang rgyal, 1487–1542), 25
Ngaripa (Snga ris pa), 205, 525n566
Ngawang Chödrak, Panchen (Paṇ chen Ngag dbang chos grags, 1572–1641), 10, 469n35
Ngawang Gelek (Ngag dbang dge legs), 54, 485n218
Ngawang Losang Gyatso (Ngag dbang blo bzang rgya mtsho, 1617–82) (Fifth Dalai Lama), 468n24
  and five ḍākinīs and statues made by Tangtong, 45–46, 482n178
  and image of Tangtong, xx
  and images at Chakpori Hill made by Tangtong, 41–42
  and levees of Lhasa, 534n656
  and longevity practice related to Tangtong's, 30
  and Nyingma Northern Treasure teachings from Tangtong, 476n104
  and Tenzin Nyima Sangpo, 16
Ngawang Losel Nyida Öbar (Ngag dbang blo gsal nyi zla 'od 'bar), 472n70
Ngawang Puntsok (Ngag dbang phun tshogs, 1648–1714), 472n70
Ngawang Sönam Lhunpo (Ngag dbang bsod nams lhun po), 336, 560n902, 561n904
Ngawang Sönam Namgyal (Ngag dbang bsod nams rnam rgyal), 336, 560n902, 561n904
Ngawang Tenzin Norbu, Dzatrul (Rdza sprul Ngag dbang bstan 'dzin nor bu, 1867–1940), 54, 485n219, 483–94n204
Ngawang Tutob Wangchuk (Ngag dbang mthu stobs dbang phyug, 1900–1950), 54

Ngawang Yongdrak (Ngag dbang yongs grags, 1714–67), 17, 18, 21, 47, 482n185
Ngödrup, the adept (Grub thob Dngos grub), 515n490
Ngödrup Gyaltsen (Dngos grub rgyal mtshan, 1337–1408). *See* Gökyi Demtruchen
Ngog Lekpai Sherab (Rngog Legs pa'i shes rab), 552n821
Ngönpo Yöndar, the mendicant (Bya gtang Sngon po yon dar), 227, 531n625
Ngor Gönsar (Ngor dgon gsar) Monastery, 279–80, 545n754, 556n851
Ngor (Ngor) subsect of Sakya tradition, 57, 545n754
Ngorchen Kunga Sangpo (Ngor chen Kun dga' bzang po, 1382–1456), 57, 486n226, 545n754
  and giving Path with the Result to Tangtong, 517n502, 545n755
  and meeting with Tangtong, 279–80
Ngurmik (Ngur mig), 167, 515n491
Niguma, 10, 472n73
  appearance of to Tangtong, 18–19, 149
  and feast at Sinpo Dzong and illusory body, 191
  and four initiations and instructions on *Vajra Lines*, 150, 508n440
  and permission to write *Collection of the Essentials*, 151
  poem of Tangtong's receiving of her transmission, 151–52
  special importance of her teachings to Tangtong, 18
  and White and Red Khecarīs, 150
  See also Six Dharmas of Niguma
nihilism, 346
Nilambhar, 574n1074
nirmāṇakāya emanated body *(sprul sku)*, 312, 500–501n380
Noble Wati ('Phags pa Wa ti), 123, 499–500n369
  See also Jowo of Kyirong
nonduality of saṃsāra and nirvāṇa, 290
nonsectarianism of Tangtong, 1, 18
nonvirtuous actions, 343
Norsangpa (Nor bzang pa, 1403–66), 431, 546n765, 581, 581n1109
Northern Treasure (Byang gter) tradition of Nyingma, 18
  and deliberate behavior practitioners, 62–63
  given to Chökyi Dronmé by Tangtong, 570n998
  and Dönyö Gyaltsen, 100, 494–95n324, 502n391
  and Great Perfection teachings, 25, 476n104
  and practices of Chöd, 19
  and Tangtong's long life, 28
  Tangtong's reception and continuation of, 24–25, 62
Nubchen Sangyé Yeshe (Gnubs chen Sangs rgyas ye shes), 549n790
Nütrawa, Omniscient (Kun mkhyen Snud kra ba), 508–9n443
Nya Ön Kunga Pal (Nya dbon Kun dga' dpal, 1285?–1379?), 508–9n443, 526n577, 563–64n934
Nyago (Nya mgo) bridge over Tsangpo River, 46, 53, 432–33, 482n182, 571n1006, 581n1112, 581n1114
  and Chökyi Dronmé, 380
  date of completion of, 433, 581–82n1115
  and ferry crossing, 40, 333
  See also Nyangpo
Nyakchu (Nyag chu) River bridge, 72, 314, 337, 488n262
Nyakpuwa Sönam Sangpo (Snyag phu ba Bsod nams bzang po, 1341–1433), 526n577
Nyal (Dmyal/Gnyal), 288, 297, 548n782
Nyal Pakmodrong (Snyal Phag mo grong), 257
Nyamkhar (Nya mkhar), 376–77
Nyang (Nyang), 259, 539n707
Nyang Nyima Öser (Nyang Nyi ma 'od zer, (1136–1204), 35, 62, 474n94, 498nn362–63, 515n490, 528n594

Nyangchu River (Nyang chu) bridge, 38, 563n928
Nyangchu (Nyang chu) and Drakchu River (Brag chu) convergence, 218, 219
Nyangpo (Nyang po), 459, 581n1115
See also Nyago
Nyemo (Snye mo), 341, 376
nyen *(gnyan)* demons, 220, 255, 530n614
See also Kharnak
Nyernyipa Chökyk Gyalpo (Nyer gnyis pa Chos kyi rgyal po, 1395–1467), 544n744, 553n826
Nyida Sangpo, Tenzin (Bstan 'dzin Nyi zla bzang po), 28, 30
Nyima Gyaltsen (Nyi ma rgyal mtshan), 543n739
Nyima Sangpo, Tenzin (Bstan 'dzin Nyi ma bzang po, b. 1436), 7, **16**, 17, 383, 472n70, 545n760
birth of at Tarpa Ling, 281
as bridge builder, 6, 12, 13, 46, 432–33
and death of Tangtong, 13, 457–59
as Dharma heir, 15–16, 380–81, 571n1009
and gold for Amitābha image at Riwoché, 384–85
investiture of, 15, 380–82
life of, 15–16
magical abilities given by Tangtong, 459
mother Khandroma Sengé, 502n390
and *Perfection of Wisdom in Eight Thousand Lines*, 514n480
projects completed by, 433
and rebirths in Chaksam tradition, 16
Tangtong's advice for at his passing, 437–38, 451, 453
work of after passing of Tangtong, 461
Nyingma (Rnying ma) tradition
and canonical lineage and treasures, 130, 503n399
mad yogins as treasure revealers, 62
mad yogins often known in, 63
and Tangtong, 23–28
and Vajrakīla, 537n685
See also treasure teachings; Northern Treasure tradition
Nyingtik Yashi (Snying thig ya bzhi), 502n392
Nyö Gyalwa Lhanangpa (Gnyos Rgyal ba Lha nang pa), 201, 523n554
Nyön *(smyon)*, "crazy," 472n71

Oathbound Protectors of the Word Who Eliminate the Arrogant, 207
Ocean of Marvels (Sherab Palden), 7–8, 463, 468nn26, 28, 493n311
and description of temples and images of Riwoché, 418
Ochu Gadrak ('O chu sga brag), blacksmiths at, 42, 254–55
"Old Father Tangtong Gyalpo" (Pha rgan Thang stong rgyal po), 475n96
Olkha Taktsé ('Ol kha stag rtse), 210, 528n591
Oṃ maṇi padme hūṃ, 23, 103, 388, 395, 523n550
and Jowo statue at Kyirong, 123
and Lo peoples, 237
reciting by Tangtong at Yungdrung Ling, 270, 543n740
See also *maṇis*
one-armspan circular residence of Tangtong, 408–9
"One Medicine for a Hundred Ills" (Nad rgya sman gcig). *See* white and red medicinal pills
Önpo Dorjé Gyaltsen (Dbon po Rdo rje rgyal mtshan) (father of Tangtong), 96, 103–4, 120, 493n311
and epidemic at Tangtong's birthplace, 109
greed of, 117–18
and inheritance of family property, 111
and military service, 110, 496n341
Tangtong paying off debt of, 169, 172
Tangtong saving from hell, 415
Önpo Namgyal Sangpo (Dbon po Rnam rgyal bzang po), 336, 571–72n1011

Opening the Door to the Sky (Nam mkha' sgo 'byed), 292, 375, 526n576, 549–50n795
Oral Transmission of Machik's Secret Behavior (Tangtong), 19–20
ordination of Tangtong, 110–11, 112–13, 128, 511n462
Orgyan Lingpa (O rgyan gling pa, 1323–ca.1360), 62, 525–26n573
Orgyan Tenzin Norbu (O rgyan Bstan 'dzin nor bu), 47
Orshö ('Or shod), 243
Ösel Dechen Ling ('Od gsal bde chen gling), 89
Otang Lake ('O thang mtsho), 50
other realms, Tangtong's service to beings in, 443, 447, 457
"overcoming perversion" posture, 311
Owa Lhatsé ('O ba lha rtse), 95, 100
  clay grotto used by Tangtong for retreat near, 153–55, 509n448
  and faithlessness of locals in recognizing Tangtong, 154–55
  prosperity of after birth of Tangtong, 106

Pacification (Zhi byed) lineage, 530–31n624
Padampa Sangyé (Pha Dam pa sangs rgyas, d. 1105), 19, 46
  meeting with Milarepa, 64–65
  and Trapa Ngönshé, 530–31n624
  and *Unwritten Mahāmudrā*, 511n462
  and White Mausoleum, 543–44n743
padma spiritual family, 229
Padmākara, 84, 266, 490n284, 543n735
  actions of leading to creation of images by Tangtong, 307–8
Padmapāṇi, 83, 490n282
Padmasambhava, Guru
  and Asura Cave, 504n405
  and bodyprint in rock in Mön, 287
  and *Bright Lamp of Prophecy*, 3–4, 187, 465n4
  Chöd practices taught by, 19
  and Chökyi Gyaltsen, 387
  and deliberate behavior and Tangtong, 66, 131
  and Dorjé Drakpotsel, 530n623
  and Drakyang Dzong meditation cave, 549n790
  and genyen mountain-gods, 509n449, 545n757
  and Glorious Copper-Colored Mountain, 98, 99, 494n322
  and Guru Saroruhavajra, 504–5n412
  and Heartdrop of the Ḍākinī teachings, 502n392
  image of at Chakpori Hill temple, 42
  image of for Master's Temple at Riwoché, 459–61
  and initiations given in Lo, 238
  and *Iron Tree* practices for immortality, 26–27
  and Kongtsun Demo, 480n161, 529n599
  and longevity of Tangtong, 445–47
  and Ngödrup Gyaltsen, 62
  and Nyang Nyima Öser, 62
  as Padmākara, 490n284
  as perfector of deliberate behavior, 59
  prophecy for Tangtong, 51, 97, 159, 176, 445–47
  return of during age of strife as Tangtong, 84–85
  and Samyé Monastery, 207–8, 525n572, 557n862
  as son of Bön sage Dranpa Namkha, 565n944
  and stūpa at Yongru in upper Tsang, 354
  and stūpa to suppress Mongol armies, 51, 185, 356, 357
  and Tangtong and terrestrial focal-points, 51
  Tangtong as mental emanation of, 1, 23, 96–97, 98, 100, 168, 187, 200, 213, 280, 443, 445, 455, 490–91n285
  and Tangtong building at Sumpa, 218–19
  and tantric initiations at Chimpu, 525n571

and treasures left in Cave of the Ḍākinīs, 230
in Uḍḍiyāna when Tangtong there, 185–86
vision of Tangtong as, 304, 377
White Stūpa of at Samyé, 571n1007
and Yama spirits at Gyala Badong, 309
See also Dorjé Drolö; Taktsang
Padmasambhava's Chronicles, 525–26n573
Pakmodru (Phag mo gru) dynasty, 13, 471n55, 526n574–5, 527n585, 559n887
and Governor Norsangpa, 546n765
and Ngagi Wangpo, 580–81n1108
Pakmodrupa Dorjé Gyalpo (Phag mo gru pa Rdo rje rgyal po, 1110–70), 494n313, 527n585, 553nn823–24, 570n997
Pakpa Palsang ('Phags pa dpal bzang, 1318–70), 563n934
Pal Khorlo Dechen (Dpal 'Khor lo bde chen), 348–49, **349**
Pal Riwoché (Dpal Ri bo che), Glorious Great Mountain, 51, 483n203
See also Riwoché Monastery
Palace of Lotus Light of Padmasambhava, 28, 185
Palchen Chöyé (Dpal chen chos ye), 523n554
Palden Chimé Drubpa (Dpal ldan 'chi med grub pa), 407, 576n1058, 577n1059
Palden Döndup (Dpal ldan don grub), 422–23, 479n1092
Palden Gyaltsen, master Ngaripa (Bla ma Mnga' ris pa Dpal ldan rgyal mtshan), 531n632
Palden Lekpa, Jonang great adept (Jo nang Sgrub chen Dpal ldan legs pa), 348, 563n933
Palden Lhamo (Dpal ldan lha mo), 523n552
Palgyi Nesar (Dpal gyi gnas gsar) Monastery. *See* Tsagong Palgyi Nesar Monastery in Kongpo
Palgyi Samyé (Dpal gyi bsam yas), 288, 548n780
Paljor Gyalpo (Dpal 'byor rgyal po). *See* Drungchen Paljor Gyalpo
Palkhor Chödé (Dpal 'khor chos sde) Monastery, 539n707
Palmo Gön (Dpal mo mgon). *See* Gyagar Lhamo
Palzin Dorjema (Dpal 'dzin rdo rje ma) (sister of Tangtong), 96, 109
Panam (Pa rnam), 348, 353, 563n927
Panchen Ngawang Chödrak (Paṇ chen Ngag dbang chos grags, 1572–1641), 10, 469n35
Panchen Shākya Chokden (Paṇ chen Shākya mchog ldan, 1428–1507), 70, 489n265
Paṇḍita Jagadānandajīvabhadra, 503n403
Paṇḍita Jivabodhi, 503–4n403
Paṇḍita Mahābodhi, 133, 503–4n403, 518–19n513
Paṇḍita Smṛtijñāna, 514n483
Pañjaranātha, 182, **183**, 519n523, 520n524, 578n1078
and ending of epidemic at Sakya, 414
seen standing to Tangtong's left, 291
Tangtong seen as, 375
Pari (Phag ri), 42, 251–52, 394, 537n682, 539n702, 574n1036
iron transported to, 257
later visits to, 539n707
Paro (Pa gro), 42, 175, 250, 252, 394
chains from bridge in, 44
and Kyewang Pakné, 256–57, 538n698
pilgrimage of people to see Tangtong, 399
and stūpa of Dumtsé, 50, 254, 255
and warning about impermanence, 399–405
See also Drakyé of Paro
Paro Taktsang (Pa gro Stag tshang), Bhutan. *See* Taktsang, Bhutan
Path of Seeing, 62, 526n579
Path with the Result (Lam 'bras), 9, 10, 410, 508–9n443, 511n462, 577n1069

and Gayadhara bringing to Tibet, 537–38n687
and Pañjaranātha, 520n524
and Virūpa, 173, 517n502
patience, 427
patrons and donors of Tangtong
from Chözong, 354
and conch shell for Avalokiteśvara, 307
Darma Kyi, 263
and Dharma king of Jang, 260, 540n711
at Karita cave in Kashmir, 266, 269
of Lhatsé, 353–54
Wangdrak, 353–54
See also Kalden Rinchen Sangmo; Namgyal Draksang
peacock, 262, 541n722
Pema Karpo, Drukchen ('Brug chen Padma dkar po, 1527–92), 485n222
Pema Lendreltsal (Padma las 'brel rtsal, 1231–59), 502n392
Pema Lingpa (Padma gling pa, 1450–1521), 62, 466–67n14, 490n284, 534n656
meeting with Nilambhar and King of Dongkha, 574n1036, 585n1146
and prophecy of Tangtong, 445
Pemaling (Padma gling), 287, 547n776
Penetration of the Intention (Gökyi Demtruchen), 25, 476n106, 495n333
penis, tying rope to Tangtong's, 69, 250
Penpo ('Phan po) (brother of Tangtong), 96, 109, 110
Penyul ('Phan yul), 75–76, 206, 525n570, 552n819
Tangtong visits during famine, 246
Perfection of Wisdom in Eight Thousand Lines, 164, 514n480
perfection of wisdom literature *(phar phyin)*, 495–96n334, 497n348, 524n558, 530–31n624
Phagö Gyaltsen Palsang (Pha rgod Rgyal mtshan dpal bzang, 1519?–1592?), 21
pilgrimage, great *(skor chen)*
from Sakya to Lhasa, 164, 245, 286, 513–14n478
Tangtong connecting with, 164, 167
poison
metaphor of use of in deliberate behavior, 77
potion of in Kāmata, 412
used against Tangtong at Nagari Dzongka, 261–63
poisonous water beneath earth, 136, 137
poisons, five coemergent, 125, 322, 423, 500n377
poisons, three, 126, 342, 388, 500–501n380
Pökya residence (Spos skya gzims khang) of Ralung Monastery, 250, 259, 536–37n679
Pönmo Chögyal (Dpon mo Chos rgyal), 567n969
possessions, 429–30
Potar Tashi Sengé, 56
Potola, 434, 535n663
sublime realm of, 267, 268
practical instructions *(dmar khrid)*, 501–2n388m, 129
Prajñāpāramitā, 116, 383
Pramāṇavārttika (Dharmakīrti), 114, 497n347, 498n357
pratimokṣa vows, 345
pratyekabuddha, 426
Prayer of Good Conduct, 286, 302, 552–53n822
Prayer of Maitreya, 415, 578n1081
precious human existence, 90, 492n297
pregnant women, Kāmata King sacrifice of, 394, 396, 398–99
preserved body *(sku dmar gdung)* of Tangtong, 54
previous and future lives of Tangtong, 555n842
as Bön teacher Tsewang Rangdrol, 352, 565n944
as the omniscient Dolpopa, 13, 14, 36, 92, 488n252, 513n472
as Drakpa Öser, King, 87–92, 313, 555n842, 555n846
and elephant skull, 266

as female dog, 288
as goat, 418
hundreds of thousands of lifetimes of, 87, 313, 317, 555n846, 579n1088
and Jamyang Khyentsé Wangpo, 31
Jatsön Nyingpo as reincarnation, 554–55n839
and making of images, 306–7
past births of including three animal births, 266
prayers as Drakpa Öser that ripened as Tangtong, 90–91
remembered after vision of Hūṃkara, 491–92n293
as Rongtön, 92
and Sangwa Düpa, 92
pride in scholarship, 114, 116
primordial awareness *(ye shes)*, 83, 116, 203, 312
fivefold, 321, 500n379
Tangtong's body of, 31, 32
Profound Path Guruyoga (Lam zab bla ma'i rnal 'byor), 174, 180, 410, 457, 519n517, 577n1069, 585n1155
prophecies by Tangtong
and Chökyi Drönmé to Tsagong, 53
and Chökyi Gyaltsen from Tang, 387
and conflict between Jang and Lho, 365, 567n970
and death of Vanaratna in Nepal, 559–60n892
and disasters in Drigung Kagyü, 304
and disciples of Nyima Sangpo, 432
and emperor of China, 323
and half see him as buddha and half as demon, 314
and Jangsem Urgyen Gema, 563n932
and longevity and service of Chökyi Dronmé, 378–79
and meditation center in Drok Megyu, 287
and Mongolian invasion of Tibet, 361, 566n958
and mountain man of Ngari, 231, 380, 525n566, 531–32n632, 559n888, 571n1007
and Nepa future, 336
for people of Jé Bodong, 353
and prophecy regarding Lhatsen Kyab's lifespan, 365, 567n969
and rebirth of Chökyi Dronmé, 406
regarding Ngamring Monastery, 363
regarding spirit-turquoise, 314, 571–72n1011
shooting arrows as augury from Lhasa, 245
and skull-cup of Chökyi Dronmé, 226, 231, 309, 380, 530n622, 571n1007
and son to Lord Dusi, 349, 564n935
spoken at his birth regarding dreams, 104
and steward at Pal Khorlo Dechen, 348
three nuns and earth, stone, and wood to spread blessing, 198–200
and war at Kharchu, 288
prophecies regarding Tangtong, 3–4
and ability to locate focal-points, 51
of achieving benefit with ḍākinīs for living beings, 176
of appearance and *Bright Lamp of Prophecy*, 97, 103, 443–45
and *Bright Lamp of Prophecy*, 3–4
of crystal-colored youth at Shalu, 165
of ḍākinīs of Uḍḍiyana, 190
of ḍākinīs regarding iron at Tsagong, 40
of Dharmaratna, 137–38
of Dönyö Gyaltsen, 105, 106, 130
of eighty-four great adepts of India, 153–54
of eleven-faced Avalokiteśvara, 200
and extending longevity through *Iron Tree* practices, 26
of gods and demons of glacial Tibet, 174–75
of image of Gampopa and Dakpo region, 213–14
for individuals who meet Tangtong, 177
Jatsön Nyingpo as reincarnation of Tangtong, 554–55n839

of Jowo of Buchu and instruction to build stūpa above Badong Dunpa, 309, 554–55n839
at Jowo to make images, 305, 306
of Kalden Dorjé Drakpa, 146–47
of Karmapa Rangjung Dorje regarding taming Lo, 234
of Khasarpaṇa at Ramadoli Charnel Ground, 179
of Kukkuripa, 145
of Kyirong Jowo, 123
of Machik Palha, 200–201
of Mañjuśrī and focal-points, 319–20, 386
and monastery at Riwoché, 51
of Niguma, 191
of Padmasambhava, 51, 97, 159, 176, 445–47
of Padmasambhava and Mongol focal-point, 186, 356
as Padmasambhava's emanation, 96
as rebirth of Subhūti, 443
regarding his longevity, 578n1075
of Rendawa, 15, 158, 159
of Shang Yudrakpa, 194–95
of Siṃhamukha, 172, 176-7
and Tangtong building at Sumpa, 218–19
of Tangtong's lifetimes, 92
of Tārā at Dongshur, 169, 239
of Vajravārāhī and bridge at Chuwori, 254
of Vajravārāhī regarding Lo, 215
See also *Bright Lamp of Prophecy*
Prophecy. See *Bright Lamp of Prophecy*
protection cords, 324
Pudé Gungyal (Spu de gung rgyal), 34
Puṇḍarīka, 546n763
Puntsok Ling (Phun tshogs gling) bridge, **5**, **36**, 479n148
Püri (Spus ri), 319

Ra Lotsāwa Dorjé Drak (Rwa Lo tsā ba Rdo rje grags, eleventh century), 512n464
Rabten Kunsang Pak (Rab brtan kun bzang 'phags, 1389–1442), 481n172, 563n928, 563n930, 563n932
and meeting with Tangtong and Vanaratna, 559–60n892
and meeting with Tangtong at Pal Khorlo Dechen, 348
and providing workers with iron to Tangtong at Pari, 42, 563n930
Rabtenpa (Rab brtan pa). *See* Rabten Kunsang Pak
Radzinsky, Edvard, xi
Rāgavaḥ, 334
Rāhu (Sgra gcan), 221, 457, 530n616, 585n1156
Rāhula, 545n756
Rāhulabhadra, 498n356
rainbow, 113, 248, 377
at passing of Tangtong, 436, 447, 449
rainbow body, 120, 150
Rājā King Doruk Naran (Ra tsa Rgyal po Rdo rug na ran), of Kāmata, 574n1036
Rakdzong iron bridge, 47
rākṣasa demon *(srin po)*, 514n481, 521n 539, 527n583, 580n1098
Ralung (Ra lung) Monastery, 250, 536–37n679
ram killed at Rinchen Ding, 415
Ramadoli Charnel Ground, 504n407, 518–19n513
Rāmeśvara cemetery, 19, 20. *See also* Charnel Ground of Rāmeśvara
Ramoché (Ra mo che) Temple, 534n656
Rangjung Dorjé (Rang byung rdo rje, 1284–1339), Third Karmapa, 35, 234, 532–33n639
Rangjung Rikpai Dorjé (Rang byung rig pa'i rdo rje, 1923–1981), Sixteenth Karmapa, 21
Rasa Trulnang (Ra sa 'phrul snang), 167, **168**, 516n494
See also Jokhang Temple
rasanā (rkyang ma), 174, 518n505
ratna spiritual family, 228–29

Ratnabhadra, Lochen (Lo chen Ratna bha dra). *See* Lochen Ratnabhadra
Ratnakāra, 138, 505n418
Ratreng (Rwa sgreng) Monastery, 302, 552n820
Raudra Cakrī (Drag po 'khor lo can), 361, 533n650, 566n963
Raven-faced Karmanātha (Las mgon Bya rog gdong can), 230, 531n631
Rechungpa Dorjé Drak (Ras chung pa Rdo rje grags, 1083–1161), 291, 549n788
reconcealed treasures *(yang gter)*, 32
Red Yamāri (Gshin rje gshed dmar), 158, 501–2n388, 512n464
relic
  of Buddha blazing with light, 304
  of dog's footbone, 288
  and Gyeré Tsarpa man, 192
Rendawa Shönu Lodrö (Red mda' ba Gzhon nu blo gros, 1349–1412), 15, 41, 510–11n461
  madhyamaka teachings of, 495–96n334
  Tangtong's meeting with, 157–59, 500n373
renewal and purification, vows of, 288, 396, 548n781
renunciation, 339–40
representations, three, 128, 501n387
retreats of Tangtong
  with Dharmaratna, 136–38
  with Draksangpa, 120–21
  and edicts in 1428, 465n5
  long during last years at Riwoché, 12, 25–26
  at Samyé Chimpu, 206, 335
  sealed in at Riwoché, 408–9, 412, 578n1075
  seven-year in clay grotto at Owa Lhatsé, 153–54
  at Shalkar Lhadong in 1434, 260
  six-year at Shalkar Lhadong meditation hut, 172–77
  year sitting immobile at Kaṃṇi Goshi, 193–94, 521n539
Ricard, Matthieu, 507n435
Rigongpa Sangyé Nyentön, 472n73
Riksum Gönpo (Rigs gsum mgon po), 56, 228, 231, 531n629, 571n1004
  arrival in Lo, 236
  and taken by emanation to meet Chökyi Dronmé, 380
  as master of Tsagong Nesar, 331
  and meeting Chökyi Dronmé in Central Tibet, 380
  and trip to Lo, 234
Rikzin Lekden Dorjé (Rig 'dzin Legs ldan rdo rje, 1500–1577), 25
Rinchen Ding (Rin chen sdings), 121, 169
  and animals protected by Tangtong, 415
  and birth of Tangtong, 103
  and epidemic during Tangtong's childhood, 109–10
  great court of and Owa village, 95
  iron suspension bridge at, 36–37, 47, 479n145
  and Shalkar Lhadong meditation hut, 172
  Tangtong's return after eighteen years, 149
  Yarlungpa Chödrak Palsang to, 297, 551n807
  See also Shalkar Lhadong
Rinchen Gang Palace (Rin chen sgang bla brang) branch of the Khön family, 531n626
Rinchen Namgyal (Rin chen rnam rgyal). *See* Lhatsun Rinchen Namgyal
Rinchen Sangpo (Rin chen bzang po), 527n584
Rinpung (Rin spungs), 282, 283, 561n904
ritual fasting *(snyung gnas)*, 198, 291, 474n92, 523n550, 533n647
  and Golden Temple of Buchu, 309
  and people at Yakdé in Rong, 341
ritual feast
  and corpse of horse at Yangal in Dra, 73–74, 209, 527n583
  at Five-Peaked Mount Wutai, 319

for pilgrims during 1437 famine, 286
presented by five ḍākinīs in Kongpo, 222–26
and pulling up of Chuwori iron bridge, 300
and woman walking nude around crowd, 209–10
rituals, necessary for Nepa rule, 336
"river-flow yoga," 153
Riwo Drasang (Ri bo bkra bzang) mountain and monastery, 130–31, 503n395
Riwoché (Ri bo che) Monastery in Chung, 5, 6, **52**, 54, **55**
bridge constructed in 1436, 42–43, 48, 273
building of temples around, 51, 483–84n204
and Circular Residence of the Sleeping Dog, 417, 579n1084
custom of offering wood and rope at, 434, 582n1120
as environmental focal-point, 33
fight with Ngamring Monastery, 370
help from Namgyal Draksang to begin, 363–64
and hereditary line of Tangtong, 17, 47
history of after death of Tangtong, 54–55
and image of Tangtong put in Master's Temple, 459
images and temples of and *An Ocean of Marvels*, 418
and investiture of Nyima Sangpo, 15, 380–82
Ka Ngapa's request for Tangtong to reside at, 278
location of, 51, 544n750
and meeting of Tangtong and Tsang Nyön, 79
not as convenient main monastery, 15
plan for and naming of, 169–72, 516n496
projects after stūpa, 383–84
Samantabhadra image and temple, 417–18, 579n1087
and Sherab Palden, 7, 8, 17
and spirit-turquoise of Lhalung Palgyi Dorjé, 314
and Tangtong and Niguma, 19
Tangtong in long retreats during last years at, 12, 25–26
and Tangtong meeting Sangyé Sangmo, 361
Tangtong sealed in residence at, 408–9, 412, 578n1075
teachings at Dzamling Gyen meditation hut, 391
and Temple of Tārā, 417, 579n1087
and Temple of the Protectors, 416–17, 421
and toll gate, 370, 433–34
trees for roofs and Tangtong's powers, 384
and verses on things not as they seem, 76–77
and white medicinal pills, 541–42n723
workers from Lho, Jang, and Ngari, 391
and Yölmo Tulku, 11, 17–18
Riwoché (Ri bo che) Monastery in Kham. *See* Taklung Matang Kham Riwoché
robbers and robberies
attempted on road to Drigung, 302–3
of Drakyul, 233
of iron from Paro at Chuwori, 43, 292
at Kyewang Pakné and Mön, 256–57
and Mön thieves at Kyewang Pakné, 256–57
at Ölkha Taktsé, 210–11
of protected animals at Rinchen Ding, 415
statues of Tangtong at Yilhung Shi, 58
Tangtong instructing disciples to in Penyul, 75–76, 246
and three thieves from Shiribum freed by Tangtong, 323
of white conch, 291
Rong River (Rong chu), 256
Rongtön Sheja Kunrik (Rong ston Shes bya kun rig, 1367–1449), 70–72, 92, 492n300, 524n558

meeting with Tangtong at Nālendra, 301–2
and Tangtong at Sangpu, 72, 488–89n263, 552n819, 568n974
Tangtong teachings given to, 524n561
roofing trees for Riwoché, 384
Root Tantra. See *Kālacakra Tantra*
Root Text for the Attainment of Immortality (Virūpa), 528n593
royal code of ten virtues *(dge ba bcu),* 237, 239, 533n646, 533n649
Ṛṣi Rāhula, 130, 503n397
rūpakāya bodies of form, 83, 87, 185

sacred commitments, 328, 345, 445
Sakha Nakpa (Sa kha nag pa), 250
Sakya (Sa skya), curing illness in, 416
Sakya Dagchen Lodrö Wangchuk (Sa skya Bdag chen Blo gros dbang phyug, 1402–81), 349, 564n936
Sakya (Sa skya) Monastery, 114, **115**, 497n348
epidemic at and Tangtong's prayer, 412–14
Great Temple of Sakya, 413
Sakya Paṇḍita (Sa skya Paṇḍi ta, 1182–1251), 487n250, 487–88n251
Sakya to Lhasa pilgrimage, 164, 245, 513–14n478
during famine year of 1437, 286
Tangtong connecting with, 164, 167
Sakya (Sa skya) tradition
and Dergé Monastery, 57
and Jang Ngamring Monastery, 497n347
and Jonang tradition, 513n471
and Lama Dampa, 227, 531n626
and Lochen Gyurmé Dechen, 9
and Pañjaranātha, 520n524
and Sakya Monastery, 497n348
and temporal power in Tibet, 333, 559n889
See also Path with the Result
Sākyaśrī, Mahāpaṇḍita (1127–1225), 46, 341, 562n916
Salmogang (Zal mo sgang), 314, 319, 556n851
Salmogang (Zal mo sgang) Stūpa, 337, 551n807
Samantabhadra, 89, 146, 206, 238, 503n396
goat horn placed in image of at Riwoché, 418
Samantabhadra Temple at Riwoché, 417–18, 459, 579n1087
sambhogakāya enjoyment body *(longs spyod rdzogs pa'i sku),* 312, 373, 500–501n380
Saṃdhinirmocana Sūtra, 320, 391
Samding Dorjé Phagmo (Bsam sdings Rdo rje phag mo) line, 482n212, 571n1007, 576n1054
Samding (Bsam sdings) Monastery, 53, 484n212, 536n678, 574n1036
Samdrup Dar (Bsam 'grub dar), 418
Samdrup Gyaltsen (Bsam grub rgyal mtshan), 508–9n443, 511n462
Samdrup Temple (Bsam grub lha khang), 6, 394, 539n707
and Könchok Dewé Jungé, 584n1140
laying foundation for, 42, 259
Samdrup Tsé (Bsam grub rtse), 265, 514n481, 542n731
sameness. *See* equal taste or sameness
saṃsāra, 146, 343, 372, 404
as laughable, 436, 447
Ngari man and instruction regarding liberation, 365
three realms of, 342, 344, 347
Samten Paljor (Bsam gtan dpal 'byor), 389
Samten Palwa (Bsam gtan dpal ba, 1291–1366), 198, 522n547
Saṃvara. *See* Cakrasaṃvara
Samyé (Bsam yas) Monastery, 206–8, **207**, 319, 557n862
and origin of ferries and bridges, 33–34
White Stūpa at, 571n1007
Samyé Chimpu (Bsam yas Mchims phu), 28, 32, 206–8, 335, 477n118, 525n571
Sanawa (Sa sna ba), 205, 525n568

Sangpo Kyong, great adept (Grub chen Bzang po skyong), 508–9n443
Sangpo Pal (Sgrub pa po Bzang po dpal), 508–9n443
Sangpu (Gsang phu), 72, 488–89n263, 524n561, 552n819
Sangri Bawachen (Zangs ri Lba ba can), 228, 231, 531n629
Sangri Khangmar (Zangs ri khang dmar), 528n589
Sangwa Düpa (Gsang ba 'dus pa), 92
Sangyé (Sangs rgyas) the blacksmith, 232
Sangyé Gyaltsen, Dharma lord (Chos rje Sangs rgyas rgyal mtshan), 513–14n478
Sangyé Gyatso (Sangs rgyas rgya mtsho), 8, 468n24
Sangyé Ön (Sangs rgyas dbon, 1251–96), 558n876
Sangyé Puntsok (Sangs rgyas phun tshogs, 1649–1705), 11
Sangyé Sangmo (Sangs rgyas bzang mo), 356–61
Sangyé Tönpa (Sangs rgyas ston pa), 472n73
Śāntideva, 111, 497n344
Sapuk (Sa phug), 287
Saraha, 115, 131, 498nn355–56, 506n428, 519n520
Sarahata, 389, 573n1028
Śāriputra, 545n752
śāsana mantra, 302–3, 553n825
Sasang Mati Panchen (Sa bzang Ma ti Paṇ chen, 1294–1376), 526n577
Satmahal Pāsāda, **141**
Śavaripa, 38, 51, 142–43, **142**, 461, 506n428
Sawang Kundrup Dega Sangpo (Sa dbang Kun grub bde dga' bzang po, 1768–90), 584–85n1142
Schaeffer, Kurtis, 470–71n49
scholar of the ten fundamental subjects *(bka' bcu pa)*, 201, 202, 288, 524n558
  Drepung, 201–4, 524n561
  Gyaltsen Sangpo, 337
  Lodrö Gyaltsen, 382
  Namkha Lekpa, 376
scholarship, pride in mere, 114, 116
scorpion-shaped mountain, 51, 170
scorpions, 215, 217
Scriptures of the Monastic Code, 443, 585n1144
secret behavior *(gsang spyod)*, 60, 159, 160, 178, 485n222
  See also deliberate behavior; mad yogins and mad behavior
secret initiation, 146, 172–74
secret mantra, 97, 145, 153, 387, 407, 507n434
Secret Treasury of the Ḍākinīs That Yields Spontaneous Enlightened Activities, 206–7
Sekhar Gutok (Sras mkhar dgu thog), 287, 547–48n778
self
  cherishing of, 343–44
  imagined fiction, 346
Semo Remo (Sras mo re mo), 261–63, 541n719
sending and taking *(gtong len)*, 344, 562n919
Sengé Puk (Seng ge phug), 254
Sengé Sangpo (Seng ge bzang po), 155
Serché, stūpa of (Gser phye 'bum pa), 288, 548n782
Sero Pal (Se ro dpal) (older brother of Tangtong), 96, 110, 111, 496n341
  greed of, 117–18
  lawsuit against, 509n447
seven-branch offering *(yan lag bdun pa)*, 90, 156
seven jewels *(rin chen bdun)*, 345, 562n921
"Seven Jewels" of Shangpa Kagyü lineage, 18, 150, 472–73n73
seven riches of a Noble One *('phags pa'i nor bdun)*, 124, 427, 500n376, 580n1104
seven siblings *(lcam dral bdun)*, 417, 578n1083
seven types of precious substances *(rin po che sna bdun)*, 90, 492n296
Severance (Gcod) tradition. *See* Chöd

sexual union, secret offering of, 225, 530n619
Shabdrung Ngawang Namgyal (Zhabs drung Ngag dbang rnam rgyal, 1594–1651), 15, 56
Shabjé Tarling (Zhabs rje thar gling), "Footprint Sanctuary of Liberation," 424
Shabkar Natsok Rangdrol (Zhabs dkar Sna tshogs rang grol, 1781–1850), 48, 54, 485n215
Shabpa Lhagyal Sangpo (Shab pa Lha rgyal bzang po), 279, 281
Shākya Palsang (Shākya dpal bzang), 412
Shākya Sangpo (Shākya bzang po), 499n363
Shākya Sengé (Shākya seng ge), 497n346
Shākya Shenyen (Shākya bshes gnyen), and red and white medicinal pills, 471n62
Shalkar Lhadong (Zhal dkar lha gdong) meditation hut and retreat, 172–77, 260, 516–17n500, 518n512, 540n710
Shalsang (Zhal bzangs), earth spirit, 118
Shalu (Zha lu) Monastery, 164, 514n482
Shambhala, 255–56, 538n695, 546n763
Shang Sambulung (Shangs Zam bu lung), 280, 545n757
Shang Tukjé Tsöndru (Zhang Thugs rje brtson 'grus, 1243–1313), 513n471
Shang Yudrakpa Tsöndru Drakpa (Zhang g.yu brag pa Brtson 'grus grags pa, 1123–93), 194–95, 522nn540–42
Shangpa Kagyü (Shangs pa bka' brgyud) tradition, 10, 469n35, 472–73n73, 495n334
  and Immortality of Body and Mind, 528n593
  Jangsem Jinpa Sangpo gives to Tangtong, 150
  and six-armed form of Mahākāla, 230, 251, 531n630, 537n681
  and Six Dharmas of Niguma, 10, 501n388, 572n1013
  Tangtong Tradition, 18–19
  See also "Seven Jewels" of Shangpa Kagyü lineage
Shar Drukha (Shar gru kha) ferry crossing and bridge, 46, 433, 582n1117
Sharkapa (Shar ka pa) family line, 563n932. *See also* Sharkhapa ruling family
Sharkhapa (Shar kha pa) ruling family, 534–35n658
Shasho Cliffs (Sha sho'i brag), 106
Shechen Drungyik Tenzin Gyaltsen (Zhe chen drung yig Bstan 'dzin rgyal mtshan). *See* Tenzin Gyaltsen
Shechen (Zhe chen) Monastery, 9
sheep, 106–7
Shekar Gyantsé (Shel dkar rgyal rtse), 283, 546n764
Sheldrak (Shel brag), 208, 525–26n573
Shelkar (Shel dkar), 364, 566n965
Shenpa, Master (Bla ma Gshen pa), 352, 353
shentong (gzhan stong) view, 30, 550n801
Shenyen Tashi Sangpo (Bshes gnyen Bkra shis bzang po), 28
shepherd, Tangtong as, 106–7
Sherab Gyaltsen (Shes rab rgyal mtshan, 1772–1847), 50, 483n196, 539n707
Sherab Palden (Shes rab dpal ldan)
  background of, 7–8, 473n77, 586n1163
  and composition of *Ocean of Marvels*, 5, 7–8
  and death of Tangtong, 7, 13, 437–38, 447, 449–51, 583n1134
  and eccentric episodes in life of Tangtong, 66–68
  and edicts from Tangtong's 1428 retreat, 465n5
  as first regent of Riwoché, 17
  magical abilities given by Tangtong, 459
  as regent for Tangtong, 438
  and Riwoché Monastery, 7, 8
  special role of, 438

and Tangtong and Jamyang Rinchen Gyaltsen, 26
Sherab Sangpo (Shes rab bzang po). *See* Lekhawa Sherab Sangpo
Shiga Neupa (Gzhis ka Sne'u pa) ruler, 298, 551n808.
See also Drungchen Drakpa Palsang
Shijé (Pacification) tradition, 19, 63, 522n547
Shinjé Dongkha (Gshin rje'i dong kha), 319
Shiribum in Minyak (Mi nyag Gzhi ri 'bum), three thieves from, 323
Shongchen Khetsun Tenpai Gyaltsen (Gshong chen Mkhas btsun bstan pa'i rgyal mtshan), 21
Shrī Götsong (Shrī Rgod tshong), 364
Shu Nyemo (Zhu Snye mo) area, 245, 535n662
Shuchen Tsultrim Rinchen (Zhu chen Tshul khrims rin chen, 1697–1774), 11, 30, 467n22
Shuna (Gzhu sna) iron bridge, 335
Siddhiratna, 139, 505n421
Siden (Gzi ldan), India, 87
Siden Dharmacakra (Gzi ldan Chos kyi 'khor lo), 89
silence, Tangtong's vow of for fourteen years, 574n1041
Siṃhamukha
appearing in Lo, 235–36
and prophecies for Tangtong, 176–77
and prophecy of Virūpa, 172
sin
and virtue in tantra, 78–79
and Yamdrok fishermen, 339
Singri (Shi gi ri), 252–53, 537n686
Sinpo Dzong (Srin po rdzong, Demon Fort) in Domé, 18, 191
Sipal (Si dpal), 287
Situ Chökyi Gyatso (Si tu Chos kyi rgya mtsho, 1880–1925), 17, 482n212
Six-armed Mahākāla or Protector (Mgon po Phyag drug pa), 230, 251, **251**, 531n630, 537n681
initiations of, 291, 508–9n443
seen standing by Tangtong, 291
Tangtong seen as, 375
Six-branch Yoga (Sbyor drug) of Kālacakra, 11, 159, 496n343, 501–2n388, 508–9n443
of Jonang tradition given to Tangtong, 159, 512n465
and Śavaripa, 506n428
Six Dharmas of Nāropa (Nā ro chos drug), 391, 501n388
Six Dharmas of Niguma (Ni gu chos drug), 25, 31, 391, 476n106, 501–2n388, 572n1013
Tangtong's guidance manuals on, 382–83, 572n1016
six fundamental treatises of Kadampa tradition *(bka' gdams gzung drug)*, 508–9n443
six limits, 173, 517–18n504
six perfections, 427–28
six-syllable *dhāraṇī-mantra. See* six syllables
six syllables, 86, 123, 124, 175, 269, 388, 491n290, 500n372
Avalokiteśvara and Tangtong's performing of, 156
and bringing benefit to living beings, 278
heard as different teachings, 410–11
six types of consciousness, 346n924
six types of living beings, 124, 289, 344, 500n374
"skull-cup, authentic" *(mtshan ldan dbu thod)*, 54, 484–85n213
to be established at Menmogang, 231, 380, 531–32n632
prophecy from Vajrayoginī regarding, 226, 530n622
Tangtong's prophecy of and Tsagong Palgyi Nesar, 309
at Tsari Machen, 231, 309, 532n633, 554n836
slate, found by Tangtong's powers, 384
smelting, origin of, 34
Smith, E. Gene, 470nn44, 48
snakes
with clinging frogs, 315

and defeat of non-Buddhists at Vajrāsana, 421
See also nāga; nāga-māra
Sodruk (So drug), earth spirits of, 214
Somanātha, 530–31n624
Sönam Drenma (Bsod nams 'dren ma), 378, 570n997
Sönam Paldren (Bsod nams dpal 'dren), 570n997
Sönam Tashi (Bsod nams bkra shis). *See* Dakpo Sönam Tashi
Songtsen Gampo (Srong btsan sgam po), 239, 474n88, 510n458, 513n475
and *Compendium of Maṇis*, 499n363
and early iron bridge, 35
and geomantic principles, 554n839
and images of Avalokiteśvara, 499–500n369
and levees of Lhasa, 534n656
and Namkha Lekpa, 438
and royal code of ten virtues, 533n649
temples built by, 49
and wives and statues in Lhasa, 521n538
"spirit-mountain" *(bla ri)*, 535n663
spiritual heroes and ḍākinīs *(dpa' bo mkha' 'gro)*, 100, 550n803
spiritual level of Delight *(sa rab dga' ba)*, 427, 580n1103
spokesman of the writing slate *(sa 'bo ra sgrog mi)*, 525n567
springs at Owa Lhatsé, 154
śrāvaka, 131, 426, 489n275
Tangtong assuming manner of, 97
two sublime, 279, 545n752
Śrāvastī, 505n419
Śrī Dharmapāla, 517n502
See also Virūpa
Śrīparvata (Dpal gyi ri bo) (=Śrīśailam?), 5, 483n203, 561n908
steel, 48
Stein, R. A., 470n44
sthaviras, 140
Sthitimalla (reign: 1382–95), 504n408
stūpa
to avert invasion by Mongols, 33, 137, 138
Badong Dunpa, 309
Bodhnāth, 133, 504n404
Bön at Yungdrung Ling, 270–71, 543n739
built by Tangtong, 1, 49–52, 311, 363–89
built in Lo, 240, 331
constructed by Tsangpa Gyaré, 263
at Drakralkha, 338
at Dumtsé, Paro, 50, 254, 255
as environmental focal-points, 33, 49
on goat horn, 418
at Gyang, 49, 51, 52, 117, 498n357, 564n937
at Jé Bodong, 50, 353
in Kāmata, 395
Kaṃṇi Goshi stūpa, 70
Kongpo Gyala, 311
Kukkuripa's instruction to Tangtong to build, 145
at Kyewang Pakné, 257
Lhungsé Kabub Stūpa at Madun Pangka, 261
liberation through contact with, 145, 506n430
of Loro, 291
in memory of Tangtong's mother, 44
at Mongolian-Tibetan border, 356–61
naturally arisen crystal in Lo, 238, 240, 331
number built by Tangtong, 50, 425
as representation of dharmakāya reality body, 189, 521n533
at Salmogang in Dokham, 337, 551n807
and Śavaripa's instruction to Tangtong to build, 143
at Serché, 288, 548n782
at Shalkar Lhadong to assist Namgyal Draksang, 260
Svayambhūnāth, 133, 134, 504n404
to tame hostile forces, 50, 261
for Tangtong's body, 7, 438, 461
at Tropu Monastery, 50–51
at Tsel Gungtang, 194–95, **195**
at Tselagang, 243
Victory, 418

Viśuddha, 252–53, 537n686
Waru Namtsel in Kongpo, 50
White Stūpa of Padmasambhava, 571n1007
in Yongru in Tsang, 354
See also Auspicious Stūpa of Many Doors; Auspicious Stūpa of Many Doors at Riwoché; Chaksam Chuwori; Jonang Stūpa of Glorious Qualities
Stūpa of Descent from the Gods (Lha babs mchod rten), 139, 505n419
Stūpa of Enlightenment (Byang chub mchod rten), 238, 395, 418
See also Chaksam Chuwori stūpa; Stūpa of Great Enlightenment
Stūpa of Great Enlightenment (Byang chub chen po'i mchod rten), 558n882
at Dartsedo, 50, 58, 316, 323
and Nyangchu River bridge, 38
and Padampa's mausoleum, 543–44n743
to subdue Lo completed, 331
See also Stūpa of Enlightenment
Stūpa of Nirvāṇa (Myang 'das mchod rten), 461
Subhūti, noble ('Phags pa Rab 'byor), 443, 585n1143
succession of Tangtong's lineage, 15–18, 431
Śuddhodana, King, 252, 537n686
Sugata, 145, 189
sugatas, eight, 44, 152
Sukhasiddhī, 528n593
Sukhāvatī, 145, 248, 269, 494n321, 507n432
and Amdruk's sword, 325
and father of Dangra boy, 415
place of attainment for Tangtong's disciples, 177, 434–35
and those involved in stūpa at Riwoché, 365, 389
Sumtön (Gsum ston), 376
Sumpa Khenpo Yeshé Paljor (Sum pa mkhan po Ye shes dpal 'byor, 1704–88), 470n44
Sumpa Lotsāwa Darma Yönten (Sum pa Lo tsā ba Dar ma yon tan, twelfth–thirteenth centuries), 548–49n787
Sunlit Central Tibet (Nyi ma Dbus), 338, 561n910
Surtso (Zur mtsho), 270
Sūtra of Excellent Golden Light, 435
Svayambhūnāth Stūpa, 133, **134**, 504n404

Tachok Chöjé (Rta mchog Chos rje), 56, 467n15, 485n224
and Chaksam tradition in Bhutan, 15, 538n699
Tachok Gang (Rta mchog sgang) Monastery, 257, 538n699. *See also* Tachok Norbugang Monastery
Tachok Khabab (Rta mchog kha bab) River, 250, 493n307, 536n677
Tachok Norbugang (Rta mchog nor bu sgang) bridge, 42, 481n170
Tachok Norbugang (Rta mchog nor bu sgang) Monastery, 6, 56, 485n224, 538n699
Tai En Namkha Tenpa (Ta'i dben Nam mkha' brtan pa, b. 1316), 497n346
Tai Situ Jangchup Gyaltsen (Ta'i si tu Byang chub rgyal mtshan, 1302–64), 38, 526n574, 559n886, 581n1113
Tai Situ Lhatsen Kyab (Ta'i si tu Lha btsan skyabs), 52, 364–65, 567n966
and help with Riwoché stūpa, 371
prophecy regarding lifespan of, 365, 567n969
Tai Situ Sönam Pak (Ta'i si tu Bsod nams 'phags), 546n764
Tai Situ (Ta'i si tu) title, 546n763
Takdrö Rong (Stag sgro'i rong), 434
Taking Happiness and Suffering as the Path, 293, 512n464
Taklung Kagyü (Stag lung bka' brgyud) tradition, 553n823
Taklung Matang Kham Riwoché (Stag lung ma thang khams ri bo che), 326–31, 558n876

Taklung (Stag lung) Monastery, 302, 409, 553n823, 557n1068
Taktsang (Stag tshang), Bhutan, 252, 253, 523n553
Taktsang Lotsāwa Ratna Sengé (Stag tshang Lo tsā ba Ratna seng ge), 11
Tamdrin (Rta mgrin), 463
Tāmradvīpa or Copper Island (Zangs gling), 5, 483n202, 506n426, 561n908
  and Auspicious Stūpa of Many Doors, 51–52, 141–42, 144, 378, 569–70n996
  Tangtong visit to, 140–45
  See also Ceylon
Tanak (Rta nag), 349–52
tangka made by Tangtong, 44
Tangtong Gyalpo (Thang stong rgyal po, 1361?–1485)
  accepting people into his retinue, 209
  appearance and pictures of, xx, 2, 3, 35, 59, 63, 71, 97, 258
  biographical sources regarding, 2–11
  and *Bright Lamp of Prophecy*, 3–4, 465n4
  as dual emanation of Hayagrīva and Mahākaruṇika, 500n371
  five hundred masters of, 18, 317
  making drawing in front of artist, 378
  and Ngorchen Kunga Sangpo, 57, 486n226
  ordination of, 110–11, 112–13, 128, 511n462
Tangtong Gyalpo (Thang stong rgyal po, 1361?–1485), as builder, 33–58
  discovery bridges could be made of iron, 221–22
  knowledge of previous iron bridges, 36
  Kyichu River abuse and decision to build bridges, 40, 196–98, 522n544
  as means to liberate beings, 38, 40
  and number of created things, 40, 50, 273, 424–25, 480n157, 564n937
  and subduing demons and spreading Buddhism, 41, 50
  temples and assembly halls built by, 46
  and three categories of construction of bridges, 40
Tangtong Gyalpo (Thang stong rgyal po, 1361?–1485), as mad adept, 2, 58–80, 296
  called "Madman of the Empty Valley," 2, 58, 65–66, 160
  difficulty to comprehend "insane" deeds of, 76–77
  and dress in only simple cloak, 66, 70, 269, 288–90
  and eating horse meat in ritual feast, 73–74, 209, 527n583
  and eating dog feces, 67
  and equal taste, 69–70
  and instruction to donkey, 66–67
  and Machik Labdrön and behavior after realization, 63
  and mad behavior as child, 65
  and meeting with Rongtön at Nālendra, 70–72
  and meeting with Tsang Nyön Heruka, 79
  Padmasambhava instructing to perform deliberate behavior, 66, 131
  and prophecy of Padmasambhava, 97
  rather experience than explain states of realization, 65
  and robbing people in Penyul, 75–76, 246
  sources of description of, 70
  and things are not always as they seem, 76–77
  and *totally good* deliberate behavior, 61–62
  and transcending dualistic consciousness, 78–79
  and tricking people to virtue, 289, 297, 432, 548n785, 581n1111
  and virtue and sin in tantric tradition, 77–78
Tangtong Gyalpo (Thang stong rgyal po, 1361?–1485), meeting with
  Aṅgaja, 164
  Avalokiteśvara, 23, 474n92

Chinese emperor Chu Ch'i-chen, 320–23, 557n867
Chökyi Drönmé, 52–53
ḍākinī at Shalu Monastery, 165–66
Delek Pal, 326–31
Delek Tashi, 349
Dharmaratna, 136–38
Dönyö Gyaltsen, 106, 494–95n324, 495n333
Dorjé Lekpa, 280, 545n756
Drakpa Gyaltsen, 208
Drigung hierarch at Drigung Monastery, 303–4, 553n826
earth spirit or nāga king Varuṇa, 215–19
five ḍākinīs in Kongpo, 222–25
Genyen Dölpa, 280–81
Jangsem Urgyen Gema, 563n932
Kadampa spiritual friends, 425–31
Kalden Dorjé Drakpa, 145–47, 247–48
King of Kāmata, 394–96
Lekhawa Sherab Sangpo, 354–55
Lord Dusi, 349
Machik Palha, 200–201
Marpa, 287
Ngorchen Kunga Sangpo, 279–80
Niguma, 18–19, 150–52, 191
Nyakpuwa Sönam Sangpo, 208–9
old woman at Kyirong, 179–81
Paṇḍita Vanaratna and Rabten Kunsang Pak, 559–60n892
Rabten Kunsang Pak at Pal Khorlo Dechen, 348
realized yogin and two consorts at Shalu Monastery, 166–67
Rendawa, 157–59, 511–12n463
Rongtön Sheja Kunrik, 70–72, 301–2, 488–89n263
Sakya Dagchen Lodrö Wangchuk, 349
Sangyé Gyaltsen, 513–14n478
and Sangyé Sangmo, 356–57, 361
Śavaripa, 142–43
and scholar of ten fundamental subjects, 201–4
Shang Yudrakpa, 194
Siddharatna at Vajrāsana, 139
Tsang Nyön Heruka, 79
Tsenden Namkhai Naljor, 164
Vajradhara at Tarpa Ling, 174
Vararuci and Pañjaranātha, 182
Virūpa, 172–74, 509–10n593
woman with tangled hair on road to Gyeré Tsarpa, 192
Tangtong Gyalpo (Thang stong rgyal po, 1361?–1485), teachings and Dharma tradition of
and Chöd practice, 19–20
and connection to Niguma and Shangpa tradition, 18–19
and *Glorious Giver of Immortality*, 28, 30
and Heartdrop of the Great Adept, 32
and meditation system of Vajravārāhī, 1
nonsectarianism of, 18
and Nyingma tradition, 23–28
Shangpa texts of, 10, 469n35
Tangtong Gyalpo (Thang stong rgyal po, 1361?–1485), visions of, 113, 505n415, 510n451
Avalokiteśvara, 256, 510n451
as Dorjé Drakpotsel, 25
during retreat with Draksangpa, 120–21
of extending ladder to higher forms of existence, 38
and Hayagrīva, 140, 510n451
and Hūṃkara, 25
of Mañjuśrī, 115, 497–98n352, 557n865
by others and their dreams, 30–31, 478n122
of people crossing water, 40
in rainbow light surrounded by women, 377
as semiwrathful adept when recovering from poison, 263
of Tārā and founding of Riwoché, 169–71
of Vajravārāhī, 19
See also abuse or nonrecognition of; childhood of; family of; longevity of; magical abilities of; names

for; previous and future lives of; prophecies regarding; retreats of; vows of
Tangtong Temple (Thang stong lha khang) of Lhundrup Teng Monastery, 57, 556n851
Tangtong Tradition (Thang lugs) of the Shangpa Kagyü lineage, 19
Tangtong's Oral Transmission (Tangtong), 19–21, 551n805
Tantra of the Direct Emergence of Vajravārāhī, 166
Tantra Trilogy of Hevajra, 166, 515n488
tantric tradition
and defining virtue and sin, 77–78
and deliberate behavior only when prepared, 74
and partners and treasure revealers, 28
Tārā, 41, 45, 170, 239, 395
image and temple of at Riwoché, 417
image of made by Tangtong in turquoise, 42, 306
and Mind Training of Sumpa Lotsāwa, 548–49n787
speaking to Tangtong at Jonang stūpa, 165
Tangtong appearing as, 286, 410
Tangtong vision of and founding of Riwoché, 169–71
teachings of received by Tangtong, 508–9n443
temple and statue at Ngurmik, 167, 515n491
Tāranātha. *See* Jonang Tāranātha
Tarpa Ling (Thar pa gling), 157
Tarpa Ling (Thar pa gling) at Rinchen Ding, 172–77, 260, 281, 425, 516–17n500, 540n710
See also Shalkar Lhadong
Tashi Dargyé (Bkra shis dar rgyas), 73, 431, 581n1110
Tashi Gomang (Bkra shis sgo mang), 255–56
Tashi Gyaltsen (Bkra shis rgyal mtshan), 103
Tashi Lungpo (Bkra shis lhun po) Monastery, 483–84n204
Tashi (Bkra shis) of Menmogang, 232
Tashi Pal (Bkra shis dpal, 1142–1210), 553n823, 577n1068
Tashi Rinchen, master artist of Jang (Byang pa'i dpon Bkra shis rin chen), 483–84n204
Tashi Sangmo (Bkra shis bzang mo), 360–61
Tashi Tsé in Jé ('Jad Bkra shis rtse)
bridge to be built at, 279, 353
Tangtong goes to, 281, 353
Tashi Tseringma (Bkra shis tshe ring ma), 271, 272, 544n746
Té (Thed), 253–54
Tekar Drosangma (Gtad dkar 'gro bzang ma), 544n746
Tekchen Chojé Kunga Tashi (Theg chen chos rje Kun dga' bkra shis, 1349–1425), 511n462, 563n933, 564n938
Tekchen Chökyi Gyalpo (Theg chen chos kyi rgyal po). *See* Tekchen Chojé Kunga Tashi
Tembu in Té (Thed Them bu), 257
ten powers *(stobs bcu)*, 405, 575–76n1051
ten royal sūtras *(rgyal po'i mdo bcu)*, 25, 476n106
ten virtues *(dge ba bcu)*, royal code of, 237, 239, 322, 533n646, 583n649
Tengtsar (Steng tsar), 221
tenma goddesses *(brtan ma bcu gnyis)*, 157, 480n161, 510n459, 523n556
Tenzin (Bstan 'dzin, Upholder of the Doctrine) title-holders, 15, 16
in residence at Chaksam Monastery on Chuwori in Central Tibet, 15, 55
Tenzin Gyaltsen (Bstan 'dzin rgyal mtshan, fl. 1759–71), 9, 468n31, 556n851, 584–85n1142
Tenzin Gyatso (Bstan 'dzin rgya mtsho, b. 1935), Fourteenth Dalai Lama, 499–500n369
Tenzin Khyenrap Tutob (Bstan 'dzin Mkhyen rab mthu stobs), 16
Tenzin Kunga Sönam Wangchuk (Bstan 'dzin Kun dga' bsod nams dbang phyug), 472n70

Tenzin Norbu. *See* Yölmo Tulku Tenzin Norbu
Tenzin Rabgyé (Bstan 'dzin rab rgyas, reign: 1680–95), 56
Tenzin Rinpoché (Bstan 'dzin rin po che). *See* Nyima Sangpo, Tenzin
Tenzin Yeshé Lhundrup (Bstan 'dzin Ye shes lhun grub). *See* Yeshé Lhundrup, Tenzin
Terdak Lingpa (Gter bdag gling pa, 1646–1714), 477n118
thirteen heroic disciples of Tangtong, 540n713
thirty-two yoga exercises for immortality *('chi med 'khrul 'khor gsum cu rtsa gnyis)*, 211, 522n540, 528n593
three bodies of enlightenment *(sku gsum)*, 290, 500–501n380
three carry-over practices *('khyer so gsum)*, 123, 345, 500n372, 562n923
Three Jewels, 126, 344, 421, 427
  and story of Drakpa Öser, 87, 88, 89, 90
  trust in, 297, 304
three nirvāṇas *(myang 'das gsum po)*, 343, 562n918
three representations *(rten gsum)*, 550n797
Three Silver Brothers (Dngul sku mched gsum), 265, 542n728
three vows *(sdom gsum)*, 79, 216, 328, 345, 427, 489n277, 519n605
Three Ways to Carry the Practice on the Path, 150
three wheels *('khor lo rnam gsum)*, 147, 198, 507n436
three white milk products, 266, 542n732
three worlds *(sa gsum/srid gsum)*, 161, 513n469
three yogas *(yo ga rnam gsum)*, 139, 475n102, 505–6n422
threefold purity *('khor gsum yongs su dag pa)*, 347, 563n925
thresholds, Tangtong's vow renouncing, 209, 292, 301, 348, 354, 355, 552n815
Tibetan landscape as body of demoness, 49, 50, 543n738, 554n839
tigers, 240
Tilopa, 64, **278**, 487–88n251, 501n388
  appearing to Tsenden Namkhai Naljor, 164
  and Dohās or vajra songs, 115–16
  dress of, 131, 209, 527n580
  and Lalitavajra, 504n411
  as same as Tangtong, 277, 278, 443, 455
Tilopa Prajñābhadra. *See* Tilopa
"time has come" instruction, 392–93
Time of the Path (Lam dus), 410, 577n1069
Tingi Shalsangma (Mthing gi zhal bzang ma), 544n746
Tirikha and its stūpa, 252–53
Tödreng Tsel (Thod 'phreng rtsal), Nepalese yoginī, 194
Tokden Drakgyal (Rtogs ldan Grags rgyal), 211
Tokden Nyakpo (Rtogs ldan Nyag po), 332, 480–81n162
Tolé Lhé (Tho le lhas), 279
Tölung (Stod lung) River and bridge, 301, 535n661
Tölung (Stod lung), 69, 249, 250, 488n257, 525n567, 536n673
Tonga (Mthong dga') geomantic focal-point of, 338
Tongwa Dönden (Mthong ba don ldan, 1416–1453), Sixth Karmapa, 211–13, 528n592, 534n653
  and meeting Tangtong at Tselagang stūpa, 243
totally good (kun tu bzang po) deliberate behavior, 60, 61
trade, Tangtong song regarding, 124–27
traders of Mangyul, 265–66
transference of consciousness, 18, 150
  and Drakpa the blacksmith, 310
  and Jonang practitioner, 292

by Kunga Sangmo for mother Dodé, 407
and Lady Kalsang, 335–36
transformation of one's body in dreams, 216, 529n606
Translated Scriptures and Translated Treatises
at Riwoché, 419
Temple at Chuwori, 250
Translated Scriptures (Bka' 'gyur), 353, 425, 511n462, 551n807
Translated Treatises (Bstan 'gyur), 250, 297, 337, 425
transmigration of the dead, 109–10
transmission, direct, 32–33
Trapa Ngönshé (Gra pa Mngon shes, 1012–90), 530–31n624
travels of Tangtong
and decision to stay at Riwoché, 369
his inability to at old age, 432
twenty-eight distant journeys of, 5, 561n908
See also magical travel
treasure-owner *(gter bdag)*, 309, 554n838
treasure teachings *(gter ma)*
and *Bright Lamp*, 3, 4, 7, 309
at Cave of the Ḍākinīs, 230
and Dawa Puk, 206
and Drakyang Dzong, 549n790
in Drok Megyu, 287
found at Drampa Gyang Red Temple, 161–62, 513n470
found in Lo, 238
and Gökyi Demtruchen, 502n391
and Kunkyong Lingpa and White Stūpa, 571n1007
and mad adepts in Nyingma tradition, 62
and Pañjaranātha, 520n524
reconcealed, 32
removed from rock face of Taktsang, 252
revealed to Tangtong at Samyé Chimpu, 206–7
Tangtong and, 1, 23–24, 86, 465n4, 475n101
and tantric partners, 28
and treasure-owner, 309
Treasury of Precious Treasure Teachings (Jamgön Kongtrul), 31
tree trunk at Ngampa Dradrok, 252
Tri Chokdrup Dé (Khri Mchog grub lde, 1371–1404), 541n718
Tri Lhawang Gyaltsen (Khri Lha dbang rgyal mtshan, 1404–64), 52, 540–41n717, 570n997
Tri Namgyal Dé (Khri Rnam rgyal sde), 540–41n717
tricking people to virtue, 289, 297, 432, 548n785, 581n1111
Tridé Tsukten (Khri lde gtsug brtan), 35
Trimkhang Lotsāwa Sönam Gyatso (Khrims khang Lo tsā ba Bsod nams rgya mtsho, 1424–82), 334, 554n836, 560nn895–96
Tringyi Shukchen (Sprin gyi shugs can), 253, 537–38n687
Tripiṭaka, 89, 492n294
Trisong Detsen (Khri srong lde btsan), King, 525n571, 536n676
and Samyé Monastery, 206–7, 525n572, 557n862
Trömo Nakmo (Khros ma nag mo), 235–36
Tropu Lotsāwa Jampa Pal (Khro phu Lo tsā ba Byams pa dpal, 1172–1236), 51, 504n411
Tropu (Khro phu) Monastery, 50–51
Trowo Palden (Khro bo dpal ldan), "Wrathful Glory," 96, 105, 111, 494n312
truth, place of, 83, 435, 490n281
Tsagong (Tsa gong)
and ḍākinīs of Uḍḍiyāna, 188–89
keys to open region of, 227–28
and Palgyi Nesar Monastery, 56
Vajrayoginī directs Tangtong to, 225–26
Tsagong Palgyi Nesar (Tsa gong Dpal gyi gnas gsar) Monastery in Kongpo, 15, 41, 56
and Chökyi Dronmé, 53, 379–80

iron factory established by Tangtong, 46, 310
and Lama Riksum Gönpo, 331, 527n582
later history of, 485n222
and skull-cup of Chökyi Dronmé, 309, 380
and Stūpa of Great Enlightenment to subdue Lo, 331
Tsami Lotsāwa (Tsa mi Lo tsā ba), 567n967
tsan *(btsan)* demons, 228, 531n627
Tsanda (Tsha mda'), 271, 543n741
Tsang (Gtsang), 353–54
Tsang Nyön Heruka (Gtsang smyon He ru ka, 1452–1507), Madman of Tsang, 58, **73**, 583–84n1136
deliberate behavior of, 72–73, 74
and Governor Horshakpa, 543n741
and Jetsun Kunga Sangmo, 576n1054, 1058
at Kaṃṇi Goshi, 521n539
in Lhasa, 488n260
and meeting with Tangtong, 12, 79
mistaken for Tangtong in crazy behavior, 70, 521n539
and Namkha Dorjé, 582n1119
and ordinary people crazy, 74
ties to Kagyü and Milarepa, 63, 64, 72
and Tsanda chieftain patron, 543n741
Tsangpa Chökyi Gyaltsen (Gtsang pa Chos kyi rgyal mtshan), 297
Tsangpa Gyaré Yeshé Dorjé (Gtsang pa rgya ras Ye shes rdo rje, 1161–1211), 263, 494n313, 523n554, 536–37n679, 542n726
See also Yeshé Dorjé
Tsangpo (Gtsang po) River, 42, 119, 245, 261, 493n307, 536n676
crossing in a coracle, 299
and iron bridge at Gangla Longka, 261
See also Tachok Khabab River
Tsangpo Yeru (Gtsang po g.yas ru) River, 108
Tsari (Tsa ri) area
opening up of, 215, 319, 523n554, 529n600
Tsari (Tsa ri) Mountain, 96, 391, 494n313, 499n364
Tsari Serchen Cave (Tsa ri'i zer chen phug), 309
Tsari Tra Sphere of Primordial Awareness (Tsa ri tra Ye shes kyi 'khor lo), 201, 434
and Tangtong and "authentic skull-cup," 231, 309, 532n633, 554n836
Tsari Tsagong (Tsa ri tsa gong), 201
Tsechen (Rtse chen) Monastery, 349, 563–64n934
Tsechu (Tshe chu) practice center at Chaksam Chuwori, 16
Tsegyal (Rtse rgyal) at Pal Korlo Dechen, 348, 563n931
Tsel Gungtang (Tshal Gung thang), 194–95, **195**, 522n540
Tselagang Stūpa (Rtse la sgang), 243
Tselmin (Mtshal min), 208–9, 526n577
Tselmin Sönam Sangpo (Mtshal min Bsod nams bzang po). *See* Nyakpuwa Sönam Sangpo
Tselpa Kagyü (Tshal pa bka' brgyud) tradition, 522n540
Tsenden Bima (Mtshan ldan Bi ma), 350–52, 564n940
Tsenden Namkhai Naljor (Mtshan ldan Nam mkha'i rnal 'byor), 164, 513n477
See also Müchen Namkhai Naljor
Tsenden Ridröma (Mtshan ldan ri khrod ma), 279, 544n751
Tsetang (Rtse thang) Monastery, 432, 559–60n892, 581n1113
Tsewang Rangdrol, Bön adept (Bon gyi grub thob Tshes dbang rang grol), 565n944
Tsewang Rikzin (Tshe dbang rig 'dzin), 565n944
Tsewang Tashi (Tshe dbang bkra shis, d. 1454/55), 52, 484n209
Tsokyé Dorjé (Mtsho skyes rdo rje, 1462–1510) of Rinpung, 431, 581n1109

Tsöndru Sangpo (Brtson 'grus bzang po), name of Tangtong, 146, 195, 443, 471n57, 511n462, 522n543
Tsöndru Sengé, "Lion of Diligence," name of Tangtong, 113
Tsongdu Gurmo (Tshong 'dus mgur mo), 164, 514n481
Tsongkhapa, lord (Rje Tsong kha pa, 1357–1419), 511–12n463, 527n586, 536n670
Tsozong (Mtsho rdzong), 219–21
Tsultrim Sangpo, great adept of Ngari (Mnga' ris grub chen Tshul khrims bzang po), 417n58
Tsurpu (Mtshur phu) Monastery, 488
Tucci, Giuseppe, 468n31, 470n44, 539n707
  and visit to Chaksam Chuwori Monastery, 56, 485n221
Tuksé Rinpoché (Thugs sras Rin po che, Precious Spiritual Son), 467n22
Tumtön Lodrö Drakpa (Gtum ston Blo gros grags pa, 1106–66), 564n939
Tupten Gyatso (Thub bstan rgya mtsho, 1876–1933), Thirteenth Dalai Lama, 31, 54
Turkic Qarlung (Gar log), 5
Turner, Samuel, 42
turquoise, 309
  constructing images from, 304–6, 553n831
  Flat Blue Sky, 314, 556n852
Tuṣita buddha field, 248, 415
twelve acts *(mdzad pa gcu gnyis)*, 436, 583n1130
twenty-four great sacred places *(gnas chen)*, 295, 520n525 550n803
twenty-ninth day offering of sacrificial cakes *(dgu gtor)*, 133, 375, 503n402
Twenty-three Verses for Fortunate People (Tangtong), 341–48, 563n926
Two-Part [Hevajra] Tantra, 165, 180, 181, 411

Ü Nyön Kunga Sangpo, Madman of Central Tibet (Dbus smyon Kun dga' bzang po, 1458–1538), 58, 63, 554n836
Uḍḍiyāna (U rgyan), 18, 24, 25, 477n117
  ḍākinīs of and advice to Tangtong, 40, 188
  and *Glorious Giver of Immortality*, 28
  as Land of Ḍākinīs, 184
  and *Mahāmāyā Tantra*, 501n386
  paradise of, 335
  portion of ritual feast from sent to Tangtong, 416
  Tangtong visit to, 182–90
Uḍḍiyāna Guru (U rgyan Gu ru), 180
  See also Padmasambhava, Guru
Uḍḍiyāna Practices of Approach and Accomplishment (U rgyan snyen sgrub), 508–9n443
Ulek (Dbu legs) Monastery, 269
Umdul Dogar ('U 'dul rdo dkar), 256, 257
Uncontrived, Naturally Arisen Vajra Words (Dzamling Dorjé), 477n121
unexcelled yoga tantras and importance of human body, 550n803
united evaṃ *(e vaṃ zung 'jug)*, 225, 530n619
untainted actions, 343
Unwritten Mahāmudrā (Vāgīśvarakīrti), 157, 511n462
upholder of the adept's hereditary line (*grub rigs 'dzin pa* and *grub rigs 'chang*), 17
Urgyen Dzong in Tanak (Rta nag U rgyan rdzong), 349–52
Urgyen Ledro Lingpa (U rgyan las 'phro gling pa), 480n161
Urgyen Tangtong Gyalpo (U rgyan Thang stong rgyal po), 24
urination, 30, 74, 315, 478n124
Urtö Chökhor Gang (Dbur stod Chos 'khor sgang), 433, 582n1117
Uṣṇiṣavijayā, 537n686
Uyuk Gong Ngön ('U yug Gong sngon), 280

Vāgīśvarakīrti, 511n462

Vairocana, 174, 461, 518n505, 537–38n687
Vairocana, sevenfold posture of, 103, 121, 152, 175, 194, 495n331
  and crossing Kyichu River, 196
  and escorting Löpon Paltsul to next life, 315
Vaiśravaṇa (Rnam sras), 249, 291, 503n394, 536n674, 549n791
  with a Red Lance, 513n475
  and yakṣa attendants, 537n680, 539n704
Vajra Cave (Rdo rje phug), in India, 145
Vajra Lines (Rdo rje'i tshig rkang) of Niguma, 18, 150, 473n75
  of Heartdrop of the Great Adept, 32, 478n134
  of Virūpa, 517–18n504
vajra-moon *(rdo rje zla ba)*, 439, 584n1139
Vajra Nairātmyā. *See* Nairātmyā
vajra songs, 115–16, 126
vajra spiritual family, 228
Vajrabhairava, 158, 501–2n388, 512n464, 538n689, 569n995
  image of at Riwoché, 383
  Tangtong as at Charnel Ground of Tumdrak, 253
  and Tangtong's residence, 378
Vajradhara, 23, 64, **175**, 388, 472n73, 505n413
  and dress of Shang Yudrakpa, 194
  essence of Tangtong is, 423
  guruyoga received from, 174, 180, 457, 519n517, 585n1155
  image of at Riwoché, 45, 306, 383
  seen by Tangtong at Drin Chuwar, 272
  as sixth buddha, 305–6, 553n830
  Tangtong seen as by Kham man, 410
  Tangtong vision at Tarpa Ling, 174
  turquoise image of given to Kongpo region, 398
Vajradhātu tradition, 497n348
Vajrakīla, 252, 504n405
Vajrāmṛta, 525–26n573
Vajrapāṇi, 41, 211, **212**, 220, 338, 530n615, 533n648
  and Chakpori Hill, 535n663
  image of made by Tangtong, 45, 307
  and Namkha Dorjé, 433
Vajrapāṇi with the Blue Robe, 129
vajras stamped in chain links, 48
Vajrāsana of Bodhgayā, 90, 134, 138–39, 334, 492n295, 505n420
  attacked by Karma Goraṇa, 421
  and heart of enlightenment, 580n1102
  Vajra Cave near, 145
  and Vararuci, 519n523
Vajrasattva, 185, 383
Vajravārāhī, 1, 167, 185, 494n323, 505n413
  and Chökyi Drönmé, 52, 378
  and Gyagar Lhamo's dream, 100
  and Heartdrop of the Great Adept, 32
  and home in Tsari mountain, 494n313
  and Mind Training of Sumpa Lotsāwa, 548–49n787
  and prophecy for Tangtong regarding Lo, 215
  and prophecy of iron bridge at Chuwori, 254
  skull-cup of, 54, 226, 484–85n213, 530n622
  and *Tangtong's Oral Transmission*, 19
  Tangtong's vision of, 19
  in union with Padmasambhava, 131
  and Yamdrok Jetsünma abbesses, 53
Vajravārāhī of the Severed Head, 528n593
Vajrayoga, 209, 354, 526n578, 565n952
  See also Six-branch Yoga of Kālacakra
Vajrayoginī, **224**, 305–6, 494n323, 585n1154
  as crazy, 64
  four initiations of, 165–66, 192
  and skull-cup of Vajravārāhī, 54, 226, 484–85n213, 530n622
  telling Tangtong to go to Tsagong, 225–26, 530n620
Vajrasattva, 238
vaṃ syllable, 83
van der Kuijp, Leonard, 466n9

Vanaratna, Mahāpaṇḍita (Paṇ chen Nags kyi rin chen, 1384–1468), 7, 334, 546n763, 559–60n892, 560n895
Vararuci, 182, 519n523
vartula script, 108, 577n1066
Varuṇa (Wa ru ṇa), 41, 215–19, 480–81n162, 529n604
vase initiation, 146
Vibhūticandra, 556–57n861
Victory Stūpa, 418
Vidāraṇa, 105
Vijayā, 252, 253, 537n686
vinaya, 114, 508–9n443
virtue, 77, 347
virtues and nonvirtues, ten, 125, 188, 339, 500n378
Virūpa, lord of yogins (Rnal 'byor dbang phyug Bi rū pa), 46, 59, 487–88n251, 517n502, 573–74n1035
  dress of, 131
  image of made for Master's Temple after Tangtong's passing, 459
  and Path with the Result to Tangtong, 173, 517n502
  and pills of the secret initiation to Tangtong, 172–74
  and prophecy of no excretions for Tangtong, 517n503, 567n967
  and Red Yamāri initiation, 512n464
  Tangtong meeting with, 172–74, 509–10n450
Virūpa (teacher of Sukhasiddhī), 528n593
Viṣṇu, 239
visual manifestation of Tangtong
  according to inclination of viewer, 376, 410
  and statues transformed to match viewer, 422–23
Viśuddha Stūpa, 252–53, 537n686
vital winds
  and action winds, 317, 556n858
  of consciousness, 317, 556n858
  of fire, 139, 314, 505n420
  in *rasanā* and *lalanā*, 174
  Tangtong bringing under control, 410
  taught by Tangtong at Ralung Monastery, 250
Vitali, Roberto, 468n28, 485n219
vows of renewal and purification, eight-branch *(bsnyen gnas yan lag brgyad)*, 288, 396, 548n781
vows of Tangtong
  made at Jonang stūpa regarding practice of Dharma, 162–63
  not to go inside ordinary buildings, 489n264
  not to pass through Chuwori door until iron bridge built, 292, 301, 552n815
  ordination, 110–11, 112–13, 128, 511n462
  permission to take from parents and king, 110, 111
  and reciting *maṇis*, 162–63
  renouncing thresholds, 209, 292, 301, 348, 354, 355, 552n815
  vow of silence for fourteen years, 574n1041
vulture, 62, 106, 259, 359, 378, 411, 423, 495n332

walking on water, Tangtong, 108, 209, 241
  across Kyichu River, 196–98
  across Yeru Tsangpo River, 208
  at Dok River, 279
Wam Tengchen (Wam Steng chen), 255, 538n694
Wang Partsam (Dbang Spar/Pa 'tshams), 465n7
Wangdrak (Dbang grags), patron, 353–54
warmth *(drod)*, 60, 61–62
Waru Namtsel (Ba ru gnam tshal), 41, 480–81n162, 529n601
  and Auspicious Stūpa of Many Doors, 332, 558–59n884
  and conversion of Varuṇa and nāga spirits, 215–19
  and stūpa built by Tangtong, 50
  Tangtong agreeing to be lord of, 219

Tangtong's instruction for temple and stūpa at, 332
Waru Seso (Wa ru se so), 215, 529n604
water
crossing over and liberating beings, 174
eight qualities of pure, 184, 520n528
one essence but many forms of, 455
Tangtong creating more at Wam Tengchen, 255
See also nāgas or water spirits; walking on water
water spirits. *See* nāgas
wealth, 124, 126, 127, 339, 342, 402
woman gone mad from theft of, 212–13
Wencheng Kongjo, 521n538
Western Mongols (Stod hor), 407, 438, 577n1060
White and Red Khecarīs, 150, 151, 508n438
white and red medicinal pills, 475n96
inspired by Avalokiteśvara, 23, 541–42n723
Tangtong's instructions relative to, 263, 541–42n723
transmission of, 471n62
white conch, 100, 104, 291, 304, 306–7
White Mausoleum (Sku gdung dkar po), 271, 543–44n743
White Old Man of Gesar legends, 2
White Stūpa (Mchod ldan dkar po) at Samyé Monastery, 571n1007
wind, edict to, 207–8
wish-fulfilling gem, 382, 388, 430
wolves, 136, 137
listening to Dharma at Kyirong, 179
Tangtong edict to, 405
Words of the Conqueror, 337, 418
writing slate *(sa 'bo ra/sa 'bor ra)*, 68, 488n253
Tangtong throwing at Dharma protectors, 406
used by Tangtong, 408–9, 577nn1065, 1067
wrong view, 339
Yakdé in Rong (Rong G.yag sde), 341–48
yakṣa horsemen, eight, 129, 291, 503n394, 539n704, 549n791
yakṣa spirits, 250, 251, 537n680
See also Gangwa Sangpo
Yama (Gshin rje) and yama spirits, 309, 404, 555n840
Yamar (G.ya' dmar), 376–77
Yamdrok Jetsünma (Ya 'brog rje btsun ma), 53–54
Yamdrok (Yar 'brog) district, 43, 250, 259
governor of, 250, 536n678
verses to fishermen at lake of, 338–40
Yangdak Heruka (Yang dag He ru ka), 475n103, 504n405
Yangtse River, 555n850
Yargyab governor (Yar rgyab Dpon chen pa), 527n584
Yari Go Nga (G.ya' ri sgo lnga), 135
Yarlung (Yar lungs), 40, 333, 433
See also Nyago (Nya mgo) bridge
Yarlung (Yar klungs) dynasty, 34
Yarlungpa Chödrak Palsang (Yar lung pa Chos drag dpal bzang), to Rinchen Ding, 297, 551n807
Yaśas, 566n963
Yatsé (Ya tshe) king, 397–98, 574n1041
Yellow River (Rma chu), 35
Yerpa (Yer pa), 204–5, **205**, 524n563
Yeru Jang (G.yas ru Byang), 278, 544n750
See also Latö Jang
Yeru Jang, Dharma King of (Chos rgyal G.yas ru Byang pa), 353, 565n948
Yeru Tsangpo (G.yas ru Gtsang po) River, 208, 218
Yeshé Dorjé (Ye shes rdo rje), 201, 523n554
Yeshé Dren (Ye shes 'dren) (paternal uncle of Tangtong), 120
Yeshé Lhundrup, Tenzin (Ye shes lhun grub, b. 1738), 16, 21
Yeshé Tsogyal (Ye shes mtsho rgyal), 502n392

Yigé Drugma (Yi ge drug ma), 502n390, 545n760
Yilhung Shi (Yid lhung gzhi) temple and statue, 57–58
Yilung Gandentsé of Gangbulé (Gangs bu le'i dbyi lung dga' ldan rtse), 157
Yoginī Ciṇṭa, 498n353
Yölmo Tulku Tenzin Norbu (Yol mo sprul sku Bstan 'dzin nor bu, 1598–1644), 10–11, **10**, 17, 469n36
Yönten Nyingpo (Yon tan snying po), 289, 291
Yongru in upper Tsang (Gtsang stod yongs ru), 353–54
Yöntsun (Yon btsun), 497n346
Yumtso Lake (G.yu mtsho), 418
Yungdrung Ling (G.yung drung gling) Monastery and stūpa, 270–71, 543n739

Six-armed Mahākāla